Everyday Encounters

An Introduction to Interpersonal Communication

FOURTH CANADIAN EDITION

Everyday Encounters

An Introduction to Interpersonal Communication

FOURTH CANADIAN EDITION

Julia Wood
University of North Carolina, Chapel Hill

Ann Schweitzer
University of Western Ontario

NELSON EDUCATION

NELSON EDUCATION

Everyday Encounters: An Introduction to Interpersonal Communication, Fourth Canadian Edition
by Julia Wood and Ann Schweitzer

Vice President, Editorial Director:
Evelyn Veitch

Editor-in-Chief, Higher Education:
Anne Williams

Acquisitions Editor:
Anne-Marie Taylor

Marketing Manager:
Amanda Henry

Developmental Editor:
Theresa Fitzgerald

Photo Researcher:
Kristiina Paul

Permissions Coordinator:
Kristiina Paul

Content Production Manager:
Christine Gilbert

Production Service:
Knowledgeworks Global Limited

Copy Editor:
June Trusty

Proofreader:
Jafar Sadique Basha

Indexer:
Knowledgeworks Global Limited

Production Coordinator:
Ferial Suleman

Design Director:
Ken Phipps

Managing Designer:
Franca Amore

Interior Design:
Peter Papyanakis

Cover Design:
Olena Sullivan

Cover Image:
© Helle Bro /iStockphoto

Compositor:
Knowledgeworks Global Limited

Printed and bound in Canada
4 5 16 15 14

For more information contact Nelson Education Ltd., 1120 Birchmount Road, Toronto, Ontario, M1K 5G4. Or you can visit our Internet site at http://www.nelson.com

Library and Archives Canada Cataloguing in Publication

Wood, Julia T.

Everyday encounters : an introduction to interpersonal communication / Julia Wood, Ann Schweitzer. — 4th Canadian ed.

Includes bibliographical references and index.

1. Interpersonal communication—Textbooks. 2. Interpersonal relations—Textbooks. I. Schweitzer, Ann. II. Title.

BF637.C45W66 2009 153.6
C2009-903719-X

ISBN-13: 978-0-17-650031-3
ISBN-10: 0-17-650031-6

Brief Table of Contents

Table of Contents

Preface

Everyday Encounters: An Introduction to Interpersonal Communication (Fourth Canadian Edition) offers a distinct alternative to existing textbooks for the introductory course in interpersonal communication. This book is unique in its emphasis on theories, research, and skills that are anchored in the field of communication and in its attention to significant trends in Canadian social life. This Canadian adaptation of the U.S. textbook brings not only the obvious changes that distinguish Canada from the United States—spelling; currency; economic, geographic, demographic, and political differences—but it also includes changes in language that represent the more subtle differences in values and approaches that mark Canadians. The cultural diversity of Canada is represented in the many voices in the text. Familiar Canadians, whether in research, art, media, politics, or sport, give the text a unique flavour, but unfamiliar voices of "common folk" also provide a regional perspective. In addition, this Canadian adaptation provides added pedagogical supports that make it very accessible to students and very helpful to teachers.

FOCUS ON COMMUNICATION RESEARCH AND THEORY

In the 1970s, when interpersonal communication was a very young intellectual area, research was limited. Because theoretical and research foundations for courses were not abundant, the content of most textbooks and courses either extended general principles of communication to interpersonal contexts or relied primarily on research in fields other than communication.

Although interpersonal communication continues to draw from other disciplines, it now is a substantive field in its own right, complete with a base of knowledge, theories, and research founded in communication. The maturation of interpersonal communication as an intellectual area is evident in the substantial original research published in academic journals, as well as in the steady stream of scholarly books. It is clear that interpersonal communication is no longer a derivative field.

Textbooks for introductory communication courses no longer need to rely primarily on research and theories developed by scholars outside the communication field. *Everyday Encounters* reflects a strong focus on research in the communication discipline. Woven into each chapter, for example, are discussions of relationships that highlight the extensive research on relational dialectics, the emergent knowledge of differences in communication that are influenced by gender, economic class, sexual orientation, ethnicity, and race.

Communication scholars' strong interest in ethics is also woven into this book. Ethical issues and choices are integral to the discussion of the range of topics that are part of interpersonal communication. These and other topics in current communication inquiry are integrated into this book. As a result, students who read it will gain an appreciation of the scope and depth of scholarship in the field of communication.

Attention to Significant Social Trends

Social diversity is not merely a timely trend, a new buzzword, or a matter of political correctness. Instead, social diversity is a basic fact of life in Canada, a country (like many others) enriched by a cornucopia of people, heritages, customs, and ways of interacting. *Everyday Encounters* reflects and addresses social diversity by weaving it into the basic fabric of interpersonal communication.

Addressing diversity adequately requires more than tacking on paragraphs on gender or race to conventional approaches to topics. Awareness of race, economic class, gender, age, and sexual orientation are woven into discussions of communication theory and skills throughout *Everyday Encounters*. For example, in exploring self-concept, detailed attention is given to race, gender, and sexual orientation as core facets of identity that shape how individuals communicate and interpret the communication of others. In examining patterns of interaction in families, research on families that are not White and middle class is included. Discussion on romantic relationships includes research on gay and lesbian relationships as well as heterosexual ones. Rather than highlighting the attention to diversity with diversity boxes or separate features, diverse social groups, customs, and lifestyles are blended into the book as a whole.

Social diversity is not the only significant social trend that affects and is affected by interpersonal communication. *Everyday Encounters* addresses communication challenges, confusions, and issues that are part of personal and social life in our era. Attention is paid to friendships, which have assumed greater importance in the face of increasing numbers of broken marriages and geographically dispersed families. Discussion of romantic relationships addresses abuse and violence between intimates, managing long-distance relationships, and the use of communication to negotiate safer sex in an era shadowed by HIV and AIDS. The final chapter examines current topics in workplace health, such as how to bring soul to the workplace and how to deal with sexual harassment and difficult people.

SPECIAL FEATURES OF *EVERYDAY ENCOUNTERS*

The emphasis on communication research and theories and attention to social diversity are two distinctive features of *Everyday Encounters*. In addition, other facets of the book are designed to make it appealing and useful to students and helpful to teachers. First, the authors have adopted a conversational tone so that students are invited to interact with ideas on a personal level. Each chapter is also enhanced by commentaries written by students in interpersonal communication classes. Their voices add a broader perspective to the scholarly material and remind the reader that the topic of interpersonal communication is about the lives of real people.

Everyday Encounters also includes pedagogical features that promote development of interpersonal communication skills. Each chapter includes several Apply the Idea exercises, which encourage students to apply concepts and principles discussed in the text to their own lives. Coupled with these exercises are Reflective Exercises that help promote reflective thinking and personal examination. Each chapter also includes a number of Communication Notes features, which highlight interesting research and examples of interpersonal communication in everyday life. Many of these are drawn from the Canadian landscape and offer a snapshot of communication ideas, foibles, and challenges in Canada.

Clusters of concepts are placed in the margin for quick reference, summary, and review. One of these sidebars is called Concepts at a Glance and the other, Review. These pedagogical features allow the student to capture key concepts in point form, which will assist study and recall. Interspersed in each chapter are photographs of people in everyday interactions. Many photographs have captions that pose questions or invite reflection. This is particularly helpful for the visual learner to capture the salient concepts of the chapter and to augment the denseness of the written text.

Following each chapter are several questions that invite students to engage in further reflection and discussion of ideas covered in the text. For most chapters, at least one question focuses specifically on ethical issues in interpersonal communication, and at least one question suggests an activity using InfoTrac® College Edition, which can be bundled with this text. For more information on this special offer, please contact your local Nelson Education Ltd. sales representative.

Additional Resources for Instructors

Accompanying *Everyday Encounters* are many instructional resources:

- An extensive *Instructor's Resource CD* (ISBN-10: 0-17-647917-1; ISBN-13: 978-0-17-647917-6) supplements the textbook and includes an *Instructor's Manual*, a *Computerized Test Bank* in ExamView® and a *PowerPoint*® presentation.

  The *Instructor's Manual* discusses philosophical and pragmatic considerations involved in teaching the introductory course in interpersonal communication. It also includes suggestions for course emphases, sample syllabuses, exercises and films appropriate for each chapter, overhead masters of diagrams in the text, a correlation chart for the *CNN Interpersonal Communication* videotapes, a list of Internet resources, journal items, panel ideas, and a bank of test items.

  The test bank for *Everyday Encounters* offers the Nelson Education Testing Advantage. NETA was created in partnership with David DiBattista, a 3M National Teaching Fellow, professor of psychology at Brock University, and researcher in the area of multiple-choice testing. NETA ensures that subject-matter experts who author test banks have had training in two areas: avoiding common errors in test construction, and developing multiple-choice test questions that "get beyond remembering" to assess higher-level thinking.

David DiBattista's guide for instructors, "Multiple Choice Tests: Getting Beyond Remembering," has been designed to assist you in using Nelson test banks to achieve your desired outcomes in your course. See the Instructor's Resource CD button "NETA Guidelines" for this valuable resource.

A text-specific Microsoft® PowerPoint® presentation includes professionally created text and images to illustrate important concepts in this book, plus a built-in flexibility that lets you add your own materials. These PowerPoint® slides can be downloaded from the text website—www.everydayencounters4e.nelson.com.

- *The Media Guide for Interpersonal Communication* is a 200-page guide containing media resource listings that provide compelling examples of interpersonal communication in an engaging format. The guide generates student interest and motivates learning through the use of film, books, plays, websites, and journal articles.

Student Resources

Student Companion Workbook

ISBN-10: 0-17-647909-0 | ISBN-13: 978-0-17-647909-1

Complements and expands students' understanding of the book. Includes a summary of each chapter, vocabulary lists, activities on perforated pages, and self-test questions. Revised activities in this Student Companion reflect the text's increased emphasis on public speaking. Can be bundled with the text.

JULIA WOOD'S ACKNOWLEDGMENTS

Many people have contributed to this book. I am especially indebted to Deirdre Cavanaugh, my editor at Wadsworth. From start to finish, she has been a full partner in this project, and her interest and insights have greatly enhanced the book. Deirdre was also most generous in providing personal support, enthusiasm, and encouragement to me.

In addition to the editorial and production team at Wadsworth, I am grateful to the many students and teachers who reviewed versions of the manuscript and whose comments and suggestions improved the final content of the book.

Writing this book was not only a professional activity but also a personal engagement that benefited from the generous support of individuals who make up my family of choice. At the top of that list is Robbie Cox, my partner in love, life, and adventure for 25 years. He cheered me on when writing was going well and bolstered my confidence when it was not. He provided a critical ear when I wanted a sounding board and privacy when I was immersed in writing. Along with Robbie, I am fortunate to have the support of my sister Carolyn and my special friends Nancy and Linda Becker. And, of course, I must acknowledge the four-footed members of my family—Madhi, Sadie Ladie, and Wicca. Unlike my two-footed companions, these three willingly keep me company when I am writing at 2 or 3 in the morning.

ANN SCHWEITZER'S ACKNOWLEDGMENTS

When I was approached by Nelson Education to author the previous edition of *Everyday Encounters*, I had been using the earlier editions with students for five years. I brought to the task a great deal of admiration for the scholarship and pedagogical style that the previous authors had infused into this text.

On starting the current edition I invited students who had recently completed the Communication course to join me as a consulting focus group. Eight students stepped forward to meet with me over a period of many weeks to go through the text page by page. Their suggestions for clarification, updates, vocabulary, and of course, Student Voices features were invaluable.

I also wish to express my appreciation to the team at Nelson Education Ltd.: Christine Gilbert, content production manager; Prasanna Sarat, project manager; and June Trusty, copy editor, whose attention to detail and deft contributions brought this edition to a polished finish.

Thank you also to the following reviewers, who provided helpful suggestions:

Grant Coleman, Mohawk College
Barbara Rice, Conestoga College
Elizabeth Skitmore, Algonquin College
Jennifer Wraight, Canadore College

I am indebted to extended family and friends who enrich my life and help me to learn more about communication on a daily basis. Special thanks to Carol Van Evera, who helped prepare this manuscript.

Skillful communication not only enriches our individual lives but is also our key to a fulfilling future for our planet and world peace.

Part 1

The Fabric of Interpersonal Communication

Chapter 1

Exploring Interpersonal Communication

Watch your thoughts; they become words.

Watch your words; they become actions.

Watch your actions; they become habits.

Watch your habits; they become character.

Watch your character; it becomes your destiny.

—Author Unknown

You've been interviewing for two months, and so far you haven't had a single job offer. After another interview that didn't go well, you run into a close friend, who asks what's wrong. Instead of just offering quick sympathy, your friend suggests that the two of you go to lunch and talk. Over pizza, you disclose that you're starting to worry that you won't find a job, and you wonder what's wrong with you.

Your friend listens closely and lets you know that he cares about your concerns. Then he tells you about other people he knows who also haven't yet had job offers. All of a sudden, you don't feel so alone. Your friend reminds you how worried you felt last term when you were struggling with your physics course and then made a B on the final.

As you listen to him, your sagging confidence begins to recover. Before leaving, he tells you about a website called *Virtual Interview* that allows you to practise interviewing skills and works with you to come up with some new strategies for interviewing. By the time you leave, you feel hopeful again.

Interpersonal communication, a selective, systemic, ongoing process in which unique individuals interact to reflect and build personal knowledge and to create meanings, is central to our everyday lives. We count on others to care about what is happening in our lives and to help us sort through problems and concerns. We want them to share our worries and our joys. In addition, we need others to encourage our personal and professional growth. Friends and romantic partners who believe in us often enable us to overcome self-defeating patterns and help us become the people we want to be. Co-workers who give us advice and feedback help us increase our effectiveness on the job. And sometimes we just want to hang out with people we like, trust, and have fun with.

We communicate to develop identities, establish connections, coordinate efforts with others, deepen ties over time, and work out problems and possibilities. In the workplace, interpersonal communication is equally important. Jerry Winsor, Dan Curtis, and Ronald Stephens (1997) asked 400 managers in a wide range of organizations to identify the applicant skills that are most important in their hiring decisions. Topping the list was oral communication. The managers said that, to get hired and to advance in careers, people needed to work effectively with others, listen well, and give feedback effectively. The importance of interpersonal communication to professional success is confirmed by other studies (Cooper, Seibold, & Suchner, 1997; Wagner, 2001; Waner, 1995). In short, interpersonal communication is central to our effectiveness and our everyday lives. It is the lifeblood of meaningful relationships in personal, social, and professional contexts.

In this chapter, we take a first look at interpersonal communication. We start by considering how communication meets important human needs. We then distinguish interpersonal communication from communication in general. Next, we examine models of communication, define interpersonal communication, and identify principles and skills of effective interpersonal communication. After reading this chapter, you should understand what interpersonal communication is (and is not), why it matters in our lives, and what skills and principles make up competent interpersonal communication.

CONCEPTS AT A GLANCE

Good Listeners

- Help us sort through problems.
- Share our feelings.
- Facilitate our growth.

A MODEL OF HOLISTIC DEVELOPMENT

Any single explanation concerning the importance of communication and interpersonal communication would be an incredible understatement. A description of our success and fulfillment as human beings brings into focus many aspects of our lives. William Huitt (1999) suggests that a description of adult success in the

FIGURE 1.1

Brilliant Star Model (Huitt, 1999)

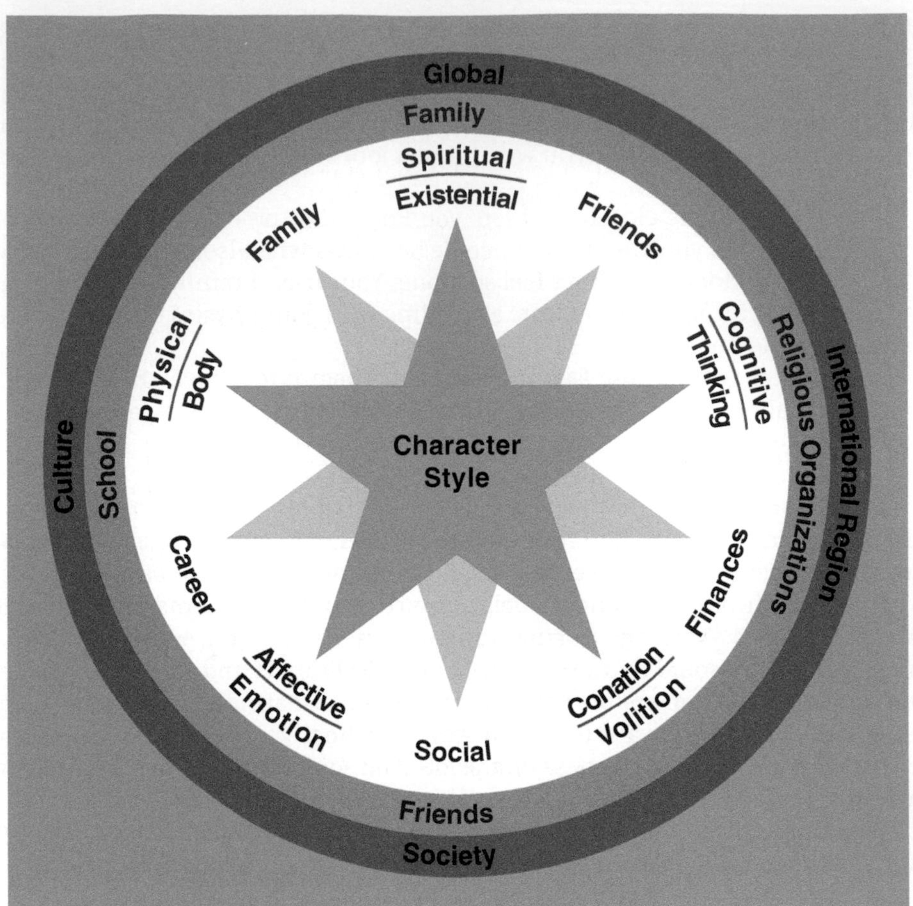

twenty-first century includes not only financial and career success, but also being happy, living a meaningful life, maintaining a support group of friends, and contributing to solving major social and cultural issues of our time.

Huitt's Brilliant Star model (Figure 1.1) indicates that to be fully ourselves, competence is needed in the intrapersonal domains of the (1) spiritual, (2) thinking, (3) volition, (4) emotion, and (5) physical. Moreover, these must be integrated into our lives along with social competencies in the interpersonal domains of (1) friends, (2) finances, (3) social (society), (4) career, and (5) family.

This model draws attention to important issues that we face every day in relation to vision, character, and competence, as described by Huitt (1999):

- "Vision has to do with dreams and goals of what is possible and desirable to do."
- "Character deals with the habits or patterns of thinking, feeling, willing, and behaving that relate to right and wrong, to justice and equity, and to morality and ethics."
- "Competence concerns the knowledge, values, attitudes, and skills that link to successful performance."

"All three issues are intertwined and difficult to isolate, although our experience suggests these can be observed separately in people."

In the next chapter, we will see how this approach helps us to understand how we develop our sense of self through communication.

THE INTERPERSONAL IMPERATIVE

Have you ever thought about why we communicate with others? Psychologist William Schutz (1966) developed *interpersonal needs theory,* which asserts that our tendency to create and sustain relationships depends on how well they meet three basic needs. The first need is for affection, the desire to give and receive love and liking. The second need is for inclusion, the desire to be social and to be included in groups. The third need is for control, which is a desire to influence the people and events in our lives.

Expanding Schutz's ideas, Abraham Maslow (1968) proposed that we communicate to meet a range of human needs. According to Maslow, basic needs must be satisfied before we can focus on those that are more abstract (Figure 1.2). Communication is a primary means of meeting needs at each level. Although Maslow's theory is now making way for more complex and holistic models, it will serve to help us understand how integrated communication is in our daily lives.

Physiological Needs

At the most basic level, humans need to survive, and communication helps us meet this need. To survive, babies must alert others when they are hungry or in pain. And others must respond to these needs, or the babies will die. Beyond survival, children need interaction if they are to thrive. Linda Mayes (2002), a physician at the Child Study Center at Yale University, reports that children can suffer lasting damage if they are traumatized early in their lives. Trauma increases the stress hormones that circulate through infants' fragile brains. One result is inhibited growth of the limbic system, which controls emotions. Adults who have suffered abuse as children often have reduced memory ability,

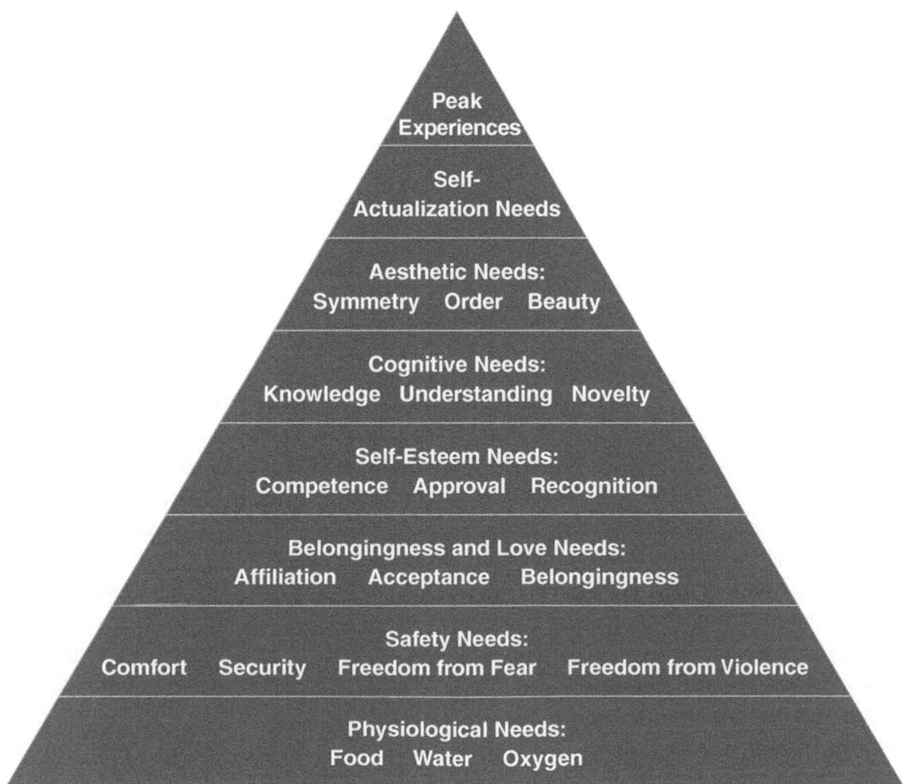

FIGURE 1.2

A Hierarchy of Needs

© John Terence Turner/Photographer's Choice/Getty Images

anxiety, hyperactivity, and impulsiveness (Begley, 1997). Further, good communication between doctors and patients is related to effective treatment and to patients' mental well-being (Fleishman, Sherbourne, & Crystal, 2000). Noted Canadian researcher Dr. Fraser Mustard (1994) has tied infant brain development to social and physical environments, stressing the impact of early infant care on learning, behaviour, and health throughout the life span.

As we grow older, we continue to rely on communication to survive and to thrive. We discuss medical problems with doctors to stay healthy and our effectiveness in communicating affects what jobs we get and how much we earn to pay for medical care, food, leisure activities, and housing. Furthermore, researchers have amassed impressive evidence to document the close link between physical health and relationships with others (Kupfer, First, & Regier, 2002; Lane, 2000; Segrin, 1998). Heart disease is more common among people who lack strong interpersonal relationships (Ornish, 1998), and arthritis patients who have strong social support experience less severe symptoms and live longer than patients without such support (Whan, 1997).

Safety Needs

We also meet safety needs through communication. If your roof is leaking or if termites have invaded your apartment, you must talk with the property manager or owner to get the problem solved so that you have safe shelter. If someone is threatening you, you need to talk with law enforcement officers to gain protection. If your friend has been drinking and you take the car keys and say, "I'll drive you home," you may save a life. We may go online to research symptoms we have or to learn about medical conditions that our friends or family members have developed. In an era when AIDS and other sexually transmitted diseases are widespread, couples must talk with each other about safer sex. The ability to discuss private and difficult issues having to do with sex is essential to our safety, although it may be embarrassing, as Aara comments.

Student Voices

Aara:

It is easier to have sex than to talk about it. I'm having to learn how to bring up the topic of safety and how to be assertive about protection. I didn't use to do that because it's embarrassing, but I'd rather be embarrassed than dead.

Communication also helps protect us from dangers and harms. When foods are determined to be unsafe, news media inform the public. Car manufacturers send owners recall messages when defects in a model are found. Workers persuade managers to do something about unsafe working conditions, and professionals communicate with each other to do their jobs. Communication is needed, too, to protect us from environmental toxins. Residents in communities with toxic waste dumps must communicate with officials and media to call attention to environmental toxins that endanger their physical survival and safety. Later, the officials and the media may communicate to compel corrective action from those responsible for dumping toxic wastes. We need only witness the staggering effects of the Walkerton water contamination in Ontario in 2000 to recognize how crucial it is to have effective and timely communication.

Belonging Needs

The third level in Maslow's hierarchy is belonging, or social, needs. All of us need others in order to be happy, to enjoy life, to feel comfortable on the job, and to fit into social groups. We want others' company, acceptance, and affirmation, and we want to give acceptance and affirmation to others.

We communicate to meet belonging needs by talking with others, sharing thoughts and feelings online, watching films together, and working on project teams. Also, interpersonal communication introduces us to ideas that broaden our perspectives. Perhaps, after talking with someone, you've thought, "I never saw it that way before" or "Gee, that really changes my attitude." In his commentary, Chad notes the importance of this type of communication.

© 2009 Jupiterimages Corporation

When in your life have you felt unsafe? How did it affect communication?

The connection between belonging needs and well-being is well established. One study found that people who lack strong social ties are 200 to 300 percent more likely to die prematurely than those whose social ties are strong (Narem, 1980). Other reports conclude that heart disease is far more prevalent in people lacking strong interpersonal relationships than in those who have healthy connections with others (Cowley, 1998; Kupfer et al., 2002; Ornish, 1999; Ruberman, 1992). Belonging is also important in our careers. We want to feel that we're a part of work groups, and we want to be part of the formal and informal communication networks in organizations.

Most of us take socialization for granted. We are born into families, and they socialize us as members of the human world of meaning and action. But what if there were no humans around to socialize you? Would you still be human?

A particularly dramatic finding is that people who are deprived of human interaction for a long time may fail to develop a concept of themselves as humans. Two such cases are documented by sociologist Kingsley Davis (1940, 1947). Anna and Isabelle, two girls who were not related to one another, received minimal human contact and care during the first six years of their lives. Authorities who discovered the children reported that both girls lived in dark, dank attics. Anna and Isabelle were so undeveloped intellectually that they behaved like six-month-olds. Anna was startlingly apathetic and unresponsive to others. She did not progress well despite care, contact, and nutrition. She died four years after she was discovered. Isabelle fared better. When she was found, she communicated by grunts and gestures and was responsive to human interaction. After two years in systematic therapy, Isabelle's intelligence approached normal levels for her age.

Student Voices

Chad:

I'm not usually a really social person, but after one of our classmates died in a freak accident, I needed to be around other people. I think a lot of my friends did. We needed to connect with others. It was almost like we felt our class had been endangered and we were trying to rebuild it by talking with others.

How do we explain the difference between these two isolated children and what happened to them? There was one major difference. Anna was left alone all the time and had no human contact. Food was periodically put in her room, but nobody talked to her or played with her. Isabelle, on the other hand, shared her space with her mother, who was deaf and mute. The family had renounced both of them and sequestered them with each other.

Although Isabelle didn't have the advantage of normal family interaction, she did have contact with a mother who loved her. Because the mother was deaf and mute, she couldn't teach Isabelle to speak, but she did teach Isabelle to interact with gestures and sounds that both of them understood. Thus, Isabelle suffered less extreme deprivation than Anna.

The need for social contact continues throughout our lives. Even people who have been raised with normal social interaction can be affected if such interaction is lacking later in life. People who have few friends are more likely to experience depression, anxiety, and fatigue (Jones & Moore, 1989; Segrin, 1998).

Self-Esteem Needs

Moving up Maslow's hierarchy, we find self-esteem needs, which involve valuing and respecting ourselves and being valued and respected by others. As we will see in Chapter 2, communication is the primary way we figure out who we are and who we can be. We gain our first sense of self from others who communicate how they see us. Parents and other family members tell children they are pretty or plain, smart or slow, good or bad, helpful or difficult. As family members communicate their perceptions, children begin to form images of themselves.

Communication Notes

INTERPERSONAL COMMUNICATION ON THE JOB

When the National Association of Colleges and Employers asked 480 companies what applicant qualities and abilities were most important to them in making hiring decisions, communication skills were at the top of the list (Schneider, 1999). According to the employers, effective job performance depends critically on skills such as expressing oneself clearly, listening well to others, creating productive working climates, and being sensitive to differences in how people perceive communication.

The employers noted that they see far too many applicants who don't know how to articulate their ideas clearly or how to interact effectively with others. Interpersonal communication skills are a key asset in applying for a job and for advancement in a career.

To find out more about the relationship between effective interpersonal communication and career success, read the 1999 Roper Starch poll results in *How Americans Communicate* at www.natcom.org/nca/index.asp?downloadid=197.

This process continues throughout life as we see ourselves reflected in others' eyes. In elementary school, our teachers and peers influence our perceptions of how smart we are, how good we are at soccer, and how attractive we are. As we date and form romantic relationships, our partners reflect their views of us as loving or unloving, generous or selfish, open or closed, and trustworthy or untrustworthy. In professional life, our co-workers and supervisors communicate in ways that suggest how much they respect us and our abilities. Through all the stages of our lives, our self-esteem is shaped by how others communicate with us.

People who lack strong interpersonal communication skills are unlikely to rise to the top of their fields, and many of them suffer lowered self-esteem as a result (Morreale, 2001).

Cognitive Needs

Maslow (1968) later inserted two more growth needs into his hierarchy—cognitive and aesthetic needs. We have a cognitive need to know, to understand, and to explore. As humans, we seek more than survival, safety, belonging, and esteem. We also thrive on growth. Each of us wants to cultivate new dimensions, enlarge our perspectives, engage in challenging and different experiences, and learn new skills.

Others also help us through inspiration and teaching. Gandhi, for instance, was a model of strength who didn't depend on aggression. Seeing him embody passive resistance with grace inspired thousands of Indians to define themselves as passive resisters. The teachings of religious leaders such as Lao-tzu, Confucius, Jesus, Muhammad, and Buddha also inspire people to grow personally. In a similar vein, consider the accomplishments of Canadians who inspire us and help create a Canadian identity—Pierre Trudeau, Margaret Atwood, Emily Carr, and Wayne Gretzky, to name a few. As we interact with teachers and leaders who inspire us, we may come to understand their visions of the world and of themselves and perhaps weave those into our own self-concepts.

Aesthetic Needs

Many individuals find that they experience a sense of personal fulfillment when they have beauty, symmetry, and order in their lives. Music, art, athletics, or an appreciation of the wonders of nature often bring a richness and joy to our spirits. Communication fosters our growth as individuals. It is often in interaction with others that we first recognize possibilities for who we can be—possibilities that hadn't occurred to us. Perhaps you can recall someone who first noticed you had a talent and encouraged you to cultivate it. Who was that person? What messages did you receive that encouraged you to nurture your talents?

Self-Actualization Needs

According to Maslow, the most abstract human need is self-actualization. Maslow defined *self-actualization* as fully developing and using our unique "talents, capacities, potentialities" (1954/1970, p. 150). To achieve this, we need to refine talents that we have already developed to some degree, while we also cultivate new potential in ourselves. As humans, we seek more than survival, safety, belonging, and esteem. We also thrive on growth. Each of us wants to cultivate new dimensions of mind, heart, and spirit. We seek to enlarge our perspectives, engage in challenging and different experiences, learn new skills, and test ourselves in unfamiliar territories. To become our fullest selves—to self-actualize—we must embrace the idea that we are always evolving, growing, changing.

Communication fosters our personal growth. Therapists can be powerful resources in helping

Student Voices

Adam:

Mr. Bentley really helped me when I had my first job. It wasn't much—just serving at a sandwich shop—but he mentored me. He noticed I was awkward interacting with people, and he said I could learn social skills. He showed me how to be more effective—how to make customers feel comfortable, how to notice subtle cues that they needed something. Before that job, I'd thought of myself as kind of an introvert, somebody not very good with people. But Mr. Bentley saw a possibility in me that I hadn't seen in myself, and, as a result, I developed social skills and confidence that I never had before.

us identify our potential. Often, therapy assists us in our quest to know, understand, and improve ourselves (Maslow, 1959/1970). In addition, friends, family, co-workers, and teachers can help us recognize promise in ourselves that we otherwise might not see. For one of the authors, one such person was her father, who told her that she had some ability as a writer. He encouraged her to write, and he taught her how to edit and rewrite so that she developed her skill as a writer. Had he not nurtured this dimension in her, she doubts that writing would be a major part of her life today. Adam recalls how such a person affected him in his first job.

Another way in which we seek personal growth is by experimenting with new versions of ourselves. For this, too, we rely on communication. Sometimes we talk with others about ways we want to grow. At other times, we try out new styles of identity without telling anyone what we're doing. Some people experiment with their identities in chat rooms, where visual cues won't expose their skin colour, gender, age, or other characteristics. For instance, some people engage in gender swapping in online communication—males present themselves as females, and females present themselves as males (Baym, 2002). Gender swapping allows us to imagine ourselves as the other sex and to try on an identity that is divorced from our physical one. In both online and face-to-face communication, we see how others respond, and we decide whether we like the effects of the new identity or whether we need to go back to the drawing board. We could not assess changes in ourselves without feedback from others. Lashelle's commentary stresses this point.

Student Voices

Lashelle:

A person who changed my life was Mrs. Dickenson, my high school history teacher. She thought I was really smart, and she helped me see myself that way. I'd never considered myself all that intelligent and I sure hadn't thought I would go to college, but Mrs. Dickenson helped me to see a whole new image of who I could be. She stayed after school a lot of days to talk to me about my future and to help me get ready for the SAT. If it weren't for her, I wouldn't be in college now.

Self-Transcendence

Self-transcendence helps us to connect to something beyond the ego or to be of assistance to others in their efforts to find self-fulfillment and realize their potential. Others also help us grow by introducing us to new experiences and ways of thinking. Conversations can enrich our perspective of ourselves and our values, relationships, events, and situations, thus enlarging us.

Peak Experiences—Participating Effectively in a Diverse Society

To the needs identified previously, we must add an eighth—peak experiences. As we navigate in this new millennium, we need to know how to live effectively in a richly diverse society. Our world includes people of different ethnicities, genders, social classes, sexual orientations, ages, and abilities. Canada is particularly diverse. Geographically, it spans an area rivalled only by Russia, China, and the United States. Socially and economically, there are vast differences from north to south and east to west. The aboriginal cultures across Canada are also as diverse as the geography. Many job applications routinely state, "Must be able to work in a cross-cultural environment." To function effectively in a world of such diversity, we rely on communication. Through interaction with others, we learn about experiences and lifestyles that differ from our own; in addition, we share our experiences and values with people who seem unlike us in certain ways. Through interaction, diverse individuals come to understand their differences and similarities, and this recognition fosters personal growth.

Participating effectively in a diverse social world is critical to success in professional life, and the multicultural mosaic of Canadian life brings many communication challenges. In a study of the most sought-after employability skills in the Canadian workforce, communication skills rank highest, particularly "the recognition and respect for people's diversity and differences" (Conference Board of Canada, 1992).

Canada is one of the few countries in the world that has a *Multiculturalism Act*. Passed in 1988, it is devoted to the preservation and enhancement of multiculturalism in Canadian communities. Like the other needs in Maslow's hierarchy, living in a diverse world becomes salient to us only when our more basic needs have been met. As long as we need food, shelter, and a sense of belonging, appreciating and supporting diversity may not be an issue to us. When the more basic needs are met, however, we recognize the importance of appreciating diversity. It's also the case, however, that learning to appreciate and support diversity may help us meet some of our more basic needs. For example, our safety may depend on communicating with someone from a different culture, and we may meet belonging needs by joining groups with people who represent a range of ethnicities, religions, sexual orientations, and so forth. One of the most vital functions of communication is to help us understand and participate in a diverse world.

Apply the Idea

COMMUNICATION AND YOUR NEEDS

How do the needs we've discussed show up in your life? To find out, try this:

- *Think about your communication over the last few days and classify each interaction according to one of the eight needs we discussed. How much of your communication focused on each need?*

  ______ physiological
  ______ safety
  ______ belonging
  ______ self-esteem
  ______ cognitive
  ______ aesthetic
  ______ self-actualization/self-transcendence
  ______ peak experiences (participating effectively in a diverse society)

Realizing that interpersonal communication is a matter of degree is a first step in understanding. Yet, we still don't have an appreciation of all that's involved in the process of interpersonal communication. To gain that, we'll now examine three models of interpersonal communication to see how interpersonal communication differs from public or social interaction.

So far, we've seen that interpersonal communication is a primary way to meet a range of human needs. Now, we need to define interpersonal communication precisely. We'll first consider three efforts to model the communication process. Following that, we'll define interpersonal communication and discuss key aspects of our definition.

CONCEPTS AT A GLANCE

Three Models of Interpersonal Communication

1. Linear
2. Interactive
3. Transactional

MODELS OF INTERPERSONAL COMMUNICATION

A **model*** is a representation of what something is and how it works. Early models of interpersonal communication were simplistic, so we will discuss them very briefly. We'll look more closely at a current model that offers sophisticated insight into the process of interpersonal communication.

Linear Models

The first model of interpersonal communication (Laswell, 1948) depicted communication as a linear, or one-way, process in which one person acts on another person. This was a verbal model that consisted of five questions describing a sequence of acts that make up communication:

Who?
Says what?
In what channel?
To whom?
With what effect?

A year later, Claude Shannon and Warren Weaver (1949) offered a revised model that added the feature of noise. **Noise** is anything that causes a loss of information as the information flows from source to destination. Noise might be static in a phone line or activities going on that distract the sender or receiver of information. Figure 1.3 shows Shannon and Weaver's model.

These early **linear models** had serious shortcomings. They portrayed communication as flowing in only one direction, from a sender to a passive receiver. This implies that listeners never send messages and that they absorb only passively what speakers say. But this isn't how communication really occurs. Listeners nod,

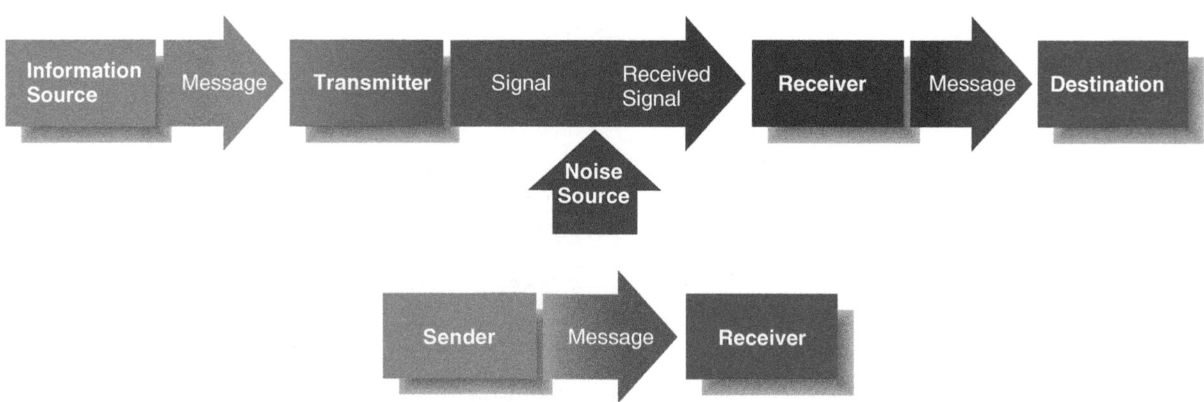

FIGURE 1.3

The Linear Model of Communication (Adapted from Shannon & Weaver, 1949)

*Boldfaced terms are defined in the glossary at the back of the book.

frown, smile, look bored or interested, and so forth, and they actively work to make sense of others' messages. Linear models also erred in representing communication as a sequence of actions in which one step (listening) follows an earlier step (talking). In actual interaction, however, speaking and listening often occur simultaneously or overlap. As you talk to friends, you notice whether they seem engaged or bored. If they nod, you're likely to continue talking; if they yawn or turn away from you, you might stop. On the job, co-workers exchange ideas, and each listens and responds while the others speak; those who are speaking are also listening for cues from others. Online, as we compose our messages, comments from others pop up on our screens. At any moment in the process of interpersonal communication, all participants are sending and receiving messages and adapting to one another.

Interactive Models

Interactive models portrayed communication as a process in which listeners give **feedback**, which is response to a message (Weiner, 1967). In addition, interactive models recognize that communicators create and interpret messages within personal fields of experience (see Figure 1.4). The more communicators' fields of experience overlap, the better they can understand each other. When fields of experience don't overlap enough, misunderstandings may occur. Lori Ann's commentary gives an example of this type of misunderstanding.

Although the interactive model is an improvement over the linear model, it still portrays communication as a sequential process in which one person is a sender and another is a receiver. In reality, everyone who is involved in communication

Student Voices

Lori Ann:

I was born in a small town, and all my life I've spoken to people whether I know them or not. I say "Hello" or something to a person I pass on the street, just to be friendly. When I went to a junior college in Toronto, I got in trouble for being so friendly. When I spoke to guys I didn't know, they thought I was coming on to them or something. And other girls would just look at me like I was odd. I'd never realized that friendliness could be misinterpreted.

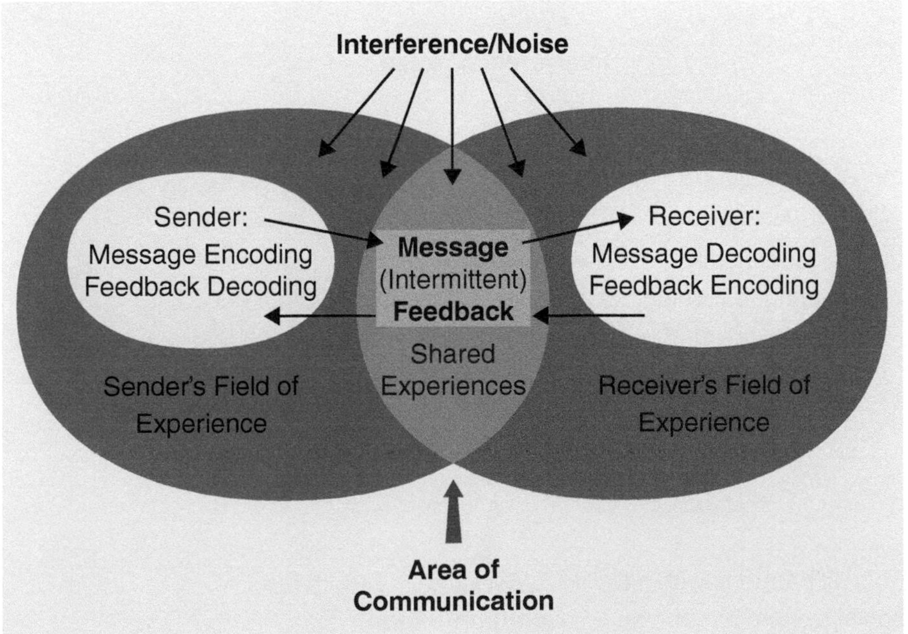

FIGURE 1.4

The Interactive Model of Communication (Adapted from Schramm, 1955)

both sends and receives messages. Interactive models also fail to capture the dynamic nature of interpersonal communication and the ways it changes over time. For example, two people communicate more openly and casually after months of exchanging e-mail messages than they did the first time they met in a chat room. Two co-workers communicate more easily and effectively after months of working together on a project team.

Transactional Models

The **transactional model** of interpersonal communication emphasizes the dynamism of interpersonal communication and the multiple roles people assume during the process. In addition, this model includes the feature of time to call our attention to the fact that messages, noise, and fields of experience vary over time (see Figure 1.5).

The transactional model recognizes that each communicator's field of experience and the shared field of experience between communicators changes over time. As we encounter new people and have new experiences that broaden us, we change how we interact with others. As we get to know others over time, relationships may become more informal and intimate. For example, people who meet online sometimes decide to get together face to face, and a serious friendship or romance may blossom.

The transactional model also makes it clear that communication occurs within systems that affect what and how people communicate and what meanings are created. Those systems, or contexts, include the shared systems of both communicators (shared campus, town, workplace, social groups, and culture) and the personal systems of each person (family, religious association, friends).

Finally, we should emphasize that the transactional model doesn't label one person a sender and the other a receiver. Instead, both people are defined as communicators who participate equally and often simultaneously in the communication process. This means that, at a given moment in communication,

FIGURE 1.5

The Transactional Model of Communication

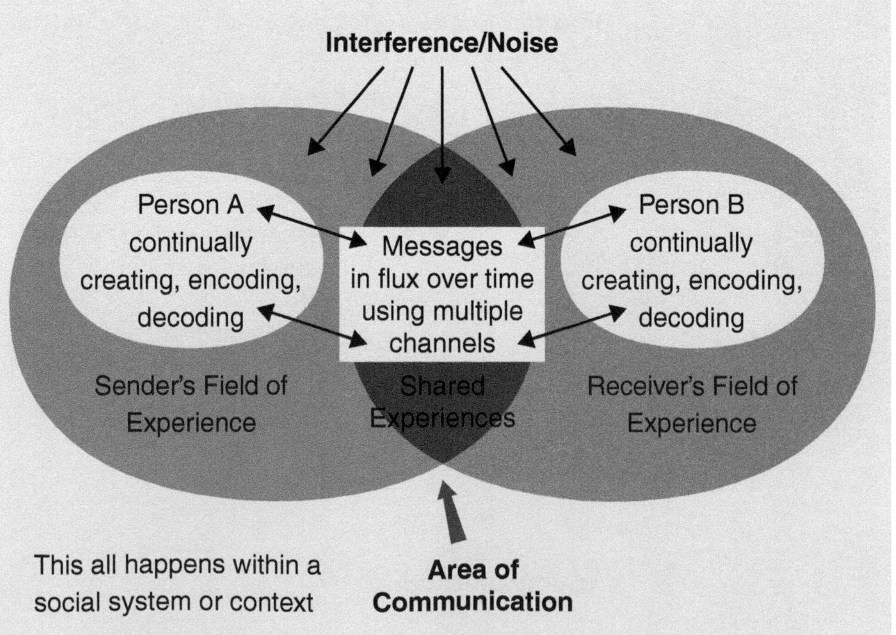

you may be sending a message (speaking or nodding your head), receiving a message, or doing both at the same time (interpreting what someone says while nodding to show you are interested). Because communicators affect each other (Rothwell, 2004), interpersonal communication involves ethical responsibilities. Our verbal and nonverbal behaviours can enhance or diminish others, just as their communication can enhance or diminish us.

Now that we have examined models of interpersonal communication and learned what is involved in the process, we're ready to develop a precise definition.

DEFINING INTERPERSONAL COMMUNICATION

When asked to distinguish interpersonal communication from communication in general, many people say that interpersonal communication involves fewer people, often just two. According to this definition, an exchange between a homeowner and a plumber would be interpersonal, but a conversation involving parents and three children would not. Although interpersonal communication often involves only two or three people, this isn't a useful definition.

Perhaps you are thinking that intimate contexts define interpersonal communication. Using this standard, we would say that a couple on a first date in a romantic restaurant engages in more interpersonal communication than an established couple in a shopping mall.

The best way to define interpersonal communication is by focusing on what happens between people, not where they are or how many are present. For starters, then, we can say that interpersonal communication is a distinct type of interaction between people.

A Communication Continuum

We can begin to understand the unique character of interpersonal communication by tracing the meaning of the word *interpersonal.* It is derived from the prefix *inter,* meaning "between," and the word *person;* interpersonal communication literally occurs between people. In one sense, all communication happens between people, yet many interactions don't involve us personally. Communication exists on a continuum from impersonal to interpersonal (see Figure 1.6).

Much of our communication involves very little personal interaction. Sometimes we don't acknowledge others as people at all but treat them as objects; they bag our groceries, direct us around highway construction, and so forth. In other instances, we do acknowledge people, yet we interact with them in terms of their social roles rather than as unique individuals. For instance, one of the authors often runs into neighbours when she is walking her dog. They engage in small talk and perhaps comment on home projects. Through this kind of interaction, they acknowledge each other as people, but they don't engage in intimate talk. With a select few people, we all communicate in deeply personal ways. These distinctions are captured in poetic terms by the philosopher Martin Buber (1970), who distinguished among three levels of communication: I–It, I–You, and I–Thou.

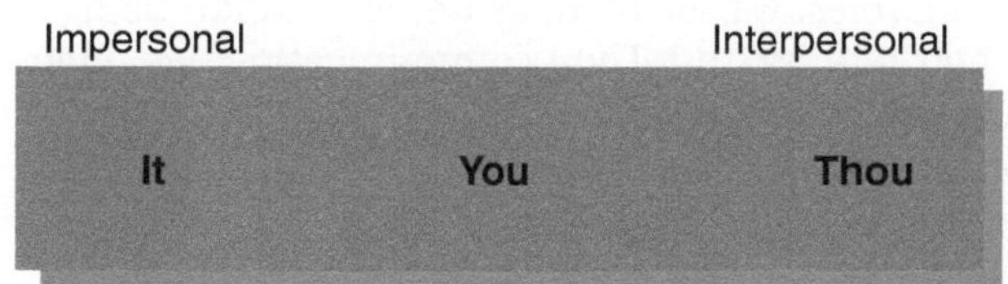

FIGURE 1.6

A Communication Continuum

Student Voices

Jason:

At this school, I get treated like a number a lot of the time. When I go to see my adviser, he asks what my identification number is—not what my name is. Most of my professors don't know my name. In high school, all the teachers called on us by name. It felt more human there. Sometimes I feel like an "it" on this campus.

I–It Communication

In an **I–It relationship**, we treat others very impersonally, almost as objects. In I–It communication, we do not acknowledge the humanity of other persons; we may not even affirm their existence. Salespeople, servers in restaurants, and clerical staff are often treated not as people but as instruments to take orders and produce what we want. We also tend not to have personal conversations with phone solicitors. In the extreme form of I–It relationships, others are not even acknowledged. When a homeless person asks for money for food, some people do not even respond, but look through and beyond the person as if she or he isn't there. In dysfunctional families, parents may ignore children, thereby treating the children as "its," not as unique individuals. Students on large campuses may also feel they are treated as "its," not as people, as Jason does.

I–You Communication

The second level that Buber (1970) identified is **I–You communication**, which accounts for the majority of our interactions. People acknowledge one another as more than objects, but they don't fully engage each other as unique individuals. For example, suppose when you're shopping, a salesclerk asks, "May I help you?" Chances are you won't have a deep conversation with the clerk, but you might treat him or her as more than an object (Wood, 2006). Perhaps you say, "I'm just browsing today. You know how it is at the end of the month—no money." The clerk might laugh and commiserate about how money gets tight by the end of each month. In this interaction, the clerk doesn't treat you as a faceless shopper, and you don't treat the clerk as just an agent of the store.

I–You relationships may also be more personal than interactions with salesclerks. For instance, we talk with others in classes, on the job, and on sports teams in ways that are somewhat personal. The same is true of interaction in chat rooms, where people meet to share ideas and common interests. Interaction is still guided by our roles as peers, as members of a class or team, and as people who have common interests, yet we do affirm the existence of others and recognize them as individuals within those roles. Teachers and students often have I–You relationships. In the workplace, the majority of our relationships are of the I–You sort. We communicate less deeply with most people in our social circles than with those we love most. Casual friends, work associates, and distant family members typically engage in I–You communication.

I–Thou Communication

The rarest kind of relationship involves **I–Thou communication**. Buber (1970) regarded this as the highest form of human dialogue because each person affirms the other as cherished and unique. When we interact on an I–Thou level, we meet others in their wholeness and individuality. Instead of dealing with them as occupants of social roles, we see them as unique human beings whom we know and accept in their totality. In I–Thou communication, we open ourselves fully, trusting others to accept us as we are, with our virtues and vices, hopes and fears, strengths and weaknesses.

Buber (1970) believed that only in I–Thou relationships do we become fully human, which for him meant that we discard the guises we use most of

Apply the Idea

COMMUNICATING IN YOUR RELATIONSHIPS

Consider how Buber's theory of communication applies to your life. Identify someone with whom you have each kind of relationship: I–It, I–You, I–Thou. Describe what needs and values each relationship satisfies.

How does communication differ in the relationships? What don't you say in I–It and I–You relationships that you do say in I–Thou relationships? How do different levels of communication affect the closeness you feel with others? Which of these three kinds of relationship can be created or sustained through e-mail and chat rooms?

the time and allow ourselves to be completely genuine (Stewart, 1986). Much of our communication involves what Buber called "seeming," in which we're preoccupied with our image and careful to manage how we present ourselves. In I–Thou relationships, however, we engage in "being," through which we reveal who we really are and how we really feel. I–Thou relationships are not common, because we can't afford to reveal ourselves totally to everyone all the time. Thus, I–Thou relationships and the communication in them are rare and special.

CONCEPTS AT A GLANCE

Features of Interpersonal Communication

- Selective
- Systemic
- Unique
- Ongoing
- Interactive
- Individual
- Personal
- Meaningful

Features of Interpersonal Communication

Building on Buber's poetic description (1970), we can define interpersonal communication as selective, systemic, unique, ongoing transactions that allow people to reflect and build personal knowledge of one another and create shared meanings. We'll discuss the key terms in this definition so that we have a common understanding of interpersonal communication.

Selective

First, as we noted earlier, we don't want to communicate intimately with the majority of people we encounter. In some cases, we neither want nor need to communicate with others even at the I–You level. For instance, if we get a phone call from a pollster, we may respond only to the questions and not engage the caller in any personal way. We invest the effort and take the risks of opening ourselves fully with only a few people. As Buber (1970) realized, most of our communication occurs on I–It or I–You levels. This is fine because I–Thou relationships take more time, energy, and courage than we are willing to offer to everyone.

Alamy/GetStock

Systemic

Interpersonal communication is also **systemic**, which means that it takes place within various systems. As the transactional model notes, communication

Communication Notes

POOR INTERPERSONAL COMMUNICATION AS THE NUMBER ONE CAUSE OF DIVORCE

Poll results reported in 1999 show that a majority of people perceive communication problems as the number one reason that marriages fail (Roper Starch poll, 1999). The research organization Roper Starch asked 1001 Americans a variety of questions about the role of communication in their lives. One finding overshadowed all others: Regardless of age, race, sex, or income level, Americans reported that communication problems are the most common cause of divorce; 53 percent of those who were polled said that ineffective communication was the principal reason for divorce.

Compare this with the frequency with which people named other causes of divorce: money problems, 29 percent; interference from family members, 7 percent; sexual problems, 5 percent; previous relationships, 3 percent; and children, 3 percent.

To read the full results of this poll, go to www.natcom.org/nca/index.asp?downloadid=197.

Use your InfoTrac® College Edition to find out more about the relationship between successful relationships and effective interpersonal communication. Conduct key word searches for these terms: *marriage and communication, intimacy and communication,* and *relationships.*

occurs in contexts that influence events and the meanings we attribute to the communication. The communication between you and the authors right now is embedded in multiple systems, including the interpersonal communication course, academic institutions, and North American society. Each of these systems influences what we expect of each other, what we write, and how you interpret what you read. The ways people communicate also vary across cultures. Whereas North Americans tend to communicate assertively and look at one another, in some traditional Asian societies assertion and eye contact are considered rude. First Nations people are traditionally less verbal than Canadians of European heritage.

Consider an example of the systemic character of communication. Suppose Ian gives Cheryl a solid gold pendant and says, "I wanted to show how much I care about you." What do his words mean? That depends in large part on the systems within which he and Cheryl interact. If Ian and Cheryl have just started dating, an expensive gift means one thing; if they have been married for 20 years, it means something different. On the other hand, if they don't have an established relationship and Cheryl is engaged to Manuel, Ian's gift may have yet another meaning. What if Ian argued with Cheryl the previous day? Then, perhaps, the gift is to apologize more than to show love. If Ian is rich, a solid gold pendant may be less impressive than if he is short of cash. Systems that affect what this communication means include Cheryl and Ian's relationship, their socioeconomic classes, cultural norms for gift-giving, and Cheryl's and Ian's personal histories. All these contexts affect their interaction and its meaning.

Because interpersonal communication is systemic, the situation, time, people, culture, personal histories, and so forth interact to affect meanings. We can't just add up the various parts of a system to understand their impact on communication. Instead, we have to recognize that all parts of a system interact;

each part affects all others. In other words, elements of communication systems are interdependent; each element is tied to all of the other elements.

Recall also that all systems include noise, which is anything that distorts communication or interferes with people's understandings of one another. Noise in communication systems is inevitable, but we can be aware that it exists and try to compensate for the difficulties it causes.

There are four kinds of noise. *Physiological noise* is distraction caused by hunger, fatigue, headaches, medications, and other factors that affect how we feel and think. *Physical noise* is interference in our environments, such as noises made by others, overly dim or bright lights, extreme temperatures, and crowded conditions. *Psychological noise* involves qualities in us that affect how we communicate and how we interpret others. For instance, if you are preoccupied with a problem, you may be inattentive. Likewise, prejudice and defensive feelings can interfere with communication. Our needs may also affect how we interpret others. For example, if we really need affirmation of our professional competence, we may be predisposed to perceive others as communicating more praise for our work than they really do.

Finally, *semantic noise* exists when words themselves are not mutually understood. Authors sometimes create semantic noise by using jargon or unnecessarily technical language. For instance, to discuss noise, the authors could have written, "Communication can be egregiously obstructed by phenomena extrinsic to an exchange that actuate misrepresentations and symbolic incongruities." Although that sentence may be accurate, it's filled with semantic noise.

In summary, when we say that communication is systemic, we mean three things. First, all communication occurs within multiple systems that affect meanings. Second, all parts and all systems of communication are interdependent, so they affect one another. Finally, all communication systems have noise, which can be physiological, physical, psychological, or semantic.

CONCEPTS AT A GLANCE

Four Kinds of Noise

1. Physical
2. Physiological
3. Psychological
4. Semantic

Student Voices

Syki:

I wish professors would learn about semantic noise. I really try to pay attention in class and to learn, but the way some faculty talk makes it impossible to understand what they mean, especially if English is a second language. I wish they would remember that we're not specialists like they are, so we don't know all the technical words.

Unique

At the deepest level, interpersonal communication is also unique. In relationships that go beyond social roles, every person is unique and is therefore irreplaceable. We can substitute people in I–It relationships and even in I–You relationships (one clerk can ring up purchases as well as another; we can get another racquetball buddy), but we can't replace intimates. When we lose intimates, we find new friends and romantic partners, but they aren't interchangeable with the ones we lost.

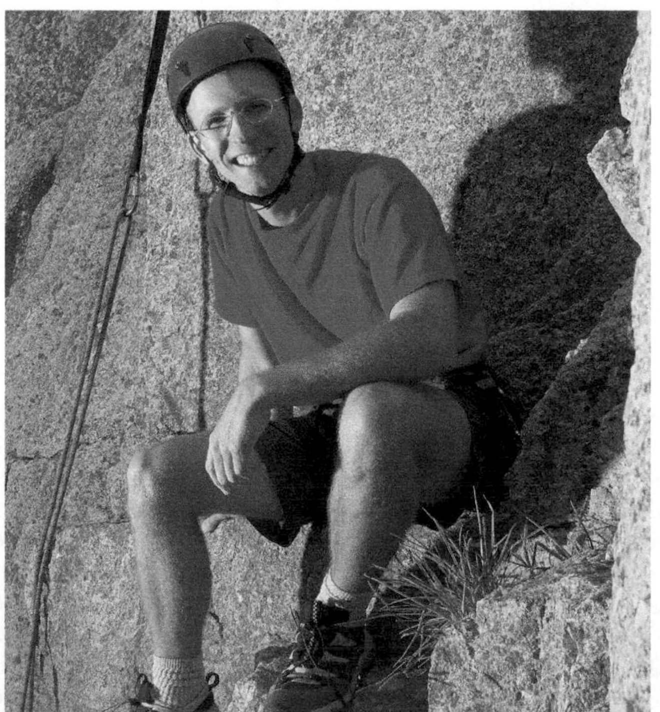

How is your uniqueness defined?

Just as every person is unique, so is each friendship and romantic relationship. Each develops its own distinctive patterns and rhythms and even special vocabulary that are not part of other interpersonal relationships. In the process of becoming close, people work out personal roles and rules for interaction, and these may deviate from general social rules and roles (Dainton, 2006; Duck, 2006; Wood, 2006). With one friend, you might go skating and get together for athletic events. With a different, equally close friend, you might talk openly about feelings. One of the authors and her sister Carolyn constantly play jokes on each other and engage in verbal duels in which they try to one-up each other. Another close friend doesn't enjoy verbal jousting, so it's not part of their interaction. As these examples show, interpersonal communication involves unique people who interact in relation to each other.

Student Voices

Jana:

My daughter is my best friend, but it wasn't always that way. As a child, she was very shy and dependent. She was a sullen teenager who resented everything I said and did. Now that she's 22, we've become really good friends. But even now, our relationship has all of the echoes of who we were with each other at different times in our lives.

Ongoing

Interpersonal communication is an ongoing, continuous **process**. This means, first, that communication evolves over time, becoming more personal as people interact. Friendships and romantic relationships gain depth and significance over the course of time, and they may also decline in quality over time. Relationships on the job also evolve over time. Ellen may mentor Craig when he starts working at her firm, but over time they may become equal colleagues. Because relationships are dynamic, they don't stay the same but continually change, just as we do.

An ongoing process also has no discrete beginnings and endings. Suppose a friend stops by and confides in you about a troubling personal problem. When did that communication begin? Although it may seem to have started when the friend came by, earlier interactions may have led the friend to feel that it was safe to talk to you and that you would care about the problem. We can't be sure, then, when this communication began. Similarly, we don't know where it will end. Perhaps it ends when the friend leaves, but perhaps it doesn't. Maybe your response to the problem helps your friend see new options. Maybe what you learn changes how you feel toward your friend. Because communication is ongoing, we can never be sure when it begins and or ends, as Kate discovered.

Student Voices

Kate:

It's really true about not knowing where communication stops. I'm a peer supporter at my college, and last year a student stopped me in the library. I started to ask her to come back later, because I was trying to finish a paper, but she looked so upset that I put the paper aside. She asked me what I planned to do when I got out of college and if things ever got so rough I just wanted to call it quits. I couldn't figure out what was bothering her, but I felt like I needed to keep listening. After an hour or so, she thanked me for my time and left. A few months later, her best friend told me that she'd been considering killing herself and talking with me was what stopped her.

Because interpersonal interaction is a process, what happens between people is linked to both past and future. In our earlier example, the meaning of Ian's gift reflects prior interactions between him and Cheryl, and their interaction about the gift will affect future interactions. All of our communication occurs in three temporal dimensions: past, which affects what happens now; present; and future, which is moulded by what occurs in this moment (Dixson & Duck, 1993; Wood, 2006). How couples handle early arguments affects how they deal with later ones. Yesterday's e-mail response from a friend influences what we write today and, in turn, what our friend may write back tomorrow. In communication, past, present, and future are always interwoven.

The ongoing quality of interpersonal communication also suggests that we can't stop the process, nor can we edit or unsay what has been said. In this sense, communication is irreversible: We can't take it back. This implies that we have an ethical responsibility to recognize the irreversibility of communication and to communicate carefully.

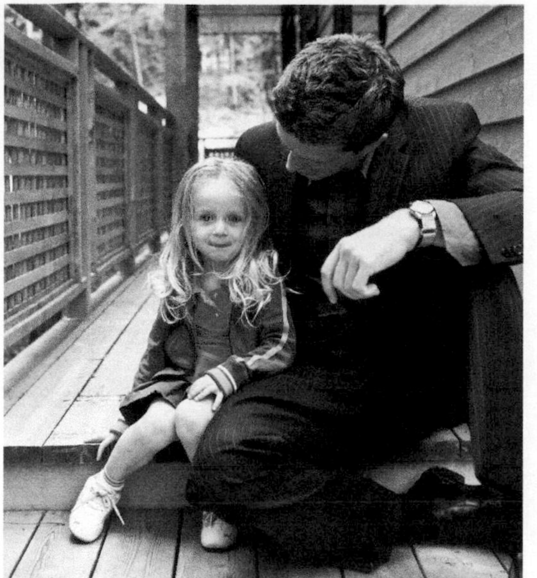

Interactive

Interpersonal communication is a process of interaction between people. As you speak to a friend, your friend smiles; while a teacher explains an idea, you nod to show you understand; as your parent scolds you, you wrinkle your brow thoughtfully or resentfully. In interpersonal encounters, all parties communicate continually and simultaneously.

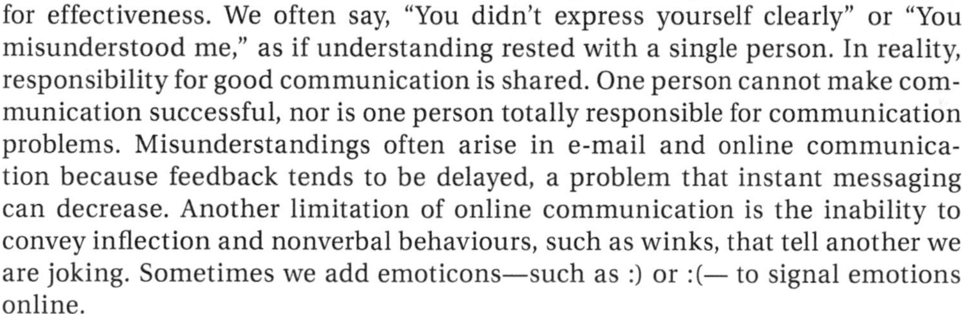

The interactive nature of interpersonal communication implies that communicators share responsibility for effectiveness. We often say, "You didn't express yourself clearly" or "You misunderstood me," as if understanding rested with a single person. In reality, responsibility for good communication is shared. One person cannot make communication successful, nor is one person totally responsible for communication problems. Misunderstandings often arise in e-mail and online communication because feedback tends to be delayed, a problem that instant messaging can decrease. Another limitation of online communication is the inability to convey inflection and nonverbal behaviours, such as winks, that tell another we are joking. Sometimes we add emoticons—such as :) or :(— to signal emotions online.

Interpersonal communication is an ongoing, interactive process, so all participants share responsibility for its effectiveness.

Individual

From Buber (1970), we learned that the deepest level of interpersonal communication involves engaging others as individuals who are unlike anyone else. When we communicate this way, we don't speak from social roles (teacher–student, boss–employee, customer–salesclerk). Instead, in I–Thou communication, we treat others, and are treated by them, as individuals. This is possible only if we learn who they are and if they, in turn, come to understand us as distinct individuals unlike anyone else. We come to understand the unique fears and hopes, problems and joys, needs and abilities of people as we interact with them meaningfully over a period of time. As trust builds, people disclose personal information that allows insight into their unique selves.

Personal

Interpersonal communication fosters personal knowledge and insights. To connect as unique individuals, we have to get to know others personally and understand their thoughts and feelings. With colleagues whom one of the authors has known for more than 25 years, the author understands some of their worries, concerns, and personal issues in ways that she didn't when they first became colleagues. Long-time friends have a history of shared experiences and knowledge that allows them to interact more fully than casual friends can.

Reflective Exercise

What is an example of unique language that you share with another person?

Student Voices

Lizelle:

What I like best about long-term relationships is all the layers that develop. I know the friends I've had since high school in so many ways. I know what they did and felt and dreamed in high school, and I know them as they are now. They have the same kind of in-depth knowledge of me. We tell each other everything, so it sometimes seems that my deepest friends know me better than I know myself.

Interpersonal communication also creates personal knowledge. As our relationships with others deepen, we build trust and learn how to communicate in ways that make each other feel comfortable and safe. The personal knowledge we gain over time in relationships encourages us to know and be known: We share secrets, fears, and experiences that we don't tell to just anyone. This is part of what Buber meant by "being" with others. Personal knowledge is a process, one that grows and builds on itself over time as people communicate interpersonally. Sometimes, we may even feel that our closest friends know us better than we know ourselves, as Lizelle explains.

Sharing personal information and experiences highlights the ethical dimension of interpersonal communication. We can use our knowledge to protect people we care about. We can also use it to hurt those people; for example, personal knowledge allows us to attack vulnerabilities others have revealed to us. Ethical communicators choose not to exploit or treat casually personal information about others.

Meaningful

The heart of interpersonal communication is shared meanings between people (Duck, 1994a, 1994b). We don't merely exchange words when we communicate. Instead, we create meanings as we figure out what each other's words and behaviours stand for, represent, or imply. Meanings grow out of histories of interaction between unique persons. For example, one of the authors and her partner are both continually overcommitted professionally, and they each worry about the pace of the other's life. Often, one of them says to the other, "*Bistari, bistari*." This phrase will mean nothing to you unless you know enough Nepalese to translate it as meaning "Go slowly, go gradually." When one of them says, "*Bistari, bistari*," they not only suggest slowing down but also remind each other of their special time living and trekking in Nepal.

Most close friends and romantic partners develop vocabularies that have meaning only to them. People who work together also develop meanings that grow out of their interactions over time. Once, some faculty members argued for 30 minutes over whether they wanted a semicolon or a dash in a sentence that was part of their mission statement. Now, whenever they start debating small issues, one of them is bound to say, "Semicolon or dash?" Usually this evokes laughter and persuades them to abandon a trivial argument.

You may have noticed that we refer to *meanings,* not just one meaning. This is because interpersonal communication involves two levels of meaning (Watzlawick, Beavin, & Jackson, 1967). The first level, called the **content meaning**, deals

CONCEPTS AT A GLANCE

Levels of Meaning for Interpersonal Communication

1. Content (literal)
2. Relational (relationship)
   Responsiveness
   Liking or affection
   Power or control

with literal, or denotative, meaning. If a parent says to a five-year-old child, "Clean your room now," the content meaning is that the room is to be cleaned immediately.

The second level is the **relationship meaning**. This refers to what communication expresses about relationships between communicators. The relationship meaning of "Clean your room now" is that the parent has the right to order the child; they have an unequal power relationship. If the parent had said, "Would you mind cleaning your room?" the relationship meaning would have reflected a more equal relationship. Suppose a friend says, "You're the only person I can talk to about this," and then discloses something that is worrying him. The content level includes the actual issue itself and the information that you're the only one with whom he will discuss this issue. But what has he told you on the relationship level? He has communicated that he trusts you, he considers you special, and he probably expects you to care about his troubles.

Student Voices

Ana:

My father needs to learn about relationship meanings. Whenever I call home, he asks me if anything's wrong. Then he asks what the news is. If I don't have news to report, he can't understand why I'm calling. Then Mom gets on the phone, and we talk for a while about stuff—nothing important, just stuff. I don't call to tell them big news. I just want to touch base and feel connected.

Scholars have identified three general dimensions or levels of relational meanings. The first dimension is responsiveness, and it refers to how aware of others and involved with them we are. Perhaps you can remember a conversation you had with someone who shuffled papers and glanced at a clock or kept looking at a computer screen while you were talking. If so, you probably felt she wasn't interested in you or what you were saying. Low responsiveness is communicated on the relationship level of meaning when people don't look at us or when they are preoccupied with something other than talking with us. Higher responsiveness is communicated by eye contact, nodding, and feedback, which indicate involvement (Richmond & McCroskey, 2000).

A second dimension of relational meaning is liking, or affection. This concerns the degree of positive or negative feeling that is communicated. Although liking may seem synonymous with responsiveness, the two are actually distinct. We may be responsive to people we don't like but to whom we must pay attention, and we are sometimes preoccupied and unresponsive to people about whom we care. We communicate that we like or dislike others by what we actually say as well as by tone of voice, facial expressions, how close we sit to them, and so forth.

Ryan McVay/Photodisc/Getty Images

What is the power balance here?

Power or control is the third dimension of relational meaning. This refers to the power balance between communicators. A parent may say to a five-year-old, "Clean your room because I say so, that's why." This communicates that the parent has greater power than the child—the power to tell the child what to do. Friends and romantic partners sometimes engage in covert power struggles on the relationship level. One person suggests going to movie X and then to dinner at the pizza parlour. The other responds by saying she doesn't want to see that movie and isn't in the mood for pizza. They could be arguing on the content level about their different preferences for the evening. If arguments over what to do are recurrent and heated, however, chances are the couple is negotiating power. In interpersonal relationships, the relationship level of meaning is often the most important, because it sets the tone for interaction and for how people feel about each other.

Apply the Idea

LEVELS OF MEANING

Reflect on relational meanings in your communication and record examples of the following:

- *Communicating responsiveness*
- *Communicating lack of responsiveness*
- *Expressing liking*
- *Expressing dislike*
- *Expressing superiority*
- *Expressing subordination*
- *Expressing equality*

What does this tell you about the relationship issues being negotiated and expressed in your relationships?

CONCEPTS AT A GLANCE

Eight Principles of Interpersonal Communication

1. We cannot *not* communicate.
2. Interpersonal communication is irreversible.
3. Interpersonal communication involves ethical choices.
4. People construct meanings in interpersonal communication.
5. Metacommunication affects meanings.
6. Interpersonal communication develops and sustains relationships.
7. Interpersonal communication is not a panacea.
8. Interpersonal communication effectiveness can be learned.

Thus far, we have seen that communication exists on a continuum, ranging from impersonal to interpersonal. We've also learned that it is best understood as a transactional process, not a linear exchange or an interaction. Based on the transactional model, we defined interpersonal communication as a selective, systemic, unique, and ongoing process of transaction between people who reflect and build personal knowledge of one another as they create meanings. Meanings, we have seen, reflect histories of interaction and involve both content and relationship levels. Building on this definition, we are now ready to identify basic principles of interpersonal communication.

PRINCIPLES OF INTERPERSONAL COMMUNICATION

A closer look at interpersonal communication suggests eight basic principles for effectiveness.

Principle 1: We Cannot *Not* Communicate

Whenever people are together, they communicate. We cannot avoid communicating when we are with others, because they interpret what we do and say as well as what we don't do and don't say. Even if we choose to be silent, we're communicating. What we mean by silence and how others interpret it depend on many social and cultural influences.

Even when we don't intend to communicate, we do so. We may be unaware of a grimace that gives away our disapproval or an eye roll that shows we dislike someone, but we are communicating nonetheless. Unconscious communication often occurs on the relationship level of meaning as we express feelings about others through subtle, often nonverbal communication. Regardless of whether we aim to communicate and whether others understand our intentions, we continuously, unavoidably communicate.

Principle 2: Interpersonal Communication Is Irreversible

Perhaps you have been in heated arguments in which you lost your temper and said something you later regretted. It could be that you hurt someone or revealed something about yourself that you meant to keep private. Later, you might have tried to repair the damage by apologizing, explaining what you said, or denying what you revealed. But you couldn't erase your communication; you couldn't unsay what you said. You may have had similar experiences when communicating by e-mail. Perhaps you read a message that made you mad, and you dashed off a pointed reply, sent it, and then wished you could unsend it. The fact that communication is irreversible reminds us that what we say and do matters. It has impact. Once we say something to another person, our words become part of the relationship.

Remembering this principle keeps us aware of the importance of choosing when to speak and what to say—or not to say!

How we communicate intimately is also irreversible. A kiss between friends can change a relationship in a moment. The kiss, as a form of communication, is irrevocable and can raise many issues within a friendship. Once the line between friendship and intimacy has been crossed, you cannot go back.

Principle 3: Interpersonal Communication Involves Ethical Choices

Ethics is the branch of philosophy that focuses on moral principles and codes of conduct. Ethical issues concern right and wrong. Because interpersonal communication is irreversible and affects others, it always has ethical implications. What we say and do affects others: how they feel, how they perceive themselves, how they think about themselves, and how they think about others. Thus, responsible people think carefully about ethical guidelines for communication. For instance, should you refrain from telling someone something that might make him less willing to do what you want? If you read a message in a chat room that makes you angry, do you fire off a nasty reply, assuming that you will never meet the person and so won't face any consequences? Do you judge another person's communication from your own individual perspective and experience? Or do you try to understand her communication on her terms and from her perspective? In work settings, should you avoid giving negative feedback because it could hurt others' feelings? In these and many other instances, we face ethical choices.

Reflective Exercise

What ethical choices have you had to make recently? What did you learn from making these choices?

Richard Johannesen (1996) has devoted most of his career to studying the ethical aspects of human communication. He says that ethical communication occurs when people create relationships of equality, when they attend mindfully to each other, and when their communication demonstrates that they are authentic, empathic, supportive, and confirming of each other. Because interpersonal communication affects us and others, ethical considerations are always part of our interactions. Throughout this book, we note ethical issues that arise when we interact with others. As you read, consider what kinds of choices you make and what moral principles guide your choices.

Principle 4: People Construct Meanings in Interpersonal Communication

Human beings construct the meanings of their communication. The significance of communication doesn't lie in words and nonverbal behaviours. Instead, meaning arises out of how we interpret communication. This calls our attention to the fact that humans use symbols, which sets us apart from other creatures.

As we will see in Chapter 5, **symbols**, such as words, have no inherent or true meanings. Instead, we must interpret them. What does it mean if someone says, "You're crazy"? To interpret the comment, you must consider the context (a counselling session, a professional meeting, after a daredevil stunt), who said it (a psychiatrist, a supervisor, a subordinate, a friend, an enemy), and the words themselves, which may mean various things (a medical diagnosis, a challenge to your professional competence, a compliment on your zaniness, disapproval).

In interpersonal communication, people continuously interpret each other. Although typically we're not aware that we assign meanings, inevitably we do so. Someone you have been dating suggests some time away from each other, a friend turns down invitations to get together, or your supervisor at work seems less open to conversations with you than in the past. The meanings of such communications are neither self-evident nor inherent in the words. Instead, we construct their significance. In close relationships, partners gradually coordinate meanings so that they share understandings of issues and feelings important to their connection. When a relationship begins, one person may regard confrontation as healthy, and the other may avoid arguments. Over time, partners come to share meanings for conflict—what it is, how to handle it, and whether it threatens the relationship or is a path to growth.

Even one person's meanings vary over time and in response to experiences and moods. If you're in a good mood, a playful gibe might strike you as funny or as an invitation to banter. The same remark might hurt or anger you if you're feeling down. The meaning of the gibe, like all communication, is not preset or absolute. Meanings are created by people as they communicate in specific contexts.

Principle 5: Metacommunication Affects Meanings

The word *metacommunication* comes from the prefix *meta,* meaning "about," and the root word *communication.* Thus, **metacommunication** is communication about communication. For example, during a conversation with your friend Pat, you notice that Pat's body seems tense and her voice is sharp. You might say, "You seem really stressed." Your statement metacommunicates about Pat's nonverbal communication.

Metacommunication may be verbal or nonverbal. We can use words to talk about other words or nonverbal behaviours. If an argument between Joe and Marc gets out of hand and Joe makes a nasty personal attack, Joe might say, "I didn't really mean what I just said. I was just so angry it came out." This metacommunication may soften the hurt caused by the attack. If Joe and Marc then have a productive conversation about their differences, Marc might conclude by saying, "This has really been a good talk. I think we understand each other a lot better now." This comment verbally metacommunicates about the conversation that preceded it.

We also metacommunicate nonverbally. Nonverbal metacommunication often reinforces verbal communication. For example, you might nod your head while saying, "I really know what you mean." Or you might move away from a person after you say, "I don't want to see you anymore." Yet, not all nonverbal metacommunication reinforces verbal messages. Sometimes, our nonverbal expressions contradict our verbal messages. When teasing a friend, you might wink to signal you don't mean the teasing to be taken seriously. Or you might smile when you say to a friend who drops by, "Oh, rats—you again!" The smile tells the friend you welcome the visit despite your comment to the contrary.

Metacommunication can increase understanding. For instance, teachers sometimes say, "The next point is really important." This comment signals students to pay special attention to what follows. A parent might tell a child, "What I said may sound harsh, but I'm only telling you because I care about you." The comment tells the child how to interpret a critical message. A manager tells a subordinate to take a comment seriously by saying, "I really mean what I said. I'm not kidding." On the other hand, if we're not really sure of what we think about an issue and we want to try out a stance, we might say, "I'm thinking this through as I go, and I'm not really wedded to this position, but what I tend to believe right now is. ..." This preface to your statement tells listeners not to assume that what you say is set in stone.

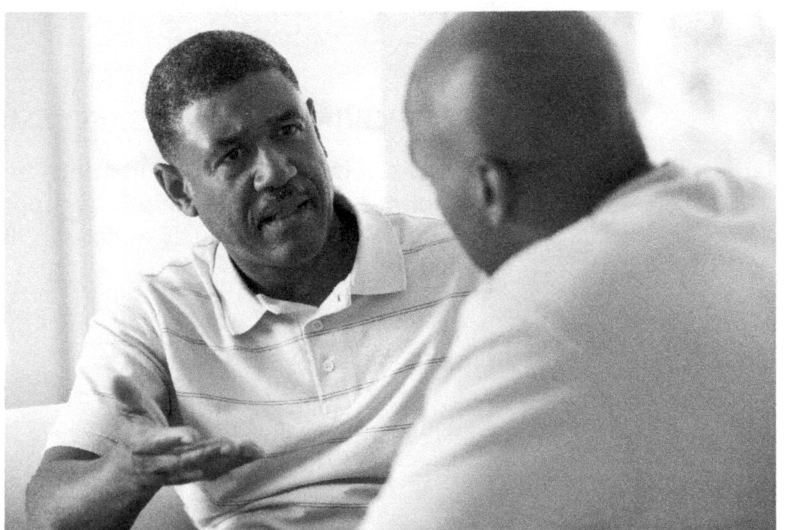
Monkey Business Images/Shutterstock

We can also metacommunicate to check on understanding: "Was I clear?" "Do you see why I feel like I do?" "Can you see why I'm confused about the problem?" Questions such as these allow you to find out whether another person understands what you intend to communicate. You may also metacommunicate to find out whether you understand what another person expresses to you. "What I think you meant is that you are worried. Is that right?" "If I follow what you said, you feel trapped between what you want to do and what your parents want you to do. Is that what you were telling me?" You may even say, "I don't understand what you just told me. Can you say it another way?" This question metacommunicates by letting the other person know you did not grasp her message and that you want to understand.

Effective metacommunication also helps friends and romantic partners express how they feel about their interactions. Linda Acitelli (1988, 1993) has studied what happens when partners in a relationship talk to each other about how they perceive and feel about their interaction. She reports that women and men alike find metacommunication helpful if there is a conflict or problem that must be addressed. Both sexes seem to appreciate knowing how the other feels about their differences; they

Student Voices

Tara:

I never feel like an argument is really over and settled until Andy and I have said that we feel better for having thrashed out whatever was the problem. It's like I want closure, and the fight isn't really behind us until we both say, "I'm glad we talked," or something to say that what we went through led us to a better place.

are also eager to learn how to communicate to resolve those differences. During a conflict, one person might say, "I feel like we're both being really stubborn. Do you think we could each back off a little from our positions?" This expresses discontent with how communication is proceeding and offers an alternative. After conflict, one partner might say, "This really cleared the air between us. I feel a lot better now."

Acitelli also found that women are more likely than men to appreciate metacommunication when there is no conflict or immediate problem to be resolved. While curled up on a sofa and watching TV, a woman might say to her male partner, "I really

Apply the Idea

IMPROVING YOUR METACOMMUNICATION

For each of the scenarios described here, write one verbal or nonverbal metacommunication that would be appropriate to express your feelings about what has been said or to clarify understanding.

1. A friend tells you about a problem with his parents, and you aren't sure whether your friend wants advice or just a safe person with whom to vent feelings.

Metacommunication

____

____

____

2. You are arguing with a person who seems more interested in winning the argument than in working things through so that both of you are satisfied. You want to change how the argument is proceeding.

Metacommunication

____

____

____

3. Your manager at work routinely gives you orders instead of making requests. You resent it when she says to you, "Take over the front room," "Clean up the storeroom now," and "I want you in early tomorrow." You want to change how your manager expresses expectations for your performance.

Metacommunication

____

____

____

Apply the Idea

4. Lately, someone who used to be a close friend seems to be avoiding you. When you do see the friend, he seems eager to cut the conversation short. He doesn't meet your eye and doesn't tell you anything about his life anymore. You want to know what is going on and how to interpret his communication.

Metacommunication

____

____

____

5. You have just spent 10 minutes telling your father why you want to study abroad next year. Earlier, your father said that studying abroad was just an extravagance, but you've tried to explain why it will broaden your education and your marketability when you look for a job next year. You aren't sure your father has understood your points.

Metacommunication

____

____

____

Reflective Exercise

What is your metacommunication like with friends and intimate partners? Are there differences in metacommunication behaviours between your male friends and their partners and your female friends and their partners?

feel comfortable snuggling with you." This comments on the relationship and on the nonverbal communication between the couple. According to research by Acitelli and others (Wood, 1997a, 1998), men generally find talk about relationships unnecessary unless there is an immediate problem to be addressed. Understanding this gender difference in preferences for metacommunication may help you interpret members of the other sex more accurately.

Principle 6: Interpersonal Communication Develops and Sustains Relationships

Interpersonal communication is the primary way we build, refine, and transform relationships. Partners talk to work out expectations and understandings of their interaction, appropriate and inappropriate topics and styles of communicating, and the nature of the relationship itself. Is it a friendship or a romantic

Student Voices

Karen:

I love talking about the future with my fiancé. Sometimes, we talk for hours about the kind of house we'll have and what our children will be like and how we'll juggle two careers and a family. I know everything won't work out exactly like we think now, but talking about it makes me feel so close to Dave and like our future is real.

relationship? How much and in what ways can we count on each other? How do we handle disagreements—by confronting them, ignoring them, or using indirect strategies to restore harmony? What are the bottom lines, the "shalt not" rules for what counts as unforgivable betrayal? What counts as caring—words, deeds, both? Because communication has no intrinsic meanings, we must generate our own in the course of interaction.

Communication also allows us to construct or reconstruct individual and joint histories. For instance, when people fall in love, they often redefine former loves as "mere infatuations" or "puppy love" but definitely not as the "real thing." When something goes wrong in a relationship, partners may work together to define what happened in a way that allows them to continue. Marriage counsellors report that couples routinely work out face-saving explanations for affairs so that they can stay together in the aftermath of infidelity (Scarf, 1987). Partners often talk about past events and experiences that challenged them and ones that were joyous. The process of reliving the past reminds partners how long they have been together and how much they have shared. As partners communicate thoughts and feelings, they generate shared meanings for themselves, their interaction, and their relationship.

Communication is also the primary means by which intimates construct a future for themselves, and a vision of shared future is one of the most powerful ties that link people (Dixson & Duck, 1993; Wood, 2006). Romantic couples often dream together by talking about the family they plan and how they'll be in 20 years. Likewise, friends discuss plans for the future and promise reunions if they must move apart. Communication allows us to express and share dreams, imaginings, and memories and to weave all of these into the joint world of relational partners.

Principle 7: Interpersonal Communication Is Not a Panacea

As we have seen, we communicate to satisfy many of our needs and to create relationships with others. Yet it would be a mistake to think communication is a cure-all. Many problems can't be solved by talk alone. Communication by itself won't end hunger, abuses of human rights around the globe, racism, intimate partner violence, or physical diseases. Nor can words alone bridge irreconcilable differences between people or erase the hurt of betrayal. Although good communication may increase understanding and help us solve problems, it will not fix everything. We should also realize that the idea of talking things through is distinctly Western. Not all societies think it's wise or useful to communicate about relationships or to talk extensively about feelings. Just as interpersonal communication has many strengths and values, it also has limits, and its effectiveness is shaped by cultural contexts.

Principle 8: Interpersonal Communication Effectiveness Can Be Learned

It is a mistake to think that effective communicators are born, that some people have a natural talent and others don't. Although some people have extraordinary talent in athletics or writing, all of us can become competent athletes and writers. Likewise, some people have an aptitude for communicating, but all of us can become competent communicators. This book and the course you are taking should sharpen your understanding of how interpersonal communication works and should help you learn skills that will enhance your effectiveness in relating to others.

GUIDELINES FOR INTERPERSONAL COMMUNICATION COMPETENCE

Sometimes we handle interactions well, and in other cases we are ineffective. What are the differences between effective and ineffective communication? Scholars define **interpersonal communication competence** as the ability to communicate effectively and appropriately. Effectiveness involves achieving the goals we have for specific interactions. In different situations, your goals might be to explain an idea, to comfort a friend, to stand up for your position, to negotiate a raise, or to persuade someone to change behaviours. The more effectively you communicate, the more likely you are to be competent in achieving your goals.

Competence also emphasizes appropriateness. This means that competent communication is adapted to particular situations and people. Language that is appropriate at a party with friends may not be appropriate in a job interview. Appropriateness also involves contexts. It may be appropriate to kiss an intimate in a private setting but not in a classroom. Similarly, many people choose not to argue in front of others but prefer to engage in conflict when they are alone.

Five skills are closely tied to competence in interpersonal communication: (1) developing a range of communication skills, (2) adapting communication appropriately, (3) engaging in dual perspective, (4) monitoring your communication, and (5) committing to effective and ethical interpersonal communication. We'll discuss each of these skills now.

CONCEPTS AT A GLANCE

Guidelines for Interpersonal Communication Competence

- Develop a range of skills.
- Adapt communication appropriately.
- Engage in dual perspective.
- Monitor your communication.
- Commit to effective and ethical communication.

Develop a Range of Skills

No one style of communication is best in all circumstances, with all people, or for pursuing all goals. Because what is effective varies, we need to have a broad repertoire of communication behaviours. Consider the different skills needed for interpersonal communication competence in several situations.

To comfort someone, we need to be soothing and compassionate. To negotiate a good deal on a car, we need to be assertive and firm. To engage constructively in conflict, we need to listen and build supportive climates. To support a friend who is depressed, we need to affirm that person, demonstrate that we care, and encourage the friend to talk about problems. To build good work relationships, we need to know how to communicate supportively, how to express our ideas clearly, and how to listen well. Because no single set of skills comprises interpersonal communication competence, we need to learn a range of communicative abilities.

© Corel

When might humour be inappropriate?

Adapt Communication Appropriately

The ability to communicate in a range of ways doesn't make us competent unless we also know which kinds of communication to use in specific interactions. For instance, knowing how to be both assertive and deferential isn't useful unless we can figure out when each style of communication is appropriate. Although there is no neat formula for adapting communication appropriately, it is generally important to consider personal goals, context, and the people with whom we communicate.

Your goals for communication are a primary guideline for selecting appropriate behaviours. If your purpose in a conversation is to give emotional support to someone, then it isn't effective to talk at length about your own experiences. On the other hand, if you want someone to understand you better, talking in depth about your life may be highly effective. If your goal is to win an argument and get your way, it may be competent to assert your point of view, point out flaws in your partner's ideas, and refuse to compromise. If you want to work through conflict in a way that doesn't harm a relationship, however, other communication choices might be more constructive. As Mary Margaret notes, she is still learning how to select appropriate behaviours.

Context is another influence on decisions of when, how, and about what to communicate. It is appropriate to ask your doctor about symptoms during an office exam, but it isn't appropriate to do so when you see the doctor in a social situation. When a friend is feeling low, that's not a good time to criticize, although at another time, criticism might be constructive. When communicating online, skilled communicators compensate for the lack of nonverbal cues by adding emoticons and expressing warmth explicitly (Baym, 2002; Parks & Roberts, 1998).

Remembering Buber's discussion of the I–Thou relationship (1970), we know it is important to adapt what we say and how we say it to particular people. As we have seen, interpersonal communication increases our knowledge of others. Thus, the more interpersonal the relationship, the more we can adapt our communication to unique partners. Abstract communicative goals, such as supporting others, call for distinct behaviours in regard to specific people. What feels supportive to one friend may not to another. One of the closest friends of one of the authors withdraws if the author challenges her ideas, but another friend relishes challenges and the discussions they prompt. What is effective in talking with them varies. We have to learn what our intimates need, what upsets and pleases them, and how they interpret various kinds of communication. Scholars use the term **person-centredness** to refer to the ability to adapt messages effectively to particular people (Bernstein, 1974; Burleson, 1987; Zorn, 1995). Appropriately adapted communication, then, is sensitive to goals, contexts, and other people.

Student Voices

Mary Margaret:

I think I need to work on figuring out when to be assertive and when not to be. For most of my life, I wasn't at all assertive, even when I should have been. Last spring, though, I was so tired of having people walk all over me that I signed up for a workshop on assertiveness training. I learned how to assert myself, and I was really proud of how much more I would stand up for myself. The problem was that I did it all the time, regardless of whether something really mattered enough to be assertive about it. Just like I was always passive before, now I'm always assertive. I need to figure out a better way to balance my behaviours.

CONCEPTS AT A GLANCE

Guidelines for Dual Perspective

- Remember, there is more than one perspective.
- Listen closely.
- Ask others for clarification.

Engage in Dual Perspective

Central to competent interpersonal communication is the ability to engage in **dual perspective**, which is understanding both our own and another person's perspective, beliefs, thoughts, or feelings (Phillips & Wood, 1983). When we adopt dual perspective, we understand how someone else thinks and feels about issues. To meet another person in genuine dialogue, we must be able to realize how that person views himself or herself, the situation, and his or her own thoughts and feelings. We may personally see things much differently, and we may want to express our perceptions. Yet, we also need to understand and respect the other person's perspective.

People who cannot take the perspectives of others are egocentric. They impose their perceptions on others and interpret others' experiences through their own eyes.

Consider an example. Roberto complains that he is having trouble writing a report for his supervisor. His co-worker Raymond responds, "All you have to do is outline the plan and provide the rationale. That's a snap." "But," says Roberto, "I've always had trouble writing. I just block when I sit down to write." Raymond says, "That's silly. Anyone can do this. It just took me an hour or so to do my report." Raymond has failed to understand how Roberto sees writing. If you have trouble writing, then composing a report isn't a snap, but Raymond can't get beyond his own comfort with writing to understand Roberto's different perspective.

Student Voices

Asha:

Sometimes it's very difficult for me to understand my daughter. She likes music that sounds terrible to me, and I don't like the way she dresses sometimes. For a long time, I judged her by my own values about music and dress, but that really pushed us apart. She kept saying, "I'm not you. Why can't you look at it from my point of view?" Finally, I heard her, and now we both try to understand each other's point of view. It isn't always easy, but you can't have a relationship on just one person's terms.

As Asha says, engaging in dual perspective isn't necessarily easy, because all of us naturally see things from our own points of view and in terms of our own experiences. Parents often have trouble understanding the perspectives of children, particularly teenagers (Fox & Frankel, 2005). Yet, we can improve our ability to engage in dual perspective (Greene & Burleson, 2003). Three guidelines can help you increase your ability to take the perspective of others:

1. Be aware of the tendency to see things from your own perspective, and resist that inclination.
2. Listen closely to how others express their thoughts and feelings, so that you gain clues of what things mean to them and how they feel.
3. Ask others to explain how they feel, what something means to them, or how they view a situation. Asking questions and probing for details communicates on the relationship level that you are interested and that you want to understand. Making a commitment to engage in dual perspective and practising the three guidelines just discussed will enhance your ability to recognize and respond to others' perspectives.

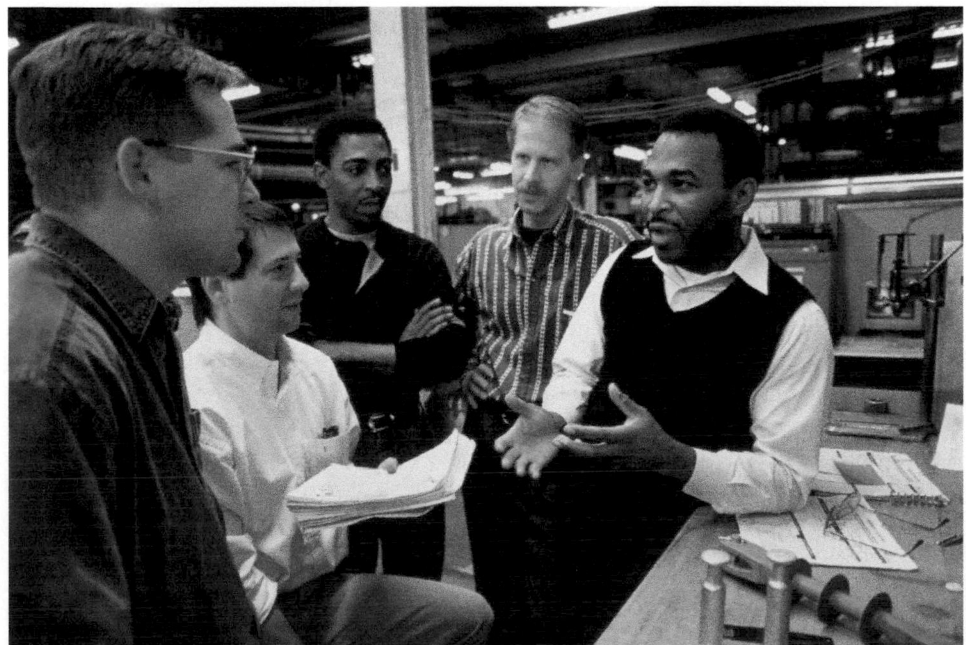

© David Joel/Stone/Getty Images

Apply the Idea

DEVELOPING DUAL PERSPECTIVE

Practise the guidelines for improving dual perspective. During the next two days, do the following in conversations:

- *Identify your own perspective on issues that others talk about. What do you think about the issues? Try not to impose your thoughts and feelings. Suspend them long enough to hear others.*
- *Pay close attention to what other people say. How do they describe feelings, thoughts, and views? Listen carefully to others without translating their communication into your own language.*
- *Ask questions such as: "What do you mean?" "How does that feel to you?" "How do you see the issue?" "What do you think about the situation?"*
- *Notice what you learn by suspending your own perspective and working to understand others.*

Monitor Your Communication

The fourth ability that affects interpersonal communication competence is **monitoring**, which is the capacity to observe and regulate your own communication. Most of us do this much of the time. Before bringing up a touchy topic, you remind yourself not to get defensive and not to get pulled into counterproductive arguing. During the discussion, Chris says something that upsets you. You think of a really good zinger but stop yourself from saying it, because you don't want to hurt Chris. In each instance, you monitored your communication.

Monitoring occurs both before and during interaction. Often, before conversations we indicate to ourselves what we do and don't want to say. During communication, we stay alert and edit our thoughts before expressing them. Online communication offers us especially effective ways to monitor our communication. We can save messages, reread them to see if they express what we really intend, and edit them before sending (Baym, 2002). Our ability to monitor allows us to adapt communication in advance and gauge our effectiveness as we interact.

Of course, we don't monitor all the time. When we are with people who understand us or when we are talking about unimportant topics, we don't necessarily need to monitor communication with great care. Sometimes, however, not monitoring can result in communication that hurts others or that leads us to regard ourselves negatively. In some cases, failure to monitor is a result of getting caught up in the dynamics of interaction. We simply forget to keep a watchful eye on ourselves, and so we say or do things we later regret. In addition, some people have poorly developed monitoring skills. They have limited awareness of how they come across to others. Communication competence involves learning to attend to feedback from others and to monitor the impact of our communication as we interact with them.

CONCEPTS AT A GLANCE

Committing to Interpersonal Communication

- Invest energy in ethical communication.
- Honour the other.
- Respect yourself.
- Deal with communication complexity.

Commit to Effective and Ethical Communication

The final requirement for interpersonal competence is commitment to effective and ethical communication. This commitment requires that you invest energy in communicating ethically with others as unique human beings. This implies that you can't treat another person as merely a member of some group, such as men, co-workers, or customers. Responding to another as a unique and valuable person also means you can't dismiss the other person's feelings as wrong, inappropriate, or silly. Instead, you must honor the person and the feelings he or she expresses, even if you feel differently.

A commitment to effective and ethical communication also includes caring about yourself and your ideas and feelings. Just as you must honour those of others, you must respect yourself and your own perspective. Finally, competent communicators are committed to the communication process itself. They realize that it is interactive and always evolving, and they are willing to deal with that complexity. In addition, they are sensitive to multiple levels of meaning and to the irreversibility of communication. Commitment, then, is vital to relationships, other people, ourselves, and communication.

In sum, interpersonal communication competence is the ability to communicate in ways that are interpersonally effective and appropriate. The five requirements for competence are (1) developing a range of communication skills; (2) adapting them appropriately to goals, other people, and situations; (3) engaging in dual perspective; (4) monitoring communication and its impact; and (5) committing to effective and ethical interpersonal communication.

Apply the Idea

IMPROVING COMMUNICATION COMPETENCE

Are you satisfied with your communication competence?

- *How competent are you in various communication skills?*
- *Describe communication situations in which you don't feel you are as competent as you'd like to be.*
- *How well do you adapt your communication to different goals, situations, and people?*
- *How consistently and effectively do you engage in dual perspective when interacting with others? How can you tell when you really understand another's point of view?*
- *How well do you monitor your communication so that you gauge how you come across to others?*
- *Describe your commitments to others, relationships, yourself, and the interpersonal communication process.*

  Consider which aspects of communication competence you would most like to improve, and make a contract with yourself to work on them during this course.

Chapter Summary

In this chapter, we launched our study of interpersonal communication. We began by noting that communication is essential to our survival and happiness. Communicating with others allows us to meet basic needs for survival and safety, as well as more abstract human needs for inclusion, esteem, self-actualization, and effective participation in a socially diverse world.

We looked at three different models of the process. The best model is the transactional one because it emphasizes the dynamic nature and the systemic quality of interpersonal communication and because it recognizes that people simultaneously send and receive messages. This model is the foundation of our definition of interpersonal communication as a selective, systemic, unique, and ongoing process of interaction between people who reflect and build personal knowledge and create meanings. We also learned that communication exists on a continuum that ranges from impersonal (I–It) to interpersonal (I–Thou). Fully interpersonal communication occurs when people engage each other as full, unique human beings who create meanings on both content and relationship levels.

We discussed eight principles of interpersonal communication. First, it is impossible *not* to communicate. Whether or not we intend to send certain messages and whether or not others understand our meanings, communication always occurs when people are together. Second, communication is irreversible because we cannot unsay or undo what passes between us and others. Third, interpersonal communication always has ethical implications. The fourth principle maintains that meanings reside not in words but rather in how we interpret them. Fifth, metacommunication affects meanings in interpersonal interaction. Sixth, we use communication to develop and sustain relationships. In fact, communication is essential to relationships because it is in the process of interacting with others that we develop expectations, understandings, and rules to guide relationships. Seventh, although communication is powerful and important, it is not a cure-all. The eighth and final principle is that effectiveness in interpersonal communication can be learned through committed study and practice of principles and skills.

Competent interpersonal communicators interact in ways that are effective and appropriate. This means that we should adapt our ways of communicating to specific goals, situations, and other people. Effectiveness and appropriateness require us to recognize and respect differences that reflect personal and cultural backgrounds. Guidelines for doing this include developing a range of communication skills, adapting communication sensitively, engaging in dual perspective, monitoring our own communication, and committing to effective and ethical interpersonal communication. In later chapters, we focus on developing the skills that enhance interpersonal communication competence.

Key Concepts

- content meaning
- dual perspective
- ethics
- feedback
- I–It communication
- interactive model
- interpersonal communication
- interpersonal communication competence
- I–Thou communication
- I–You communication
- linear model
- metacommunication
- model
- monitoring
- noise
- person-centredness
- process
- relationship meaning
- symbols
- systemic
- transactional model

For Further Thought and Discussion

1. Use each of the three models presented in this chapter to describe an interpersonal communication encounter. What does each model highlight? What does each model neglect or ignore? Which model best explains the process of interpersonal communication?
2. Interview a professional in the field you plan to enter. Ask him or her to explain the communication skills needed for success and advancement in the field. Which skills do you already have? Which ones do you need to develop or improve? Write out a personal action plan for using this book and the course it accompanies to enhance your effectiveness in interpersonal communication.
3. Go to the placement office on your campus and read descriptions of job openings. Record the number of job descriptions that call for communication skills. Share your findings with others in your class.
4. Identify a relationship of yours that has become closer over time. Describe the earliest stage of the relationship. Was it an I–It or an I–You relationship at that time? During that early stage of the relationship, what did you talk about? Were there topics or kinds of talk you avoided? Now, describe the current relationship. What do you now talk about? Can you identify differences over time in your own and the other person's shared fields of experience?
5. Use your InfoTrac® College Edition to read *Psychological Health and Change in Closeness in Platonic and Romantic Relationships* by Duncan Cramer and Marie Donachie. Which aspects of interpersonal communication does this article suggest are related to psychological health and closeness in relationships?

Chapter 2

Communication and the Creation of Self

To venture causes anxiety, but not to venture is to lose one's self.

—Søren Kierkegaard

It is our choices that make us who we are.

—Professor Dumbledore, *Harry Potter*

I am a singer. I am short. I am shy. I am a sister. I am a brother. I am a parent. I am a goalie. I am a student. I am a woman. I am a man. I am gay. I am straight. I am a Christian. I am White. I am Black. I am First Nations.

Who am I? Throughout our lives we ponder this question. We answer it one way at one time, then change our answer as we ourselves change. At the age of five, perhaps you defined yourself as your parents' daughter or son. That view of yourself implicitly recognized sex, race, and social class as parts of your identity. In high school, you may have described yourself in terms of academic strengths ("I'm good at math and science"), athletic endeavours ("I'm a forward on the team"), leadership positions ("I'm president of the Photography Club"), friends and romantic partners ("I'm going steady with Cam"), or future plans ("I'm starting college next year"; "I'm going to be a lawyer"). Now that you're in college or university, it's likely you see yourself in terms of a major, a career path, and perhaps a relationship you hope will span the years ahead. You've probably also made some decisions about your sexual orientation, spiritual commitments, and political beliefs.

As you think about the different ways you've defined yourself over the years, you'll realize that the self is not a constant entity that is fixed early and then remains stable. Instead, the *self* is a process that evolves and changes continuously. The self emerges and is reborn throughout our lives. The influences that shape who we are include interactions with others and our reflections on them. In this chapter, we will explore how the self is formed and changed in the process of communicating with others.

WHAT IS THE SELF?

The **self** arises in communication and is a multidimensional process of internalizing and acting from social perspectives. Although this is a complicated way to describe the self, it directs our attention to some important propositions about this very complicated concept.

CONCEPTS AT A GLANCE

Defining the Self

- The self arises in communication with others.
- The self is multidimensional.
- The self is a process.
- The self internalizes social perspectives.
- Social perspectives on the self are constructed and variable.

The Self Arises in Communication with Others

As babies, we don't have a clear understanding of our values and who we are. Instead, we develop a sense of self in the process of communicating with others who tell us who we are.

From the moment we enter the world, we interact with others. As we do, we learn how they see us, and we take their perspectives inside ourselves. This process usually begins in the family, as we learn how our parents, siblings, and other relatives view us. Later, as we interact with peers and teachers, we gain additional perspectives on ourselves. Still later, when we take jobs, we learn how co-workers and supervisors see us as employees. We also tune into media, which give us additional perspectives on ourselves. We internalize many of these views, and they become part of who we are and how we see ourselves. Thus, how we perceive ourselves is based largely on the people with whom we interact.

George Herbert Mead (1934) devoted his career to understanding how the self develops through communication. According to Mead, we develop selves by internalizing two kinds of perspectives that are communicated to us: the perspectives of *particular others* and the perspective of the *generalized other*. Let's now look more closely at these two types of social perspectives on which we rely to define ourselves and to guide how we think, act, and feel.

Particular Others

The first perspectives that affect us are those of particular others. **Particular others** are specific people who are significant to us. They include family members, peers, teachers, and other individuals who are especially important in our lives. As babies interact with particular others in their world, they learn how others see them. This is the beginning of a self-concept. Notice that the self starts from outside—from how particular others view us. For most of us, family members are the first major influence on how we see ourselves. Mothers, fathers, siblings, and often day-care providers are particular others who are significant to most infants. In addition, some families include aunts, uncles, grandparents, and others who live together.

Parents and other individuals who matter to us communicate who we are and what we are worth through direct definitions, reflected appraisals, scripts, and attachment styles (see Figure 2.1). If parents communicate to children that they are special and cherished, the children are likely to see themselves as worthy of love. On the other hand, children whose parents communicate that the children are not wanted or loved may come to think of themselves as unlovable.

Direct Definition

As the term implies, **direct definition** is communication that tells us who we are by explicitly labelling us and our behaviours. Family members, as well as peers, teachers, and other individuals, define us by how they describe us. For instance, parents often communicate gender roles directly by telling us what boys and girls do and don't do. "Nice girls don't play rough," "You should help Mom around the house," and "Don't get your clothes dirty." Sons, on the other hand, are more likely to be told, "Go out and get 'em," "Stick up for yourself," and "Don't cry." As we hear these messages, we pick up our parents' and our society's gender expectations.

Positive direct definitions enhance our self-esteem: "You're smart," "You're strong," "You're great at soccer." Negative direct definitions can damage children's self-esteem (Brooks & Goldstein, 2001): "You're a troublemaker," "You're stupid," "You're impossible." Negative messages can demolish a child's sense of self-worth. Andrew Vachss (1994), who fights for children's rights, believes that emotional abuse is just as damaging as other forms of abuse (see the Communication Notes feature, "Emotional Abuse").

FIGURE 2.1

Family Influences on Self-Concept

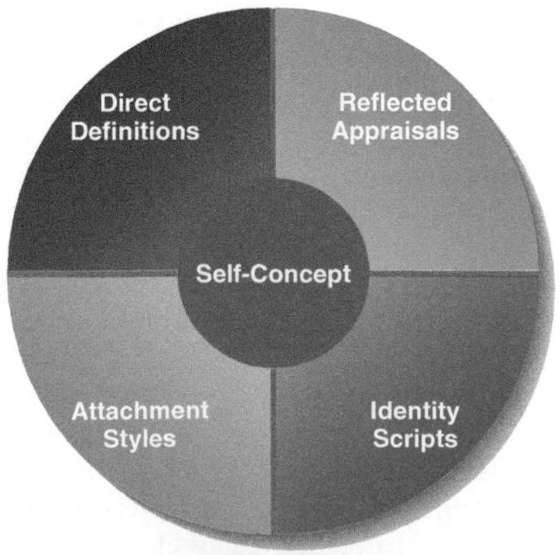

Communication Notes

EMOTIONAL ABUSE

Andrew Vachss is an attorney and author who has devoted his life to helping children who have been abused. He has worked with children who have been sexually assaulted, physically maimed, abandoned, starved, and otherwise tortured. Yet Vachss (1994) regards emotional abuse as the worst harm of all. He says, "Of all the many forms of child abuse, emotional abuse may be the cruelest and longest-lasting of all. Emotional abuse is the systematic diminishment of another. It may be intentional or subconscious (or both), but it is always ... designed to reduce a child's self-concept to the point where the victim considers himself unworthy—unworthy of respect, unworthy of friendship, unworthy of the natural birthright of all children: love and protection. ... [T]here is no real difference between physical, sexual, and emotional abuse. All that distinguishes one from the other is the abuser's choice of weapons."

Particular others often provide us with direct definitions of our racial and ethnic identities. In cultures with a majority race, members of minority races often make special efforts to impart racial identity to children. According to Susan Mosley-Howard and Cheryl Burgan Evans (1997), many African American parents and grandparents teach children to take pride in the strength and struggle that are part of African Americans' history. Many African American families also feel they must teach children that racism still exists in the United States (Mosley-Howard & Evans, 1997). Thus, the ethnic training in many African American families stresses both positive identification with Black heritage and awareness of prejudice on the part of people who are not Black.

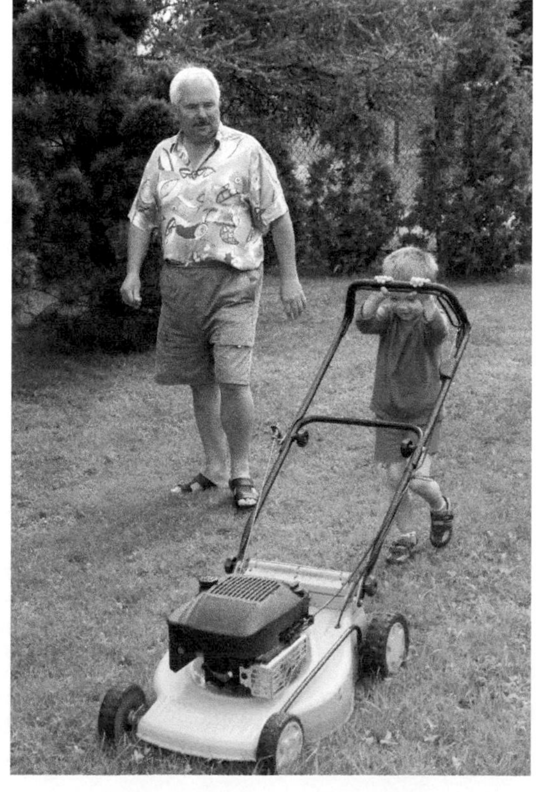
PKruger/Shutterstock

Direct definition also takes place as particular others respond to children's behaviours. If a child clowns around and parents respond by saying, "What a cut-up; you really are funny," the child learns to see herself or himself as funny. If a child dusts furniture and receives praise ("You're great to help clean the house"), helpfulness is reinforced as part of the child's self-concept. From direct definition, children learn what others value in them, and this shapes what they come to value in themselves. Through explicit labels and responses to our behaviours, family members and others who matter to us provide direct definitions of who we are and—just as important—who we are supposed to be.

Family members also offer us direct definitions of our ethnic identities. Most Canadians define themselves in two ways, first as Canadian and second as an ethnic subgroup. The challenge of modern parenting lies in not only helping children identify with their unique cultural heritage, such as Métis or Scottish or Pakistani, but also providing them with the skills to function in diverse communities.

© 2009 Jupiterimages Corporation

Berry Brazelton is a renowned pediatrician and a professor emeritus of pediatrics at Harvard Medical School. According to Brazelton (1997), parents and other family members boost or impair children's self-esteem by their responses to children's behaviour. Especially important is responding with enthusiasm to a child's accomplishments. When a baby masters walking, she or he will show a look of delight at this new achievement. For that feeling to be complete, however, the child needs positive responses from others. Family members need to smile and say, "Wow, you did it!" Brazelton says that how a child is treated in the first eight months of life sets the child's expectation of success or failure in life. If the child's accomplishments are noticed and praised, the child progressively gains self-confidence and undertakes increasingly difficult challenges. On the other hand, if the child's achievements are not noted and affirmed, the child is a candidate for low self-expectations and defeating self-fulfilling prophecies.

Student Voices

Talmidge:

During high school, a lot of my friends thought I was too religious. They would kid me about being "Goody Two-Shoes" because I didn't drink or do other things that most of them did. In college, I've found more Christian friends who respect what I stand for. They make me feel better about myself.

Reflected Appraisal

If we do not perceive or accept particular others' direct definitions of us, these definitions might not become part of how we see ourselves. **Reflected appraisal** is another's view of us, which affects how we see ourselves. This concept is similar to the *looking glass self,* based on Charles Cooley's poetic comment, "Each to each a looking glass / Reflects the other that doth pass" (1961, p. 5). Others are mirrors for us—the views of ourselves that we see in them (our mirrors) shape how we perceive ourselves. If others communicate that they think we are smart, we are likely to reflect that appraisal in how we act and think about ourselves. If family members communicate that they see us as dumb or unlikable, we may reflect their appraisals by seeing ourselves in those ways.

The appraisals of us that parents express let us know when our behaviours are not acceptable. Did your parents ever tell you that something you said or did was inappropriate? Did they ever punish you for misbehaving? If so, you know how effectively others' appraisals can communicate that they regard our behaviours as unacceptable.

Anatoliy Samara/Shutterstock

Peers also communicate their perceptions of us. When we accept them, peers' reflected appraisals affect how we see ourselves. The importance of peers' reflected appraisals is illustrated by this amusing example from Don Monkerud's (1990) research. Jeremy Bem was raised by parents who were committed to nonsexist child-rearing. When Jeremy put barrettes in his hair, his parents expressed neither surprise nor disapproval. But a different response greeted Jeremy when he wore his barrettes to nursery school. His male peers repeatedly told him that "only girls wear barrettes." Jeremy tried to tell them that wearing barrettes had nothing to do with being a boy or a girl, but his peers were adamant that he couldn't be a boy if he wore barrettes. Finally, in frustration, Jeremy pulled down his pants and declared that, because he had a penis, he was a boy. The other boys laughed at this and informed Jeremy, "Everybody has a penis; only girls wear barrettes" (1990, p. 83).

We don't have a record of how Jeremy and his barrettes fared after this incident, but we do know that Jeremy, like all of us, was affected by his peers' appraisals of him. The reflected appraisals of peers join with those of family members and shape the images we have of ourselves.

Communication Notes

THE ROLE OF FATHERS IN SOCIALIZING CHILDREN

For years, mothers have been regarded as essential to children's development. We've all heard about "maternal instinct" and "mothers' intuition." Yet, mothers are only half the picture. Fathers play important roles in children's development, and the roles they play tend to be distinct from those of mothers.

Fathers seem more likely than mothers to challenge and stretch children to achieve more. Fathers urge children to take initiative, to tolerate risks, and to experiment with unfamiliar activities and situations. Fathers also tend to focus on playing with their children, and fathers' play generally is physically stimulating. Roughhousing with fathers seems to develop children's courage and willingness to take risks.

Mothers, in contrast, seem to specialize in protecting children and emotionally reassuring them. Mothers, more than fathers, accept children at their current levels and don't push them to go further. Mothers also spend more of their time with children in care-taking activities than in play.

Researchers who have studied parents' interactions with children conclude that fathers and mothers typically contribute in unique and valuable ways to their children's development and self-esteem (Popenoe, 1996; Stacey, 1996). Fathers especially seem prepared to help their sons and daughters develop confidence, autonomy, and high expectations of themselves. Mothers are more likely to provide children with a sense of self-acceptance and to teach them to be sensitive to others. Researchers conclude that both mothers and fathers make substantial and unique contributions to the full development of children.

A number of groups support active fathering and provide information about the impact fathers can have on children. Two websites you might want to visit are the National Fatherhood Initiative at www.fatherhood.org and the Fatherhood Project at www.fatherhoodproject.org.

One way to think about reflected appraisals is to realize that others can behave as uppers, downers, and vultures. People act as **uppers** when they communicate positively about us and reflect positive appraisals of our self-worth. They notice our strengths, see our progress, and accept our weaknesses and problems without discounting us. When we're around uppers, we feel more upbeat and positive about ourselves. Uppers aren't necessarily unconditionally positive in their communication. A true friend can be an upper by recognizing our weaknesses and helping us work on them. Instead of putting us down, an upper believes in us and helps us believe in ourselves and our capacity to change. *Identify two uppers in your life.*

People act as **downers** when they communicate negatively about us and our self-worth. They call attention to our flaws, emphasize our problems, and put down our dreams and goals. When we're around downers, we tend to feel down about ourselves. Reflecting their perspectives, when we're around downers, we're more aware of our weaknesses and are less confident of what we can accomplish. *Identify two downers in your life.*

Vultures are extreme downers. When people act as vultures, they not only communicate negative images of us but also attack our self-concepts just as actual vultures prey on their victims (Simon, 1977). Sometimes vultures initiate harsh criticism. They say, "You don't measure up to the other people hired when you were," or "You'll never look professional at your weight."

Vultures pick up on our own self-doubts and magnify them. They find our weak spots and exploit them; they pick us apart by focusing on sensitive areas in our self-concept. For example, a friend of mine manages his time inefficiently and is very sensitive about it. I once observed a co-worker pick him apart just as a vulture picks apart its prey. The co-worker said, "I can't believe this is all you've done. You're the most unproductive person I've ever known. What a waste! Your output doesn't justify your salary." That harangue typifies the sort of attack on self-worth that vultures enjoy. By telling us we are inadequate, vultures demolish our self-esteem. *Can you identify vultures in your life?*

Think about how you feel about yourself when you're with people who act as uppers, downers, and vultures. Can you see how powerfully others' communication affects your self-concept? You might also think about the people for whom you act as an upper, a downer, or a vulture.

Reflected appraisals are not confined to childhood but continue throughout our lives. Sometimes, teachers are the first to see potential in students that the students have not recognized in themselves. When teachers communicate that

Apply the Idea

To understand how reflected appraisals have influenced your self-concept, try this exercise.

1. First, list five words that describe ways you see yourself. Examples are responsible, ambitious, introverted, clumsy, funny, intelligent, shy, and athletic.
2. Next, identify the particular people who have been and are especially significant in your life. Try to list at least five people who matter to you.
3. Now, think about how these special people communicated to you about the traits you listed in Step 1. How did they express their appraisals of what you defined as important parts of yourself?

Can you trace how you see yourself to the appraisals reflected by particular others in your life?

students are talented in a particular area, the students may come to see themselves that way. Later, as you enter professional life, you will encounter co-workers and bosses who reflect their appraisals of you: you're on the fast track, average, or not suited to your position. The appraisals of us that others communicate shape our sense of ourselves.

One particularly powerful way in which reflected appraisals can affect our self-concept is through **self-fulfilling prophecies**, which is acting in ways that embody our internalization of others' expectations or judgments about us. If you have done poorly in classes where teachers didn't seem to respect you, and you have done well with teachers who thought you were smart, then you know what a self-fulfilling prophecy is. The prophecies we act to fulfill usually are first communicated by others. However, because we internalize others' perspectives, we may allow their definitions and prophecies for us to become our own.

Communication Notes

INTERNALIZING RACIAL STEREOTYPES

According to Stanford University researcher Claude Steele, groups that are negatively stereotyped by others may internalize those negative stereotypes, thereby creating a self-fulfilling prophecy. Steele says that groups that are victims of widely held negative perceptions often fear that the stereotypes about them are true (Woo, 1995).

To test his idea, Steele designed an experiment. He told undergraduate students that they would be taking a test to measure their verbal reasoning. Half the students were asked to identify their race before taking the test. The other half were not asked to identify their race. Steele's results were dramatic. When students were required to state their race, Blacks tested significantly lower than Whites. When students weren't asked to identify their race, scores for Blacks and Whites were equivalent.

Many of us believe things about ourselves that are inaccurate. Sometimes, labels that were once true aren't any longer, but we continue to believe them. In other cases, the labels may never have been valid, but we believe them anyway. Unfortunately, children often are called "slow" or "stupid" when they have physiological difficulties, such as impaired vision or hearing, or when they are struggling with a second language. Even when the real source of difficulty is discovered, the children already may have internalized a destructive self-fulfilling prophecy.

Student Voices

Renee:

I now see that I labelled myself because of others' perspectives. Since I was in first grade, my grandmother said I was fat and that I would never lose weight. Well, you can imagine what this did to my self-esteem. I felt there was nothing I could do about being fat. At one point, I weighed 82 kilograms—pretty heavy for a girl who's 165 centimetres tall. Then, I got with some other people who were overweight, and we convinced ourselves to shape up. I lost 23 kilograms, but I still thought of myself as fat. That's only started to change lately as friends and my family comment on how slim I am. Guess I'm still seeing myself through others' eyes.

Identity Scripts

Psychologists define **identity scripts** as rules for living and identity (Berne, 1964; Harris, 1969).

Communication Notes

CHALLENGING THE DEFINITION OF DANCER

Internationally acclaimed British Columbia choreographer Lynda Raino created "Big Dance," a modern dance class for large people. All of the participants believed that they could never dance because of how they saw themselves and how "dancer" is portrayed in our culture. Raino describes the overwhelming transformation that occurs in the women when they don dance leotards and celebrate their large bodies in movement instead of hiding in shame. Raino says these women have to reinvent themselves as dancers and their journey challenges the definition of "dancer" for all of us. "It is a renovation of the spirit that takes place, and it is truly awesome to witness" (personal communication, March 10, 2001).

Photo: J. Hoadley

How do you respond to this picture of dancers? (Big Dance, Victoria, BC)

Like the scripts for plays, identity scripts define our roles, how we are to play them, and the basic elements in the plots of our lives. Think back to your childhood and identify some of the principal scripts that operated in your family. Did you hear any of these scripts from family members: "We are responsible people," "Our family always helps those in need," "A good education is the key to success," or "Live by God's word." These are examples of identity scripts people learn in families.

Most psychologists believe that the basic identity scripts for our lives are formed very early, probably by age five. This means that fundamental understandings of who we are and how we are supposed to live are forged when we have almost no control. Adults have the power, and children unconsciously internalize the scripts that others write. As adults, however, we have the capacity to review the identity scripts that were given to us and to challenge and change those that do not fit the selves we now choose to be.

Attachment Styles

Finally, parents and others who care for young children communicate through **attachment styles**, which are patterns of caregiving that teach us who we and others are and how to approach relationships. From extensive studies of interaction between parents and children, John Bowlby (1973, 1988) developed a theory that we learn attachment styles in our earliest relationships. In these formative relationships, caregivers communicate how they see us, others, and relationships.

Most children form their first human bond with a parent—usually the mother, because women typically take primary care of children. Clinicians who have studied attachment styles believe that the first bond is especially important because it forms the child's expectations for later relationships (Ainsworth et al., 1978; Bartholomew & Horowitz, 1991; Miller, 1993). Four distinct attachment styles have been identified, as shown in Figure 2.2.

A **secure attachment style** is the most positive. This style develops when the caregiver responds in a consistently attentive and loving way to the child. In response, the child develops a positive sense of self-worth ("I am lovable") and a positive view of others ("People are loving and can be trusted"). People with secure attachment styles tend to be outgoing, affectionate and able to handle the challenges and disappointments of close relationships without losing self-esteem. Equally important, people who have secure attachment styles usually are comfortable with themselves when they are not involved in close relationships. Their security enables them to engage in intimacy with others without depending on relationships for their self-worth.

A **fearful attachment style** is cultivated when the caregiver in the first bond communicates in negative, rejecting, or even abusive ways to the child. Children who are treated this way often infer that they are unworthy of love and that others are not loving. Thus, they learn to see themselves as unlovable and others as rejecting. Not surprisingly, people with a fearful attachment style tend to be apprehensive about relationships. Although they often want close bonds with others, they sometimes

Student Voices

Grace:

In my family, intelligence was a primary value: To be smart was good, and to be less than smart was unacceptable. I was great at outdoor activities such as building tree houses and leading "jungle expeditions" through the woods behind our home. Yet my parents were indifferent to my aptitudes for adventures and physical activity. What they stressed was learning and reading. I still have vivid memories of being shamed for a B in reading on my first-grade report card. Just as intensely, I recall the excessive praise heaped on me when I won a reading contest in fourth grade. By then I had learned what I had to be to get approval from my family.

© Bill Aron/PhotoEdit

Apply the Idea

REFLECTING ON YOUR IDENTITY SCRIPTS

To take control of our own lives, we must first understand the influences that currently shape them. Identify identity scripts your parents taught you.

1. First, recall explicit messages your parents gave you about "who we are" and "who you are." Can you hear their voices telling you codes that you were expected to follow?
2. Next, write down the scripts. Try to capture the language your parents used as they communicated the scripts to you.
3. Now, review each script. Which ones make sense to you today? Are you following any that are not constructive for you today? Do you disagree with any of them?
4. Finally, commit to changing scripts that aren't productive for you or that conflict with values you hold.

We can rewrite scripts once we are adults. To do so, we must become aware of what our families have taught us and take responsibility for scripting our own lives.

FIGURE 2.2

Styles of Attachment

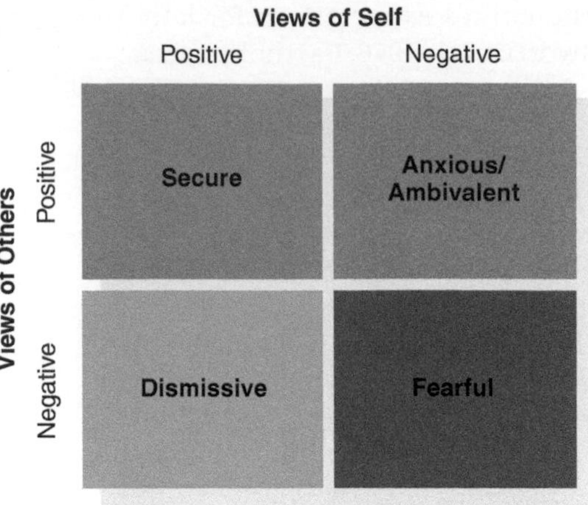

fear others will not love them and that they are not lovable. Thus, as adults they may avoid others or feel insecure in relationships.

A **dismissive attachment style** is also promoted by caregivers who are disinterested in, rejecting of, or abusive toward children. Yet people who develop this style do not accept the caregiver's view of them as unlovable. Instead, they typically dismiss others as unworthy. Consequently, children develop a positive view of themselves and a low regard for others and relationships. Those with a dismissive attachment style often develop a defensive view of relationships and regard them as unnecessary or undesirable.

A final pattern is the **anxious/ambivalent attachment style**, which is the most complex of the four. Each of the other three styles results from a consistent pattern of treatment by a caregiver. The anxious/ambivalent style, however, is fostered by inconsistent treatment from the caregiver. Sometimes the person who cares for a child is loving and attentive; at other times, the caregiver is indifferent or rejecting. The caregiver's communication is not only inconsistent but also unpredictable. He or she may respond positively to something a child does on Monday but react negatively to the same behaviour on Tuesday. Naturally, this unpredictability can cause anxiety for the child who depends on the caregiver (Miller, 1993). Because children tend to assume that adults are always right, they believe themselves to be the source of any problem—that they are unlovable or deserve abuse.

In adult life, people who have anxious/ambivalent attachment styles tend to be preoccupied with relationships. On one hand, they know others can be loving and affirming. On the other hand, they realize that others can hurt them and

Student Voices

Zondi:

In South Africa where I was born, I learned that I was not important. Most daughters learn this. My full name is Zondomini, which means between happiness and sadness. The happiness is because a child was born. The sadness is because I am a girl, not a boy. I am struggling now to see myself as worthy.

Student Voices

Noreen:

When I was little, my father was an alcoholic, but I didn't know that then. All I knew was that sometimes he loved me and played with me and sometimes he would shout at me for nothing. Once he told me I was his sunshine, but later that same night he told me he wished I'd never been born. Even though now I understand the alcohol made him act that way, it's still hard to feel I'm okay.

be unloving. Reflecting the pattern displayed by the caregiver, people with an anxious/ambivalent attachment style often are inconsistent themselves. One day, they invite affection; the next day, they rebuff it and deny needing or wanting closeness.

Our probability for developing a particular attachment style is affected by socioeconomic class, as clinical psychiatrist Robert Karen reports (in Greenberg, 1997). Poor families face serious hardships brought on by poverty: lack of adequate and nutritious food, poor shelter or homelessness, and inadequate medical care. These hardships can preoccupy and depress parents, making it difficult for them to be as responsive and loving to children as parents who have more material resources (Greenberg, 1997).

The attachment styles we learned in our first close relationship tend to persist (Bartholomew & Horowitz, 1991; Belsky & Pensky, 1988; Bowlby, 1988; Guerrero, 1996). However, this is not inevitable. We can modify our attachment styles by challenging the disconfirming self-perceptions communicated in our early years and by forming relationships that foster secure connections.

A study by Beth LePoire, Carolyn Shepard, and Ashley Duggan (1999) provides evidence that attachment styles can change. They found that the influence of parental attachment style was modified by romantic partners later in life, as did Franz Neyer (2002). In other words, the people we choose to have relationships with affect our attachment styles.

Apply the Idea

DETERMINING YOUR ATTACHMENT STYLE

Using the four descriptors below taken from Griffin and Bartholomew (1994), choose the relationship style that most accurately describes you in your romantic relationships.

A. *It is easy for me to become emotionally close to others. I am comfortable depending on others and having others depend on me. I don't worry about being alone or having others not accept me.*

B. *I am uncomfortable getting close to others. I want emotionally close relationships, but I find it difficult to trust others completely, or to depend on them. I worry that I will be hurt if I allow myself to become too close to others.*

C. *I want to be completely emotionally intimate with others, but I often find that others are reluctant to get as close as I would like. I am uncomfortable being without close relationships, but I sometimes worry that others don't value me as much as I value them.*

D. *I am comfortable without close emotional relationships. It is very important to me to feel independent and self-sufficient, and I prefer not to depend on others or have others depend on me.*

A = Secure; B = Fearful; C = Preoccupied (or Anxious/Ambivalent); D = Dismissing

What accounts for the relationship style you chose?

The Generalized Other

The perspectives of the **generalized other** reflect the views generally held by others in a society. Every society and social group has a generalized other, which reflects the shared values, experiences, and understandings of the particular society or social group (Sorrentino et al., 2005). The perspectives of the generalized other are revealed to us in two ways. First, we learn them as we interact with others, who have internalized cultural values and pass them on to us. For instance, most of us are exposed to the generalized other's perspective on gender in the process of playing with childhood friends. A study by Carol Martin and her colleagues (2000) showed that children three-and-a-half to seven years old have strong preferences for playing with other children of the same sex. This study also showed that young boys and girls thought peers were more likely to approve of their behaviour if they played with others of the same sex.

In Canadian culture, the perspective of the generalized other views murder, rape, robbery, and embezzlement as wrong, and each of us learns that as we participate in the society. In addition, we learn which aspects of identity society considers important, how society views various social groups, and, by extension, how it views us as members of specific groups. Researchers have identified four elements that are central to personal identity in modern

Apply the Idea

IDENTIFYING SOCIAL VALUES IN MEDIA

Select four popular magazines. Record the focus of their articles and advertisements. What do the articles and ads convey about what is valued in Canada? Identify themes and types of people that are emphasized. What cultural values about gender do the magazines communicate? What do articles convey about how women or men are regarded and what they are expected to be and to do? Ask the same questions about advertisements. How many ads aimed at women focus on being beautiful, looking young, losing weight, taking care of others, and attracting men? How many ads aimed at men emphasize strength, virility, success, and independence?

To extend this exercise, identify cultural values conveyed by television, movies, and news stories. Pay attention to who is highlighted and how different genders, races, and professions are represented.

The institutions that organize our society also communicate the generalized other's perspective by the values they uphold. For example, our judicial system reminds us that, as a society, we value laws and punish those who break them. In Western culture, the institution of marriage communicates society's view that, when people marry, they become a single unit, which is why joint ownership of property is assumed for married couples. Our institutions inevitably reflect prevailing social prejudices. For instance, we may be a lawful society, but wealthy defendants often can buy better "justice" than poor ones can. These and other values are woven into the fabric of our culture, and we learn them with little effort or awareness. The generalized other in modern Western culture emphasizes race, gender, sexual orientation, and socioeconomic class as central to personal identity (Andersen & Collins, 1998).

Western culture: race and ethnicity, gender, sexual orientation, and socioeconomic status (Andersen & Collins, 1992; James, 1999; Wood, 1995b, 1996).

jimchou/Shutterstock

Race and Ethnicity

Race and ethnicity are considered primary aspects of personal identity. The word "race" has often been used to categorize and identify the peoples of the world. Seen in the four colours of red, white, black, and yellow, race focused upon skin colour as the defining measure. Now, with our multicultural communities, the distinctions between colour are blurred and so is the importance placed on those differences.

The uniqueness of our ethnic communities, however, is cause to celebrate. It may be seen in the Chinese New Year in Vancouver or a ceilidh in Nova Scotia. Rich and diverse cultural customs are part of the fabric of Canadian life. The large cosmopolitan cities of Toronto and Vancouver are clear examples of multicultural communities, while in smaller communities, an ethnic majority may still predominate the social landscape. Wherever we live, our ethnicity is one way to define ourselves. "The Construction of Race in North America" explores the origins of race and ethnicity.

Student Voices

Leona:

I was a child of the adoption scoops of the '50s and '60s in BC and Alberta. I was taken from my First Nations home and raised by White adoptive parents. When I became an adult, I not only began my search for my biological parents as so many adopted children do, I also began my search for my ethnic identity. In finding my family and ancestors, I reclaimed my aboriginal roots and redefined my ethnicity. I am a First Nations woman!

Communication Notes

THE CONSTRUCTION OF RACE IN NORTH AMERICA

The word "white" wasn't used to describe race or identity until Europeans colonized the United States. They invented the label "White" as a way to increase solidarity among European settlers who actually had diverse ethnic backgrounds. By calling themselves "White," these diverse groups could gloss over differences among them and use their common skin hue to distinguish themselves from people of colour. White, in other words, is a term that was created to legitimize slavery.

During the time when slavery was an institution in the United States, Southern plantation owners invented a system of racial classification known as "the one-drop rule." According to this system, a person with as little as one drop of African blood was classified as Black. Thus, racial divisions were established, although arbitrarily. Social demographer William Petersen (1997) says that ethnicity is incredibly difficult to measure reliably. Increasing numbers of people have multiple racial and ethnic identities. For example, if a woman is one-fourth Black, one-fourth Chinese, one-fourth Thai, one-eighth White, and one-eighth First Nations, what race is she?

Gender

Gender is another important category in Western culture. Historically, men have been more valued and considered more rational, competent, and entitled to privilege than women. In the 1800s, women were not allowed to own property, gain professional training, or vote. It was considered appropriate for a husband to beat his wife; the phrase "rule of thumb" comes from the law that stated a man could beat his wife as long as he used a stick no thicker than his thumb.

On October 18, 1929, the Privy Council of England, at the time Canada's highest court, decided that women were "persons" under Section 24 of the *BNA Act*. This case came to be known as the "Persons Case," brought forward by five Canadian women who challenged the interpretation of "person" as "he." These courageous women—Emily Murphy, Nellie McClung, Irene Parlby, Louise McKinney, and Henrietta Muir Edwards—became known as the "Famous Five."

Even now, near the beginning of the twenty-first century, women and men are still not considered equals in many societies. Some scholars argue that gender is the most important aspect of personal identity in Western culture (Fox-Genovese, 1991). From the pink and blue blankets hospitals wrap around newborns to differential salaries earned by women and men, gender is a major facet of identity. Given the importance our society places on gender, it is no wonder that one of the first ways children learn to identify themselves is by their sex (Wood, 1996).

Western cultures have had strong gender prescriptions. Girls and women were expected to be caring, deferential, and cooperative, whereas boys and men were supposed to be independent, assertive, and competitive (Wood, 1994d). Consequently, women who asserted themselves or competed were likely to receive social disapproval, be called "bitches," and otherwise reprimanded for violating gender prescriptions. Men who refused to conform to social views of masculinity and who were gentle and caring risked being labelled "wimps." Views on gender prescriptions are changing, but there is still great variability in how the roles of men and women are perceived. Our gender, then, makes a great deal of difference in how others view us and how we come to see ourselves.

Student Voices

Allison:

When I was really young, I was outside playing in a little swimming pool one day. It was hot, and my brothers had their shirts off, so I took mine off too. When my mother looked up and saw me, she went berserk. She told me to get my shirt back on and act like a lady. That's when I knew that girls have to hide and protect their bodies, but boys don't.

Student Voices

David:

I'm gay, and many people think that gay is all I am. Once they find out I'm gay, nothing else about me seems relevant to them. They can't see all the ways in which we are alike and that we have more similarities than differences. They don't see that I am a student (just like them), that I am working my way through school (just like them), that I worry about tests and papers (just like them), that I love hockey (just like them). All they see is that I am gay, and that I am not like them.

Sexual Orientation

Sexual orientation is a third aspect of identity. Historically, heterosexuality was viewed as the normal sexual orientation, and lesbians, bisexuals and gays were regarded as abnormal. Society continues to communicate this viewpoint not only directly in some cases, but also through privileges given to heterosexuals but denied to gays, lesbians, and bisexuals.

Communication Notes

An Inclusive Self-Concept

Sexual orientation is an important influence on self-concept, as are the opportunities and material conditions of our lives. Yet, it is difficult to find good sources of information on how gay men, lesbians, transsexuals, and bisexuals view themselves and society. Egale Canada (égale being the French word for equal) is a national organization that advances equality and justice for lesbian, gay, bisexual, and trans-identified people and their families across Canada. See www.egale.ca/index.asp.

Another useful source is the website of the Gay & Lesbian Alliance Against Defamation (GLAAD: www.glaad.org), which offers extensive information on self-concept and other issues that affect individuals.

For example, a woman and man who love each other can be married and have their commitment recognized religiously and legally. However, two men or two women who love each other and want to be life partners are often denied social and legal recognition (Wood, 1995c). Heterosexuals can cover partners on insurance policies and inherit from them without paying taxes, but people with other sexual orientations are frequently excluded. To be homosexual or bisexual in modern Western culture is to be socially devalued. However, many gays and lesbians reject negative social views of their identity; instead, they form communities that support positive self-images.

Socioeconomic Status

Socioeconomic status is a fourth important aspect of identity in our society. Even though Canada is relatively open with regard to class (unlike India and South Africa, as discussed in the Communication Notes feature "Caste Counts"), the strata of society we belong to affects everything from how much money we make to the kinds of jobs and lifestyle choices we see as possibilities for ourselves. Class, as defined by Langston (1992) is difficult to point to because, unlike sex and ethnicity, it is not visible. Class isn't just the amount of money a person has. It's a basic part of how we understand the world and how we think, feel, and act. Class affects which stores, restaurants, and schools are part of our life. It influences who our friends are, where we live and work, and even the kind of car we drive.

Galina Barskaya/Shutterstock

In a 1995 book edited by Barney Dews and Carolyn Law, *This Fine Place So Far from Home: Voices of Academics from the Working Class,* a number of academics say that they have entered a middle-class world where they don't feel at ease or fully accepted. Many report wrenching identity conflicts as they interact with their working-class families and

Communication Notes

CASTE COUNTS

Societies around the world have created systems of classifying people (Ferrante, 1992). One of the most rigid is the caste system in India. Within this system, a person's class is hereditary: One is born into a particular caste and cannot move out of it in the current life. The Brahmans are the highest caste; they are priests and lawmakers. Next are the Kshatriyas, the warriors. The third caste, the Vaisyas, are farmers and merchants. Sudras, or labourers, make up the fourth caste. Until very recently, there was a fifth caste: Harijans, also known as untouchables, who were considered to be entirely outside the social order. This caste was abolished by a specific clause added to India's constitution. The remaining four classes are progressively subdivided, producing finer and finer distinctions among people (Human Rights Watch, 1999).

Rigid class distinctions are also part of South Africa's history (Wren, 1990). Apartheid, an Afrikaans word that means "apartness," has prevailed in South Africa for hundreds of years and was made the official policy of the country in 1948. Once the Nationalists, a conservative White political party, seized power, they passed hundreds of laws to enforce rigid racial separation in almost every area of life and to support domination of the country by the White minority. In 1990, South Africa abolished the Separate Amenities Act, which had mandated separate and unequal cemeteries, parks, trains, hotels, hospitals, and so forth for Whites and Blacks. Other discriminatory practices and laws are gradually being dismantled in South Africa. Visit the Human Rights Watch website to learn more about the caste system and other ways people are restricted by class memberships: www.hrw.org.

Student Voices

Geneva:

I may be in a first-class university, but I don't fit with most of the folks here. That hits me in the face every day. I walk across campus and see girls wearing shoes that cost more than all four pairs I own. I hear students talking about restaurants and trips that I can't afford. Last week, I heard a guy complaining about being too broke to get a GPS for his car. I don't own a car. I don't know how to relate to these people who have so much money. I do know they see the world differently than I do.

their middle-class colleagues. "Torn between two worlds and two identities" is how they describe themselves. The values and self-concepts that they grew up endorsing are at odds with the values and identities regarded as appropriate where they now live and work.

People with economic security have the resources and leisure time to focus on therapy, yoga, spiritual development, and spas to condition their bodies. These are not feasible for people who are a step away from poverty. Members of the middle and upper classes assume they will attend college or university and enter good professions, yet often these options are not realistic for working-class people (Langston, 1992). Guidance counsellors may encourage academically gifted working-class students to go to work or pursue vocational education after high school, whereas middle-class students of average ability are routinely steered toward good colleges or universities and status careers. In patterns such as these, we see how the perspective of the generalized other shapes our identities and our concrete lives.

Low social class and its concurrent poverty restrict the lives of many Canadians. Most Canadians agree that families should have at least a subsistence income—enough money for the food, clothing, and shelter needed to survive. Some, but not all, argue that our obligations to children go further than subsistence to include social inclusion—full participation in society. To facilitate inclusion, funds would be needed for a wider range of goods: school field trips, sports team membership, clothing that not only keeps you warm but also doesn't attract ridicule, and access to education based on ability, not income. Low socioeconomic status impacts on children's health and education, and thus can affect their subsequent income potential. In addition, many disadvantaged Canadians are subject to prejudice because of the preconceived notions by the generalized other about low-income people being lazy or careless. This challenge to their sense of self-worth further restricts their choices (Shillington, 2000).

It's important to realize that these aspects of identity intersect. Race interacts with gender, so women of colour experience double oppression and devaluation in our culture (Lorde, 1992; McIntosh, 1995). Socioeconomic class and sexual orientation also interact: Homophobia, or fear of homosexuals, is particularly pronounced in the working class, so a lesbian or gay person in a poor community may be socially ostracized (Langston, 1992). Socioeconomic class and gender

Reflective Exercise

Do you think class is evident in your community? In what ways are you affected by the demarcations between people in your job or at your school? Is the difference largely one of available money and resources or is it a deeper difference? Is "class" alive and well in Canada?

Apply the Idea

INTERNALIZING THE GENERALIZED OTHER

Which views of the generalized other have you internalized?

- *How do you evaluate women? How important is physical appearance to your judgments?*
- *How do you evaluate men? To what extent do strength and ambitiousness affect your judgments?*
- *What were you taught about First Nations people, Francophones, Anglophones, or members of Asian cultures? Which of those views have you imported into yourself?*
- *How do you see heterosexuals, bisexuals, gays, and lesbians? How did you develop these views?*

Are there social perspectives and attitudes that you hold but don't really respect or like? If so, consider challenging them and re-forming those parts of yourself.

also are interlinked; women are far more likely to live at the poverty level than are men (Ehrenreich, 1995; Roux, 2001). Gender and race intersect, so Black men have burdens and barriers not faced by White men (Dyson, 1995). All facets of our identity interact.

Social Comparison

As we learn the generalized other's perspective, we come to ask how we measure up to others. **Social comparison** is assessing ourselves in relation to others to form judgments of our own talents, abilities, qualities, and so forth. Whereas reflected appraisals are based on how we think others view us, social comparisons are our own use of others as measuring sticks for ourselves. We gauge ourselves in relation to others in two ways.

First, we compare ourselves with others to decide whether we are like them or different from them. Are we the same sex, age, colour, religion? Do we hang out with the same people? Do we have similar backgrounds, political beliefs, and social commitments? Assessing similarity and difference allows us to decide with whom we fit. Research shows that most people are more comfortable with others who are like them, so we tend to gravitate toward those we regard as similar (Pettigrew, 1967; Whitbeck & Hoyt, 1994). However, this can deprive us of the perspectives of people whose experiences and beliefs differ from our own.

We also use social comparison to measure ourselves and our abilities in relation to others. Am I

Student Voices

Sandi:

I baby-sit three children. A big thing for them is when the mail comes each day. The older two children sometimes get letters, but the youngest one, Harrison, never does. He always asks if there are any letters for him, and when I tell him no, he just looks so disappointed. So I've started writing to him once a week. It's helped him feel more equal to his older brother and sister.

Apply the Idea

REVIEWING YOUR SOCIAL COMPARISONS

Find out whether your social comparisons are realistic. First, write "I am" six times. Complete the first three sentences with words that reflect positive views of yourself. Complete the fourth through sixth sentences with words that express negative views of yourself. For example, you might write, "I am kind," "I am smart," "I am responsible," "I am clumsy," "I am selfish," and "I am impatient."

Next, beside each sentence write the names of two people in comparison to whom you judge yourself for each quality. For "I am kind," you would list people you use as standards of kindness. List your social comparisons for all self-descriptions.

Now, review the names and qualities. Are any of the people unrealistic standards of comparison for you? If so, whom might you select for more realistic social comparisons?

as good a guard as Lazlo? Do I play the guitar as well as Chris? Am I as smart as Serena? Am I as attractive as Toshika? Comparing ourselves to others is normal, and it helps us develop realistic self-concepts. However, we should be wary of using inappropriate standards of comparison. It isn't realistic to judge our attractiveness in relation to stars and models or our athletic ability in relation to professional players.

The Self Is Multidimensional

There are many dimensions, or aspects, of the human self. You have an image of your physical self: how large, attractive, and athletic you are. In addition, you have perceptions of your cognitive self, including your intelligence and aptitudes. You also have an emotional self-concept. Are you sensitive or not? Are you generally upbeat or cynical? Then there is your social self, which involves how you are with others. Some of us are extroverted and joke around a lot or dominate interactions, whereas others prefer to be less prominent.

Our social selves also include our social roles: daughter or son, student, worker, parent, or partner in a committed relationship. Each of us also has a moral self that consists of our ethical and spiritual beliefs, the principles we believe in, and our overall sense of morality. Although we use the word *self* as though it referred to a single entity, in reality the self is made up of many dimensions. The multiple dimensions of self are shaped by direct definitions, reflected appraisals, identity scripts, attachment styles, the perspectives of the generalized other, and social comparisons.

The Self Is a Process

The self develops gradually and changes throughout our lives. We do not enter the world with fully formed identities. Newborn babies have no **ego boundaries**, which define where an individual stops and the rest of the world begins (Chodorow, 1989). To an infant, nursing is a single sensation in which the boundary between itself and the mother is blurred. A baby perceives no boundaries between its foot and the tickle by a father. Over time, infants gradually begin to distinguish themselves from the external environment. This is the beginning of a self-concept: the realization that one is a separate entity.

Within the first year or two of life, as infants start to differentiate themselves from the rest of the world, the self begins to develop. Babies, then toddlers, then children devote enormous energy to understanding who they are. They actively seek to define themselves and to become competent in the identities they claim (Kohlberg, 1958; Piaget, 1932/1965). For instance, early on, little girls and boys start working to become competent females and males. They scan the environment, find models of females and males, and imitate and refine their performances of gender (Levy, 1999).

In like manner, children figure out what it takes to be smart, strong, attractive, and responsible, and they work to become competent in each area. Throughout our lives we continue the process of defining and presenting our identities. The ways we define ourselves vary as we mature. Struggling to be a swimmer at age four gives way to striving to be popular in high school and being a successful professional and partner in adult life. The fact that we change again and again during our lives is evidence of our capacity for self-renewal and continual growth.

SOCIAL PERSPECTIVES ON THE SELF ARE CONSTRUCTED AND VARIABLE

We have seen that we gain a sense of personal identity and an understanding of social life by encountering and internalizing the social perspectives of significant others and the generalized other. This could lead you to think that our self-concepts are determined by fixed social values. As we will see, however, this isn't the case. Social views are constructed and variable, so they can be changed. An example of the variability of social values is examined in the *Communication Notes* feature "A Cross-Cultural Look at Sexual Identity."

Communication Notes

A CROSS-CULTURAL LOOK AT SEXUAL IDENTITY

In Canada, First Nations peoples confer a special name to gay, lesbian, or bisexual members. They are called "Two-Spirited." "The aboriginal concept of gender assignment and identity is somewhat more complex than the binary opposites of male and female in Anglo-American Society" says Gordon de Frane, who addresses the nature and limitations of the term "Two-Spirited" (2000, p. 3). Today, the term applies not only to sexual orientation but also to a larger, more encompassing view of the world or a truer integration of the male and female in all of us. Two-spirited members of tribes were once revered and exalted to the status of shaman because of the gift they bore.

Constructed Social Views

Social perspectives are constructed in particular cultures at specific times. What a society values does not reflect divine law, absolute truth, or the natural order of things. The values that are endorsed in any society are arbitrary and designed to support dominant ideologies or the beliefs of those in power. For example, it was to men's advantage to deny women the right to vote, because doing so preserved men's power to control the laws of the land. Similarly, it was to the European settlers' advantage to force the aboriginal people of Canada onto reserves. By approving of heterosexuality and not homosexuality, the culture supports a particular arbitrary family ideal. When we reflect on widely endorsed social values, we realize that they tend to serve the interests of those who are privileged by the status quo.

Differing Social Views

The constructed and arbitrary nature of social values becomes especially obvious when we consider how widely values differ from culture to culture. For example, in Sweden, Denmark, and Norway, same-sex partnerships are allowed and are given full legal recognition and Canada and some U.S. states now permit same-sex marriages. There are also cultures in which heterosexuality is not the only sexual orientation regarded as normal. Some cultures even recognize more than two genders.

Prescriptions for femininity and masculinity also vary substantially across cultures. In some places, men are emotional and dependent, and women are assertive and emotionally controlled. The individualistic ethic so prominent in the West is not valued or considered normal in many other countries, particularly Asian and African ones (Gaines, 1995).

The frail, pale appearance considered feminine in the 1800s gave way to more robust, well-rounded ideals in the mid-1900s, as embodied by Marilyn Monroe. Today, a more athletic body is one of the ideals prescribed for women. Magazines reflect and encourage the current view that strength and athletic ability are also desirable feminine attributes.

Social meanings also vary across time within single cultures. For example, in the 1700s and 1800s, women in Europe and North America were often viewed as too delicate to engage in hard labour. During the World Wars, however, women were expected to do "men's work" while men were at war. When the men returned home, society once again decreed that women were too weak to perform in the labour market, and they were reassigned to home and hearth.

Social prescriptions for men have also varied. The rugged he-man who was the ideal in the 1800s relied on his physical strength to farm wild lands. After the Industrial Revolution, physical strength and bravado gave way to business acumen, and money replaced muscle as a sign of manliness. Today, as our society struggles with changes in women, men, and families, the ideals of manhood are being revised yet again. Increasingly, men are expected to be involved in caring for children and to be sensitive as well as independent and strong.

The meaning of homosexuality has also been revised over time in Western culture. Until fairly recently, our society strongly disapproved of gays, lesbians, and bisexuals, so most nonheterosexuals did not publicly acknowledge their sexual orientation. Although much prejudice still exists, it is gradually diminishing. Marriage laws in Canada have also changed. In 2005, Canada joined Belgium, the Netherlands, and Spain in legalizing same-sex marriages; couples can now obtain marriage licenses and register their marriages legally. Some U.S. states have followed suit. As social views of homosexuality change, more and more gays and lesbians are openly acknowledging their sexual orientation.

The meaning our society assigns to different ethnic groups has also varied markedly over our history as a nation. Although ignorance and prejudice still haunt our nation, they are lessening. Today, inclusive curricula in

Student Voices

Hannah:

Because I'm an older student, I have a good understanding of how views change in society. Forty years ago when I first started college, women were not taken very seriously. I had no female professors, and there wasn't a Women's Studies department at my college. Our teachers, and all of us, just expected that most women at the college would become wives and mothers who either worked little part-time jobs or didn't work outside the home. Any woman who said she wanted to pursue a full-time career was considered kind of strange.

Attitudes on campus are so different today. There are lots of female professors who are role models for young women—they are living proof that women can have careers and families. And this generation of students doesn't assume women are going to school to get their "Mrs. degree." A majority of the female students I know have serious career ambitions, and most of the male students seem to assume that their female classmates and girlfriends will work full-time for most of their lives. What a difference 40 years has made in how women are viewed.

How has the concept of femininity changed in the twenty-first century?

Apply the Idea

SOCIAL DEFINITIONS OF MASCULINITY AND FEMININITY

To find out how society in general (the generalized other) defines ideals for women and men today, review five current popular Canadian magazines. You may review them in the library or online, using your InfoTrac® College Edition. Select magazines that aim at postsecondary-age readers. While reviewing the magazines, answer the following questions:

- *How many females are shown actively involved in pursuits such as sports or manual labour?*
- *How many females are shown in passive roles such as relaxing, eating, or waiting for others?*
- *How many females are shown in domestic settings or engaged in domestic activities such as preparing meals and caring for children?*
- *How many males are shown actively involved in pursuits such as sports or manual labour?*
- *How many males are shown in passive roles such as relaxing, eating, or waiting for others?*
- *How many males are shown in domestic settings and/or engaged in domestic activities such as preparing meals and caring for children?*
- *How many females are slender?*
- *How many males are muscular and strong-looking?*
- *How many members of minorities are shown?*
- *How many members of the minorities shown have physical features that are more typical of Caucasians than of their own ethnic groups?*

Communication Notes

THE REALITY OF RACE

For centuries, race has been used as a primary way of classifying people. Yet, most scientists now reject the concept of race as a valid means of defining individual and group identities. According to Jonathan Marks, a biologist at Yale University, "race has no biological reality."

Increasingly, scientists assert that race is only a socially constructed category. DNA research reveals that there is no scientific basis for the racial categories widely used in society. According to DNA studies, there is actually far more genetic variation within a single African population than in all non-African populations put together.

Loring Brace, an anthropologist at the University of Michigan, reports that intelligence is one human trait that doesn't vary from population to population. According to Brace, the differences among people grouped into different races that show up on intelligence tests reflect environmental and cultural factors, including differing levels of nutrition and quality of education, and don't reflect innate intellectual capacity.

schools recognize and celebrate the strengths of students of various abilities and ethnic origins. Professional development conferences for teachers frequently have a focus of "diversity and multiple perspectives." As the generalized other's perspective on diverse ethnicities enlarges, people of all strata of society gain more positive reflected appraisals of their identity than was the case years ago. The Communication Notes feature "The Reality of Race" discusses the issue of race as a social, not biological, reality.

Other socially constructed views are also variable. In the 1950s and 1960s, people with disabilities were often confined to their homes or put into institutions. Today, many schools endorse inclusion, which places students with physical or mental disabilities in regular classrooms. Sensitivity to people who have special needs grows as fully able students become more familiar with people with disabilities.

The meaning of age has also varied throughout our history. In the 1800s, the average life span was less than 60 years, and it was not uncommon for people to die in their 40s or 50s. Then, unlike today, 50 was considered old. The average life span today is nearly 80, making 50 seem considerably less old. In the 1800s, people typically married in their teens, and they often had five or more children before reaching 30. Today, many people wait until their 30s to begin having children, and parents in their 40s aren't considered "too old."

Student Voices

Michiko:

After the internment of the Japanese in British Columbia during World War II, my parents were afraid to openly demonstrate any of our Japanese customs. We only ate rice and used chopsticks at home, and only if no one would witness it. It's taken a long time for my parents to trust that their Japanese customs and heritage are once again valued. I am gradually changing the way they think by voicing my views. It's wonderful to see my father proud once again to be a Japanese Canadian in public.

Changing Social Views

Social perspectives are changeable and, in fact, have changed significantly over time. Social perspectives are fluid and respond to individual and collective efforts to weave new meanings into the fabric of social life. Each of us has the responsibility to speak out against social perspectives that we perceive as wrong or harmful. By doing so we participate in the ongoing process of refining who we are as a society.

GUIDELINES FOR IMPROVING SELF-CONCEPT

So far, we have explored how we form our self-concepts as we interact with particular others and as we encounter the perspective of the generalized other. Now, we want to know how we can enhance our self-concepts.

CONCEPTS AT A GLANCE

To Improve Self-Concept

- Make a firm commitment to personal growth.
- Gain and use knowledge to support personal growth.
- Set goals that are realistic and fair.
- Seek contexts that support personal growth.

Make a Firm Commitment to Personal Growth

The first principle for changing self-concept is the most difficult and the most important. You must make a firm commitment to cultivating personal growth. This isn't as easy as it might sound. A firm commitment involves more than saying, "I want to be more open to others." Saying this sentence is simple. What is more difficult is investing energy and effort to bring about change. From the start, realize that changing how you think of yourself is a major project.

There are two reasons why it is challenging to change our self-concept. First, doing so takes continual effort. Because the self is a process, it is not formed in one fell swoop, and it cannot be changed in a moment of decision. We must realize at the outset that there will be setbacks, and we can't let them derail our resolution to change. Last year, a student said she wanted to be more assertive, so she began to speak up more often in class. When a professor criticized one of her contributions, her resolution folded. Changing how we see ourselves is a long-term process, so we can't let setbacks undermine our commitment to change.

A second reason that makes it difficult to change self-concept is that the self resists change. Morris Rosenberg (1979), a psychologist who studied self-concept extensively, said that most humans tend to resist change and that we also seek esteem or a positive view of ourselves. The good news is that we want esteem or a positive self-image; the bad news is that we find it difficult to change, even in positive directions. Interestingly, Rosenberg and others have found that we are as likely to hold on to negative self-images as we are positive ones. Apparently, consistency itself is comforting. If you realize in advance that you may struggle against change, you'll be prepared for the tension that accompanies personal growth.

Student Voices

Tina:

One social value I do not accept is that it's good to be as thin as a rail if you're female. A lot of my girlfriends are always dieting. Even when they get weak from not eating enough, they won't eat, because they'll gain weight. I know several girls who are bulimic, which is really dangerous, but they are more scared of gaining a pound than of dying. I refuse to buy into this social value. I'm not fat, but I'm not skinny either. I'm not as thin as models, and I'm not aiming to be. It's just stupid to go around hungry all the time because society has sick views of beauty for women.

Gain and Use Knowledge to Support Personal Growth

Commitment alone is insufficient to bring about constructive changes in your self-concept. In addition, you need several types of knowledge. First, you need to understand how your self-concept was formed. In this chapter, we've seen that much of how we see ourselves results from socially constructed perspectives. Based on what you've learned, you can exercise critical judgment about which social perspectives to accept and which to reject. For instance, you should critically reflect on the generalized other's views of race, gender, sexual orientation, and socioeconomic class to decide whether you want to accept these views as part of your own perspective.

Second, you need information about yourself. One way to get this information is through **self-disclosure**, which is revealing information about ourselves that others are unlikely to discover on their own. Self-disclosure is an important way to learn about ourselves. As we reveal our hopes, fears, dreams, and feelings, we get responses from others that give us new perspectives on who we are. In addition, we gain insight into ourselves by seeing how we interact with others in new situations.

A number of years ago, Joseph Luft and Harry Ingham (Luft, 1969) created a model of different sorts of knowledge that affect self-development. They called the model the **Johari Window** (Figure 2.3), which is a combination of their first names, Joe and Harry.

Four types of information are relevant to the self. Open, or public, information is known both to us and to others. Your name, height, major, and tastes in music probably are open information that you share easily with others. The blind area contains information that others know about us but we don't know about ourselves. For example, others may see that we are insecure even though we think

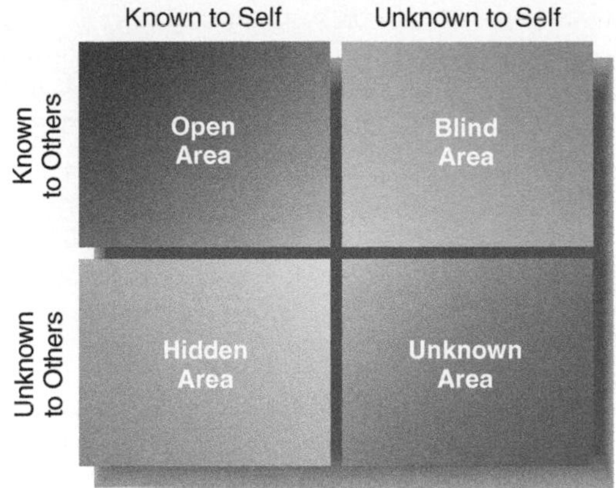

FIGURE 2.3

The Johari Window

we've hidden that well. Others may also recognize needs or feelings that we haven't acknowledged to ourselves.

The third area includes hidden information, which we know about ourselves but choose not to reveal to most others. You might not tell many people about your vulnerabilities or about traumas in your past because you consider this private information. The unknown area is made up of information about ourselves that neither we nor others know. This consists of your untapped resources, your untried talents, and your reactions to experiences you've never had. You don't know how you will manage a crisis until you've been in one, and you can't tell what kind of parent you would be unless you've had a child.

It is important to gain access to information in our blind and unknown areas. One way to do this is to expand our experiences by entering unfamiliar situations, trying novel things, and experimenting with new kinds of communication. Another way to increase self-knowledge is to interact with others to learn how they see us. We can gain insight into ourselves by reflecting on their perceptions. Others are likely to offer us insights into ourselves only if we make it safe for them to do so. If a friend states a perception of you that you dislike and you become defensive, the friend may not risk sharing other perceptions in the future. If we learn to respond nondefensively to others' perceptions of us, including criticism, then we pave the way for honest appraisals from them.

Although self-disclosure has many potential values, it is not always advisable. Self-disclosure necessarily involves risks, such as the risk that others will not accept what we reveal or that they might use it against us. Appropriate self-disclosure minimizes these risks by proceeding slowly and in relationships in which trust has been established. It's wise to test the waters gradually before plunging into major self-disclosures. Begin by revealing information that is personal but not highly intimate or damaging if exploited. Before disclosing further, observe how the other person responds to your communication and what she or he does with it. You might also pay attention to whether the other person reciprocates by disclosing personal information to you. Because self-disclosures involve risk, we need to be cautious about when and to whom we reveal ourselves. Table 2.1 lists key benefits and risks of self-disclosing communication.

In addition to reading this book and learning from your class, there are other ways to gain knowledge to help you set and achieve personal goals, including books and websites that focus on personal growth. Other people are another source of knowledge. Talking with others is a way to learn about relationships and what people want in them. Others can also provide useful feedback about your

TABLE 2.1

BENEFITS AND RISKS OF SELF-DISCLOSING COMMUNICATION

Benefits	Risks
May increase trust. May increase closeness. May enhance self-esteem. May increase security. May enhance self-growth.	Others may reject us. Others may think less of us. Others may violate our confidences.

interpersonal skills and your progress in the process of change. Finally, others can serve as models. If someone you know is particularly skillful in supporting others, observe her or him carefully to identify particular communication skills. You may not want to imitate this person exactly, but observing will make you more aware of concrete skills involved in supporting others. You can then tailor some of the skills others display to suit your personal style.

Set Goals That Are Realistic and Fair

Efforts to change how we see ourselves work best when we set realistic and fair goals. In a culture that emphasizes perfectionism, it's easy to be trapped into expecting more than is humanly possible.

Western society urges us to expect more, more, more of ourselves—more successes, more productivity, more possessions, more everything (Lacher, 2005). This is unrealistic and can only make us unhappy, because we can never achieve or have or be enough.

Being realistic also involves making fair assessments of ourselves. This requires us to place judgments in context and to see ourselves as being in process. To assess ourselves effectively, we need to understand not only our discrete qualities and abilities but also how all of our parts fit together to form the whole self. One of the ways we treat ourselves unfairly is to judge particular abilities out of context. We have to appreciate our particular skills and weaknesses in the overall context of who we are.

For example, if an accomplished young writer compares herself to only national literary greats such as Margaret Atwood or Ann-Marie MacDonald, she will never recognize her own achievements in writing. Her self-assessment is unrealistic because she compares herself to people who are extremely successful in particular spheres of life, yet she doesn't notice that her models might not be especially impressive in other areas. As a result, she mistakenly feels she is inadequate in most ways. In our efforts to improve self-concept, then, we should acknowledge our strengths and virtues as well as parts of ourselves we wish to change.

If you define a goal as becoming a totally perfect communicator in all situations, you are

Student Voices

Kendrick:

I really got bummed out my freshman year. I had been the star on my high school basketball team, so I came to college expecting to be a star here, too. The first day of practice, I saw a lot of guys who were better than I was. They were incredible. I felt like nothing. When I got back to my room, I called my mom and told her I was no good at basketball here. She told me I couldn't expect to compete with guys who had been on the team for a while and who had gotten coaching. She asked how I stacked up against just the other first-year players, and I said pretty good. She told me they were the ones to compare myself to.

setting yourself up for failure. It's more reasonable and constructive to establish a series of realistic small goals that you can meet. You might focus on improving one of the skills of communication competence we discussed in Chapter 1. When you are satisfied with your ability at that skill, you can move on to a second one. Kendrick's and Timoteo's reflections reminds us that we should be fair in judging ourselves. We often judge our abilities and set our goals with reference to unfair standards.

Being fair to yourself also requires you to accept that you are in process. Earlier in this chapter, we saw that one characteristic of the human self is that it is continually in process, always becoming. This implies several things. First, it means you need to accept who you are now as a starting point. You don't have to like or admire everything about yourself, but it is important to accept who you are now as a basis for going forward. The self that you are results from all the interactions, reflected appraisals, and social comparisons you have made during your life. You cannot change your past, but you do not have to let it define your future.

Accepting yourself as in process also implies that you realize you can change. Who you are is not who you will be in five or ten years. Don't let yourself be

Student Voices

Timoteo:

I've really struggled with my academic goals. It's very important to me and my whole family that I do well in school. I am the first in my family to go to college, so I must succeed. I've felt bad when I make Bs and Cs and others in my classes make As. For a long time, I said to myself, "I am not as smart as they are if they make better grades." But I work 35 hours a week to pay for school. Most of the others in my classes either don't have to work or work fewer hours than I do. They have more time to spend writing papers and studying for tests. I think better of my academic abilities when I compare myself to other students who work as much as I do. That is a more fair comparison than comparing myself to students who don't work.

Communication Notes

IF AT FIRST YOU DON'T SUCCEED

Achieving goals for self-development is hard. If you don't succeed at first, it's easy to become discouraged and to quit trying. One way to keep yourself motivated to work toward your goals is to remember that a lot of people we consider very successful weren't always so:

- Isaac Newton did so poorly in his early school years that his teachers labelled him "unpromising."
- One of Ludwig van Beethoven's early music teachers said that he was hopeless as a composer.
- Michael Jordan was cut from his high school basketball team. The same is true of Boston Celtics' Bob Cousy. Both players are now in the Basketball Hall of Fame.
- One of Thomas Jefferson's grade school teachers told him he was stupid and should go into some line of work where his pleasant personality, not his mind, might allow him to succeed.
- Walt Disney was fired from his job on a newspaper because, according to his editor, he "lacked imagination and had no good ideas."
- Winston Churchill failed sixth grade and had to repeat it.
- Babe Ruth struck out 1300 times, which remains the record for strikeouts in the major leagues.

hindered by defeating, self-fulfilling prophecies or the false idea that you cannot change (Rusk & Rusk, 1988). You can change if you set realistic goals, make a genuine commitment, and then work for the changes you want.

Seek Contexts That Support Personal Growth

Just as it is easier to swim with the tide than against it, it is easier to change our views of ourselves when we have some support for our efforts. You can do a lot to create an environment that supports your growth by choosing contexts and people who help you realize your goals. First, think about settings. If you want to become more extroverted, put yourself in social situations rather than in libraries. But libraries are a better context than parties if your goal is to improve your academic performance.

Second, think about the people whose appraisals of you will help you move toward changes you desire. You can put yourself in supportive contexts by consciously choosing to be around people who believe in you and encourage your personal growth. It's equally important to steer clear of people who pull us down or say we can't change. In other words, people who reflect positive appraisals of us enhance our ability to improve.

Others aren't the only ones whose communication affects our self-concepts. We also communicate with ourselves, and our own messages influence our esteem. One of the most crippling kinds of self-talk we can engage in is **self-sabotage**. This involves telling ourselves we are no good, we can't do something, there's no point in trying to change, and so forth. We may be repeating judgments others have made of us, or we may be inventing our own negative self-fulfilling prophecies. Either way, self-sabotage defeats us because it undermines belief in ourselves. Self-sabotage is poisonous; it destroys our motivation to change and grow. We can act as downers or even vultures, just as others can. In fact, we can probably do more damage to our self-concepts than others can because we are most aware of our vulnerabilities and fears. This may explain why vultures originally were described as people who put themselves down.

We can also act as uppers for ourselves. We can affirm our strengths, encourage our growth, and fortify our sense of self-worth. Positive self-talk builds motivation and belief in yourself. It is also a useful strategy to interrupt and challenge negative messages from yourself and others. The next time you hear yourself saying, "I can't do this" or someone else says, "You'll never change," challenge the negative message with self-talk. Say out loud to yourself, "I can do it. I will change." Use positive self-talk to resist counterproductive communication about yourself.

Before leaving this discussion, we should make it clear that improving your self-concept is not facilitated by uncritical positive communication. None of us grows and improves when we listen only to praise, particularly if it is less than honest. The true uppers in our lives offer constructive criticism to encourage us to reach for better versions of ourselves.

Student Voices

Bob:

I never drank much until I got into this one group at school. All of them drank all the time. It was easy to join them. In fact, it was pretty hard not to drink and still be one of the guys. This year, I decided I was drinking too much, and I wanted to stop. It was hard enough not to keep drinking, because the guys were always doing it, but what really made it hard was the way the guys got on me for abstaining. They let me know I was being uncool and made me feel like a jerk. Finally, to stop drinking, I had to get a different apartment.

Apply the Idea

IMPROVING YOUR SELF-CONCEPT

1. Define one change you would like to make in yourself. It might be a behaviour or a self-fulfilling prophecy or anything about yourself you would like to alter.
2. Write down the change you want to make. Use strong, affirmative language to motivate yourself: "I will listen more carefully to friends" or "I will start speaking up in classes," for example.
3. Refine your general goal by making sure it is realistic and fair. Write out your refined goal using specific language: "I want to show my two best friends that I am paying attention when they talk to me" or "I want to make one comment in each meeting of one class this week," for example.
4. Place the card or paper where you will see it often. Each time you see it, repeat the message aloud to yourself. This should help sustain your commitment to making the change.
5. Observe others who are models for what you want to be. Write down what they do. Use specific language to describe how they communicate: "Tracy nods a lot and repeats back what others say so they know she is listening" or "Anton provides examples of concepts in class so that the ideas are more concrete," for example.
6. Select contexts that assist you in reaching your goal: "I will talk with my friends in private settings where there are no distractions that interfere with listening well" or "I will begin speaking up in class in my Communication 100 course because it is the most discussion-oriented and because other students make a lot of comments there. Later, I will speak up in my sociology course, which is more lecture-oriented," for example.

To learn more about the self and ways of changing yourself, go to mentalhelp.net.

Chapter Summary

In this chapter, we explored the self as a process that evolves over the course of our lives. We saw that the self is not present at birth but develops as we interact with others. Through communication, we learn and import social perspectives—those of particular others and those of the generalized other, or society as a whole. Reflected appraisals, direct definitions, and social comparisons are communication processes that shape how we see ourselves and how we change over time. The perspective of the generalized other includes social views of aspects of identity, including race, gender, sexual preference, and class. However, these are arbitrary social constructions that we may challenge once we are adults. When we resist counterproductive social views, we promote change in society.

The final section of the chapter focused on ways to improve self-concept. Guidelines for doing this are to make a firm commitment to personal growth; to acquire and use knowledge about desired changes and concrete skills; to set realistic goals, assessing yourself fairly; and to create contexts that support the changes you seek. Transforming how we see ourselves is not easy, but it is possible. We can make amazing changes in who we are and how we feel about ourselves when we embrace our human capacity to make choices.

Key Concepts

- anxious/ambivalent attachment style
- attachment style
- direct definition
- dismissive attachment style
- downers
- ego boundaries
- fearful attachment style
- generalized other
- identity scripts
- Johari Window
- particular others
- reflected appraisal
- secure attachment style
- self
- self-disclosure
- self-fulfilling prophecy
- self-sabotage
- social comparison
- uppers
- vultures

For Further Thought and Discussion

1. Set a specific, fair, realistic goal for improving your interpersonal communication. For the next two weeks, focus on making progress toward that goal, following the guidelines in this chapter. Share the results of your work with others in your class.
2. Talk with one man and one woman who are 20 years older than you. Talk with one man and one woman who are 40 years older than you. In each conversation, ask them to explain how men and women were expected to be when they were 20 years old. Ask them to describe how women and men were expected to act and dress. Ask them to explain what behaviours, goals, and attitudes were considered inappropriate for women and men when they were 20 years old. Compare their responses with views held by 20-year-olds today.
3. Use your InfoTrac® College Edition to access the last four issues of *Sex Roles: A Journal of Research*. Select two articles that focus on self-concept (also look for words in the titles such as *identity, self, self-esteem*, and *personality*) and read both articles. How does what you learn expand the discussion of self-concept presented in this chapter?
4. Discuss the idea of race with members of your class. You may want to reread the section on race and identity in this chapter. What is race? Is race a useful way to classify people? Why or why not? Do you think Statistics Canada should allow people who are filling out forms to checkmark multiple races to define themselves?
5. Think about a time when you tried to create some change in yourself and were not successful. Review what happened by applying the four principles for improving self-concept presented in the last section of this chapter. Now that you understand these principles, how might you be more effective if you wanted to create that same change in yourself today?
6. Use your InfoTrac® College Edition to read *Race and Gender as Components of Working Self-Concept* by Elizabeth Aries and her colleagues. Are their findings consistent with your own experiences in being aware of your race and gender?

7. George Herbert Mead was a philosopher and scholar who first developed many of the ideas about self presented in this chapter. To learn more about Mead's life and work, visit www.sociologyprofessor.com/socialtheorists/georgeherbertmead.php; www.iep.utm.edu/m/mead.htm; plato.stanford.edu/entries/mead.
8. To learn more about how attachment styles affect children, Type "attachment styles" into the Google search window to find information on current research.

Chapter 3

Perception and Communication

The eye sees only what the mind is prepared to comprehend.

—Henri Bergson

The social world that we share with others is a world we have imagined together and agreed with each other to believe in.

—Elizabeth Janeway

paul prescott/Shutterstock

This chapter focuses on meaning, which is the heart of communication. To understand how humans create meanings for themselves and their activities, we need to understand how perception and communication interact. As we will see, perception shapes how we understand others' communication and how we ourselves communicate. At the same time, communication influences our perceptions of people and situations. Before reading further, try to connect the nine dots at the right without lifting your pencil from the paper. You may use no more than four lines, the lines must be straight, and the lines must be connected to one another.

CONCEPTS AT A GLANCE

Perception and Communication

- Perception shapes communication.
- Communication influences perception.

To understand how perception and communication interact, we'll first discuss the three-part process of perception. Next, we'll consider factors that affect our perceptions. Finally, we'll identify guidelines for improving perception so we can communicate more effectively.

Before we explore those topics, let's return to the nine dots problem. Could you solve it? Most people have trouble solving the problem because they label the nine dots a square, and they try to connect the dots staying within the boundaries of a square. However, it's impossible to connect the dots with four straight lines if you define the dots as a square. One solution (there are several) appears at the end of the chapter, on page 98.

This exercise makes an important point about the relationship between labels and human perception. The label *square* affects how you perceive the nine dots. In everyday communication, our words affect how we perceive others, situations, events, behaviours, and ourselves. At the same time, our perceptions, which are always incomplete and subjective, shape what things mean to us and hence the labels we use to name them. As long as we perceive the nine dots as a square, we can't solve the problem. Similarly, we communicate with others according to how we perceive and define them, and we may miss opportunities when our labels limit what we perceive. In the pages that follow, we want to unravel the complex relationships between perception and communication.

Labels limit what we perceive.

© Corbis

THE PROCESS OF HUMAN PERCEPTION

Perception is the active process of creating meaning by selecting, organizing, and interpreting people, objects, events, situations, and other phenomena. Note that perception is defined as an active process. We do not passively receive what is "out there" in the external world. Instead, we actively work to make sense of ourselves, others, and interactions. To do so, we select only certain things to notice, and then we organize and interpret what we have selectively noticed. What anything means to us depends on the aspects of it that we notice and on our organization and interpretation of those aspects. Thus, perception is not a simple matter of recording external reality. Instead, we invest a lot of energy in constructing the meanings of phenomena.

Perception consists of three processes: selecting, organizing, and interpreting (see Figure 3.1). These processes are continuous, so they blend into one another. They are also interactive, so each of them affects the other two. For example, what we select to perceive in a particular situation affects how

FIGURE 3.1

The Process of Human Perception

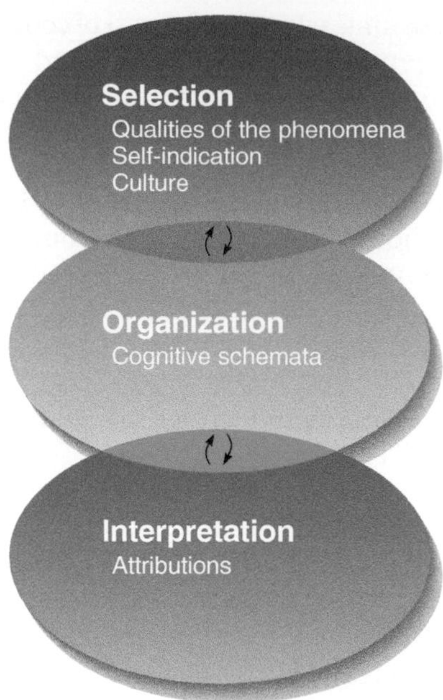

we organize and interpret the situation. At the same time, how we organize and interpret a situation affects our subsequent selections of what to perceive in the situation.

Selection

Stop for a moment and notice what is going on around you right now. Is there music in the background? Is the room warm or cold, messy or neat, large or small, light or dark? Is there laundry in the corner waiting to be washed? Can you smell anything—food being cooked, the stale odour of last night's popcorn, traces of cologne? Can you hear muted sounds of activities outside? Now, think about what's happening inside you: Are you sleepy, hungry, comfortable? Do you have a headache or an itch anywhere? On what kind of paper is your book printed? Is the type large, small, easy to read? How do you like the size of the book, the colours used, the design of the pages?

Photodisc/Getty Images

Probably you weren't conscious of most of these phenomena when you began reading the chapter. Instead, you focused on understanding the material in the book. You narrowed your attention to what you defined as important, and you were unaware of other aspects of the book and your surroundings. This is typical of how we live our lives. We can't attend to everything in our environment, because there is far too much going on in and around us, and we don't view most of it as relevant to us in any given moment.

We select to attend to certain stimuli based on a number of factors. First, some qualities of phenomena draw attention. For instance, we notice things that **STAND OUT**, because they are larger, more intense, or more unusual than other phenomena. So we're more likely to hear a loud voice than a soft one and to notice someone in a bright shirt than someone in a drab one. In the photo on the previous page, your eyes are probably drawn to the figure wearing the white shirt, because it stands out from all of the others. Change also compels attention, which is why we may take for granted all the pleasant interactions with a friend and notice only the tense moments.

Sometimes, we deliberately influence what we notice by indicating things to ourselves (Mead, 1934). In fact, in many ways, education is a process of learning to point out to ourselves things we hadn't seen before. Right now, you're learning to be more conscious of the selectivity of your perceptions, so in the future you will notice this more on your own. In English courses, you learn to notice how authors craft characters and use words to create images. In science courses, you learn to attend to molecular structures and chemical reactions. Classes in business teach you to notice assets, liabilities, and gross and net profits. Look at the vase in Figure 3.2. Look again at Figure 3.2, knowing that it is not a vase but profiles of two faces. Do you see the faces now?

What we select to notice is also influenced by who we are and what is going on within us. Our motives and needs affect what we see and don't see. If you have recently ended a romantic relationship, you're more likely to notice attractive people at a party than if you are committed to someone. Motives also explain the oasis phenomenon, in which thirsty people stranded in the desert see water although none really exists. Our expectations also affect what we notice (Bargh, 1999). This explains the self-fulfilling prophecy discussed in Chapter 2. A child who is told she is unlovable may notice rejecting, but not affirming, communication from others. An employee who is told he has leadership potential is likely to notice all of his professional successes and strengths and to be less aware of his shortcomings. Suzanne illustrates how we can use selective perception to our advantage.

Student Voices

Suzanne:

I decided to use the information about selective attention to stop smoking. Usually when I smoked, I noticed how relaxing it was to puff a cigarette and how much I liked the flavour. But this week when I lit up, I would focus on the burning smell of the match. Then I would notice how the smoke hurt my eyes when it rose from the cigarette. I also noticed how nasty ashtrays look with butts in them and how bad a room smells when I've been smoking in it. Once I really paid attention to everything I disliked about cigarettes, I was able to stop. I haven't had one in six days!

FIGURE 3.2

Perception: What do you see?

REVIEW

Selection is the process of focusing on

- The phenomena around us
- Our self-interest
- The culturally familiar

Cultures also influence what we selectively perceive. Assertiveness and competitiveness are encouraged and considered good in individualistic cultures such as Canada, so we don't find it odd when people compete and try to best each other. By contrast, collectivist cultures emphasize group loyalty, cooperation, and not causing others to lose face. Thus, in many Asian societies, competitive individuality is noticed and considered negatively. In Korea, for example, age is a very important aspect of individuals—the older a person is, the more he or she is to be respected. Many Koreans also place priority on family relations. Consequently, Koreans are more likely than Westerners to perceive the ages and family roles of people with whom they communicate. The Korean language reflects the cultural value of age and family ties through its different word forms used for people of different ages and different family status: *gahndah,* meaning "to go," is used when speaking to a teenage peer; *gah* to a parent; and *gahneh* to a grandparent (Ferrante, 1995).

Student Voices

Camille:

The person who is my ideal of a friend is Jaden. When my relationship broke up, I was devastated. She stayed by me, making sure I ate and got outside once in a while, and listened endlessly to my crying and negativity. She reminded me that yes it is wonderful to have someone to sweep you off your feet, but it's also good to have someone to sweep the floor occasionally. I eventually began to feel like life as a single woman wasn't intolerable. She stood by me.

Organization

Once we have selected what to notice, we must make sense of it. We organize what we have noticed and attribute meaning to it. A useful theory for explaining how we organize experience is **constructivism**, which states that we organize and interpret experience by applying cognitive structures called *schemata* (see Figure 3.3 and Table 3.1). We rely on four schemata to make sense of interpersonal phenomena: prototypes, personal constructs, stereotypes, and scripts (Hewes, 1995; Kelly, 1955).

Prototypes

A **prototype** defines the clearest or most representative example of some category (Fehr, 1993).

FIGURE 3.3

Cognitive Schemata Used to Organize and Interpret Experience

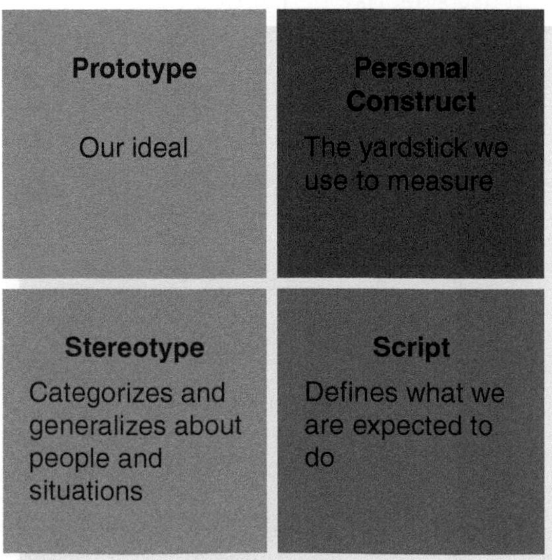

Prototype
Our ideal
Personal Construct
The yardstick we use to measure
Stereotype
Categorizes and generalizes about people and situations
Script
Defines what we are expected to do

TABLE 3.1

EXAMPLES OF COGNITIVE SCHEMATA USED TO ORGANIZE AND INTERPRET EXPERIENCE

	Scholastic	Courage	Food	Beauty
Prototypes	Einstein	Terry Fox	dessert	supermodel
Personal Constructs	smart↔dumb	courageous↔ cowardly	delicious↔yucky	beautiful↔homely
Stereotypes	nerd, genius	strong, good	fattening	airhead
Scripts	Study hard.	Act bravely.	Be a good cook.	Always look good.

For example, you probably have a prototype of the great teacher, the excellent supervisor, the true friend, and the perfect romantic partner. Each of these categories is exemplified by a person who is the ideal; that's the prototype.

For example, if Jaden is the best friend you've ever known, then Jaden is your prototype of a good friend. The prototype (Jaden) helps you decide who else fits into a particular category (good friend). You get to know Chris, and question how closely he resembles Jaden. If you view him as resembling her, then you would put Chris into the category Jaden exemplifies: good friend. Prototypes organize our perceptions by allowing us to place people and other phenomena into broad categories. We then consider how close they are to our prototype, or exemplar, of that category.

We also have prototypes of relationships (Fehr, 1993; Fehr & Russell, 1991; Hasserbrauck & Aaron, 2001). Most prototypes of romantic relationships emphasize trust, caring, honesty, friendship, and respect. Although passion may come to mind when we think of love, it seems less central to our prototype of love than companionship and caring.

Student Voices

Damion:

The person who is my ideal of a friend is my buddy Jackson. He stood by me when I got into a lot of trouble a couple of years ago. I got mixed up with some guys who used drugs, and I started using them, too. Pretty soon the coach figured out what was going on, and he suspended me from the team. I felt like I was finished when he did that, and then I really got into drugs. But Jackson wouldn't give up on me, and he wouldn't let me give up either. He took me to a drug centre and went there with me every day for three weeks. He never turned away when I was sick or even when I cried most of one night when I was getting off the drugs. He just stood by me. Once I was straight, Jackson went with me to see the coach about getting back on the team.

Personal Constructs

A **personal construct** is a "mental yardstick" that we use to measure a person or situation along a bipolar dimension of judgment (Kelly, 1955). Examples of personal constructs are *intelligent–unintelligent, kind–unkind, responsible–irresponsible, assertive–unassertive,* and *attractive–unattractive.* We rely on personal constructs to size up people and other phenomena. How intelligent, kind, or attractive is this person? Whereas prototypes help us decide into which

Our personal constructs create a kind of picture frame through which we view every new person we meet. If they don't fall within the boundaries of our "frame" we may not notice them.

broad category a phenomenon fits, personal constructs let us make more detailed assessments of particular qualities of people and other phenomena.

Diversity

The personal constructs we rely on shape our perceptions because we define things only in the terms of the constructs we use. Notice that we structure what we perceive and what it means by the constructs we choose to use. Thus, we may not notice qualities of people that aren't covered by the constructs we apply.

Student Voices

Nai Lee:

One of the ways I look at people is by whether they are independent or related to others. That is one of the first judgments I make of others. In Korea, we are not so individualistic or independent as people in the West. We think of ourselves more as members of families and communities than as individuals. The emphasis on independent identity was the first thing I noticed when I came to this country, and it is still an important way I look at people.

Stereotypes

A **stereotype** is a predictive generalization about a person or situation. Based on the category into which we place someone or something and how that person or thing measures up against the personal constructs we apply, we predict what he, she, or it will do. For instance, if you define someone as "right wing," you might stereotype her or him as likely to vote for the Conservative Party of Canada and to hold traditional family values. You may have stereotypes of fraternity and sorority members, military personnel, athletes, and people from other cultures.

Stereotypes don't necessarily reflect actual similarities between people. Instead, stereotypes are based on our perceptions of similarities between people or on social perspectives that

Apply the Idea

CHANGING CONSTRUCTS—CHANGING PERCEPTIONS

Use the left-hand column below to list five adjectives that are important in how you perceive potential romantic partners. These are your personal constructs.

1. ______________	1. ______________
2. ______________	2. ______________
3. ______________	3. ______________
4. ______________	4. ______________
5. ______________	5. ______________

Now, use the right-hand column to list five other constructs that you could use when you are perceiving potential romantic partners.

How would using the constructs on the right alter or enlarge your perceptions of people you are considering as romantic partners? ______________

____

we've internalized. We may perceive similarities that others don't, and we may fail to perceive commonalities that are obvious to others.

Statistics Canada has moved away from use of the term "race" and instead categorizes people in terms of their ethnic origins. But this is problematic also. Is the term *Asian*, for instance, useful for describing people? Racial and ethnic stereotypes can lead us to not see differences among people we place into a particular category. The broad label *Asian* doesn't distinguish among people from varied cultures, including Japan, Malaysia, Nepal, and China. It is not the idea of a group designation that is offensive, but the prejudicial, stereotypical predictions that we might make about individuals in any specific group *are* offensive. *Native American* is another very broad category that includes diverse Native American tribes (Vickers, 1999), and Mahicans thinks that the term *First Nations* also leads people to not notice the differences among tribes.

Stereotypes may be accurate or inaccurate. In some cases, we have incorrect understandings of a group, and in other cases, individual members of a group don't conform to the behaviours typical of a group as a whole. Although we need stereotypes to predict what will happen around us, they can be harmful if we forget that they are based not on objective reality but instead on our prototypes and our application of personal constructs.

Student Voices

Phyllis:

I'll tell you what stereotype really gets to me: the older student. I'm 48 and working on my degree, and everyone at this college treats me like their mother, not a peer. They believe I'm dabbling in courses like a hobby instead of seriously planning a career. They expect I won't understand what the workplace is like nowadays. It's as if I was from another planet instead of another generation.

Shannon:

I hate the way people stereotype me because of the way I talk. I grew up in Newfoundland, and say things in a different way—at least that's what people at this school say. They act like I'm stupid because of my "Newfie" accent. And then, some of them ask me to talk—I mean, really—they ask me to talk and then say, "Isn't that the funniest accent you ever heard?" It's like they're so busy listening to my accent they don't listen to WHAT I have to say. I knew, when I decided to attend a college halfway across the country, I'd run into some differences. But I didn't know that the way I talk would lead others to label me as slow and unintellectual.

Scripts

The final cognitive schema we use to organize perceptions is the script. A script is a guide to action. Scripts consist of sequences of activities that are expected of us and others in particular situations. They are based on our experiences and observations of interaction in various contexts. Many of our daily activities are governed by scripts, although we're typically not aware of them. We have a script for greeting casual acquaintances on campus ("Hey, what's up?" "Not much"). We also have scripts for dating, managing conflict, talking with professors, dealing with clerks, and interacting with co-workers on the job.

Scripts organize perceptions into lines of action and are useful in guiding us through many of our interactions. However, they are not always accurate or constructive, so we shouldn't accept them uncritically. For instance, if your parents often engaged in bitter, destructive quarrelling, you may have learned a script for conflict that will undermine your relationships. Similarly, if you grew up in a community that treated people of

Student Voices

Mahicans:

People have a stereotype of First Nations people. Non-aboriginals think we are all alike—how we look, how we act, what we believe, what our traditions are. But that isn't true. The Coast Salish and Cree are as different as people from Kenya and Winnipeg. Some tribes have a history of aggression and violence; others have traditions of peace and harmony. We pray to different spirits and have different tribal rituals and customs. All of these differences are lost when people stereotype us all into one group.

Communication Notes

"I CAN'T UNDERSTAND THE TEACHER'S ACCENT."

It's not unusual to hear North American students complain that international teachers are hard to understand because of heavy accents, faulty pronunciation of English words, and so forth. In response to student complaints, more than a dozen U.S. states have passed laws to establish standards for English for international teaching assistants. According to John Gravois (2005), such laws may be solving the wrong problem.

Gravois asks whether the problem is that some international teaching assistants don't speak English clearly or that some American students don't listen well because they stereotype international teaching assistants as lacking proficiency in English. According to Gravois, Don Rubin, a professor of education and speech communication at the University of Georgia, designed an experiment in 1988 to answer that question.

Rubin audiotaped an American man from central Ohio delivering a lecture. He then played that lecture to students. To half the students, the lecturer was identified as "John Smith from Portland," and the image of an American man was projected in the classroom. The same tape was played to the other half the students, but the lecturer was identified as "Li Wenshu from Beijing," and the image of an Asian man was projected in the classroom.

After hearing the lecture, students were asked to fill in the missing words from a printed transcript of the lecture. The students who thought the lecturer was Asian made 20 percent more errors than students who thought the lecturer was American. Rubin concluded that students stereotype international teachers as less proficient at English than American teachers. They "heard" Li Wenshu as being less proficient in English than John Smith, even though the two were the same person giving the same lecture.

Tim Macpherson/Stone/Getty Images

What stereotype and personal constructs would you have of the people in this photo?

certain races negatively, you may want to assess that script critically before using it to direct your own activities.

Prototypes, personal constructs, stereotypes, and scripts are cognitive schemata that we use to organize our perceptions of people and other phenomena. These cognitive schemata reflect the perspectives of particular others and the generalized other. As we interact with people, we internalize our culture's ways of classifying, measuring, and predicting phenomena and its norms for acting in various situations.

Interpretation

Even after we have selectively perceived phenomena and organized our perceptions, what they mean to us is not clear. There are no intrinsic meanings in phenomena.

Communication Notes

A SCRIPT FOR ROMANCE

Researchers Christine Bachen and Eva Illouz (1996) wanted to know to what extent mass media influence young people's ideas about romance. To find out, they asked students in the fourth, seventh, tenth, and eleventh grades to pick three out of six photos shown to them that represented a man and a woman in love. They then asked the students to select the single photo that best exemplified a man and a woman in love. Next, the researchers asked the students to use their own words to describe a romantic dinner and a typical first date. Finally, the researchers asked the students to tell an ideal love story.

There was a high rate of agreement among students. For the first task, they overwhelmingly chose photos of couples in exotic locales who were looking directly at each other and touching or kissing. For the second task, the majority of students selected a photo showing a couple on a boat, the most exotic of the photos they had been shown. Descriptions of romantic dinners emphasized atmosphere and the visual features of settings: soft lighting, music, exquisite food. Students also agreed on the script for a first date: going out to dinner, although not necessarily a romantic dinner, or to a movie.

Most interesting to the researchers was what students offered as ideal love stories: The stories involved falling in love and getting married, but that wasn't the end. The final focus of students' stories was having children and acquiring the material means to give them comfortable lives.

After analyzing the data, Bachen and Illouz concluded that students' perceptions of love and romance reflect media ideals. Advertising and broadcast media link romance to leisure, consumption, and exotic places and activities—the very things the students in their study associated with love and romance.

Instead, we assign meaning by interpreting what we have noticed and organized. **Interpretation** is the subjective process of explaining our perceptions in ways that make sense to us. To interpret the meaning of another's actions, we construct explanations for them.

Communication Notes

THE "BI-RACIAL BEAUTY"

Alicia Keys was first recognized for the songs she wrote for her hit album "Songs in A Minor." Sometimes called the "bi-racial beauty," Keys is half African American and half Italian, and was born and raised in Harlem, New York. Keys explains that while growing up in Harlem, she was exposed to a lot of different types of music, from rock (Nirvana), R&B, and jazz (Miles Davis), to classical. Keys says, "I think it was inevitable that I would merge all of them in what I do now." Keys is also multiracial mentally, combining many musical and cultural aspects to create her own independent identity. She has made being multiracial a positive and beautiful attribute.

There are more and more people who do not fit into one racial category. Race has become an inaccurate method to distinguish individuals, because many races are closely interacting and merging together to form new forms of ethnicity.

REVIEW

We use four cognitive schemata to organize our thinking about people and situations:

- Prototypes
- Personal constructs
- Stereotypes
- Scripts

Apply the Idea

SIZING UP OTHERS

Pay attention to the cognitive schemata you use the next time you meet a new person. First, notice how you classify the person. Do you categorize her or him as a potential friend, date, co-worker, or neighbour? Next, identify the constructs you use to assess the person. Do you focus on physical characteristics (attractive–unattractive), mental qualities (intelligent–unintelligent), psychological features (secure–insecure), or interpersonal qualities (friendly–unfriendly)? Would different constructs be prominent if you used a different prototype to classify the person? Now, note how you stereotype the person. What do you expect him or her to do, based on the prototype and constructs you've applied? Finally, identify your script, or how you expect interaction to unfold between you.

Extend your thinking about how our classifications of people affect our perceptions of them by reading Nancy Shute's brief 2001 article, "A Black and White World," available in your InfoTrac® College Edition.

Attributions

An **attribution** is an explanation of why something happened or why someone acts a certain way (Heider, 1958; Kelley, 1967). Attributions have four dimensions, as shown in Figure 3.4. The first is locus, which attributes a person's actions to internal factors ("He has no patience with people who are late") or external factors ("The traffic jam frustrated him"). The second dimension is stability, which explains actions as the result of stable factors that won't change over time ("She's a Type A personality") or unstable factors that may or will be different at another time ("She acted that way because she has a headache right now").

FIGURE 3.4

Dimensions of Attributions

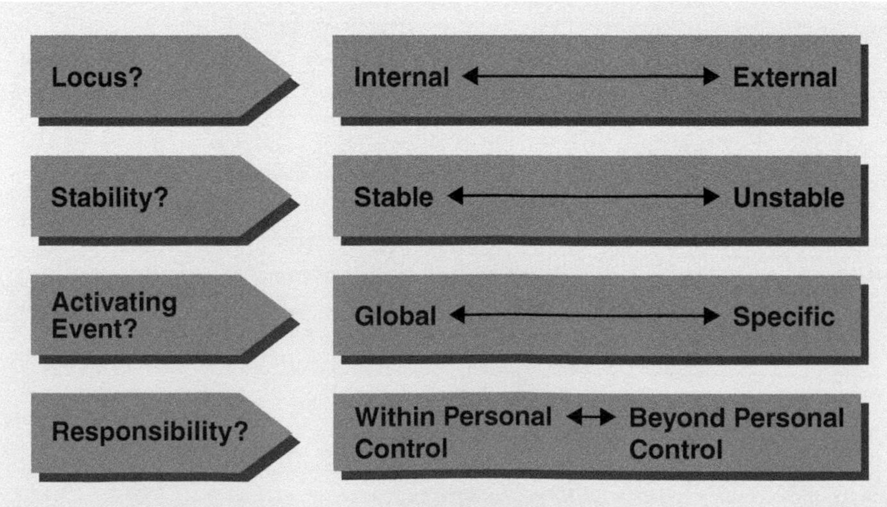

Specificity is the third dimension, and it explains behaviour in terms of whether the behaviour has global implications that apply in most or all situations ("He's an introvert") or specific implications that apply only in certain situations or under certain conditions ("He gets quiet whenever he needs to think"). Many people think stability and specificity are similar, but really they are distinct dimensions. Stability concerns time (whether the reason is temporary or enduring), whereas specificity concerns the breadth of the explanation (all situations, events, and places, or particular or limited situations and places). Here are examples of how we might combine these two dimensions to explain why Angela yelled at Fred:

- Stable and specific: She yelled at Fred (specific) because she is short-tempered (stable).
- Stable and global: She yells at everyone (global) because she is short-tempered (stable).
- Unstable and specific: She yelled at Fred (specific) because she was in a hurry that day (temporary, unstable factor that could change).
- Unstable and global: She yells at everyone (global) when she is in a hurry (unstable).

The dimensions of stable–unstable, global–specific, and internal–external lead us to explain phenomena on a fourth dimension, which is responsibility. Do we hold a person responsible for a particular behaviour? We're more likely to hold someone responsible if we think she or he could control the behaviour. If we attribute Angela's yelling to her lack of effort to control her temper, we're more likely to judge her harshly than if we attribute her yelling to lack of sleep or to a medication she's taking for a short time (unstable). How we account for others' actions affects our feelings about them and our relationships with them. We can be more or less positive toward others, depending on how we explain what they do.

Our attributions influence the meanings we attach to others and to their communication. For example, how do you account for the fact that your supervisor at work shouts orders gruffly? Does she have an authoritarian personality? Or is she insecure because she is new in the role of supervisor? Or is she reacting to a medication? Each of these three attributions invites a distinct understanding of why the supervisor shouts.

CONCEPTS AT A GLANCE

Two Common Attribution Errors

1. Self-serving bias
2. Fundamental attribution error

Attribution Errors

Researchers have identified two common errors that people make in their attributions. The first is the **self-serving bias**. As the term implies, this is a bias toward ourselves and our interests. Research indicates that we tend to construct attributions that serve our personal interests (Hamachek, 1992; Sypher, 1984). Thus, we are inclined to make internal, stable, and global attributions for our positive actions and our successes. We're also likely to claim that good results come about because of personal control we exerted. For example, you might say that you did well on a test because you are a smart (internal and stable) person who is always responsible (global) and studies hard (personal control).

Student Voices

Jen:

When I do badly on a test or paper, I usually say that either the professor was unfair or I had too much to do that week and couldn't study like I wanted to. But when my friends do badly on a test, I tend to think they're not good in that subject or they aren't disciplined or whatever.

The self-serving bias also works in a second way. We tend to avoid taking responsibility for negative actions and failures by attributing them to external, unstable, and specific factors that are beyond personal control (Schutz, 1999). To explain a failing grade on a test, you might say that you did poorly because the professor (external) put a lot of tricky questions on that test (unstable, specific factor), so all your studying didn't help (outside of personal control). In other words, our misconduct results from outside forces that we can't help, but all the good we do reflects our personal qualities and efforts. This self-serving bias can distort our perceptions, leading us to take excessive personal credit for what we do well and to abdicate responsibility for what we do poorly. When the self-serving bias shapes how we interpret our behaviours, we form an unrealistic image of ourselves and our activities.

In a 1996 interview with *Newsweek*'s John McCormick and Sharon Begley, Tiger Woods described how his father taught him to accept responsibility for his bad shots in golf. When he was a preschooler and hit a bad shot, he slammed his club on the ground. His father would ask him, "Who's responsible for that bad shot? The crow that made the noise during your backswing? The bag somebody dropped? Whose responsibility was that?" (McCormick & Begley, 1996, p. 55). Woods learned to say it was his responsibility. As he took responsibility for his bad shots, Woods learned that he could control his skill.

Communication Notes

THINKING YOUR WAY TO A GOOD RELATIONSHIP

What makes a relationship work? Obviously, lots of things are involved, but one that most people don't recognize is how we think about what our friends and romantic partners do and don't do (Bradbury & Fincham, 1990; Fletcher & Fincham, 1991; Friesen, Fletcher, & Overall, 2005; Seligman, 2002). Partners in happy relationships tend to think in positive ways about each other. People attribute nice things a partner does to internal, stable, and global reasons. "He got the film for us because he is a good person who always does sweet things for us." Happy couples attribute unpleasant things a partner does to external, unstable, and specific factors. "She yelled at me because all the stress of the past few days made her not herself."

In contrast, unhappy couples tend to think negatively. They tend to attribute a partner's nice actions to external, unstable, and specific factors. "She got the tape because she had some extra time this particular day." Negative actions are seen as stemming from internal, stable, and global factors. "He yelled at me because he is a nasty person who never shows any consideration for anybody else." Negative attributions fix pessimistic views and undermine motivation to improve a relationship. Whether positive or negative, attributions may be self-fulfilling prophecies.

Related research demonstrates that attributional patterns are linked to marital quality and forgiveness. We are less likely to forgive a partner if we attribute his or her transgression to personal irresponsibility (Fincham, 2000; Fincham, Paleari, & Regalia, 2002; Finkel et al., 2002; McCullough & Hoyt, 2002).

The second kind of attributional error is so common it is called the **fundamental attribution error.** This involves how we use the dimension of locus. We tend to overestimate the internal causes of others' undesirable behaviours and underestimate the external causes. Conversely, we are likely to underestimate the internal causes of our own misdeeds and failures and overestimate the external causes (Schutz, 1999; Sedikides et al., 1998).

Communication Notes

SELF-SERVING ATTRIBUTIONS AND SPORTS

Our team is always better, right? If the other team wins, it's due to luck, right? It turns out that the self-serving bias shows up not just in judgments of people but also in judgments of sports. Curious to know whether sports fans would fall victim to the fundamental attributional error, Daniel Wann and Michael Schrader designed an experiment. They asked 59 undergraduate women and 55 undergraduate men to view athletic contests and explain why their teams won or lost. Consistently, students who identified strongly with their teams attributed their teams' victories to internal, controllable, and stable causes. Just as consistently, they attributed their teams' losses to external factors for which the teams couldn't be blamed.

Read the full text of Wann and Schrader's 2000 article in your InfoTrac® College Edition. Go to the key word search and enter *attributions*. You may want to read some of the other articles your search produces.

The fundamental attributional error was obvious in a legal case on which one of the authors consulted a few years ago. A woman sued her employer for transferring her. She alleged that he did so because he was biased against women. Her boss denied being biased against women. He claimed that he transferred her because her poor performance made her the most expendable person in his department. Written records, such as yearly performance reviews, and the woman's own testimony revealed that she had not met all of her job responsibilities, and she had been told this repeatedly. Furthermore, her boss's record of hiring and promotions showed that nearly 50 percent of his hires and promotions over the past decade had been women and minorities.

At the trial, the plaintiff was asked whether it was possible that her performance had influenced her boss's decision to transfer her. "No, he did it because he doesn't want to work with women," she replied. Thus, she totally discounted external factors that could explain his decision and placed full responsibility on internal qualities (his alleged gender bias). When asked whether she thought her performance might have made her more expendable than others who worked in her former department, she said, "No, the only problems with my performance were due to interruptions and lack of cooperation from others." Thus, she rejected any personal responsibility for errors in her work and laid full responsibility on circumstances beyond her control. In court, the author explained the fundamental attribution error to the jury and showed how it surfaced in the woman's testimony. The jury found in favour of the woman's boss.

We've seen that perception involves three interrelated processes. The first of these, selection, involves noticing certain things and ignoring others out of the total complexity of what is going on. The second process is organization, whereby we use prototypes, personal constructs, stereotypes, and scripts to organize what we have selectively perceived. Finally, we engage in interpretation to make sense of the perceptions we have gathered and organized. Attributions are a primary way we explain what we and others do.

Although we've discussed selection, organization, and interpretation separately, in reality they may occur in a different order or simultaneously. Thus, our interpretations shape the cognitive schemata we use to organize experiences, and the ways we organize perceptions affect what we notice and interpret. For instance, in her commentary earlier in this chapter, Nai Lee's interpretations of Westerners' individualism were shaped by the schemata she learned in her homeland of Korea. Also, reliance on the individualistic–communal construct shaped what she noticed about North Americans. Now that we understand the complex processes involved in perception, we're ready to consider a range of factors that influence what and how we perceive.

CONCEPTS AT A GLANCE

Factors That Influence Our Perceptions

- Physiology
- Age
- Culture
- Roles
- Cognitive abilities
- Self

INFLUENCES ON PERCEPTION

Individuals differ in how they perceive situations and people. In this section, we consider some of the influences on our perceptions.

Physiology

One reason perceptions vary among people is that we differ in our sensory abilities and physiologies. One of the authors has a keener sense of hearing than her partner does; he can barely hear music at the volume that she finds comfortable. The hot, spicy foods that she perceives as delicious are painful to her partner. Such differences in sensory abilities affect our perceptions.

Our physiological states also influence perception. If you are tired or stressed, you're likely to perceive things more negatively than you normally would. For instance, a playful insult from a co-worker might anger you if you were feeling down but wouldn't bother you if you were feeling good. Each of us has our own biorhythm, which influences the times of day when we tend to be alert and fuzzy. One of the authors is a morning person, so that's when she prefers to teach classes and write. She is less alert and less creative later in the day. Thus, she perceives things in the morning that she simply doesn't notice when her energy level declines.

Are you a morning, afternoon, or evening person?

Medical conditions are another physiological influence on perceptions. If you've ever taken drugs that affected your thinking, you know how dramatically they can alter perceptions. People may become severely depressed, paranoid, or uncharacteristically happy under the influence of hormones or drugs. Changes in our bodies caused by medical conditions may also affect what we selectively perceive. One of the authors has a back disorder that periodically renders her immobile or dependent on canes. When her back is out of order, she is far more aware of stairs, uneven ground, and any activities that require her to bend. When her back is working well, she doesn't notice these things any more than someone without back problems does.

Age

Age is another factor that influences our perceptions. Compared with a person of 20, a 60-year-old has a more complex fund of experiences to draw on in perceiving situations and people. When one of the authors was 22 years old and in graduate school, she mentioned to her father that it was hard to get by on the salary from her teaching assistantship. He said that, during the early 1930s, he would have been very happy to have had enough money just to eat. Because her father had lived through the Great Depression, he had a broader perspective than she did on how hard life can be.

Reflective Exercise

Consider the cost of each of these ordinary purchases:

- A cup of coffee
- A glass of beer
- Parking
- Bus fare
- A litre of milk
- The cost of a movie

Now ask a person in his or her 40s to remember the cost of these when he or she was 20. Ask the same of people in their 60s and 80s. How do these people perceive the cost of living today? Does that perception alter what they choose to do with their money? How does a point of comparison alter their decisions? Does it alter yours?

Age also influences our perceptions of time. The seven-year-old nephew of one of the authors perceives a year as being much longer than the author does. A year is a full seventh of his life but less than a fiftieth of hers; a year really is longer in his life than hers. As we grow older and have more experiences, our perspective on many things changes. For example, one of the authors used to feel down if her teaching didn't go well on a given day or if she had an unexpected expense. When her father died when she was 36, she gained a wholly new perspective on what is bad and what is worth feeling down about.

How does age affect our perceptions?

Age and the wealth of experiences it brings can also change our perceptions of social issues. The extent of discrimination still experienced by women and minorities understandably frustrates many college and university students. The authors are more hopeful than some of these students because we have seen many changes in our lifetime. For example, women were not admitted to colleges or universities on an equal basis with men. When we entered the job market, few laws protected women and minorities against discrimination in hiring, pay, and advancement. The substantial progress made during our lifetime leads us to perceive substantial progress in lessening discrimination and to perceive current inequities as changeable.

Culture

A **culture** is the totality of beliefs, values, understandings, practices, and ways of interpreting experience that are shared by a number of people. Culture forms the pattern of our lives and guides how we think, feel, and communicate (Lee, 2000). The influence of culture is so pervasive that it's hard to realize how powerfully it shapes our perceptions. We will discuss the influence of culture in greater detail in Chapter 7.

Standpoint

In recent years, scholars have realized that we are affected by the culture as a whole as well as by particular social groups to which we belong (Hallstein, 2000; Haraway, 1988; Harding, 1991). A **standpoint** is a point of view shaped by awareness of the material, social, and symbolic conditions common for members of a social group. People who belong to powerful, high-status social groups have a vested interest in preserving the system that gives them privileges; thus, they are unlikely to perceive its flaws and inequities. On the other hand, those who belong to less privileged groups are able to see inequities and discrimination (Collins, 1998; Harding, 1991).

Women and men often have different standpoints, although not every individual man and woman shares the standpoint that is typical of his or her sex. For instance, the caregiving we generally associate with women results less from any maternal instinct than from the social role of mother, which teaches women to care for others, to notice who needs what, and to defer their own needs (Ruddick, 1989). Other researchers have discovered that men who are in caregiving roles become nurturing, accommodative, and sensitive to others' needs as a consequence of being in the social role of caregiver (Kaye & Applegate, 1990).

Gendered standpoints also are evident in marital conflict. Researchers have found that conflict lessens wives' love for husbands more than it lessens husbands' love for wives (Huston, McHale, & Crouter, 1985; Kelly, Huston, & Cate, 1985). From early childhood, many young girls are socialized to attend to relationships, preserve interpersonal harmony, and avoid conflict. In contrast, young boys typically are socialized to engage in conflict, resolve it, and then go on with their activities. It makes sense that, in general, conflict with a spouse might be more upsetting and disruptive to women than men.

Gendered standpoints also are obvious in the effort women and men in general invest in maintaining relationships. Socialized into the role of relationship expert, many women are expected by others and themselves to take care of relationships (Tavris, 1992; Wood, 1993, 1994d, 1998). They are supposed to know when something is wrong and to resolve the tension. This may explain why women tend to be more aware than men of problems in relationships (Brehm, 1992; Wood, 1998).

Student Voices

Janice:

I'll vouch for the idea of standpoint affecting how we communicate. I was always a pretty independent person. Some people even thought I was kind of selfish, because I really would prioritize myself. Then I had my first baby, and I stayed home with him for a year. I really changed—and I mean in basic ways. I believed that my most important job was to be there for Timmy, and so my whole day focused on him. He was the person I thought about first, not myself. I learned to hear the slightest difference in his cries, so I could tell when he was hungry or needed his diapers changed or wanted company.

When I went back to work after a year, a lot of my former colleagues said I was different—much more attentive and sensitive to what they said and more generous with my time than I had been. I guess I developed new patterns of communicating as a result of mothering.

Other standpoints also influence our perceptions. Ethnicity, for example, affects how we perceive ourselves and our families. Many cultures are less individualistic than the majority of Canadians. Yet, even within this country, there are differences among distinct social groups. These differences are exhibited in our perceptions of how we care for our children, our elderly, and our sick. Ethnicity will dictate the kind of attention we pay to our families and the responsibility we feel toward them.

Apply the Idea

IDENTIFYING DIVERSE PERSPECTIVES

To become more aware of diverse perspectives on social life, talk with someone whose standpoint differs from your own. Discuss how you and the other person think about families, careers, and attending college or university. Explore how the individual perceives his or her relationship with his or her family, the financing of his or her education, and his or her expectations after graduation. How do these perceptions differ from your own? Does interaction with this person give you new perspectives on familiar things in your life?

Roles

Our perceptions also are shaped by roles. Both the training we receive to fulfill a role and the actual demands of the role affect what we notice and how we interpret and evaluate the role. The authors perceive classes in terms of how interested students seem, whether they appear to have read the material, and whether what they're learning is useful in their lives. Students have told us that they perceive classes in terms of time of day, number and difficulty of tests, whether papers are required, and whether the professor is interesting. We have different perceptions of classes.

Sarah Salmela/Shutterstock

The professions that people enter influence what they notice and how they think and act. For example, before her professional training, one young woman did not have highly developed analytical thinking skills. However, after she completed law school, she was extremely analytic; her conversational style changed, becoming more analytical, logical, and probing. Here is another example: Physicians are trained to be highly observant of physical symptoms. Once, at a social gathering, a physician asked one of the authors how long she had had a herniated disk. Shocked, she told him she didn't have one. "You do," he insisted, and, sure enough, a few weeks later a disk ruptured. His medical training had enabled him to perceive subtle changes in posture and walk that the author hadn't noticed.

Social roles can also influence how we perceive communication about our feelings. Professions that call for detachment and objectivity may encourage

Student Voices

Rebecca:

I was stunned at the impact training can have on the way we take part in the simplest things. I was at the beach with my friend Stan last summer, and his eyes kept darting around the waterfront. At one point he jumped up and ran into the water, reached down and pulled up a coughing, sputtering toddler, much to the shock and gratitude of the parent standing a metre away.

Stan is a lifeguard and, although he wasn't on duty that day, he is trained to notice the subtle changes in the splashing water and the looks on people's faces. Me, I was just taking in a beautiful scene at the beach and focusing on the sun, the colour of the water, and the sailboats. I hadn't even noticed the distressed child.

members not to express their emotions and to be uncomfortable when others do. We'll discuss the relationship between social roles and communication about emotions more fully in Chapter 4.

Cognitive Abilities

In addition to physiological, cultural, and social influences, perception is also shaped by cognitive abilities. How elaborately we think about situations and people, and our personal knowledge of others, affect how we select, organize, and interpret experiences.

Cognitive Complexity

People differ in the number and type of cognitive schemata they use to perceive, organize, and interpret people and situations. **Cognitive complexity** refers to the number of personal constructs used (remember, these are bipolar dimensions of judgment), how abstract they are, and how elaborately they interact to shape perceptions. Most children have fairly simple cognitive systems: They rely on few personal constructs, focus more on concrete categories than abstract and psychological ones, and often are unaware of relationships between different perceptions.

CONCEPTS AT A GLANCE

Two Aspects of Cognitive Abilities That Affect Communication

1. Cognitive complexity
2. Person-centredness

In general, adults are more cognitively complex than children. However, adults have different degrees of cognitive complexity, and this affects perceptions. If you think of people only as nice or mean, you have a limited range for perceiving others. Similarly, people who focus on concrete data tend to have less sophisticated understandings than people who also perceive psychological data. For example, you might notice that a person is attractive, tells jokes, and talks to others easily. These are concrete perceptions. At a more abstract, psychological level, you might reason that the concrete behaviours you observe reflect a secure, self-confident personality. This is a more sophisticated perception because it offers an explanation of why the person acts as she or he does.

©2009 Jupiterimages Corporation

What if you later find out that the person is very quiet in classes? Someone with low cognitive complexity would have difficulty integrating the new information into prior observations. Either the new information would be dismissed because it doesn't fit, or it would replace the former perception and the person would be redefined as shy (Crockett, 1965; Delia, Clark, & Switzer, 1974). A more cognitively complex person would integrate all of the information into a coherent account. Perhaps a cognitively complex person would conclude that the person is very confident in social situations but less secure in academic ones.

Person-Centredness

Person-centredness is related to cognitive complexity because it entails abstract thinking and use of a wide range of schemata. As discussed in Chapter 1, person-centredness is the ability to perceive another as a unique individual. Our ability to perceive others as unique depends first on how well we make cognitive distinctions. People who are cognitively complex rely on more numerous and more abstract schemata to interpret others. Second, person-centred communicators use knowledge of particular others to guide their communication. Thus, they tailor vocabulary, nonverbal behaviours, and language to the experiences, values, and interests of others. The result is person-centred communication.

Recalling the discussion of I–Thou relationships in Chapter 1, you may remember that these are relationships in which people know and value each other as unique individuals. To do so, we must learn about another, and this entails much time and interaction. As we get to know another better, we gain insight into how she or he differs from others in a group ("Rob's not obsessive like other political activists I've known," "Ellen's more interested in people than most computer science majors"). The more we interact with another and the greater the variety of experiences we have together, the more insight we gain into the other's motives, feelings, and behaviours. As we come to understand others as individuals, we fine-tune our perceptions of them. Consequently, we're less likely to rely on stereotypes. This is why we often communicate more effectively with people we know well than with strangers or casual acquaintances.

Person-centredness, the ability to *perceive* others as unique, is not empathy. **Empathy** is the ability to feel with another person, to feel what she or he feels in a situation. Feeling with another is an *emotional* response. Our feelings tend to be guided by our own emotional tendencies and experiences, so it may be impossible to feel exactly what another person feels. In Steve's case, he may not be able feel Sherry's sadness about her father, but he recognizes that this is very emotional for her. What we can do is realize that another is feeling something and connect as well as we can, based on our own different experiences. With commitment and effort, we can learn a lot about how others see the world, even if that differs from how we see it. This knowledge, along with cognitive complexity, allows us to be person-centred communicators.

When we take the perspective of another, we try to grasp what something means to that person and how he or she perceives things. This involves suspending judgment, at least temporarily. We can't appreciate someone else's perspective when we're imposing our evaluations of whether it is right or wrong, sensible or crazy. Instead, we must let go of our own perspective and perceptions long enough to enter the world of another person. Doing this allows us to understand issues from the other person's point of view so that we can communicate more effectively. At a later point in interaction, we may choose to express our own perspective or to disagree with the other. This is appropriate, but voicing our own views is not a substitute for the equally important skill of recognizing others' perspectives.

Student Voices

Steve:

You really have to know somebody on an individual basis to know what she or he likes and wants. When I first started dating Sherry, I sent her red roses to let her know I thought she was special. That's the "lovers' flower," right? It turns out that was the only flower her father liked, and they had a million red roses at his funeral. Now they make Sherry sad because they remind her he's dead. I also took her chocolates once, then later found out she's allergic to chocolate. By now, I know what flowers and things she likes, but my experience shows that the general rules don't always apply to individuals.

© Ariel Skelley/CORBIS

The self influences perception.

Self

A final influence on our perceptions is ourselves. Consider how differently people with the four attachment styles we discussed in Chapter 2 would perceive and approach close relationships. People with secure attachment styles assume that they are lovable and that others are trustworthy. Thus, they tend to perceive others and relationships in positive ways. In contrast, people with fearful attachment styles perceive themselves as unlovable and others as not loving. Consequently, they may perceive relationships as dangerous and potentially harmful. The dismissive attachment style inclines people to perceive themselves positively, others negatively, and close relationships as undesirable. People who have anxious/ambivalent attachment styles often are preoccupied with relationships and perceive others in unpredictable ways.

Implicit personality theory helps explain how the self influences interpersonal perceptions. An implicit personality theory is a collection of unspoken and sometimes unconscious assumptions about how various qualities fit together in human personalities. Most of us think certain qualities go together in people. For instance, you might think that people who are outgoing are also friendly, confident, and fun. The assumption that outgoing people are friendly, confident, and fun is not based on direct knowledge; instead, it is an inference based on your implicit personality theory of the qualities that accompany outgoingness.

Apply the Idea

DISCOVERING YOUR IMPLICIT PERSONALITY THEORIES

Following are three descriptions of people. After reading each one, list other qualities you would expect to find in the person described.

- *Belinda is highly intelligent and analytical, and she is planning a career as a trial attorney. She loves to argue issues and enjoys being with others who have sharp reasoning and verbal skills.*
- *Andrew is a loner. He spends a lot of his time in his room reading or surfing the Internet. At first, others in the dorm invited him to parties, but he never went, so they stopped asking him. He is always polite and pleasant to others, but he doesn't seek out company.*
- *Gilles loves jokes, including pranks. Those around him have learned to expect practical jokes and know that Gilles enjoys being the recipient of pranks. He studies enough to get decent grades, but academics aren't a priority. Seldom seen alone, Gilles is a sociable person who likes to have a good time.*

In the Apply the Idea exercise, you made inferences about Belinda, Andrew, and Gilles based on what you already knew about them. What is the basis of your inferences? If you're like most people, your inferences are based on experiences with others you have known or observed. So, how you perceive Belinda, Andrew, and Gilles reflects as much about you and your experiences as it does about those individuals. This underlines the fact that how we perceive others and relationships is based not only on what is external to us but also on what is internal.

In sum, physiology, age, culture and standpoint, roles, cognitive abilities, and we ourselves affect what we perceive and how we interpret others and experiences. In the final section of the chapter, we'll consider ways to improve the accuracy of our perceptions.

GUIDELINES FOR IMPROVING PERCEPTION AND COMMUNICATION

Because perception is a foundation of interpersonal communication, it's important to form perceptions carefully and check their accuracy. Here, we discuss seven guidelines for improving the accuracy of perceptions and, ultimately, the quality of interpersonal communication.

CONCEPTS AT A GLANCE

Guidelines for Improving the Accuracy of Perceptions

- Recognize that all perceptions are partial and subjective.
- Avoid mind-reading.
- Check perceptions with others.
- Distinguish between facts and inferences.
- Guard against the self-serving bias.
- Guard against fundamental attribution error.
- Monitor labels.

Recognize That All Perceptions Are Partial and Subjective

Our perceptions are always partial and subjective. They are partial because we cannot perceive everything. They are subjective because they are influenced by factors such as physiology, age, culture and standpoint, roles, cognitive abilities, and ourselves and our experiences.

Objective features of reality have no meaning until we notice, organize, and interpret them. It is our perceptions that construct meanings for the people and experiences in our lives. An outfit perceived as elegant by one person may appear cheap to another. A teacher regarded as fascinating by one student may put another student to sleep.

The subjective and partial nature of perceptions has implications for interpersonal communication. One implication is that when you and another person disagree about something, neither of you is necessarily wrong. It's more likely that you have previously paid attention to different things and that there are differences in your personal, social, cultural, cognitive, and physiological resources for perceiving.

A second implication is that it's wise to remind ourselves that our perceptions are based at least as much on ourselves as on anything external to us. If you perceive another person as domineering, there's a chance that you are feeling insecure in your ability to interact with that person. If you perceive others as unfriendly toward you, it may be that you think of yourself as unworthy of friends. Remembering that perceptions are partial and subjective curbs the tendency to think that our perceptions are the only valid ones or that they are based exclusively on what lies outside us.

Student Voices

Joelle:

So this girl I met a few weeks ago said she was having a party, and it would be lots of fun with some cool people. She asked if I wanted to come, so I said, "Sure, why not?" When I got there everybody was drinking—I mean seriously drinking. They were playing this weird music—sort of morbid—and they had a DVD of *Friday The 13th* going nonstop. They got so loud that the neighbours came over and told us to hold it down. In a couple of hours, most of the people there were totally wasted. That's not my idea of fun. That's not my idea of cool people.

Avoid Mind-Reading

Mind-reading is assuming that we understand what another person thinks, feels, or perceives. When we mind-read, we act as though we know what is on another's mind, and this can get us into trouble. Marriage counsellors and communication scholars say mind-reading contributes to conflict between people (Dickson, 1995; Gottman, 1993; Gottman, Notarius, Gonso, & Markman, 1976). The danger of mind-reading is that we may misinterpret others.

Consider a few examples. One person says to her partner, "I know you didn't plan anything for our anniversary because it's not important to you." A supervisor notices that an employee is late for work several days in a row and assumes that the employee isn't committed to the job. Gina is late meeting her friend Alex, who assumes she is late because she's still mad about something that happened earlier. Alex is guessing at the reason for Gina's tardiness and could well be wrong.

Mind-reading also occurs when we say or think, "I know why you're upset" (Has the person said she or he is upset? What makes you think you know why that person is upset if she or he actually is?) or "You don't care about me anymore" (maybe the other person is too preoccupied or worried to be as attentive as usual). We also mind-read when we tell ourselves we know how somebody else will feel or react or what he or she will do. The truth is that we don't really know; we're only guessing. When we mind-read, we impose our perspectives on others instead of allowing them to say what they think. This can cause misunderstandings and resentment, because most of us prefer to speak for ourselves.

Student Voices

Adriana:

Mind-reading drives me crazy. My boyfriend does it all the time, and he's wrong as often as he's right. Last week he got tickets to a concert because he "knew" I'd want to go. Maybe I would have if I hadn't already planned a trip that weekend, but he never checked on my schedule. A lot of times when we're talking, he'll say something, then before I can answer he says, "I know what you're thinking." Then he proceeds to run through his ideas about what I'm thinking. Usually he's off-base, and then we get into a sideline argument about why he keeps assuming what I'm thinking instead of asking me. I really wish he would ask me what I think.

CONCEPTS AT A GLANCE

Three Steps for Perception-Checking

1. State what it is that you have observed.
2. Check to see whether the other perceives the same thing.
3. If so, request clarification of the behaviour.
4. If not, give one or two possible interpretations of the behaviour.

Check Perceptions with Others

The third guideline follows directly from the first two. Because perceptions are subjective and partial, and because mind-reading is an ineffective way to figure out what others think, we need to check our perceptions with others. In the anniversary example mentioned earlier, an effective communicator might ask, "Did you forget our anniversary?" If the partner did forget, then the speaker might ask, "Why do you think you forgot?" The person may not know why, or the reasons may not be satisfactory, but asking is more likely to open a productive dialogue than attributing bad motives is.

Perception-checking is an important communication skill because it helps people arrive at a mutual understanding of each other and their relationship. To check perceptions, you should first state what you have noticed. For example, a person might say to a co-worker, "Lately, I've thought you were less talkative in team meetings." Then, the person should check to see whether the other perceives the same thing: "Do you feel you've been less talkative?"

Apply the Idea

CHECKING PERCEPTIONS

To gain skill in perception-checking (and all communication behaviours), you need to practise. Try these exercises:

- *Monitor your tendencies to mind-read, especially in established relationships in which you feel you know the other person well.*
- *The next time you catch yourself mind-reading—stop. Instead, tell the other person what you are noticing and invite her or him to explain how she or he perceives what's happening. First, find out whether the other person agrees with you about what you noticed. Second, if the two of you agree, find out how the other person interprets and evaluates the issue.*
- *Engage in perception-checking for two or three days so that you have lots of chances to see what happens. When you're done, reflect on the number of times your mind-reading was inaccurate.*
- *How did perception-checking affect interaction with friends, co-workers, and romantic partners? Did you find out things you wouldn't have known if you'd engaged in mind-reading?*

Finally, it's appropriate to ask the other person to explain her or his behaviour. In the example, the person might ask, "Why do you think you're less talkative?" (If the other person doesn't perceive that he or she is less talkative, the question might be, "Why have you been reading memos and not saying much during our team meetings?")

When checking perceptions, it's important to use a tentative tone rather than a dogmatic or accusatory one. This minimizes defensiveness and encourages good discussion. Just let the other person know you've noticed something and would like to know his or her perceptions of what is happening and what it means.

Distinguish Between Facts and Inferences

Competent interpersonal communication also depends on distinguishing facts from inferences. A fact is an objective statement based on observation. An inference involves an interpretation that goes beyond the facts. For example, suppose that a person is consistently late reporting to work and sometimes dozes off during discussions. Co-workers might think, "That person is lazy and unmotivated." The facts are that the person comes in late and sometimes falls asleep. Defining the person as lazy and unmotivated is an inference that goes beyond the facts. It's possible that the co-worker is tired because he or she has a second job or is taking medication that induces drowsiness.

It's easy to confuse facts and inferences because we sometimes treat the latter as the former. When we say, "That employee is lazy," we've made a

Communication Notes

THE TRUTH, THE WHOLE TRUTH, AND NOTHING BUT THE TRUTH

Ronnie Bullock was serving a 60-year sentence for kidnapping and raping a woman when DNA tests revealed that he could not have committed the crime. Like a number of other prisoners, Bullock was convicted largely on the basis of eyewitness testimony. "That's the man; I'll never forget his face" tends to be highly convincing to jurors. The problem is that eyewitness testimony isn't always accurate.

Based on extensive studies, Brian Cutler and Steven Penrod (1995) estimate that eyewitness testimony may have led to the conviction and imprisonment of more than 4500 innocent people. Why is eyewitness testimony not always reliable? One reason is that witnesses' perceptions are shaped by the language that attorneys use. In one experiment, viewers were shown a film of a traffic accident and then were asked, "How fast were the cars going when they smashed into each other?" Other viewers were asked how fast the cars were going when they "bumped" or "collided." Viewers testified to significantly different speeds depending on which word was used.

Lawyers' language can also influence jurors' perceptions (Feigenson, 2000). In a separate experiment (Trotter, 1975), viewers were shown a film of a traffic accident, after which they filled out a questionnaire that included questions about things that had not actually been in the film. Viewers who were asked, "Did you see the broken headlight?" more frequently testified that they had seen it than did viewers who were asked, "Did you see a broken headlight?"

Roy Malpass, a psychologist at the University of Texas, notes another reason for inaccurate eyewitness testimony: selective perception (Miller, 2000). Research shows that witnesses focus selectively on weapons, a phenomenon that scholars call "weapon focus." When perception is riveted on a weapon, it's not focused on the person holding the weapon (Miller, 2000). Thus, recall of that person's appearance may be flawed.

Eyewitness Evidence: A Guide for Law Enforcement, a U.S. Department of Justice publication, summarizes research on eyewitness testimony and offers guidelines for improving its reliability. You can access this publication and others about eyewitness evidence by going to the U.S. Department of Justice's website at www.usdoj.gov and entering *eyewitness evidence* in the search window.

Apply the Idea

USING TENTATIVE LANGUAGE

To become more sensitive to our tendencies to confuse facts and inferences, for the next 24 hours, pay attention to the language you use to describe people and interactions. Listen for words such as "is" and "are" that imply factual information. Do you find instances in which tentative language would be more accurate?

Now, extend your observations to other people and the language they use. When you hear others say, "she is," "they are," or "he is," are they really making factual statements, or are they making inferences?

statement that sounds factual, and we may then perceive it as factual. To avoid this tendency, substitute more tentative words. For instance, "That employee seems unmotivated" or "That employee may be lazy" are more tentative statements that keep the speaker from treating an inference as a fact. We must make inferences to function in the world, yet we risk misperceptions and misunderstandings if we don't distinguish our inferences from facts.

Student Voices

Janet:

For years, my husband and I argued about housework. I was always criticizing him for not doing enough, and felt resentful about how much I did. He always said that he did a lot, but I just didn't notice. After studying the self-serving bias in class, I did an "experiment" at home. I watched him for a week and kept a list of all the things he did. Sure enough, he was—is—doing a lot more than I thought. I never noticed that he sorted laundry or walked the dog four times a day or wiped the kitchen counters after we'd finished fixing dinner. I noticed everything I did but only the big things he did, like vacuuming. I simply wasn't seeing a lot of his contributions to keep our home in order.

Guard against the Self-Serving Bias

Because the self-serving bias can distort perceptions, we need to monitor it carefully. Monitor yourself to see whether you attribute your failures or your adverse behaviours to factors beyond your control and whether you attribute your accomplishments to your own efforts. The self-serving bias also inclines us to notice what we do and to be less aware of what others do. Obviously, this can affect how we feel about others, as Janet's comments illustrate.

Monitoring the self-serving bias also has implications for how we perceive others. Just as we tend to judge ourselves generously, we may also be inclined to judge others too harshly. Monitor your perceptions to see whether you attribute others' successes and admirable actions to external factors beyond their control and their shortcomings and blunders to internal factors they can (should) control. If you do this, substitute more generous explanations for others' behaviours, and notice how that affects your perceptions of them.

Guard against the Fundamental Attribution Error

We've also discussed a second error in interpretation: the fundamental attribution error. This occurs when we overestimate the internal causes of others' undesirable behaviour and underestimate the external causes, and when we underestimate the internal causes of our own failings or bad behaviours and overestimate the external causes. We need to guard against this error because it distorts our perceptions of ourselves and others.

To reduce your chances of falling victim to the fundamental attribution error, prompt yourself to look for external causes of others' behaviours that you may not have thought of or appreciated. Instead of assuming that the unwanted behaviour reflects another's motives or personality, ask yourself, "What factors in the person's situation might lead to this behaviour?" You can ask the converse question to avoid underestimating internal influences on your own undesirable actions. Instead of letting yourself off the hook by explaining a misdeed as caused by circumstances you couldn't control, ask yourself, "What factor inside of me, that is my responsibility, influenced what I did?" Looking for external factors that influence others' communication and internal factors that influence our own communication checks our tendency to make fundamental attribution errors.

Apply the Idea

GUARDING AGAINST FUNDAMENTAL ATTRIBUTION ERROR

For each scenario described below, write an alternative explanation based on external factors that might account for the other person's behaviour.

- *The person you've been dating for a while is late meeting you. It is the third time this month you've had to wait, and you are angry that your date is so inconsiderate.*
- *You're talking with a friend about your serious concerns about what you will do after you graduate. You notice that your friend seems uninterested and keeps looking at her watch. You think to yourself, "If you are so self-centred that you can't make time for me, I don't need you for a friend."*
- *For each scenario described below, write an alternative explanation based on internal factors that could influence your behaviour.*
- *You are running late, so when a friend stops by to chat, you don't invite him in and don't encourage conversation. Your friend says, "You're being a real jerk." You think to yourself, "This has nothing to do with me. It has to do with all of the pressures I'm facing."*
- *During an argument with your roommate about who is going to do grocery shopping, you get really angry. Without thinking, you blurt out, "With all of the weight you've gained, you should stop thinking about groceries." Your roommate looks hurt and leaves the room. Afterward, you think, "Well, I wouldn't have said that if she hadn't been so belligerent."*

Monitor Labels

In giving names to our perceptions, we clarify them to ourselves. But just as words crystallize experiences, they can also freeze thought. Once we label our perceptions, we may respond to our own labels rather than to actual phenomena. If this happens, we may communicate in insensitive and inappropriate ways.

Consider this situation. Suppose you get together with five others in a study group, and a student named Andrea monopolizes the whole meeting with her questions and concerns. Leaving the meeting, one person says, "Gee, Andrea is so selfish and immature! I'll never work with her again." Another person responds, "She's not really selfish. She's just insecure about her grades in this course, so she was hyper in the meeting." Chances are that these two people will perceive and treat Andrea differently depending on whether they've labelled her "selfish" or "insecure." Once the two people have labelled Andrea's behaviour based on their subjective and partial perceptions, they may act toward Andrea based on their labels.

When we engage in interpersonal communication, we abstract only certain aspects of the total reality around us. Our perceptions are one step away from reality because they are always partial and subjective. We move a second step from reality when we label a perception. We move even farther from the actual reality when we respond not to behaviours or our perceptions of them but instead to the label we impose.

We should also monitor our labels to adapt our communication to particular people. Competent interpersonal communicators are sensitive to others and their preferences and choose their words accordingly. This is especially important when we are talking about identities. Many adult females resent being called *girls* and prefer to be called *women*. Most gays and lesbians reject the label *homosexual*, and they may resent hearing themselves labelled as such. Many people who have disabilities feel that the term *disabled people* suggests that they are disabled as people simply because they have some physical or mental condition. They prefer the term *person with disabilities* to the term *disabled person* (Braithwaite, 1996).

Is effective, sensitive communication possible when there are no universal guidelines for what to call people? Yes, if we are willing to invest thought and effort in our interactions. We begin by assuming that we may not know how others want to be labelled and that not all members of a group have the same preferences. Just because my friend Marsha wants to be called *Black*, I shouldn't assume that others share that preference. It's appropriate to ask others how they identify themselves. Asking shows that we care about their preferences and want to respect them. This is the heart of person-centred communication.

Perceiving accurately is neither magic nor an ability that some people naturally possess. Instead, it is a communication skill that can be developed and practised. Following the seven guidelines we have discussed will allow you to form perceptions more carefully and more accurately in interpersonal communication.

Chapter Summary

In this chapter, we've explored human perception, a process that involves selecting, organizing, and interpreting experiences. These three processes are not separate in practice; instead, they interact such that each one affects the others. What we selectively notice affects what we interpret and evaluate. At the same time, our interpretations become a lens that influences what we notice in the world around us. Selection, interpretation, and evaluation interact continuously in the process of perception.

We have seen that perception is influenced by many factors. Our sensory capacities, age, and physiological condition affect what we notice and how astutely we recognize stimuli around us. In addition, our cultural backgrounds and standpoints in society shape how we see and interact with the world. Roles, cognitive abilities, and who we are also influence perception. Thus, interpersonal perceptions reflect both what is inside of us and what is outside of us.

Understanding how perception works provides a foundation for improving our perceptual capacities. We discussed seven guidelines for improving the accuracy of perceptions. First, realize that all perceptions are subjective and partial, so there is no absolutely correct or best understanding of a situation or a person. Second, because people perceive differently, we should avoid mind-reading or assuming that we know what others perceive or what their actions mean. Third, it's a good idea to check perceptions, which involves stating how you perceive something and asking how another person does.

A fourth guideline is to distinguish facts from inferences. Avoiding the self-serving bias is also important because it can lead us to perceive ourselves too charitably and to perceive others too harshly. We should also guard against the fundamental attribution error, which can undermine the accuracy of our explanations of our own and others' communication. Finally, it's important to monitor the labels we use. This involves awareness that our labels reflect our perceptions of phenomena and sensitivity to the language others prefer, especially when we describe their identities. Just as we can't see how to solve the nine dots problem if we consider the dots a square, so we cannot see aspects of ourselves and others when our labels limit our perceptions. The following figure shows the solution to the problem on page 71.

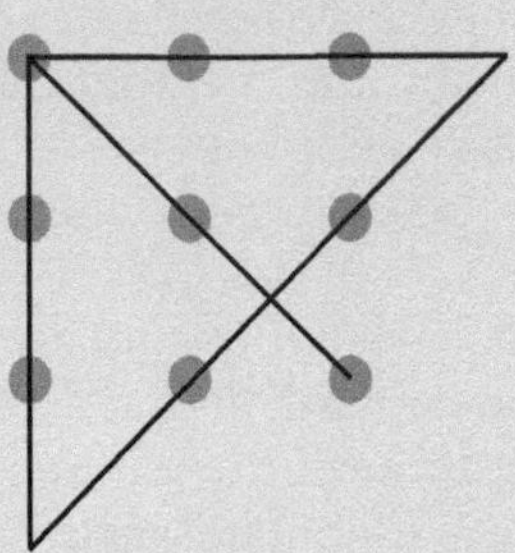

Key Concepts

- attribution
- cognitive complexity
- constructivism
- culture
- empathy
- fundamental attribution error
- implicit personality theory
- interpretation
- mind-reading
- perception
- personal constructs
- prototype
- scripts
- self-serving bias
- standpoint
- stereotypes

For Further Thought and Discussion

1. To understand how your standpoint influences your perceptions, visit a social group that is different from your own. If you are White, you might attend services at a Black church. If you are Christian, you could go to a Jewish synagogue or a Buddhist temple. In the unfamiliar setting, what stands out to you? What verbal and nonverbal communications do you notice? Do they stand out because they are not present in your usual settings? What does your standpoint highlight and what does it obscure?
2. Think of two situations, one in which you perceive that the majority of people are like you (same gender, race, sexual orientation, age) and one in which you perceive that you are a minority. How does your sense of being a majority or a minority influence your perceptions of the others present?
3. Identify an example of the self-serving bias in your interpersonal perceptions. Describe how you explained your own behaviour and that of others. Then, revise your explanation in such a way that the self-serving bias is eliminated.
4. Identify an example of the fundamental attribution error in your interpersonal perceptions. Describe how you explained

your own behaviour and that of others. Then, revise your explanation in such a way that it no longer reflects the fundamental attribution error.

5. Use your InfoTrac® College Edition to read David DeCremer's 2000 article, "Effect of Group Identification on the Use of Attributions," published in the *Journal of Social Psychology*. Describe what DeCremer means by the "group-serving bias" and who is most likely to have it. Does DeCremer's finding of a group-serving bias fit your personal experiences?
6. Use your InfoTrac® College Edition to find articles dealing with how race is defined. Describe the controversy among scholars regarding how races are perceived. Conduct a survey to determine the most current politically correct terminology to define different ethnic groups.

Chapter 4

Emotions and Communication

The best and most beautiful things in the world cannot be seen or even touched. They must be felt with the heart.

—Helen Keller

The truth is that our finest moments are most likely to occur when we are feeling deeply uncomfortable, unhappy, or unfulfilled. For it is only in such moments, propelled by our discomfort, that we are likely to step out of our ruts and start searching for different ways or truer answers.

—M. Scott Peck (2000)

© Corbis

Anthony's Story

My live-in partner of a year, Natasha, brought a kitten home. At first, we were thrilled with the new addition to "our family." Soon after, I began to feel distant. I'd sit for long periods, not engaging my partner in conversation. Anxious, Natasha would ask me what was wrong. I didn't know. I only knew that something uncomfortable was happening to me. She asked me if it was the cat. I said "No." She asked if I wanted to be alone. I said "Sometimes." Insightfully, she asked, "Is this too much like marriage?" I said, "Yes." She asked if I wanted her to leave. I could only answer "Not really."

It took some time and a lot of talking for me to sort out the confusing mix of feelings I was experiencing. On the one hand, Natasha was right. This was all getting very domestic. I was panicking. On the other hand, the option of being alone again was not attractive nor was it what I wanted. I did however feel overwhelmed with what appeared like an escalation of responsibilities and commitment and yet I didn't believe I had a choice. To speak up about feeling crowded and pressured was unthinkable. I couldn't bear for Natasha to leave. On the other hand, I wasn't sure I could put everything on hold and "start a family." The kitten was a symbol.

Although we experience and express feelings, we don't always do so effectively. Sometimes, like Anthony, we aren't able to identify exactly what we feel. Even if we can recognize our emotions, we aren't always sure how to express them clearly and constructively. We may not realize what goal we have for expressing emotions. Do we just want to get feelings out, or do we want another person to comfort us, reassure us, or behave differently toward us? In order to communicate well, we need to develop skill in identifying and expressing our feelings in ways that support particular communication goals.

EMOTIONS

Emotions, or feelings, are part of our lives. We feel happiness, sadness, shame, pride, embarrassment, envy, disappointment, and a host of other emotions. And we express our emotions in interpersonal communication. We may express emotions nonverbally (smiling, trembling, blushing) or verbally ("I'm enjoying this," "I'm scared," "I feel anxious about the interview"). Sometimes we express emotions through complex verbal messages such as metaphors and similes (Kovecses, 1990). For instance, you might say, "I feel like a plane that's soaring," or "I am a bomb, just waiting to explode." And, of course, in many situations, we communicate emotions both verbally and nonverbally, for example, saying, "I'm so happy right now" while smiling.

To open this chapter, we'll discuss *emotional intelligence,* which is distinct from cognitive intelligence. Next we define emotions and examine different theories that attempt to explain emotions and their causes. Then we explore why we sometimes fail to express our feelings and how we can learn to express them effectively. Finally we discuss guidelines for communicating emotions in ways that foster our individual growth and the quality of our relationships with others.

Ryan McVay/Photodisc/Getty Images

EMOTIONAL INTELLIGENCE

In his 1995 book *Emotional Intelligence,* Daniel Goleman (1995a) explored a kind of intelligence distinct from the type that standard IQ tests measure. In 2002, Goleman and his colleagues Richard Boyatzis and Annie McKee co-authored *Primal Leadership: Realizing the Power of Emotional Intelligence.* Goleman highlighted the critical role that emotional intelligence plays in organizational leadership.

Goleman popularized an idea that Carol Saarni (1990) originated. In her early work, Saarni emphasized a quality she called "emotional competence," which involves awareness of our own emotions, including multiple emotions experienced simultaneously, the ability to recognize and empathize with others' emotions, awareness of the impact of our expression of emotions on others, and sensitivity to cultural rules for expressing emotions.

Emotional intelligence is the ability to recognize feelings, to judge which feelings are appropriate in which situations, and to communicate those feelings effectively. According to Goleman (1995a, 1995b; Goleman, Boyatzis, & McKee, 2002), people who have high emotional intelligence quotients (EQs) are more likely than people with lower EQs to create satisfying relationships, to be comfortable with themselves, and to work effectively with others.

To learn more about EQ and to take an online EQ test, go the Institute for Health and Human Potential website at www.ihhp.com/quiz.php.

Emotional intelligence consists of qualities that aren't assessed by standard intelligence tests:

- Being aware of your feelings
- Dealing with emotions without being overcome by them

Communication Notes

EMOTIONAL INTELLIGENCE ON THE JOB

The value of emotional intelligence is not limited to intimate relationships. It is equally relevant to the workplace and job success. Psychologist Daniel Goleman (Goleman, Boyatzis, & McKee, 2002) reports that EQ, or emotional intelligence, is a critical factor in career advancement. To reach this conclusion, Goleman collected data from 150 firms to learn what distinguishes mediocre employees from superstars. He reports that conventional IQ accounts for no more than 25 percent of success on the job, whether the job is copier repairperson, CEO, or scientist. The greater difference comes from EQ. Furthermore, claims Goleman, the importance of conventional IQ decreases, and the importance of EQ increases, as jobs become more difficult and higher in company rank.

Goleman is careful to point out that cognitive abilities, including those measured by IQ tests, are important to getting a job—most people get jobs because they have the necessary cognitive qualifications. But advancement depends on other factors, including EQ.

EQ is not just being nice to others. In the workplace, EQ is the ability to manage your own emotions and handle relationships with others constructively. Among the emotional competencies Goleman sees as critical to career advancement are self-control, initiative, empathy, political savvy, and supportive, cooperative communication.

Several websites offer additional materials on emotional intelligence. One is the Consortium for Research on Emotional Intelligence in Organizations at www.eiconsortium.org. This site provides background information on EQ, resources that discuss EQ's relevance to specific topics such as the workplace and parenting, and answers to frequently asked questions about EQ.

Another site is the EQ Institute at www.eqi.org. This site provides definitions of EQ, self-tests for EQ, references, and suggestions for college and university students writing papers on emotional intelligence.

- Not letting setbacks and disappointments derail you
- Channelling your feelings to assist you in achieving your goals
- Being able to understand how others feel without their spelling it out
- Listening to your feelings and those of others so you can learn from them
- Having a strong yet realistic sense of optimism

UNDERSTANDING EMOTIONS

Although emotions are basic to humans and communication, they are difficult to define precisely. Some researchers assert that humans experience two kinds of emotions: some that are based in biology and thus instinctual and universal, and others that we learn in social interaction (Kemper, 1987). Yet, scholars don't agree on which emotions are basic (Izard, 1991; Shaver et al., 1987; Shaver, Wu, & Schwartz, 1992). Also, many scholars don't think it's useful to distinguish between basic emotions and learned emotions (Ekman & Davidson, 1994).

Many scholars think that most or all emotions are socially constructed to a substantial degree. For example, we learn when and for what to feel guilty or proud. We learn from particular others and the generalized other when to feel gratitude, embarrassment, and so forth. In her 1989 book *Anger: The Misunderstood Emotion,* Carol Tavris argues that anger is not entirely basic or instinctual. She shows that our ability to experience anger is influenced by social interaction, through which we learn whether and when we are supposed to feel angry.

Explore the patterns of emotions represented in Figure 4.1. What qualities do you see in the "petals" that are opposite to each other? Have you experienced

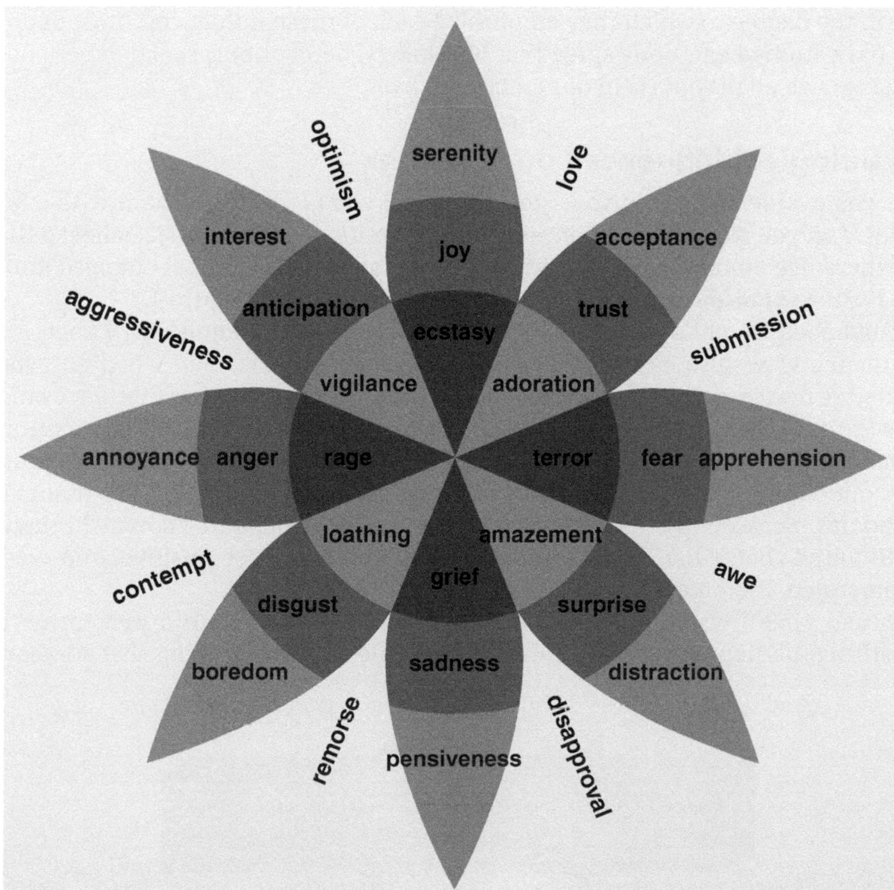

FIGURE 4.1

What is your emotional range?

emotional shifts from the tips of the petals toward the centre and back out again? What about the words between the petals—might they be combinations of the two adjoining sets of emotion? The concept of emotional intelligence highlights the importance of emotions to our everyday communication and our relationships. All aspects of our lives are affected by what we feel, how skillfully we identify our feelings, and how effectively we communicate them to others.

So far, we've discussed emotions without defining exactly what they are. In the next section, we will pin down the nature of emotions by defining them and identifying their diverse components.

Student Voices

Kenneth:

Last year when I got married, I've never felt so many things in one moment. As I watched my bride walk down the aisle and take my arm, I felt happiness as well as a sense of loss about my independence, hope and anxiety about our future, and even confidence in our ability to make a new life together.

Most scholars also agree that we experience emotions holistically, not individually. In many instances, what we feel is not a single emotion but several mingled together. Paul Ekman and Richard Davidson (1994) surveyed research on emotions and concluded that blends of emotion are common. For instance, you might feel both sad and happy at your graduation or both grateful and resentful when someone helps you.

We can define **emotions** as our experience and interpretation of internal sensations as those are shaped by physiology, perceptions, language, and social experiences. It's important to realize that emotions are processes rather than fixed states of being. Physiological, perceptual, linguistic, and social influences are not independent. Instead, they interact continuously to shape our experience of emotions. Although researchers vary in the degree to which they emphasize each of these influences, most people who have studied emotions agree that physiology, perceptions, social experience, and language all play parts in our emotional lives.

CONCEPTS AT A GLANCE

Influences on Emotions

Physiological influences on emotion

- Organismic view

Perceptual influences on emotion

- Perceptual view
- Cognitive-labelling view

Social influences on emotions

- Interactive view
  - Framing rules
  - Feeling rules
  - Emotional work

Physiological Influences on Emotions

Have you ever felt a knot in your stomach when you got back an exam with a low grade? If so, you experienced a physiological reaction. Early theorists believed that we experience emotion when external stimuli cause physiological changes in us. This is the **organismic view of emotions**, and it is shown in Figure 4.2.

Advanced by philosopher William James and his colleague Carl Lange, the organismic view, also called the *James–Lange view,* asserts that, when an event occurs, we first respond physiologically, and only after that do we experience emotions (James, 1890; James & Lange, 1922). This perspective assumes that emotions are reflexes that follow from physiological arousal. In other words, from the organismic outlook, emotions are both the product and the expression of occurrences in our bodies. For example, Chris Kleinke, Thomas Peterson, and Thomas Rutledge (1998) found that, when people smile, their moods are more positive, and when people frown, their moods are more negative.

James (1890) wrote that emotional expression begins with a perception of something, perhaps seeing a gift with your name on it or noticing that someone

FIGURE 4.2

The Organismic View of Emotions

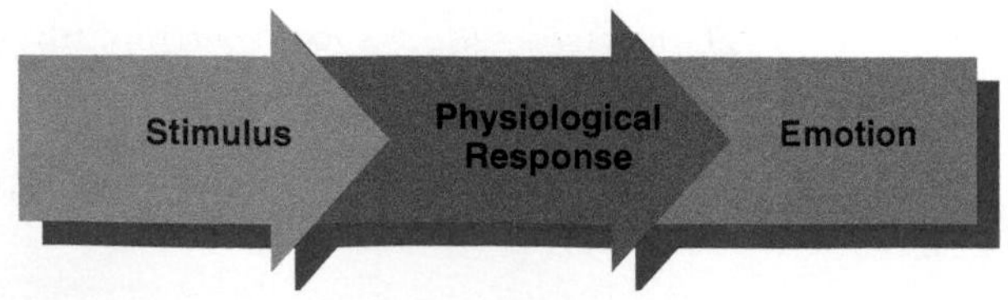

with a weapon is running toward you. After the perception, James believed, we experience changes in our bodies: We smile on seeing the gift; adrenaline surges when we are approached by someone with a weapon. Finally, said James, we experience emotion: We feel joy at the gift, fear at the aggressor.

The organismic view regards emotions as instinctual responses to physiological arousal caused by external stimuli. James specifically discounted what he called "intellectual mind stuff" (Finkelstein, 1980) as having nothing to do with our perceptions of stimuli and, by extension, our emotions. For James and others who shared his view, emotions result from physiological factors that are instinctual and beyond conscious control.

Perceptual Influences on Emotions

James's view of the relationship between bodily states and feelings is no longer widely accepted (Ekman & Davidson, 1994; Frijda, 1986; McLemee, 2003; Reisenzaum, 1983). Today, most researchers think the physiological influences are less important than other factors in shaping emotions.

The **perceptual view of emotions**, which is also called *appraisal theory*, asserts that subjective perceptions shape what external phenomena mean to us. External objects and events, as well as physiological reactions, have no intrinsic meaning. Instead, they gain meaning only as we attribute significance to them. We might interpret trembling hands as a symbol of fear, a raised fist as a threat, and a knot in the stomach as anxiety. Alternatively, we might interpret trembling hands as signifying joy on graduation day; a raised fist as power and racial pride, as it was during the U.S. civil rights movement of the 1960s and 1970s; and a knot in the stomach as excitement about receiving a major award. These different interpretations would lead us to define our emotions quite distinctly. That's the key to the perceptual view of emotions: We act on the basis of our interpretation of phenomena, not the actual phenomena (trembling hands, raised fist, a knot in the stomach).

The ancient Greek philosopher Epictetus observed that people are disturbed not by things but by the views we take of them. Buddha observed that we are what we think; with our thoughts, we make the world. In other words, how we view things leads us to feel disturbed, pleased, sad, joyous, afraid, and so forth. Thus, our perceptions filter our experiences, and it is the filtered experiences that influence what we feel and how we respond.

We respond differently to the same phenomenon, depending on the meaning we attribute to it. For example, if you earn a low score on a test, you might interpret it as evidence that you are not smart. This interpretation could lead you to feel shame or disappointment or other unpleasant emotions. On the other hand, you might view the low score as the result of a tricky or overly rigorous exam, an interpretation that might lead you to feel anger at the teacher or resentment at the situation. Anger is very different from shame. Which one you feel depends on how you perceive the score and the meaning you attribute to it. The perceptual view of emotions is represented in Figure 4.3.

A slight modification of the perceptual view is the **cognitive labelling view of emotions**, which claims that our labels for our physiological responses

Student Voices

Harihar:

Buddhism teaches us that our feelings arise not from things themselves but from what we attach to them. In my life, this is true. If I find myself upset about how a conversation is going, I ask myself, "Harihar, what is it that you were expecting to happen? Can you let go of that and enter into what is actually happening here?" That helps me realize that I must let go of my attachment to certain expected outcomes of the conversation.

FIGURE 4.3

The Perceptual View of Emotions

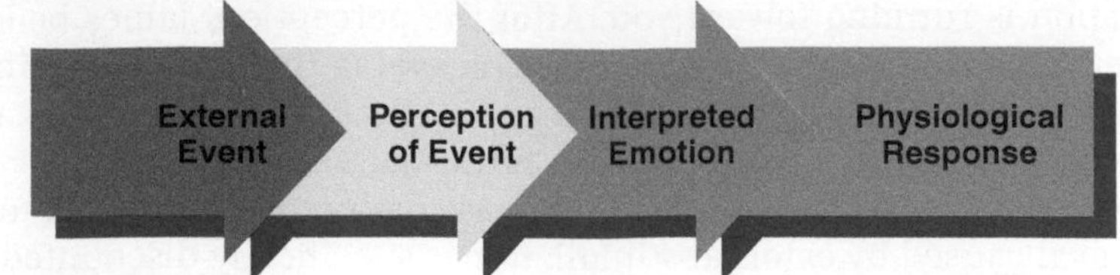

Student Voices

Shinobu:

The most important lesson I learned when my family first moved to Canada was that a bad grade on a test is not a judgment that I am stupid. It is a challenge for me to do better. My English teacher taught me that. He said that if I saw a bad grade as saying I am dumb or a failure, I would never learn English. He taught me to see grades as challenges that I could meet. That attitude made it possible for me not to give up and to keep learning.

influence our interpretations of and responses to events (Schachter, 1964; Schachter & Singer, 1962). Phrased another way, what we feel may be shaped by how we label physiological responses. For example, if you feel a knot in your stomach when you see that you received a low grade on an exam, you might label the knot as evidence of anxiety. Thus, what you felt would not result directly from either the event itself (the grade) or your perceptions of the event. Instead, it would be shaped by how you labelled your physiological response to the event. See Figure 4.4.

One of the authors witnessed how our labels for events and our responses to them influence what we feel. Her two-year-old niece, Michelle, who weighed less than 14 kilograms, was greeted at the door by the author's 30-kilogram dog, Madhi, who ran up and started licking Michelle. Immediately, Michelle started crying, saying, "Mommy, Mommy, I'm scared. My heart is going fast because she came after me and made me scared." Her mother cuddled Michelle and said, "Your heart isn't going fast because you're scared, sweetheart. It's because Madhi surprised you and you were startled. Madhi was telling you how much she loves you. Dogs are our friends." Michelle's mother and the author then petted Madhi and let the dog lick them, saying repeatedly, "Oh, Madhi licked me because she loves me. She startled me."

Michelle quickly picked up on the language and began to laugh, not cry, when Madhi bowled her over. By the end of the day, Michelle and Madhi were fast friends. Before she went to bed that night, Michelle announced, "Madhi makes my heart beat faster because I love her." What happened here? Madhi's exuberance didn't diminish, nor did Michelle's physiological response of increased heart rate. What did change was how Michelle labelled her physiological response. Her mother and the author had taught her to interpret Madhi's behaviour as friendly and exciting instead of threatening. Michelle's label for her emotion also changed: *scared* became *startled*.

There is probably some validity to each view of emotions that we've explored. The organismic view calls our attention to the physiological aspects of emotions; we do have bodily responses to what happens around us. The perceptual view reminds

FIGURE 4.4

The Cognitive Labelling View of Emotions

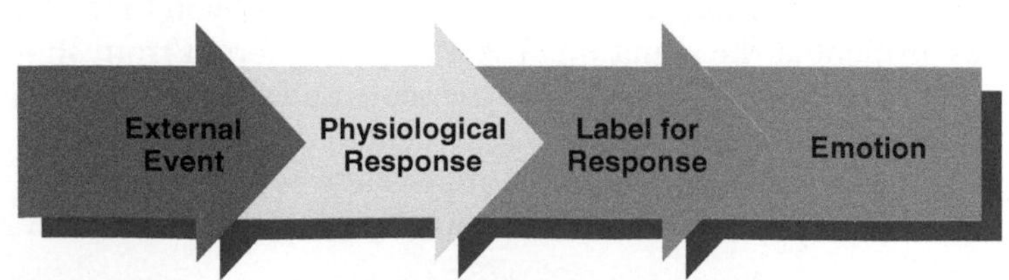

us that how we perceive external events and our physiological reactions influences the meanings we attach to experiences and the emotions we think are appropriate. Finally, the cognitive labelling view emphasizes the role of language in shaping our interpretation of events, our physiological responses, appropriate emotions, or all three. Each of the models we've considered so far gives us insight into emotions. Yet, none of these models is complete, because none adequately accounts for the critical influence of culture in shaping emotions and how we communicate them.

© Dennis Galante/Corbis

What emotions are beyond our conscious control? Have you ever laughed and cried at the same time?

Social Influences on Emotions

As we learned in Chapter 3, perception is influenced by the culture and the social groups to which we belong. Historian Barbara Rosenwein (1998) considers the groups we identify with to be "emotional communities" because they teach us how to understand and express emotions. Examples of emotional communities are families, neighbourhoods, gangs, monasteries, and religious groups. The society and communities in which we live influence our beliefs about which emotions are good or bad, which emotions we should express or repress, and with whom we can appropriately communicate which emotions. For example, the emotion of shame is emphasized much more in traditional Asian societies than in Western societies. This may explain why 95 percent of Chinese parents report that their children understand the meaning of shame by age three, whereas only 10 percent of American parents report this (Sedgwick, 1995; Shaver, Schwartz, Kirson, & O'Connor, 1987; Shaver, Wu, & Schwartz, 1992).

Insight into social influences on emotions and our expression of them is fairly new. Beginning in the 1970s, some scholars began to advance the **interactive view of emotions**, which proposes that social rules and understandings shape what people feel and how they do or don't express their feelings. Arlie Hochschild (1979, 1983, 1990) pioneered in this area by investigating the ways that people experience, control, and express feelings. The interactive view of emotions rests on three key concepts: framing rules, feeling rules, and emotion work. This model of emotions is represented in Figure 4.5.

Framing Rules

Framing rules define the emotional meaning of situations. For instance, Western culture defines funerals as sad and respectful occasions and weddings as joyful events. Within any single culture, however, there are multiple social groups and resulting standpoints. Different social groups may teach members distinct

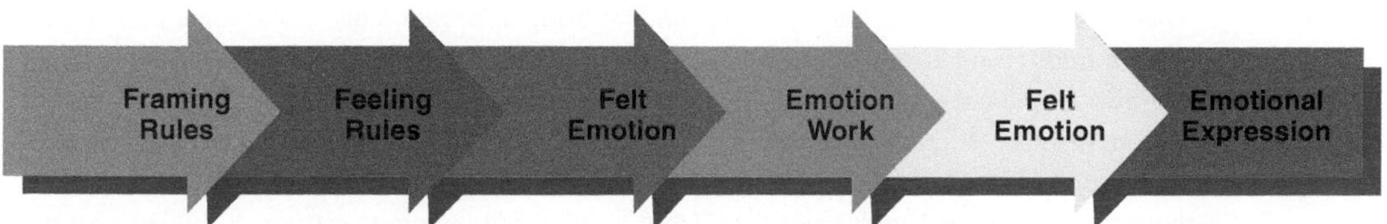

FIGURE 4.5

The Interactive View of Emotions

©Robert A. Sabo/Getty Images

framing rules for the same situations. For example, many Irish people, including many in North America, hold a wake when a person dies. A wake is a festive occasion during which people tell stories about the departed person and celebrate his or her life. Other groups define funerals and the receptions following them as sombre occasions at which any mirth or festivity would be perceived as disrespectful and inappropriate. During the Jewish practice of sitting *shiva,* family members do not engage others in routine ways such as talking on the phone.

Feeling Rules

Feeling rules tell us what we have a right to feel or what we are expected to feel in particular situations. Feeling rules reflect and perpetuate the values of cultures and social groups. For example, cultures that emphasize individuality promote the feeling rule that it is appropriate to feel pride in personal accomplishments, whereas cultures that emphasize collectivism teach members that accomplishments grow out of membership in groups and reflect well on those groups, not on individuals (Johnson, 2000). Thus, in such cultures a feeling rule might be that it is appropriate for a person to feel gratitude to family and community for personal accomplishments.

A newspaper story that shows how feeling rules differ between cultures reported that teachers didn't realize that parents and students from collectivist cultures are dismayed when report cards state that students "speak up in class"—a good thing from a teacher's standpoint. But, because collectivist cultures emphasize the overall community, an individual who stands out may be perceived as showing off and inappropriately calling attention to himself or herself ("Teachers' Words," 2000).

Communication Notes

THE SOCIAL SHAPING OF GRIEF

Cultures have distinct framing rules about death (Lofland, 1985; Miller, 1993, 1998). In some African tribes, death is regarded as cause to celebrate a person's passage to a better form of life. Buddhists do not regard the death of a body as the end of a person, because the person is assumed to continue in other forms. In some cultures, people feel deep grief over the loss of cousins to whom they have deep and lasting attachments. In contrast, other cultures define cousins as distant relations whose death seldom provokes deep sadness.

Framing rules for death also vary over time in a single culture. Modern Western cultures enjoy a low infant mortality rate (in Canada, approximately 5.2 deaths per 1000 infants) and a long life expectancy. Today, the average life expectancy for people living in Canada is 81 years for women and 75 years for men. In earlier times, the infant mortality rate in Western societies ranged from 50 to 400 deaths per 1000 infants, and the life expectancy was decades shorter than it is today. Scholars who have studied historical and diary research from earlier times report that death was viewed as a normal, routine part of life that did not call for intense and prolonged mourning.

All social communities have rules that specify acceptable and unacceptable ways to feel.

Feeling rules are sometimes explicated in terms of rights and duties. The following common phrases highlight the language of duty and rights that infuses feeling rules:

I'm entitled to feel sad.
You have no right to feel unhappy.
She should be grateful to me for what I did.
My disappointment in you is justified.
I ought to feel happy my friend got a job.
I shouldn't feel angry at my father.

Hochschild perceives a strong connection between feeling rules and social order. She (1990) claimed that one way a society attempts to control people is through feeling rules that uphold broad social values and structures. For example, teaching people that they should feel pride in their personal accomplishments reinforces the value that Western culture places on individualism and ambition. Teaching people to regard accomplishments as communal, not individual, upholds the value that many non-Western cultures place on groups. Philosopher Jerome Kagan (1998) points out that morality is not innate but learned as people internalize the moral values of their cultures.

In Canada, the teachers of morality have typically been the family and the church. Now that role is shifting to schools. Many Canadian schools teach empathy in elementary grades to improve the abilities of **deep acting**, which involves learning what they should and should not feel. Children are shown pictures that depict emotionally laden moments. The children are then asked, "How would you feel if this were you?" and "What would you like people to do or say to you if this were you?" This activity allows children to learn about empathy and to expand their repertoire of feelings.

Apply the Idea

RELIGIONS AND FEELING RULES

Religions urge people to follow particular feeling rules. For example, Judeo-Christian commandments direct people to "honour thy father and thy mother" and to "not covet thy neighbour's house, nor his wife." Buddhism commands people to feel compassion for all living beings and to do what one can to alleviate suffering. Hinduism commands followers to accept their place (caste) in this life.

Make a list of all the feeling rules you can identify that are proposed by your spiritual or religious affiliation. Be sure to list both what you are supposed to feel and what you are not supposed to feel.

1. ______________________________
2. ______________________________
3. ______________________________
4. ______________________________

Compare your responses with those of students who have different religious or spiritual beliefs. What similarities and differences in feeling rules can you identify?

Communication Notes

CULTURAL CODES FOR ANGER

Anthropologists tell us that how we express anger is influenced by the society in which we live. In North America and many other Western cultures, anger is viewed as healthy and something we express so that it doesn't fester inside us (Nanda & Warms, 1998). In some societies, however, anger is almost absent. For example, the Semai of Malaysia are a nonviolent people who do not perceive anger as a healthy or appropriate emotion. the Semai believe that a person who stays angry will have misfortune. Because it is the angry person who gets hurt, the Semai try to avoid anger. Not a single murder among the Semai has ever been recorded (Dentan, 1995; Robarchek & Dentan, 1987).

Other societies view anger differently. For instance, one group that lives in the New Guinea highlands has a well-established custom for venting aggression. People who feel aggressive are defined as wild pigs who are out of control. Because they are out of control, they are allowed to behave in bizarre ways that would never be condoned in a normal person. Wild pigs are said to "run amok." They are able to vent aggression without being judged as deviant. After all, when they are in the agitated state, they aren't people—they're wild pigs. By running amok, the person expresses aggressive feelings and can then return to normal identity. Thus, these New Guinea communities have created a safety valve for people who feel overcome by unruly impulses (Newman, 1964; Shott, 1979; Winzeler, 1990).

A second way in which feeling rules uphold social structure is by permitting the expression of negative feelings and of bad-mannered means of expressing them toward people with limited power. Hochschild's (1983) studies of people in service industries reveal that the less power employees have, the more they tend to be targets of negative emotional expressions from others. People who have more power may learn they have a right to express anger, offence, frustration, and so forth, whereas people who have less power may learn that it isn't acceptable for them to express such emotions. To test the validity of this idea, ask yourself who is the target of more complaints and greater hostility: servers or restaurant managers, flight attendants or pilots, receptionists or CEOs?

Parents differ in how they teach children to deal with feelings. Some parents encourage children to control their inner feelings through deep acting, which involves learning what they should and should not feel. For instance, children may be taught that they should feel grateful when given a gift even if they don't like the gift. Many children are taught that they should not feel angry when a sibling takes a toy. Deep acting requires changing how we perceive and label events and phenomena.

Other parents emphasize **surface acting**, which involves controlling the outward expression of emotions rather than controlling feelings. Parents who emphasize surface acting teach children to control their outward behaviours, not necessarily their inner feelings. For example, children learn that they should say "thank you" when they receive a gift and that they should not hit a sibling who takes a toy. Expressing gratitude is emphasized more than feeling grateful, and refraining from hitting someone who takes a toy is stressed more than being willing to share toys.

Emotion Work

The final concept is **emotion work**, which is the effort to curb feelings we think we shouldn't have or to generate feelings we think we should have. We do emotion work to suppress or eliminate feelings we think are wrong. For example, you might think it is wrong to feel gleeful when someone you dislike is hurt. Hochschild (1979, 1983) refers to this as "the pinch," which is a discrepancy between what we feel and what we think we should feel. If you feel gleeful about another's bad luck, you might engage in emotion work in an effort to make yourself feel sad. We also engage in emotion work to cultivate feelings we think we should have, such as prodding ourselves to feel joy for our friend's good fortune.

Communication Notes

FAKING IT

"It happened again today: I was bluffing my way through material in my Property class [a standard course in law school], about which I knew no more than what the teaching manual told me...." That's how law professor William Miller begins his book *Faking It* (2003, p. 1).

This isn't Miller's first foray into the world of self-presentation. For years, he has studied emotions—those of the Vikings, particularly Viking warriors (Miller, 1993, 1998). Now, Miller turns his attention to modern-day warriors like you and me as we bluff and fake our way through surface acting: pretending to be happy for a colleague who wins a major award, feigning pleasure when someone you dislike enters your space, acting informed when we know little. His book *Faking It* takes note of how we bluff our way through life and work. The book is not only informative but also wonderfully funny and interesting.

As Donna Vocate (1994) notes, much of our emotion work takes place through self-talk—we try to talk ourselves into feeling what we think is appropriate and out of feeling what we think is inappropriate. In addition, we often talk to friends to figure out whether our feelings are appropriate—we rely on friends to help us reduce uncertainty about feelings (Heise, 1999; Milardo, 1986; Parks & Adelman, 1983).

Typically, what we think we should feel is based on what we've learned from our social groups and the larger culture. Social groups teach us what feelings are appropriate in particular situations. For example, Clifton Scott and Karen Meyers (2005) found that firefighters engage in emotion work to manage feelings such as fear and disgust, which can interfere with controlling damage and providing medical help to victims of fires. People who have been socialized in multiple cultures with different values may be especially vulnerable to feeling "the pinch." For example, Kimberly Gangwish (1999) describes Asian American women as "living in two worlds" in terms of their emotions and how they express them. First-generation Asian American women said they knew that, in the United States, it was acceptable to feel angry and upset, but they couldn't express those feelings because Asian cultures frown on expressing negative emotions.

Student Voices

Andrea:

Last week in the emergency ward waiting room I could not help but notice that a person who clearly arrived after me was taken before me, even though that person's injuries appeared less severe! I was so annoyed and felt ignored by the health workers. Even though I know that those feelings were there, I had to repress my frustration, remain courteous, and accept the wait. After all, maybe their problem was more severe than mine.

Student Voices

Huang:

In my native country, students are supposed to be respectful of teachers and never speak out in class. It has been hard for me to learn to feel I have a right to ask questions of a professor here. Sometimes I have a question or I do not agree with a professor, but I have to work to tell myself it is okay to assert myself. To me, it still feels disrespectful to speak up.

Framing rules, feeling rules, and emotion work are interrelated (refer back to Figure 4.5). Framing rules that define the emotional meaning of situations lead to feeling rules that tell us what we should feel or have a right to feel in a given context. If we don't feel what our feeling rules designate we should, we may engage in emotion work to squelch inappropriate feelings or to bring about feelings that we think suit the circumstances. We then express our feelings by following rules for appropriate expression of particular emotions in specific contexts.

The interactive view of emotions emphasizes the impact of social factors on how we perceive, label, and respond emotionally to experiences in our lives. A strength of this model is its acknowledgment of cultural differences in feelings and their expression.

How we think about emotions affects how much we believe we can control what we experience and express in everyday life. If you agree with William James that feelings are instinctual, then you will assume that feelings cannot be managed. Whatever you feel, you feel. That's it. On the other hand, if you accept the interactive view of emotions, you are more likely to think you can analyze your feelings and perhaps change them and your expression of them through emotion work. The interactive view assumes we have some power over how we feel and act. If you agree with this perspective, you are more likely to monitor your feelings and to make choices about how to communicate them.

We may not have total control over what we feel, but usually we can exert some control. Furthermore, we can exercise substantial control over how we do or don't express our feelings and to whom we express them. Taking personal responsibility for when, how, and to whom you express feelings is a cornerstone of ethical interpersonal communication.

There is no clear dividing line between what we feel and how we express feelings. The two interact in the emotional process. What we feel influences how we express (or don't express) our emotions. It's equally true that how we express

Communication Notes

THE GIFT OF FEAR

Don't ignore your fear. That's the message of Gavin de Becker's book, *The Gift of Fear* (1997). For years, de Becker has worked as a security consultant to celebrities. He notes that many people have been taught to dismiss feelings of fear by labelling them "silly" or "stupid." They invest emotion work in talking themselves out of feeling fear. Big mistake, says de Becker. If you're waiting for an elevator, and when the door opens, you have a strong, fearful reaction to a person in the elevator, what do you do? De Becker says many people try to talk themselves out of the fear with thoughts such as, "There's nothing to be afraid of." Wrong, says de Becker. He advises us to wait for the next elevator. If you have a feeling that someone is lurking in a parking lot, don't dismiss it as paranoia; heed it, and find someone to walk with you. De Becker believes that fear often arises in response to subtle cues in an environment—cues of which we are not consciously aware but to which we respond anyway.

Reflective Exercise

Examine your family's feeling rules. When you were a child, which emotions were allowed expression and in what way? What gender rules for feelings were evident in your family? How did this experience prepare you for managing emotions in intimate relationships? In work relationships? Are you satisfied with the range of emotions you feel and with your expression of them?

our feelings is echoed back to us, affecting how we interpret our feelings (Anderson & Guerrero, 1998; Fridlund, 1994; Philippot & Feldman, 2004).

In the Student Voices example, Mae is displaying a high degree of what Goleman calls "emotional intelligence," as described earlier.

Student Voices

Mae:

Sometimes during an argument with my partner, my body begins to shake out of nowhere. I know when this happens that I have tapped into deep old feelings of fear and mistrust from the past. I know that I don't feel psychologically safe. I have learned to honour this sign and to ask for some space and time to think about what is being asked of me. It's as if I have to discharge the feelings of panic and get back to the present. Sometimes I just have to leave. I tell my partner, "I don't feel comfortable right now. I'm going to leave and think about what has gone on here before continuing.

OBSTACLES TO THE EFFECTIVE COMMUNICATION OF EMOTIONS

Skill in recognizing and expressing emotions is important to interpersonal competence, yet many of us repress feelings or express them inappropriately. Let's consider reasons we may not express emotions, and then ask how we can learn to express emotions effectively.

Reasons We May Not Express Emotions

We can identify four common reasons people don't communicate emotions. As we discuss each reason, reflect on whether you rely on it in your own emotional expression.

CONCEPTS AT A GLANCE

Four Reasons Why We May Not Express Emotions

1. Social expectations
2. Vulnerability
3. Protecting others
4. Social and professional roles

Social Expectations

As we have noted, what we feel and how we express it are influenced by the culture and social groups to which we belong. Gender socialization seems particularly important in shaping feelings and the expression of them. In North America, men are expected to be more restrained than women in expressing emotions—at least most emotions. Men are allowed to express anger, which is often disapproved of in women. Anger and other emotions regarded as powerful are allowed and often admired in men.

In other ways, however, men in Western societies are expected to be emotionally restrained. The expression of hurt, fear, depression, and many other emotions is often neither encouraged nor admired in men. This social expectation is not universal. For example, Italian men routinely express a range of emotions dramatically and openly. In North American society, however, most men learn the feeling rule that they should not feel or express a great many emotions. This can lead some men to deny feelings or avoid expressing how they feel. Over time, men who do this may become alienated from their feelings, unable to recognize what they do feel because society has taught them that they aren't allowed to experience a great many feelings.

Women face different restrictions than men on the feelings society allows them. Women are generally taught that they should not feel or express anger. Our culture considers anger unattractive and undesirable in women (Tavris, 1989). Thus, many women are constrained by the feeling rule that they should not feel anger and that, if they do, they should not express it. This discourages women from acknowledging legitimate anger and expressing it assertively.

Other feeling rules are learned by many Western women. Most women in our society are encouraged from childhood to care about others (Eisenberg, 2002; Taylor, 2002). Many women learn the feeling rule that they should care about and care for others all the time (Eichenbaum & Orbach, 1987; Rubin, 1985). Thus, many women engage in emotion work in an attempt to make themselves feel (deep acting) caring when they don't naturally feel that way.

Communication Notes

SUGAR AND SPICE AND BULLYING!

"Sugar and spice and everything nice" is not the whole picture about girls. Recently, scholars' tracking of adolescent girls' bullying (Simmons, 2002, 2004; Underwood, 2003) shows that many young girls engage in social aggression toward other girls, and they do so using distinctly feminine rules for expressing aggression. Unlike physical aggression, which is standard in boys' aggression, social aggression is usually indirect, even covert. It takes forms such as spreading hurtful rumours, social exclusion, and encouraging others to turn against a particular girl.

Why do young girls rely on indirect and social strategies of aggression? One reason appears to be that, even at young ages, girls understand that they are supposed to be nice to everyone, so they fear that being overtly mean to others would lead to disapproval or punishment. Instead of learning how to work through feelings of anger and dislike, young girls learn to hide such feelings and express them only indirectly.

Student Voices

Sadie:

The other night, I got home after working the dinner shift at my restaurant. I was dead tired. The phone rang, and I almost didn't answer. Now, I wish I hadn't. It was my friend Brooke, and she was upset about a fight with her boyfriend. I tried to cut the call short, but she said, "I'm really hurting, and I need to talk." And so I reminded myself that I do care about Brooke. I told myself that my fatigue wasn't as important as Brooke's problem. So we stayed on the phone for over an hour, and we talked through what was happening. Sometimes I wish I could just say, "I'm not available for you now," but I'd feel like a real jerk if I did that.

Even more often, report researchers, women squelch feelings of jealousy toward friends and feelings of competitiveness in personal and professional relationships. Because most Western women are taught that they should support others, they often feel that they shouldn't experience or express envy or competitiveness. Not being able to express or even acknowledge such feelings can interfere with honest communication in interpersonal relationships.

When women squelch these feelings, there can be undesirable personal and relationship effects. Denying or refusing to act on competitive feelings can limit women's career advancement. Not dealing openly with feelings of jealousy or envy in friendships can create barriers and distance. For women, demanding of themselves that they always be emotionally available and caring to anyone who wants their help can be overwhelming. Conversely, women in male-dominated roles or roles traditionally played by men may find that they suppress their feelings of vulnerability in favour of the more aggressive, action-oriented behaviours of their workplace, giving rise to feelings of competitiveness, detachment, and anger. Also, as men take on more caregiving and nurturing roles, the restrictiveness of the social expectations around expression offeelings loosens. As our workplace and community roles become more gender-mixed, the strict social definitions of emotional expression become more lax.

Vladimir Mucibabic/Shutterstock

What feeling rules were you taught?

Vulnerability

A second reason we may not express our feelings is that we don't want to give others information that could affect how they perceive us. We fear that someone will like us less if we disclose that we feel angry with him or her. We worry that someone will lose respect for us if our nonverbal behaviours show that we feel weak or scared. We fear that if we disclose how deeply we feel about another person, she or he will reject us. Furthermore, we may be concerned that others could use knowledge of our vulnerabilities against us. To protect ourselves from being vulnerable to others, we may not express feelings verbally or nonverbally

Protecting Others

Another reason we often choose not to express feelings is that we fear we could hurt or upset others. Sometimes we make an ethical choice not to express emotions that would hurt another person without achieving any positive outcome. Choosing not to express emotions in some situations or to some people can be constructive and generous, as Tara's commentary illustrates.

The tendency to restrain emotional expression to protect others is particularly strong in many Asian cultures because they view hurting others as shameful (Johnson, 2000; Min, 1995; Ting-Toomey & Oetzel, 2002; Yamamoto, 1995). Traditional Asian cultures also view conflict as damaging to social relationships, so they discourage emotional expressions that might lead to conflict (Johnson, 2000; Servaes, 1988; Ting-Toomey & Oetzel, 2002; Yum, 1987).

Student Voices

Chuck:

I guess I fell prey to the idea that real men don't whine or give in to problems. It took a nervous breakdown to teach me otherwise. Two years ago, I was going to school part-time and working full-time. My company downsized, which meant that those of us who weren't fired had to pick up the work of those who were. I began putting in more hours at the job. Then I gave up my daily workout to create more time for studying and working. I just kept stuffing down all I felt—the resentment, the stress, the anxiety about getting everything done. I didn't talk to my girlfriend or brother or co-workers or anyone. I didn't want anyone to think I couldn't take the heat.

One day, I couldn't get up. I just couldn't get out of bed. I stayed there all day and the next day and the next. Finally, my brother hauled me to a hospital where I was diagnosed with acute stress. By that time, I also had an ulcer and my blood pressure was really elevated. My doctor said I needed counselling. I said no. He asked whether I'd rather learn how to deal with my emotions or die in the next year. Given that choice, I went into counselling. What I discovered was that I've spent my whole life stuffing emotions down. I had to learn what I should have learned as a child—that it's okay to feel things and that it really helps to talk about what I'm feeling.

Student Voices

Tara:

My best friend, Fran, is a marriage saver. When I'm really angry with my husband, I vent to her. If there's a really serious problem between me and Al, I talk with him. But a lot of times I'm upset over little stuff. I know what I'm feeling isn't going to last and isn't any serious problem in our marriage, but I may be seething anyway. Letting those feelings out to Fran gets them off my chest without hurting Al or our marriage.

Yet, Asians and people of Asian descent are not the only ones who want to protect relationships from emotional expression. If a friend of yours behaves in ways that you consider irresponsible, you may refrain from expressing your disapproval because to do so might cause tension between you. Yet, it isn't healthy to consistently avoid expressing emotions. The physical and psychological impact of denying or repressing emotions can harm you and devastate your relationships (Pennebaker, 1997; Schmanoff, 1985, 1987).

Totally open and unrestrained expression of feeling isn't necessarily a good idea. Sometimes it is both wise and kind not to express feelings. It's often not productive to vent minor frustrations and annoyances. If someone we care about is already overburdened with anxiety or emotional problems, we may choose to monitor our communication so that the other person doesn't have to respond to our feelings at the moment. Thus, there can be good reasons not to show or discuss feelings or not to show or discuss them at a given time.

Communication Notes

"JE T'AIME, PAPA"

The funeral of Pierre Elliott Trudeau on October 4, 2000, transfixed a nation. The parting words of Justin Trudeau's eulogy touched everyone, regardless of political affiliation. They were the words of a son in grief: "I love you, Papa." His public display of tears riveted audiences all over the country. Justin's articulate account of his father as a loving family man was profoundly moving. We all grieved for the loss of this father. As Justin painted the picture of "Dad" to us all, an intimate portrait not visible in the public figure, we all grieved for the loss of the "father" in our own lives.

This confident, warm, engaging son rewrote the rules of emotional expression for a nation. The wave of mourning that ensued was unprecedented in Canada. It was as if our very definition of a nation was tied up in the character of Trudeau, who advocated in his life for Canadian unity and assertiveness. His death and the words of his son took us beyond partisan politics to the human heart. Men cried openly. Foes prayed together. The nation wept.

Nasr's commentary on the following page provides a good example of an instance in which it is caring not to express feelings. Yet, we would be mistaken to think it's always a good idea to keep feelings to ourselves. Avoiding the expression of negative or upsetting feelings can be harmful if such feelings directly affect relationships with others or if doing so may threaten our own health. Susan Schmanoff (1987) found that intimacy wanes when couples' communication consistently lacks emotional disclosures, even unpleasant ones. If not expressing feelings is likely to create barriers in relationships or to cause us serious personal distress, then we should try to find a context and mode of expression that allow us to communicate our emotions.

Social and Professional Roles

A final reason why we may not express some feelings is that our roles make it inappropriate. The queen of England, for example, must always monitor her expression of feelings so that she does not act in ways that are incongruent with her role as the queen. An attorney who cried when hearing a sad story from a witness might be perceived as unprofessional. A doctor or nurse who expressed anger toward a patient might be regarded as unprofessional. Police officers and social workers might be judged to be out of line if they expressed animosity instead of objective detachment when investigating a crime or working with people in need of help.

When one of the authors testifies as an expert witness in trials, the lawyers questioning her often try to rattle her with personal attacks or trick questions, or by deliberately twisting what she has said. These are routine, normal tactics in cross-examinations. If the author were to respond emotionally—perhaps with an angry outburst—she would lose credibility with the jury. To be effective in the role of an expert witness, she must restrain highly emotional reactions.

We've identified four common reasons we may not express our emotions. Although we can understand all of them, they are not equally constructive in their consequences. There is no simple rule for when to express feelings. Instead, we must exercise judgment. We have an ethical obligation to make thoughtful choices about whether, when, and how to express our feelings. As a responsible communicator, you should strive to decide when it is necessary, appropriate, and constructive to express your feelings, keeping in mind that you, others, and relationships will be affected by your decision.

© Kwame Zikomo/SuperStock

Children need to be heard.

Student Voices

Nasr:

Last week, I was rejected by the law school that was my top choice. Normally, I would have gone over to Jason's apartment to hang out with him and let him boost me up. Ever since we met in freshman year, we've been tight friends, and we talk about everything in our lives. But right now, Jason's struggling with his own stuff. His mother just got diagnosed with cancer, and his father is out of work. I know we'll talk about my disappointment sometime, but I figured it could wait until he gets into a better place.

Ineffective Expression of Emotions

We don't always deny or repress our emotions. Sometimes we realize we have feelings and we try to express them, but we don't do so effectively. We'll look at three of the most common forms of ineffective emotional expression

Speaking in Generalities

"I feel bad." "I'm happy." "I'm sad." Statements such as these do express emotional states, but they do so ineffectively. Why? Because they are so general and abstract that they don't clearly communicate what the speaker feels. Does "I feel bad" mean the person feels depressed, angry, guilty, ashamed, or anxious? Does "I'm happy" mean the speaker is in love, pleased with a grade, satisfied at having received a promotion, delighted to be eating chocolate, or excited about an upcoming vacation? When we use highly general, abstract emotional language, we aren't communicating effectively about what we feel.

CONCEPTS AT A GLANCE

Ineffective Expression of Emotions

- Speaking in generalities
- Not owning feelings
- Counterfeit emotional language

Also, our nonverbal repertoire for expressing emotions may be limited. Withdrawing from interaction may be an expression of sadness, anger, depression,

Apply the Idea

ENLARGING YOUR EMOTIONAL VOCABULARY

A key aspect of emotional competence is an adequate emotional vocabulary. Reflect on your emotional vocabulary and how and when you use particular words to describe emotions.

Listed here are some of the more common emotion words people that use. For each one, write out three other emotion words that describe subtle distinctions in feeling.

Example: resentment outrage irritation

anger

____

sadness

____

happiness

____

fear

____

anxiety

____

love

____

or fear. Lowering our head and eyes may express a range of emotions, including reverence, shame, and thoughtfulness. We are capable of experiencing many, many emotions, yet most of us recognize or express only a small number.

In *Anger: The Struggle for Emotional Control in America's History* (1986), Carol Stearns and Peter Stearns report that people in the United States recognize only `a few of the emotions humans can experience, and they express those emotions whenever they feel something. For example, a person might say, "I'm frustrated" when he is angry, confused, hurt, anxious, disappointed, and so forth. A limited emotional vocabulary restricts our ability to communicate clearly with others (Saarni, 1999). There are many similarities between Canadian and U.S. cultures in this respect. Some people routinely describe what they feel by relying on only one or a few emotions.

For the next week, extend this exercise by trying to be more precise in how you describe your feelings. Does expanding your emotional vocabulary give you and others more understanding of what you feel?

CONCEPTS AT A GLANCE

Key Points for Expressing Anger

- Don't damage relationships.
- Don't damage yourself.
- Don't damage property.

Not Owning Feelings

Stating a feeling in a way that disowns personal responsibility for the feeling is one of the most common obstacles to effective expression of emotions (Proctor, 1991). "You make me angry" states a feeling (although the word *angry* may be overly general), yet this statement relies on *you* language, which suggests that somebody other than the speaker is the source or cause of the angry feeling. Others certainly say and do things that affect us; they may even do things *to* us. But we—not anyone else—decide what their actions mean, and we—not anyone else—are responsible for our feelings.

How could we use *I* language to revise the statement, "You make me angry"? We could change it to: "I feel angry when you don't call when you say you will." The statement would be even more effective—clearer and more precise—if the speaker said, "I feel hurt and insecure when you don't call when you say you will." And the statement would be still more effective if it included information about what the speaker wants from the other person: "I feel hurt and insecure when you don't call when you say you will. Would you be willing to call if we agree that it's okay for calls to be short sometimes?" This statement accepts responsibility for a feeling, communicates clearly what is felt, and offers a solution that could help the relationship.

Student Voices

Annie:

My mother exploded when she was angry. I became afraid of anyone's anger including my own. Anger was a dangerous emotion.

Takeshi:

My parents refused to talk when they felt angry. In my family, refusing to talk—silence—is the message of anger.

Aaron:

There was so much passive-aggressive behaviour in my family that now, as an adult, when there is no apparent conflict, I am still uneasy and never feel at peace in a relationship.

Counterfeit Emotional Language

A third ineffective form of emotional communication is relying on **counterfeit emotional language.** This is language that seems to express emotions but does not actually describe what a person is feeling. For example, shouting "Why can't you leave me alone?" certainly reveals that the speaker is feeling something, but it doesn't describe what he or she is feeling. Is it anger at a particular person, frustration at being interrupted, stress at having to meet a deadline, or the need for time alone? We can't tell what feeling the speaker is experiencing.

Reflective Exercise

How do you usually express anger? What is the impact of expressions of anger on the people around you? What are your family scripts around feeling and expressing anger? What changes, if any, would you like to make around expressing anger?

Effective communicators provide clear descriptions of their feelings and the connection between their feelings and others' behaviours. "I feel frustrated when I'm working and you walk in, because I lose my train of thought" is a more constructive statement than "Why can't you leave me alone?" The first statement communicates what is troubling you and states that it is situation-specific.

It's also counterfeit and unproductive not to explain feelings. "That's just how I feel" doesn't tell a person how her or his behaviour is related to your feelings or what you would like her or him to do. Sometimes, we say, "That's just how I feel" because we haven't really figured out why we feel as we do or what we want from another person. In such cases, we should take responsibility for understanding what's going on inside ourselves before we ask others to understand. Only when you can identify situations and your emotional reactions to them can you communicate clearly to others (Planalp, 1997).

Another form of counterfeit emotional language uses feeling words but really expresses thoughts: "I feel this discussion is getting sidetracked." The perception that a discussion is going off on a tangent is a thought, not a feeling. Maybe the speaker feels frustrated that the discussion seems to be wandering, but that feeling is not communicated by the statement.

The three types of ineffective emotional communication we've considered give us insight into some of the more common ways we may evade—consciously or not—clear and honest communication about our feelings. In the final section of this chapter, we consider specific ways to communicate our feelings effectively and constructively and to respond sensitively to others' communication about their emotions.

Apply the Idea

AVOIDING COUNTERFEIT EMOTIONAL LANGUAGE

Listed here are five statements that include counterfeit emotional language. Rewrite each statement so that it describes a feeling or an emotional state. Make sure you also rely on I language, not you language, and offer precise, clear descriptions, not vague ones. Avoid "I feel that ..." when what you mean is "I believe that ..." What follows "I feel" should be a feeling word or description.

1. Shut up! I don't want to hear anything else from you.
2. You're a wonderful person.
3. I feel like we should get started on our group project.
4. I can't believe you were here all day and didn't clean up this mess.
5. Can't you see I'm working now? Leave me alone.

GUIDELINES FOR COMMUNICATING EMOTIONS EFFECTIVELY

What we've explored so far in this chapter suggests several guidelines for becoming skilled at communicating our feelings. In this section, we extend our discussion to identify six guidelines for effective communication of emotions. This process is summarized in Figure 4.6.

Identify Your Emotions

Before you can communicate emotions effectively, you must be able to identify what you feel. As we have seen, this isn't always easy. For reasons we've discussed, people may be alienated from their emotions or unclear about what they feel, especially if they experience multiple emotions at once. To become more aware of your emotions, give mindful attention to your inner self. Just as we can learn to ignore our feelings, we can teach ourselves to notice and heed them.

Sometimes, identifying our emotions requires us to sort out complex mixtures of feeling. For example, we sometimes feel both anxious and hopeful. To recognize only that you feel hopeful is to overlook the anxiety. To realize only that you feel anxious is to ignore the hope you also feel. Recognizing the existence of both feelings allows you to tune in to yourself and to communicate accurately to others what you are experiencing.

When sorting out intermingled feelings, it's useful to identify the primary or main feeling—the one or ones that are dominant at the moment. Doing this allows you to communicate clearly to others what is most important in your

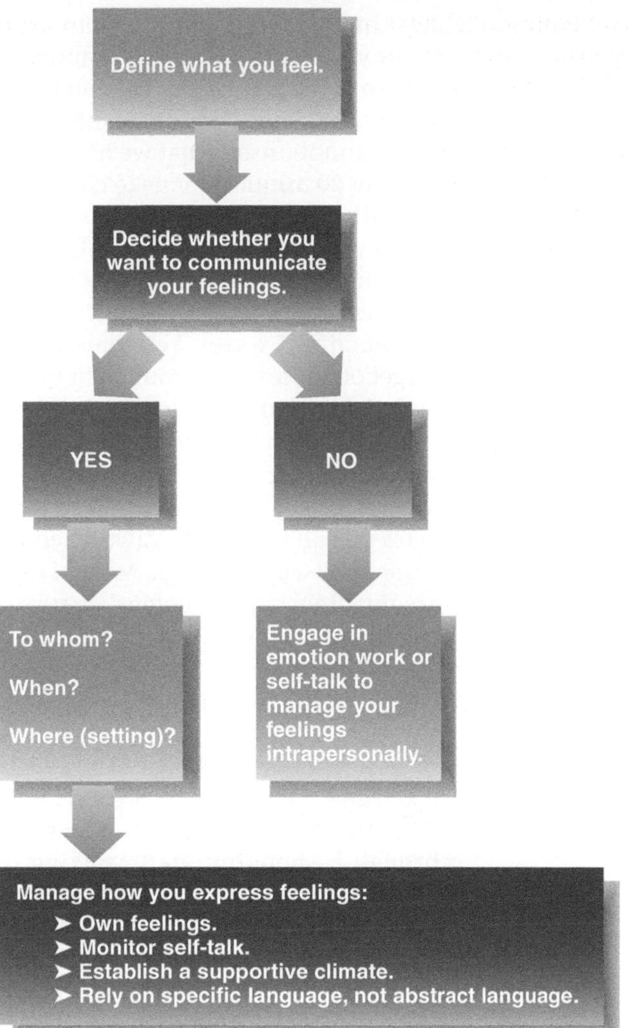

FIGURE 4.6

Effective Communication of Emotions

emotional state. Think back to the example that opened this chapter. Anthony felt overwhelmed, trapped, and scared. But he also felt love for his partner. By deciding which one was primary, he gave Natasha a chance to be a real support.

Choose How to Express Emotions

Once you know what you feel, you'll want to consider how to express your emotions. The first choice facing you is whether you want to communicate your emotions to particular people. As we noted in the previous section, sometimes it is both wise and compassionate not to tell someone what you feel. You may decide that expressing particular emotions would hurt others and would not accomplish anything positive. This is not the same thing as not expressing emotions just to avoid tension, because tension between people can foster growth in individuals and relationships.

We may also decide not to communicate emotions because we prefer to keep some of our feelings private. This is a reasonable choice if the feelings we keep to ourselves are not ones that others need to know in order to understand us and to be in satisfying relationships with us. We don't have a responsibility to bare our souls to everyone, nor are we required to tell all of our feelings, even to our intimates.

If you decide you do want to communicate your emotions, then you should assess the different ways you might do that and select the one that seems likely to be most effective. Four guidelines can help you decide how to express emotions. First, evaluate your current state. If you are really upset, you may not be able to express yourself clearly and fairly. In moments of extreme emotion, our perceptions may be distorted, and we may say things we don't mean. Remember that communication is irreversible—we cannot unsay what we have said. According to Daniel Goleman (1995b), it takes about 20 minutes for us to cleanse our minds and bodies of anger. Thus, if you are really angry, you may want to wait until you've cooled down so that you can discuss your feelings more fruitfully.

The second step is to decide to whom you want to express your feelings. Often, we want to communicate our emotions to the people they concern—the person with whom we are upset or whose understanding we seek. Yet, sometimes we don't want to talk to the person who is the target of our feelings. You might be too upset to talk productively, or you might not think the person can help you. In cases such as these, it may be useful to find someone to whom you can safely express your feelings without harming the person about whom you have them. Venting can be healthy because it allows us to acknowledge strong feelings without imposing them on others who might be hurt. A good friend can be a safety valve when we want to vent.

Next, select an appropriate time to discuss feelings. Most of us are better able to listen and respond when we are not preoccupied, defensive, stressed, rushed, or tired. Generally, it's not productive to launch a discussion of feelings when we lack the time or energy to focus on the conversation. It may be better to defer discussion until you and the other person have the psychological and physical resources to engage mindfully.

Finally, select an appropriate setting for discussing feelings. Many feelings can be expressed well in a variety of settings. For instance, it would be appropriate to tell a friend you felt happy while strolling with him through a shopping mall, walking on campus, or in a private conversation. However, it might not be constructive to tell a friend you feel angry with her or disappointed in her in a public setting. Doing so could make the other person feel on display, which is likely to arouse defensiveness, making it less likely that the two of you can have a constructive, open discussion of feelings. Many people report that they feel freer to express emotions honestly online than in face-to-face communication (Baym, 2002). However, some people really dislike communicating about personal topics online. So, before choosing to discuss emotions in cyberspace, make sure the other person is comfortable with that.

Student Voices

Bob:

When I didn't get a promotion, I was ready to blow my top. But I knew better than to blow it around my boss or anyone at the company. Nope, I said I was sick and left for the day and called a friend who works at home. We met for lunch, and she let me just blow off steam with her in a place where no one from work would see me venting.

Own Your Feelings

Owning your feelings is so important to effective communication that the guideline bears repeating. Using *I* language to express feelings reminds us that we—not anyone else—have responsibility for our feelings. When we rely on *you* language ("You hurt me"), we risk misleading ourselves about our accountability for our emotions.

I language also reduces the potential for defensiveness by focusing on specific behaviours that we would like changed ("I feel hurt when I am interrupted") instead of criticizing another's basic self ("You are so rude"). Criticisms of specific behaviours are less face-threatening than criticisms of our personality or self (Cupach & Carlson, 2002). Thus, when we use *I* language to describe how we feel when another behaves in particular ways, the other person is more able to listen thoughtfully and respond sensitively to our expression of emotion. We expand the possibility for healthy, rich interpersonal relationships when we take responsibility for our own feelings by using *I* language. We will visit these concepts further in Chapter 5.

Communication Notes

VIRTUAL EMOTIONS

Most of the time, we're not highly conscious of our need to express emotions, because most communication media don't constrain our ability to do so. But when we enter cyberspace, things change. Have you ever had a friend misunderstand an e-mail message because the text you typed didn't covey that you were being sarcastic, ironic, or just plain joking?

The potential for misunderstanding because nonverbal cues of emotion are missing on the Internet probably is why emoticons are so popular (Netspeak, 2000). The word *emoticon* is a combination of two words: *emotion* and *icon*. Thus, emoticons are icons that represent facial expressions that show what feeling we mean to convey with our written message.

:D grin	;) wink	:> devilish grin	:/ frustrated
:*) kiss	:) smile	{name} hug	:O surprise
:(frown	:'(crying/sad	::(::):: Band-Aid	

Monitor Your Self-Talk

A fourth guideline is to monitor your self-talk. You'll recall from Chapter 2 that the ways we communicate with ourselves affect how we feel and act. **Self-talk** is communication with ourselves. We engage in self-talk when we do emotion work. We might say, "I shouldn't feel angry" or "I don't want to come across as a wimp by showing how much that hurt." Thus, we may talk ourselves out of or into feelings and out of or into ways of expressing feelings.

Psychologist Martin Seligman (1990) believes that "our thoughts are not merely reactions to events; they change what ensues" (p. 9). In other words, the thoughts we communicate to ourselves affect what happens in our lives. Self-talk can work for us or against us, depending on whether we manage it or it manages us. This point is stressed by Tom Rusk and Natalie Rusk in their book *Mind Traps* (1988). They point out that many people have self-defeating ideas that get in the way of their effectiveness and happiness. According to the Rusks, unless we learn to manage our feelings effectively, we cannot change patterns of behaviour that leave us stuck in ruts. Tuning in to your self-talk and learning to monitor it helps you manage your emotions.

Adopt a Rational–Emotive Approach to Feelings

Monitoring your self-talk allows you to appreciate the connections between thoughts and feelings. As Sally Planalp and Julie Fitness (2000) point out, "Cognition relies on emotion, emotion relies on cognition" (p. 732). Thus, how we think about feelings affects our feelings. The relationship between thoughts and feelings led therapist Albert Ellis (1962) to develop the **rational–emotive approach to feelings**. This approach uses rational thinking and self-talk to challenge debilitating thoughts about emotions that undermine healthy self-concepts and relationships. The rational–emotive approach to feelings proceeds through four steps, as shown in Figure 4.7.

The first step is to monitor your emotional reactions to events and experiences that distress you. Notice what's happening in your body; notice your nonverbal behaviour. Does your stomach tighten? Are you clenching your teeth? Is your heart racing? Do you feel nauseated?

The second step is to identify the events and situations to which you have unpleasant responses. Look for commonalities between situations. For example, perhaps you notice that your heart races and your palms get clammy when you talk with professors, supervisors, and academic advisers, but you don't have these physiological responses when you interact with friends, co-workers, or people whom you supervise. You label your emotions as *insecurity* in the former cases and *security* in the latter ones. One commonality between the situations in which you feel insecure is the greater power of the other person. This could suggest that you feel insecure when talking with someone who has more power than you.

The third step is to tune in to your self-talk (Vocate, 1994). Listen to what's happening in your head. What is your *Me* saying? Is it telling you that you shouldn't feel certain emotions ("It's stupid to feel anxious," "Don't be a wimp")? Is it telling you to hide your feelings ("Don't let on that you're insecure")? Is it telling you that you should feel something you don't ("You're supposed to feel confident and in command")? We need to identify and challenge debilitating ways of thinking about our emotions and, by extension, ourselves. These irrational beliefs, or fallacies, hinder our ability to manage and express emotions effectively. Table 4.1 lists some of the most common fallacies that sabotage realistic appraisals of ourselves and our feelings.

We can use our self-talk to challenge the debilitating fallacies. For example, assume that Tyronne has been working well at his job and thinks his boss should give him a raise. He tunes in to his self-talk (Step 3) and hears himself saying, "Well, maybe I shouldn't ask for a raise, because, after all, I have made some mistakes. I could do better." This self-talk reflects the fallacy of perfectionism. Tyronne listens further to himself and hears this message: "If I ask him for a raise, and he gets angry, he might fire me, and then I wouldn't have a job and couldn't stay in school. Without a degree, I have no future." This self-talk exemplifies the fear of catastrophic failure.

How might Tyronne dispute these fallacies? To challenge the perfectionism fallacy, he could say, "True, I'm not perfect, but I'm doing more and better work than the other employees hired at the same time I was." To dispute the fallacy of catastrophic failure, Tyronne might say to himself, "Well, he's not likely to fire me, because I do my job well, and training someone new would be a lot of trouble. And what if he does fire me? It's not like this is the only job in the world. I could get

FIGURE 4.7

The Rational–Emotive Approach to Feelings

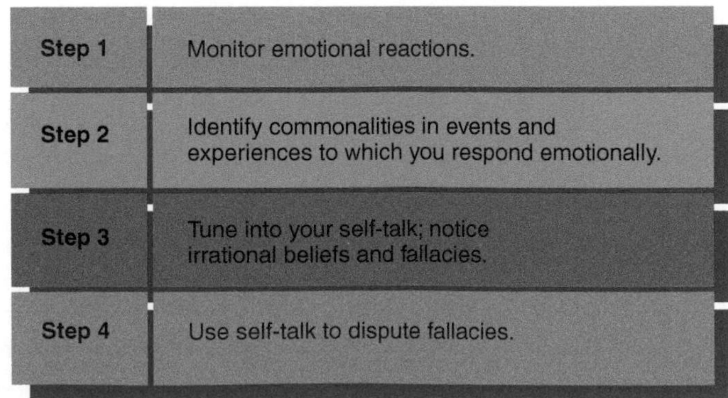

Step 1
Monitor emotional reactions.
Step 2
Identify commonalities in events and experiences to which you respond emotionally.
Step 3
Tune into your self-talk; notice irrational beliefs and fallacies.
Step 4
Use self-talk to dispute fallacies.

TABLE 4.1

COMMON FALLACIES ABOUT EMOTIONS

Fallacy	Typical Effects
Perfectionism	Unrealistically low self-concept Stress Chronic dissatisfaction with self Jealousy and envy of others
Obsession with "shoulds"	Saps energy for constructive work Can make others defensive Can alienate self from feelings Unrealistic standards set the self up for failure
Overgeneralization	Perceives one failure as typical of self Generalizes inadequacies in some domains to total self
Taking responsibility for others	Thinking you are responsible for others' feelings Feeling guilt for how others feel Depriving others of taking responsibility for selves
Helplessness	Believing that there is nothing you can do to change how you feel Resignation, depression
Fear of catastrophic failure	Extreme negative fantasies and scenarios of what could happen Inability to do things because of what might happen

Communication Notes

TALKING YOURSELF INTO—OR OUT OF—A JOB

Imagine that you have a really important job interview coming up. It's kind of scary to think about, isn't it? Now, imagine that you are someone who is generally anxious in communication situations, and you have a big job interview coming up. That's even scarier.

Research shows that communication anxiety affects people before, during, and after job interviews (Ayres et al., 1998). People with communication anxiety fuel their anxiety with negative self-talk. In addition, these people create self-fulfilling prophecies that undermine their effectiveness in job interviews. Examples of negative self-talk that impairs interviewing competence are "There's not a chance I'll get an offer," "I should have stayed home," or "There's no point in being here." When people repeat these messages to themselves before and during interviews, they tend to talk themselves into ineffectiveness.

another job pretty fast." Instead of letting debilitating fallacies defeat us, we can use our self-talk to question and challenge the irrational thinking that undermines us.

Respond Sensitively When Others Communicate Emotions

A final guideline is to respond sensitively when others express their feelings to you. Learning to communicate your emotions effectively is only half the process of communicating about emotions. You also want to become skilled in listening and responding to others when they share feelings with you.

When others express feelings, our first tendency may be to respond with general statements, such as "Time heals all wounds," "You shouldn't feel bad," "You'll be fine," or "You'll feel better once you get this into perspective." Although such statements may be intended to provide reassurance, in effect they tell others that they aren't allowed to feel what they feel or that they will be okay (right, normal) once they stop feeling what they are feeling.

Communication Notes

ALBERT ELLIS IN ACTION

Albert Ellis was not a mild-mannered sort of therapist, nor did he want to be. He was known for his dramatic style and for pushing, pushing, pushing his clients. He firmly believed that people whom many clinicians diagnosed as neurotics were not neurotic but only suffering from irrational thinking. He often described this as stupid thinking on the part of nonstupid people.

Ellis was convinced that we can unlearn stupid behaviours and function more effectively (Ellis, 1962; Ellis & Harper, 1975; Seligman, 1990). In dealing with clients, Ellis would berate them for stupid thinking, all the while insisting that they were not stupid people. He wanted his clients to learn new and better ways of thinking. "You're living under a tyranny of shoulds. Stop shoulding yourself to death," he would demand. "Quit thinking wrong and start thinking right," he urged. His clients responded to Ellis's unorthodox style and therapy. Many learned to think differently, and this led them to feel and act differently and more effectively in their lives.

Visit the Albert Ellis Institute at www.rebt.org. The site provides background information on rational-emotive therapy and features Albert Ellis's answers to questions from visitors to the site.

Another common mistake in responding to others' expression of feelings is to try to solve the other person's problem so the feelings will go away. Research suggests that the tendency to try to solve others' problems is more common in men than women (Swain, 1989; Tannen, 1990). Helping another solve a problem may be appreciated, but usually it's not the first support a person needs when she or he is expressing strong emotions. What many people need first is just the freedom to say what they are feeling and have those feelings accepted by others. Probably because of socialization, women are generally more skilled than men at providing solace, comfort, and emotional support (Basow & Rubenfeld, 2003; MacGeorge et al., 2003; MacGeorge et al., 2004).

When others express emotions to you, it's supportive to begin by showing you are willing to discuss emotional topics (Steiner-Pappalardo & Gurung, 2002).

Communication Notes

MANAGING ANGER

In their book *Anger Kills* (1998), Redford Williams and Virginia Williams summarize years of research and clinical studies that show that anger harms our physical and mental health. Convinced by evidence that anger is dangerous, they developed a test to measure how dangerous a person's level of anger is. Here are a few items adapted from the test:

1. When I get stuck in a traffic jam,
   a. I am usually not particularly upset.
   b. I start to feel irritated and annoyed quickly.
2. When someone treats me unfairly,
   a. I usually forget the incident fairly quickly.
   b. I tend to keep thinking about the incident for hours.
3. When I am caught in a slow-moving line at the grocery store,
   a. I seldom notice or mind the wait.
   b. I fume at people who dawdle ahead of me.
4. When I hear or read about another terrorist attack,
   a. I wonder why some people are so cruel to others.
   b. I feel like lashing out.

The more (b) answers a person has, the more anger he or she feels. The authors recommend strategies for controlling anger that include the communication skills we've discussed:

- Use self-talk to reason with yourself about your anger.
- Learn to assert yourself firmly but not aggressively.
- Develop your ability to empathize with others.
- Develop one or more strong friendships in which you can confide feelings.
- Listen!
- Use the rational-emotive approach to feelings to stop angry thoughts.

The test items are adapted from the test on pages 5–11 of *Anger Kills*.

Next, accept where they are as a starting place (Goldsmith & Fitch, 1997). You don't have to agree or approve to accept what another is feeling. While listening, it's helpful to interject a few minimal encouragers, which will be discussed in more detail in Chapter 6. Saying "I understand" or "Go on" conveys that you accept the other person's feelings and want him or her to continue talking. It's appropriate to mention your own experiences briefly to show that you empathize. However, it's not supportive to refocus the conversation on you and your experiences.

Paraphrasing, which we will discuss more in Chapter 8, is another way to show that you understand what another feels. When you mirror back not just the content but the feeling of what another says, it confirms the other person and what he or she feels. "So, it sounds as if you were really surprised by what happened. Is that right?" "What I'm hearing is that you are more hurt than angry. Does that sound right to you?" These examples of paraphrasing allow you to check on your perception of the speaker's feelings and also show that you are listening actively.

The guidelines we've identified may not always make emotional communication easy and comfortable. However, following them will help you understand and express your feelings and respond effectively when others discuss their feelings.

Chapter Summary

In this chapter, we explored the complex world of emotions and our communication about them. We considered different views of what's involved in experiencing and expressing emotions. From our review of theories, we learned that emotions have physiological, perceptual, linguistic, and social dimensions. We also examined some of the reasons people don't express feelings or express them ineffectively. The final focus of our attention was on guidelines for effective communication about emotions.

We identified six guidelines that can help us be effective in expressing our feelings and responding to the feelings of others. Because these guidelines are critical to interpersonal communication, we'll close the chapter by restating them:

1. Identify your emotions.
2. Choose how to communicate your emotions.
3. Own your feelings.
4. Monitor your self-talk.
5. Adopt a rational–emotive approach to emotions.
6. Respond sensitively when others communicate emotions.

Key Concepts

- cognitive labelling view of emotions
- counterfeit emotional language
- deep acting
- emotional intelligence
- emotions
- emotion work
- feeling rules
- framing rules
- interactive view of emotions
- organismic view of emotions
- perceptual view of emotions
- rational–emotive approach to feelings
- self-talk
- surface acting

For Further Thought and Discussion

1. Use your InfoTrac® College Edition to read Sherri Widen and James Russell's 2002 article, "Gender and Preschoolers' Perception of Emotion," published in the *Merrill-Palmer Quarterly.* What do the authors report about differences in emotions attributed to males and females? How might you explain their findings based on the discussion of influences on perception in Chapter 3?
2. Do you rely on only a few emotional words to express your feelings? If so, monitor your emotional language and work to enlarge your emotional vocabulary. Can you generate more precise words to describe your feelings?
3. Use your InfoTrac® College Edition to survey advice about communicating emotions that is published in popular magazines. Survey articles in magazines such as *Chatelaine* or *Maclean's*. How does advice in popular magazines compare with what you read in this chapter?
4. Review the fallacies discussed in the last section of this chapter. Do any of these fallacies show up in your intrapersonal communication? After reading about the fallacies and ways to challenge them, can you monitor and revise your intrapersonal communication?
5. We discussed different perspectives on emotions. Which perspective—or what combination of several perspectives—makes the most sense to you? Why? Explain how the perspective you favour gives you insight into emotions that you don't get from other perspectives.
6. What ethical principles can you identify to guide when and how people express emotions to others? Is honesty always the best policy? Is it ethical for one person to decide what another should know or can handle? How might ethical principles vary across cultures?

Chapter 5

The World of Words

The limits of my language mean the limits of my world.

– Ludwig Wittgenstein (1922)

Our language has wisely sensed the two sides of being alone. It has created the word *loneliness* to express the pain of being alone. And it has created the word *solitude* to express the glory of being alone.

– Paul Tillich (1963)

© Jeff Greenberg/The Image Works

In Poland in the 1980s, the trade union Solidarity was born. The birth was not a dramatic event. There were no fireworks. There was no grand announcement of a powerful new union. Instead, the union grew out of words—simple, face-to-face conversations among 10 or so workers in a Gdansk shipyard. They talked with each other about wanting freedom from oppressive conditions, about the need for change. Then this handful of individuals talked with other workers and others and others. Within just a few months, the Solidarity trade union had more than 9 million members (Wheatley, 2002). Language is powerful. It can create enormous changes in all spheres of life—personal, interpersonal, professional, social, and political.

The human world is a world of words and meanings. Just as weavers intertwine individual threads together to create fabric, so do we weave words together to create meaning in our lives. We use words to express ourselves and to give meaning to our identities, relationships, and activities. This chapter focuses on the verbal dimension of communication and its impact on our lives. We begin by defining symbols and symbolic abilities. Next we explore different communication communities to appreciate differences in how distinct social groups use language. We close the chapter by discussing guidelines for effective verbal communication.

THE SYMBOLIC NATURE OF LANGUAGE

Symbols are arbitrary, ambiguous, abstract representations of other phenomena. For instance, your name is a symbol that represents you. *House* is a symbol that stands for a particular kind of building. *Love* is a symbol that represents certain intense feelings. All language is symbolic, but not all symbols are language. Art, music, and much nonverbal behaviour are symbolic representations of feelings, thoughts, and experiences. To better understand symbols, we'll consider three characteristics of symbols: arbitrariness, ambiguity, and abstraction (see Figure 5.1).

Language Is Arbitrary

Language is **arbitrary,** which means that words are not intrinsically connected to what they represent. For instance, the word *book* has no necessary or natural

FIGURE 5.1

Symbols

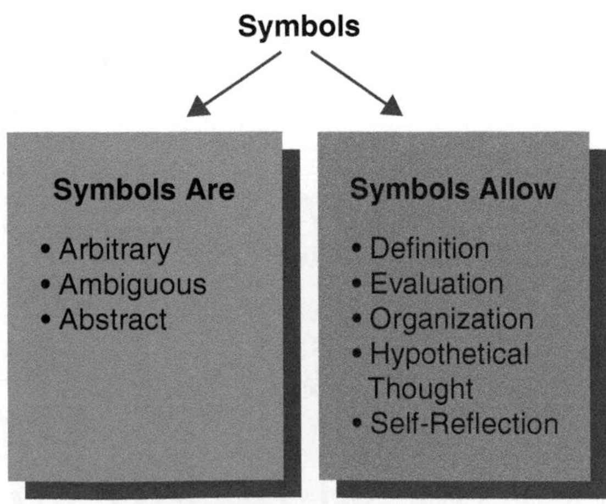

connection to what you are reading now. All our symbols are arbitrary because we could easily use other symbols as long as we all agreed on their meanings. Certain words seem right because members of a particular society or social group agree to use them in particular ways, but they have no natural correspondence with their referents. The arbitrary nature of language becomes obvious—sometimes humorously so—when we discover that our words don't mean the same thing in another culture. The manufacturer of Dr. Pepper learned this lesson when marketing plans for the soft drink didn't work in the United Kingdom. There, "I'm a pepper" means "I'm a prostitute" (Leaper, 1999).

Because language is arbitrary, the meanings of words can change over time. In other words, language is dynamic. In the 1950s, *gay* meant "lighthearted" and "merry"; today, it is generally understood to refer to homosexuals. The words *geek* and *nerd* used to be insults, but today they often convey admiration of someone's technological expertise. Our language also changes as we invent new words. Some Jamaicans began using *disrespect* as a verb to describe behaviours that demean someone. Now, the term *disrespect* and its abbreviated forms, *dis* or *diss*, are widely used and are in many dictionaries: In the *Nelson Canadian Dictionary*, *dis* and *diss* appear, along with the definition "to insult or show disrespect for someone."

Language Is Ambiguous

Language is **ambiguous** because the meanings of words aren't clear-cut or fixed. To one person, a *good friend* is someone to hang out with; to another, it is someone to confide in. The term *affordable clothes* means different things to people who earn the minimum wage and to people who are affluent. The words are the same, but their meaning varies according to people's unique experiences and circumstances.

Although words don't mean exactly the same thing to everyone, many symbols have an agreed-upon range of meanings within a culture. Thus, all of us know that dogs are four-footed creatures, but *dog* has personal meanings for each of us that are based on dogs we have known and our experiences with them. In learning language, we learn not only words but also the meanings and values attributed to them by our society. In Canada, most children learn not only that dogs are four-footed creatures but also that they are friends, members of the family, or useful in guarding, herding, and so forth. In some other countries, children learn that dogs are four-footed creatures that can be killed and eaten. We tend to assume that words mean the same thing to others that they do to us. Because symbols are ambiguous, however, there is no guarantee that people will agree on meanings.

Ambiguous language is a common problem between friends and romantic partners (Beck, 1988). A wife asks her husband to be more sensitive, but she and he have different understandings of what "being more sensitive" means. Martina tells her friend that he's not being attentive, meaning that she wants him to listen more closely to what she says. However, he infers that she wants him to call more often and open doors for her.

Ambiguity in language can also create confusion in the workplace. When the CEO of a company tells employees to restrict computer usage to their jobs, the CEO means employees should not use their computers to chat with family and friends. However, some employees could interpret the message as telling them not to send or respond to e-mails about company issues that are outside their specific job descriptions. Similarly, telling a supervisor that you'd appreciate feedback on your job performance

Communication Notes

TECHNOSPEAK

In 1991, Random House published the first *Computer and Internet Dictionary.* In 1999, the third edition appeared, expanded by 3000 new terms. Editor Philip Margolis (1999) says it's almost impossible to keep up with all the new words that are invented to refer to our computerized lives, including *blog, cybering, cyberspace, cybernaut, cyperpunk, chat room, flaming, fan site, hyperlink, URL, instant message, real-time quote, real-time chat, netiquette,* and *netlet.*

As technology races ahead, no doubt more new words will enter the language, but not all will survive the test of time. Mechanical transportation invigorated the English language in the early twentieth century, much as the computer is doing today, giving us some words that have survived, such as *dashboard, speedometer,* and *carsick.* Yet many words that were coined in response to new modes of transportation did not endure; *aerodrome* was replaced by *airport,* for example (Ayto, 1999).

James Kilpatrick (2000), who studies and writes about the use of English, notes that "the English language functions in the fashion of a great tree. It sheds dead limbs, and it produces green shoots" (p. 11A).

doesn't identify the kind of feedback you want or which aspects of your job performance you want your supervisor to assess. It would be more effective to say, "I would like you to give me your assessment of the thoroughness of my written reports."

Language Is Abstract

Finally, language is **abstract,** which means that it is not concrete or tangible. Words stand for ideas, people, events, objects, feelings, and so forth, but they are not the things they represent. In Chapter 3, we discussed the process of abstraction, whereby we move farther and farther away from concrete reality. As our symbols become increasingly abstract, the potential for confusion mushrooms. One way this happens is through overgeneralization. Couples counsellor Aaron Beck (1988) reports that overly general language distorts how partners think about a relationship. They may make broad, negative statements, such as, "You always interrupt me." In most cases, such statements are overgeneralizations and hence not accurate. Yet, by symbolizing experience this way, partners frame how they think about it.

Researchers have shown that we are more likely to recall behaviours that are consistent with our labels for people than behaviours that are inconsistent (Fincham & Bradbury, 1987). When we say that a friend is always insensitive, we cue ourselves to remember all the occasions in which the friend was insensitive and to overlook times when she or he was sensitive. When we call a co-worker uncooperative, we're likely to notice uncooperative behaviours rather than cooperative ones.

We can lessen the potential for misunderstanding by using specific language. It's clearer to say, "I wish you wouldn't interrupt when I'm talking" than to say, "Don't be so dominating." It's clearer to say, "On Fridays, men don't need to wear ties, and women don't need to wear heels" than to say, "Casual dress is okay on Fridays."

Student Voices

Dammon:

A while ago I told my girlfriend I needed more independence. She got all upset because she thought I didn't love her anymore and was pulling away. All I meant was that I need some time with the guys and some for just myself. She said that the last time a guy said he wanted more independence, she found out he was dating others.

Apply the Idea

COMMUNICATING CLEARLY

To express yourself clearly, it's important to learn to translate ambiguous words into concrete language. Practise translating with the statements below.

Example:
Ambiguous language: You are rude.
Clear language: I don't like it when you interrupt me.

Ambiguous Language	Clear Language
You're conceited.	________________
I want more freedom.	________________
Casual dress is okay on Fridays.	________________
I want us to be closer.	________________
Your work is sloppy.	________________

PRINCIPLES OF VERBAL COMMUNICATION

CONCEPTS AT A GLANCE

The Four Principles of Communication

1. Language and culture reflect each other.
2. Meanings of language are subjective.
3. Language use is rule-guided.
4. Communication devices shape meaning.

We've seen that language is arbitrary and ambiguous and that words are abstract representations of other phenomena. We're now ready to explore how language works. We'll discuss four principles of verbal communication.

Language and Culture Reflect Each Other

Communication reflects cultural values and perspectives. It also creates or reproduces culture by naming and normalizing practices valued by the culture. The words in a language reflect what the mainstream in a culture regards as worth naming. The dominant values of a culture are reflected in calendars, in which important days are named. Look at a calendar. Are Christmas, Thanksgiving, New Year's Day, and Passover recognized? Are Kwanzaa, Saka, Seleicodae, Elderly Day, and Ramadan on the calendar? Most Western calendars reflect the Judeo-Christian heritage of the mainstream culture. We do not name what we consider unimportant. Cultures don't give symbolic reality to practices of which the majority of members disapprove. Antagonists to same-sex marriage fight against the use of the word "marriage" to apply to enduring relationships between members of the same gender.

To understand further how cultural values are woven into language, consider the cultural values that adages express. What is meant by the common North American saying, "Every man for himself"? Does it reflect the idea that men, and not women, are the standard? Does it reflect individualism as a value? What is meant by "The early bird gets the worm"?

Different values are expressed in adages from other cultures. What values are expressed in the Mexican proverb, "He who lives a hurried life will soon dic"? How is this view of time different from dominant views of time in Canada? In Africa, two popular adages are "The child has no owner" and "It takes a whole village to raise a child," and in China a common saying is "No need to know the person, only the family" (Samovar & Porter, 2000). A Japanese adage states that "It is the nail that sticks out that gets hammered down" (Gudykunst & Lee, 2002). What values are expressed by these sayings? How are they different from mainstream Western values and the language that embodies them?

Many Asian languages include specific words to describe numerous particular relationships, such as "my grandfather's sister," "my mother's uncle," or "my youngest son." These words reflect traditional Asian cultures' emphasis on family relationships (Ferrante, 1995). The English language has far fewer words to represent specific kinship bonds, which suggests that Western culture places less priority on ties beyond those in the immediate family.

Imagine this scenario: A North American businessperson travels to Japan to negotiate a deal. After the North American has made the proposal, the Japanese executive responds, "I see you have put much thought into this idea." Assuming that this indicates the Japanese executive is pleased with the proposal, the North American says, "Then, shall we sign the contract and be on our way?" The Japanese executive replies, "I think we have much to talk about on your good proposal." What's happening here? If you are unfamiliar with Japanese communication styles, you might assume that the Japanese executive is being evasive or is not putting all the cards on the table. However, Japanese culture prioritizes cooperation, politeness, and not causing others to lose face. The Japanese business person's communication reflects the rules of the speech community that require not saying "no" directly to another person (Cathcart & Cathcart, 1997; Dolan & Worden, 1992).

Scholars of language and culture maintain that the language we learn shapes how we categorize the world and even how we perceive and think about our world (Fantini, 1991; Hakuta, 1986; Lim, 2002). For example, Hopi Indians have one word

Communication Notes

THE WHORF–SAPIR VIEW OF LANGUAGE

Linguist Benjamin Whorf and anthropologist Edwin Sapir (Whorf, 1956) advanced the theory of linguistic determinism, which states that language determines what we can perceive and think (Hoijer, 1994). According to this theory, we cannot perceive or think about things for which we don't have words. Initially, this theory was widely accepted. Examples from languages of non-Western cultures were used to support the theory. For instance, the language of the Hopi Indians makes no distinction between stationary objects and moving processes, whereas English uses nouns and verbs, respectively. The language that Hopi Indians learn and use teaches them to perceive people and events as highly processual rather than static.

Over time, however, linguistic determinism has been discredited. Numerous examples show that members of a culture can perceive phenomena that have no specific names. For example, Geoff Nunberg (2003) notes that, although Arabic does not have a single word for *compromise,* the language has many phrases that capture the idea of compromise.

Although linguistic determinism is no longer accepted by most scholars, there is acceptance of the less extreme claim that language reflects and shapes perception and thought. This notion helps us understand why some words and phrases can't be translated into other languages without losing meaning. *Tsuris* is a Yiddish word that is best translated as "trouble upon trouble." For instance, *tsuris* might describe a homeowner who experiences drenching rains followed by the breaking of a dam that floods the property.

The language of the Muscogee (Creek) Nation includes a word that designates the unique kind of love between parents and children (Seay, 2004), and Pacific Islanders' language, which is now disappearing, includes names for many species of fish that are unnamed in the languages of cultures less dependent on fish for survival (Nettle & Romaine, 2000).

for "water in open space" and another word for "water in a container." The English language has only the one noun, *water*. Some of us perceive saying good-bye to guests as a single event. In contrast, in Japan saying good-bye is a process. Hosts and guests typically say good-bye in the living room and again at the front door. Guests walk a distance from the house, then turn and wave good-bye to the hosts, who are waiting at their gate or door to wave the third good-bye.

© iStockphoto.com/Lokibaho

Communication also changes cultures, as is clear from the example of the Solidarity trade union that opened this chapter. A primary way in which communication changes cultural values and perspectives is by naming things in ways that alter understandings. For example, the term *date rape* was coined in the late 1980s. Although probably many women had been forced to have sex with their dates before that time, until the term was coined there was no concise and commonly understood way to describe such an occurrence as a violent and criminal act (Wood, 1992b). Cultural understandings of other sexual activities have been similarly re-formed by the coining of terms such as *sexual harassment* and *marital rape*, both of which characterize activities previously perceived as acceptable. As society has become more aware and accepting of gay and lesbian relationships, the term *domestic partnership* has gained acceptance.

Language is a primary tool of social movements in their efforts to change cultural life and meanings. In the 1960s, the civil rights movement in the United States relied on communication to transform public laws and, more gradually, public views of Blacks. Powerful speakers, such as the Reverend Martin Luther King, Jr., and Malcolm X, praised Black Americans' heritage and identity.

Language has also been influential in altering social views of people with disabilities. Whereas *disabled person* was a commonly accepted phrase for many years, most people are now aware that this label can offend, and they know that the preferred phrase is *person with a disability* (Braithwaite, 1996). The gay rights movement has increased awareness of multiple sexual orientations by increasing use of words such as *transsexual* and *transgender*. Social views of deaf people have also been altered in recent times. The term *deaf*, a medical condition, is distinguished from *Deaf*, a culture with rich linguistic resources (Carl, 1998).

The Meanings of Language Are Subjective

Because symbols are abstract, ambiguous, and arbitrary, the meanings of words are never self-evident or absolute. Instead, we construct meanings in the process of interacting with others and through dialogues we carry on in our own heads (Duck, 1994a, 1994b; Shotter, 1993). The process of constructing meaning is itself symbolic because we rely on words to think about what words and other things mean.

For humans, words are layered with multiple meanings. Although we're usually not conscious of

Student Voices

Dirk:

It took me a long time to understand certain words in my fiancée's family. When I first met them, I heard them talk about the wife's career, but I knew she did not work. In the family, they say her career is keeping track of all the children. They also talked about the husband's hobby of being broke. I thought this meant he spent a lot of money on a hobby or something, but what they mean is he likes to give to causes and this takes a lot of money. It took several visits for me to understand the family vocabulary.

the effort we invest to interpret words, we continuously engage in the process of constructing meanings. When somebody says, "Get lost," you have to think about the comment and the person who made it to decide whether it's an insult, friendly needling, or a demand that you leave. You might take it as a joke from a friend but as criticism from an employer. What the words mean to you also depends on your self-esteem and previous experiences. People who are secure and have high self-esteem are not as likely to be hurt as people who have less self-confidence.

CONCEPTS AT A GLANCE

Two Kinds of Communication Rules

1. Regulative rules
2. Constitutive rules

Language Use Is Rule-Guided

Verbal communication is patterned by unspoken but broadly understood rules (Argyle & Henderson, 1985; Schiminoff, 1980). **Communication rules** are shared understandings of what communication means and what kinds of communication are appropriate in particular situations. For example, we understand that people take turns speaking, that flaming can get us kicked out of some chat rooms, and that we should speak softly in libraries. In the course of interacting with our families and others, we unconsciously absorb rules that guide how we communicate and how we interpret others' communication. According to Judi Miller (1993), children begin to understand and follow communication rules as early as one to two years of age.

Communication Notes

CHAT ROOM ETIQUETTE

What are the rules and norms for communicating online? At the moment, that's uncharted water. Many people think chat rooms and discussion newsgroups are uncivil: One person can flame another with angry, demeaning insults. People can ignore others and even block their communication. Another kind of problem is that people can misrepresent themselves by saying they are Asian when they are Hispanic, male when they are female, and so forth. Who regulates what is allowable on the Internet?

For more information about rules for communicating online, go to www.essortment.com/all/chatroomsetiqu_rixx.htm.

Two kinds of rules govern communication (Cronen, Pearce, & Snavely, 1979; Pearce, Cronen, & Conklin, 1979). **Regulative rules** regulate interaction by specifying when, how, where, and with whom to talk about certain things. For instance, Westerners know not to interrupt when someone else is speaking in a formal setting, but in more casual situations, interruptions may be appropriate. In other cultures, there are strong rules against interrupting in any context.

Some families have a rule that people cannot argue at the dinner table. Families also teach us rules about how to communicate in conflict situations (Honeycutt, Woods, & Fontenot, 1993; Jones & Gallois, 1989; Yerby, Buerkel-Rothfuss, & Bochner, 1990). In Chapter 4, we learned that our family experiences around emotions taught us the rules about expression of certain feelings.

Regulative rules also define when, where and with whom it's appropriate to show affection and disclose private information. Regulative rules vary across cultures so that what is considered appropriate in one society may be regarded as impolite or offensive elsewhere.

Constitutive rules define what communication means by specifying how to count, or interpret, specific kinds of communication. We learn what counts as respect (paying attention), friendliness (smiles or smiley emoticons in online communication), affection (kisses, hugs), and professionalism (dressing well, demonstrating expertise). We also learn what communication is expected if we want to be perceived as a good friend (showing support, being loyal), a responsible employee (meeting deadlines, making confident oral presentations), and a desirable romantic partner (showing respect and trust, being faithful, sharing confidences). We learn constitutive and regulative rules from particular others and the generalized other. Likc regulative rules, constitutive rules are shaped by cultures. Among traditional Arabs, smelling another person's cheeks counts as a customary form of greeting (Almany & Alwan, 1982).

What regulative rules did you learn in school?

Apply the Idea

COMMUNICATION RULES

Think about the regulative and constitutive rules that you follow in your communication. For each item, identify two rules you have learned.

After you've identified your rules, talk with others in your class about the rules they follow. Are there commonalities among your rules that reflect broad cultural norms? What explains differences in individuals' rules?

Regulative Rules

list rules that regulate how you:

- *Talk with elders*
- *Interact at dinner time*
- *Have first exchanges in the morning*
- *Respond to criticism from your supervisor*
- *Greet casual friends on campus*
- *Talk with professors*

Constitutive Rules

How do you communicate to show:

- *Respect*
- *Love*
- *Disrespect*
- *Support*
- *Professional ambition*
- *Contempt*

Student Voices

Yumiko:

I try to teach my children to follow the customs of my native Japan, but they are learning to be Canadian. I scold my daughter, who is seven this year, for talking loudly and speaking when she has not been addressed, but she tells me all the other kids talk loudly and talk when they wish to talk. I tell her it is not polite to look directly at others, but she says everyone looks at others here. She communicates as a Canadian, not a Japanese.

The meaning of verbal communication arises out of cultural teachings, subjective interpretations, communication rules, and punctuation. These four principles highlight the creativity involved in constructing meaning. We're now ready to probe how verbal communication affects us and our relationships.

Everyday interaction is guided by rules that tell us when to speak, what to say, and how to interpret others' communication. Our social interactions, which involve I–It and I–You relationships, tend to adhere to rules that are widely shared in our society. Interaction between intimates also follows rules, but these may not be broadly shared by members of the culture. Intimate partners negotiate private rules to guide how they communicate and what certain things mean (Wood, 1982, 1995c). Couples craft personal rules for whether and how to argue, express love, make decisions, and spend time together (Beck, 1988; Fitzpatrick, 1988).

It's important to understand that we don't have to be aware of communication rules in order to follow them. For the most part, we're not conscious of the rules that guide how, when, where, and with whom we communicate about various things. We may not realize we have rules until one is broken and we become aware that we had an expectation. A study by Victoria DeFrancisco (1991) revealed that between spouses there was a clear pattern in which husbands interrupted wives and were unresponsive to topics that wives initiated. Both husbands and wives were unaware of the rules, but their communication nonetheless sustained the pattern. Becoming aware of communication rules empowers you to change those that don't promote good interaction, as Emily's commentary illustrates.

Student Voices

Emily:

My boyfriend and I had this really frustrating pattern about planning what to do. He'd say, "What do you want to do this weekend?" And I'd say, "I don't know. What do you want to do?" Then he'd suggest two or three things and ask me which of them sounded good. I would say they were all fine with me, even if they weren't. And this would keep on forever. Both of us had a rule not to impose on the other, and it kept us from stating our preferences, so we just went in circles about any decision.

Well, two weekends ago, I talked to him about rules, and he agreed we had one that was frustrating. So we invented a new rule that says each of us has to state what we want to do, but the other has to say if that is not okay. It's a lot less frustrating to figure out what we want to do since we agreed on this rule.

Communication Devices Shape Meaning

We format communication to decide what it means. In interpersonal communication, certain signals define beginnings and endings of interaction episodes. Debra Tannen (2001, 2002) describes conversational signals that are strongly affected by ethnic background, regional background, age, class, and gender.

To decide what a communication means, we must establish common meanings for **communication devices** such as speed, pacing, pausing, overlap, and interruption. When we don't agree on these devices, problems may arise. A common example of conflicting patterns in the use of communication devices used to punctuate our interactions can be seen when we look at pacing and pausing. If two people who are conversing have even slight differences in the amount of time each one finds as a comfortable pause between comments, difficulties may arise. When the person accustomed to shorter pauses is confronted by longer pauses, that person is likely to think, "I guess you have nothing more to say, so since I want to keep the conversation going, I'll need to say something else." On the other hand, the person whose style is marked by longer pauses may feel that he or she never gets a chance to say anything! There is not a right or wrong way to pace a conversation, but if such a discrepancy is not recognized and the individuals don't work on finding a mutually agreeable pace, the relationship may not be very satisfying.

Communication Notes

FRENCH LANGUAGE AND FRENCH CANADIAN IDENTITY

Language is a symbol of ethnic pride and distinctiveness. The fight in Quebec for French language dominance is an issue of identity, marking a linguistic journey in Canada that has not been easy. In 1982, Canada finally established English and French as the official languages of the country. Prior to that, Bill 101, *The Charter of the French Language,* was passed in 1977, requiring that all signs in Quebec must be displayed in French. Any English words have to appear in a smaller size than the French ones.

In April of 2000, the Quebec Superior Court upheld Quebec's French language sign laws when a grocery storeowner and his wife were fined for having the French and English words the same size. It was a matter of identity.

According to Tannen (2001) the communication devices of overlap and interruption are noticed when two people are talking at the same time. Some individuals are accustomed to "talking along"—interjecting phrases or questions to show that they are connected with what the other person is saying. Other people find this style of conversation rude and distracting. Again, one style of turn-taking is not always preferred, but if participants in a conversation do not agree on the use of these devices, the communication will not be satisfying or effective. This reminds us of a guideline discussed in Chapter 1: Dual perspective is essential to effective communication.

There are no objectively correct communication devices, because they depend on subjective perceptions. When partners don't agree on communication devices, they don't share meanings for what is happening between them. To break out of unconstructive cycles, partners need, first, to realize they may use communication devices differently and, second, to discuss how each of them experiences the pattern.

REVIEW

The meaning of verbal communication arises out of:

- Cultural teachings
- Subjective interpretations
- Communication rules
- Communication devices

These four principles highlight the creativity involved in constructing meaning.

FUNCTIONS OF SYMBOLS

The ability to use symbols allows humans to live in a world of ideas and meanings. Instead of just reacting to our concrete environments, we think about them and sometimes transform them. Philosophers of language have identified five ways in which symbols affect our lives (Cassirer, 1944; Langer, 1953, 1979). As we discuss each, we'll consider how to realize the constructive power of symbols and minimize the problems they can prompt.

CONCEPTS AT A GLANCE

Five Ways Symbols Affect Our Lives

1. Symbols define.
2. Symbols evaluate.
3. Symbols organize perceptions.
4. Symbols allow hypothetical thought.
5. Symbols allow self-reflection.

Symbols Define

We use symbols to define experiences, people, relationships, feelings, and thoughts. As we saw in Chapter 3, the definitions we impose shape what things mean to us.

Labels Shape Perceptions

When we label someone, we focus attention on particular aspects of a person and that person's activities, and we necessarily obscure other aspects of who that person is. We might define a person as an environmentalist, a teacher, a gourmet cook, or a father. Each definition directs our attention to certain aspects of the person. We might talk with the environmentalist about wilderness legislation, discuss class assignments with the teacher, swap recipes with the chef, and exchange stories about children with the father. If we define someone as an Asian, a Buddhist, or a Canadian, then that may be all we notice about that person, although there are many other aspects. We tend to perceive and interact with people according to how we define them.

Our language reflects our subjective perceptions and, at the same time, it shapes and fixes our perceptions. If you saw a person eat a very large meal, how would you describe what you saw? If the person was a teenaged boy, you might describe him as being a growing boy. If the person was a slender woman, you might describe her as having a healthy appetite. If the person was overweight, you might describe him as a glutton. Notice that the amount of food and the act of eating don't change, but our perceptions and labels do.

The labels that we apply to people and things shape how we evaluate and respond to them. According to Joel Best (1989), the impact of labels is especially evident in language about AIDS. Calling it a "moral problem" defines people with the disease as having behaved badly and suggests the solution is to change behaviour. By contrast, calling AIDS a "medical problem" defines people with the disease as having certain biological processes that are not the fault of individuals. Consequently, the solution to AIDS as a "medical problem" lies in medical treatment.

Labels Can Totalize

Totalizing occurs when we respond to a person as if one label (one we have chosen or accepted from others) totally represents who he or she is. We fix on one symbol to define someone and fail to recognize many other aspects of who that person is (Wood, 1998). Some individuals totalize gays and lesbians as if sexual orientation is their only important facet. Interestingly, we don't totalize heterosexuals on the basis of their sexual orientation. Totalizing also occurs when we dismiss people by saying, "He's a Liberal," "She's old," or "He's just a jock." Totalizing is not the same as stereotyping. When we stereotype someone, we define him or her in terms of characteristics of a group. When we totalize others, we negate most of who they are by spotlighting a single aspect of their identity.

Student Voices

Indira:

I know all about totalizing. A teacher in a sociology class was referring to the immigrant population of Canada. She turned toward me and said, "We have one in our class. What is it like?" I turned to see who she was talking about. I see myself as an Indo-Canadian, female, premed student whose family has been here for two generations. She saw me only as an immigrant from India.

Labels Affect Relationships

The symbols we use to define experiences in our relationships affect how we think and feel about those relationships. In a study, romantic couples were asked how they defined differences between them (Wood et al., 1994). Some individuals defined differences as positive forces that energize a relationship and keep it interesting. Others defined

Apply the Idea

SAYINGS AND EXPRESSIONS

Many common expressions and sayings are phrased exclusively in male terms, thus excluding women. Rephrasing them in gender-neutral terms will help make them more inclusive, without changing the essential wisdom of the saying. Below are some examples of common sayings that have been rephrased to be gender-neutral (University College Cork). How would you rephrase the other ones?

Instead of:	**Try:**
Everything comes to him who waits	Everything comes to those who wait
To each his own	To each one's own
One man's meat is another man's poison	What is food to one is poison to another
Time waits for no man	Time waits for no one
Peace on earth; goodwill to men	______________________
Policemen are your friends	______________________
I'll order the businessman's special for lunch	______________________
The soldiers manhandled the prisoners	______________________

For more examples of gender-neutral terms, go to the University College Cork website: www.ucc.ie/equalcom/language.html.

differences as problems or barriers to closeness. The study found a direct connection between how partners defined differences and how they acted. Partners who viewed differences as constructive approached disagreements with curiosity, interest, and a hope for growth through discussion. On the other hand, partners who labelled differences as "problems" tended to deny differences and to avoid talking about them.

A number of communication scholars have shown that the language we use to think about relationships affects what happens in them (Duck, 1985, 1994a, 1994b; Honeycutt, 1993; Spencer, 1994). People who consistently use negative labels to describe their relationships heighten awareness of what they don't like and diminish perceptions of what they do like (Cloven & Roloff, 1991). It's also been shown that partners who focus on good facets of their relationships are more conscious of virtues in partners and relationships and less bothered by imperfections (Bradbury & Fincham, 1990; Fletcher & Fincham, 1991).

These studies show us that our definitions of relationships can create self-fulfilling prophecies. Because verbal language is ambiguous, arbitrary, and abstract, there are multiple ways in which we can define any experience. Once we select a label, we tend to see the experience in line with our label. This suggests we should reconsider definitions that undermine healthy self-concepts and interpersonal relationships.

Symbols Evaluate

Symbols are not neutral or objective descriptions. They are laden with values, which is an intrinsic quality of symbols. In fact, it's impossible to find words that are completely neutral or objective.

Values in Language Reflect and Shape Perceptions

We describe people we like with language that accentuates their good qualities and downplays their flaws. Just the reverse is true of our descriptions for people we don't like. Restaurants use positive words to heighten the attractiveness of menu entrées. A dish described as "tender London broil gently sautéed in its natural juices and topped with succulent mushrooms" sounds more appetizing than one described as "cow carcass cooked in blood and topped with fungus grown in compost and manure."

Perhaps you've seen humorous illustrations of how differently we describe the same behaviours enacted by ourselves, people we like, and people we don't like: I am casual, you are messy, she's a slob. I am organized, you are methodical, he is obsessive-compulsive. I am assertive, you are aggressive, she's a bully. Although these are funny, they also reflect our tendencies to use labels with different evaluations to describe behaviour.

Of course, there are degrees of evaluation in language. We might describe people who speak their minds as assertive, outspoken, courageous, or authoritarian. Each word has a distinct connotation. In recent years, we have become more sensitive to how symbols can hurt people. Most individuals with disabilities prefer not to be called disabled, because that totalizes them in terms of a disability.

Designations for homosexuals are currently in transition. The term *homosexual* has negative connotations and words such as *fairy, dyke,* and *faggot* are considered by some to be offensive (but see the Communication Notes feature "Reappropriating Language"). Some gays and lesbians use the term *sexual orientation* to suggest they didn't choose their sexual pattern, while others use the term *sexual preference* to indicate their sexual orientation is a matter of choice, not genetics. Still others speak of *affectional preference* to signal that their commitment concerns the entire realm of affection, not just sexual activity.

Communication Notes

REAPPROPRIATING LANGUAGE

An interesting communicative phenomenon is the reappropriation of language. This happens when a group reclaims terms used by others to degrade it and treats those terms as positive self-descriptions.

The intention of reappropriation is to take the sting out of a term that others use pejoratively. Some feminists and women musicians have reappropriated the term *girl* to define themselves and to resist the general connotations of childishness. Some gays have reappropriated the term *queer* and are using it as a positive description of who they are.

Writer Reynolds Price (1994) developed cancer of the spine that left him paralyzed. He scoffs at terms such as *differently abled* and *physically challenged* and refers to himself as a "cripple" and others as "temporarily able-bodied."

Language Can Be Negatively Loaded

Language is powerful. It shapes our perceptions and those of others. This implies that each of us has an ethical responsibility to recognize the impact of language and to guard against engaging in uncivil speech ourselves as well as refusing to tolerate it from others.

Loaded language comprises words that strongly slant perceptions and thus meanings. For example, American radio personality Rush Limbaugh referred to feminists as "Feminazis," which implies feminists are also Nazis. The city of Vancouver, BC, is called "Hongcouver" by those few disturbed by the increasing Asian population. Loaded language also encourages negative views of older people. Terms such as "geezers" and "raisins" or "the blue-rinse brigade" incline us to regard older people with contempt or pity. Alternatives such as "senior citizen" and "elder" reflect more respectful attitudes.

Probably many of us have sympathy with Raymond, in the Student Voices feature, who was 54 years old when he took a communication course. It is hard to keep up with changes in language, and it's inevitable that we will occasionally offend someone unintentionally. Nonetheless, we should try to learn what terms hurt or insult others and avoid using those. It's also advisable for us to tell others when they've referred to us with a term that we dislike. As long as we speak assertively but not confrontationally, it's likely that others will respect our ideas.

Student Voices

Raymond:

I'm as sensitive as the next guy, but I just can't keep up with what language offends what people anymore. When I was younger, "Indian" was an accepted term, then it was "Native," and now it's "First Nations." Sometimes I forget and say "Indian," and I get accused of being racist. It used to be polite to call females "girls," but now that offends a lot of the women I work with. Just this year, I heard that we aren't supposed to say "blind" or "disabled" anymore; we're supposed to say "a person with a visual impairment" and "differently abled." I just can't keep up.

Language Can Degrade Others

Haig Bosmajian is a scholar of communication and ethics. Throughout his career, he has been concerned about the ways in which language is used to degrade and dehumanize others. Bosmajian notes that how we see ourselves is profoundly influenced by the names we are called (1974). One form of degrading language is **hate speech,** which is language that radically dehumanizes others. Malicious and abusive messages scrawled on the cars and homes of minority citizens and offensive graffiti in public washrooms and on public buildings are insulting to the targeted social groups.

Language is powerful. The values inherent in the words we use shape our perceptions and those of others. This implies that each of us has an ethical responsibility to recognize the impact of language and to guard against engaging in uncivil speech ourselves, as well as not tolerating it from others.

Symbols Organize Perceptions

We use symbols to organize our perceptions. As we saw in Chapter 3, we rely on cognitive schemata to classify and evaluate experiences. How we organize experiences affects what they mean to us. For example, your prototype of a good friend affects how you judge particular friends. When we place someone in the category of friend, the category influences how we interpret the friend and her or his communication. An insult is likely to be viewed as teasing if made by a friend, but a call to battle if made by an enemy. The words don't change, but their meaning varies depending on how we organize our perceptions of words and those who speak them.

R. Morley/Photolink/Photodisc/Getty Images

Do you speak Canadian?

Language Allows Abstract Thought

The organizational quality of language also allows us to think about abstract concepts, such as justice, integrity, and healthy family life. We use broad concepts to transcend specific, concrete activities and to enter the world of conceptual thought and ideals. Because we think abstractly, we don't have to consider every specific object and experience individually. Instead, we can think in general terms.

Language Can Stereotype

Our capacity to abstract can also distort thinking. A primary way this occurs is through stereotyping, which is thinking in broad generalizations about a whole class of people or experiences. Examples of stereotypes are "teachers are smart," "jocks are dumb," "feminists hate men," "religious people are kind," and "conflict is bad." Notice that stereotypes can be positive or negative.

Common to all stereotypes is classifying an experience or person based on general perceptions of some category. When we use terms such as "WASP," "lesbian," and "working class," we may see what members of each group have in common and may not perceive differences between individuals. We may not perceive the uniqueness of the individual person if we label that person only as a member of one group. Stereotyping is related to totalizing, because when we stereotype someone, we may not perceive other aspects of that person—those not represented in the stereotype. For example, if we stereotype someone as a jock, we may see only what she has in common with other athletes or physical education students. We may not notice her other aspects, such as her political stands, individual values, ethnic background, and so forth.

Clearly, we have to generalize. We simply cannot think about each and every thing in our lives as a specific instance. However, stereotypes can blind us to important differences among phenomena we lump together. Thus, it's important to reflect on stereotypes and to stay alert to differences among people and things we place into any category. We should also remind ourselves that when we place others into categories, the categories are our tools—they are not objective descriptions.

Symbols Allow Hypothetical Thought

Where do you hope to be five years from now? What would you do if you were in a friend's position? To answer these questions, you must think hypothetically, which means thinking about experiences and ideas that are not part of your concrete, present situation. Because we can think hypothetically, we can plan, dream, remember, set goals, consider alternative courses of action, and imagine possibilities.

We Can Think Beyond Immediate, Concrete Situations

Hypothetical thought is possible because we use symbols. When we symbolize, we name ideas so that we can hold them in our minds and reflect on them. We can contemplate things that currently have no real existence, and we can remember ourselves in the past and project ourselves into the future. Our ability to live simultaneously in all three dimensions of time explains why we can set goals and work toward them, even though there is nothing tangible about them in the moment (Dixson & Duck, 1993). For example, you've invested many hours studying and writing papers because you have the idea of yourself as someone with a university degree. The degree is not real now, nor is the self that you will become once you have the degree. Yet the idea is sufficiently real to motivate you to work hard for many years.

We Live in Three Dimensions of Time

Hypothetical thought also allows us to live in more than just the present moment. We infuse our present lives with knowledge of our histories and plans for our futures. Both past and future affect our experience in the present. In the context of work, we often remember past interactions with a colleague and anticipate future ones, and both of these affect how we communicate in the present.

Close relationships rely on ideas of past and future. One of the strongest "glues" for intimacy is a history of shared experiences (Bellah et al., 1985; Bruess & Hoefs, 2006; Wood, 2006). Just knowing that they have weathered rough times in the past helps partners get through trials in the present. Belief in a future also sustains intimacy. With people we don't expect to see again, we interact differently from the way we interact with people who are continuing parts of our lives. Talking about the future also knits intimates together because it makes real the idea that more is ahead (Acitelli, 1993; Duck, 1990; Wood, 2006).

> **Student Voices**
>
> **Raad:**
>
> Sometimes I get very discouraged that I do not yet know English perfectly and that there is much I still do not understand about customs in this country. It helps me to remember that when I came here two years ago I did not speak English at all, and I knew nothing about how people act here. Seeing how much progress I have made helps me not to be discouraged with what I do not know yet.

We Can Foster Personal Growth

Thinking hypothetically helps us grow personally. In Chapter 2, we noted that one guideline for improving self-concept is to accept yourself as being in process. To fuel continued self-improvement requires you to remember who you were at an earlier time, to appreciate progress you've made, and to keep an ideal image of the person you want to become. If you want to become more outgoing, you imagine yourself talking easily to others, going to parties, and so forth. If you want to be more effective in presenting ideas to members of your work team, you imagine yourself preparing your ideas, speaking confidently, and responding to questions from colleagues.

Symbols Allow Self-Reflection

Just as we use language to reflect on what goes on outside of us, we also use it to reflect on ourselves. Humans don't simply exist and act. Instead, we think about our existence and reflect on our actions. Mead (1934) considered self-reflection to be the basis for human selfhood. He believed that our capacity to look at ourselves and our activities was responsible for civilized society.

According to Mead, there are two aspects to the self. First, there is the *I*, which is the spontaneous, creative self. The *I* acts impulsively in response to inner needs and desires, regardless of social norms. The *Me* is the socially conscious part of the self that monitors and moderates the *I*'s impulses. The

> **Student Voices**
>
> **Elyse:**
>
> I volunteer at the homeless shelter. Sometimes, when I'm talking to the people who come there for food or to sleep, I feel like shaking them and telling them to get their lives in order. I get so frustrated with the ones who don't seem to make any effort to change their situations. But I know that everybody puts them down all the time—the last thing they need is to hear more of that from a college kid who probably never experienced real hardships. So I keep my frustration to myself. I guess that's the *Me* part of me controlling my *I*.

© Randy M. Ury/CORBIS

Writing can inspire self-reflection.

Student Voices

Rachael:

During the first week of college, I went to a mixer and got drunk. I didn't drink in high school, so I didn't know what alcohol could do to me. I was a mess—throwing up, passing out. The next morning I hated myself for how I'd been. But in the long run, I think it was good that it happened. Whenever I feel like having more to drink than I should, I just remember what I was like that night and how much I hated myself that way, and that stops me from having anything more to drink.

Me reflects on the *I* from the social perspectives of others. The *I* is impervious to social conventions and expectations, but the *Me* is keenly aware of them. In an argument, your *I* may want to hurl a biting insult at someone you don't like, but your *Me* censors that impulse and reminds you that it's impolite to put others down. The *Me* reflects on the *I* by analyzing the *I*'s actions. This means we can think about who we want to be and set goals for becoming the self we desire. The *Me* can feel shame, pride, and regret for the *I*'s actions, an emotion that is possible because we self-reflect. We can control what we do in the present by casting ourselves forward in time to consider how we might later feel about our actions. Elyse makes this point in her commentary.

Self-Reflection Allows Us to Monitor Communication

Self-reflection also empowers us to monitor ourselves, a skill we discussed in Chapter 1 and again in Chapter 4. When we monitor ourselves, we (the *ME*) notice and evaluate our (the *I*'s) actions and may modify them based on our judgments (Phillips & Wood, 1983; Wood, 1992a). For instance, during a discussion with a friend you might say to yourself, "Gee, I've been talking nonstop about me and my worries, and I haven't even asked how she's doing." Based on your monitoring, you might inquire about your friend's life.

Apply the Idea

I–ME DIALOGUES

To see how the I and the Me work together, monitor your internal dialogues. These are conversations in your head as you consider different things you might say and do.

Monitor your I–Me dialogues as you talk with a professor, a close friend, and a romantic partner. What creative ideas and desires does your I initiate? What social controls does your Me impose? What urges and whims occur to your I? What social norms does your Me remind you of?

How do the I and the Me work together? Does one sometimes muffle the other? What would be lost if your I became silent? What would be missing if your Me disappeared?

When interacting with people from different cultures, we monitor by reminding ourselves that they may have different values and communication rules from ours. Self-reflection allows us to monitor our communication and adjust it to be effective.

> **Student Voices**
>
> **Myrella:**
>
> I have a really bad temper that can get me into serious trouble if I'm not careful. Sometimes I feel like telling someone off or exploding or whatever, but I stop myself by thinking about how bad I'll look if I do it. I remind myself that others might see me as hysterical or crazy or something, and that helps me to check my temper.

Self-Reflection Allows Us to Manage Our Image

Our image is the identity we present to others. Because we reflect on ourselves from social perspectives, we are able to consider how we appear in others' eyes. When talking with teachers, you may consciously present yourself as respectful, attentive, and studious. When interacting with parents, you may repress some of the language and topics that surface in discussions with your friends. When talking with someone you'd like to date, you may choose to be more attentive than you are in other circumstances. We continuously adjust our communication to fit particular situations and people.

We use symbols to define, classify, and evaluate experiences; to organize perceptions; to think hypothetically; and to self-reflect. Each of these abilities helps us create meaning in our personal and interpersonal lives. Each of them also carries with it ethical responsibilities for how we use communication and the impact it has on ourselves and others.

SPEECH COMMUNITIES

Although all humans use symbols, we don't all use them in the same way. As we have seen, symbols are social conventions whose meanings we learn in the process of interacting with others. For this reason, people from different social groups use communication in different ways and attach different meanings to particular communicative acts.

A **speech community** exists when people share norms about how to use talk and what purposes it serves (Labov, 1972). Members of speech communities share perspectives on communication that outsiders do not have. Conversely, members of particular speech communities may not understand how communication is used in other speech communities. This explains why misunderstandings often arise between members of different social groups.

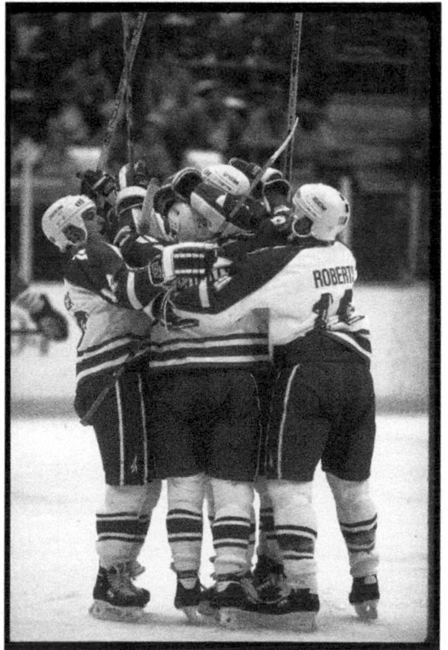

© Corel

To what speech communities do you belong?

Speech communities are not defined by countries or geographic locations, but by shared understandings of how to communicate. In Western society there are numerous speech communities, including First Nations, gay men, lesbian women, deaf individuals, and people with disabilities. Each of these groups has distinct understandings of communication and ways of using it—ways that are not familiar to people outside the group. Some speech communities engage in more dramatic and elaborate verbal play than others. Some are very restrained, and language is minimal. Canada has a unique linguistic heritage. Our two official languages define

Communication Notes

CANADIANISMS, EH?

Long before "The Rant," Canadians were known by their linguistic anomaly of "eh." It is a tag on a statement or a question that is as distinctive as "Y'all" is to the southern United States. There are several other linguistic anomalies that identify Canada as a distinct linguistic community. Check these out:

Poutine	A Québécois specialty of French fries covered in cheese curds and gravy
Screech	A Newfoundland dark rum
Loonie	The one-dollar coin with a loon on the back
Rez	A First Nations reservation
Robertson screw	The square-holed screw and screwdriver invented by Ontario's P. L. Robertson in 1908, highly coveted by the international market because of its resistance to being stripped.
Snowbird	A Canadian who flies south during the winter to vacation
Nanaimo bar	A chocolate custard square originating in Nanaimo, BC
Skookum	The word for "big" in Salish. Skookumchuck Narrows is a treacherous channel of water on the west coast of BC.
Liver-in	A Newfoundland live-in maid
Ceilidh	A Cape Breton dance party (borrowed from the Gaelic)

us as distinct. See other distinctly Canadian turns of phrase in the Communication Notes feature "Canadianisms, eh?"

Gender Speech Communities

Of the many speech communities that exist, gender has received particularly extensive study. Because we know more about it than about other speech communities, we'll explore gender as a specific example of speech communities and the misunderstandings that surface between members of different speech communities. Researchers have investigated both the way in which women and men are socialized into some different understandings of how communication functions and the way their communication differs in practice.

Socialization into Gender Speech Communities

One of the earliest studies showing that children's games are a primary agent of gender socialization was by Maltz & Borker in 1982. Since that landmark study, many other researchers have studied gender socialization in children's play groups (Clark, 1998; Leaper, 1994, 1996; Martin et al., 2000). They report that children's play is usually sex-segregated, and there are notable differences between the games the sexes tend to play. These differences seem to teach boys and girls some distinct rules for using communication and interpreting the communication of others.

Games that are traditionally favoured by girls, such as house and school, involve few players, include talk to negotiate how to play (because there aren't clear-cut guidelines), and depend on cooperation and sensitivity between players. Baseball, soccer, and war, which are typical boys' games, require more players and have clear goals and rules, so less talk is needed to play. Most boys' games are highly competitive, both between teams and for individual status within teams. Interaction in games teaches boys and girls distinct understandings of why, when, and how to use talk.

Children also learn gender-stereotyped roles through the content of children's television cartoons (Leaper et al., 2002). Television often portrays males as being more prominent and more aggressive, displaying more leadership capabilities. Female roles often involve compassion, affection, romance, and support. The differences in how girls and boys are portrayed can impact their communication and interpretation skills throughout life.

Gendered Communication in Practice

Research on women's and men's communication reveals that the rules taught through childhood play are evident in adult interaction. For instance, women's talk generally is more expressive and focused on feelings and personal issues, whereas men's talk tends to be more instrumental and competitive (Aries, 1987; Beck, 1988; Coates & Cameron, 1989; Johnson, 1989; Martin et al., 2000; Treichler & Kramarae, 1983; Wood, 1994c, 1994d, 1998).

Another general difference between the sexes involves what members of each sex tend to perceive as the primary foundation of close relationships. For most men, activities tend to be the primary foundation of close friendships and romantic relationships (Inman, 1996; Metts, 2006; Swain, 1989; Wood & Inman, 1993). Thus, men typically cement friendships by doing things together and for one another. For many women, communication usually is a primary foundation of relationships. Women also do things with and for people they care about, yet most women see talk as an essential foundation for intimacy. For many women, communicating is the essence of building and sustaining closeness (Aries, 1987; Becker, 1987; Braithwaite & Kellas, 2006; Metts, 2006; Riessman, 1990).

Notice that differences between men and women are matters of degree. They are not absolute dichotomies (MacNeil & Byers, 2005). Men sometimes use talk expressively, and women sometimes use talk instrumentally. Also, keep in mind that not all women follow rules of feminine communication communities, and not all men follow rules of masculine ones.

Reflective Exercise

Examine Table 5.1 and identify how closely your own experience and that of your specific speech community conforms to the generalizations of feminine and masculine speech rules.

TABLE 5.1

RULES OF GENDER SPEECH COMMUNITIES

Feminine Communication Rules	Masculine Communication Rules
1. Include others. Use talk to show interest in others, and respond to their needs.	1. Assert yourself. Use talk to establish your identity, expertise, knowledge, and so on.
2. Use talk cooperatively. Communication is a joint activity, so people have to work together. It's important to invite others into conversation, wait your turn to speak, and respond to what others say.	2. Use talk competitively. Communication is an arena for proving yourself. Use talk to gain and hold attention, to wrest the talk stage from others; interrupt and reroute topics to keep you and your ideas spotlighted.
3. Use talk expressively. Talk should deal with feelings, personal ideas, and problems and should build relationships with others.	3. Use talk instrumentally. Talk should accomplish something, such as solving a problem, giving advice, or taking a stand on issues.

Misunderstandings between Gender Speech Communities

Socialization in different gender communities accounts for some common misunderstandings between women and men. One such misunderstanding occurs when women and men discuss problems. Often, when a woman tells a man about something that is troubling her, he offers advice or a solution (Duck, 2006; Tannen, 1990; Wood, 1994d, 1996, 1998). His view of communication as primarily instrumental leads him to show support by doing something. Because feminine communities see communication as a way to build connections with others, however, women often want empathy and discussion of feelings before advice is useful. Thus, women sometimes feel that men's responses to their concerns are uncaring and insensitive. On the other hand, men may feel frustrated when women offer empathy and support instead of advice for solving problems.

Research also indicates that men tend to be less comfortable than women about making personal disclosures (Aries, 1987; Wood & Inman, 1993). Another conundrum in interaction between men and women concerns different styles of listening. Socialized to be responsive and expressive, women tend to make listening noises such as "um hm," "yeah," and "I know what you mean" when others are talking (Tannen, 1990; Wood, 1996, 1998). This is how they show that they are attentive and interested. Yet, masculine communities don't emphasize using communication responsively, so men tend to make fewer listening noises when another is talking. Thus, women sometimes feel that men aren't listening to them because men don't symbolize their attention

Student Voices

Suzie:

Gender speech communities explain a big fight my boyfriend and I had. We've been dating for three years and we're pretty serious, so I wanted our anniversary to be really special. I suggested going out for a romantic dinner where we could talk about the relationship. Andy said that sounded dull, and he wanted to go to a concert where there would be zillions of people. At the time, I thought that meant he didn't care about us like I do, but maybe he feels close when we do things together instead of when we just are together.

in the ways women have learned and expect. Notice that this does not mean that men don't listen well. Rather, the ways in which many men listen aren't perceived as listening carefully by some women, because women and men tend to have different regulative and constitutive rules for listening. Recall from Chapter 3 that perception shapes meaning.

Monika Gniot/Shutterstock

A very common misunderstanding occurs when a woman says, "Let's talk about us." To many men, this often means trouble because they interpret the request as implying that there is a problem in the relationship. For women, however, this is not the only—or even the main—reason to talk about a relationship. Feminine speech communities regard talking as the primary way to create relationships and build closeness (Riessman, 1990). In general, women view talking about a relationship as a way to celebrate and increase intimacy. Socialized to use communication instrumentally, however, men tend to think that talking about a relationship is useful only if there is some problem to be resolved (Acitelli, 1988, 1993). For many men, the preferred mode of enhancing closeness is to do things together. Suzie's commentary illustrates this gender difference.

CONCEPTS AT A GLANCE

Guidelines for Improving Verbal Communication

- Engage in dual perspective.
- Own your own feelings and thoughts.
- Respect what others say about their feelings and thoughts.
- Strive for accuracy and clarity.

GUIDELINES FOR IMPROVING VERBAL COMMUNICATION

We've explored what symbols are and how they may be used differently in distinct speech communities. Building on these understandings, we will now consider guidelines for improving effectiveness in verbal communication.

Engage in Dual Perspective

A critical guideline for effective verbal communication is to engage in dual perspective. This involves recognizing another person's perspective and taking that into account as you communicate. Effective interpersonal communication is not a solo performance, but a relationship between people. Awareness of others and their viewpoints should be reflected in how we speak.

We don't need to abandon our own perspectives to accommodate those of others. In fact, it would be as unhealthy to stifle your own views as to ignore those of others. Dual perspective, as the term implies, consists of two perspectives. It requires honouring both our own point of view and another's when we communicate. Most of us can accept and grow from differences, but we seldom feel affirmed if we are unheard or disregarded. Acknowledging others' viewpoints in your communication paves the way for affirming relationships.

Student Voices

Acques:

For so long, my mother and I have argued with each other. I have always felt she was overly protective of me and tried to intrude in my life with all the questions she asked about what I'm doing, who I'm seeing, and everything. For years, almost any discussion between us wound up in an argument. I would just resist and challenge her.

But for the last month, I've been trying to understand where she's coming from. When she asks who I'm seeing, I don't just say "None of your business" or "Get off my case" like I used to. Now I ask her why she wants to know. What she says is she's interested in who I hang with and why I like them. That's kind of cool, I think—that my mom is really interested in my life. That's a lot different than seeing her questions as coming from a mother hen who wants to run my life. Trying to understand her perspective has been really, really tough, but it has made an incredible difference in our relationship.

Student Voices

Neely:

I thought that the idea of *I* language was kind of silly, but I did the exercise assigned in class anyway. Surprise. I found out I was using a lot of *you* language, and it had the effect of letting me off the hook for what I felt and did. Like, I would say, "You pushed me to say that" when really I had control over whether to say it or not. But when I said, "You pushed me," I could dismiss what I said as not my fault. I've continued to focus on not using *you* language even though the assignment is over.

Own Your Feelings and Thoughts

We often use language in ways that obscure our responsibility for how we feel and what we think. For instance, we say, "You made me mad" or "You hurt me," as if what we feel was caused by someone else. On a more subtle level, we sometimes blame others for our responses to what they say. "You're so demanding" really means that you are irritated by what someone else wants or expects. The irritation is *your* feeling.

Although how we interpret what others say may lead us to feel certain ways, others do not directly cause our responses. In certain contexts, such as abusive relationships, others may powerfully shape how we think and feel. Yet even in these extreme situations, we need to remember that we, not others, are responsible for our feelings. Telling others they make you feel some way denies your responsibility for your own feelings and is likely to arouse defensiveness, which doesn't facilitate healthy interpersonal relationships. In Chapter 4, we discussed this as the fallacy of taking responsibility for others. We do not cause another's feelings.

Effective communicators take responsibility for themselves by using language that owns their thoughts and feelings. They claim their feelings and do not blame others for what happens within themselves. To take responsibility for your own feelings, rely on *I* language, rather than *you* language. *I* language owns thoughts and feelings and does not blame them on others. Table 5.2 gives examples of the difference.

There are two differences between *I* language and *you* language. First, *I* language takes responsibility, whereas *you* language projects it onto another person. Second, *I* language is more descriptive than *you* language. *You* language tends to

TABLE 5.2

YOU LANGUAGE AND *I* LANGUAGE

***You* Language**	***I* Language**
You hurt me.	I feel hurt when what I say is ignored.
You make me feel small.	I feel small when I am called selfish.
You're so domineering.	When you shout, I feel dominated.
You humiliated me.	I felt humiliated when my problems were aired in front of our friends.
You made me fall in love with you.	I have fallen in love with you.
You make me laugh.	I feel happy when I am with you.

be accusatory and abstract. This is one of the reasons it's ineffective in promoting change. *I* language, on the other hand, provides concrete descriptions of behaviours that we dislike without directly blaming the other person for how we feel.

Monkey Business Images/SnapVillage

Some people feel awkward when they first start using *I* language. This is natural because most of us have learned to rely on *you* language. With commitment and practice, however, you can learn to communicate with *I* language.

Once you feel comfortable using *I* language, you will find that it has many advantages. First, it is less likely than *you* language to make others defensive, so *I* language opens the doors for dialogue. *You* language is particularly likely to arouse defensiveness or anger when it is used to express criticism or dissatisfaction. In a recent study, however, Amy Bippus and Stacy Young (2005) found that some people reacted positively when they were targets of positive *you* language (e.g., "You make me feel wonderful").

Second, *I* language is more honest. We misrepresent our responsibility when we say "You made me feel ..." because others don't control how we feel. Finally, *I* language is more empowering than *you* language. When we say you did this or you made me feel that, we give control of our emotions to others. This reduces our personal power and, by extension, our motivation to change what is happening. Using *I* language allows you to own your own feelings while explaining to others how you interpret their behaviours.

Apply the Idea

USING *I* LANGUAGE

For the next three days, whenever you use *you* language, try to rephrase what you said or thought in *I* language. How does this change how you think and feel about what's happening? How does using *I* language affect interaction with others? Are others less defensive when you own your feelings and describe, but don't evaluate, their behaviours? Does *I* language facilitate working out constructive changes?

Now that you're tuned into *I* and *you* language, monitor how you feel when others use *you* language about you. When a friend or romantic partner says "You make me feel ...," do you feel defensive or guilty? Try teaching others to use *I* language so that your relationships can be more honest and open. Remember the rule from Chapter 4: A statement that begins with "I feel that ..." is not a statement of feeling but a statement of belief.

Respect What Others Say About Their Feelings and Thoughts

Has anyone ever said to you, "You shouldn't feel that way"? If so, you know how infuriating it can be to be told that your feelings aren't valid, appropriate, or acceptable. It's equally destructive to be told our thoughts are wrong. We feel disconfirmed when someone says, "How can you think something so stupid?"

Student Voices

Thelma:

I go crazy when someone tells me I shouldn't feel what I'm feeling. I can't help what I feel. Feelings aren't something we control. They just are. When someone tells me I should feel a certain way, I get so angry and I just shut up. I think that they're not even trying to understand me. They are just evaluating how I feel as wrong. That is totally toxic to me! There's no point in talking to someone who says and thinks that.

Effective communicators don't dispute or disparage what others say about what they feel and think. Even if you don't feel or think the same way, you can still respect another person as the expert on her or his own thoughts and emotions.

One of the most disconfirming forms of communication is speaking for others when they are able to speak for themselves. We shouldn't assume we understand how they feel or think. As we have seen, our distinct experiences and ways of interpreting life make each of us unique. We seldom, if ever, completely grasp what another person feels or thinks. Although it is supportive to engage in dual perspective, it isn't supportive to presume we fully grasp what's happening in someone else and can speak for them.

It's particularly important not to assume we understand people from other cultures, including those distinct communities within our society. Recently, an Asian Indian woman in a class commented on the discrimination she faces, and a White man in the class said, "I know what you mean. Prejudice really hurts." Although he meant to be supportive, his response angered the woman, who retorted, "You have no idea how I feel, and you have no right to act like you do until you've been female and non-White." It's careless to say, "I know what you mean" unless we have had the exact experiences. It becomes especially poignant when someone speaks of painful experiences such as discrimination. When we claim to share what we haven't experienced, we take away from others' lives and identities.

Respecting what others say about what they feel and think is a cornerstone of effective interpersonal communication. We also grow when we open ourselves to perspectives, feelings, and thoughts that differ from our own. If you don't understand what others say, ask them to elaborate. This shows you are interested and respect their expertise or experience. Inviting others to clarify, extend, or explain their communication enlarges understanding between people.

Strive for Accuracy and Clarity

Because symbols are arbitrary, abstract, and ambiguous, the potential for misunderstanding always exists. In addition, individual and cultural differences foster varying interpretations of words. Although we can't completely eliminate misunderstandings, we can minimize them.

Be Aware of Levels of Abstraction

Misunderstanding is less likely when we are conscious of levels of abstraction. Much confusion results from language that is excessively abstract. For instance, suppose a professor says, "Your papers should demonstrate a sophisticated conceptual grasp of material and its pragmatic implications." Would you know how to write a paper to satisfy the professor? Probably not, because the language is abstract. Here's a more concrete description: "Your papers should include definitions of the concepts and specific examples that show how they apply in real life." With this more concrete statement, you would have a clear idea of what the professor expected.

Apply the Idea

USING CONCRETE LANGUAGE

Rewrite each statement, replacing abstract language with more concrete language.

Example: I want to be more responsible.
Rewrite: I want to be on time for work and classes, and I want to live within my budget each month and not run up charges on my credit card.

1. I get really angry when people are rude.
2. I like teachers who are flexible and open-minded.
3. My roommate is such a slob.
4. I believe intimate relationships are based on unconditional love and acceptance.
5. I resent it when my supervisor has unrealistic expectations of me.
6. I think the media in this country are irresponsible.

Sometimes, however, abstract language is appropriate. As we have seen, abstract language allows us to generalize, which is necessary and useful. The goal is to use a level of abstraction that suits particular communication objectives and situations. Abstract words are appropriate when speakers and listeners have similar concrete knowledge about what is being discussed. For example, an established couple might talk about "lighthearted comedies" and "heavy movies" as shorthand ways to refer to two kinds of films. Because they have seen many movies together, they have shared referents for the abstract terms *lighthearted* and *heavy,* so confusion is unlikely. Similarly, long-term friends can say, "Let's just hang out" and understand the activities implied by the abstract term *hang out.*

More concrete language is useful when communicators don't have shared experiences and interpretations. For example, early in a friendship the suggestion to "hang out" would be more effective if it included specifics: "Let's hang out today—maybe watch the game and go out for pizza." In a new dating relationship, saying "Let's have a casual evening" would be less clear than "Let's rent a movie and fix dinner at my place tonight."

Abstract language is particularly likely to lead to misunderstandings when people talk about changes they want in one another. Concrete language and specific examples help people have similar understandings of which behaviours are unwelcome and which ones are wanted. For example, "I want you to be more helpful around the house" does not explain what would count as being more helpful. Is it vacuuming and doing laundry? Shopping for groceries? Fixing half the meals? It won't be clear what the speaker wants unless more concrete descriptions are supplied. Saying, "I want our team to be more efficient" could mean that the person wants meetings to start promptly, wants all members of a team to be on time for meetings, or wants more accomplished at each meeting. Likewise, "I want to be closer" could mean that the speaker wants to spend more time together, to talk about the relationship, to do things together, to have a more adventurous sex life, or any number of other things.

CONCEPTS AT A GLANCE

Qualify Language by

- Undoing static evaluations
- Using mental indexing

Another strategy for increasing the clarity of communication is to qualify language. Two types of language should be qualified. First, we should qualify generalizations so that we don't mislead ourselves or others into mistaking a general statement for an absolute one. "Politicians are crooked" is a false statement because it overgeneralizes. A more accurate statement would be "A number of politicians have been shown to be dishonest." Qualifying reminds us of the limitations of what we say.

Apply the Idea

USING QUALIFIED LANGUAGE

Study the unqualified and qualified statements below.

Unqualified	Qualified
Foreign cars are better than domestic ones.	Hondas and Toyotas generally require less maintenance than Fords and Chevys.
Science courses are harder than humanities courses.	Most students find chemistry tougher than music.
Television is violent.	Many commercial programs include a lot of violence.

Practise your skill in qualifying language by providing appropriate restrictions for the overgeneralizations below.

Unqualified: Women make better doctors.
Qualified: ________________________________

Unqualified: Affirmative action gives jobs to unqualified people.
Qualified: ________________________________

Unqualified: Men are more competitive than women.
Qualified: ________________________________

Unqualified: Textbooks are boring.
Qualified: ________________________________

We should also qualify language when describing and evaluating people. A **static evaluation** is an assessment that suggests that something is unchanging. Such an evaluation is particularly troublesome when applied to people: "Anne is selfish," "Don is irresponsible," "Bob is generous," "Vy is dependent." Whenever we use the word *is,* we suggest that something is inherent and fixed. In reality, we aren't static but are continuously changing. A person who is selfish at one time may not be at another. A person who is irresponsible on one occasion may be responsible in other situations.

Indexing is a technique developed by early communication scholars to remind us that our evaluations apply only to specific times and circumstances

(Korzybski, 1958). To index, we would say "Anne acted selfishly," "Don was irresponsible," "Bob was generous," and "Vy was dependent on others for self-esteem." See how indexing ties description to a specific time and circumstance? Mental indexing reminds us that we and others are able to change in remarkable ways.

Effective interpersonal communication is accurate and clear. We've considered four principles for improving the effectiveness of verbal communication. Engaging in dual perspective is the first principle and a foundation for all others. A second guideline is to take responsibility for our own feelings and thoughts by using *I* language. Third, we should respect others as the experts on what they feel and think and not presume we know what they mean or share their experiences. The fourth principle is to strive for clarity by choosing appropriate degrees of abstraction, qualifying generalizations, and indexing evaluations, particularly those applied to people.

Student Voices

Ken:

Parents are the worst for static evaluations. When I first got my licence seven years ago, I had a fender-bender and then got a speeding ticket. Since then I've had a perfect record, but you'd never know it from what they say. Dad's always calling me "hot-rodder," and Mom goes through this safety spiel every time I get ready to drive somewhere. You'd think I was the same now as when I was sixteen.

Chapter Summary

In this chapter, we discussed the world of words and meaning, the uniquely human universe that we inhabit because we are symbol users. Because symbols are arbitrary, ambiguous and abstract, they have no inherent meanings. Instead, we actively construct meaning by interpreting symbols based on perspectives and values that are endorsed in our culture and social groups and based on interaction with others and our personal experiences. We also punctuate to create meaning in communication.

Instead of existing only in the physical world of the here and now, we use symbols to define, evaluate, and classify ourselves, others, and our experiences in the world. In addition, we use symbols to think hypothetically, so that we can consider alternatives and simultaneously inhabit all three dimensions of time. Finally, symbols allow us to self-reflect so that we can monitor our own behaviours.

Although members of a society share a common language, we don't all use it the same way. Different groups, or speech communities, which exist both within and between countries, teach us rules for talking and for interpreting communication. Because communication rules vary among social groups, we shouldn't assume that others use words just as we do. Likewise, we shouldn't assume that others share our rules for communicating.

The final section of this chapter discussed principles for improving effectiveness in verbal communication. Because words can mean different things to various people and because different social groups instill some distinct rules for interacting, misunderstandings are always possible. To minimize them, we should engage in dual perspective, own our thoughts and feelings, respect what others say about how they think and feel, and monitor abstractness, generalizations, and static evaluations. In the next chapter, we continue our discussion of the world of human communication by exploring the fascinating realm of nonverbal behaviour.

Key Concepts

- abstract
- ambiguous
- arbitrary
- communication devices
- communication rules
- constitutive rules
- hate speech
- indexing
- loaded language
- regulative rules
- speech community
- static evaluation
- totalizing

For Further Thought and Discussion

1. Think about different metaphors for Canadian society. Discuss the difference between the metaphors of "the cultural mosaic" and "the cultural melting pot" as they relate to the differences in Canadian and American culture. What metaphors would you propose that would capture the diversity and richness of Canadian culture?
2. Use your InfoTrac® College Edition to read two articles in journals that focus on experiences and perspectives of minority groups in Canada. What does reading these articles teach you about the perspectives of minority groups in Canada? Focus on the language used in the articles to describe minority and majority cultures. What definitions and evaluations are in the language?
3. To appreciate the importance of hypothetical thought, enabled by symbols, try to imagine the following: living only in the present with no memories and no anticipations of the future; having no goals for yourself; knowing only the concrete, immediate reality. How would not having hypothetical thought affect your life?
4. In this chapter we learned that language changes. We coin new words when we feel the need to represent something that is not currently named in our language. Can you think of experiences, situations, or relationships that are not currently named? What names would you give them?
5. Check out the graffiti on your campus. Do you see examples of loaded language, stereotyping, and hate speech? Share your findings with your classmates.
6. What should be done about hate speech? Should we censor it? Would doing so violate our constitutional right to freedom of speech? Are there other, perhaps less formal, ways to reduce hate speech?
7. What labels that you dislike have been applied to you or to groups to which you belong? Explain how the labels affect you.
8. Does your school have a code or policy on hate speech? If so, what limits does the policy impose on freedom of speech?
9. Notice how media describe Canada's ethnic and racial diversity in the news. Do television programs, newspapers, and other media spotlight race when the person is not White? How often are minorities described in terms of their races? Are people ever described as being White?

Chapter 6

Nonverbal Communication

The eyes have one language everywhere.

—George Herbert

The reality of the other person is not in what he reveals to you, but in what he cannot reveal to you. Therefore, if you would understand him, listen not to what he says but rather to what he does not say.

—Kahlil Gibran (1926)

This chapter examines how we send messages without words. This nonverbal communication is a major dimension of human interaction. Consider the following two scenarios.

> Jay and Emma gaze into each other's eyes as they nibble their beautifully prepared salads topped with marinated mushrooms and herb croutons. They can hear only muffled sounds from people at the other tables spread sparsely throughout the lavish dining area. The comfortable upholstered chairs, subtle lighting, and soft music add to the leisurely, intimate mood of the evening. Fifteen minutes after bringing the salads, the server returns with their entreés and asks whether they would like anything else.
>
> Amy's and Ted's eyes meet across the Formica table in the diner. They speak loudly to be heard above the clamour of rock music, conversations at other tables crowded around them in the bright room, and order announcements shouted from the grill. Less than five minutes after they order, the server plops loaded plates in front of them and leaves the check. Ted and Amy eat their burritos quickly and leave, spending less than 20 minutes on the entire meal.

These two couples had very different dining experiences. The restaurant where Jay and Emma dined featured low lighting, carefully arranged spaces, soft music, and a gracious pace of service that encouraged lingering and intimate conversation. In contrast, Ted's and Amy's restaurant was crowded, bright, and loud, and the service was fast and functional, all of which discouraged lingering or intimate conversation. These aspects of nonverbal communication account for much of the difference in the dining experiences.

Compare the difference in the use of space and time in these eating experiences.

Nonverbal communication is the fascinating world beyond words that is central to interpersonal communication. To launch our discussion, we'll examine the nature of nonverbal communication and how it differs from verbal communication. Next, we will identify four principles of nonverbal communication. The third section of the chapter discusses different types of nonverbal behaviour. We complete the chapter with guidelines for improving personal effectiveness in nonverbal communication.

DEFINING NONVERBAL COMMUNICATION

Nonverbal communication is all aspects of communication other than words themselves. It includes not only gestures and body language, but also how we utter words: inflection, pauses, tone, volume, and accent. These nonverbal features affect the meanings of our words. Nonverbal communication also includes features of environments that affect interaction, personal objects such as jewellery and clothes, physical appearance, and facial expressions.

Scholars estimate that nonverbal behaviours account for 65 to 93 percent of the total meaning of communication (Birdwhistell, 1970; Hickson, Stacks, & Moore, 2004; Mehrabian, 1981). To understand verbal and nonverbal dimensions of communication, we identify similarities as well as differences between verbal and nonverbal communication.

Similarities between Verbal and Nonverbal Communication

Nonverbal communication is similar to verbal communication in four respects: it is symbolic, it is rule-guided, it may be intentional or nonintentional, and it reflects culture.

Nonverbal Communication Is Symbolic

Like verbal communication, much nonverbal communication is symbolic, which means that it represents other things. To represent different moods, we shrug our shoulders, lower our eyes, and move away from or toward others. We smile to symbolize pleasure in seeing a friend, frown to show anger or irritation, and widen our eyes to indicate surprise.

Because nonverbal communication is symbolic, it is arbitrary, ambiguous, and abstract. Thus, we cannot be sure what a wink or a hand movement means. Depending on the context and the people involved, a wink might express romantic interest, signal that the person winking is joking, or mean that the person winking has something in her or his eye. Also, we can't guarantee that others will perceive the meanings we intend to communicate with our nonverbal actions. You might move closer to someone to indicate that you like the person, but he or she may feel that you are rude and imposing.

Nonverbal Communication Is Rule-Guided

Another similarity between the two kinds of communication is that both are rule-guided. Within particular societies, we share general understandings of what specific nonverbal behaviours are appropriate in various situations and what they mean. For example, in Canada, as well as many other countries, handshakes are the conventional method of beginning and ending business meetings. Smiles are generally understood to express friendliness, and scowls are generally perceived as indicating displeasure of some type.

We follow rules (often unconsciously) to create different interaction climates. For instance, people dress differently to attend a funeral than to attend a soccer game. A formal speaking occasion might call for a podium placed at a distance from listeners' chairs, which are arranged in neat rows. Flags, banners, or other ceremonial symbols might be displayed near the podium. To symbolize a less formal speaking occasion, the podium might be omitted, chairs might be arranged in a circle, and the person speaking might be seated. The different spatial arrangements symbolize different moods and set the stage for distinct kinds of interaction.

Nonverbal Communication May be Intentional or Unintentional

Both verbal and nonverbal communication may be deliberately controlled or unintentional. For example, you may carefully select clothes to create a professional impression when you are going to a job interview. You may also deliberately control your verbal language in the interview to present yourself as assertive, articulate, and respectful. We exert conscious control over much of our nonverbal communication.

Sometimes, however, both nonverbal and verbal communication are unconscious and unplanned. Without awareness, you may wince when asked a tough question by the interviewer. Without knowing it, you may use incorrect grammar when speaking. Thus, both nonverbal and verbal communication are sometimes controlled and sometimes inadvertent.

Nonverbal Communication Reflects Culture

Like verbal communication, nonverbal behaviour is shaped by cultural ideas, values, customs, and history (Andersen et al., 2002; Emmons, 1998). Just as we learn our culture's language, we also learn its nonverbal codes. For example, in Canada, most people use knives, forks, and spoons to eat. In Korea, Japan, China, Nepal, and other Asian countries, chopsticks often are the primary eating utensil. In Canada, it is common for friends and romantic partners to sample food from each other's plate, but Germans consider this extremely rude. Dress, as we will learn, is a statement we make about ourselves. Most Western women wear slacks, shirts, dresses, and suits for business, whereas saris are traditional dress in India. Later in this chapter, we'll look more closely at cultural influences on nonverbal behaviour as one of the principles of the nonverbal communication system.

Differences between Verbal and Nonverbal Communication

There are also differences between verbal and nonverbal communication and the meanings we attach to each. We consider three distinctions between the two kinds of communication.

Nonverbal Communication Is Perceived as More Believable

One major difference is that most people believe that nonverbal communication is more reliable than verbal communication in expressing true feelings (Andersen, 1999). This is especially the case when verbal and nonverbal messages are inconsistent. If someone glares and says, "I'm glad to see you," you are likely to believe the nonverbal message, which communicates that the speaker is *not* pleased to see you. If you say you feel fine, but you are slumping and the corners of your mouth are turned down, others probably will not believe your verbal message.

The fact that people tend to believe nonverbal behaviours doesn't mean that nonverbal behaviours actually are honest or that we really can interpret them reliably. It's also possible for us to manipulate nonverbal communication, just as we manipulate our verbal communication. Politicians are coached not only in how to speak but also in how to use nonverbal communication to bolster images.

Nonverbal Communication Is Multichanneled

Nonverbal communication often occurs simultaneously in two or more channels, whereas verbal communication tends to take place in a single channel. Nonverbal communication may be seen, felt, heard, smelled, and tasted, and we may receive nonverbal communication through several of these channels at the same time. If you touch a person while smiling and whispering an endearment, nonverbal communication occurs in three channels at once. In contrast, vocal verbal communication is received through hearing, whereas written verbal communication and American Sign Language are received through sight—in each case, a single channel.

One implication of the multichanneled nature of nonverbal communication is that selective perception is likely to operate. If you are visually oriented, you may tune in more to visual cues than to smell or touch. On the other hand, if you are touch-oriented, you may pay particular attention to tactile cues.

Nonverbal Communication Is Continuous

Finally, nonverbal communication is more continuous than verbal communication. Verbal symbols start and stop. We say something or write something, and then we stop talking or writing. Yet it is difficult, if not impossible, to stop nonverbal communication. As long as two people are together, they are engaging in nonverbal behaviours, deliberately or unintentionally. How we enter and leave rooms, how we move, even how we tilt our head may affect others' interpretations of us. Further, nonverbal features of environment, such as lighting or temperature, are ongoing influences on interaction and meaning. Understanding similarities and differences between verbal and nonverbal behaviour gives us insight into each form of communication and helps us appreciate how they work together in providing communication.

CONCEPTS AT A GLANCE

Four Principles of Nonverbal Communication

1. Nonverbal communication may supplement or replace verbal communication.
2. Nonverbal communication may regulate interaction.
3. Nonverbal communication often establishes relationship-level meanings.

PRINCIPLES OF NONVERBAL COMMUNICATION

Now that we have defined nonverbal communication and compared and contrasted it with verbal communication, let's explore how nonverbal communication actually works. Three principles of nonverbal communication enhance understanding of how it affects meaning in human interaction.

Nonverbal Communication May Supplement or Replace Verbal Communication

Communication researchers have identified five ways in which nonverbal behaviours interact with verbal communication (Andersen, 1999; Malandro & Barker, 1983). First, nonverbal behaviours may repeat verbal messages. For example, you might say "yes" while nodding your head. Second, nonverbal behaviours may highlight verbal communication. For instance, you can emphasize particular words by speaking louder. Third, you can use nonverbal behaviour to complement or add to words. When you see a friend, you might say, "I'm glad to see you" and underline the verbal message with a warm embrace. Lyrics (verbal) and music (nonverbal) often work together (Sellnow & Sellnow, 2001).

Fourth, nonverbal behaviours may contradict verbal messages, as when someone says, "Nothing's wrong" in a frosty, hostile tone of voice. Finally, we sometimes substitute nonverbal behaviours for verbal ones. For instance, you might roll your eyes to indicate you disapprove of something. In all of these ways, nonverbal behaviours augment or replace verbal communication. The Communication Notes feature "The Case of Clever Hans" illustrates the impact of nonverbal communication.

Nonverbal Communication May Regulate Interaction

More than verbal cues, nonverbal behaviours regulate the flow of communication between people. In conversations, we generally know when someone else is through speaking and when it is our turn to talk. We also sense when a

Communication Notes

THE CASE OF CLEVER HANS

In the 1900s, Herr von Osten trained his horse Hans to count by tapping his front hoof. Hans learned quickly and was soon able to multiply, add, divide, subtract, and perform complex mathematical calculations. He could even count the number of people in a room or the number of people wearing eyeglasses. Herr von Osten took Hans on a promotional tour. At shows, he would ask Hans to add 5 and 8, divide 100 by 10, and do other computations. In every case, Hans performed flawlessly, leading others to call him "Clever Hans." Because some doubters thought Clever Hans's feats involved deceit, proof of his mathematical abilities was demanded.

The first test involved computing numbers that were stated on stage by people other than von Osten. Using his hoof, Hans pounded out the correct answers. However, he didn't fare so well on the second test in which one person whispered a number into Hans's left ear and a different person whispered a number into his right ear. Hans was told to add the two numbers and pound out the sum, an answer not known by anyone present. Hans couldn't solve the problem.

On further investigation, it was deduced that Hans could solve problems only if someone he could see knew the answer. When Hans was given numbers and asked to compute them, viewers leaned forward and tensed their bodies as Hans began tapping his hoof. When Hans tapped the correct number, onlookers relaxed their body postures and nodded their heads, which Hans took as a signal to stop tapping.

Hans was clever, not because he could calculate but because he could read people's nonverbal communication.

© Mary Evans Picture Library/Alamy

professor welcomes discussion from students and when the professor is in a lecture mode. Seldom do explicit verbal cues tell us when to speak and when to keep silent. When talking, friends typically don't say, "Your turn to talk" or hold up signs saying "I am through now." Instead, taking turns in conversation usually is regulated nonverbally (Malandro & Barker, 1983). We signal that we don't want to be interrupted by averting our eyes or by maintaining a speaking volume and rate that thwarts interruption. When we're through talking, we look back to others to signal, "Okay, now somebody else can

Reflective Exercise

Watch a conversation from a distance and record the number and kinds of nonverbal behaviours that speakers and listeners use when speaking and when indicating the desire to speak.

speak." We invite specific people to speak by looking directly at them. Although we aren't usually aware of nonverbal actions that regulate interaction, we rely on them to know when to speak and when to remain silent.

CONCEPTS AT A GLANCE

Interaction of Nonverbal with Verbal Communication

- Repeating
- Highlighting
- Complementing
- Contradicting
- Substituting

Nonverbal Communication Often Establishes Relationship-Level Meanings

You'll recall that, in Chapter 1, we discussed two levels of meaning in communication. To review, the content level of meaning is the literal message. The relationship (or relational) level of meaning defines communicators' identities and relationships between them. Nonverbal communication often acts as "relationship language" that expresses the overall feeling of relationships (Burgoon et al., 1984; Keeley & Hart, 1994; Sallinen-Kuparinen, 1992). Nonverbal communication can convey three dimensions of relationship-level meanings (Mehrabian, 1981).

Responsiveness

One dimension of relationship-level meaning is responsiveness. Through eye contact, facial expressions, and body posture, we indicate our interest in others' communication. Online, we may communicate responsiveness by responding immediately to an instant message or to comments in a chat room. In face-to-face interaction, Westerners signal interest by holding eye contact and assuming an attentive posture. To express lack of interest or boredom, we may slouch or decrease visual contact.

CONCEPTS AT A GLANCE

Three Dimensions of Relationship-Level Meanings

1. Responsiveness
2. Liking
3. Power

Synchronicity, or harmony, between people's postures and facial expressions may reflect how comfortable they are with each other (Berg, 1987; Burgoon, Stern, & Dillman, 1995; Capella, 1991). We're more likely to perceive co-workers as being interested in our ideas if they look at us, nod, and lean forward than if they gaze around the room, look bored, and fiddle with papers as we speak (Miller & Parks, 1982).

As Allan's commentary illustrates, different speech communities teach members distinct rules for showing responsiveness. Because feminine speech communities tend to emphasize building relationships by expressing interest in others, women generally display greater nonverbal responsiveness than men (Montgomery, 1988; Ueland, 1992). In addition to communicating their own feelings nonverbally, women generally are more skilled than men in interpreting others' emotions (Hall, 1978; Hall, Carter, & Horgan, 2000; Noller, 1986). Prisoners, another subordinate group, also show strong decoding capacity (Wood, 1994d), which suggests that decoding may be a learned sur-

Simone van den Berg/Shutterstock

Are women more emotionally expressive than men?

Student Voices

Allan:

The most useful professional development seminar I've ever attended was on listening. Our instructor showed us how to sit and look at people to show that we were interested. We learned that most men don't show their interest with head nods and eye contact. That explained to me why some of the women I supervised at a part-time job complained that I never seemed interested when they came to talk to me. It wasn't that I wasn't interested. I just didn't show it with my nonverbal behaviour.

vival strategy for people with limited power. The well-being and sometimes physical safety of those with less power depend on being able to decipher the feelings and intentions of those with more power.

A second dimension of relationship meaning is liking. Nonverbal behaviours often are keen indicators of how positively or negatively we feel toward others. Smiles and friendly touching tend to indicate positive feelings, whereas frowns and belligerent postures express antagonism (Keeley & Hart, 1994). Opening your arms to someone signals affection and welcome, whereas turning your back on someone indicates dislike.

In addition to these general rules shared in Western society, more specific rules are instilled by particular speech communities. Masculine speech communities tend to emphasize emotional control and independence, so men are less likely than women to use nonverbal behaviours to reveal how they feel. Reflecting the values of feminine socialization, women, in general, sit closer to others, smile more, and engage in greater eye contact than men (Hall, Carter, & Horgan, 2000; Montgomery, 1988; Reis, Senchak, & Solomon, 1985). With intimate partners, women are more likely than men to initiate hand-holding and touch. Women also tend to be more nonverbally expressive of their inner feelings because that is encouraged in feminine speech communities.

Nonverbal behaviours also tend to reflect feelings between marriage partners. Happy couples tend to sit closer together and engage in more eye contact than unhappy couples do. Furthermore, people who like each other tend to touch often and to orient their body postures toward each other (Burgoon, Stern, & Dillman 1995; Miller & Parks, 1982; Noller, 1986).

Student Voices

Carla:

I swear, it's so hard to figure out what guys think of you. When you're around a guy, he's like Mr. Stone Face, so he doesn't give away anything about how he feels. I can't tell by how he acts if a guy likes me or is interested. My girlfriends say the same thing—guys are just inscrutable. Girls aren't like that at all. If we like someone, we smile and let him or her know, instead of acting distant and aloof.

Power is the third dimension of relationship-level meaning. We use nonverbal behaviours to assert dominance and to negotiate for status and influence (Burgoon & LePoire, 1999; Henley, 1977; Remland, 2000). Given what we have learned about gender socialization, it is not surprising that men generally assume greater amounts of space than women and use greater volume and more forceful gestures to assert themselves (Hall, 1987; Henley, 1977; Leathers, 1986; Major, Schmidlin, & Williams, 1990).

Status also affects tendencies to communicate power nonverbally. The prerogative to touch another reflects power, so people with power tend to touch those with less power. For instance, bosses touch secretaries far more often than secretaries touch bosses (Spain, 1992). Time is also linked to people's status. People who are considered important can keep others waiting. How often have you waited for your appointment at a doctor's office? People with high status can also be late to appointments and events without risking serious repercussions. Yet, if someone with lower power is late, she or he may suffer disapproval, penalties, or cancellation of the appointment.

As Jerry's observations on the following page indicate, space also expresses power relations. People who have power usually have more space than those who have little or no power. Most executives have large, spacious offices, whereas their secretaries often have smaller offices or workstations. As people move up the organizational ladder, they tend to have larger offices. Homes also reflect power differences among family members. Adults usually have more space than children, and men more often than women have their own rooms, chairs, or other special spaces.

Responsiveness, liking, and power are dimensions of relationship-level meanings that are often expressed through nonverbal communication. This is why communication researchers Judee Burgoon and Beth LePoire (1999) conclude that "nonverbal cues are laden with relationship meaning" (p. 121).

Power may also be exerted through silence, a forceful form of nonverbal communication. By not responding, we can discourage others from speaking and clear the way to talk about our own preferred topics. DeFrancisco (1991) found that some husbands respond with silence to their wives' communication, a behaviour that discourages wives from further interaction. Conversational control is also maintained by a continuous flow of words and vocalizations, forcing everyone to wait for a break

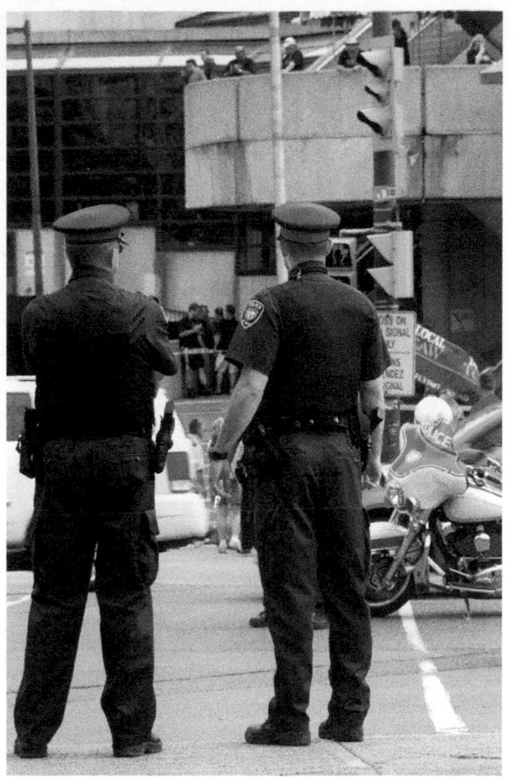

David P. Lewis/Shutterstock

Would you find this intimidating? What are the communication challenges for these officers?

Communication Notes

"I'LL MOVE WHEN I'M READY AND NOT BEFORE!"

Have you ever felt that a driver was really slow in pulling out of a parking space for which you were waiting? It turns out that your imagination may not be playing tricks on you. A recent study of 400 drivers in a shopping mall found that drivers took longer to pull out of a space if someone was waiting than if nobody was there to claim the space (Raphael, 1997).

On average, if nobody was waiting for the space, drivers took 32.2 seconds to pull out of a spot after opening a car door. If someone was waiting, drivers took about 39 seconds. And woe to the person who honks to hurry a driver: Drivers took 43 seconds to pull out of a space when the waiting driver honked!

Reflective Exercise

What do you think of the notion that subordinated groups of people are more skilled at reading nonverbal communication than those in superordinate positions? In what situations would you probably need to be more aware of nonverbal behaviour to protect yourself?

Student Voices

Jerry:

Last summer, I had an internship with a big accounting firm, and space really told the story on status. Interns like me worked together in two large rooms on the first floor, with partitions to separate our desks. New employees worked on the second floor in little cubicles. The higher up you were in the hierarchy of the firm, the higher up your office was—literally. I mean, the president and vice presidents—six of them—had the whole top floor, while there were 40 or more interns crowded together on my floor.

in the speech. This effectively maintains power over the group of listeners. In its extreme form, power is nonverbally enacted through violence and abuse, both of which reflect and sustain dominance (Wood, 1994d).

In sum, three principles provide a foundation for understanding nonverbal communication. First, nonverbal behaviour may supplement or replace verbal communication. Second, nonverbal behaviours may regulate interaction. Finally, nonverbal behaviour is more powerful than verbal behaviour in expressing relationship-level meanings. We're now ready to explore the types of nonverbal behaviour that make up this intricate communication system.

Communication Notes

MULTITASKING TIME

Technology is shifting our sense of time (Potter, 2001; Urgo, 2000). Computers encourage multitasking, which is engaging in multiple tasks simultaneously or in overlapping and interactive ways. Windows technology was designed to make it possible for a user to do multiple tasks at once. While you are writing an essay, the e-mail program running behind your word-processing program alerts you when new messages arrive. As you type, the Office Assistant function pops up occasionally to offer you formatting options, and red and green squiggles alert you that the spell-checker is questioning your spelling, spacing, or whatever.

Multitasking goes beyond what we do with computers. People interrupt conversations or other activities to answer cellphones and check pagers. Drivers talk on phones while navigating traffic. Students bring laptops to class and, when not taking notes, check e-mail or work on other tasks. The buzz of call-waiting prompts a person to suspend the present telephone conversation.

So what's wrong with multitasking? One obvious problem is that, when we attend to several tasks at once, we're likely to do each one less well than if we concentrated on one thing at a time (Brooks, 2001). Another problem is that over time multitasking may diminish our ability to give sustained attention to any single topic or activity (Healy, 1990; Honoré, 2005). It appears that the continuously shifting images and messages in computer games and online communication shape our neural maps such that we expect new images or stimulation frequently, so we learn to sustain attention for only short spans of time.

TYPES OF NONVERBAL COMMUNICATION

Because so much of our interaction is nonverbal, this system includes many types of communication. In this section, we will consider nine forms of nonverbal behaviour, and we will point out how we use each to establish relationships and to express personal identity and cultural values.

Kinesics

Kinesics refers to body position and body motions, including those of the face. Clearly, we signal a great deal about how we feel and see ourselves by how we hold our bodies. Someone who stands erectly and walks confidently is likely to be perceived as self-assured, whereas someone who slouches and shuffles may be seen as lacking confidence. A person who walks quickly with a resolute facial expression will be perceived as more determined than someone who saunters along with an unfocused gaze.

Student Voices

Kelly:

A friend of mine never relinquished conversational power. It made perfect sense to me once I'd heard that term. Daryl was a great guy, but he would always fill in the spaces between his sentences with a long "ah-h-h" or he'd say, "and so-oo," and then he'd carry right on into his next thought. No one could get a word in edgewise. He always had the floor. Yikes, it was infuriating!

Body postures may signal whether we are open to interaction. In classes, students often look downward to dissuade teachers from calling on them. To invite interaction, Westerners look at others and smile, signalling that conversation is welcome. Yet, in many traditional Asian societies, direct eye contact and smiling at someone who is not an intimate might be considered disrespectful.

Gestures are important nonverbally. Humans communicated by gesture long before they learned to communicate verbally (Corballis, 2002). Many people "talk with their hands," which psychology professor Susan Goldin-Meadow (2004) says actually helps us think. We use gestures to emphasize verbal language and to express feelings. We use one hand gesture to indicate "okay" and a different hand gesture to communicate contempt. But gestures don't always translate across cultures. For example, the hand gesture that stands for "okay" in North America is the gesture for worthlessness in France and is regarded as obscene in Iraq (Word for Word, 2005).

CONCEPTS AT A GLANCE

Nine Types of Nonverbal Communication

1. Kinesics (movement)
2. Haptics (touch)
3. Physical appearance
4. Artifacts
5. Environmental factors
6. Proxemics (space)
7. Chronemics (time)
8. Paralanguage (vocalizations)
9. Silence

Our faces are intricate messengers. The face alone is capable of more than a thousand distinct expressions that result from variations in tilt of the head and movements of the eyebrows, eyes, and mouth (Eckman, Friesen, & Ellsworth, 1971). Our eyes can shoot daggers of anger, issue challenges, or radiate feelings of love. With our faces, we can indicate disapproval (scowls), doubt (raised eyebrows), admiration (warm eye gazes), and resistance (stares). The face is particularly powerful in conveying responsiveness and liking (Keeley & Hart, 1994; Patterson, 1992).

One of the most important aspects of kinesics concerns how we position ourselves relative to others and what our positions say about our feelings toward them. Couples communicate dissatisfaction by increasing the physical distance between themselves and by smiling less and looking away from each other (Miller & Parks, 1982). We also use nonverbal behaviours such as smiles, close seating, and warm gazes to signal that we like others and are happy with them (Gueguen & De Gail, 2003; Walker & Trimboli, 1989).

For good reason, poets call the eyes the "windows to the soul." Our eyes communicate some of the most important and complex messages about how we feel about others. If you watch infants, you'll notice that they focus on others' eyes. Even as adults, we tend to look at eyes to judge others' honesty, interest, friendliness, and self-confidence. Virginia Richmond and James McCroskey (2000) found that eye contact, along with other nonverbal behaviours, affects relationships between supervisors and subordinates. Supervisors who look at subordinates, smile, and incline their heads toward subordinates are perceived by subordinates as more credible and interpersonally attractive. Furthermore, these nonverbal behaviours from supervisors are positively related to subordinates' motivation and job satisfaction. It's also the case that customers leave larger tips for servers who maintain eye contact than for servers who don't (Davis & Kieffer, 1998).

Communication Notes

HOW TO DISCOURAGE ASSAULT

Many criminals are highly skilled at interpreting nonverbal behaviour. Their success in getting away with crimes depends on their ability to read others. Convicted thieves report that they don't pick victims randomly but instead carefully select whom to rob. They look for people whose walk signals unsureness and whose posture and face suggest passivity. Some people announce they're good targets, declared one career thief. The best way to avoid being picked as a victim is to walk confidently, hold your head upright, and meet others' eyes without staring. Above all, never appear to be unsure or lost—particularly if you are!

Fearful body language can attract predators.

These nonverbal clues are so important that computer text messaging has created emoticons—emotional icons (e.g., "smileys")—used to compensate for the inability to convey voice inflections, facial expressions, and bodily gestures in written communication. Emoticons can be very effective in avoiding misinterpretation of the writer's intentions. Most manually produced emoticons look like faces (eyes, nose, and mouth) when rotated 90 degrees clockwise. A recent browse of the Internet located collections of thousands of ready-made emoticons for downloading.

For years, many lawyers have used body language to sway jurors' feelings and impressions of cases. For example, to suggest that a witness is lying, lawyers sometimes roll their eyes in full sight of jurors. Standing farther away from witnesses during questioning enhances the witnesses' credibility with jurors. Some lawyers look conspicuously at their watches to signal jurors that the opposition's arguments are boring or ridiculous. Recently, some judges have tried to set limits on lawyers' nonverbal behaviour. A growing number of judges now require lawyers to stand at lecterns, which restricts face and body motions that might influence jurors.

Gestures are the special interest of David McNeill, a professor of linguistics and psychology at the University of Chicago. According to McNeill (1992), much of what we want to communicate involves imagery, and imagery is not well conveyed by words. Thus, to communicate the images we have, we rely heavily on gestures, especially hand movements. In an interview (Mahany, 1997), McNeill offered the interesting observation that the gesture of the extended middle finger, which some

Apply the Idea

COMMUNICATING CLOSENESS

To become more aware of nonverbal cues of intimacy, watch a television show that features interaction between characters, and keep a record of characters' kinesic communication.

- *How close to each other do characters who are intimate stand or sit? How close do characters who are antagonistic stand or sit? What is the distance between characters who are just meeting or who have casual relationships?*
- *What patterns of eye contact do you notice between characters who are intimates, characters who are enemies, and characters who are casual acquaintances? How often do they look at each other? How long is eye gaze maintained in each type of relationship?*
- *What facial expressions signal characters who do and don't like each other? How often do they smile or stare?*

What do your observations reveal about kinesics and relationship-level meanings?

Westerners use to convey contempt, was used for the same message more than 2000 years ago by ancient Romans.

Haptics

Haptics, the sense of touch, is the first of our five senses to develop (Leathers, 1976), and many scholars believe that touching and being touched are essential to a healthy life (Benjamin & Werner, 2004). Research on dysfunctional families reveals that mothers touch babies less often and less affectionately than mothers in healthy families. In disturbed families, mothers tend to push children away, nonverbally signalling rejection (Birdwhistell, 1970). In contrast, babies who are held closely and tenderly tend to develop into self-confident adults who have secure attachment styles (Main, 1981; Mwakalye & DeAngelis, 1995).

© iStockphoto.com/vm

Touching also communicates power and status. People with high status touch others and invade others' spaces more than people with less status do (Henley, 1977). Cultural views of women as being more touchable than men are reflected in gendered patterns of contact. In general, parents touch sons less often and more roughly than they touch daughters (Condry, Condry, & Pogatshnik, 1983). Exposure to these patterns early in life teaches the sexes different rules for using touch and interpreting touches from others.

As adults, women tend to use touch to show liking and intimacy (Montgomery, 1988), whereas men are more likely than women to use touch to assert power and

Communication Notes

FREEDOM OF (NONVERBAL) SPEECH

Nonverbal communication has been costly for some sports stars. When German midfielder Stefan Effenberg made an obscene gesture to fans during a World Cup match in the summer of 1994, his coach promptly kicked him off the squad ("Be Civil," 1994).

Private companies such as athletic teams can make their own rules. For example, Basketball Nova Scotia, among others, adopted a zero tolerance for disrespect to officials (Basketball, 2009). This includes directing nonverbal insults at an official. However, in Canada, the *Canadian Charter of Rights and Freedoms* protects nonverbal behaviour, so it is unlikely that we could be prosecuted for making obscene gestures in public.

Reflective Exercise

What is the importance of kinesics right now in your life as a part of communication? How would the gestures you now use change if you used American Sign Language, some examples of which are shown in Figure 6.1?

control (Henley, 1977; Jhally & Katz, 2001; Leathers, 1986). For example, women frequently hug others and touch the hands and arms of friends during conversation. Men are more likely than women to use touch aggressively to exert power over others or to repel physical aggression. Because many females are taught to be nice to others and preserve relationships, women may be reluctant to object to touching, even if it is unwanted. These gendered patterns contribute to sexual harassment, where women are often the targets of unwelcome touch (LePoire, Burgoon, & Parrott, 1992), as Claire's commentary illustrates.

Student Voices

Claire:

There's a guy where I work who really bothers me. He doesn't really cross a clear line, but it seems like he's always brushing against me. Like when he comes to my desk, he leans over just enough that his chest presses against me. Sometimes he touches my arm or hand when he's showing me a paper, and the other day he stood behind me to show me how to run a new spreadsheet program. He had both arms around me when it would have been easier to work the mouse if he'd sat beside me. I've never said anything because I don't want to hurt his feelings or seem hysterical or something, but it really bothers me.

Physical Appearance

Western culture places an extremely high value on physical appearance. For this reason, in face-to-face interactions, most of us notice how others look, and we often base our initial evaluations of others on their appearance, over which they have limited control. The excessive emphasis that Western culture places on physical attractiveness and youthful appearance contributes to eating disorders, abuse of steroids and other drugs, and the popularity of cosmetic surgery.

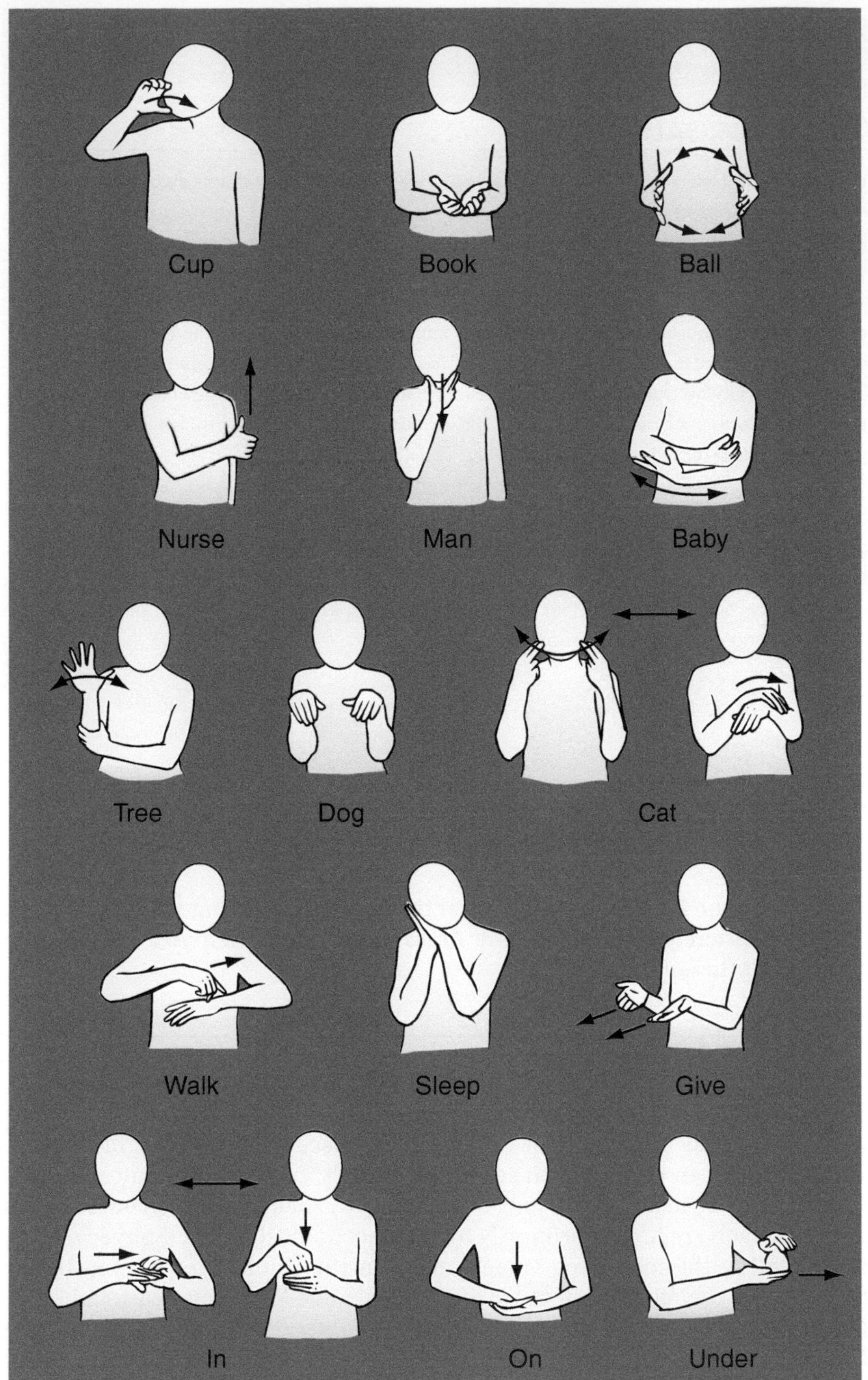

FIGURE 6.1

American Sign Language Hand Signals

Does physical appearance affect what people earn? It may. A study of 2500 male and female lawyers revealed a relationship between physical attractiveness and earning power: The attorneys who were judged more attractive earned as much as 14 percent more than attorneys who were judged less attractive ("Good-Looking Lawyers," 1996).

Communication Notes

BEAUTY FOR SALE

Sander Gilman (1999a, 1999b) studies people who have surgery that is strictly cosmetic. People want larger or smaller breasts, noses, and chins. They want less fat here and more there. They want hair put on their bald heads and varicose veins removed from legs. They want skin tightened, eyelids lifted, wrinkles removed.

Aesthetic surgery isn't just for women or Americans. In the United States, the most popular cosmetic surgeries for men are hair implants, face lifts, and, increasingly, penis enlargements (Bordo, 1999). In the Far East, "eye straightening" is nearly as common as nose surgery is in the United States. And cosmetic surgery is no longer restricted to wealthy people—65 percent of people who have plastic surgery in the United States have annual family incomes of less than $50 000 (Gross, 2000; Sharlet, 1999).

Trends in plastic surgery tend to mirror trends in cultural views of physical attractiveness. When fuller body styles were idealized in women, there were few surgeries to reduce fat and many to increase breast size. As thinner, more athletic bodies have become cultural ideals for women, liposuction and breast reduction surgeries have increased. Likewise, as the culture increasingly emphasizes leanness and muscularity as masculine ideals, more men are having pectoral implants and liposuction.

Reflective Exercise

What is your experience with attractiveness and earning power? Are you treated differently when you are dressed up than when you are wearing casual clothes or are untidy?

Cultures stipulate ideals for physical form. Currently, Western cultural ideals emphasize thinness and youth in women and muscularity and height in men. Heterosexual women and gay men seem particularly vulnerable to cultural pressures to be thin because they are judged so keenly by their attractiveness, whereas heterosexual men are judged primarily by their accomplishments (Spitzack, 1990, 1993). Reflecting the increasing value placed on the thinness of women in the United States is the fact that in the 1950s, the average Miss America weighed 61 kilograms, but by the early 1980s her weight had dropped to 53 kilograms. Also, in 1962, leading fashion models weighed only 8 percent less than average women; by 1992, they weighed 25 percent less (Mazur, 1989). The cultural emphasis on thinness is so great that many people consider being seriously overweight a greater social stigma than a criminal record, cancer, a facial scar, or a missing hand (Harris, Walters, & Waschall, 1991).

These cultural pressures can lead to serious problems but, fortunately, help is available from organizations such as the National Eating Disorder Information Centre (see the Communication Notes feature "Help for Eating

Disorders"). This culture's value of thinness is qualified by ethnic identity. Browse the Internet and take a look in high-end fashion stores across Canada where there is an ethnic concentration, and compare the look of one ethnic group to another's.

Communication Notes

HELP FOR EATING DISORDERS

Preoccupation with weight can rob you of vitality and possibly endanger your life. If your weight is really bothering you or if you have an eating disorder, help is available from the National Eating Disorder Information Centre (NEDIC) in Toronto (toll-free: 1-866-633-4220 or www.nedic.ca). You could also check with your municipal or provincial health department to find out what programs might be available in your area.

Thinness in women is not prized or encouraged in all cultures and social communities. In traditional African societies, full-figured bodies are perceived as symbolizing health, prosperity, and wealth, which are all desirable (Villarosa, 1994). African Americans who embrace this value accept or prefer women who weigh more than the current ideal for Caucasians (Molloy & Herzberger, 1998; Root, 1990; Thomas, 1989; Vobejda & Perlstein, 1998).

Class membership further modifies ethnic values concerning weight. In 1994, *Essence* magazine reported that African American women who were either affluent or poor were likely to have strong Black identities that allowed them to resist White preoccupations with thinness. On the other hand, middle-class African American women who were upwardly mobile were more inclined to deemphasize their ethnic identities to get ahead, and they were more susceptible to obsessions with weight and eating disorders (Villarosa, 1994). Another example of how weight and ethnicity are linked is evidenced in traditional Inuit culture, where a woman would not be considered good marriage material if she was too thin, because she would not have enough fat to endure the cold.

Student Voices

Iliana:

In Rio de Janeiro, large, full hips on women are considered voluptuous and attractive, and are emphasized by cinched-in waists. The large women here in Vancouver wear loose clothes to hide their size. It's hard to get used to.

Artifacts

Artifacts are personal objects that we use to announce our identities and heritage and to personalize our environments. Many people use avatars to symbolize identities in online communication. In face-to-face communication, we craft our image by how we dress and what objects we carry and use. Nurses and physicians wear white and often drape stethoscopes around their necks; professors travel with briefcases, whereas students more often tote backpacks. White-collar professionals tend to wear tailored outfits and dress shoes, whereas blue-collar workers more often dress in jeans or uniforms and boots.

What do your clothes say about you?

The military requires uniforms that define individuals in terms of the group; in addition, stripes and medals signify rank and accomplishments.

One study (Morris et al., 1996) showed that undergraduate students tend to perceive graduate teaching assistants as having greater expertise if the teaching assistants dress professionally than if they dress casually. However, the same study showed that the undergraduate students perceived casually dressed teaching assistants as more extroverted and sociable than those who dressed formally.

Artifacts may also define personal territories. To claim our spaces, we fill them with objects that matter to us and that reflect our experiences and values. Lovers of art adorn their homes with paintings and sculptures that announce their interests and personalize their private space. Religious families often express their commitment by displaying pictures of holy scenes and the Bible, the Koran, or other sacred texts. Lohmann, Arriga, and Goodfriend (2003) studied artifacts in homes. They found that couples with more objects depicting the couple as a couple rather than as individuals—wedding photos, for example—have greater closeness than couples who have fewer artifacts that define them as a couple. The researchers concluded that "the environment in which much of a couple's joint life unfolds—their home—is imbued with their couple identity" (p. 447).

In her book *Composing a Life,* Mary Catherine Bateson (1990) comments that we turn houses into homes by filling them with what matters to us. We make impersonal spaces familiar and comfortable by adorning them with artifacts that express our experiences, relationships, values, and personalities. We use mugs given to us by special people, surround ourselves with books and magazines that announce our interests, and sprinkle our world with objects that reflect what we care about.

Artifacts communicate important relationship meanings. We use them to announce our identities (see the Communication Notes feature "Piercing Punishment") and to express how we perceive and feel about others. Although clothing has become more unisex in recent years, once you venture off campus, gendered styles are evident. To declare gender, we dress to meet the cultural expectations of men and women. Thus, women sometimes wear makeup, dresses that may have lace or other softening touches, skirts, high-heeled shoes, jewellery, and hose, all of which conform to the cultural ideal of women as decorative objects. Typically, men wear little, if any, jewellery, and their clothes and shoes are functional. Flat shoes allow a person to walk comfortably or run if necessary; high heels don't. Men's clothing is looser and less binding, and it includes pockets for wallets, keys, and so forth. In contrast, women's

Student Voices

Jenetta:

Whenever I move, the first thing I have to do is get out the quilt that my grandmother made. Even if it is summer and I won't use the quilt, I have to unpack it first and put it out where I can see it. She brought me up, and seeing that quilt is my way of keeping her in my life.

Communication Notes

PIERCING PUNISHMENT

According to a 1996 "Business Bulletin," it seems not everyone appreciates the rage for body piercing. A nursing student at Camosun College in Victoria, BC, was asked to remove three of the four earrings she wore in each ear because of the *perception* of lack of professionalism. Restaurants seem most sensitive to piercing. Some employers set limits on which body parts can be pierced or how many piercings an employee may have. Starbucks draws the line at two piercings per ear, and those are okay only if the earrings match.

An online poll conducted by Starbucks in October 2008 indicated that 74 percent of respondents would visit Starbucks the same number of times if employees had visible but unobtrusive tattoos, but that only 56 percent of respondents would continue to patronize Starbucks if employees had more than two visible piercings (blogs.starbucks.com/blogs/customer/archive/2008/10/06/poll-results-tattoos-piercings.aspx).

clothing tends to be more tailored and often doesn't include pockets, making a purse necessary.

We also use artifacts to establish racial identity. Jewellery and clothing are a common way to express a distinctive cultural heritage. Note the increase of ethnic artifacts that have reached the fashion markets in Canada. Artifacts communicate our identity from an early age. Many hospitals still swaddle newborns in blue and pink blankets to designate gender, and even though many parents today try to be nonsexist, many still send gender messages through the toys they give their children. In general, parents (especially fathers) give sons toys that encourage rough and active play (balls, trains) and competitiveness (baseball gloves, toy weapons), whereas they give daughters toys that cultivate nurturing (dolls, toy kitchens) and attention to appearance (makeup kits, frilly clothes) (Caldera, Huston, & O'Brien, 1989; Lytton & Romney, 1991; Pomerleau et al., 1990).

Some employers set limits on which body parts can be pierced.

We use artifacts to announce our identities and to project a particular image to others. Jeans and a grungy shirt convey one image; a business suit conveys a very different one. Body piercings are increasingly popular, but not everyone appreciates them (Forbes, 2001). Customers in some restaurants have been offended by wait staff with multiple piercings, so management has policies that regulate piercings ("Business Bulletin," 1996). Tattoos are also used to announce identity. In his amusing (and also serious) book *The T-Shirt Book,* Scott Fresener (1995) profiles people who own thousands of T-shirts, each important for defining some aspect of who they are or have been.

Cultures, as well as social groups within a single culture, have artifacts that are especially important reflections of heritage and values. For example, many Jewish people light candles in a menorah to symbolize sacred values. Christians rely on crosses and manger replicas to symbolize reverence for Jesus.

In 1966, Kwanzaa was designated a time for African Americans to remember their African heritage and values. Now, more than 20 million people celebrate

Apply the Idea

ARTIFACTS AND IDENTITY

Did childhood artifacts contribute to your gender identity? What kinds of toys did your parents give you? Did they ever discourage you from playing with particular kinds of toys? Did you ask for toys that aren't prescribed by society for your gender? Did your parents let you have those toys?

Now think about the clothing your parents gave you. If you're a woman, did your parents expect you to wear frilly dresses and stay clean? If you're a man, did your parents give you clothes meant for rough play and getting dirty?

Do you have artifacts that reflect your ethnic identity? What objects are part of your culture's celebrations and spiritual observances? Do you have any jewellery or clothes that reflect your ethnic heritage?

Kwanzaa in Canada, the United States, England, the Caribbean, and Africa. Kwanzaa is observed from December 26 through January 1. A kinara holds seven candles that symbolize seven distinct principles rooted in African culture. On the sixth day of Kwanzaa, a magnificent feast, the karamu, draws together whole communities to celebrate their heritage and their connections (see the

Communication Notes

KWANZAA

Rituals allow people to acknowledge and celebrate important values (Otnes & Lowrey, 2004). One such ritual is associated with Kwanzaa, which in 1966 was designated a time for individuals to honour their African heritage and the everyday activities of keeping a home. In this way, Kwanzaa symbolizes the centrality of home and family to those of African ancestry, historically and today (Bellamy, 1996; George, 1995).

The kinara is a branched candleholder that holds seven candles, one to be lit on each day of the Kwanzaa observance (*Kwanzaa*, 2009). Three red candles, which symbolize struggles, are placed on the left for days two, four, and six of the celebration. The day-two candle symbolizes the principle of *kujichagulia,* or self-determination. The day-four candle symbolizes *ujamaa,* cooperative economics within communities. The day-six candle represents *kuumba,* or creativity.

On the right side of the kinara are placed three green candles to symbolize the future. The day-three candle on the far right represents *ujima,* collective work and responsibility. The day-five candle symbolizes *nia,* or purpose. The day-seven candle represents *imani,* or faith. The middle candle is black to stand for *umoja,* unity among Black people.

On the sixth day of Kwanzaa, there is a feast called Karamu. During the feast, traditional African foods and family favourites are featured. Thus, Kwanzaa celebrates foods that have been passed down through generations of African descendants.

For more information about Kwanzaa, go to *Kwanzaa*: www.officialkwanzaawebsite.org/index.shtml.

Communication Notes feature "Kwanzaa"). Thus, artifacts are an important way that we adorn not only our bodies but also our environments and make a statement about what we value.

David Cooper/GetStock.com

Environmental Factors

Environmental factors are another nonverbal influence on interpersonal interaction. Environmental factors are elements of settings that affect how we feel and act. For instance, we respond to architecture, colours (see the Communication Notes feature "How Colours Affect Mood"), room design, temperature, sounds, smells, and lighting. Rooms with comfortable chairs invite relaxation, whereas rooms with stiff chairs induce formality. Dimly lit rooms can set a romantic mood, although dark rooms can be depressing. We feel solemn in churches and synagogues with their sombre colours and sacred symbols.

We tend to feel more lethargic on sultry summer days and more alert on crisp fall ones. Delicious smells can make us hungry, even if we weren't previously interested in food. Our bodies synchronize themselves to patterns of light, so we feel more alert during daylight than during the evening. In settings where people work during the night, extra lighting and even artificial skylights are used to simulate daylight so that workers stay alert. Even Walmart wants to bring natural light into its stores because a test showed that workers were more productive and customers bought more when natural light was used instead of artificial light (Pierson, 1995).

Communication Notes

HOW COLOURS AFFECT MOOD

How much is mood influenced by colour? Research reports the following relationships between colours and moods (Varkonyi, 1996; Wexner, 1954):

Red	Exciting, stimulating
Blue	Secure, comfortable, soothing
Orange	Distressed, upset, disturbed
Brown	Dejected, unhappy, melancholy
Green	Calm, serene, peaceful
Black	Powerful, strong, defiant
Yellow	Cheerful, joyful, jovial
Purple	Dignified, stately

The effects of colour are not limited to their visual impact. Rebecca Ewing (Varkonyi, 1996), a colour consultant, reported that she learned about the power of colour from three women—all of whom were blind. The blind women could identify different colours, a phenomenon that has been documented, by sensing distinct vibrations from different colours; these vibrations affected feelings and moods. Ewing compared the blind women's responses to colours with those of sighted people, and she found the same reactions to colours. So, how does colour affect our feelings? Says Ewing, red stimulates the appetite, blue stifles conversation, black evokes reverence, and green is calming.

© 2009 Jupiterimages Corporation

As the examples that opened this chapter illustrate, the environments of most fast-food restaurants encourage customers to eat quickly and move on, whereas more expensive restaurants are designed to promote longer stays and extra spending on wines and desserts. Even background music can affect diners' behaviour. Studies show that people eat faster when fast music is played in an eating area ("Bites," 1998; Bozzi, 1986).

An interesting illustration of the relationship between culture and environmental factors is *feng shui* (which means "wind and water" and is pronounced "fung shway"). Dating back more than 3000 years, feng shui is rooted in Taoism and aims to balance life energy, or *chi* (Spear, 1995). Feng shui consultants help homeowners and businesspeople arrange spaces to promote a smooth flow of energy and a harmony with nature. Some of the feng shui principles are consistent with Western research on nonverbal communication: Don't put large furniture in the path to the front door; a stairway should never directly face the front door; use green to increase good fortune; use mirrors where you want to stimulate creativity (Cozart, 1996; O'Neill, 1997).

Communication Notes

LET THE SUN SHINE IN

Have you ever felt tired when working under fluorescent lights? Have you ever felt the need to take a break and get outside into the sunlight? If so, join the crowd. All light, it seems, is not equal. A study by the Rocky Mountain Institute in Colorado (Pierson, 1995) reports that increased daylight in workspaces results in less absenteeism and fewer worker errors. Walmart opened a prototype daylit store. The company used skylights in half of the store, with artificial lighting in the other half. Not only were workers more productive and comfortable in the areas lit by natural light, but customers were also more productive—they spent more money.

Student Voices

Gary:

Part of our training for management was to learn how to manage turf. We were taught we should always try to get competitors into our offices—not go to theirs. This gives us the advantage, just like playing on the home court gives a team an advantage. We also learned that we should go to subordinates' offices if we needed to criticize them so that they would feel less threatened and more willing to improve their performance. The trainers also stressed the importance of meeting on neutral ground when we had to negotiate a deal with another company. They warned us never to meet on the other guys' turf because that would give them the advantage.

Proxemics

Proxemics refers to space and how we use it (Hall, 1968). Every culture has norms for using space and for how close people should be to one another. In Western culture, we interact with social acquaintances from a distance of 1 to 6 metres but are comfortable with 50 centimetres or less between us and close friends and romantic partners (Hall, 1966). When we are angry with someone, we tend to move away and to resent it if she or he approaches us. People who want to even out power in business negotiations often seek neutral territories for interaction. Gary makes this point in his commentary.

The amount of space we think we need to be comfortable is not strictly individual. There are notable cultural differences in the amount of space with which people feel comfortable. In China, for example, the average person has about 4 square metres of space, which amounts to a 2-metre by 2-metre room. In addition, members of Chinese families often sleep in the same room and also share bathrooms and kitchens with other families (Butterfield, 1982).

Reflective Exercise

Who sits at the head of the table at family dinners? Who has the most physical space in your household? How were those decisions made?

Space also indicates status, with greater space being assumed by those with higher status (Henley, 1977). Substantial research shows that women and minorities generally have less space than White men in Western society (Spain, 1992). The prerogative to invade someone else's personal space is also linked to power, with those having greater power also being most likely to trespass into others' territory (Henley, 1977). Responses to invasions of space also reflect power, with men likely to respond aggressively when their space is invaded (Fisher & Byrne, 1975). This suggests gendered socialization, which encourages women to defer and accommodate, and men to vie for status. The Communication Notes feature "Environmental Racism" reveals another connection between space and power.

Communication Notes

ENVIRONMENTAL RACISM

The term ***environmental racism*** is used to describe a pattern whereby toxic waste dumps and hazardous plants are disproportionately located in low-income neighbourhoods. Whether this is deliberately planned or not, many industries expose our most vulnerable communities to pollutants and carcinogens that seldom affect middle- and upper-class neighbourhoods. The pattern is very clear: The space of minorities and poor people can be invaded and contaminated, but the territory of more affluent citizens cannot.

How people arrange space reflects how close household members are and whether they want interaction. Couples who are very interdependent tend to have greater amounts of common space and less individual space in their homes than do couples who are more independent (Fitzpatrick, 1988; Fitzpatrick & Best, 1979; Werner, Altman, & Oxley, 1985; Werner & Haggard, 1985). Similarly, families who value interaction arrange furniture to invite conversation and eye contact. Less interactive families arrange furniture to discourage conversation. Chairs may be far apart and may face televisions instead of one another (Burgoon, Buller, & Woodhall, 1989; Keeley & Hart, 1994). Our use of space is a statement we make about what we value and what the culture values.

People also invite or discourage interaction by how they arrange office spaces. Some of your professors may have desks that face the door, with chairs placed beside their desks for open communication with students; other professors may have desks turned away from the door and may position chairs in front of their desks to preserve status and distance.

The effects of proxemics on behaviour have not gone unnoticed by companies that make money by keeping people on the move. At McDonald's around the world, seats tilt forward at a 10-degree angle to discourage customers from lingering. The fast-food giant further fosters quick eating by placing seats at the two-person tables only 67 centimetres apart, when it has been established that the distance most people find comfortable for interaction is about a metre apart (Eaves & Leathers, 1991).

Apply the Idea

WHAT DOES YOUR SPACE SAY?

Survey your room or apartment. Is furniture arranged to promote or discourage interaction? How much space is common, and how much is reserved for individuals? Is space divided evenly between you and your roommate(s), or do some people have more space than others?

Now, think about the home where you grew up. How was the space arranged there? Was there a living room or family room? If so, was furniture set up to invite interaction? Was there a lot, a little, or a moderate amount of common space?

Next, think about a place where you work or have worked in the past. How was space arranged in the workplace? Who had more and less space? Who had spaces where doors could be closed to ensure privacy?

How do spatial arrangements in your home, your current living quarters, and your workplace regulate interaction and reflect the styles and status of people who live there?

Chronemics

Chronemics refers to how we perceive and use time to define identities and interaction. In Western culture, there is a norm that important people with high status can keep others waiting (Hickson, Stacks, & Moore, 2004). Conversely, people with low status are expected to be punctual. It is standard practice to have to wait, sometimes a good while, to see a physician, even if you have an appointment. This carries the message that the physician's time is more valuable than yours. Professors can be late to class and students are expected to wait, but students may be reprimanded if they appear after a class has begun. Subordinates are expected to report punctually to meetings, but bosses are allowed to be tardy.

GetStock

In Western societies, time is important, so speed is highly valued (Honoré, 2005; Keyes, 1992; Schwartz, 1989). Linguists (Lakoff & Johnson, 1980) have noted many everyday North American phrases that reflect the cultural view that time is very valuable: "Don't waste time," "Save time," "Spend time," "Can't spare time," "Invest time," "Run out of time," "Budget time," "Borrowed time," "Lose time," "Use time profitably." Many other cultures have more relaxed attitudes toward time (Levine & Norenzayan, 1999).

The West's emphasis on speed is reflected in how we go about daily activities. We replace computer hardware and software as soon as faster models

Communication Notes

THE TIME BIND

Sociologist Arlie Hochschild claims that time is the central issue in American corporate life today. In her book *The Time Bind: When Work Becomes Home and Home Becomes Work* (1997), Hochschild reports that many professionals today feel compelled to force home and family time into an industrial, time-saving model that, ironically, is less and less endorsed in workplaces. Children often are allotted 20 or 30 minutes of time at the end of the day when two working parents get home. Dinner is restricted to 15 minutes so that there is enough time to drive the kids to their soccer game. Breakfasts are made and eaten assembly-line style. Tasks that families used to share are increasingly outsourced as busy parents hire a birthday party service, a personal shopper, and a cleaning service. There just isn't enough time for parents to do all the homemaking and child-rearing activities themselves.

Where has the time gone? Hochschild says it goes more and more into paid jobs. Many professionals work 9, 10, or more hours a day, including weekends. Perhaps most disturbing is Hochschild's conclusion that many people prefer to be in the workplace than at home; they stretch their on-the-job hours and condense their time at home. Why? Because for many people, the workplace is more pleasant, less frenzied and rushed, with time to socialize and relax on breaks. The bottom line, according to Hochschild, is that home and work have switched places; for many, work is a sanctuary, and home is a site of stress and agitation.

But, says Hochschild, that is not acceptable. She urges people to demand a workplace that doesn't compromise their families. She also feels that businesses should encourage workers to leave at the end of a reasonable-length work day and reward employees who do so.

and programs hit the market. We often try to do several things at once to get more done, rely on the microwave to cook faster, and take for granted speed systems such as instant copying and photo processing. Many other cultures have far more relaxed attitudes toward time and punctuality. It's not impolite in many South American countries to come late to meetings or classes, for example, and it's not assumed that people will leave at the scheduled time for ending. Whether time is savoured or compulsively counted and hoarded reflects larger cultural attitudes toward living.

The amount of time we spend with different individuals reflects our interpersonal priorities. When possible, we spend more time with people we like than with those we don't like or who bore us. Researchers report that increasing contact is one of the most important ways in which college and university students intensify relationships, and reduced time together signals decreasing interest (Baxter, 1985; Dindia, 1994; Tolhuizen, 1989). Time is also related to status in work settings. Bankers spend more time with important clients who have major accounts; brokers spend more time with clients who have a lot of money than with clients who have less; architects meet more often and for longer periods with companies that are building a series of large structures than with individuals who want to build a single home; and fund-raisers invest greater amounts of time in well-off donors than in moderate contributors.

Chronemics also involve expectations of time, which are established by cultural norms. For example, you expect a class to last 50 or 75 minutes. Several minutes before the end of a class period, students often close notebooks and start gathering their belongings, signalling the teacher that time is up. Similarly, we expect weekly religious services to last approximately an hour, and we might be upset if a spiritual leader talked beyond the time we've allowed. These expectations reflect our culture's general orientation toward time, which is that it is a precious commodity that we should not give away readily.

Paralanguage

Paralanguage is communication that is vocal but does not use words. It includes sounds such as murmurs and gasps, and vocal qualities such as volume, pitch, and inflection. Paralanguage also includes accents, pronunciation, and the complexity of sentences.

Our voices are versatile instruments that give others, including friends and romantic partners, cues about how to interpret us. Whispering, for instance, signals secrecy and intimacy, whereas shouting conveys anger. Depending on the context, sighing may communicate empathy, boredom, or contentment. Negative paralanguage, such as sneering and ridiculing by tone of voice, is closely associated with dissatisfaction in marriage (Gottman, Markman, & Notarius, 1977; Noller, 1987). A derisive or sarcastic tone communicates scorn or dislike more emphatically than words. The reverse is also true: A warm voice underlines feelings of love, and a playful lilt invites frolic and fun.

Our voices affect how others perceive us. To some extent, we control vocal cues that influence image. For instance, we can deliberately sound firm and sure of ourselves in job interviews when we want to project self-confidence. Similarly, we can consciously make ourselves sound self-righteous, seductive, and unapproachable when those images suit our purposes. Even when we don't intentionally manipulate our vocal qualities, they may still project an image.

Apply the Idea

PARALINGUISTIC CUES

Say "Oh, really" to express the following meanings:

- *I don't believe what you just said.*
- *Wow! That's interesting.*
- *I find your comment boring.*
- *That's juicy gossip!*
- *I can't believe you think I can get the report done that soon.*

Now, say "You love me" to convey these meanings:

- *You really do? I hadn't realized that.*
- *That ploy won't work. I told you we're through.*
- *You couldn't possibly love me after what you did!*
- *Me? I'm the one you love?*
- *You? I didn't think you loved anyone.*

Reflective Exercise

Consider the distinctive sounds of Canada. What are the involuntary inflections and vocal qualities that distinguish the speech of Newfoundlanders, French Canadians, Albertans, Caribbean Canadians, Asian Canadians, and First Nations peoples? What assumptions do you make when you hear these sounds? How is the paralanguage part of the overall message being communicated in these cases?

For example, although we may wish to appear accepting, we may inadvertently convey shock or surprise in response to a friend's personal disclosure about past experiences.

We modulate our voices to reflect our cultural heritage and to announce we are members of specific cultures. Ryan, for example, would use casual slang and tonal inflections that were part of his skateboarding culture. We also use paralanguage to declare gender by behaving in a masculine or feminine manner. To appear masculine, men use strong volume, low pitch, and limited inflection, all of which conform to cultural prescriptions for men to be assertive

Student Voices

Ryan:

I got an excellent job interview with Club Med, eh! My teacher told me my language style might limit me. I hadn't even thought of my language before. She was right. I use a lot of slang and say "yup," "nope," and "eh" a lot. It doesn't leave the impression I want. I had to learn a classier language style to win my interview.

Note the gender differences in body language.

and emotionally controlled. To enact femininity, women tend to use higher pitch, less volume, and more vocal inflection—features that reflect cultural views of women as deferential and polite. Men and women both, however, use masculine or feminine paralanguage to demonstrate control or receptivity. Consider the circumstances where you wish to sound more masculine or more feminine.

We also enact class by how we pronounce words, the accents we use, and the complexity of our sentences. Class is expressed by vocabulary (greater vocabulary is generally associated with higher education) and by grammar. Ryan discovered this in his Club Med interview. In addition to paralinguistic cues, other nonverbal behaviours communicate class. For example, artifacts generally differ in the homes of working-class and upper-class people. Affluent individuals possess more books, expensive art, and valuable jewellery than do less affluent individuals.

Silence

A final type of nonverbal behaviour is silence, which can communicate powerful messages. "I'm not speaking to you" actually speaks volumes. We use silence to communicate different meanings. For instance, it can symbolize contentment when intimates are so comfortable they don't need to talk. Silence can also communicate awkwardness, as you know if you've ever had trouble keeping conversation going with a new acquaintance—we feel pressured to fill the void. In some cultures, including many Eastern (Lim, 2002) and First Nations (Braithwaite, 1990) ones, silence indicates respect and thoughtfulness.

Silence soothes seriously ill babies. Hospital intensive-care nurseries have found that special headphones that block noise reduce the stress caused by the sounds of respirators, ventilators, and other hospital machinery. Within the headphones is a mini-microphone that detects irritating low-frequency noises and eliminates them by generating anti-noise waves. In trials of the headphones, babies who wore them had fewer sleep disturbances and less change in blood pressure ("Cyberscope," 1996).

Yet, silence isn't always comforting. It is sometimes used to disconfirm others. In some families, children are disciplined by being ignored. No matter what the child says or does, parents refuse to acknowledge his or her existence. In later life, the silencing strategy may also surface. You know how disconfirming silence can be if you've ever said "Hello" to someone and did not receive a reply. Even if the other person didn't deliberately ignore you, you feel slighted. We sometimes deliberately freeze out intimates and refuse to answer e-mails from friends with whom we're angry.

Organizations such as military academies and religious groups use silencing or excommunication to punish those who err or disobey. It is a powerful way to strip someone of personhood.

The complex system of nonverbal communication includes kinesics, haptics, physical appearance, artifacts, environmental factors, proxemics, chronemics, paralanguage, and silence. In the final section of this chapter, we consider guidelines for improving the effectiveness of our nonverbal communication.

Student Voices

Michael:

Silencing is the cruellest thing you can do to a person. That was how my parents disciplined all of us. They told us we were bad and then refused to speak to us—sometimes for several hours. I can't describe how awful it felt to get no response from them, to be a nonperson. I would have preferred physical punishment. I'll never use silencing with my kids.

GUIDELINES FOR IMPROVING NONVERBAL COMMUNICATION

The following guidelines should decrease the chance that you will misunderstand others' nonverbal behaviours or that others will misperceive yours.

CONCEPTS AT A GLANCE

Guidelines for Improving Nonverbal Communication

- Monitor your nonverbal communication.
- Be tentative when interpreting others' nonverbal communication.
- Consider the person.
- Consider the context.
- Use *I* language when interpreting nonverbal communication.

Monitor Your Nonverbal Communication

Think about the previous discussion of ways we use nonverbal behaviours to announce our identities. Are you projecting the image you desire? Do friends ever tell you that you seem uninterested or far away when they are talking to you? If so, you can monitor your nonverbal actions so that you convey greater involvement and interest in conversations.

Have you set up your living and working spaces so that they invite the kind of interaction you prefer, or are they arranged to interfere with good communication? Paying attention to nonverbal dimensions of your world can empower you to use them more effectively to achieve your interpersonal goals.

Be Tentative When Interpreting Others' Nonverbal Communication

Although stores are filled with popular advice books that promise to show you how to read nonverbal communication, there really aren't any sure-fire formulas. It's naive to think we can precisely decode something that is as complex and ambiguous as nonverbal communication. When we believe that we can, we risk misjudging others.

While people attach meaning to nonverbal behaviours, it's important to realize these are only generalizations about conclusions that people draw. We have not and cannot state what any particular behaviour means to specific individuals in a given context. For instance, we've said that satisfied couples tend to sit closer together than unhappy couples. As a general rule, this is true, at least in Western societies. However, sometimes very contented couples prefer autonomy and like to keep distance between them some of the time. In addition, someone may maintain distance because of a cold and not wanting a partner to catch it.

Be tentative when interpreting nonverbal communication.

In work settings, people who don't look at us may be preoccupied with solving a problem and do not intend to ignore us. Different cultures teach members different rules for expressing and interpreting nonverbal behaviour (Matsumoto et al., 2002). Because nonverbal communication is ambiguous and personal, we should not assume we can interpret it with absolute precision. Effective communicators qualify interpretations of nonverbal communication with awareness of personal and contextual factors.

Consider the Person

Generalizations about nonverbal behaviour tell us only what is generally the case. They don't tell us about the exceptions to the rule. Nonverbal patterns that accurately describe most people may not apply to particular individuals. Although eye contact generally indicates responsiveness in Western culture, some individuals close their eyes or look down to concentrate when listening. In such cases, it would be inaccurate to conclude a person who doesn't look at us isn't listening. Similarly, people who cross their arms and have a rigid posture are often expressing hostility or lack of interest in interaction. However, the same behaviours might mean a person is cold and trying to conserve body heat. Many people use less inflection, fewer gestures, and a slack posture when they're not really interested in a conversation. However, we all exhibit these same behaviours when we are tired.

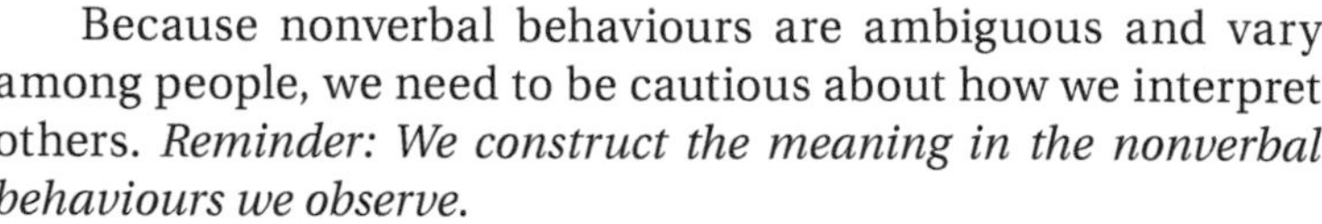

Because nonverbal behaviours are ambiguous and vary among people, we need to be cautious about how we interpret others. *Reminder: We construct the meaning in the nonverbal behaviours we observe.*

Consider the Context

Our nonverbal communication reflects not only how we see ourselves but how we feel. In addition, it reflects the various settings we inhabit. Most people are more at ease on their own turf than on someone else's, so we tend to be friendlier and more outgoing in our homes than in business meetings and public places.

We also dress according to context. Students who see professors in professional clothing on campus are often surprised to see them in jeans or running clothes at home or in town. Like everyone, professors dress differently for various occasions and contexts.

Immediate physical setting is not the only context that affects nonverbal communication. As we have seen, all communication, including the nonverbal dimension, reflects the values and understandings of particular cultures (Andersen et al., 2002). We are likely to misinterpret people from other cultures when we impose the norms and rules of our own.

Even in our own country, we have diverse speech communities, and each has its own rules for nonverbal behaviour. We run the risk of misinterpreting men if we judge them by the norms of feminine speech communities. A man who doesn't make "listening noises" may well be listening intently according to the rules of masculine speech communities. Similarly, men often misperceive women as agreeing when they nod and make listening noises while another is talking. According to feminine speech communities, ongoing feedback is a way to signal interest, not necessarily approval.

We should try to adopt a dual perspective when interpreting others, especially when different social groups are involved. We can become more effective nonverbal communicators if we monitor our own nonverbal behaviours and qualify our interpretation of others by keeping personal and contextual considerations in mind.

Student Voices

Mei-Ling:

I often have been misinterpreted in this country. My first semester here, a professor told me he wanted me to be more assertive and to speak up in class. I could not do that, I told him. He said I should put myself forward, but I have been brought up not to do that. In Taiwan, that is very rude and ugly, and all of us are taught not to speak up to teachers. Now that I have been here for three years, I sometimes speak in classes, but I am still more quiet than Canadian students. I know my professors think I am not so smart because I am quiet, but that is the teaching of my country.

Apply the Idea

USING *I* LANGUAGE ABOUT NONVERBAL BEHAVIOURS

I language makes communication about nonverbal behaviours more responsible and clear. Practise the skill of translating you language into *I* language to describe nonverbal behaviour.

Example:

You language: You're staring at me.
I language: When you look at me so intensely, I feel uneasy.

CONVERT YOU LANGUAGE TO I LANGUAGE

I hate it when you give me that know-it-all look. ____________________
I can tell you don't believe me by your expression. ____________________
Don't crowd me. ____________________
Your T-shirt is offensive. ____________________

Chapter Summary

In this chapter, we've explored the fascinating world beyond words. We began by noting both the similarities and the differences between verbal and nonverbal communication. Next, we discussed how nonverbal communication functions to supplement or replace verbal messages, to regulate interaction, and often to establish relationship-level meanings.

We discussed nine types of nonverbal communication. These are kinesics (face and body motion), haptics (use of touch), physical appearance, artifacts, environmental factors, proxemics (use of space), chronemics (use of and orientations to time), paralanguage, and silence. Each type of nonverbal communication reflects cultural understandings and values and also expresses our personal identities and feelings toward others. In this sense, nonverbal communication has a theatrical dimension because it is a primary way we create and present images of ourselves.

Because nonverbal communication, like its verbal cousin, is symbolic, it has no inherent meaning that is fixed for all time. Instead, its meaning is something we construct as we notice, organize, and interpret nonverbal behaviours that we and others enact. Effectiveness requires that we learn to monitor our own nonverbal communication and to exercise caution in interpreting that of others.

Key Concepts

- artifacts
- chronemics
- environmental racism
- haptics
- kinesics
- nonverbal communication
- paralanguage
- proxemics

For Further Thought and Discussion

1. Think about the information on lawyers' nonverbal communication provided earlier in the "Kinesics" section. What ethical issues are involved in lawyers' use of nonverbal behaviours in an effort to influence jurors? What ethical issues are involved in judges' restrictions of lawyers' nonverbal communication? Is this a violation of the right to free speech?
2. Visit six restaurants near your campus. Describe the seating arrangements, lighting, music (if any), distance between tables, and the colours used in the decor. Do you find any relationship between nonverbal communication patterns and the expensiveness of restaurants?
3. Read an online journal that is devoted exclusively to research on haptic communication: *Haptics-e* at www.haptics-e.org.
4. Describe the spatial arrangements in the family in which you grew up. How large was your home? How many people lived there? Did each member of the family have his or her own bedroom? Did anyone in the family have a separate work or hobby room or a special chair in which others did not sit? Did the proxemic patterns in your home reflect status differences among family members?
5. Use your InfoTrac® College Edition to skim articles and advertisements in *Better Homes and Gardens*, which has a predominantly White readership, and *Essence*, which has a predominantly Black readership. How many articles and advertisements that focus on weight (losing it, controlling it) do you find in each of these magazines? What can you conclude about different racial groups' views of weight?

6. Is it ethical to interpret others' nonverbal communication without recognizing their cultural perspective? If not, how does doing this reflect unethical behaviour and/or attitudes?
7. Founded in 1997, the Center for Nonverbal Studies is located in Spokane, Washington, and La Jolla, California. It publishes *The Nonverbal Dictionary of Gestures, Signs, and Body Language Cues* and presents essays on nonverbal behaviours by anthropologists, archeologists, biologists, linguists, and communication scholars. Although the full dictionary was not yet available when this book was written, you can read selected entries, complete with usage notes and research references, on the center's website at center-for-nonverbal-studies.org.
8. What does silence mean to you? Does its meaning differ in various contexts? What do you mean when you are silent? Do you ever use silence strategically?
9. For thousands of years, colours have been used in Oriental rugs to represent important religious and cultural concepts. For instance, blue symbolizes truth or solitude; green, sacred; and yellow, power or glory. Learn more about the history or Oriental rugs and the significance of the use of colours and symbols by visiting www.arearugfacts.com/parts_of_a_rug_design.php.
10. Use your InfoTrac® College Edition to skim articles and advertisements in two Canadian magazines. How many articles and advertisements that focus on weight (losing, controlling) do you find in each of these magazines? What can you conclude about the body image of men and women in Canada? Are there ethnic differences?
11. Use your InfoTrac® College Edition to review the tables of contents for the last four issues of *Environmental Action Magazine*. Is the topic of environmental justice (also called *environmental racism*) discussed in any of the issues? Do you find any recent reports on patterns in location of toxic waste dumps and other environmental dangers?

Chapter 7

Cultural Diversity and Communication

Human diversity makes tolerance more than a virtue; it makes it a requirement for survival.

—Rene Dubos (1981)

I know there is strength in the differences between us. I know there is comfort where we overlap.

—Ani DiFranco (1994)

© iStockphoto.com/Lorado

Local businesses and property owners perceive graffiti as a serious and pervasive urban blight. It engenders community fear as a sign of criminal and gang activity; it is an eyesore that gives a neighbourhood a bad image. Ryan has a different perspective. He considers himself a graffiti artist. He uses his medium to do more than just vandalize public buildings; it's his way of objecting to oppressive social and economic control by waging a cultural war and declaring independence from society's restrictions. He is serious about his work and creates large, carefully executed, intricate, and detailed designs that will bring him respect from other artists. He and his artist friends search out buildings that are suited to their purpose of being visible to as many people as possible, thus reaching a wide audience.

The graffiti artists and the owners of these buildings clearly have different values and beliefs about this situation. Most people grow up assuming that their values and beliefs are better. Is there any awareness of each other's meanings or motivations in this case? In what ways is the viewpoint of each misread or misunderstood? How can such a strong cultural gap be bridged?

THINKING LIKE AN ANTHROPOLOGIST

In this chapter, we will reflect on cultural diversity and the wide variations of human behaviours, values, and beliefs. This is vitally important in a world of increasing connection and interaction that requires us to be informed and responsible citizens of the world. Even when we are not travelling abroad, we increasingly encounter people from other cultures in our home communities. By learning to free ourselves from provincial and ethnocentric thinking, we can develop the mind-set and communication skills to appreciate the richness and value of other people's points of view. **Cultural anthropology** describes and seeks to explain similarities and differences in thought and behaviour among groups of humans.

On the way to reaching our goals, we will use the following questions from cultural anthropology (Omohundro, 2008) in order to consider and understand transcultural communication:

1. What is culture? Subculture? Ethnic group?
2. How does the context of people's lives influence their communication?
3. How does culture affect individualistic interactions and relationships?
4. How do we understand cultural characteristics in communication?
5. How do we respond to these patterns?
6. How might we best accommodate differences in cross-cultural communication?

Once we have answered these questions, we will be better able to appreciate, respect, and interpret humanity in all its diversity. We will be able to increase our fluency and mobility in a multicultural world, in our personal lives, and in our work.

Culture is the learned and shared understandings among a group of people about how to behave and what has meaning in our lives. Culture forms the pattern of our lives and guides how we think, feel, act, and communicate (Lee, 2000; Omohundro, 2008). The influence of culture is so pervasive that it's hard to realize how powerfully it shapes our perceptions.

Subculture is a particular mix of shared understandings held by groups within a larger society. What distinguishes one subculture from another in a society might be language, dress, religion, work habits, food preferences, and child-rearing practices, to mention just a few. People engaged in fishing in the Canadian Maritimes, home-schooling, and vegetarianism represent some of these subcultures. Other subcultures derive from common residence location, work, or interests, such as graffiti artists in urban areas or pipeline industry workers in Alberta. Subcultures include different ethnic groups and social classes of differing ages, genders religious and spiritual beliefs, and professions, and even groups with specific issues common to each member, such as cancer survivor support groups.

Communication Notes

EBONICS

A word has been coined to identify the language of the Black community as a unique speech community. What was termed "Black English" is now called "Ebonics," a blend of the words "ebony," meaning *black*, and "phonics," the *sounds of speech*. Children from Black communities, such as one near Halifax, Nova Scotia, are provided language support in English classes because they are regarded as coming from a different language culture. Standard English or "the Queen's English" is only a dialect.

Author Alice Travis (2007) states, "Studies have repeatedly demonstrated that immigrants who have mastered their native languages in standard form are advantaged in learning Standard English. Dialect speakers are severely disadvantaged in acquiring fluency in English because of a lack of familiarity with formal grammatical constructs. The traditional pedagogical approach to teaching Standard English to speakers of Ebonics has been to apply different rules to students academically handicapped by Black English as their first language.

Many school districts treat Ebonics as a sacrosanct cultural trait while requiring students who speak other foreign languages to enrol in English as a Second Language courses. Such classes are not mandatory for Black English speakers, widening the racial achievement gap as students move through elementary and secondary grades."

An **ethnic group** functions within society to maintain a subculture based on religion, language, common origin, or ancestral traditions. Typically, an ethnic group invests effort to distinguish itself from others in the wider society. In North America, First Nations people are renewing their commitment to learning and preserving their languages and traditions. Francophones in Canada are very aware of their group identity, and they devote energy to fostering awareness of their distinctiveness. *Little Mosque on the Prairie* and *Monsoon House* are two examples of media programs that bring greater visibility to the growing diversity in Canada.

Adolescence as an Example of a Subculture

Adolescence comprises its own distinct subculture, or more descriptively, *counter-culture*. The hormonal changes during this period bring about enormous shifts in

Communication Notes

DIVERSITY IN CANADA

Canada's 32 million inhabitants reflect a cultural, ethnic, and linguistic makeup found nowhere else on earth. Data from the 2006 census show that more than 200 different ethnic origins are currently reported, indicating that the Canadian population is increasingly diverse (*Multiculturalism Act*). According to projections, this trend will continue. These changes present new challenges as the needs of Canadians also change with the diverse population. (See Figure 7.1).

body size, shape, and sexual and brain development. In general, early adolescence is characterized by a growing ability to use abstract thought; social and emotional growth, including awareness of others; increasing development of a sense of fairness, social consciousness, purpose, and personal identity (Who am I?); peer bonding; separation from family; sudden, intense emotions; and a strong sense of recognition of no longer being a child but still not yet fully an adult.

Of course, collectively, teenagers are in fact the replacement generation that eventually inherits the world that the previous generation has created. They begin to try on more adult roles and can now put "brain power" behind the prior decade of learning communication skills, physical mastery, and emotional awareness. By rejecting the old ways, they seek to re-create reality as a clearer reflection of themselves. The 1960s is an example of this. The so-called "hippie" generation collectively changed the Western world with defiant protests against war, sexism, and racism; a focus on back-to-earth mentality; and experimentation with mind-altering substances and sexual

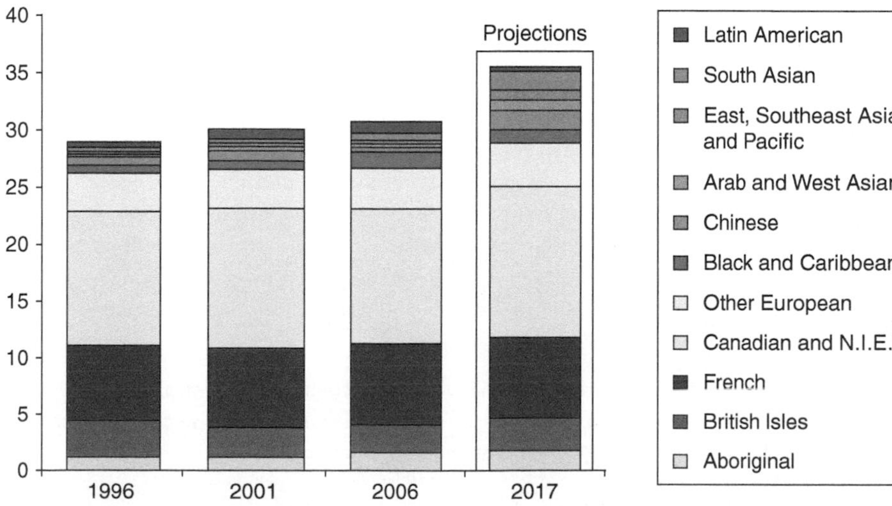

FIGURE 7.1

The Cultural Mosaic of Canada

Source: Citizenship and Immigration Canada. *Annual Report on the Operation of the Canadian Multiculturalism Act.* 2007–2008, "Diversity in Canada 1996–2006 and 2017 projections."

*not included elsewhere

"freedom." Feminism, diversity recognition, and awareness of the world as a "global village"; the "green revolution"; as well as the AIDS epidemic, all ensued. In contrast, children born in the new millennium will begin to reach their teens in 2013. How will they construct the values of their generation?

Reflective Exercise

What are some of the unique characteristics of your generation as they pertain to the following?

Food ____________________

Fashion ____________________

Science and technology____________________

Social networking____________________

Travel ____________________

Threats to health____________________

How might your parents answer these questions? Would their answers have been different when they were your age?

Communication Notes

ADOLESCENT CHARACTERISTICS

Recent brain research explains more about how adolescents learn. Dr. Jay Giedd is a neuroscientist at the National Institute of Mental Health in the United States and one of the pioneers in brain research using magnetic resonance imaging (MRI). After noting that there is "exuberant growth" of brain cells during the prepuberty years and then a "pruning" time during adolescence, Dr. Giedd and others hypothesize that stimulating brain activity during these years is critical (California Department of Education):

> The capacity to be skilled in many different areas is building up during those times.... But the pruning-down phase is perhaps even more interesting, because our leading hypothesis for that is the "Use it or lose it" principle. Those cells and connections that are used will survive and flourish. Those cells and connections that are not used will wither and die. So if a teen is doing music or sports or academics, those are the cells and connections that will be hard-wired. If the teen is lying on the couch or playing video games or watching MTV, those are the cells and connections that are going [to] survive.

In short, for students to learn to think critically, solve complex problems, and be successful with a wide variety of tasks, schools must challenge them to practise complex tasks and strengthen the brain's capacity to engage in those thinking activities.

Characteristics of a Culture

There are seven primary characteristics of a culture. It is (1) integrated; (2) a product of history; (3) changing; (4) strengthened by values; (5) an influence on behaviours; (6) symbolically transmitted; and (7) unique, complex, and variable. There is widespread consensus among anthropologists that these seven characteristics describe all cultural groups. In order for a culture to be sustained, interdependence among its members is necessary; each person contributes to the culture through beliefs and behaviours.

There are also numerous interactions and relationships among the many facets of a society, a country, or a group. No culture is static. What affects one member will set off a ripple effect to others, and changes in one area can bring about changes in another. One example of this is how the violent opposition to apartheid in South Africa in the 1980s resulted in major changes toward multiracial democracy. This was reflected in the election of Nelson Mandela as the first Black president in that country. To what extent do you think the election of Barack Obama in 2008 in the United States also reflects changes toward a multiracial democracy?

Another example is how the global increase in environmental awareness has brought new economic opportunities in such directions as transportation (hybrid and battery-operated vehicles), education (curriculum that includes the three Rs—reduce, reuse, recycle), "green" jobs (such as organic farming and energy-efficient construction work), and energy consumption (alternatives such as water, wind, and solar power instead of reliance on fossil fuels). Languages can also reflect these changes, as when "garbage disposal" becomes "waste resource management."

When there is contact with other cultures, changes can sometimes occur rapidly, as in the case of September 11, 2001, when the clash of cultures literally exploded in the face of America as the World Trade Center Towers collapsed, allegedly at the hands of the al Qaeda. Or when explorers and missionaries colonized the "new worlds," and European diseases became rampant among indigenous populations, upsetting their delicate balance of health and wiping out entire villages.

Values and the acceptance of what is considered important, good and bad, or right and wrong can determine how a society functions together to promote itself. A belief in similar standards or morals can produce behaviour that adds to the cohesiveness of the whole. Jewish cultures, for example, centre around the synagogue and religious rites of passage.

Symbols and symbolic objects and actions carry an agreed-upon meaning within a culture. While a cross may denote a Christian belief, a pentacle might refer to Wiccan traditions. In Canada, the maple leaf symbolizes the country, and in most places, a pictogram of a woman or a man on a door in a public place indicates a gendered toilet facility. On roads, vehicles stop at intersections marked by red lights or octagonal signs. The action of winking can indicate levity, flirtatiousness, or a shared inside joke, depending on the context. Language itself is a symbolic communication, as we learned in Chapter 5.

A culture is also affected by climate and geography. Coastal fishing villages, desert nomads, equatorial tribes, and polar communities will each have different historical traditions, styles of apparel, and diet and nutrition.

Globalization has brought about awareness that the perception of societies as discreet, unrelated units is an outmoded notion. Like the food we eat that crosses continents and oceans, and the air we breathe that circulates the planet, we cannot escape our connections with each other.

CONCEPTS AT A GLANCE

The Seven Characteristics of Cultures

1. Cultures are integrated.
2. Cultures are products of history.
3. Cultures can be changed, and they can cause change.
4. Cultures are strengthened by values.
5. Cultures are powerful influences on behaviour.
6. Cultures are largely composed of and transmitted by symbols.
7. Cultures are unique in their complexity and variability.

Communication Notes

COMMUNICATING IN A MULTICULTURAL WORLD

Communicating effectively with diverse people begins with learning metacommunication, that is, how people in different cultures view communication and actually practise it. One excellent resource for learning more is the website of the Society for Cross-Cultural Research (www.sccr.org). In addition to presenting a wealth of good information, this site provides links to many other intercultural communication sources.

Nonverbal Communication Reflects and Expresses Cultural Values

In Chapter 6, we noted that nonverbal communication is similar to verbal communication in expressing cultural values. Like verbal communication, nonverbal patterns reflect specific cultures. This implies that most nonverbal behaviour is not instinctive but learned in the process of socialization. In addition to diversity among groups in our country, nonverbal behaviours vary from one country to another. As you might expect, dissimilarities reflect distinct cultural values.

Have you ever seen the bumper sticker "If you can read this, you're too close"? That slogan proclaims North Americans' fierce territoriality. We prize private space and we resent—and sometimes fight—anyone who trespasses on what we consider our turf. The German culture also emphasizes private space. Germans often build walls and hedges to insulate themselves from neighbours. In other cultures, people are less territorial. For instance, many Brazilians stand close together in shops, buses, and elevators, and when they bump into one another, they don't apologize or draw back (Andersen et al, 2002; Wiemann & Harrison, 1983). In many Middle Eastern countries, men often walk with their arms around other men, but in North America, touching between male friends is uncommon except during sports events.

Norms for touching also reflect cultural values. In one study, North Americans, who are relatively reserved, were observed engaging in an average of only two touches an hour. The emotionally restrained British averaged zero touches an hour. Parisians, long known for their emotional expressiveness, touched 110 times an hour. Puerto Ricans touched most, averaging 180 touches an hour (Knapp, 1972). Iraqis don't want or expect the amount of personal space that most Americans do and, in fact, consider it offensive if one steps or leans away from a male. To help American soldiers stationed in Iraq, the Marine Corps distributes the *Iraq Culture Smart Card*, which include advice such as never touch another person with your left hand do not expose the soles of your shoes or feet ("Word for Word," 2005).

arabianEye/Getty Images

Patterns of eye contact also reflect cultural values. In North America, frankness and assertion are valued, so meeting another's eyes is considered appropriate and a demonstration of personal honesty. Eye contact is also valued among most Hispanics. Yet, in many Asian and northern European countries, direct eye contact is considered abrasive and disrespectful (Axtell, 1990a, 1990b; Hall, 1968; Samovar & Porter, 2000). In Brazil, on the other hand, eye contact often is so intense that many North Americans consider it rude. Imagine the confusion this causes in intercultural business negotiations!

Cultural training also influences which emotions we express and how we express them (Matsumoto et al., 2002). For example, many people raised in traditional Italian and Jewish communities are more emotionally expressive than people raised in English or German communities. In Japan and many other Asian cultures, it is generally considered rude to express negative feelings toward others. In North America, the display of negative feelings is less constrained.

Student Voices

Diana:

I was so uncomfortable when I travelled to Mexico last year. People just crammed into buses, even when all the seats were taken. They pushed up together and pressed against each other. I felt they were really being rude, and I was uptight about having people on top of me like that. I guess it was a learned cultural difference, but it sure made me uneasy at the time. I never knew how territorial I was until I felt my space was being invaded.

Communication Notes

HANDSHAKES AROUND THE WORLD

Although the handshake is one of the most commonly known haptic symbols, its duration and style varies across cultural settings. Handshakes also take different forms and meanings in a business setting than in a social setting.

Generally in North America, a good firm handshake, where the webs of each person's hand touch, is an appropriate way to close a business deal. In fact, a handshake is a common business gesture internationally.

However, in social settings, the handshake varies widely. Latin cultures are more open to frequent touching and, as a result, their greetings often go beyond the conventional handshake and may include expressive embraces and kissing of the air beside the cheek. In Mexico, greetings often include smiles, nods, and friendly handshakes. A firm handshake is preferred in Germany, while in France, handshakes tend to be light and quick. In Japan, the traditional greeting is a bow, not a handshake.

Each form of handshake or greeting reflects the culture's values and must be recognized. Consider what the implications are for multinational corporation team-building, for example, and for negotiation strategies for various purposes when culturally different groups are involved!

For more information about the customs of various countries related to their business practices and social interaction, go to faculty.css.edu/dswenson/web/CULTURE/CULTMAPS.HTM.

Cultural Differences Regarding Conflict

The majority of Mediterranean cultures regard conflict as a normal, valuable part of everyday life. In these cultures, people routinely argue and wrangle, and nobody gets upset or angry. In France and in Arabic countries, men debate one another for the sheer fun of it. It doesn't matter who wins the debate—the argument itself is enjoyable (Copeland & Griggs, 1985). Many Hispanic cultures also regard conflict as both normal and interesting. Because Hispanic cultures tend to value emotions, conflicts are opportunities for emotional expression.

Chinese people have a very different view of conflict. Yan Bing Zhang, Jake Harwood, and Mary Hummert (2005) asked Chinese adults to evaluate transcripts in which an older worker criticized a younger worker. Older participants in this study favoured an accommodating style that emphasized relational harmony. Younger adults preferred a problem-solving style, emphasizing assertiveness and cooperation, or they perceived the two styles as being equally desirable. Both groups had less positive perceptions of the avoiding style, which was perceived as disrespectful of others, and the competing style, which was regarded as being driven by self-interest. In contrast, many Westerners prefer the competing style (Bergstrom & Nussbaum, 1996).

Mainstream culture in North America emphasizes assertiveness and individuality, so many Westerners are competitive and reluctant to give in to others. In more communal societies, people have less individualistic perspectives and are less likely to focus on winning conflicts (Ting-Toomey, 1991; Vanyperen & Buunk, 1991). In Japan and many other Asian cultures, open disagreement is strongly condemned (Gangwish, 1999), and great effort is made to avoid winning at the cost of causing another person to lose face (Rowland, 1985; Weiss, 1987). In Japanese sports, the ideal is not for one team to win but for a tie to occur so that neither team loses face. When there is to be a winner, Japanese athletes try to win by only a slim margin so that the losing team is not humiliated (Ferrante, 1992, p. 102).

Listening competence includes being sensitive to differences in listening and speaking styles. Because others may speak and listen differently than we do, we shouldn't automatically impose our rules and interpretations on them. Instead, we should try to understand and respect their styles. By exercising dual perspective, we are more likely to listen effectively to others on their terms.

APPROACHES TO THE STUDY OF CULTURES

In general, cultural diversity has been studied by focusing on cultural values and cultural practices. This is termed an *aggregate approach*. The field of cross-cultural management has been dominated by research on cultural values. In recent years, another approach has emphasized analysis of cultural practices at the individualistic level. A person is a conduit through which all environmental influences flow—cultural, subcultural, and ethnic.

Aggregate Approach

Edward Hall and Geert Hofstede are examples of researchers using a values-based approach to culture, drawing from an anthropological tradition emphasizing both the identification and classification of core cultural values. These authors have developed typologies of various countries' cultural values and include such dimensions as power orientation, individualism, and time orientation.

Time is an aspect of our lives that takes on very different meanings in different cultures. Hall (1983), an anthropologist, found that the cross-cultural experience of time varied enormously. In Northern Europe, most of North America, and Japan, people organize time as separate items—one thing at a time. In North America, for many of us, our social and business lives, even our sex lives, are commonly schedule-dominated. We speak of time being spent, wasted, or lost. On the other hand, Mediterranean and Latin American cultures model time as an involvement in several things at once. Time in these cultures stresses the involvement of people and the completion of transactions—schedules seem to be in a constant state of flux.

Consider a few aspects of modern Western culture that influence our perceptions. Western culture emphasizes technology and its offspring, speed. Most Westerners expect things to happen fast, almost instantly. Whether it's instant photos, accessing websites, or one-hour dry cleaning, we live at an accelerated pace (Wood, 2000a). We text-message friends, we jet across the country, and we microwave meals. In countries such as Nepal and Mexico, life often proceeds at a more leisurely pace, and people spend more time talking, relaxing, and engaging in low-key activities.

Communication Notes

CULTURAL VIEWS OF TIME

North Americans and Germans differ in the time they invest in work (Benjamin & Horwitz, 1994). The typical job in Germany requires 37 hours per week, with a minimum of five weeks' paid leave annually, guaranteed by law. Stores close on weekends and on four of five weeknights so that workers can have leisure time. In the United States, jobs typically require 44 to 80 hours per week, and many workers can't take more than a week's leave at a time.

Further, many North Americans take second jobs even when their first jobs allow a comfortable standard of living. Germans can't understand this, remarking that "Free time can't be paid for." Personal time is considered so precious in Germany that it is illegal to work more than one job during holidays, which are meant to allow people to restore themselves.

Some cultures have monochronic orientations toward time while others have polychronic orientations. Monochronic (one time) cultures, such as Canada, view time as a valuable commodity to be saved, scheduled and carefully guarded. In monochronic cultures, punctuality and efficiency are valued. Thus, people are expected to be on time for appointments and classes, and they are expected to complete work quickly (Hall, 1976; Honoré, 2004, 2005).

In contrast, polychronic (many times) cultures take a more holistic, systemic view of time. Members of these cultures assume that many things are happening simultaneously. Thus, punctuality is seldom stressed. Meetings may start late, with people joining in after discussions begin. Tangential discussions and social conversations are part of normal meetings in polychronic cultures. People may even cancel meetings without the dramatic reasons expected for cancelling in monochronic cultures.

The belief that time is holistic leads members of polychronic cultures to assume that the rhythms of life—working, socializing, attending to personal matters—are interrelated and often overlapping. A faculty member at a U.S.

Student Voices

Louanne:

When I first came to the city to attend college, I thought I had come to a different planet. I had grown up on a reservation of 300 people and even though I understood there would be many adjustments, I wasn't prepared for everyone's preoccupation with time and being "on time." Everyone seemed anxious. They were always in a hurry. Coming late to a class or a meeting was unheard of. In my village, no one berated someone for being late like they do here. There was trust that everything would get done in time. I hated that first year of college.

university discovered how differently cultures view time when he accepted a teaching position in Brazil (Levine, 1988). Some of his students didn't show up until halfway through the class period, and many students were in no hurry to leave when the class ended. Instead, they wanted to stay to ask questions and discuss ideas.

Hall (1976) also described societies as having "high" or "low" context distinctions, creating broad cultural differences. ***High context*** refers to societies or groups with close connections over a long period of time, and where relationships are more important than tasks. Great emphasis is put on holistic understanding of meanings. Words themselves have little meaning until placed in the context of particular people, relationships, and histories. Many aspects of behaviour are not made explicit because most members know what to do and what to think from years of interaction with each other (family gatherings, long-standing group membership, childhood friendships), and much of the information is gleaned from nonverbal or environmental cues.

Low context refers to societies and groups where people tend to have many connections but of shorter duration or for some specific reason. In these societies, cultural behaviour and beliefs tend to be more explicit, rule-oriented, and task-centred. They may need to be spelled out explicitly so that those coming into the cultural environment know how to behave. The content level of meaning is given greater priority. Words and literal meaning are emphasized. Examples of low-context groups include groups of passengers at large airports, patrons in a cafeteria, spectators at a sports events, or participants in a study groups. North America is considered to have mainly low-context cultures, whereas many Asian cultures are more high-context ones (Hall, 1976; Lim, 2002).

While these terms are sometimes useful in describing some aspects of a culture, one can never say a culture is "high" or "low," because all societies contain both modes. These terms are more useful to describe and understand particular situations and environments ("Culture at Work").

Dutch academic Geert Hofstede developed markers that reflect the national cultural characteristics or dimensions of a given country. These cultural differences describe averages or tendencies and not characteristics of individuals. His "5D" model includes five major dimensions: power distance; individualism; masculinity; uncertainty avoidance; and time orientation (Hofstede, 1991, 2001).

Power distance (high versus low) describes how a society handles inequalities, and is defined by Hofstede as "the extent to which the less powerful members of institutions and organizations within a country expect and accept that power is distributed unequally." This dimension represents inequality as it is defined from below, not from above. It suggests that a society's level of inequality is endorsed by the followers as much as by the leaders. In low power distance nations such as the United Kingdom, inequalities among people will tend to be minimized, decentralization of activities is more likely, subordinates expect to be consulted by superiors, and privileges and status symbols are less evident. Conversely, in high power distance nations, inequalities among people are considered desirable. There is greater reliance by the less powerful on those who hold power, centralization of power is more normal, and subordinates are likely to be separated from their bosses by wide differentials in salary, privileges, and status symbols.

Individualism versus its opposite, **collectivism**, is the degree to which individuals are integrated into groups. On the individualistic side, we find societies in which the ties between individuals are loose; everyone is expected to look after oneself and one's immediate family. Individualistic goals and achievements are encouraged, and individual rights are seen as most important. Rules promote independence, choices, and freedom of speech. Canada, the United States, Australia, and Ireland are countries with generally individualistic cultures.

On the collectivist side, we find societies in which people from birth onward are integrated into strong, cohesive in-groups, often extended families. Continued and ongoing protection is provided in exchange for unquestioning loyalty. Each person is expected to conform, to do what is best for the group, and to avoid expressing opinions that go against it. Rules promote order, obedience, and cooperation with others. Japan, Egypt, Greece, and Brazil have largely collectivist cultures.

While Canada is largely an individualistic culture in which personal initiative is expected and rewarded, other cultures, particularly many Asian ones, are more collectivist, and identity is defined in terms of one's family, rather than as an individualistic quality. Because families are more valued in collectivist cultures, elders are given greater respect and care in those cultures.

Communication Notes

COLLECTIVIST AND INDIVIDUALISTIC CHILD-CARE PRACTICES

The difference between collectivist and individualistic cultures is evident in child-care practices. More communal countries have policies that reflect the value they place on families. In every developed country except the United States, new parents, including adoptive parents, are given at least six weeks of paid parental leave (Wood, 1994d). In Canada, since December 31, 2000, maternity and parental leave with Employment Insurance benefits has been extended to 50 weeks (15 weeks maternity and 35 weeks parental). Parental leave can be shared by the parenting partners.

Check out the Human Resources and Skills Development Canada website for particulars: www.hrsdc.gc.ca. On the site's home page, enter "parental and adoption leaves" in the search window and then scroll down to the same words in the resulting list.

Masculinity refers to the distribution of roles between the genders and pertains to societies in which social gender roles are clearly distinct. Its opposite, *femininity*, pertains to societies in which social gender roles overlap and tend to be more androgynous. The extent to which a culture is conducive to dominance, assertiveness, and acquisition of things indicates masculinity, while a culture that is more conducive to people, feelings, and the quality of life indicates femininity.

In a masculine society such as the United Kingdom, there is a division of labour where the more assertive tasks are given to men. There is a stress on academic success, competition, and achievement in careers. According to Hofstede (2001), in a feminine society such as France, the emphasis is on relationships, compromise, life skills, and social performance. The last 10 to 15 years have seen changes toward a "feminization" process to the behaviour of Western democracies.

The characteristic of **uncertainty avoidance** deals with society's tolerance for uncertainty and ambiguity; it indicates to what extent a culture programs its members to feel either uncomfortable or comfortable in unstructured situations. Unstructured situations are novel, unknown, surprising, or different from the usual. In order to avoid uncertainty, cultures try to minimize the possibility of such situations by strict laws and rules, along with safety and security measures. People in countries that avoid uncertainty are also more emotional and motivated by inner nervous energy. The opposite types, *uncertainty acceptance* cultures, are more tolerant of different opinions; they try to have as few rules as possible. These cultures are more indifferent and contemplative, and not so disposed to express emotions.

The fifth dimension, **long-term orientation,** versus *short-term orientation*, describes the degree to which a society does or does not value long-term commitments and respect for tradition. Long-term traditions and commitments tend to hamper institutional change and include values oriented toward the future, such as thrift, industriousness, and perseverance, as opposed to short-term values, such as fulfilling social obligations, living for the day, and protecting one's "face" (Hofstede, 1980, 2001; Longatan, 2008).

Individualistic Approach

In Chapter 2, we saw how our individualistic sense of *self* develops from the cultural environment in which we are raised. We learn to adapt our behaviour in order to survive and thrive in the surroundings in which we find ourselves. The ethnic background of our parents and the social class to which we belong affect our sense of self. We are strongly influenced in the creation of self by the many facets of our culture.

What are our possible responses to others who are culturally diverse or different from us? We need to navigate the twin misconceptions of "we are all the same" and "we are each unique." As we explore the richness and intense effect of culture on the construction of self, the implications of cultural diversity on communication will become more evident. See aces1 comments below.

In the individualistic approach, each person has a unique, psychological "fingerprint" that makes everyone different. Consequently, knowing whether a person comes from an individualistic culture may be less useful than knowing whether the person embraces individualistic beliefs and values. This psychological fingerprint is the complex set of memories, thoughts, ways of thinking, and feelings that we each have about the world around us (Earley & Mosakowski, 2004).

David Suzuki's Communication Notes feature, "A Japanese Canadian Perspective," also illuminates some of the assumptions we make about culture and the impact that culture has on our perceptions. Suzuki's experience is a good example of Earley & Mosakowski's (2004) individualistic approach to culture.

Student Voices

ACES1:

I do it (graffiti) cause it fun. also when im doing graff im in my own world where no one can bother me and all my problems are gone. when i had my college interview i took some of my pieces an told my tutor my inspiration is street art and she into that typa stuff so that shud be trill.

Communication Notes

A JAPANESE CANADIAN PERSPECTIVE

by David Suzuki

My genes can be traced in a direct line to Japan. I am a pure-blooded member of the Japanese race. And whenever I go there, I am always astonished to see the power of that biological connection. In subways in Tokyo, I catch familiar glimpses of the eyes, hairline, or smile of my Japanese relatives. Yet when those same people open their mouths to communicate, the vast cultural gulf that separates them from me becomes obvious: English is my language, Shakespeare is my literature, British history is what I learned, and Beethoven is my music.

Each time I visit Japan, I am reminded of how Canadian I am and how little the racial connection matters. I first visited Japan to attend the International Congress of Genetics in Tokyo. For the first time in my life, I was surrounded by people who all looked like me. While sitting in a train and looking at the reflections in the window, I found that it was hard to pick out my own image in the crowd. I had grown up in a Caucasian society in which I was a minority member. My whole sense of self had developed with that perspective of looking different. All my life I had wanted large eyes and brown hair so I could be like everyone else. Yet on that train, where I did fit in, I didn't like it.

Cultural Intelligence Quotient

Cultural intelligence (CQ) improves cultural understanding at an individual level (Earley & Mosakowski, 2004). Earley and Mosakowski proposed that if we understand why people from different backgrounds act as they do, we can improve how we relate to one another. These ideas stem largely from the field of psychology. They emphasize an aspect of intelligence as a person's capacity to solve problems and adapt to changing situations in cultural contexts.

In Chapter 4, we explored the concept of emotional intelligence (Goleman, 1995a) as distinct from the traditional academic skills often thought to underlie intelligence. Both emotional and cultural intelligence go beyond the traditional views of IQ as evaluating problem-solving, mathematical, or reading skills. Instead, they reflect how well people are able to empathize, work with, direct, and interact with other people.

In their examination of the influence of culture on emotional intelligence, Gangopadhyay and Mandal (2008) conclude that basic emotions are perceived similarly around the world, but display rules governing emotional expression vary from culture to culture.

Cultural intelligence is related to emotional intelligence, but it picks up where emotional intelligence leaves off. A person with high emotional intelligence grasps what makes us human and at the same time what makes each of us different from one another. A person with high cultural intelligence can somehow tease out of a person's or group's behaviour those features that would be true of all people and all groups, those peculiar to this person or this group. The vast realm that lies between those two poles is culture (Earley & Mosakowski, 2004).

Communication Notes

CULTURAL INTELLIGENCE

According to Earley & Mosakowski (2004), cultural intelligence has the following three dimensions:

Head: Rote learning about the beliefs, customs, and taboos of foreign cultures will never completely prepare a person for every situation that arises. However a newcomer will devise *learning strategies*. Although most people find it difficult to discover a point of entry into alien cultures, the very coherence of which can make them seem like separate, parallel worlds, an individual with high cognitive CQ notices clues to a culture's shared understandings.

Body: You cannot simply say that you understand another culture; your actions and demeanour must prove that you are ready to some extent to enter their world. Whether it's the way you shake hands or order a coffee, evidence of an ability to mirror the customs and gestures of the people around you will prove that you esteem them well enough to want to be like them. This won't happen if a person suffers from a deep-seated reservation about the called-for behaviour or lacks the physical poise to pull it off.

Heart: Adapting to a new culture involves overcoming obstacles and setbacks. People can do that only if they believe in their own efficacy. A person who doesn't believe himself or herself capable of understanding people from unfamiliar cultures will often give up after any efforts meet with hostility or incomprehension. By contrast, a person with high motivation will, upon confronting obstacles, setbacks, or even failure, reengage with greater vigour.

GUIDELINES FOR IMPROVING CULTURAL INTELLIGENCE

Diversity is the Canadian reality. It embraces a multitude of ethnicities, races, religions, languages, cultures and subcultures. The acknowledgement of this reality, however, demands a deliberate response. In recent years, at the constitutional, legal, and policy levels, that response has been very emphatic and dramatic. Diversity has become a dynamic concept that is redefining the Canadian social landscape (see Figure 7.2).

At the practical level we recognize that diversity is not only ethically correct, it is the law, it leads to personal enrichment, and it also makes good policy and business sense. We have many reasons to increase cultural competence in our communication. Figure 7.3 illustrates four perspectives.

Through interaction with others, we learn about experiences, values, customs, and lifestyles that differ from our own. In addition, we share our experiences and values with people who seem unlike us in certain ways. Through

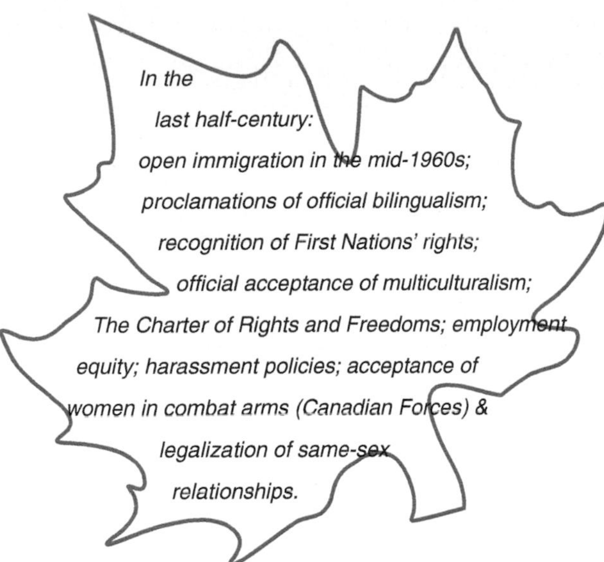

In the
last half-century:
open immigration in the mid-1960s;
proclamations of official bilingualism;
recognition of First Nations' rights;
official acceptance of multiculturalism;
The Charter of Rights and Freedoms; employment
equity; harassment policies; acceptance of
women in combat arms (Canadian Forces) &
legalization of same-sex
relationships.

FIGURE 7.2

Diversity has become a dynamic concept that is redefining the Canadian social landscape.

interaction, people come to understand their differences and similarities, and this fosters personal growth. Friendships between people with different cultural backgrounds enlarge perspectives and appreciation of the range of human values and viewpoints (Bernard, 2004). Interacting with a range of people allows us to notice not only differences between others and ourselves but also our similarities. This idea is expressed by poet Maya Angelou (1990) in the poem "Human Family," in which she writes, "We are more alike, my friends, than we are unalike."

Cultural Intellligence Profiles

Earley & Mosakowski (2004) describe six profiles that may be present in an individual in varying combinations or degrees during different times or contexts. The profiles differ in the strength or source of the kinds of intelligence being used and the ways in which they can be applied (see Table 7.1).

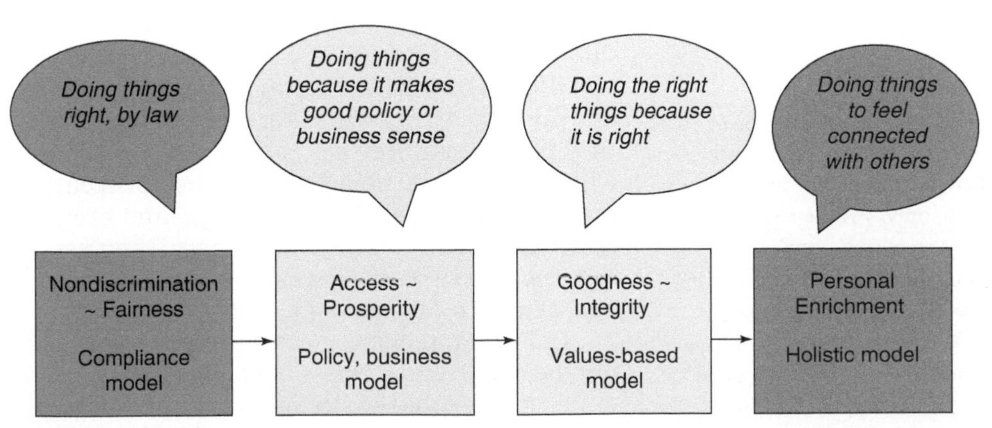

FIGURE 7.3

Why embrace diversity?

Source: Adapted from "Diversity Best Practices in Military Organizations in Canada, Australia, the United Kingdom, and the United States," *Canadian Forces Journal*, Vol. 9, No. 3, March 1, 2009.

TABLE 7.1

CULTURAL INTELLIGENCE PROFILES

Cultural Intelligence Profiles	Head CQ	Body CQ	Heart CQ
The *provincial* can be quite effective when working with people of similar background but runs into trouble when venturing farther afield.	low	low	low
The *analyst* methodically deciphers a foreign culture's rules and expectations by resorting to a variety of elaborate learning strategies.	high	low	low
The *natural* relies entirely on intuition rather than on a systematic learning style. A natural is rarely steered wrongly by first impressions.	high	low	low
The *ambassador*, like many political appointees, may not know much about the culture he or she has just entered, but convincingly communicates a certainty that he or she belongs there.	low	low	high
The *mimic* has a high degree of control over his or her actions and behaviour, if not a great deal of insight into the significance of the cultural cues he or she picks up.	low	high	low
The *chameleon* possesses high levels of all three CQ components and is very uncommon. A chameleon may even be mistaken for a native of the culture.	high	high	high

Cultivating Your Cultural Intelligence

Why can some people act appropriately and effectively in new cultures or among people with unfamiliar backgrounds while others flounder? A person with high CQ whether cultivated or innate, can understand and master cross-cultural encounters as needed. Sometimes individuals who fit in smoothly with their peers often have great difficulty making sense of, and then being accepted by, cultural strangers. They may embody the habits and norms of their own culture, but feel alien when they enter a culture that is not their own. People who are somewhat detached from their own culture may more easily adopt the customs and even the body language of an unfamiliar host. They're used to being observers and making a conscious effort to fit in (Earley & Mosakowski, 2004).

Cultural intelligence can be developed in both our personal and professional lives. We need to examine our own CQ strengths and weaknesses in order to establish a starting point, thereby selecting an area that we wish to develop.

Student Voices

Roberto:

One of the hardest adjustments for me in Canada has been keeping my voice down. In Italy, people shout all the time and wave their arms. No one avoids conflict there. It is the normal way of communicating where I come from. When my girlfriend visits my family, she is always alarmed at the shouting and thinks everyone is fighting. I tell her that we just disagree noisily and 10 minutes later we will be singing or laughing.

Apply the Idea

CULTURAL VALUES

How do values in Western culture affect your everyday perceptions and activities? See whether you can trace concrete implications of these cultural values.

Example: Competition: This value is evident in concrete practices such as competitive sports, grading policies, and attempts to have the last word in casual conversations.

Productivity

___

Individualism

___

Speed

___

Youth

___

Wealth

___

A person high in **cognitive CQ** has extensive rote learning about the beliefs, customs, and taboos of other cultures. To improve your cognitive CQ, you might work on developing **analogical and inductive reasoning** by reading several cross-cultural case studies and distilling common principles. Seek information about the culture or subculture that you are interested in knowing more about. Go as close to the source as possible; don't overlook media representations and first-hand interactions, remembering to ask open-ended questions and to listen effectively.

A person high in **motivational CQ** is confident of being able to understand people from unfamiliar cultures. If your motivational CQ is low, develop cultural mindfulness by performing simple awareness exercises, such as placing yourself in an unknown setting and trying to find out where to buy a newspaper, get something to eat, or how to get somewhere. Consciously become aware of any cultural patterns that are different from yours. Notice any sense of personal discomfort this causes you. How might you respond in a different way than you automatically would?

Actions and demeanour that show how ready we are to enter the world of another culture describes our **physical CQ**. Someone having difficulty with physical CQ might enroll in acting classes to develop flexibility in a repertoire of responses. Any activities that help us enrich our ability to adapt our interactions in culturally sensitive ways will promote physical CQ. Try watching a movie with the volume off: What are the nonverbal culturally coded messages? The next time you are at an airport or other gathering place where there are many people, observe the various ways in which people relate physically to each other. Notice eye contact, touching, physical gestures, movements, even clothing or dress style. Notice how familiar or foreign these seem to you.

Apply the Idea

DIAGNOSING YOUR CULTURAL INTELLIGENCE

The statements below reflect different facets of cultural intelligence (Earley & Mosakowski, 2004). For each set, add up your scores and divide by four to produce an average. For purposes of your own development, it is most useful to think about your three scores in comparison to one another. Generally, an average of less than 3 would indicate an area calling for improvement, while an average of greater than 4.5 reflects a true CQ strength.

Rate the extent to which you agree with each statement, using the scale:

1 = Strongly disagree; 2 = Disagree; 3 = Neutral; 4 = Agree; 5 = Strongly agree

Cognitive CQ

_______ Before I interact with people from a new culture, I ask myself what I hope to achieve.
_______ If I encounter something unexpected while working in a new culture, I use this experience to figure out new ways to approach other cultures in the future.
_______ I plan how I'm going to relate to people from a different culture before I meet them.
_______ When I come into a new cultural situation, I can immediately sense whether something is going well or something is wrong.
Total _______ ÷ 4 = Cognitive CQ

Physical CQ

_______ It's easy for me to change my body language (for example, eye contact or posture) to suit people from a different culture.
_______ I can alter my expression when a cultural encounter requires it.
_______ I modify my speech style (for example, accent or tone) to suit people from a different culture.
_______ I easily change the way I act when a cross-cultural encounter seems to require it.
Total _______ ÷ 4 = Physical CQ

Emotional/Motivational CQ

_______ I have confidence that I can deal well with people from a different culture.
_______ I am certain that I can befriend people whose cultural backgrounds are different from mine.
_______ I can adapt to the lifestyle of a different culture with relative ease.
_______ I am confident that I can deal with a cultural situation that's unfamiliar.
Total _______ ÷ 4 = Emotional/motivational CQ

As we see from the Student Voice features in this chapter, all of our personal experiences stem from, and are embedded in, the particular familiar culture in which we were raised and live. By recognizing the power of culture and expanding our awareness, we can each navigate our place in the world with more ease and have a greater array of choices and strategies with which to respond in any given situation, no matter how foreign it may initially seem. As we refine these responses, we also develop a stronger sense of self, and our lives can become enriched by the diversity of other cultures. The skills we develop through cultural intelligence will enable us to embrace diversity, not only because it is legal, moral, and practical, but also because it creates more meaningful connections with others (refer back to Figure 7.3).

Student Voices

Byron:

Sometimes my buddies and I will call each other "boy" or even "Black boy," and we know we're just kidding around. But if a White calls me "boy," I get real mad. It doesn't mean the same thing when they call us "boy" that it does when we call ourselves "boy."

Nolea:

Last week I was at the store choosing which fashion magazine to buy. As I was looking over the selection, the manager of the store came up to me and informed me in no uncertain terms that these magazines were there to be purchased and not to be read in the store. His tone was loud, rude, and condescending. I felt that he had discriminated against me because I am a teenager. He never would have spoken to an older person that way.

Cultural Competence in Organizations

Definitions of cultural competence have evolved from diverse perspectives, interests, and needs. They have now been incorporated in legislation, federal statutes and programs, health and mental health organization structures, and academic settings. The National Center for Cultural Competence (NCCC) embraces a conceptual framework and model for achieving cultural competence in organizations adapted from the definitions developed by Cross et al. (1989) as shown in Figure 7.4.

Cultural Competence in Health Care

At many Canadian universities, medicine is taught in a setting of problem-based learning. One of the inclusions in the curriculum is a goal of developing awareness of the patient's culture and the beliefs and values related to healing in that culture. In hospitals and other medical facilities, this alters the approach taken by doctors in communication, diagnosis, and treatment. Because culture affects perception, Western doctors lacking in cultural intelligence may misdiagnose or inappropriately prescribe treatment for their patients. A Chinese Canadian living in Vancouver might be taking shark cartilage supplements for the treatment of arthritis, and may be dismissed as ignorant or superstitious if the doctor is not familiar with alternative views of healing.

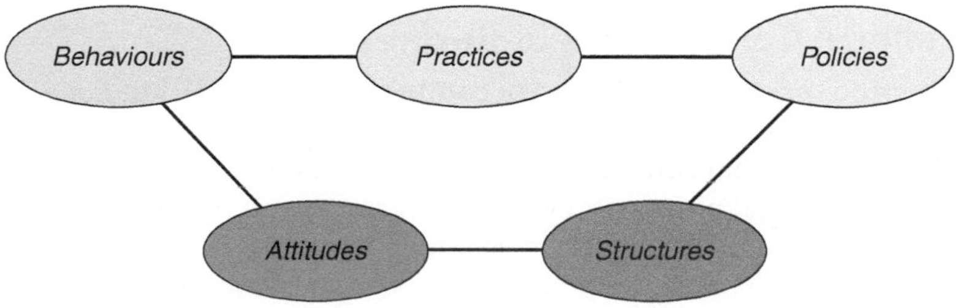

FIGURE 7.4

Cultural Competence Conceptual Framework

Source: National Center for Cultural Competence: www.commonwealthfund.org.

Communication Notes

CULTURAL COMPETENCE

Cultural competence is a developmental process that evolves over an extended period. Individuals and organizations will demonstrate various levels of competence in any given situation. Cultural competence requires that organizations:

- Have a defined, congruent set of values and principles, and demonstrate behaviours, attitudes, policies, and structures that enable them and their personnel to work effectively cross-culturally;
- Have the capacity to value diversity, conduct self-assessment, manage the dynamics of difference, acquire and institutionalize cultural knowledge, and adapt to diversity and the cultural contexts of the communities they serve;
- Incorporate the above in all aspects of policymaking, administration, practice, and service delivery, and systematically involve patients, families, and their communities.

Many doctors in North America are encouraged to attend workshops that teach them about the cultural practices and folk beliefs of immigrants from other countries (Anders, 1997; Mangan, 2002). Researchers cite the case of one doctor, Jeffrey Syme, who found an immediate application for what he learned in a workshop. A number of his patients had emigrated from Cape Verde, a string of islands off West Africa. Many of these patients asked him for Valium, but refused to discuss their problems with him. Syme knew, of course, that Valium is a medication that should be prescribed only for specific conditions. In the workshop, however, Syme learned that in Cape Verde, Valium is an over-the-counter treatment that people routinely take for everyday blues. So, they perceived Valium as a mild medication that they could take as casually as many people take common headache remedies.

In another case, ignorance of folk beliefs led a doctor to faulty perceptions of a patient (Anders, 1997; Mangan, 2002). A folk belief among many Guatemalans is that giant worms in the stomach govern well-being. One doctor attending the workshop said, "I just had a patient like that." What had the doctor done when her patient complained that giant worms in his stomach were making him feel bad? She referred him to mental health specialists because she perceived his statement to indicate that he was mentally unbalanced. In both cases, the doctors misperceived patients by not taking into account the patients' cultural customs and beliefs.

Cultural Competence in Business

More and more companies are becoming international, but not all workers who are transferred to another country or who do business with international colleagues find it easy to understand and adapt to the nonverbal norms of the new cultures (Axtell, 1990a, 1990b). For instance, in Germany it is considered very rude to cough in concerts and in many other public areas. In India, whistling tunes is highly offensive.

Gift-giving holds many opportunities for misunderstandings. A gift wrapped in blue and black might offend many Asians because those colours symbolize death in their cultures. An American might take offence if a Japanese person does not open a presented gift. In Japan, however, it is customary not to open gifts in front of the giver. An American might bring an extravagant gift to make a good impression on a Singaporean manager with whom he hopes to do business. Unfortunately for the American, the Singaporean manager probably would view an extravagant gift as an attempt at bribery—not exactly a good impression (Axtell, 1990a, 1990b).

B-C Images/Gallo Images/Getty Images

Imagine this scenario: A Western businessman goes to Japan to negotiate a deal. When the Westerner makes his proposal, the Japanese businessman responds, "I see you have put much thought into this idea." Assuming this indicates that the Japanese executive is pleased with the proposal, the Westerner says, "Then, shall we sign the contract and be on our way?" The Japanese executive replies, "I think we have much to talk about on your good proposal." What's happening here? If you are unfamiliar with Japanese communication styles, you might assume that the Japanese businessman is being evasive. However, Japanese culture holds in high priority cooperation, politeness, and not causing others to lose face. The Japanese businessman's communication reflects the rules of his culture that require him not to say no directly to another person (Cathcart & Cathcart, 1997; Dolan & Worden, 1992).

How much time does a good worker invest in his or her work? That may depend on where one works. In Canada, jobs typically require 30 to 44 hours a week. Vacation time is two to three weeks per year for most Canadian workers. Many other countries have laws that ensure more vacation time for workers. According to the Economic Policy Institute (Robinson, 2000), laws guarantee the following numbers of vacation days: Spain, 30; France, 30; Ireland, 28; Japan, 25; Portugal, 25; Belgium, 24; Norway, 21; Germany, 18; United States, 0.

Putting Ethnocentricity into Perspective

The term *ethnocentrism* is the combination of two Greek words: *ethnos*, meaning *nation*, and *kentron*, meaning *centre*. One views reality as if one's own group is the centre of everything, and all others are scaled and rated with reference to it. Ethnocentrism is a normal tendency for people to fill individual and collective needs for identity and predictability. While ethnocentrism in low levels can be very important for in-group development, high ethnocentric levels can be innately damaging for intercultural communication (Neuliep & McCroskey, 1997).

Ethnocentrism's "in-group" may be any of the cultural/subcultural groups that we noted earlier in the chapter: age, language, social class, gender, sexual preference, disability, race, religion or ethnicity. When the in-group's ethnocentrism reaches a high level leading to intolerance and discrimination, we use terms such as *racism, sexism, ageism, classism,* or *bigotry* (Wrench et al., 2006).

Of these subcultures, religious fundamentalism is one group that deserves special exploration in regard to ethnocentrism. Gordon Allport (1954) first questioned the role of religion in the creation of prejudice when he wrote, "The role of religion is paradoxical. It makes prejudice and it unmakes prejudice. While the creeds of the great religions are universalistic, all stressing brotherhood, the practice of these creeds is frequently divisive and brutal. The solemnity of religious ideals is offset by the horrors of persecution in the name of these same ideals" (p. 444).

Altemeyer and Hunsberger (1992) also believed that the variable accounting for a number of prejudicial beliefs was "religious fundamentalism," which they defined as:

> ... the belief that there is one set of religious teachings that clearly contains the fundamental, basic, intrinsic, essential, inerrant truth about humanity and deity; that this essential truth is fundamentally opposed by forces of evil which must be vigorously fought; that this truth must be followed today according to the fundamental, unchangeable practices of the past; and that those who believe and follow these teachings have a special relationship with the deity. (p. 118)

They found that the variables that were key when examining the influence of religion on prejudice were "the covariation of authoritarian submission, authoritarian aggression, and conventionalism" (p. 114).

Hunsberger (1996) also examined how religious fundamentalism functioned across various cultural contexts. Members of the Hindu, Islamic, Judaic, and Christian religious faiths were sought out for participation in his study. The commonalities across the four religious traditions yielded surprisingly similar patterns.

Intercultural communication apprehension is "the fear or anxiety associated with either real or anticipated communication with people from different groups, especially cultural and/or ethnic groups" (Neuliep & McCroskey, 1997). In essence, people who have high levels of intercultural communication apprehension will innately have communication problems stemming from their fear or anxiety. As we have studied, this would cause havoc with an individual's physical CQ and emotional/motivational CQ.

In a study conducted by Wrench and McCroskey (2003), the researchers found that homophobia and ethnocentrism were highly related constructs. Homonegativity is the degree to which an individual has prejudicial biases against gay, lesbian, bisexual, and transgendered/transsexual people.

Ethnocentrism and homonegativity were strongly and positively related constructs and both were moderately negatively related to responsiveness. In essence, the more someone considers other people's feelings, listens to what others have to say, and recognizes the needs of other people, the less likely that one will be ethnocentric or homonegative.

Figure 7.5 examines the effects of tolerance for disagreements and attitudes about heterogeneity on cross-cultural perceptions. McCroskey, Richmond, and McCroskey (2006) define tolerance for disagreement as "the degree to which we can deal with disagreement from another person before we take it personally" (p. 125). The question then becomes: How much tolerance for disagreements will people have when they are certain that their particular cultural position is the one that is best and that all others are inferior? The more we perceive these differences as being personally threatening, the less we are able to see them simply as issues that may be viewed from varying perspectives.

The notion of "zealous" originates from the same root word as "jealousy." We jealously protect our world view and put down all others who do not agree with us. Unfortunately, at the far end of the spectrum, zealous personal defensiveness is manifest; fear, hatred, and violence are rampant. Celebration of diversity can be expanded in any situation where we are able to embrace a "live and let live" attitude about heterogeneity; we do not all need to be the same. It is our diversity, in fact, that makes life delightful!

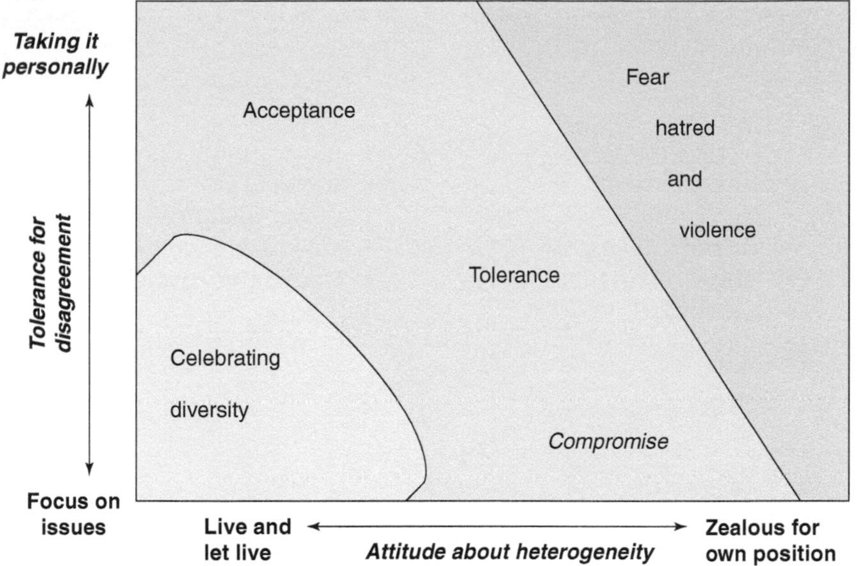

FIGURE 7.5

Beliefs, Feelings, and Values as They Relate to Cross-Cultural Perceptions

Chapter Summary

In this chapter, we began by thinking of culture as an anthropologist would, by describing and seeking to explain similarities and differences in thought and behaviour among groups of humans. We learned that the seven primary characteristics of a culture are that it is: (1) integrated; (2) a product of history; (3) changing; (4) strengthened by values; (5) an influence on behaviours; (6) symbolically transmitted; and (7) unique, complex, and variable. We explored the myriad manifestations of nonverbal communication as they reflect or express cultural values. We also discussed cultural differences regarding conflict.

Two approaches to the study of culture have been examined. The aggregate approach is values-based and includes the meaning of time, high- and low-context distinctions, and Hofstede's five dimensions of power distance, individualism/collectivism, masculinity/femininity, uncertainty avoidance/acceptance and long-term and short-term orientation (1991, 2001). The individualistic approach recognizes that each person has a unique psychological "fingerprint" comprised of a complex set of memories, thoughts, and ways of thinking and feeling.

We have learned that cultural intelligence is an understanding of why people of different backgrounds act as they do, and how we can improve the way we relate to each other by developing our CQ related to the head, body, and heart. We have seen evidence of why diversity has become a dynamic concept in defining the Canadian social landscape, through the compliance, policy/business, values-based, and holistic models. Earley & Mosakowski (2004) described six profiles of sources of strength used in cultural intelligence. We had the opportunity to diagnose our personal CQ and learn how to strengthen areas that need development.

Cultural competence is also required in organizations. We found examples of the importance and implications of organizational CQ in health care and business. Finally, we examined the qualities of tolerance for disagreement and attitudes about heterogeneity that require a strong personal focus in order to put ethnocentricity into perspective.

Key Concepts

- analogical and inductive reasoning
- cognitive CQ
- collectivism
- cultural anthropology
- cultural intelligence (CQ)
- culture
- ethnic group
- ethnocentrism
- high context
- individualism
- long-term orientation
- low context
- masculinity
- motivational CQ
- physical CQ
- power distance
- subculture
- uncertainty avoidance

For Further Thought and Discussion

1. A group called "Style in Progress" (www.styleinprogress.ca) took over an alley in Toronto for a 24-hour period of legal graffiti painting in the summer of 2008 (for some photos of the results, go to www.youtube.com/watch?v=tltSZDRJxyE). In what ways was this group dealing with ethnocentric tendencies?
2. Browse the Internet using the words *cultural communication, high vs. low context cultures, diversity in Canada,* and *intercultural communication,* to name a few. See where this leads!
3. Read about what is appropriate in various cultures for business dress, gifts, and interaction norms at the *Executive Planet* website at www.executiveplanet.com.
4. Communicating comfortably and effectively with diverse people is essential to career success as organizations become increasingly global and diverse. Go to Cornell University's website at www.ilr.cornell.edu/library/subjectGuides/workplaceDiversity.html, which focuses on workplace diversity and offers good information and links to other sites.
5. Talk with three or four people who are as culturally diverse as possible. Ask them how their childhood illnesses were treated. What was the experience of being sick like for them?
6. Compare your answers from the Apply the Idea exercise "Cultural Values" with those of your classmates. Discuss the impact of cultural values on your day-to-day perceptions and activities.

Part 2

Weaving Communication into Relationships

Chapter 8

Mindful Listening

You can't fake listening. It shows.

—Raquel Welch, actor

The most basic and powerful way to connect to another person is to listen. Just listen. Perhaps the most important thing we ever give each other is our attention. ... A loving silence often has far more power to heal and to connect than the most well-intentioned words.

—Rachel Naomi Remen (1997)

Meet Anna Deavere Smith. She's a playwright, an artist in residence at MTV, a recipient of the MacArthur Foundation "genius" award, a performance studies teacher at Tisch School of the Arts, and a professor at New York University. She's won high praise for her one-woman shows, *Fires in the Mirror,* which dealt with ethnic turmoil in Crown Heights, Brooklyn, and *Twilight: Los Angeles,* which focused on the riots that erupted following the acquittal of the police officers accused of beating Rodney King. She also played the president's secretary in *The American President* and a paralegal in *Philadelphia,* and she had a continuing role on the television series *The West Wing.*

© CORBIS SYGMA

Anna Deavere Smith has added another title to her résumé—teaching medical students at Yale and law students at New York University. You might wonder what qualifies her to instruct medical and law students. After all, she's not a doctor or lawyer.

Anna Deavere Smith is a virtuoso listener. That's why she was hired to teach medical and law students. "No one listens better ... than Anna Deavere Smith," says Dr. Ralph Horat, chair of the Department of Internal Medicine at Yale's School of Medicine (Arenson, 2002, p. 34). Doctors and lawyers need to listen, and conventional medical and legal training doesn't teach them how to listen well. That's why the school turned to Anna Deavere Smith. She says, "Listening is not just hearing what someone tells you word for word. You have to listen with a heart.... It's very hard work" (Arenson, 2002, p. 35). In teaching prospective doctors and lawyers how to listen well to patients and clients, Smith emphasizes the need to be "wide awake" (2005).

Doctors and lawyers aren't the only ones who need to listen well. We all do. If you think about your normal day, you'll realize that listening—or trying to—takes up at least half of your waking time. Attending to others' communication—by listening, reading lips, or using American Sign Language—takes up more of our time than any other communication.

Usually when we think about communication, we think about talking. Yet, talking is not the only or even the greatest part of communication. For people to interact and share meaning, they must also listen to one another. As obvious as this is, few of us devote as much energy to effective listening as we do to effective talking. If you think about your normal day, you'll realize that listening—or trying to—takes up about half of your waking time.

Listening is the single greatest communication activity in which we engage. We spend more time listening than talking, reading, or writing. This point is well made by Marilyn Buckley, who says, "Students listen to the equivalent of a book a day; talk the equivalent of a book a week; read the equivalent of a book a month; and write the equivalent of a book a year" (1992, p. 622).

Studies of a range of people from college students to professionals indicate that the average person spends at least 50 percent of waking time listening to others (Barker et al., 1981; Wagner, 2001). You listen in classes, listen to acquaintances in casual conversation, listen to your parents, listen to clerks in stores, listen to your supervisor and customers when you're at work, and listen to friends when they talk to you about important concerns or issues in their lives. If we don't attend to others' communication effectively, we're communicating poorly about half of the time. This point was well made in an advertisement sponsored by the Unisys Corporation: "How can we expect him to learn when we haven't taught him how to listen?" (cited in Berko, Wolvin, & Wolvin, 1995, p. 81). If we can't listen, we can't learn.

The costs of poor listening can be very high. Doctors who don't listen fully to patients may misdiagnose or mistreat medical problems (Nyquist, 1992; Underwood & Adler, 2005). For this reason, an increasing number of medical practices hire communication specialists to provide listening workshops for medical practitioners. They'd rather pay the consultants' fees than the legal fees for malpractice suits that can result from poor listening (Crossen, 1997).

In this chapter, we explore listening and how to listen effectively. First, we consider what's involved in listening (it's more than most of us realize). Next, we discuss obstacles to effective listening and how we can minimize them. We also consider some common forms of nonlistening. The fourth section of the chapter explains different types of listening and the distinct skills needed for each. To wrap up the chapter, we identify guidelines for improving listening effectiveness.

Communication Notes

"THE SPIRIT CATCHES YOU, AND YOU FALL DOWN."

That's how the parents of three-month-old Lia Lee explained why she fainted. Doctors diagnosed the problem as epilepsy, but Lia's Hmong parents disagreed. They told the doctors that the soul can temporarily disappear from the body. When it does, evil spirits catch you and make you fall down (Fadiman, 1997). The doctors didn't listen to the Lees, dismissing their ideas as superstitious folklore. And the Lees didn't listen to the doctors, dismissing them as not understanding why their daughter fainted. The doctors prescribed anti-seizure medications, but the Lees didn't give Lia the medication regularly. Instead, they treated her with sacred amulets and visits to a shaman, and they changed her name to fool the evil spirits. Lia suffered a massive seizure that left her in a vegetative state, where she has been for 18 years (Underwood & Adler, 2005). Had the doctors and the Lees listened more mindfully, Lia's situation might be totally different.

Or consider the case of Mohammad Kochi, an Afghan immigrant, who developed stomach cancer. Kochi had the recommended surgery but refused to undergo the recommended chemotherapy. The doctors assumed that Kochi refused because he didn't want to endure the unpleasantness of chemotherapy, so they didn't communicate with him about his reasons for refusing. Later—too late to help Kochi—the doctors learned that he refused because, as a Muslim, he could not allow fluids to enter his body after he had cleansed himself for prayer. A continuous IV drip, which the doctors had proposed, would have required him to disrespect his religion (Underwood & Adler, 2005). If the doctors had asked Kochi why he refused and then had listened to his answer, they could have told him about other ways that chemotherapy can be administered.

CONCEPTS AT A GLANCE

Effective Listening

- The listening process
- Obstacles to effective listening
- Forms of nonlistening
- Adapting listening to communication goals
- Guidelines for effective listening

THE LISTENING PROCESS

Listening is a complex process that involves far more than our ears. To listen well, we rely on our ears, minds, and hearts. Although we often use the words *listening* and *hearing* as if they were synonyms, actually they are different. **Hearing** is a physiological activity that occurs when sound waves hit our eardrums. People who are deaf or hearing-impaired receive messages visually through lip-reading or sign language.

Listening is far more complex than hearing or otherwise physically receiving messages. Listening has psychological and cognitive dimensions that mere hearing,

FIGURE 8.1

Chinese for "Listening"

or physically receiving messages, does not. The multifaceted aspects of listening are reflected in the Chinese character in Figure 8.1, which includes the symbols for the eyes, ears, and heart. We can define **listening** as an active, complex process that consists of being mindful; hearing, selecting, and organizing information; interpreting communication; responding; and remembering.

Listening, then, is more than hearing. It also requires us to interpret, remember, and respond to what others communicate. The International Listening Association (ILA) (1995; see the ILA website at listen.org) emphasizes that listening is an active process, which means we must exert effort to listen well. We must be involved with our ears and hearts and minds if we want to listen effectively. Figure 8.2 outlines the listening process.

Student Voices

Talyn:

I always thought I was a good listener, until I spent two years living in Japan. In that culture there is a much deeper meaning to listening. I realized that most of the time I was only hearing others. Often I was thinking of my responses while they were still talking. I had not been listening with my mind and heart. When I spoke to a Japanese person, he listened so thoughtfully. I was embarrassed one day to realize that every time I made a noise or gesture, everyone was silent and allowed me to speak. I hadn't been giving them that same graciousness.

Mindfulness

The first step in listening is to make a decision to be mindful. **Mindfulness** is a concept from Zen Buddhism that refers to being fully present in the moment. The Reverend Jisho Perry says that "to pay attention is to stop putting our own ideas and opinions on the situation" (1996, p. 22). It's what Anna Deavere Smith (2005) calls "wide awakeness." When we are mindful, we don't let our thoughts drift to what we did yesterday or plan to do this weekend, nor do we focus on our own feelings and responses. Instead, when we listen mindfully, we tune in fully to another person and try to understand what that person is communicating, without imposing our own ideas, judgments, or feelings.

Mindfulness starts with the decision to attend fully to another. Physically, this is signified by paying attention, adopting an involved posture, keeping eye contact, and indicating interest in what the other person says

1. Mindfulness
2. Attending
3. Hearing
4. Selecting and organizing information
5. Interpreting communication
6. Responding to others
7. Remembering communication

FIGURE 8.2

The Listening Process

(Bolton, 1986). These behaviours are called "attending." Mindfulness is the first step in effective listening, and it is the foundation for all other parts of the process.

Because mindful listening involves taking the perspective of another, it fosters dual perspective—a cornerstone of effective communication. In addition, mindfulness enhances the effectiveness of another's communication. When people sense we are really listening, they tend to elaborate on their ideas and express themselves in more depth.

Mindfulness is a choice. It is not a talent that some people have and others don't. No amount of skill will make you a good listener if you don't make a commitment to attend to another person fully and without diversion. Thus, effective listening begins with the choice to be mindful.

Apply the Idea

BEING MINDFUL

To develop your ability to be mindful, follow these guidelines in a situation that calls for you to listen:

- *Empty your mind of thoughts, ideas, plans, and concerns so that you are open to the other person.*
- *Concentrate on the person with whom you are interacting. Say to yourself, "I want to focus on this person and on what she or he is feeling and thinking."*
- *If you find yourself framing responses to the other person, try to push those aside; they interfere with your concentration on the other person's words.*
- *If your mind wanders, don't criticize yourself; that's distracting. Instead, gently refocus on the person you are with and on what that person is communicating to you. It's natural for other thoughts to intrude, so just push them away and stay focused on the other person.*
- *Let the other person know you are attending mindfully: Give nonverbal responses (nods, facial expressions), ask questions to encourage elaboration, and keep eye contact.*
- *Evaluate how mindfully you listened. Did you understand the other person's thoughts and feelings? Did you feel more focused on that person than you usually do when you listen to others?*

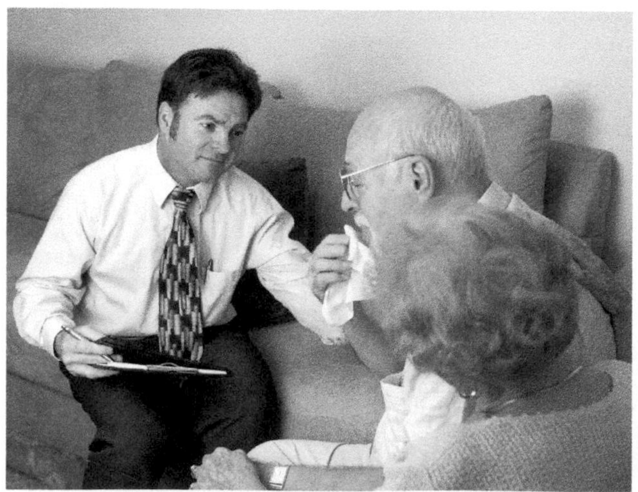

Lisa F. Young/Shutterstock

Attending describes the specific behaviours of being mindful. In North America, most people show that they are listening actively through certain behaviours. These actions can easily be remembered by the acronym FELOR:

F = Face the speaker
E = Eye contact
L = Lean forward
O = Open posture
R = Relax

Once you have decided to be mindful and then "attended" to the person speaking, you are ready to receive messages.

Communication Notes

GOOD LISTENING = CAREER ADVANCEMENT

What monetary value would you attach to good listening? It turns out that effective listening can be worth a lot in your paycheque. Listening skill is ranked as the single most important feature of effective managers (Winsor, Curtis, & Stephens, 1997). It's also the top-ranked communication skill for accountants (Morreale, 2004). Just as listening skill is associated with career advancement, poor listening is a leading reason that some people don't advance in careers (Deal & Kennedy, 1999; Waner, 1995).

Physically Receiving Messages

The second process involved in listening is physically receiving messages. As we noted earlier, hearing is a physiological process in which sound waves hit our eardrums so that we become aware of noises, such as music, traffic, or human voices. For people who have hearing impairments, messages are received in other ways, such as writing, lip-reading, and ASL.

Receiving messages is a prerequisite for listening. For most of us, hearing is automatic and unhindered. However, people with hearing impairments may have difficulty receiving oral messages. When we speak with someone who has a hearing disability, we should face the person and ask if we are coming across clearly.

Hearing impairments are not the only restriction on physically receiving messages. Hearing

Student Voices

Nicole:

As a bank teller, I find it increasingly difficult to do my job properly when clients are using their cellphones. My responsibilities include listening to the client and offering suggestions—but when they're talking away to someone on the phone, I am unable to confirm their needs and I have to wait for a pause in their conversation in order to ensure there is nothing else to do. Sometimes, if they want something more, they will even go to great lengths to find a pen and a piece of paper to write down instructions while continuing to talk on the phone! In the end, the interaction is cold and I have to complete the transaction in silence. In this case, the client is certainly not being mindful, and communication is complicated by technology.

Communication Notes

SIGNING AS A RECOGNIZED LANGUAGE

Canadian Sign Language (CSL), French Canadian Sign Language (FCSL), and American Sign Language (ASL) are recognized by governments as real languages (Manning, 1996). Sign language interpreters are required for deaf people in the Canadian courts.

The first lesson that students learn is that these sign languages are not just a visual form of English (Carl, 1988). Rather, they are complex linguistic systems with their own syntactical and grammatical structure. CSL, FCSL, and ASL are also more conceptual than spoken English. There are signs for distinct concepts such as walking quickly and walking slowly, and being smart and being very smart. Spoken English relies on modifiers to make these distinctions: The word "walking" is modified by "quickly" or "slowly"; the word "smart" is modified by "very."

As with any language, learning ASL and its derivatives introduces students not just to words but also to the values of the deaf culture. For example, students learn that in ASL there is only one word for music—a sweeping gesture with the right hand under the left arm. Because deaf individuals cannot hear, they don't need the many terms hearing individuals use to describe different kinds of music.

Robert Koene/Photodisc Green/Getty Images

Are mindfulness and technology compatible?

ability tends to decline when we are fatigued from concentrating on communication. You may have noticed that it's harder to pay attention in classes that run 75 minutes than in classes that run 50 minutes. Background noise can also interfere with hearing. It's difficult to hear well if loud music is playing, a television is blaring, cellphones are beeping, or others are talking nearby.

Women and men seem to differ somewhat in their listening behaviours. As a rule, women are more attentive than men to the whole of communication. Thus, many men tend to focus their hearing on specific content aspects of communication, whereas women generally are more likely to attend to the whole of communication, noticing details, tangents, and relationship-level meanings. Judy Pearson (1985), a prominent communication scholar, suggests that this could result from the brain's hemispheric specializations. Women usually have better-developed right lobes, which govern creative and holistic thinking, whereas men typically have better-developed left lobes, which control analytic and linear information processing.

Student Voices

Heather:

My parents are so strange! To watch them, you'd think they were deliberately trying to make it impossible to hear each other. Here's what happens: Dad will turn on the radio, and then Mom will start talking. He won't hear part of what she says, and then she'll get into a huff that he ignored her. Or sometimes Mom will have the television on, and Dad will say something from the other room. When she doesn't hear him, he'll get on her case about caring more about whatever program is on than about him. They do this all the time—no wonder they can't hear each other!

Mark:

My girlfriend amazes me. We'll have a conversation, and then later one of us will bring it up again. What I remember is what we decided in the talk. She remembers that too, but she also remembers all the details about where we were and what was going on in the background and particular things one of us said in the conversation. I never notice all of that stuff, and I sure don't remember it later.

Selecting and Organizing Material

The third element of listening is selecting and organizing material. As we noted in Chapter 3, we don't perceive everything around us. Instead, we selectively attend only to some messages and elements of our environments. What we attend to depends on many factors, including our interests, cognitive structures, and expectations. Selective listening is also influenced by culture; as early as age one, babies distinguish the sounds of their language, but they don't learn to recognize sounds in other languages. Thus, people who learn a second language later in life may not be able to recognize sounds that weren't in their first language (Monastersky, 2001).

We can monitor our tendencies to attend selectively by remembering that we are more likely to notice stimuli that are intense, loud, or unusual or that otherwise stand out from the flow of communication. This implies that we may overlook communicators who speak quietly and don't call attention to themselves. Youngae, a visiting student from Taiwan, observes that most Canadian students often ignore what she says because she speaks softly and unassertively. Westerners who are accustomed to outspoken, individualistic speaking styles may not attend to speaking styles that are less bold. If we're aware of the tendency not to notice people who speak quietly, we can guard against it so that we don't miss out on people and messages that may be important. The Communication Notes feature "Hard Times for Listening" explores the effect of our rushed lifestyles on listening.

Communication Notes

HARD TIMES FOR LISTENING

Have you noticed that there's a lot more talk than listening going on these days? Television talk shows, call-in radio programs, and hotlines encourage people to talk, talk, talk. But is anyone listening?

Scholars of communication point to several factors that have reduced listening skills. First, there is the fast pace of everyday life. Hurrying is a national pastime in the West. Even when we don't need to hurry, we seem habituated to do so. In conversations, we're thinking, "Get to the point."

Another contributor to poor listening is media. Television and radio encourage passive attention, not active listening. Further, says communication consultant Sheila Bentley, the constant interruption of commercials decreases our skill in sustaining attention for periods of time (Crossen, 1997).

Poor listening causes mistakes and problems, which explains why many companies now require employees to attend listening workshops. Starbucks, for instance, requires employees to learn to listen to orders and rearrange customers' requests in the sequence of size, flavouring, milk, and caffeine. That's helpful when customers often spurt out "Double-shot decaf grande" or "Iced, skim, cappuccino, small."

Once we've selected what to notice, we then organize the stimuli to which we've attended. As you'll recall from Chapter 3, we organize our perceptions by relying on cognitive schemata, which include prototypes, personal constructs, stereotypes, and scripts. As we listen to others, we decide how to categorize them by asking which of our prototypes they most closely resemble: good friend, person in trouble, student, teacher, and so forth. We then apply personal constructs to define in more detail others and their messages. We evaluate whether they are upset or calm, open to advice or closed to it, and so on. Based on our construction of others, we then apply stereotypes that predict what they will do. When friends are clearly distraught, we can reasonably predict that they will want to vent and that they may not want advice until after they have had a chance to express their feelings. Finally, we apply scripts, which specify how interaction should proceed, including how we should act.

Student Voices

Chad:

I had to have outpatient surgery on my knee last year. My doctor told me to bring an adult with me for the surgery. I said my friend Jake was going to bring me and come back to pick me up. The doctor said, "No, he must stay here with you the whole time." The doctor explained that I wouldn't be able to listen carefully to instructions because of anxiety and the anesthetic. I thought he was wrong, but he wasn't. After the surgery, I thought I was alert and normal when the doctor explained how to take care of the knee and what was normal and not normal after this surgery. By the time Jake drove me home, I couldn't remember a thing the doctor had said.

Student Voices

Tonya:

I work as a volunteer counsellor at a women's centre, and the other day, something happened that shows how wrong a script we can have. This woman came in, a student about my age, and she told me she was pregnant. She was very upset and having trouble talking, so I tried to help out by going into the discussion most pregnant women who come to the centre want. I told her a lot of people have untimely pregnancies and that it doesn't have to interfere with her life. Then I said that I could recommend several doctors who could perform abortions.

By then she was crying even harder, and I started trying to tell her that abortions weren't a serious medical procedure. Finally, she managed to get out that she wanted to have the baby and needed help working out that decision. Well, that's a whole different script than abortion counselling. I had misperceived her, and that led me to adopt an inappropriate script.

Student Voices

Bart:

I'd been married and working for years when I decided I wanted to come back to school and finish my degree. When I mentioned it to the guys I worked with, they all came down hard on me. They said I was looking for an easy life as a career student and trying to get above them. My dad said it would be irresponsible to quit work when I had a wife and child, and he said no self-respecting man would do that. It seemed like everyone had a view of what I was doing and why, and their views had nothing to do with mine.

The only person who really listened to me was Evangeline, my wife. When I told her I was thinking about going back to school, the first thing out of her mouth was "What would that mean to you?" She didn't presume she knew my reasons, and she didn't start off arguing with me. She just asked what it meant to me, then listened for a long, long time while I talked about how I felt. She focused completely on understanding me, and that made it easy to talk. Maybe that's why we're married.

The schemata we use to organize our perceptions (see Chapter 3) help us figure out how to respond to others. It's important to remember that *we construct others and their communication* when we use our schemata to make sense of situations and people. In other words, we create meaning by how we select and organize communication. Remembering this reminds us to keep perceptions tentative and open to revision. In the course of interaction, we may want to modify perceptions.

Interpreting Communication

The fourth step in listening is interpreting others' communication. The most important principle for effective interpretation is to engage in dual perspective so that you interpret others on their terms. Certainly, you won't always agree with other people or how they see themselves, others, and situations. Engaging in dual perspective doesn't require you to share, or agree with, others' perspectives; however, it does require you to make an earnest effort to understand them.

To interpret others on their own terms is one of the greatest gifts we can give. Too often, we impose our meanings on others, try to correct or argue with them about what they feel, or crowd out their words with our own. As listening expert Robert Bolton (1986, p. 167) observes, good listeners "stay out of the other's way" so they can learn what others think and feel.

Responding

Effective listening also involves **responding,** which is communicating attention and interest. As we noted in Chapter 1, interpersonal communication is a transactional process in which we simultaneously listen and speak. Skillful listeners show that they are following the communication and are interested. In North America, signs of responsive listening include eye contact, nodding, attentive posture, and questions and comments that invite others to elaborate. These behaviours signal that we are involved in what is happening in the moment.

We all tend to communicate more clearly and interestingly when we feel that others are committed to us and our communication (Deal & Kennedy, 1999). The Communication Notes feature "The Impact of Responsive Listening" describes an experiment that shows the power of this type of listening skill.

Good listeners let others know they are interested during a conversation. They attend. They adopt a posture of involvement, nod their heads, make eye contact, and give vocal responses such as "um hmm," "okay," and "go on." All of these behaviours show we are attentive, interested, and ready to hear more. These responses are used in varying degrees, depending on our communication goal. Responding also includes several other very effective skills: paraphrasing, encouraging, questioning, summarizing, and supporting. We'll look more specifically at these skills when we discuss how to adapt our listening to the communication goal. On the relationship level of meaning, responsiveness communicates that we care about the other person and what she or he says.

Scott Milless/Shutterstock

Communication Notes

THE IMPACT OF RESPONSIVE LISTENING

Two researchers decided to test the impact of responsive listening on a speaker (Bolton, 1986). They taught students in a college psychology course to respond with nonverbal communication cues. The professor in the class was a boring lecturer who read his notes in a monotone voice, seldom gestured, and did little to engage students. After the first few minutes of class, the students who had been trained in responsiveness began to show interest in the lecturer. They changed their postures, kept greater eye contact, nodded their interest, and so forth. Within half a minute after the students began to respond, the lecturer started to use gestures, his speaking rate and inflection increased, and he began to interact with students visually and verbally.

Then, at a prearranged signal, the students stopped responding and communicated disinterest. For a few awkward minutes, the lecturer sought responses, but then he lapsed back into his monotone lecture, not engaging the students. Simply by demonstrating interest in the teacher's communication, the students were able to make him more effective and the class more exciting for everyone.

Apply the Idea

RESPONSIVE LISTENING

The next time a friend or co-worker starts to talk with you, express disinterest by slouching, avoiding eye contact, and withholding vocal feedback. You might want to look at something else, such as a paper or book, while your friend is talking. Note what happens as you communicate a lack of interest. How does the other person act? What happens to his or her communication? Does he or she criticize you for not listening?

Now, reverse the experiment. When somebody starts to talk to you, show interest. Put aside what you were doing, incline your body slightly forward, make eye contact, and give vocal feedback to indicate that you are following. Note what happens as you listen responsively. Does the other person continue talking? Does he or she become more engaging?

Finally, try varying your listening style during a single conversation. Begin by listening responsively, then lapse into a passive mode that expresses disinterest. What happens when you vary your listening style?

SW Productions/Photodisc Green/Getty Images

Listening is the gift we give to those we respect.

Remembering

The final aspect of listening is **remembering,** which is the process of retaining what you have heard. According to communication teachers Ron Adler and Neil Towne (1993), we remember less than half of a message immediately after we hear it. As time goes by, retention decreases further: We recall only about 35 percent of a message eight hours after hearing it. Because we forget about two-thirds of what we hear, it's important to make sure we retain the most important third. Effective listeners let go of a lot of details to retain the more important content (Cooper, Seibold, & Suchner, 1997; Fisher, 1987). By being selective about what to remember, we enhance our listening competence. Later in this chapter, we discuss strategies for retaining material.

OBSTACLES TO EFFECTIVE LISTENING

We've seen that a lot is involved in effective listening. Adding to the complexity are hindrances to effective listening. There are two broad types of barriers to effective listening: obstacles in the communication situation and obstacles in the communicators. (Did you notice that this series of ideas to be discussed was organized into two broad classes to aid your retention of the basic content?). See Figure 8.3 for a description of the external obstacles to listening.

External Obstacles

Many barriers to effective listening are present in communication situations. Although we can't always control external obstacles, knowing what situational factors hinder effective listening can help us guard against them or at least compensate for the noise they create.

Message Overload

The sheer amount of communication we engage in makes it difficult to listen fully all the time. Think about your typical day. You go to classes for three

FIGURE 8.3

External Obstacles to Listening

External Obstacles

- Message overload
- Message complexity
- Noise (physical, psychological, and semantic)

hours. How much you learn and how well you do on examinations depend on your ability to listen mindfully to material that is often difficult. After listening for 50 minutes in a history class, you listen for 50 minutes in a communication class and 50 more minutes in a business class. A great deal of information comes your way in those three lectures. After class, you check your voice mail and find three messages from friends—you need to remember them and respond before the day ends. You start doing research on the Web and find more than 300 sites for your topic—how can you possibly process all the information they offer? Then you go to work, and your supervisor informs you of new procedures. Feeling a need to get on to other matters, your supervisor describes the procedure quickly, and you are expected to understand and follow it.

Student Voices

Desmond:

I've been married for nearly 30 years, so I've figured out when I have to listen sharply to Edna and when I can just let her talk flow in one ear and out the other. She's a talker, but most of what she talks about isn't important to me. But if I hear code words, I know to listen up. If Edna says, "I'm really upset about such and such," or if she says, "We have a problem," my ears perk up and I listen carefully. It's not very fair to Edna, but it's the only way I can cope sometimes with her constant talk.

Naturally, we feel overwhelmed by the amount of information we are supposed to understand and retain. To deal with the overload, we often screen the talk around us, much as we screen calls on our answering machines, to decide when to listen carefully.

Message Complexity

The more detailed and complicated the message, the more difficult it is to follow and retain it. People for whom English is a second language often find it hard to understand English speakers who use complex sentences with multiple clauses or slang expressions (Lee, 1994, 2000). Even native speakers of English often feel overwhelmed by the complexity of some messages. It's tempting to tune out messages that are filled with technical words, detailed information, and complex sentences. If we let message complexity overwhelm us, however, we may perform poorly in school or on the job, and we may let down friends and intimates.

There are ways to manage complex messages to maximize how much we understand and retain. When we have to listen to messages that are dense with information, we should summon up extra energy. In addition, taking notes and asking questions for clarification may help us understand and retain difficult information. A third strategy is to group material as you listen, organizing the ideas in ways that make later recall easier.

Noise

A third impediment to effective listening is physical noise. Perhaps you've been part of a crowd at a rally or a game. If so, you probably had to shout to the person next to you just to be heard. Although most noise is not as overwhelming as the roar of crowds, there is always some noise in communication situations. It might be music or television in the background, other conversations nearby, pagers that are beeping, or thunder or traffic sounds from outside.

Gregory reminds us that allowing distractions communicates, on the relationship level of meaning, that we're not responsive. Good listeners do what they can to minimize environmental distractions. It's considerate to turn off a television or lower the volume of music if someone wants to talk with you.

Student Voices

Gregory:

I've been a salesman for a long time, and I know when clients are really interested and when they're not. If someone answers a phone when I'm in his or her office, I know they aren't focused on what I'm saying. Taking calls or leaving the door open for people to drop in communicates that they're not interested in me or the service I represent.

Likewise, it's courteous to turn off the sound of cellphones and pagers when attending lectures, concerts, or other events in which a buzzing phone could distract others who have come to listen. Professionals often ask that their calls be held when they want to give undivided attention to a conversation with a client or business associate. It's also appropriate to move from a noisy area to cut down on distractions. Even if we can't always eliminate noise, we can usually reduce it or change our location to one that is more conducive to effective listening.

Communication Notes

TECHNOLOGICAL OVERLOAD

Our era is dominated by technologies of communication. We can reach others faster than ever before. We can find people we want to talk with in their homes, offices, or cars or when they're in meetings or at restaurants, movies, or the beach. Many people feel overloaded by the relentless stream of information that technology makes possible (Hymowitz, 2000; Imperato, 1999; Salopek, 1999; Shenk, 1997).

You don't have to be hopelessly outdated to wonder whether communication technologies impede meaningful communication between people. Does being wired all the time diminish how we interact with people in any given moment? Author Jonathan Coleman (2000) recalls a summer evening when he attended his daughter's lacrosse practice. He writes, "Standing next to me was a father more intent on the cellphone conversation he was having than on watching his daughter play. Time and again she would look toward him, craving his attention, but he never saw her. Nor, for that matter, did another girl's mother see her child, focused as she was on her laptop, merrily tapping away."

Can we really engage others if we have a cellphone handy and will answer it if it rings? Can we listen well to any conversation—in person or on a phone—if we are actually or potentially involved in more than one conversation? If we can't, then does technology, as Coleman suggests, "create the illusion of intimacy" while it actually "makes us intimate strangers"?

Internal Obstacles

In addition to external obstacles, five barriers inside us can hinder listening: preoccupation; prejudgment, including reacting to emotionally loaded language; lack of effort; not recognizing and adapting to diverse listening styles; and our desire to "fix" things (see Figure 8.4).

Preoccupation

When we are absorbed in our own thoughts and concerns, we can't focus on what someone else is saying. Perhaps you've attended a lecture right before you had a

Internal Obstacles

- Preoccupation
- Prejudgment
- Lack of effort
- Not recognizing diverse listening styles
- Our desire to "fix"

FIGURE 8.4

Internal Obstacles to Listening

test in another class and later realized you got almost nothing out of the lecture. That's because you were preoccupied with the upcoming test. Or maybe you've been in conversations with co-workers and realized that you weren't listening at all because you were thinking about your own concerns.

©iStockphoto.com/Joseph C. Justice Jr.

When we are preoccupied with our own thoughts, we aren't fully present for others. We're not being mindful. In describing how she stays mindful in intense interviews, Anna Deavere Smith says, "I empty out myself. While I'm listening, my own judgments and prejudices certainly come up. But I know I won't get anything unless I get those things out of the way" (Arenson, 2002, p. 35). It's natural for our thoughts to wander occasionally. When they do, we should note that our focus has wandered and actively call our minds back to the person who is speaking and the meaning of the message.

Prejudgment

Another reason we may not listen effectively is that we prejudge others or their communication. Sometimes we think we already know what is going to be said, so we don't listen carefully. At other times, we decide in advance that others have nothing to offer us, so we tune them out. When we prejudge others' communication, we sacrifice learning new perspectives that might enlarge our thinking (Van Styke, 1999).

Melea's commentary demonstrates that we prejudge when we impose our preconceptions about a message. When this happens, we assume we know what another feels, thinks, and will say, and we then assimilate her or his message into our preconceptions. In the workplace, we may not pay close attention to what a co-worker says because

Student Voices

Dawn:

I think my biggest problem as a listener is preoccupation. Like, my friend Marta came to me the other day and said she wanted to talk about her relationship with her boyfriend. I followed her for a few minutes, but then I started thinking about my relationship with Ted. After a while—I don't know how long—Marta said to me, "You're not listening at all. Where is your head?" She was right. My head was in a totally different place.

Student Voices

Melea:

My parents are so busy prejudging what I'm going to say that they absolutely cannot listen to me. Like last weekend, I went home and was trying to explain why I am having difficulty with my physics class. My dad interrupted before I'd even described the problem with his take on it: he said I couldn't help it because girls have trouble with the sciences. Thanks a lot, but that's not the problem. I've done fine in other science classes, but he conveniently forgets that. The problem here is the teacher, but dad will never know that because he won't listen.

we think we already know what is being expressed. Recalling our earlier discussion of mind reading, you'll realize that it's unwise to assume we know what others think and feel. When we mind read, misunderstandings are likely. We may misinterpret what the person means because we haven't really listened on her or his terms.

When we prejudge, we disconfirm others because we deny them their own voices. Instead of listening openly to others, we force their words into our own preconceived mind-set. This devalues them. Prejudgments also reduce what we learn in communication with others. If we decide in advance that others have nothing worthwhile to say, we foreclose the possibility of learning something new. Melea's father foreclosed learning what was troubling her about her physics class.

The tendency to react to emotionally loaded language—words that evoke very strong responses, positive or negative—can lead to prejudgment. You may find some words and phrases very soothing or pleasant, while certain other words and phrases may summon up negative feelings and images for you. When we react to words that are emotionally loaded for us, we may fail to grasp another person's meaning (Wagner, 2001). For example, some people respond very negatively and emotionally to any statement that begins, "You should. . . ." As soon as they hear that phrase, they feel that the speaker is judging them and telling them what she should feel, think, or do. And they stop listening.

When we react to emotionally loaded language, we don't learn what another person has to say. We give up our responsibility to think critically about what others say, to consider their words carefully instead of reacting unthinkingly to particular words. One way to guard against this is to be aware of words and phrases that tend to trigger strong emotional reactions in us. If we bring these to a conscious level, then we can monitor our tendencies prejudge the message and to respond unthinkingly.

Lack of Effort

It is hard work to listen effectively—to focus closely on what others are saying, to grasp their meanings, to ask questions, and to give responses so that they know we are interested and involved. It's also hard to control situational noise and perhaps fight fatigue, hunger, or other physiological conditions that can impede listening (Isaacs, 1999).

Because active listening takes so much effort, we can't always do it well. We may want to listen but have trouble marshalling the energy needed. When this happens, you might ask the other person to postpone interaction until a time when you will have the energy to listen mindfully. If you explain that you want to defer communication because you really are interested and want to be able to listen well, she or he is likely to appreciate your honesty and commitment to listening.

Not Recognizing Diverse Listening Styles

Another internal hindrance to effective listening is not recognizing and adjusting to the need for different listening styles. How we listen should vary, for two reasons. First, different skills are needed when we listen for pleasure, for information, and to support others. We discuss these kinds of listening later in the chapter. A second reason for having diverse listening styles is differences between cultures and speech communities. In some cultures, listening means quietly attending to others. In other cultures, listening means participating while others are talking.

The more we understand about different people's rules for listening, the more effectively we can signal our attention in ways others understand. For example, Nepalese citizens give little vocal feedback when another is speaking. In that culture, it would be considered rude and disrespectful to make sounds while someone else is talking. Cultures also vary in what they teach members about eye contact. In the West, it is considered polite to make frequent, but not constant, eye contact with someone who is speaking. In other cultures, continuous eye contact is normative, and still others frown on virtually any eye contact.

Even in Canada, there are differences in listening rules based on membership in gender, racial, and other speech communities. Because feminine socialization emphasizes conversation as a way to form and develop relationships, women tend to maintain eye contact, give substantial vocal and verbal feedback, and use nods and facial expressions to signal interest (Tannen, 1990; Wood, 1994d, 1998). Masculine speech communities, with their focus on emotional control, teach most men to provide fewer verbal and nonverbal signs of interest and attentiveness. If you understand these general differences, you can adapt your listening style to provide appropriate responses to women and to men.

Because speech communities cultivate different communication styles, we shouldn't automatically impose our rules and interpretations on others. Instead, we should try to understand and respect their styles and listen effectively to them on their terms, not ours.

Student Voices

Jennifer:

I used to get irritated at my boyfriend because I thought he wasn't listening to me. I'd tell him stuff, and he'd just sit there and not say anything. He didn't react to what I was saying by showing emotions in his face or anything. Several times, I accused him of not listening, and he said back to me exactly what I'd said. He was listening, just not my way. I've learned not to expect him to show a lot of emotion or respond to what I say as I'm talking. That's just not his way, but he *is* listening.

Communication Notes

LISTENING IN A WORLD DOMINATED BY SIGHT

Does the visual orientation of Western culture make listening more difficult? Writer William Isaacs thinks it does. In his 1999 book *Dialogue and the Art of Thinking Together,* Isaacs notes that light moves at 186 000 miles per second, whereas sound moves at 1088 feet per second. If we watch television for a few minutes, we're exposed to thousands of images. We see at least as many images if we spend the same amount of time on the Internet. Isaacs thinks that we've become habituated to the pace of visual stimuli such that we are impatient with the pace of aural stimuli. His advice? If you want to listen better, slow down!

CONCEPTS AT A GLANCE

Forms of Nonlistening

- Pseudolistening
- Monopolizing
- Selective listening
- Defensive listening
- Ambushing
- Literal listening

Our Desire to "Fix"

The final way we hinder our listening effectiveness comes from our desire to fix what is wrong with those who share with us. Too quickly, we can fall into advising, directing, and taking charge when what is needed is our attentive, mindful, empathic listening. Our desire to "fix" frequently comes from our own discomfort with witnessing someone in distress. We'd rather do something than watch someone go through pain or anguish. Yet, when we step in unbidden, we give a very clear message that we don't trust the other person to solve his or her own problems. Our help becomes a hindrance by disempowering the people we care about. Consider that it is likely our own pain we wish to avoid.

FORMS OF NONLISTENING

Now that we've discussed obstacles to effective listening, let's consider forms of nonlistening. We call these patterns *nonlistening* because they don't involve real listening. We discuss six kinds of nonlistening that may seem familiar to you because most of us engage in them at times.

Pseudolistening

Pseudolistening is pretending to listen. When we pseudolisten, we appear to be attentive, but really our minds are elsewhere. We engage in pseudolistening when we want to appear conscientious, although we really aren't interested. Sometimes we pseudolisten because we don't want to hurt someone who is sharing experiences.

We also pseudolisten when communication bores us but we have to appear engaged. Superficial social conversations and dull lectures are two communication situations in which we may consciously choose to pseudolisten so that we seem polite even though we really aren't interested. Although it may be appropriate to pseudolisten in some situations, there is a cost: We run the risk of missing information because we really aren't attending.

Pseudolisteners often give themselves away when their responses reveal that they weren't paying attention. Common indicators of pseudolistening are responses that are tangential or irrelevant to what was said. For example, if Martin talks to Charlotte about his job interviews, she might respond tangentially by asking about the cities he visits: "Did you like New York or Atlanta better?" Although this is related to the topic of Martin's job interviews, it is tangential to the main issue. An irrelevant response would be, "Where do you want to go for dinner tonight?" That response is completely unrelated to what Martin said.

Student Voices

Renee:

Pseudolistening should be in the training manual for flight attendants. I had that job for six years, and you wouldn't believe the kinds of things passengers told me about—everything from love affairs to family problems. At first I tried to listen, because I wanted to be a good attendant. After a year, though, I learned just to appear to be listening and to let my mind be elsewhere.

Student Voices

Bellino:

I get into a lot of trouble because I pseudolisten. Often I slip into pretending to listen in classes. I'll start off paying attention and then just drift off and not even realize I've stopped listening until the teacher asks me a question and I don't even know what we're discussing. That's humiliating!

Monopolizing

Monopolizing is continuously focusing communication on ourselves instead of listening to the person who is talking. Two tactics are typical of monopolizing. One is conversational rerouting, in which a person shifts the topic back to himself or herself. For example, Ellen tells her friend Marla that she's having trouble with her roommate, and Marla reroutes the conversation with this response: "I know what you mean. My roommate is a real slob. And that's just one of her problems. Let me tell you what I have to live with. . . ." Rerouting takes the conversation away from the person who is talking and focuses it on the self.

Another monopolizing tactic is interrupting to divert attention to ourselves or to topics that interest us. Interrupting can occur in combination with rerouting, so that a person interrupts and then directs the conversation to a new topic. In other cases, diversionary interrupting involves questions and challenges that are not intended to support the person who is speaking, as illustrated in the Communication Notes feature "Doctor, Are You Listening?" Monopolizers may fire questions that express doubt about what a speaker says ("What makes you think that?" "How can you be sure?" "Did anyone else see what you did?") or prematurely offer advice to establish their own command of the situation and possibly to put down the other person ("What you should do is ... ," "You really blew that," "What I would have done is ... ,").

Communication Notes

DOCTOR, ARE YOU LISTENING?

If you've ever been frustrated by doctors who didn't listen well, you're not alone. Communication researcher Michael Nyquist (1992) studied doctor-patient interaction and found that, on average, patients had only 18 seconds to describe their problems before doctors interrupted them. Once the doctor interrupted, she or he tended to ask specific, closed questions that discouraged patients from explaining symptoms, life situations, and so forth that might affect diagnosis and treatment. Once interrupted, only 1 of 52 patients asserted themselves to complete what they had originally wanted to tell the doctor.

Sheila Bentley (Crossen, 1997) presents communication workshops to medical practitioners. Listening is a primary focus in her training because she has found that many of the mistakes doctors make—ones that often lead to expensive malpractice suits—result from poor listening on the part of doctors.

Both rerouting and diversionary interrupting are techniques to monopolize a conversation. They are the antithesis of good listening. The following conversation illustrates monopolizing and also shows how disconfirming of others it can be:

Chuck: I'm really bummed about my Econ class. I just can't seem to get the stuff.

Sally: Well, I know what you mean. Econ was a real struggle for me too, but it's nothing compared to the stats course I'm taking now. I mean, this one is going to destroy me totally.

Chuck: I remember how frustrated you got in Econ, but you finally did get it. I just can't seem to, and I need the course for my major. I've tried going to review sessions, but ... .

Sally: I didn't find the review sessions helpful. Why don't you focus on your other classes and use them to pull up your average?

Chuck: That's not the point. I want to get this stuff.

Sally: You think you've got problems? Do you know that right now I have three papers and one exam hanging over my head?

Chuck: I wonder if I should hire a tutor.

Sally shows no interest in Chuck's concerns, and she pushes her own conversational agenda. Chances are good that she doesn't even understand what he is feeling, because she isn't really focusing on what he says; she isn't really listening

Monopolizing is costly not only to those who are neglected but also to the monopolizers. A person who dominates communication has much less opportunity to learn from others than does a person who listens to what others think and feel. We already know what we think and feel, so there's little we can learn from hearing ourselves!

It's important to realize that not all interruptions are attempts to monopolize. We also interrupt to show interest, to voice support, and to ask for elaboration. Interrupting for these reasons doesn't divert attention from the person speaking; instead, it affirms that person and keeps the focus on her or him. Research indicates that women are more likely than men to interrupt to show interest and support (Anderson & Leaper, 1998; Aries, 1987; Beck, 1988; Mulac et al., 1988; Stewart et al., 1990). Some studies suggest that men are more likely than women to interrupt to gain control of conversations, but more research is needed to verify or disconfirm this (Aries, 1996; Goldsmith & Fulfs, 1999).

Selective Listening

A third form of nonlistening is **selective listening,** which involves focusing on only particular parts of communication. As we've noted, all listening is selective to an extent because we can't attend to everything around us. With selective listening, however, we screen out parts of a message that don't interest us and rivet attention on topics that do interest us. For example, students might be pseudolistening to a lecture but become highly attentive when a teacher says, "This will be on the test." Employees zero in on communication about raises, layoffs, and holidays. People who own beach property become highly attentive to information about hurricanes.

Selective listening also occurs when we reject communication that makes us uneasy. For instance, smokers may selectively not attend to a radio report on the dangers of smoking and secondhand smoke. We may also screen out communication that is critical of us. You may not take in a friend's comment that you are really judgmental; you may selectively tune out your boyfriend's or girlfriend's observation that you can be selfish. We all have subjects that bore us or disturb us, yet it's unwise to listen selectively when doing so could deprive us of information or insights that could be valuable.

Defensive Listening

After taking cooking lessons, Thelma bakes a cake for her friend Louise's birthday. When Louise sees the cake, she says, "Wow, that's so sweet. My Mom always made a special cake for my birthday, and she would decorate it so elaborately." Thelma replies, "Well I'm sorry that I didn't decorate the cake extravagantly. I guess I still have a lot to learn about cooking." Thelma's response illustrates **defensive listening,** which is perceiving personal attacks, criticism, or hostility in communication that is not critical or mean-spirited. When we listen defensively, we assume others don't like, trust, or respect us, and we read these motives into whatever they say, no matter how innocent their communication may be.

Some people are generally defensive, expecting criticism from all quarters. They perceive negative judgments in almost anything said to them. In other instances, defensive listening is confined to specific topics or vulnerable times when we judge ourselves to be inadequate. A worker who fears she is not performing well may hear criticism in benign comments from co-workers; a student who fails a test may hear doubts about his intelligence in an innocent question about how school is going.

Defensive listening can deprive us of information and insights that might be valuable, even if not pleasant. In addition, responding defensively to honest feedback may discourage others from being honest with us.

> **Student Voices**
>
> **Dan:**
>
> I remember a time when I was a defensive listener. I had just gotten laid off from work—the recession, you know—and I felt like nothing. I couldn't support my family, and I couldn't stand the idea of going on unemployment. Nobody in my family ever did that. Once when my son asked me for a few bucks for a school outing, I just lit into him about how irresponsible he was about money. My wife mentioned the car needed some repair work and I shouted at her that I wasn't a money machine. I'd never been like that before, but I was just so sensitive to being out of work that I had a chip on my shoulder. You couldn't talk to me about money without my taking it as a personal attack.

Ambushing

Ambushing is listening carefully for the purpose of attacking a speaker. Unlike the other kinds of nonlistening we've discussed, ambushing involves very careful listening but it isn't motivated by a genuine desire to understand another. Instead, ambushers listen intently to gather ammunition they can use to attack a speaker. Krista listens very carefully to her teammate Carl as he describes a marketing campaign. When Carl finishes, Krista pounces: "You said we could get a rough draft of the whole campaign by the end of the month. You forgot that we lose two workdays for the annual retreat next week. Besides, your plan calls for some outsourcing. Where are you getting the funds for that?" Krista's response shows that she listened to Carl's ideas not to understand them and work with him but to identify weak spots and attack them.

Not surprisingly, people who engage in ambushing tend to arouse defensiveness in others. Few of us want to speak up when we feel we are going to be attacked. In Chapter 10, we look more closely at communication that fosters defensiveness in others.

> **Student Voices**
>
> **Kralyn:**
>
> My first husband was a real ambusher. If I tried to talk to him about a dress I'd bought, he'd listen just long enough to find out what it cost and then attack me for spending money. Once I told him about a problem I was having with one of my co-workers, and he came back at me with all of the things I'd done wrong and didn't mention any of the things the other person had done. Talking to him was like setting myself up to be assaulted.

Literal Listening

The final form of nonlistening is **literal listening,** which involves listening only for content and ignoring the relationship level of meaning. As we have seen, all communication includes content or literal meaning as well as relationship meaning, which pertains to power, responsiveness, and liking between people. When we listen literally, we attend only to the content level and overlook what's being communicated on the relationship level. When we listen only literally, we are insensitive to others' feelings and to our connections with them. Cammy's commentary provides a good illustration of literal listening that deals only with content-level meaning. Literal listening may disconfirm others. When we listen literally, we don't make the effort to understand how others feel about what they say or to endorse them as people.

We have seen that there are many obstacles to effective listening. Situational obstacles include message overload, message complexity, and noise. In addition to these, there are five potential interferences inside of us: preoccupation; prejudgment, including unthinking reactions to emotionally loaded language; lack of

Student Voices

Cammy:

My sister Lannie is a literal listener. I swear, she just doesn't get all of the meaning that is between words. The last time we were home together, Mom was talking about how bad she felt that she didn't seem to have any interest in cleaning the house as it should be done and making elaborate meals. Lannie heard that, and her response to Mom was that the house wasn't clean and that Mom needed to either devote more time to it or hire someone. Then Lannie told her she ought to plan the week's dinners on Sunday so that she could shop and set aside time to make nice meals.

Give her a break! Mom just had a double radical mastectomy a month ago, and she's really depressed. She feels bad about losing her breasts, and she's worried that they didn't get all of the cancer. Who would feel like scrubbing floors and fixing gourmet food after going through that? What Mom needed was for us to hear that she was worried and unhappy and for us to tell her the house and fancy meals didn't matter. Anybody with an ounce of sensitivity could figure that out.

effort; failure to recognize diverse listening styles; and our desire to "fix" people.

The obstacles to effective listening combine to create six types of nonlistening: pseudolistening, monopolizing, selective listening, defensive listening, ambushing, and literal listening. What you've learned prepares you to think now about how you can listen more mindfully.

ADAPTING LISTENING TO COMMUNICATION GOALS

The first requirement for listening effectively is to determine your reason for listening. We listen differently when we listen for pleasure, to gain information, and to support others. We'll discuss the particular attitudes and skills that contribute to each type of effective listening.

Listening for Pleasure

Often, we engage in **listening for pleasure.** We listen to music for pleasure. We may listen to some radio programs for enjoyment. Because listening for pleasure doesn't require us to remember or respond to communication, the only guidelines are to be mindful and control distractions. Just as being mindful in lectures allows us to gain information, being mindful when listening for pleasure allows us to derive full enjoyment from what we hear. Controlling interferences is also important when we are listening for pleasure. A beautifully rendered Mozart concerto can be wonderfully satisfying but not if a television is on in the background.

CONCEPTS AT A GLANCE

Snapshot of Listening for Pleasure

- Be mindful.
- Control obstacles.

Apply the Idea

IDENTIFYING YOUR NONLISTENING HABITS

Apply the material we've just discussed by identifying times when you've engaged in nonlistening.

- *Describe a situation in which you pseudolistened.*
- *Describe an instance in which you monopolized communication.*
- *Describe a time when you listened defensively.*
- *Describe an example of ambushing someone else.*
- *Describe an instance when you listened selectively.*
- *Describe a time when you listened literally.*

Now repeat this exercise, but this time focus on examples of others who engage in each of the six types of ineffective listening.

CONCEPTS AT A GLANCE

Snapshot of Listening for Information

- Be mindful.
- Control obstacles.
- Ask questions.
- Use aids to recall.
- Organize information.

Listening for Information

Monkey Business Images/Shutterstock

Much of the time, we are **listening for information.** At such times, our goal is to gain and evaluate information. We listen for information in classes, at political debates, when important news stories are reported, and when we need guidance on everything from medical treatments to directions to a new place. In each case, we listen to gain and understand information in order to act appropriately. To do this, we need to use skills for critical thinking and for organizing and retaining information.

Be Mindful

First, it's important to choose to be mindful. Don't let your mind wander when information gets complicated or confusing. Instead, stay focused on the information, and take in as much as you can. Later, you may want to ask questions about material that wasn't clear even when you listened mindfully.

Control Obstacles

You can also minimize noise in communication situations. You might shut a window to mute traffic noises or adjust a thermostat so that the room's temperature is comfortable. You should also try to minimize psychological distractions by emptying your mind of concerns and ideas that can divert your attention. Let go of preoccupations and prejudgments that can interfere with effective listening. In addition, it's important to monitor the tendency to react to emotionally loaded language. As William Isaacs (1999) notes, we must make a very deliberate effort to cultivate an inner silence that allows us to listen thoughtfully to others.

Ask Questions

Also important is posing questions to speakers. Asking a speaker to clarify or elaborate the message may help you understand information you didn't grasp at first; it also enhances insight into content that you did comprehend. "Could you explain what you meant by ...?" and "Can you clarify the distinction between ...?" are questions that allow you to deepen your grasp of content. Questions compliment a speaker because they indicate that you are interested and want to know more.

Use Aids to Recall

To understand and remember important information, we can apply the principles of perception we discussed in Chapter 3. For instance, we learned that we tend to notice and recall stimuli that are repeated. To use this principle in everyday communication, repeat important ideas to yourself immediately after hearing them (Estes, 1989). Repetition can save you the embarrassment of having to ask people you've just met to repeat their names.

Another way to increase retention is to use mnemonic (pronounced "new-monic") devices, which are formulas or rhymes used as an aid in remembering. They can be used for a list of items that may or may not have to be remembered in a certain order. Keep the cue words or phrases as simple as possible. "Sam's Horse Must Eat Oats" would help you remember the Great Lakes in order of size: Superior, Huron, Michigan, Erie, Ontario. "Every Good Boy Deserves Fun" assists in remembering the order of notes in music—E, G, B, D, F. Random letters and numbers that you need to remember, such as on a licence plate, can be easily recalled by adding detail to each letter or number. For example, a British Columbia licence plate of BTR430 can be remembered as "Big Trouble at 4:30."

Acronyms (pronounced *ak'ra-nim*) are words or phrases made from the initial letter or letters of each of the parts of a term. For example, the acronym RAM stands for "random access memory," and NATO comprises the first letters of "North Atlantic Treaty Organization." If your supervisor asks you to code and log all incoming messages, you might remember the instruction by using the acronym CLAIM. You can also invent acronyms to help you recall personal information; for example, PAL is an acronym to remember that "Peter from Alberta is going into Law."

Organize Information

REVIEW

By choosing to be mindful, minimizing distractions, asking questions, repeating, using mnemonic devices, and organizing ideas, we can increase our ability to understand and remember informational communication.

Another technique to increase retention is to organize what you hear. When communicating informally, most people don't order their ideas carefully. The result is a flow of information that isn't coherently organized, and so is hard to retain. We can impose order by regrouping what we hear. For example, suppose a friend tells you he's confused about long-range goals, then says he doesn't know what he can do with a math major, wants to locate in the North, wonders if graduate school is necessary, likes small towns, needs some internships to try out different options, and wants a family eventually. You could regroup this stream of concerns into two categories: academic information (careers for math majors, graduate school, internship opportunities) and lifestyle preferences (North, small town, family). Remembering those two categories allows you to retain the essence of your friend's concerns, even if you forget many of the specifics. Repetition, mnemonics to create patterns, and regrouping are ways to enhance what we remember.

Apply the Idea

IMPROVING YOUR RETENTION

Apply the principles we've discussed to enhance memory.

- *The next time you meet someone, repeat his or her name to yourself three times in a row after you are introduced. Do you remember the name better when you do this?*
- *After your next interpersonal communication class, take 15 minutes to review your notes. Try reading them aloud so that you hear as well as see the main ideas. Does this increase your retention of material covered in class?*
- *Invent mnemonics to help you remember basic information in communication.*
- *Organize complex ideas by grouping them into categories. Try this first in relation to material presented in classes. To remember the main ideas of this chapter, you might use major subheadings to form categories: the listening process, obstacles to listening, forms of nonlistening, listening goals, and guidelines. The mnemonic PONGG (process, obstacles, nonlistening, goals, guidelines) could help you remember those categories.*

Listening to Support Others

We engage in relationship listening, **listening to support others,** when we listen to a friend's worries, hear a romantic partner discuss our relationship, or help a co-worker sort through a problem. Specific attitudes and skills enhance relationship listening.

CONCEPTS AT A GLANCE

Snapshot of Listening to Support

- Be mindful.
- Control obstacles.
- Attend.
- Suspend judgment.
- Understand the other's perspective.
- Paraphrase.
- Use minimal encouragers.
- Question.
- Summarize.
- Express support.

Be Mindful

The first requirement for effective relationship listening is mindfulness. You'll recall that this was also the first step in listening for information and pleasure. When we're interested in relationship-level meanings, however, a different kind of mindfulness is needed. Instead of focusing on information, we concentrate on what lies between and behind the content in order to understand what another is feeling, thinking, needing, or wanting in a conversation.

Control Obstacles

It is particularly important to control the external and internal obstacles when we are called on to listen empathically to someone. Our decision to turn off a TV or music, not answer a phone, or ask someone to watch the children are important acts of respect to our speaker. If it is not a convenient time for you to be completely mindful, it is more honest and kind to reschedule so you can be an undistracted listener.

Attend

Once you've controlled the obstacles to your ability to listen effectively, it is time to let your speaker know that you are paying attention and that his or her thoughts and feelings are important to you. We do this by using the attending behaviours described earlier, FELOR. Turn and face your speaker; maintain appropriate eye contact; lean forward so there is not a great distance between your faces, as opposed to lounging back; open your posture; and relax.

Be Careful of Expressing Judgments

When listening to help another person, it's usually wise to avoid judgmental responses, at least initially. Imposing our own judgments separates us from others and their feelings. We've inserted something between us. Yet, there are times when it is appropriate and supportive to offer opinions and to make evaluative statements. Sometimes, people we care about genuinely want our judgments, and in those cases, we should be honest about how we feel. Particularly when others are confronting ethical dilemmas, they may seek the judgments of people they trust.

If someone asks our opinion, we should try to present it in a way that doesn't disconfirm the other person. Margaret could have said to Cordelia, "How can you even think of breaking your word? That would be immoral." Whew—pretty disconfirming. Many times, people excuse cruel comments by saying, "Well, you asked me to be honest" or "I mean

Student Voices

Margaret:

Once my friend Cordelia was asked to work for an MLA, but she had agreed to take a job at a large law firm. She talked to me about her quandary and asked me what I thought she should do. Although it was clear to me that she wanted to join the MLA's election campaign, I couldn't honestly tell her I approved of that. I told her that, for me, it would be wrong to go back on my word. I then offered to think with her about ways she might approach her future employer about starting at a later date. After a long talk, Cordelia thanked me for being honest. Part of being a real friend in this instance was making a judgment. That's appropriate only if someone invites our evaluation or if we think another person is in danger of making a serious mistake.

Student Voices

Logan:

I hate the term "constructive criticism." Every time my dad says it, what follows is a put-down. By now, I've learned not to go to him when I have problems or when I'm worried about something in my life. He always judges what I'm feeling and tells me what I ought to feel and do. All that does is make me feel worse than I did before.

this as constructive criticism." Too often, however, the judgments are harsher than candour requires. If we are committed to supporting others, we use honesty to support them, not to tear them down.

Understand the Other Person's Perspective

We can't respond effectively to others until we understand their perspective and meanings. To do this, we must focus on the words and nonverbal behaviours that give us clues about how others feel and think.

Paraphrasing is a method of clarifying others' meaning or needs by reflecting our interpretations

Apply the Idea

PRACTISING SUSPENDING JUDGMENT

It's very difficult to refrain from giving advice or judging. Remember our discussion earlier about wanting to "fix" the dilemmas of our friends and partners? In responding to the statements below, avoid advising and judging. Try to turn the focus back onto the speaker to encourage that person to find his or her own solutions. As a guideline, don't advise or judge until a person has asked three times for help.

Your friend is talking about breaking up a long-term relationship.

- *"What should I do?"*

Your response:

___

- *"You've been through this before, tell me what you did."*

Your response:

___

- *"I have no idea what to do."*

Your response:

___

of their communication back to them. For example, a friend might confide, "I think my kid brother is messing around with drugs." We could paraphrase this way: "So you're really worried that your brother's experimenting with drugs." This allows us to clarify whether the friend has any evidence of the brother's drug involvement and also whether the friend is, in fact, worried about the possibility.

The response might be, "No, I don't have any real reason to suspect him, but I just worry, because drugs are so pervasive in high schools now." This clarifies by telling us the friend's worries are more the issue than any evidence that the brother is experimenting with drugs. Paraphrasing also helps us figure out what others feel. If a friend screams, "This situation is really getting to me," it's not clear whether your friend is angry, hurt, upset, or frustrated. We could find out which emotion prevails by saying, "You seem really angry." If anger is the emotion, your friend would agree; if not, she would clarify what she is feeling.

Apply the Idea

LEARNING TO PARAPHRASE

Practise effective listening by paraphrasing the following statements.

- *I've got so many pressures closing in on me right now.*
- *I'm worried about all of the money I've borrowed to get through school.*
- *I'm nervous about telling my parents that I'm gay when I see them next weekend.*
- *I don't know if Kim and I can keep the relationship together once she moves away for her job.*

Use Minimal Encouragers

Minimal encouragers prompt the speaker to go on. Minimal encouragers increase understanding of the other's thoughts and feelings by soliciting more information. These communications gently invite another person to elaborate by expressing interest in hearing more. Examples of minimal encouragers are "Tell me more," "Really?" "Go on," "I'm with you," "Then what happened?" "Yeah?" and "I see." We can also use nonverbal minimal encouragers such as a raised eyebrow to show involvement, a head motion to indicate we understand, or widened eyes to indicate we're fascinated.

Minimal encouragers indicate we are listening, following, and interested. They encourage others to keep talking so that we can more fully understand what

Apply the Idea

USING MINIMAL ENCOURAGERS

Practise encouraging others to elaborate on their thoughts and feelings by developing minimal encouragers in response to each of these comments:

- *I'm really worried about getting into grad school.*
- *I'm not sure whether I'm measuring up to my boss's expectations for new employees.*
- *I just learned that I'm a finalist for a scholarship next year.*
- *I think my girlfriend is cheating on me.*
- *I haven't had any job offers yet and I've been interviewing for four months. I'm beginning to wonder whether I'll get a job at all.*
- *I'm so excited about how this relationship is going. I've never been with someone as attentive and thoughtful as Enrico.*

Nicholas Sutcliffe/Shutterstock

Monkey Business Images/Shutterstock

Are there gender differences in the way we listen?

they mean. Keep in mind that these are *minimal* encouragers. They should not interrupt or take the talk stage away from another. Instead, effective minimal encouragers are very brief interjections that prompt, rather than interfere with, the flow of another's talk.

Question

Asking questions is a third way to enhance understanding of what another feels or needs. Sometimes it's helpful to ask questions that yield insight into what a speaker thinks or feels. For instance, we might ask, "How do you feel about that?" "What do you plan to do?" or "How are you working this through?" Another reason we ask questions is to find out what a person wants from us. Sometimes it isn't clear whether someone wants advice, a shoulder to cry on, or a safe place to vent feelings. If we can't figure out what's wanted, we can ask the other person, "Are you looking for advice or a sounding board?" "Do you want to talk about how to handle the situation or just air the issues?"

Asking direct questions signals that we want to help and allows others to tell us how we can best do that. Avoid "why" questions like "Why did you do that?" They tend to force people to defend their position instead of exploring it. As well, a question like "Why do you think she did that?" calls for too much speculation about a third party's intentions. It takes away from the speaker's feelings.

REVIEW

Listening Skills for Understanding the Other's Perspective

- Paraphrase
- Use minimal encouragers
- Ask questions
- Summarize

Summarize

Summarizing is the fourth skill of understanding and helping. When we offer a summary of what we have heard others say, it is as if we are holding a mirror up for them to see themselves in a new way. A summary is a long paraphrase that captures all the thoughts, feelings, and actions that the speaker has shared. A good summary can lay out the complexities of what the speaker is struggling with and perhaps provide some insight into feelings and wants. We might say something like "It sounds like you have a lot on your plate right now. You're trying to make a decision about university in the fall and manage a part-time job, four courses, and a full-time relationship. You describe feeling overwhelmed, pressured, and a little resentful. Am I right?" Summarizing assists others to sort through and put into priority what is most important to them. It allows them to feel truly heard and understood. Notice how the example does not try to "fix" the dilemma, it just provides good listening.

Express Support

Once we understand another's meanings and perspective, it's important to communicate support. This doesn't necessarily require us to agree with the other person's perspective or feelings, but it does require that we express support for the person. We may express support in a number of ways without agreeing. For example, you can say that you appreciate the difficulty of a friend's situation, you realize what a tough decision this is, and you understand your friend's feelings (even if your feelings are different). Perhaps the most basic way to support another is by listening mindfully, which shows that you care enough to attend fully to the other person. To illustrate how we can support a person even if we don't agree with his or her position, consider the following dialogue:

Janice: I just don't see how I can have a baby right now.

Marita: Tell me more about what you're feeling. (minimal encourager)

Janice: I feel trapped. I mean, I've still got two years of school, and we're not ready to get married.

Marita: So? (minimal encourager)

Janice: (Silence, then) I hate the thought, but I guess I'll have to get an abortion.

Marita: Sounds as if you don't feel very comfortable with that choice. (paraphrase)

Janice: I'm not, but it seems like the only answer.

Marita: What other options have you considered?

Janice: Well, I guess I really don't know of any other answers. Do you?

Marita: You could have the baby and place it for adoption or maybe even work out an arrangement with a couple that can't have a baby of their own. (advising)

Janice: No, I really can't afford to give up nine months of my life right now. Besides, I don't think I could give away a baby after carrying it all that time. Don't you think I should have an abortion?

Marita: Gee, I don't want to tell you what to do. I'm not comfortable endorsing abortion, but you may not feel the same way. (nonjudgmental, supporting)

Janice: I don't endorse abortion either, but I don't feel like I have a realistic choice.

Marita: I respect you for the way you're going about making this choice. It's a good idea to talk with people like we're doing now. (supporting)

Janice: I just hate the idea of having an abortion.

Marita: It sounds like you're not very sure that's the right answer for you. (paraphrase)

Janice: I don't know.

Marita: Let's talk a little more. How do you think you'd feel if you did have an abortion? (minimal encourager, open question)

This dialogue illustrates several principles of effective relational listening. First, notice that Marita's first two comments are minimal encouragers, designed to nudge Janice to elaborate on her perspective. Marita's third response is a paraphrase to make sure she understands what Janice is feeling. Marita then tries suggesting alternatives to abortion, but when Janice rejects those, Marita doesn't push her. Advising can road-block the flow of speaking and listening. Marita then validates Janice's feelings by expressing support. Marita makes her own position on abortion clear—she doesn't condone it—but she separates her personal stance from her respect for Janice and the way Janice is thinking through the decision.

Particularly important in this conversation is Marita's effort to collaborate with Janice in problem solving. By showing that she's willing to talk further and that she wants to help Janice work out the problem, Marita behaves as an active

Student Voices

Sheryl:

I think the greatest gift my mother ever gave me was when I told her I was going to marry Bruce. He isn't Jewish, and nobody in my family has ever married out of the faith before. I could tell my mother was disappointed, and she didn't try to hide that. She asked me if I understood how that would complicate things like family relationships and rearing kids. We talked for a while, and she realized I had thought through what it means to marry out of the faith. Then she sighed and said she had hoped I would find a nice Jewish man. But then she said she supported me whatever I did, and Bruce was welcome in our family. She told me she'd raised me to think for myself, and that's what I was doing. I just felt so loved and accepted by how she responded.

listener and a committed friend. Marita's listening style allows Janice to talk through a very tough issue without Marita imposing her own judgments. Sometimes it's difficult to listen openly and nonjudgmentally, particularly if we don't agree with the person speaking. However, if your goal is to support another person, then sensitive, responsive involvement including collaboration, if appropriate, is an ideal listening style.

GUIDELINES FOR EFFECTIVE LISTENING

Three guidelines summarize our discussion and foster effective listening: be mindful, adapt listening appropriately, and listen actively.

Be Mindful

By now, you've read this suggestion many times. Because it is so central to effective listening, however, it bears repeating. Mindfulness is a choice to be wholly present in an experience. It requires that we put aside preoccupations and preconceptions to attend fully to what is happening in the moment. Mindful listening is one of the highest compliments we can pay to others because it conveys the relationship-level meaning that they matter to us. Being mindful requires discipline and commitment. We have to discipline our tendencies to judge others, to dominate the talk stage, and to let our minds wander. Mindfulness also requires commitment to another person and to the integrity of the interpersonal communication process. Being mindful is the first and most important principle of effective listening.

Communication Notes

MORE ON DEVELOPING LISTENING SKILLS

Many good resources can help you improve your listening skills. One good book is Madelyn Burley-Allen's *Listening: The Forgotten Skill* (1995), which offers a self-teaching guide for recognizing listening styles, including your own, and learning to listen more effectively. In addition, the Internet offers a number of sites that provide concrete, practical suggestions for improving your skill at listening. Many of the sites elaborate on guidelines offered in this chapter, including those on creating and using mnemonics and taking notes effectively.

To develop skill in creating and using mnemonics and other techniques for improving recall, visit www.mindtools.com/memory.html.

Adapt Listening Appropriately

Like all communication activities, listening varies according to goals, situations, and people. What's effective depends on our purpose for listening, the context in which we are listening, and the needs and circumstances of the person to whom we are listening.

When we listen for pleasure, we should be mindful and minimize distractions so that we derive as much enjoyment as possible from listening. When we listen for information, a critical attitude, evaluation of material, and a focus on the content level of meaning enhance listening. Yet when we engage in relationship listening, very different skills are needed. We want to communicate openness and caring, and the relationship level of meaning is at least as important as the content level of meaning. Thus, we need to adapt our listening styles and attitudes to different goals.

Effective listening is listening that is adapted to others. Some people need prompting and encouragement to express themselves, whereas others need us only to be silent and attentive. Paraphrasing helps some people clarify what they think or feel, whereas others don't need that kind of assistance. We need to be skilled in a variety of listening behaviours and to know when each is appropriate. Recall from Chapter 1 that the ability to use a range of skills and to exercise judgment about which ones are called for is fundamental to interpersonal communication.

Listen Actively

When we realize all that's involved in listening, we appreciate what an active effort it is. To listen effectively, we must be willing to focus our minds, to organize and interpret others' ideas and feelings, to express our interest on both the content level and the relationship level of meaning, and to retain what a speaker says. In some situations, we also become active partners by listening collaboratively and engaging in problem solving. Doing this is hard work! Recognizing that mindful listening is an active process prepares us to invest the effort needed to do it effectively.

Chapter Summary

Zeno of Citium, an ancient philosopher, said, "We have been given two ears and but a single mouth in order that we may hear more and talk less." His wry observation is as relevant today as it was thousands of years ago. Similar wisdom came from Mother Teresa in an interview with Dan Rather (Bailey, 1998, p. C5):

Rather: What do you say to God when you pray?

Mother Teresa: I listen.

Rather: Well, what does God say?

Mother Teresa: He listens.

In this chapter, we've explored the complex and demanding process of mindful listening. We began by distinguishing hearing and listening. Hearing is a physiological process that doesn't entail effort on our part. Listening, in contrast, is a complicated process involving physically receiving messages, selecting, organizing, interpreting, responding, and remembering. To do it well takes commitment and skill.

There are many obstacles to effective listening. External obstacles include message overload, complexity of material, and external noise in communication contexts. In addition, listening can be hampered by preoccupations and prejudgments, including reactions to emotionally loaded language; lack of effort; failure to recognize and adapt to diverse listening styles; and our desire to "fix" things. These obstacles give rise to various types of nonlistening, including pseudolistening, monopolizing, selective listening, defensive listening, ambushing, and literal listening.

We've identified skills and attitudes appropriate to different listening goals. Listening for pleasure is supported by mindfulness and efforts to minimize distractions and noise. Informational listening requires us to adopt a mindful attitude and to think critically, organize and evaluate information, clarify understanding by asking questions, and develop aids for retention of complex material. Listening to support others (relationship listening) also involves mindfulness, but it calls for different listening skills: suspending judgment, paraphrasing, giving minimal encouragers, and expressing support enhance the effectiveness of relationship listening.

The ideas we've discussed yield three guidelines for effective listening. First, we must be mindful. Second, we should adapt our listening skills and style to accommodate differences in listening purpose and individuals. Finally, we should remember that listening is an active process and be prepared to invest energy and effort in doing it skillfully. Because listening is important in all speech communities, in later chapters we'll revisit some of the ideas covered here as we discuss dynamics in relationships.

Key Concepts

- ambushing
- attending
- defensive listening
- hearing
- listening
- listening for information
- listening for pleasure
- listening to support others
- literal listening
- mindfulness
- minimal encouragers
- monopolizing
- paraphrasing
- pseudolistening
- remembering
- responding
- selective listening
- summarizing

For Further Thought and Discussion

1. Review the six types of nonlistening discussed in this chapter. Are any of them common in your communication? Select one of your nonlistening practices and work to reduce its occurrence.
2. What ethical principles can you identify to guide the three kinds of listening? Are different ethical principles appropriate when listening for information and listening to support others?
3. Keep a record of your listening for the next two days. How much time do you spend listening for information, listening to support others, and listening for pleasure?
4. Use your InfoTrac® College Edition to read pamphlets and articles published by professional associations. Also skim articles in recent issues of *The Globe and Mail* or *Business Quarterly*. Is the importance of listening mentioned in these publications? Discuss your findings with others in your class.
5. Apply the strategies for remembering that we discussed in this chapter. Create mnemonics, organize material as you listen, and review material immediately after listening. Do you find that using these strategies increases your listening effectiveness?

6. Who is your prototype, or model, for an effective listener? Describe what the person does that makes her or him effective. How do the person's behaviours fit with guidelines for effective listening discussed in this chapter?
7. The International Listening Association is a rich resource for learning more about listening and networking with others who recognize its importance in everyday life. Its website (www.listen.org) features exercises to test and improve listening, factoids about listening, Internet discussion groups, quotes about the nature and value of listening, and a bibliography for those who want to read more.

Chapter 9

Communication Climate: The Foundation of Personal Relationships

In a full heart there is room for everything, and in an empty heart there is room for nothing.

—Antonio Porchia (1943)

You may be deceived if you trust too much, but you will live in torment if you don't trust enough.

—Frank Crane (1927)

Do you feel foggy-headed or down when the sky is overcast and upbeat when it's sunny? Does your mood ever shift as the weather changes? Most of us respond to climate. We feel more or less positive depending on the conditions around us. In much the same way that we react to physical climates, we also respond to interpersonal climates.

© iStockphoto.com/Eliza Snow

Interpersonal climate is the overall feeling or emotional mood between people—warm or cold, safe or anxious, comfortable or awkward, accepting or rejecting, open or guarded. Understanding interpersonal climates will give you insight into why you feel relaxed and comfortable in some of your relationships and uneasy and defensive in others. Further, learning how communication shapes interpersonal climates will empower you to create and sustain the climates that you want in your relationships.

This chapter explores communication as a primary influence on building and sustaining interpersonal climates in personal, social, and professional relationships. We begin by discussing features of satisfying interpersonal relationships. Next, we examine the kinds of communication that build confirming, supportive interpersonal climates. Finally, we discuss guidelines for creating and sustaining healthy interpersonal climates. In the next chapter, we'll see how confirming, supportive climates assist us in managing conflict when it arises.

Student Voices

Fiona:

The worst time in my whole life was my first semester here. I felt so lonely being away from my family and all my friends at home. Back there we were really close, and there was always somebody to be with and talk to, but I didn't know anybody on this campus. I felt all alone and like nobody cared about me. I became depressed and almost left school, but then I started seeing a guy and I made a couple of friends. Everything got better once I had some people to talk to and be with.

FEATURES OF SATISFYING PERSONAL RELATIONSHIPS

As we saw in Chapter 1, we relate to others to fulfill human needs for survival, safety, belonging, esteem, and self-actualization in a diverse social world. When we are involved in satisfying relationships, we feel more positive about our lives and ourselves.

CONCEPTS AT A GLANCE

Features of Close Relationships

- Investment
- Commitment
- Trust
- Comfort with relational dialectics

Many people feel as Fiona does. Research indicates that in North America, loneliness during the first year of college or university depends more on whether a person has friends than on whether a person has good family ties (Cutrona, 1982). North Americans rely more on friends than do Russians, Koreans, or Turks (Ryan et al., 2005). We rely on friends to satisfy our needs for belonging and acceptance, especially after we have moved away from home.

Personal relationships are very complex and are shaped by numerous factors. Of the many influences, four are particularly critical for building and sustaining satisfying close relationships: investment, commitment, trust, and comfort with relational dialectics. As we discuss each of these influences, realize that members of different speech communities may have distinct rules for what each feature includes and how it is communicated. For example, in general, Westerners rely heavily on verbal disclosures to build trust, whereas most traditional Asians are less verbally revealing and depend on actions to build trust. Caucasians tend to regard commitment as a tie between two people,

Monkey Business Images/Shutterstock

Student Voices

Tris:

I dated this one guy for a long time before I finally had to cut my losses. He said he loved me, but he wouldn't put anything into the relationship. I gave so much—always accommodating him, doing things for him, loving him, but there just wasn't any reciprocity. It was a one-way street with him, and I felt like he didn't value me very much at all.

Student Voices

Terry:

I was really crazy about this girl my first year, but I just didn't trust that she really cared about me. I was always doing little things to show her I cared, like taking her a flower or changing the oil in her car. But she never did little things for me. As long as I was taking care of her, she was great. But when I needed to feel she was there for me, things didn't work very well. I just didn't trust her to look out for me.

whereas other ethnic groups often perceive commitment as including links between families and communities (Gaines, 1995).

Investment

A **relationship investment** is what we put into a relationship that we could not retrieve if the relationship were to end. When we care about another person, we invest time, energy, thought, and feelings in interaction. We may also invest materially by spending money, giving gifts, and so forth. In workplace relationships, we also invest time, energy, thought, and feeling and often give material assistance to co-workers.

Relationship investments cannot be recovered, so the only way to reap the benefits of your investments is to stick with a relationship (Brehm, 1992). We can't get back the time, feelings, and energy we invest in a relationship. We cannot recover the history we have shared with another person. Thus, to leave is to lose the investment we've made.

Perceived equality of relationship investment affects satisfaction with romantic relationships. The happiest dating and married partners feel that they invest equally (Fletcher et al., 1987; Hecht, Marston, & Larkey, 1994). When we perceive ourselves as investing more than our partner, we tend to be dissatisfied and resentful. When we perceive our partner as investing more than we are, we may feel guilty. Thus, perceived inequity erodes satisfaction (Brehm, 1992) and communication. Partners

Apply the Idea

YOUR INVESTMENT IN RELATIONSHIPS

What have you invested in your closest friendship, romantic relationship, and workplace relationship?

- *How much time have you spent in each relationship?*
- *How many decisions have you made to accommodate the other person?*
- *How much money have you spent on each person?*
- *To what extent is your history entwined with that of the other person?*
- *How much trust have you given each person?*
- *How much support have you given each person?*
- *Do the other person's investments roughly equal yours?*
- *What would be lost if these relationships ended? Could you recover your investment?*

who feel they are investing unequally tend to have limited disclosures and engage in little supportive communication (Brehm, 1992).

Commitment

Commitment is a decision to remain in a relationship. Notice that commitment is defined as a decision, not a feeling (Etcheverry & Le, 2005). The hallmark of commitment is the intention to share the future. In committed relationships, partners assume that they will continue together. Unlike passion or attraction, which arise in the present, commitment links partners together in the future. Because partners in committed relationships view their connection as continuing, they are unlikely to bail out during the inevitable rough times. Problems and tensions aren't seen as reasons to end the relationship.

Whereas love is a feeling we can't control, commitment is a decision. It is a choice to maintain a relationship. Cognitive therapist Aaron Beck (1988) believes that the decision to commit injects responsibility into relationships. When partners make a commitment, they take responsibility for continuing to invest in and care for their bond. Without responsibility, relationships are subject to the whims of feeling and fortune, which are not a stable basis for the long term.

What challenges do you face in personal relationships?

Communication Notes

WHAT KEEPS RELATIONSHIPS TOGETHER?

Imagine that the person you have been seeing for a long time says, "I love you." Would you assume that meant that the person wants to spend his or her life with you? You wouldn't if you were familiar with research on what holds relationships together over time.

To find out what holds a relationship together, Mary Lund (1985) studied heterosexual college seniors. She measured their love for partners by asking how they felt about their partners. To measure commitment, Lund asked them to rate the strength of their intention to stay in the relationship. She found that the continuation of relationships depended more on commitment than on love. Couples who had high levels of love but low commitment to a shared future were less likely to remain together than couples who were highly committed to a joint future. Thus, the intention to stay together is a more powerful glue than positive feelings between partners.

It seems that, once people decide to stay in a relationship, they are more likely to invest in it. In turn, their investments enrich the relationship so that staying is rewarding. Summarizing her findings, Lund said that, although love usually accompanies commitment, commitment and investment have more to do with whether a relationship lasts than do love and rewards.

Lund's findings provide insight into one reason arranged marriages often are strong and enduring (Nanda & Warms, 1998). In societies where marriages are arranged, bride and groom enter the marriage without love (sometimes they have not even met) but with a steadfast commitment to the permanence of the marriage. Love may come later.

Student Voices

Erin:

I've been married for six years, and it has been a very difficult relationship. We were married right out of high school because I was pregnant. This set our marriage off to a rocky start. We separated twice, which tells you that we weren't totally committed. The last time we separated and got back together, we agreed this would be our last try at making the marriage work. We decided that if it was going to have a chance of working, both of us had to put everything we have into it. We also decided to get the words "separation" and "divorce" out of our vocabulary. I can't believe the change that we have had in our relationship since we decided to put everything into it and not to talk about breaking up. We now have a true commitment.

Trust

A third cornerstone of satisfying personal relationships is a high degree of trust between partners (Brehm, 1992; Steiner-Pappalardo & Gurung, 2002; Veroff, 1999). **Trust** involves believing in another's reliability (that he or she will do as promised) and emotionally relying on another to look out for our welfare and our relationship. Trust doesn't come automatically in relationships. Usually, it is earned over time. We learn to trust others as they prove that they are reliable, show that they care, and make the investments to enrich the relationship. When trust is established, we feel psychologically safe in the relationship. One reason trust is so important to relationships is that it allows us to take risks with others. We open ourselves to others only if we feel we can count on them to protect our confidences and to care about us and our well-being.

Self-Disclosure

Self-disclosure can both build and reflect trust between people. **Self-disclosure** is the revelation of personal information about ourselves that others are unlikely to discover in other ways. According to researchers who have studied communication between intimates, self-disclosure is a key gauge of closeness, at least among Westerners (Derlega & Berg, 1987; Hansen & Schuldt, 1984; Meeks, Hendrick, & Hendrick, 1998).

Student Voices

Phillip:

When Denny and I decided to go out on our own, we'd worked together in a tech firm for two years, and neither of us felt like that was where we wanted to be for life, or even for another three years. So we started our own company. It was really scary because we didn't have any guarantees or any safety net. All we had was each other, and that really changed our relationship. We spent a lot more time together, talked for hours about every detail of our business, travelled together to evaluate new software and business-to-business companies. We took risks with each other, learned to trust each other to the max. And we spent a lot of time dreaming about what could happen with our company and how we could bring that about. In a way, I think the dreaming and planning together was like a real cement for us. After a year of working together that closely, we were more like brothers than partners in a business.

Self-disclosure should take place gradually and with appropriate caution. We begin by disclosing superficial information ("I'm worried that I won't find a job," "I'm afraid of heights"). If a person responds with empathy to early and limited disclosures, we're likely to reveal progressively more intimate information ("My father served time in prison," "I was fired from my last job," "I take medication for depression"). If these disclosures are also met with understanding and confidentiality, trust continues to grow.

In the early stages of relationship development, reciprocity of disclosures is important. We're willing to disclose our private feelings only as long as the other person also reveals personal information (Cunningham, Strassberg, & Haan, 1986). When a relationship is just beginning, we feel vulnerable; the other could betray a confidence or reject us because we disclose something negative. Our feeling of vulnerability is reduced if the other person is also allowing vulnerability by making self-disclosures to us.

Reciprocity of disclosures becomes less important as a relationship grows and stabilizes. In most stable relationships, people don't feel the need to reciprocate disclosures immediately. Unlike new acquaintances, they have the time to reciprocate on a more leisurely schedule. Thus, in established relationships, disclosure is more likely to be greeted with a response to what has been revealed than with an immediate, equivalent disclosure.

Monkey Business Images/Shutterstock

Although all of us disclose some personal information in close relationships, not everyone discloses equally or in the same ways. People vary in how much they want to self-disclose, so an absolute amount of disclosure is not a surefire measure of trust or relationship health. Also, cultural differences shape our tendencies to self-disclose. People raised in a traditional Chinese society tend to disclose less personal information than most Westerners do. Among Pakistanis, disclosures between parents and children are much rarer than among Canadian-born families.

Gender also seems to affect how and how much people disclose, as discussed in the Communication Notes feature "Different Modes of Closeness." In general, women make more verbal disclosures both to other women and to men. Women also tend to place greater value on verbal disclosures than most men (Floyd & Parks, 1995). Men generally talk less about personal feelings, especially their shortcomings or self-doubts (Johnson, 2000). Many men self-disclose more often with actions than with words. Sorell's comments make this point.

Communication Notes

DIFFERENT MODES OF CLOSENESS

Research indicates that women and men generally place equal value on closeness, but they tend to differ somewhat in how they create and express it. Many researchers trace these differences to childhood play (Benenson, Apostoleris, & Parnass, 1997; Rose & Asher, 2000).

Young boys typically interact with their friends by doing things in groups (playing sports or engaging in rough-and-tumble play). As a result, boys tend to bond with others by doing things together. Carrying the lessons of childhood play into adult friendships, many men do not regard intimate or emotional conversation and self-disclosure as the only, or even the primary, path to closeness. Instead, their preferred path to intimacy is activity (doing things with and for others). This mode is called *closeness in the doing*.

Young girls tend to interact with friends through dialogue (socializing in dyads or triads in which face-to-face communication is central). As a result, many girls learn to form intimate connections through talking. As adults, women tend to favour dialogue (sharing personal disclosures and intimate communication) as a path to intimacy. This is called *closeness in dialogue*.

Both women and men travel both paths to intimacy. What differs is the degree of emphasis that women and men, in general, place on each path. Recent studies indicate that both women and men do things for people they care about. Instrumental shows of affection, or closeness in the doing, are part of most women's friendships, although they are usually not as central as in men's friendships. Both ways of expressing and experiencing closeness are valid, and both should be respected. Research also indicates that men sometimes express closeness through dialogue, just not as frequently as most women (Canary & Dindia, 1998; Metts, 2006; Wood & Inman, 1993).

Student Voices

Sorell:

When I really need some support from my girlfriend, I don't just come out and say, "I need you." What I do is go over to her place or call her to see if she wants to come to my place. Sometimes we just sit together watching TV or something. And that helps. I know she knows that I am down and need her, but I don't have to say it. I do the same thing when I think she is feeling low. It's hard for me to say "I love you and I'm sorry you feel bad." But I can be with her, and I can hug her and let her know through my actions that I care.

Student Voices

Kalen:

I think what first clued me in that Shelby was losing interest was that she stopped telling me private stuff about herself. For the first couple of months we dated, she shared so much about her dreams, plans, and fears. The more she told me about herself and the more I told her, the closer I felt. But then she seemed to withdraw and not want to share her private thoughts. That was really the start of the end.

Different modes of expressing closeness are not confined to personal relationships. They also show up in the workplace. Women generally rely more than men on talk to form and sustain close working relationships, whereas men generally rely more than women on doing things for and with co-workers to establish and develop close working relationships (Tannen, 1995).

Although self-disclosing is important early in the process of developing intimacy, for most relationships it is not a primary communication dynamic over the long haul. Although disclosure wanes over time, partners continue to reap the benefits of the trust and depth of personal knowledge created by early disclosures. Radical decreases in disclosures may signal trouble in a relationship (Baxter, 1987), as Kalen discovered.

Comfort with Relational Dialectics

A final quality of healthy relationships is understanding and being comfortable with **relational dialectics,** which are opposing forces, or tensions, that are normal in relationships. Although these tensions are normal, they can be frustrating if we don't understand them and if we don't label them as normal. Table 9.1 illustrates three relational dialectics that have been identified by researchers (Baxter, 1988, 1990, 1993; Baxter & Simon, 1993; Erbert, 2000).

Autonomy/Connection

All of us experience tension between the desire to be autonomous, or independent, and the desire to be close, or connected to others. Friends and romantic partners want to spend time with each other, to have joint interests, and to talk personally.

TABLE 9.1

RELATIONAL DIALECTICS

Autonomy/Connection	I need my own space. I want to be close.
Novelty/Predictability	We need to do something new and different. I like the familiar rhythms we have.
Openness/Closedness	I like sharing so much with you. There are some things I don't want to talk about with you.

At the same time, they need to feel that their individuality is not swallowed up by relationships. Tension between the need for autonomy and the need for connection also marks relationships on the job. We may enjoy being part of teams and like the sense of community in our workplace. At the same time, we may want to do some solo projects and work independently.

Relationship counsellors agree that the most central and continuous friction in most close relationships arises from the opposing needs for autonomy and for connection (Beck, 1988; Scarf, 1987). Both autonomy and closeness are natural human needs. The challenge is to preserve individuality while also nurturing connection in a relationship. For example, when partners in a relationship take vacations, they might eat all meals together, engage in shared activities, and sleep and interact in confined spaces where privacy is limited. When they return home after a vacation, however, they might interact less than usual for several days. Having been immersed in togetherness, they both seek distance to reestablish their autonomous identities.

Student Voices

Max:

Dialectics explains something that has really confused me. I've never understood how I could want so much to be with Ashley for a while and then feel suffocated and need to get away. I've worried that it means I don't love her anymore or there is something wrong between us. But now I see how both needs are normal and okay.

Novelty/Predictability

The second dialectic is the tension between wanting routine or familiarity and wanting novelty in a relationship. All of us like a certain amount of routine to provide security and predictability in our lives. For example, you and a friend might have long ago agreed to get together at a particular restaurant on Sundays for lunch and visiting. You count on that as a steady, habitual time to see each other. Yet, too much routine becomes boring, so it's also natural to seek novel experiences. Every so often, you and your friend might decide to explore a new restaurant or make a day trip, just to introduce variety into your friendship.

On-the-job relationships also feel the tension between the desire for predictability and the desire for novelty. We want enough routine at work to feel competent and familiar with our responsibilities, but we also want enough novelty and change to keep us stimulated. However, as Dennis points out, too much novelty in the workplace can be overwhelming.

Student Voices

Dennis:

Last year was extremely difficult for my wife Katie. It seemed like everything at her job changed at once. First, the company was bought by a large corporation. Then, the CEO Katie had worked under for 10 years was fired and a new one brought on board. The new guy implemented all kinds of changes in company policies and procedures. A lot of the staff got frustrated and quit, so that led to changes in Katie's co-workers.

Openness/Closedness

The third dialectic is a tension between wanting open communication and needing a degree of privacy, even with intimates. With our closest partners, we self-disclose in ways we don't with co-workers and casual acquaintances. Yet, we also desire some privacy, and we want our intimates to respect that. Completely unrestrained

Student Voices

Andy:

My girlfriend has trouble accepting the fact that I won't talk to her about my brother Jacob. He died when I was eight, and I still can't deal with all my feelings, especially with feeling guilty that he died and I'm alive. I just can't talk about that to anybody. With my girlfriend, I talk about lots of personal stuff, but Jacob is just too private and too hard.

© 2009 Jupiterimages Corporation

Respectful negotiation is crucial to resolving differences.

expressiveness would be intolerable (Baxter, 1993; Petronio, 1991). There is nothing wrong with seeking privacy; it doesn't mean that a relationship is in trouble. It means only that we have normal needs for both openness and closedness.

The three dialectics create ongoing tensions in healthy relationships. This is a problem only if partners don't understand that dialectics and the tension they generate are natural parts of relationships. Once we realize that dialectics are normal in all relationships, we can accept and grow from the tensions they generate (Baxter & Montgomery, 1996; Metts, 2006).

Dialectics are interrelated. For instance, friends who are highly open are also likely to be very connected, whereas more closed friends tend to favour greater autonomy (Aries, 1987). Relational dialectics also interact with other facets of interpersonal communication. For instance, partners who prefer a high degree of individuality tend to create more individual spaces and fewer common ones in their homes than do partners who favour greater connection (Fitzpatrick, 1988; Fitzpatrick & Best, 1979). Likewise, some workplaces have lots of open spaces and few doors (or few closed doors), whereas other work sites feature separate offices, closed doors, and few common spaces for interaction.

CONCEPTS AT A GLANCE

Responding to Dialectics

- Neutralize the two poles.
- Prioritize dialectics.
- Separate dialectics.
- Reframe needs.

Negotiating Dialectical Tensions

Baxter (1990) has identified four ways in which partners handle the tension generated by opposing needs. One response, called *neutralization,* is to negotiate a balance between two dialectical needs. Each need is met to an extent, but neither is fully satisfied. A couple might have a fairly consistent equilibrium between the amount of novelty and the amount of routine in their relationship.

A second response is *prioritize,* in which we give priority to one dialectical need and neglect the other. For example, co-workers might be very closed about all topics. Some partners cycle between dialectical needs, favouring each one alternately. A couple could be continuously together for a period and then be autonomous for a time.

A third way to manage dialectics is *separation.* When we separate dialectics, we assign one dialectical need to certain spheres of interaction and the opposing dialectical need to other aspects of interaction. For instance, friends might be open about many topics but respect each other's privacy in one or two areas. Employees might work independently on most tasks but operate very interactively and openly on specific teams. Many dual-career couples are autonomous professionally, relying little on each other for advice, although they are very connected about family matters.

The final method of dealing with dialectics is *reframing.* This is a complex and transformative

Student Voices

Beverly:

My folks are so funny. They plod along in the same old rut for ages and ages, and my sister and I can't get them to do anything different. Mom won't try a new recipe for chicken, because "we like ours like I always fix it." Dad won't try a new style of shirt because "that's not the kind of shirt I wear." Dynamite wouldn't blow them out of their ruts. But then, all of a sudden, they'll do a whole bunch of unusual things. Like once they went out to three movies in a day, and the next day they went for a picnic at the zoo. This kind of zaniness goes on for a while, then it's back to humdrum for months and months. I guess they get all of their novelty in occasional bursts.

strategy in which partners redefine contradictory needs as not being in opposition. In other words, they reframe their perceptions by redefining what is happening. One of the authors and her colleagues found an example of this when they studied differences between intimate partners (Wood et al., 1994). Some partners transcended the opposition between autonomy and connection by defining differences and disagreements (which emphasize individuals) as enhancing intimacy (which emphasizes the relationship). Another example of reframing is deciding that novelty and predictability are not opposites, but allies. One couple commented that their routines make novelty interesting, and novelty makes routines comforting.

Apply the Idea

APPLYING RELATIONAL DIALECTICS

How do relational dialectics operate in your life? To find out, select three of your relationships: a close friendship, a current or past romantic relationship, and an on-the-job relationship. For each relationship, answer these questions:

- *How are needs for autonomy expressed and met?*
- *How are needs for connection expressed and met?*
- *How are needs for novelty expressed and met?*
- *How are needs for predictability expressed and met?*
- *How are needs for openness expressed and met?*
- *How are needs for closedness expressed and met?*

Now, think about how you manage the tension between opposing needs in each dialectic. When do you rely on neutralization, selection, separation, and reframing? How satisfied are you with your responses? Experiment with new ways to manage dialectical tensions.

Research indicates that, in general, the least effective and least satisfying response is selection, in which one dialectical need is neglected (Baxter, 1990). Squelching any natural human impulse diminishes us. The challenge is to find ways to accommodate all our needs, even when they seem contradictory.

Healthy relationships exist when the people in them create a satisfying interpersonal climate by investing, making a commitment, developing trust, and learning to understand and negotiate dialectical tensions. Underlying these four features is *confirmation,* which we discuss in the next section of the chapter.

CONFIRMING AND DISCONFIRMING CLIMATES

We first encountered philosopher Martin Buber in Chapter 1 when we discussed I–It, I–You, and I–Thou relationships. Buber (1957) believed that all of us need confirmation to be healthy and to grow. The essence of confirmation is feeling known and valued as an individual. In relationships that have a confirming climate, we feel personally cherished and respected.

Interpersonal climates exist on a continuum from confirming to disconfirming (Figure 9.1). Few relationships are purely confirming or disconfirming; most fall somewhere between the two extremes. Some interactions are confirming and others are disconfirming—communication cycles between basically confirming and basically disconfirming.

Relationships usually don't move abruptly from one spot on the continuum to a different spot. Usually, one level of confirmation flows into the next in a gradual way. You might not feel very confirmed by a person you have just met. As the two of you talk and interact, the other person may communicate that he or she values you, so you begin to feel more confirmed. Over time, you move on to feeling that the relationship is basically confirming.

CONCEPTS AT A GLANCE

Elements of Confirming Climates

- Recognition
- Acknowledgment
- Endorsement

Levels of Confirmation and Disconfirmation

Building on Buber's ideas as well as those of psychiatrist R. D. Laing (1961), communication scholars have extended insight into confirming and disconfirming climates (Cissna & Sieburg, 1986). They have identified three levels of communication that confirm or disconfirm others. As we discuss these, you'll notice that confirming communication involves person-centredness, which we discussed in Chapter 1. Highly person-centred communication recognizes another's feelings and ideas as legitimate. Low person-centred communication denies, ignores, or challenges another's feelings and ideas (Burleson, 1994; Jones & Burleson, 2003).

Recognition

The most basic form of confirmation is *recognizing that another person exists.* We do this with nonverbal behaviours (a smile or touch) and verbal communication ("Hello," "Good to meet you"). We disconfirm others at a fundamental level when

FIGURE 9.1

Interpersonal climates exist on a continuum and are frequently in flux.

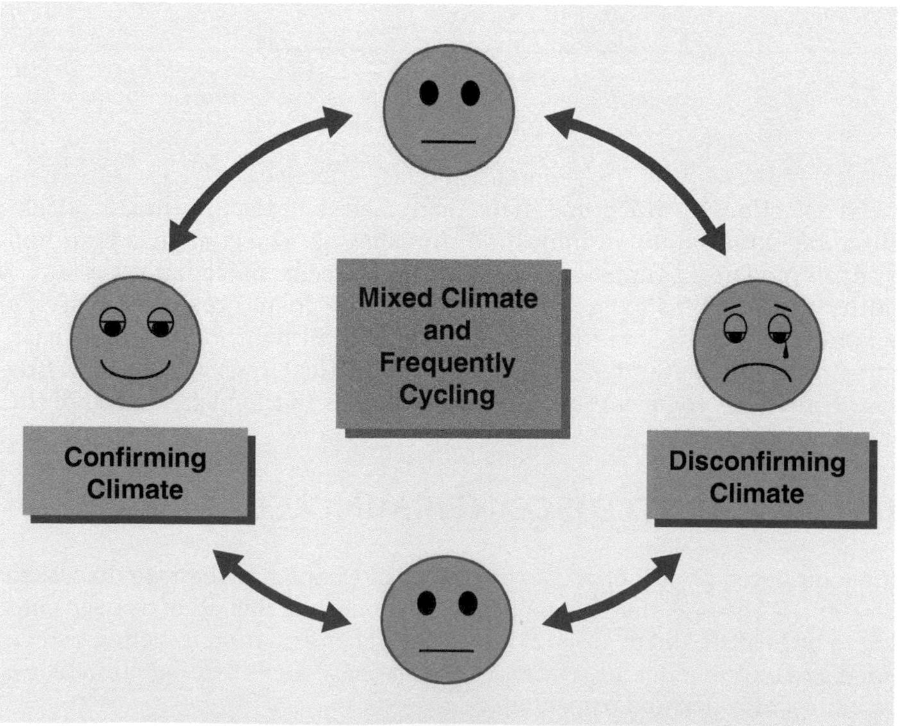

we don't acknowledge their existence. For example, you might not speak or look up when a co-worker enters your office. A parent who punishes a child by refusing to speak to her or him disconfirms the child.

Student Voices

Kingston:

You'd think that Canada would be a place with no discrimination since Canadians always brag about our diversity. But I can tell you that discrimination and racism is alive and well in Canada. If I walk the streets late at night with my non-Black friends, we are never bothered, but if I am out alone I am suddenly seen as a potentially dangerous Black.

Acknowledgment

A second and more positive level of confirmation is acknowledgment of what another feels, thinks, or says. Nonverbally, we acknowledge others by nodding our heads or by making eye contact to show we are listening. Verbal acknowledgments are direct responses to others' communication. If a friend says, "I'm really worried that I blew the LSAT exam," you could acknowledge that by paraphrasing: "So you're scared that you didn't do well on it, huh?" This paraphrasing response acknowledges both the thoughts and the feelings of the other person.

Communication Notes

RACIAL PROFILING

The October 20, 2002, issue of the *Toronto Star* carried an article entitled "Police target black drivers," which suggested that police were stopping more Blacks than any other race and called it "racial profiling" (Rankin et al., 2002). Of some randomly selected 1300 people in Toronto who were asked about their contacts with the police, 28 percent of the Blacks reported being stopped within the last two years, compared to only 14.6 percent of the Whites. This alleged tendency of the police to stop more Blacks than Whites has created a disconfirming climate toward Blacks.

One 17-year-old Black man reported, "When I'm driving with my brother and he sees a cop in the rearview mirror, he's shook. But when I'm with a White friend and he sees a cop in the rearview mirror, he's still chilling."

We disconfirm others when we don't acknowledge their feelings or thoughts. Reponses that are tangential, irrelevant, or impersonal don't acknowledge what another has said. For instance, a tangential response to your friend's statement about the LSAT would be, "Yeah, the LSAT's a killer. The people who design those standardized tests must be real sadists. Have you ever wondered what kind of person would do that for a living? Want to go out and shoot some darts tonight?" would be an irrelevant response that ignores the friend's comment.

© Photo Network/Alamy GetStock

A disconfirming climate is established in this scene by the act of turning away.

Student Voices

Lori:

You'd be amazed by how often people refuse to acknowledge what differently abled people say. A hundred times I've been walking across campus and someone has come up and offered to guide me. I tell them I know the way and don't need help, and they still put an arm under my elbow to guide me. I may be blind, but there's nothing wrong with my mind. I know if I need help. Why won't others acknowledge that?

An impersonal response that fails to acknowledge your friend individually would be, "Everybody feels that after taking the test." A denial response would be, "You did fine on the LSAT." Notice that each type of disconfirmation is not person-centred.

Lori makes an important point. It is fundamentally disconfirming to have others ignore what we say and think. Especially when we deal with people who differ from us in important ways, we should take time to learn what they perceive as confirming and disconfirming. This idea is illustrated in the Communication Notes feature "Guidelines for Communicating with People with Disabilities."

Communication Notes

GUIDELINES FOR COMMUNICATING WITH PEOPLE WITH DISABILITIES

Like all of us, people with disabilities value confirming communication that demonstrates that we respect them and their abilities. The following guidelines provide advice for communicating confirmation when interacting with people who have disabilities.

- When you talk with someone who has a disability, speak directly to the person, not to a companion or interpreter.
- When you are introduced to a person with a disability, offer to shake hands. People who have limited hand use or who have artificial limbs usually can shake hands.
- When you meet a person who has a visual impairment, identify yourself and anyone who is with you. If a person with a visual impairment is part of a group, preface your comments to that person with his or her name.
- You may offer assistance, but don't provide it unless your offer is accepted. Then, ask the person how you can best assist (ask for instructions).
- Treat adults as adults. Don't patronize people in wheelchairs by patting them on the shoulder or head; don't use childish language when speaking to people who do not have a mental disability.
- Respect the personal space of people with disabilities. It is rude to lean on a wheelchair, because that is part of someone's personal territory.
- Listen mindfully when you talk with someone who has difficulty speaking. Don't interrupt or supply words to others. Just be patient and let them finish. Don't pretend to understand if you don't. Instead, explain what you didn't understand, and ask the person to respond.
- When you talk with people who use a wheelchair or crutches, try to position yourself at their eye level and in front of them to allow good eye contact.
- It is appropriate to wave your hand or tap the shoulder of people with hearing impairments as a way to get their attention. Look directly at the person and speak clearly, slowly, and expressively. Face those who lip-read, place yourself in a good light source, and keep your hands away from your mouth. Do not chew gum.
- Relax. Don't be afraid to use common expressions, such as "See you later" to someone with a visual impairment, or "Did you hear the news?" to someone with a hearing difficulty. They're unlikely to be offended and may turn the irony into a joke.

Endorsement

The strongest level of confirmation is *endorsement*. Endorsement involves accepting another's feelings or thoughts. For example, you could endorse by saying, "It's natural to be worried about the LSAT when you have so much riding on it. I know how much going to law school means to you." We disconfirm others when we don't accept their thoughts and feelings. If you respond to the friend by saying, "How can you worry about the LSAT when the country is on the verge of war?" you reject the validity of the expressed feelings.

Endorsement isn't always possible if we are trying to be honest with others. Sometimes we cannot accept what another feels or thinks, so we can't give an endorsing response. A few years ago, one of the authors spent a lot of time with a 15-year-old. Bobby and the author found many things to do and talk about, and she continually looked for ways to confirm him. Gradually, trust between them grew, and they shared more and more personal information. One day, he told the author that he had tried acid and was looking forward to doing more acid in the future. She couldn't endorse what Bobby had done and couldn't support his desire to continue using acid. She told Bobby that she cared about him but couldn't approve of this behaviour. She informed him of some of the long-term consequences of acid and the dangers of its being mixed with other drugs. Bobby hadn't been aware of this information. In this situation, the author was able to confirm him as a person without endorsing a particular behaviour. The trust they had built up and the confirming climate they had established allowed them to talk honestly about the dangers of drugs.

Disconfirmation is not mere disagreement. After all, disagreements can be productive and healthy, and they imply that people matter enough to each other to argue. What is disconfirming is to be told that we are crazy, wrong, stupid, or unimportant. If you think about what we've discussed, you'll probably find that the relationships in which you feel most valued and comfortable are those with high levels of confirmation. Table 9.2 illustrates the different levels on which confirmation and disconfirmation occur.

Endorsement isn't always possible if we are trying to be honest with others. Sometimes we cannot accept what another feels or thinks, so we can't make an

TABLE 9.2

CONFIRMING AND DISCONFIRMING MESSAGES

	Confirming Messages	Disconfirming Messages
Recognition	"You exist." "Hello."	"You don't exist." Silence.
Acknowledgment	"You matter to me." "We have a relationship." "I'm sorry you're hurt."	"You don't matter." "We are not a team." "You'll get over it."
Endorsement	"What you think is true." "What you feel is okay." "I feel the same way."	"You are wrong." "You shouldn't feel what you do." "Your feeling doesn't make sense."

MANDY GODBEHEAR/Shutterstock

Being ignored is the most disconfirming message of all.

endorsing response. University of Victoria researcher Sibylle Artz, in her landmark research on violence in schoolgirls (1998), makes an important distinction between judgment and condemnation. Because so many of the girls she researched had poor models around them for moral reasoning, Artz found it important to judge a violent act without condemning the person. In this way, she could provide a moral response and yet still maintain the confidence of the girls. Artz could *acknowledge* the fears but not necessarily *endorse* the behaviour. This is a very important approach in dealing with youth at risk.

Even in the healthiest and most supportive relationships, there are usually some defensive moments and some situations in which we don't feel comfortable. Yet, in most satisfying relationships, the overall climate is generally supportive and confirming.

Confirming and disconfirming messages are important influences on the climate of personal relationships. In addition, other kinds of communication contribute to the overall feelingof a relationship. We'll now consider specific forms of communication that shape the interpersonal atmosphere between friends and romantic partners.

Reflective Exercise

Analyzing Your Relationships

Think about two relationships in your life: one in which you feel good about yourself and safe in the connection and one in which you feel disregarded or not valued. Identify instances of each level of confirmation in the satisfying relationship and instances of each level of disconfirmation in the unpleasant one. Recognizing confirming and disconfirming communication should give you insight into why these relationships are so different.

Defensive and Supportive Climates

Communication researcher Jack Gibb (1961, 1964, 1970) studied the relationship between communication and interpersonal climates. He began by noting that with some people we feel defensive and on guard, so we are unlikely to communicate openly with them. Gibb called these "defensive climates." Gibb also noted that with some other people we feel supported and comfortable, so we are likely to communicate freely with them. Gibb referred to these as "supportive climates." The two kinds of feelings, and the interpersonal climates that foster them, are not typically pure in form. Even in the most healthy and supportive relationships, there are usually some defensive moments and some situations in which we don't feel comfortable. Yet, most established relationships have a fairly stable climate.

Gibb believed that the different feelings we have around various people are due largely to communication that promotes feeling defensive or feeling supported. Gibb identified six types of communication that promote defensive climates and six opposite types of communication that foster supportive climates, as shown in Table 9.3.

Evaluation versus Description

Few of us feel what Gibb called "psychologically safe" when we are the targets of judgments. Communication researchers report that evaluative communication evokes defensiveness (Conrad & Poole, 2002; Eadie, 1982; Stephenson & D'Angelo, 1973). It's not surprising that Wayne felt judged by his family when he told them he was gay. His parents and brother made evaluations—very negative ones of him and of being gay.

We are also less likely to self-disclose to someone we think is judgmental (Caughlin et al., 2005). As we noted in Chapter 8, even positive evaluations can sometimes make us defensive because they carry the relationship-level meaning that another person feels entitled to judge us (Cupach & Carlson, 2002). Here are several examples of evaluative statements: "It's dumb to feel that way," "You shouldn't have done that," "I approve of what you did," "That's a stupid idea."

Descriptive communication doesn't evaluate others or what they think and feel. Instead, it describes behaviours without passing judgment. I language, which we learned about in Chapter 5, describes what the person speaking feels or thinks, but it doesn't evaluate another. (You language does

Student Voices

Wayne:

I've experienced a lot of disconfirmation since I came out. When I told my parents I was gay, Mom said, "No, you're not." I told her I was, and she and Dad both said I was just confused, but I wasn't gay. They refuse to acknowledge I'm gay, which means they reject who I am. My older brother isn't any better. His view is that I'm sinful and headed for hell. Now what could be more disconfirming than that?

John Bailey/Shutterstock

Is your criticism filled with You language?

TABLE 9.3

COMMUNICATION AND CLIMATE

Defensive Communication	Supportive Communication
Evaluation	Description
Certainty	Provisionalism
Strategy	Spontaneity
Control	Problem orientation
Neutrality	Empathy
Superiority	Equality

evaluate). Descriptive language may refer to another, but it does so by describing, not evaluating, the other's behaviour: "You seem to be sleeping more lately" versus "You're sleeping too much," "You seem to have more stuff on your desk than usual" versus "Your desk is a mess."

Apply the Idea

USING DESCRIPTIVE LANGUAGE

To develop skill in supportive communication, translate the following evaluative statements into descriptive ones.

Example:
Evaluative: This report is poorly done.
Descriptive: This report doesn't include background information.

Evaluative

You're lazy.

____

I hate the way you dominate conversations with me.

____

Stop obsessing about the problem.

____

You're too involved.

____

Your work isn't up to par.

____

Certainty versus Provisionalism

We communicate certainty by using language that is absolute and often dogmatic. This kind of language suggests that there is one and only one answer, valid point of view, or reasonable course of action. Because certainty proclaims one absolutely correct position, it slams the door on further discussion. There's no point in talking with people whose minds are made up and who demean any point of view other than their own. Sometimes certainty is expressed by restating a position over and over instead of responding to alternative ideas from others (Alexander, 1979).

Perhaps you've been in a conversation with someone who says, "I don't want to hear it," "You can't change my mind," or "I've already figured out what I'm going to do, so just save your breath." These comments reflect certainty and an unwillingness to consider other points of view. When confronted with such statements, we're likely to feel disconfirmed and to follow the advice to "save our breath." We're also likely to be uninterested in communicating with people who imply that our ideas are wrong because our ideas don't agree with their ideas. "I know what I'm talking about; you don't" is a disconfirming comment that squelches motivation to continue interacting.

One form of certainty communication is **ethnocentrism**, which is the assumption that our culture and its norms are the only right ones. If a speaker assumes that Western Anglo communication styles are the only correct ones, he or she makes a serious communication error. Dogmatically asserting, "It's disrespectful to be late" reveals a lack of awareness of cultures that are less obsessed with speed and efficiency than some White Canadian cultures. Aboriginal cultures, for example, have a much more relaxed notion of time. Additional examples of certainty statements are "This is the only idea that makes sense," "My mind can't be changed because I'm right," "Only a fool would vote for that person," and "Any intelligent person would agree with me."

Although Canada is one of the very few countries that have legislated for multiculturalism, that has not always controlled racism against ethnoracial minorities (Henry, 2002). The blind ignorance of ethnocentrism provides the context for a situation in which everyone loses. For example, if health care professionals do not provide a culturally sensitive environment, all health goals will be compromised. Health care workers will be frustrated in providing effective care and the people whom they wish to help will not be able to involve themselves in promoting their own health (Davidhizar & Giger, 1998).

> **Student Voices**
>
> **Monika:**
>
> My father is a classic case of closed-mindedness. He has his ideas, and everything else is crazy. I told him I was majoring in communication studies, and he hit the roof. He said there was no future in learning to write speeches, and he told me I should go into business so that I could get a good job. He never even asked me what communication studies is. If he had, I would have told him it's a lot more than speechwriting. He starts off sure that he knows everything about whatever is being discussed. He has no interest in other points of view or learning something new. He just locks his mind and throws away the key. We've all learned just to keep our ideas to ourselves around him—there's no communication.

An alternative to certainty is provisionalism, which communicates openness to other points of view. When we speak provisionally, or tentatively, we suggest that our minds aren't sealed. We signal that we're willing to consider what others have to say, and this encourages others to voice their ideas. Provisional communication includes statements such as "The way I tend to see the issue is ...," "One way to look at this is ...," and "Probably what I would do in that situation is...." Notice how each of these comments signals that the speaker realizes there could be other positions that are also reasonable. Tentativeness signals an open mind, which is why it invites continued communication.

Strategy versus Spontaneity

Most of us feel on guard when we think others are manipulating us or being less than open about what's on their minds. An example of strategic communication is this: "Would you do something for me if I told you it really mattered?" If the speaker doesn't tell us what we're expected to do, it feels like a setup.

We're also likely to feel that another is trying to manipulate us with a comment such as, "Remember when I helped you with your math last term and when I did your chores last week because you were busy?" With a preamble like that, we can smell a trap. When employees think supervisors are trying to manipulate them, they become defensive (Conrad & Poole, 2002). Nonverbal behaviours may also convey strategy, as when a person pauses for a long time before answering or refuses to look at us when she or he speaks. A sense of deception pollutes the communication climate.

Spontaneity is the counterpoint to strategy. Spontaneous communication feels open, honest, and unpremeditated. "I really need your help with this computer glitch" is a more spontaneous comment than "Would you do something for me if I told you it really matters?" Likewise, it is more spontaneous to ask for a favour in a straightforward way ("Would you help me?") than to

> **Student Voices**
>
> **Jana:**
>
> Last year, I worked for someone who was always using strategies on me. She'd come to my workstation on Monday and ask, "How does your week look?" At first, I'd give her a straight answer, but after a few times I realized she was setting me up. If I said, "Not too bad," she'd give me another assignment. I wouldn't have minded if she'd just asked me straight up if I could do a particular thing.

Monkey Business Images/Shutterstock

Strategy or spontaneity? What do you choose when you are in conflict?

preface a request by reciting all we have done for someone else. Strategic communication is contrived and devious, whereas spontaneous interaction is authentic.

Control versus Problem Orientation

Like strategies, controlling communication attempts to manipulate others. Unlike strategies, controlling communication tends to be relatively overt. A common instance of controlling communication is a person's insistence that his or her solution or preference should prevail. Whether the issue is trivial (what movie to see) or serious (whether to move to a new part of the country), controllers try to impose their point of view on others. This disconfirms and disrespects others.

Defensiveness arises because the relationship level of meaning is that the person exerting control thinks she or he has greater power, rights, or intelligence than others. It's disconfirming to be told that our opinions are wrong, that our preferences don't matter, or that we aren't smart enough to have good ideas. Supervisors who micromanage subordinates communicate that they don't trust others to do the job right (Conrad & Poole, 2002). A wife who earns a higher salary might say to her husband, "Well, I like the Honda more than the Ford you want, and it's my money that's going to pay for it." The speaker not only pushes her preference but also tells her husband that she has more power than he does because she makes more money.

Student Voices

Pat:

My roommate last year was a real jerk. Her goal in life was to control me and everyone else around her. Sometimes she'd say she felt like going out for dinner and I'd agree, and then she'd ask me where I wanted to go. Even if I picked her favourite place, she would insist on going somewhere else. She just had to be in charge. Once I moved things around in the room and she fussed a lot and moved them back. Later, she moved things the way I had, but then it was her choice. She didn't care about issues or working things through. All she cared about was being in control.

Problem-oriented communication tends to cultivate supportive, confirming interpersonal climates. Problem-oriented communication focuses on finding a solution that all parties find acceptable. Here's an example of problem-oriented communication between co-workers: "It seems that we have really different ideas about how to tackle this new project. Let's talk through what each of us has in mind and see how we can connect our goals." Notice how this statement invites collaboration and emphasizes the goal of meeting both people's needs. Problem-oriented behaviours tend to reduce conflict and keep lines of communication open (Alexander, 1979; Civickly, Pace, & Krause, 1977; McKinney, Kelly, & Duran, 1997).

One of the benefits of problem-oriented communication is that the relationship level of meaning emphasizes the importance of the relationship between communicators. When we convey that we want to collaborate with another person to resolve some mutual problem, we let the other know that we care more about the relationship than about getting our own way. In contrast, controlling behaviours aim for one person to triumph over the other, an outcome that undercuts the other person and the relationship.

Neutrality versus Empathy

People tend to become defensive when others respond to them in a neutral or detached manner. Research on interview climates indicates that defensiveness arises when an interviewer appears withdrawn and distant (Civickly, Pace, & Krause, 1977). Neutral communication implies a lack of regard and caring for others. Consequently, it disconfirms their worth.

In contrast to neutrality, empathic communication confirms the worth of others and our concern for them. Empathic communication is illustrated by these examples: "I can understand why you feel that way. It's an entirely reasonable way to feel in your situation" and "Wow, it must have really stung when your supervisor said that to you." Empathy doesn't necessarily mean agreement; instead, it conveys acceptance of other people and respect for their perspectives. Especially when we don't agree with others, it's important to communicate that we value them as people.

Student Voices

Faye:

My brother never responds to what I say. He listens, but he just gives me nothing back. Sometimes I push him and ask, "What do you think?" or "Does what I'm saying make sense to you?" All he does is shrug or say, "Whatever." He simply won't show any involvement. So I say, why bother talking to him?

Superiority versus Equality

Like many of the other communication behaviours we've discussed, the final pair of behaviours that affect climate is the one most pertinent to the relationship level of meaning. Communication that conveys superiority says, "I'm better." Understandably, we feel on guard when people act as if they are better than we are.

Consider several messages that convey superiority: "I know a lot more about this than you do," "You just don't have my experience," "I know a better way to do this," "You really should go to my hairstylist." Each of these messages clearly says, "You aren't as good (smart, savvy, competent, attractive) as I am." Predictably, the result is that we protect our self-esteem by trying to avoid people who belittle us.

Communication that conveys equality is confirming and fosters a supportive interpersonal climate. We feel more relaxed and comfortable communicating with people who treat us as equals. At the relationship level of meaning, expressed equality communicates respect and equivalent status. We can have exceptional experience or ability in certain areas and still show regard for others and their contribution to interaction. Creating a climate of equality allows everyone to be involved without fear of being judged inadequate.

Apply the Idea

ASSESSING COMMUNICATION CLIMATES

Use the behaviours we've discussed as a checklist for assessing communication climates. The next time you feel defensive, ask whether communication reflects superiority, control, strategy, certainty, neutrality, or evaluation. Chances are that one or more of these are present in communication.

For a communication climate you find supportive and open, check to see whether the communication reflects spontaneity, equality, provisionalism, problem orientation, empathy, and description. To improve defensive climates, try modelling supportive communication. Resist the normal tendencies to respond defensively when a climate feels disconfirming. Instead, focus on being empathic, descriptive, and spontaneous, showing equality and tentativeness, and solving problems.

We've seen that confirmation, which may include recognizing, acknowledging, and endorsing others, is the basis of healthy communication climates. Our discussion of defensive and supportive forms of communication enlightens us about the specific behaviours that tend to make us feel confirmed or disconfirmed.

GUIDELINES FOR CREATING AND SUSTAINING HEALTHY CLIMATES

CONCEPTS AT A GLANCE

Guidelines for Creating and Sustaining Healthy Climates

- Actively use communication to build confirming climates.
- Accept and confirm others.
- Affirm and assert yourself.
- Respect diversity in relationships.
- Respond to criticism constructively.

Now that we understand how communication creates interpersonal climates, we're ready to identify five guidelines for building and sustaining healthy climates.

Actively Use Communication to Build Confirming Climates

The first principle is to use what you've learned in this chapter to enhance the climates in your relationships. Now that you know what generates defensive and supportive climates, you can identify and curb disconfirming patterns of talk, such as evaluation and superiority. In addition, you can actively work to use supportive communication such as problem orientation and tentativeness.

You can also enhance interpersonal climates by accepting and growing from the tension generated by relational dialectics. Growth in individuals and relationships depends on honouring our needs for autonomy and connection, novelty and routine, and openness and closedness. Thus, the friction between contradictory needs keeps us aware of our multiple needs and the importance of fulfilling each of them.

Accept and Confirm Others

Throughout this chapter, we've seen that confirmation is central to healthy climates and fulfilling relationships. Although we can understand how important it is, it isn't always easy to give confirmation. Sometimes we disagree with others or don't like certain things they do. Being honest with others is important because we expect real friends to be sources of honest feedback, even if it isn't always pleasant to hear (Rawlins, 1994). This implies that we should express honest misgivings about our friends and their behaviours. We can offer honest feedback within a context that assures others that we value and respect them, as Houston's commentary explains.

Student Voices

Houston:

The best thing my friend Jack ever did for me was to get on my case about experimenting with drugs. He told me it was stupid to play with my mind and to risk my health just for kicks, and he kept at me until I tapered off. What made it work was that Jack made it clear that he thought too much of me to stand by when I was hurting myself. A lot of my other so-called friends just stood by and said nothing. Jack is the only one who was a real friend.

For a relationship to work, people in it must feel confirmed. Confirmation begins with acknowledging others and accepting the validity of their needs and preferences. Dual perspective is a primary tool for accepting others because it calls on us to consider them on their own terms. Although intimate talk may be what makes you feel closest to another person, that person may experience greater closeness when you do things together. To meet the needs of both of you, you could take turns honouring each other's preferred paths to closeness. Alternatively, you might combine the two styles of intimacy by doing things together that invite conversation. For example, backpacking is an activity in which talking naturally occurs.

Affirm and Assert Yourself

It is just as important to affirm yourself as it is to affirm others. You are no less valuable, your needs are no less important, and your preferences are no less valid than those of others. It is a misunderstanding to think that the interpersonal communication principles we've discussed concern only how we behave toward others. Equally, they pertain to how we should treat ourselves. Thus, the principle of confirming people's worth applies just as much to oneself as to others. Likewise, we should respect and honour both our own and others' needs, preferences, and ways of creating intimacy.

Although we can't always meet the needs of all parties in relationships, it is possible to give voice to everyone, including yourself. If your partner favours greater autonomy than you do, you need to recognize that preference and also assert your own. If you don't express your feelings, there's no way others can confirm you. Thus, you should assert your feelings and preferences while simultaneously honouring different ones in others.

Unlike aggression, assertion doesn't involve putting your needs above those of others. At the same time, assertion doesn't subordinate your needs to those of others as does deference. **Assertion** is a matter of clearly and nonjudgmentally stating what you feel, need, or want (see Table 9.4). You can do this without disparaging others or what they want. You should simply state your feelings clearly in an open, descriptive manner.

The meaning of assertion varies between cultures. For instance, directly asserting your own ideas is considered disrespectful by many Koreans and Chinese. Because African Americans are generally more assertive than European Americans, an African American may have a more direct, more pointed style of asserting himself or herself (Houston, 2004; Orbuch & Veroff, 2002).

To communicate effectively with others, we need to learn how they affirm themselves and how they express their feelings directly or indirectly. When each person states her or his feelings and expresses awareness of the other's perspective,

Student Voices

Laquanda:

It took me a long time to learn to look out for myself as well as I look out for others. I was always taught to put others first, probably because I'm a girl. I mean, neither of my brothers had that drilled into them. But I did, and for years I would just muffle my needs and whatever I wanted. I concentrated on pleasing others. I thought I was taking care of relationships, but really I was hurting them, because I felt neglected and I resented that. What I'm working on now is learning to take care of myself and others at the same time.

TABLE 9.4

AGGRESSION, ASSERTION, AND DEFERENCE

Aggressive	Assertive	Deferential
We're going to spend time together.	I'd like to create more time for us.	It's okay with me not to spend time with each other.
Tell me what you're feeling; I insist.	I would like to understand more about how you feel.	If you don't want to talk about how you feel, okay.
I don't care what you want; I'm not going to a movie.	I'm really not up for a movie tonight.	It's fine with me to go to a movie if you want to.

Student Voices

Eleanor:

About a year after George and I married, he was offered a promotion if he'd move to Halifax. We were living in Calgary at the time, and that's where our families and friends were. I didn't want to move because I was rooted with my people, but we could both see how important the move was to George's career. The week before we moved, George gave me the greatest present of our lives. He handed me two tickets—one for a round-trip flight from Halifax to Calgary so that I could visit my family, and a second ticket he'd gotten for my best friend so that she could visit me after we moved. I felt he really understood me and had found a way to take care of my needs. I still have the ticket stubs in my box of special memories.

the parties are likely to find a way to acknowledge both viewpoints. Eleanor's commentary illustrates acknowledging another's needs.

Respect Diversity in Relationships

Just as individuals differ, so do relationships. There is tremendous variety in what people find comfortable, affirming, and satisfying in interpersonal interaction. For example, you might have one friend who enjoys a lot of verbal disclosure and another who prefers less. There's no reason to try to persuade the first friend to disclose less or the second one to be more revealing. Similarly you may be comfortable with greater closeness in some of your relationships and with more autonomy in others. Differences between people create a rich variety of relationships.

Even a single relationship varies over time. Because dialectics generate constant tension, people continuously shift their patterns and ways of honouring contradictory needs in their relationships. It's natural to want more closeness at some times and more distance at other times over the life of a relationship. It's also advisable to experiment with different responses to dialectical tensions. You may find that it's effective to compromise between closeness and autonomy and to satisfy your desire for openness by sharing certain topics while meeting your need for privacy by not discussing other topics.

Because people and relationships are diverse, we should strive to respect a range of communicative choices and relationship patterns. In addition, we should be cautious about imposing our meaning on others' communication. People from various cultures, including ones within North America have learned different communication styles. What Westerners consider openness and healthy self-disclosure may feel offensively intrusive to people from some Asian

Apply the Idea

COMMUNICATING ASSERTIVELY

The following statements are deferential or aggressive. Revise each one so that it is assertive.

1. I guess your preference for going to the party is more important than my studying.
2. I don't need your permission to go out. I'll do what I please.
3. I suppose I could work extra next week if you really need a loan.
4. I don't like it when you spend time with Tim. Either stop seeing him, or we're through.

societies. The dramatic, assertive speaking style of many African Americans can be misinterpreted as abrasive or confrontational from a Western Caucasian perspective (Orbuch & Veroff, 2002). The best way to understand what others' behaviour means is to ask them about it. This conveys the relational message that they matter to you, and it allows you to gain insight into the interesting diversity around us.

Respond Constructively to Criticism

A fifth guideline is to learn to respond effectively when others offer constructive criticism. Sometimes, others communicate criticism in language that fosters defensiveness: "You are so inconsiderate!" "You're selfish." We tend to react defensively to such judgmental language, and we may dismiss the criticism (think that it isn't true) or just think that the other person is being mean. These are natural and understandable responses, but they aren't necessarily constructive ways to deal with criticism. The problem with denying or dismissing criticism is that it deprives us of a chance to learn more about how others see us and to reevaluate our own actions. Refusing to acknowledge others' criticism is also likely to erect barriers in relationships.

A more constructive response to criticism is to begin by seeking more information: "What do you mean when you say that I'm inconsiderate?" "What do I do that you see as selfish?" Asking these questions allows you to get concrete information. Remember that others may not have your understanding of how to communicate effectively. Thus, they may use abstract terms that you can help them translate into specifics to be addressed. They may also use you language ("You hurt me") that you can explore to determine whether there is something you do to which they respond by feeling hurt.

A second step in responding constructively to criticism is to consider it thoughtfully. Is the criticism valid? Are you inconsiderate in some ways? Are you selfish in some respects? If, after reflection, you don't think the criticism is accurate, offer your interpretation of the behaviours the other perceived as inconsiderate or selfish. You might say, "I can see how you might feel it's selfish of me to go out with my friends so often, but to me it's because I care about them, just like I spend time with you because I care about you." Notice that this response not only offers an alternative interpretation of particular behaviour, but also affirms the other person.

Student Voices

Betsy:

I didn't appreciate it when my roommate called me a slob. But because of what I've learned in this course, I didn't just ignore what Marie said or fire back an insult to her. Instead, I asked her what she meant. She told me she hated coming home to our apartment and finding my clothes on the bathroom floor and dishes in the sink. Well, I could deal with that. So I resolved to pick up my clothes and wash my dishes before I left each day. Before, if this had happened, I would have felt hurt and probably wouldn't have done anything differently. But I felt less hurt and more in control because of how I responded to Marie's criticism, and I know she's a lot happier living with me now!

If you decide that the criticism is valid, then consider whether you want to change how you act. Do you want to be perceived by others as inconsiderate or selfish? If not, you can choose to change how you act. For suggestions on how to bring about changes in yourself, you may want to review the guidelines offered at the end of Chapter 2.

The guidelines we've discussed combine respect for self, others, and relationships with communication that fosters healthy, affirming climates for connections with others. We can transform our relationships when we take responsibility for shaping interpersonal climates and when we develop the knowledge and communication skills to do so.

Chapter Summary

In this chapter, we've explored personal relationships and the communication climates that make them more or less satisfying. The four elements of healthy interpersonal relationships are investment, commitment, trust, and comfort with relational dialectics.

Perhaps the most basic requirement for healthy communication climates is confirmation. Each of us wants to feel valued, especially by those who matter most to us. When partners recognize, acknowledge, and endorse each other, they communicate, "You matter to me." We discussed particular kinds of communication that foster supportive and defensive climates in relationships. Defensiveness is bred by evaluation, certainty, superiority, strategies, control, and neutrality. More supportive climates arise from communication that is descriptive, provisional, equal, spontaneous, empathic, and problem oriented.

To close the chapter, we considered five guidelines for building healthy communication climates. The first is to use your communication to enhance the mood of a relationship. Second, we should accept and confirm our friends and romantic partners, communicating that we respect them, even though we may not always agree with them or feel as they do. The third guideline is a companion to the second one: We should accept and confirm ourselves just as fully as we do others. Each of us is entitled to assert his or her own thoughts, feelings, and needs. Doing so allows us to honour ourselves and to help our partners understand us. Fourth, we should realize that diversity in relationships is a source of personal and interpersonal growth. People vary widely, as do the relationship patterns and forms they prefer. By respecting differences among us, we all expand our insights into the fascinating array of ways that humans form and sustain intimate relationships. Finally, personal growth and healthy relationships are fostered by dealing constructively with criticism.

In the next three chapters, we look in greater detail at personal relationships. Chapter 10 extends our discussion of climate by examining how we can create constructive relationship contexts for dealing effectively with conflict. Chapter 11 discusses friendships and romantic relationships, and Chapter 12 focuses on communication in the workplace. In each chapter, we consider what these relationships are, how communication affects them, and how we might cope with some of the inevitable problems and challenges of sustaining close relationships over time. What we have learned about climate, as well as what we've learned about other facets of interpersonal communication in earlier chapters, will serve as a foundation for a deeper look at the dynamics of close relationships.

Key Concepts

- assertion
- commitment
- ethnocentrism
- interpersonal climate
- investment
- relational dialectics
- self-disclosure
- trust

For Further Thought and Discussion

1. Have you found it difficult to confirm others when you disagree with them? If so, does reading this chapter help you distinguish between recognition, acknowledgment, and endorsement? Can you distinguish between confirming others as people and endorsing particular ideas or behaviours?

2. What ethical principles are implied in communication that confirms and disconfirms others? Is it wrong to disconfirm others? All others? Intimates?
3. To what extent do you honour yourself and others in communication situations? Do you give equal attention to both your needs and those of others? If not, focus on balancing your efforts to confirm yourself and others in future interactions.
4. Think of an interaction in which you felt disconfirmed or defensive. Describe how others in the situation communicated toward you. How many of Gibb's defensiveness-producing communication behaviours can you identify as present in the situation?
5. How often are you deferential, assertive, and aggressive in your communication? What are the situations and relationships in which each kind of behaviour is most likely for you? Do the behaviours you select advance your own goals and your relationships?
6. Use your InfoTrac® College Edition to locate recent reports on assertion. How do researchers define assertion? Do they advocate any guidelines for when assertiveness is appropriate and inappropriate?
7. Practise applying this chapter's guidelines for responding to criticism. What happens when you listen to criticism without becoming angry and when you express appreciation to others for their feedback?

Chapter 10

Managing Conflict in Relationships

Sometimes it's worse to win a fight than to lose.

—Billie Holiday, jazz singer

You can't shake hands with a clenched fist.

—Indira Gandhi (prime minister of India, 1966–1977, 1980–1984)

© iStockphoto.com/Li Kim Goh

Joseph: You really made me angry when you flirted with other guys at the party last night.

Carmen: I'm surprised you could even see I was flirting, you were drinking so much.

Joseph: Maybe I was drinking because my girlfriend was too busy dancing with other guys to pay any attention to me.

Carmen: Did it ever occur to you that maybe I'd pay more attention to you if you'd clean up your act? Why don't you get serious about graduate school and start acting responsibly?

Joseph: I'll do that right after you quit smoking and spend some time with me instead of always burying yourself in readings for your classes.

Carmen: You just say that because you're jealous that I'm in a graduate program and you're not.

Joseph: I wouldn't exactly call social work much of a graduate program.

Carmen: It's more than you have. At least I'm planning for a profession. Why don't you?

Joseph: You never do anything but complain, complain, complain. You really are a drag.

Carmen: It takes one to know one.

Joseph and Carmen have a problem, and it isn't just the issues they're discussing. Their larger problem is that they are not handling their conflict constructively. From previous chapters, we've learned enough to understand how negative communication fuels discord between them. For example, Joseph launched the conversation with *you* language. Instead of owning his anger, he blamed Carmen for it. In turn, she didn't own her anger. Joseph may also have misidentified what he was feeling. Is he really feeling angry at Carmen, or is he hurt or jealous that she spent more time with other men at the party than with him?

Both Joseph and Carmen disconfirmed the other with personal attacks. Furthermore, neither of them engaged in dual perspective: Neither recognized and acknowledged the other's point of view. Each of them listened defensively and ambushed the other. Carmen and Joseph pursued their individual agendas and failed to connect with each other. As a result, Carmen and Joseph clash. Their argument did nothing for either of them or for the climate of their relationship.

Let's start the conversation again, and see how positive communication might improve things.

Joseph: I felt hurt when you flirted with other guys at the party last night, and then I felt angry. [Joseph identifies hurt as the more basic feeling. He also owns his feelings.]

Carmen: I can understand that. I know you don't like me to pay attention to other men. [She acknowledges Joseph's feelings.] I got upset when you drank a lot, and I want you to understand how I feel about that. [Carmen owns her feelings and asserts her needs in the situation.]

Joseph: You're right about my drinking and your talking with other men. I know you hate it when I drink too much. [He acknowledges her concern.]

Carmen: Well, I guess neither of us was at our best last night. I was really tired, so I probably got more irritated than I usually would. [She shares responsibility for what happened.]

Joseph: And I've been feeling kind of down because you're so focused on your graduate program, and I can't seem to get started. [Because an affirming climate has been created, Joseph can disclose his deeper worries to Carmen.]

Carmen: I know you feel discouraged right now. [She again acknowledges his feelings.] I would too. [She shows empathy.] But you're so smart, and you'll do great once you settle on a course of action. [She confirms him by showing that she believes in him. She focuses their discussion on a single issue, which may allow them to address it effectively.] Why don't we put our heads together to sort through some of the options and try to figure out how you can proceed? [She offers support and shows commitment to his welfare.]

Joseph: That would really help me. I just need to talk through a lot of possibilities. [He acknowledges her offer of help.] I'd really like to get your perspective on some ideas I've got. [He shows he values her viewpoint.]

Carmen: I've got all the time you want. [She confirms his value and her commitment to the relationship. Her comment also addresses Joseph's relationship-level concern that she may not want to spend time with him.]

Joseph: (smile) Okay, and I promise I won't drink while we're talking. [He uses humour to restore good climate. On the relationship level of meaning, he is asking, "Are we okay now?"]

Carmen: (smile) And I promise I won't flirt with other guys while we're talking. [She reciprocates his relationship-level message by signalling that she, too, feels friendly again.]

The conflict proceeded very differently in the second instance. Both Carmen and Joseph owned their feelings and confirmed each other by acknowledging expressed feelings and concerns. The supportive climate they established enabled Joseph to reveal deeper worries that lay below his opening complaint about Carmen's flirting, and Carmen responded supportively to his disclosure. They also came up with a plan to address Joseph's worries. Especially important, they communicated effectively at the relationship level of meaning. Their relationship would be strengthened by how they managed their conflict in the second scenario.

© iStockphoto.com/Tatiana Gladskikh

The expressed struggle is the "topic" but not always the "issue" in a relationship. What topics do you argue about? What might the real issues be?

Unlike Carmen and Joseph, we usually don't get a chance to go back and redo a conflict we've already had. Instead, we have to live with the consequences, which may be unpleasant. Because we can't hit an instant replay button for our conflicts, it's wise to learn how to manage conflict effectively so we're ready to do so when the need arises.

There is no magic bullet for handling conflict constructively. However, communication is one of the most important influences on conflict and its effect on relationships. Research shows that communication problems contribute to dissatisfaction with relationships and to breakups (Dindia & Fitzpatrick, 1985). We also know that positive, supportive communication is one of the strongest influences on long-term satisfaction with relationships (Gottman & Silver, 2000; Markman, 1981).

© iStockphoto.com/digitalskillet

In this chapter, we explore conflict in interpersonal relationships. We begin by defining conflict. Next, we consider principles of conflict to add depth to our understanding of it. Third, we discuss different ways to approach conflict. The fourth section of the chapter focuses on specific communication patterns that affect the process of conflict and its impact on individuals and relationships. We conclude by identifying guidelines for communicating effectively when engaging in conflict.

DEFINING INTERPERSONAL CONFLICT

Interpersonal **conflict** exists when people who depend on each other express different views, interests, or goals that they perceive as incompatible or opposed. Let's look more closely at each part of this definition.

Expressed Disagreement

Interpersonal conflict is expressed disagreement, struggle, or discord. Thus, it is not conflict if we don't recognize disagreement or anger or if we repress it so completely that it is not expressed directly or indirectly. Conflict exists only if disagreements or tensions are expressed in some way.

We express disagreement in various ways. Shooting daggers with your eyes nonverbally communicates anger and discord just as clearly as saying, "I'm angry with you." Walking out on a conversation and slamming a door express hostility, as does refusing to talk to someone. Sometimes, we express disagreement overtly or directly, such as by saying, "I'm furious with you." Other modes of communicating conflict are more covert or indirect, such as deliberately not answering the phone because you are angry with the caller. In both cases, people realize they are in conflict, and they express their conflict, although in different ways.

CONCEPTS AT A GLANCE

Some Elements of Conflict

- Expressed disagreement
- Interdependence
- The felt need for resolution

Interdependence

Interpersonal conflict can occur only between people who depend on each other in the area of the conflict. Differences need not be resolved between people who don't affect each other. Stefan's food preferences differ from those of most of his colleagues. Because he and his colleagues don't need to agree about food, they are not in conflict over this issue. We may disagree with others and even judge them negatively, but that alone doesn't mean conflict will occur. Interpersonal conflict exists only when it is expressed by people who affect one another. If you don't, why bother?

The Felt Need for Resolution

Conflict is more than just having differences. We differ with people about many things, but this doesn't invariably lead to conflict. For example, suppose that one of your friends doesn't like large dogs and you don't like small ones, or your best friend dislikes cats but you adore them. As long as you don't live together, these differences don't spark conflict. Conflict involves tensions between goals, preferences, or decisions that we feel we need to reconcile. In other words, conflict involves two perceptions: the perception that our concerns are at odds with those of another person, and the perception that we and that other person must resolve our differences.

Student Voices

Lenore:

It's kind of strange, but you really don't fight with people who don't matter. With a lot of guys I dated, if I didn't like something they did, I'd just let it go because they weren't important enough for the hassle. But Rod and I argue a lot, because we do affect each other. Maybe fighting is a sign that people care about each other.

PRINCIPLES OF CONFLICT

Many people view conflict as inherently negative (Turner & Shutter, 2004), but that is a misunderstanding. To address this misunderstanding as well as others, we discuss five principles of conflict.

CONCEPTS AT A GLANCE

Principles of Conflict

- Conflict is natural.
- Conflict may be overt or covert.
- Conflict is shaped by social groups
- Conflict may be managed well or poorly.
- Conflict may be good.

Principle 1: Conflict Is Natural in Relationships

Conflict is a normal, inevitable part of most interpersonal relationships. When people matter to each other and affect each other, disagreements are unavoidable. You like meat, and your friend is a strict vegetarian. You like to work alone, and your co-workers like to interact in teams. You think money should be enjoyed, and your partner believes in saving for a rainy day. You want to move to a place where there's

Student Voices

Ron:

It sounds funny, but the biggest thing my fiancée and I fight about is whether it's okay to fight. I was brought up not to argue and to think that conflict is bad. In her family, people did argue a lot, and she thinks it is healthy. What I'm coming to realize is that there is a lot of conflict in my family but it's hidden, so it never gets dealt with very well. I've seen her and her parents really go at it but, I have to admit, they work through their differences, and people in my family don't.

a great job for you, but the location has no career prospects for your partner. Again and again, we find ourselves at odds with people who matter to us. When this happens, we have to resolve the differences, preferably in a way that doesn't harm the relationship.

The presence of conflict does not indicate that a relationship is unhealthy or in trouble, although how partners manage conflict does influence relational health. Actually, engaging in conflict indicates that people are involved with each other. If they weren't, there would be no need to resolve differences. This is a good point to keep in mind when conflicts arise, because it reminds us that a strong connection underlies even disagreement.

Most of us have attitudes about conflict that reflect scripts we learned in our families. Like Ron, some of us were taught that conflict is bad and should be avoided, whereas others learned that airing differences is healthy. Because conflict is inevitable in interpersonal relationships, we should develop constructive ways to deal with it.

Apply the Idea

UNDERSTANDING YOUR CONFLICT SCRIPT

What conflict script did you learn in your family? Think back to your childhood and adolescence and try to remember what implicit rules for conflict your family modelled and perhaps taught.

- *Did people disagree openly with each other?*
- *What was said or done when disagreements surfaced? Was the reaction verbal? Was it physical? Was it respectful? Did your parents encourage open discussion of differences?*
- *How do you currently reflect your family's conflict script? Now that you can edit family scripts and author your own, how would you like to deal with conflict?*

Read on in this chapter to consider ways you might write a conflict script that is constructive and reflects your values.

© iStockphoto.com/mammamaart

Is your conflict style overt or covert?

Principle 2: Conflict May Be Overt or Covert

When we defined conflict, we noted that disagreement can be expressed either overtly or covertly. Overt conflict is out in the open and explicit. It exists when people deal with their differences in a direct, straightforward manner. They might calmly discuss their disagreement, intensely argue about ideas, or engage in a shouting match. Overt conflict can also involve physical attacks, although of course that's neither healthy nor constructive. Physical violence is never acceptable in an enduring relationship with someone whom you care about, and it is rarely appropriate even in less close relationships.

Yet, conflict isn't always overt. Covert conflict exists when people express their feelings about disagreements indirectly. When angry, a person may deliberately do something to hurt or upset another person. Angry that his supervisor is requiring employees to make up a day missed for snow, Andy spends half the day surfing the net. Knowing that Elliott hates to be kept waiting, his wife intentionally arrives 20 minutes late for a dinner date because he chose a restaurant she doesn't like. These people are expressing their anger indirectly, and the conflict is covert.

A common form of covert conflict is **passive aggression,** which is acting aggressively while denying feeling or acting aggressive. If Dedra doesn't call her mother every week, her mother "forgets" to send Dedra a cheque for spending money. When Arlene won't forgo studying to go out dancing, Clem coincidentally decides to play music at high volume in the room adjacent to Arlene. Passive aggression punishes another person without accepting responsibility for the punishment. It undercuts the possibility of honest, healthy relationships.

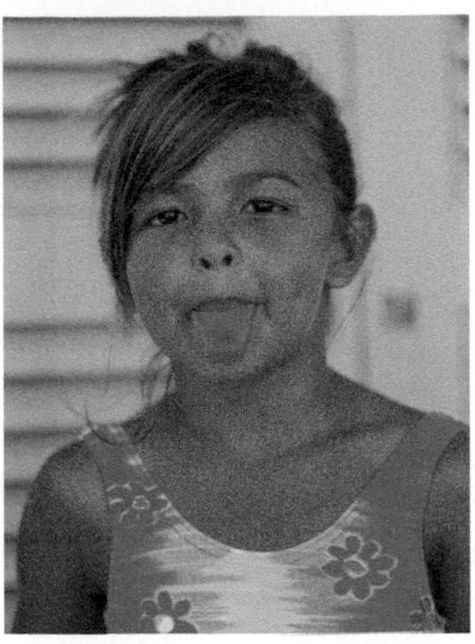

Hoby Finn/Photodisc/Getty Images

Is this an example of overt or covert conflict?

Much covert conflict takes place through **games,** highly patterned interactions in which the real conflicts are hidden or denied and a counterfeit excuse created for arguing or criticizing (Berne, 1964). Games also involve cooperation between players.

The nature of games will become clear if we discuss a few specific ones. In a game called "Blemish," one person pretends to be complimentary but actually puts another down. Ann asks her friend whether she looks okay for an important interview. The friend, who is angry that she herself doesn't have any interviews lined up, responds, "The new suit looks really great. There's just this one little thing. You seem to have gained weight. Your stomach and hips look big, and that suit doesn't hide the extra pounds." The friend is playing "Blemish"; she focuses on one thing that is wrong and downplays all that is right. Her anger or resentment is expressed indirectly.

Another game is "NIGYYSOB" ("Now I've Got You, You Son of a B——"). In this one, a person deliberately sets another person up for a fall. Knowing that her husband is not a good cook, Ellie asks him to fix dinner one evening. When he overcooks the main dish, and the sauce is lumpy, she criticizes him for preparing a bad meal. Ellie worked to find a way to make him fail and then pounced on him when he did.

"Mine Is Worse Than Yours" is another commonly played game. Suppose you tell a friend that you have two tests and a paper due next week, and your friend says, "You think that's bad? Listen to this: I have two tests, three papers, and an oral report all due in the next two weeks." Your friend expressed no concern for your plight; rather, he told you that his situation is worse. In this game, people try to monopolize rather than listen and respond to each other.

"Yes, But" is a game in which a person pretends to be asking for help but then refuses all help that's offered. Doing this allows the person who initiates the game to attempt to make the other person feel inadequate for being unable to help. Lorna asks her boyfriend to help her figure out how to better manage her money. When he suggests that she should spend less, Lorna says, "Yes, but I don't buy anything I don't need." When he suggests she might work extra hours at her job, she responds,

Student Voices

Staci:

I was recently in a relationship that I thought was the greatest ever, strictly because we never fought. I've had relationships with lots of arguments, so I thought it was fabulous that Steve and I never fought. I grew up with a twice-divorced mom, and I've seen her and my father and then my stepfather really go at it. All I ever wanted was a conflict-free relationship because I thought that would be a good relationship.

One time, Steve called me to say he had to break our date to cover at work for another guy. All I did was sigh and say, "Fine, if that is what you need to do." But it wasn't fine with me; I resented his putting the other guy ahead of me. A little later, he called me back to say he'd changed his mind and would join me and two friends of ours. So, what happened? He sat at the table all night and barely said two words. I was so mad, but I didn't say a word about the evening and neither did he. Just a month later, we broke up. Even then, there was no overt conflict.

CONCEPTS AT A GLANCE

Destructive Games

- Blemish
- NIGYYSOB
- Mine Is Worse Than Yours
- Yes, But

Student Voices

Chuck:

My parents specialize in games. Dad likes to set Mom up by asking her to take care of some financial business or get the car fixed. Then he explodes about what she does. I think he is just trying to find excuses for chewing her out. Mom also plays games. Her favourite is "Blemish." She always finds something wrong with an idea or a paper I've written or a vacation or whatever. Then she just harps and harps on the defect. Sometimes being around them is like being in a minefield.

"Yes, but that would cut into my free time." When he mentions she could get a better-paying job, Lorna says, "Yes, but I really like the people where I work now." When he points out that she could save a lot by packing lunches instead of buying them, she replies, "Yes, but I'd have to get up earlier." "Yes, But" continues until the person trying to help finally gives up in defeat. Then, the initiator of the game can complain, "You didn't help me."

Games and passive aggression are dishonest, ineffective ways to manage conflict. They are dishonest because they camouflage the real issues. They are ineffective because, as long as conflict remains hidden or disguised, it's almost impossible for people to recognize and resolve it.

Apply the Idea

IDENTIFYING GAMES IN YOUR COMMUNICATION

Apply what you've read about covert conflict to your own life. Describe an example of when you or someone with whom you have a relationship played each of these games:

- *Blemish*
- *NIGYYSOB*
- *Mine Is Worse Than Yours*
- *Yes, But*

What was accomplished by playing the game? Were the real conflicts addressed?

Principle 3: Social Groups Shape the Meaning of Conflict Behaviours

Our cultural membership and socialization in particular social communities affect how we view and respond to conflict.

Cultural Differences Regarding Conflict

The majority of Mediterranean cultures regard conflict as a normal, valuable part of everyday life. In these cultures, people routinely argue and wrangle, and nobody gets upset or angry. In France and in Arabic countries, men debate one another for the sheer fun of it. It doesn't matter who wins the debate—the argument itself is enjoyable (Copeland & Griggs, 1985). Many Hispanic cultures also regard conflict as both normal and interesting. Because Hispanic cultures tend to value emotions, conflicts are opportunities for emotional expression.

Chinese people have a very different view of conflict. Yan Bing Zhang, Jake Harwood, and Mary Hummert (2005) asked Chinese adults to evaluate transcripts in which an older worker criticized a younger worker. Older participants favoured an accommodating style. Younger adults preferred a problem-solving style (assertive and cooperative) to an accommodating style (emphasizes relational harmony) or perceived the two styles as equally desirable. Older and younger participants alike had less positive perceptions of the avoiding style, which was perceived as disrespectful of others, and the competing (driven by self-interest) style of dealing with conflict. In contrast, many Westerners prefer the competing style (Bergstrom & Nussbaum, 1996).

Mainstream culture in North America emphasizes assertiveness and individuality, so many Westerners are competitive and reluctant to give in to others. In more communal societies, people have less individualistic perspectives and are less likely to focus on winning conflicts (Ting-Toomey, 1991; Vanyperen & Buunk, 1991). Similarly, in Japan and many other Asian cultures, open disagreement is strongly condemned (Gangwish, 1999). Great effort is made to avoid winning at the cost of causing another person to lose face (Rowland, 1985; Weiss, 1987). In Japanese sports, the ideal is not for one team to win but for a tie to occur so that neither team loses face. When there is to be a winner, Japanese athletes try to win by only a slim margin so that the losing team is not humiliated (Ferrante, 1992).

> **Student Voices**
>
> **Roberto:**
>
> One of the hardest adjustments for me in Canada has been keeping my voice down. In Italy, people shout all the time and wave their arms. No one avoids conflict there. It is the normal way of communicating where I come from. When my girlfriend visits my family, she is always alarmed at the shouting and thinks everyone is fighting. I tell her that we just disagree noisily and 10 minutes later we will be singing or laughing.

Differences among Social Communities

Our orientations toward conflict are influenced not only by culture but also by social communities based on gender, sexual orientation, and race/ethnicity. There are some general differences in how women and men respond to conflict, although the generalizations don't apply to all women and men (Stafford, Dutton & Haas, 2000; Wood, 2005). In general, women are more likely to want to discuss conflictual issues, whereas many men tend to avoid conflict. Women are also more likely than men to defer and compromise, both of which reflect gendered prescriptions for women to accommodate others.

Men are more likely than women to feel overwhelmed when asked to engage in communication about differences. Women sometimes feel that men are unwilling to discuss anything about relationships. Of course, these are broad generalizations that overstate how men and women act. Nonetheless, women and men often find themselves responding very differently to relationship tensions and not understanding each other's perspective.

Masculine socialization places less emphasis on talk as a means to intimacy; as a group, men are less likely than women to see discussion as a good way to handle conflict in personal relationships. In professional situations and athletics, men may be very vocal in dealing with conflict. Yet, in their personal lives, men often deny or minimize problems rather than deal openly with them. Long-term studies of marriage indicate that husbands are more inclined than wives to withdraw from conflict and

> **Student Voices**
>
> **Kristo:**
>
> My girlfriend drives me crazy. She thinks anytime the slightest thing is wrong in our relationship, we have to have a long, drawn-out analysis of it. I just don't want to spend all that time dissecting the relationship.
>
> **Genevieve:**
>
> My boyfriend is a world-class avoider. When something is wrong between us, I naturally want to talk about it and get things right again. But he will evade, tell me everything's fine when it's not, say the problem is too minor to talk about, and use any other tactic he can come up with to avoid facing the problem. He seems to think if you don't deal with problems, they somehow solve themselves.

that stonewalling by husbands is a strong predictor of divorce (Bass, 1993). Men are more likely than women to use coercive tactics, both verbal and physical, to avoid discussing problems and to force their resolutions on others (Johnson, in press; Snell, Hawkins, & Belk, 1988; White, 1989).

Communication Notes

THE WHITE RIBBON CAMPAIGN

In Canada, the White Ribbon Campaign was begun by a group of men deeply concerned about violence against women. Most violent acts are committed by men. From November 25 to December 6, the anniversary of the 1989 Montreal Massacre, men and boys are encouraged to wear white ribbons to symbolize their opposition to violence against women. Today, the White Ribbon Campaign is celebrated by both men and women across Canada. For more information, check out the website at www.whiteribbon.ca or contact:

White Ribbon Campaign
365 Bloor Street East, Suite 203
Toronto, Ontario M4W 3L4
Toll-free: 1–800–328–2228

Before leaving our discussion of gender, we should note one other important finding. Psychologist John Gottman (1993; Jacobson & Gottman, 1998) reports that, in general, men experience greater and longer-lasting physical responses to interpersonal conflict than women do. Compared with women, during conflict men's heart rates rise more quickly and to higher levels and stay elevated for a longer period of time. Because conflict tends to be more physically and psychologically painful to men than to women, men may be motivated to deny, avoid, or minimize issues that could cause conflict.

Sexual orientation doesn't seem to be a major influence on how people see and deal with conflict. Caryl Rusbult and her colleagues (Rusbult, Johnson, & Morrow, 1986; Rusbult, Zembrodt, & Iwaniszek, 1986; Wood, 1986, 1994b) report that, in their responses to conflict, gay men are much like heterosexual men, and lesbians are similar to heterosexual women. Similarly, a major national study reported that gender explains far more of the differences between partners than does sexual orientation (Blumstein & Schwartz, 1983). Most children, regardless of sexual orientation, are socialized on the basis of their sex. Thus, boys, both gay and heterosexual, tend to learn masculine orientations toward interaction, whereas lesbian and heterosexual girls are socialized toward feminine styles of interaction.

Recent research indicates that race/ethnicity is related to conflict styles and to interpretations of them. Terri Orbuch and Joseph Veroff and their colleagues (Orbuch & Eyster, 1997; Orbuch & Veroff, 2002; Orbuch, Veroff, & Hunter, 1999) report that open, verbal arguing is destructive for White couples but not necessarily for Black couples. They also report that Black wives are more likely than White wives to believe that airing conflicts can lead to positive resolution.

Principle 4: Conflict Can Be Managed Well or Poorly

People respond to conflict in a variety of ways, from physical attack to verbal aggression to collaborative problem solving. Although each method may resolve differences, some are clearly preferable to others. Depending on how we handle disagreements, conflict can either promote continuing closeness or tear a relationship apart.

One of the main reasons conflict is handled poorly is that it often involves intense feelings, which many people do not know how to identify or express. We may feel deep disappointment, resentment, or anger toward someone we care about, and this is difficult to manage. Our discussion in Chapter 4 should have helped you identify your feelings and choose effective ways to communicate your emotions in conflict situations. Other skills we've discussed—such as using *I* language and monitoring the self-serving bias—will also help you manage the feelings that often accompany conflict.

Conflict can be managed well or poorly.

Learning how different kinds of communication affect relationships, individuals, and conflict resolution empowers you to make informed choices about dealing with conflict in your relationships. The ideas and skills we cover in this chapter and throughout this book will help you manage interpersonal conflict to cultivate personal growth and relationship maturity.

Principle 5: Conflict Can Be Good for Individuals and Relationships

Although we tend to think of conflict negatively, it can be beneficial in a number of ways. When managed constructively, conflict provides opportunities for us to grow as individuals and to strengthen our relationships. Conflict also allows us to consider points of view different from our own. A perceived crisis can actually afford us an opportunity, as we deepen our insight into our ideas and feelings when we express them and get responses from others. (See Figure 10.1.) Based on what we learn, we may change our own views.

Conflict can also enhance relationships by enlarging partners' understandings of each other. What begins as a discussion of a particular issue usually winds up providing broader information about why partners feel as they do and what meanings they attach to the issue. In the example that opened this chapter, the original complaint about Carmen's flirting led to the discovery that Joseph felt insecure about his identity and Carmen's respect for him because she was succeeding in graduate work, and he wasn't advancing in school or a career. Once his concern emerged, the couple could address deeper issues in their relationship.

Lack of conflict isn't necessarily a symptom of a healthy relationship (Arnett, 1986). Low levels

Student Voices

Jens:

We were arguing in class about whether nursing and teaching should be declared essential services in Canada and therefore exempt from strikes. I was very opposed to strikes and job action, especially in health care, but after listening to two of the nursing students in my class talk about inequity, I really saw a different point of view. I thought our positions were irresolvable, but the argument was actually pretty enlightening.

FIGURE 10.1

Chinese for "Crisis"

Student Voices

Jana:

Geoff and I have a pretty intense relationship. We fight a lot, and we fight hard. Some of my friends think this is bad, but we don't. Nothing is swept under the carpet in our relationship. If either of us is angry or upset about something, we hash it out then and there. But we are just as intense in positive ways. Geoff lets me know all the time that he loves me, and I am always hugging and kissing him. I guess you could just say our relationship is passionate—in bad moments and good ones.

of conflict could reflect limited emotional depth between partners or unwillingness to engage in communication about differences. Researchers report that there is no direct association between marital happiness and the number of arguments that spouses have (Howard & Dawes, 1976; Muehlhoff & Wood, 2002). Instead, the key is to have a greater number of positive, affirming interactions than negative ones. One group of researchers refers to this as "keeping a positive balance in the marital bank account" (Gottman et al., 1976; Gottman & Silver, 2000).

To review, we've discussed five principles of interpersonal conflict. First, we noted that conflict is both natural and inevitable in int erpersonal relationships. Second, we discovered that conflict can be directly communicated or covertly expressed through indirect communication or games that camouflage real issues. Third, we saw that conflict styles and meanings are shaped by social location—membership in cultures and social communities. Fourth, we emphasized that how we manage conflict influences its resolution and its impact on interpersonal climates. Finally, we saw that conflict can be constructive for individuals and relationships. We can now build on these principles by discussing diverse ways people approach and respond to conflict.

ORIENTATIONS TO CONFLICT

We've noted that conflict can be managed in various ways, some more effective than others. We now look at three basic orientations that affect how we approach conflict situations. In the next section of the chapter, we'll see how these different approaches shape our patterns of responding during conflict. Each way of approaching conflict is appropriate in some relationships and situations; the challenge is to know when a particular approach is constructive.

Lose–Lose

A **lose–lose** orientation assumes that conflict results in losses for everyone and that it is unhealthy and destructive for relationships. A wife might feel that conflicts about money hurt her, her husband, and the marriage. Similarly, a person may refrain from arguing with a friend, believing the result would be wounded pride for both of them. Because the lose–lose orientation assumes that conflict is inevitably negative, people who adopt it typically try to avoid conflict at all costs. Yet, seeking to avoid conflict at all costs may be very costly indeed. We may have to defer our own needs or rights, and we may feel unable to give honest feedback to others.

Although the lose–lose orientation is not usually beneficial in dealing with conflicts in close relationships, it has merit in some circumstances. One obvious value of this approach is that it prompts us to ask whether we want or need to engage in

Student Voices

Theo:

I hate to fight with friends. I do just about anything to avoid an argument. But sometimes what I have to do is sacrifice my preferences or even my rights just to avoid conflict. And sometimes I have to go along with something I don't believe in or think is right. I'm starting to think that maybe conflict would be better than avoiding it—at least in some cases.

conflict. Some issues aren't worth the energy and the discomfort that conflict arouses. Sometimes two people are better off choosing the inevitable loss of their relationship as well as their stake in the issue of conflict in order to for each maintain her or his personal sense of equilibrium. We might have a more peaceful planet if national leaders believed that war produces only losers, regardless of whether one side officially wins.

Win–Lose

Win–lose orientations assume one person wins at the expense of the other. A person who sees conflict as a win–lose matter thinks disagreements are battles that can have only one victor. What one person gains is at the other's loss; what one person loses benefits the other. Disagreements are seen as zero-sum games in which there is no possibility for everyone to benefit.

The win–lose orientation is cultivated in cultures that place value on individualism, self-assertion, and competition. We know that Canada is largely an individualistic society that values those qualities. Other cultures, such as Japan, place priority on quite different values: cooperation, keeping others from failing, and finding areas of agreement. Not surprisingly, the win–lose orientation to conflict is more common in the West than in Japan. Examine the interesting American account of the Communication Notes feature "Japanese and American Styles of Negotiation."

Communication Notes

JAPANESE AND AMERICAN STYLES OF NEGOTIATION

The differences between Japanese and American views of conflict shape specific communication patterns during business negotiations (McDaniel & Quasha, 2000; Weiss, 1987). Consider how each of the following negotiation strategies reflects values typical of Japanese or American society.

Japanese Style

- Understate your own initial position or state it vaguely to allow the other room to state his or her position.
- Find informal ways to let the other person know your bottom line to move agreement forward without directly confronting the other with your bottom line.
- Look for areas of agreement, and focus talk on them.
- Avoid confrontation or explicit disagreement.
- Work to make sure that neither you nor the other person fails.
- Plan to spend a long time discussing issues before even moving toward a decision.

American Style

- Overstate initial position to establish a strong image.
- Keep your bottom line secret from the other person to preserve your power and gain the most.
- Where there are differences, assert your position and attempt to win the other's assent.
- Be adversarial.
- Work to win all you can.
- Push to reach decisions as rapidly as possible.

Reflective Exercise

In what way are Canadians different from and similar to Americans in their approach to business abroad? What assumptions do you make when you are in another country?

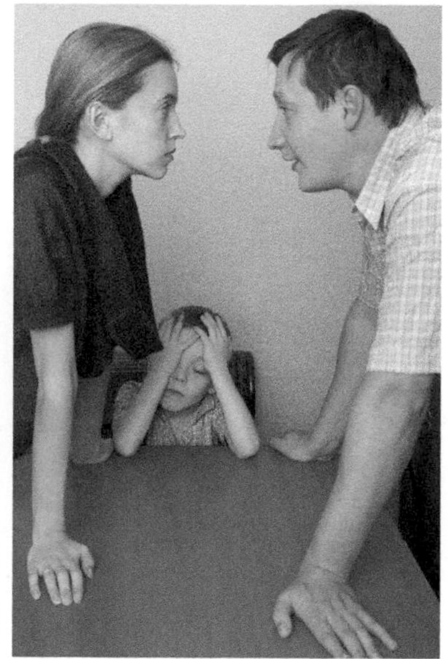

Tatiana Gladskikh/Shutterstock

Partners who disagree about whether to move to a new location might adopt a win–lose orientation. In turn, this would lock them into a yes–no view in which only two alternatives are seen: move or stay put. The win–lose orientation almost guarantees that the partners won't work to find or create a mutually acceptable solution, such as moving to a third place that meets both partners' needs, or having a long-distance relationship so that each person can have the best location. The more person A argues for moving, the more person B argues for not moving. Eventually one of them "wins" but at the cost of the other and the relationship. A win–lose orientation toward conflict tends to undermine relationships because someone has to lose.

A win–lose approach can be appropriate when we have a high desire for our position to prevail, low commitment to a relationship, and little desire to take care of the person with whom we disagree. When you're buying a car, for instance, you want the best deal you can get, and you probably have little concern for the dealer's profit and little commitment to continuing the relationship. One of the authors adopted a win–lose approach to conflict with doctors when her father was dying. The doctors weren't doing all they could to help him, because they saw little value in investing in someone who was dying. On the other hand, the author wanted the doctors to do everything possible to help her father. The doctors and she had opposing views, and she cared less about whether the doctors were happy and liked her than about winning the best medical care for her father.

Student Voices

Tess:

One of the roughest issues for Jerry and me was when he started working most nights. The time after dinner had always been "our time." When Jerry took the new job, he had to stay in constant contact with the Vancouver office. Jerry and I used to do something together at 6 p.m., but because of the time difference, it's only 3 p.m. on the west coast, and the business day is still going. I was hurt that he no longer had time for us, and he was angry that I wanted time he needed for business. We kept talking and came up with the idea of spending a day together each weekend, which we'd never done. Although my ideal would still be to share evenings, this solution keeps us in touch with each other.

Win–Win

Win–win orientations assume that there are usually ways to resolve differences so that everyone gains. A good solution is one that everyone finds satisfactory. When all people are committed to finding a solution that satisfies everyone, a win–win resolution is often possible.

Sometimes people can't find or create a solution that is each person's ideal. In such cases, each person may make some accommodations to build a solution that lets the other win as well. When partners adopt win–win views of conflict, they often discover solutions that neither had thought of previously. This happens because they are committed to their own and the other's satisfaction. Sometimes, win–win attitudes result in compromises that satisfy enough of each person's needs to provide confirmation and to protect the health of the relationship.

In Chapter 3, we learned that how we perceive things has a powerful impact on what they mean to us and on the possibilities of resolution that we imagine. Remember how you couldn't solve the nine dots problem in Chapter 3 if you perceived it as a square? In a similar way, we're unlikely to find a win–win solution if we perceive conflict as win–lose or lose–lose.

Apply the Idea

IDENTIFYING ORIENTATIONS TOWARD CONFLICT

For each statement below, decide which of the three orientations to conflict it reflects.

_____ 1. We can't both be satisfied on this issue.
_____ 2. Since we disagree about which movie to see, let's just not go out tonight.
_____ 3. We're never going to see eye to eye on this, so I'll just defer to you.
_____ 4. If we keep talking, I think we'll figure out something that will work for both of us.
_____ 5. I can't stand fighting. Nobody ever wins.
_____ 6. No matter what you say, I'm not giving any ground on this issue. I feel very strongly about it, so you'll just have to go along with me.
_____ 7. We may not have a solution yet, but I think we're finding some areas of agreement. Let's try to build on those.

Key: 1 = Win–lose; 2 = Lose–lose; 3 = Win–lose; 4 = Win–win; 5 = Lose–lose; 6 = Win–lose; 7 = Win–win

Apply the Idea

IDENTIFYING YOUR CONFLICT TENDENCIES

Could you identify your orientation to conflict from this discussion? To check, answer these questions:

1. *When conflict seems about to occur, do you:*
   a. *Marshall arguments for your solution?*
   b. *Feel everyone is going to get hurt?*
   c. *Feel there's probably a way to satisfy everyone?*
2. *When involved in conflict, do you feel:*
   a. *Competitive urges?*
   b. *Resigned that everyone will lose?*
   c. *Committed to finding a mutual solution?*
3. *When you disagree with another person, do you assume:*
   a. *The other person is wrong?*
   b. *Neither of you is right?*
   c. *There are good reasons for what each of you thinks and feels?*

Key: (a) answers indicate a win–lose orientation; (b) answers suggest a lose–lose orientation; (c) answers reflect a win–win orientation.

RESPONSES TO CONFLICT

Roger is correct that physical violence can sometimes stop an argument—at least temporarily. Physical force may be an unfortunate necessity in some situations, such as combat or self-protection. In interpersonal relationships, however, it is a very poor way to deal with conflict. A great deal of research demonstrates that violence in families harms both perpetrators and victims, and it violates the trust on which close relationships are built (Jacobson & Gottman, 1998; Johnson, in press). In Chapter 11, we'll look more closely at the dynamics of violence between intimate partners. In this section, we'll consider ways of responding to conflict other than with violence.

> **Student Voices**
>
> **Roger:**
>
> One thing I learned when I was serving in the military is that a fist will stop an argument a lot faster than words. You can talk all day long and never reach resolution, but a good pop in the face ends conflict real fast.

Our approach to conflict shapes how we respond when conflict occurs. A series of studies identified four distinct ways North Americans respond to relational distress (Rusbult, 1987; Rusbult, Johnson, & Morrow, 1986; Rusbult & Zembrodt, 1983; Rusbult, Zembrodt, & Iwaniszek, 1986). These are represented in Figure 10.2. According to this model, responses to conflict can be either active or passive, depending on how overtly they address problems. Responses can also be constructive or destructive in their capacity to resolve tension and to preserve relationships.

> **Student Voices**
>
> **Chai:**
>
> A friend of mine uses the exit strategy on e-mail. Whenever we get into an argument, she stops replying to my e-mail messages. I know she reads them, because she's on e-mail several times every day. But if we're having an argument, she just won't reply. It's like she's not there, and I can't make her talk to me.

The Exit Response

The **exit response** involves physically walking out or psychologically withdrawing. Refusing to talk about a problem is an example of psychological exit. Ending a relationship and leaving when conflict arises are examples of literal exit. Because

FIGURE 10.2

Responses to Conflict in Relationships

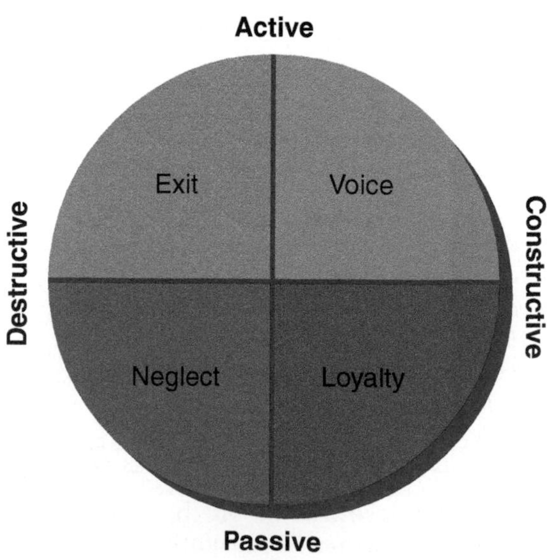

exit doesn't address problems, it tends to be destructive. Because it is a forceful way to avoid conflict, it is active.

Exit responses are associated with lose–lose and win–lose orientations toward conflict. People who have a lose–lose orientation assume that nobody can benefit if conflict takes place, so they see no point in engaging in conflict and prefer to avoid it. For different reasons, the win–lose orientation may promote the exit response. People who see conflicts as win–lose situations may exit physically or psychologically if they think they will lose should the conflict become overt.

When is an exit response appropriate?

The Neglect Response

The **neglect response** denies or minimizes problems, disagreements, anger, tension, or other matters that could lead to overt conflict. People communicate that they prefer to neglect conflicts by saying, "There isn't a disagreement here," "You're creating a problem where none exists," or "You're making a mountain out of a molehill." These statements deny that a problem exists or that a problem is important. Neglect generally is destructive because it doesn't resolve tension. It is passive because it avoids discussion. In some situations, however, neglect may be an effective response to conflict. For instance, if an issue can't be resolved, discussing it may further harm a relationship. Also, if a conflict isn't important to a relationship's health, it may be appropriate not to deal with it.

The lose–lose and win–lose orientations may prompt the neglect response for the same reasons that each of those orientations is associated with the exit response. Either the person thinks that escalating the disagreement will harm everyone, or the person thinks that she or he will lose if the conflict is allowed to progress.

The Loyalty Response

The **loyalty response** is staying committed to a relationship despite differences. In other words, the person who adopts loyalty as a response to conflict decides to stay in a relationship and tolerate the differences. Loyalty may be desirable if tolerating differences isn't too costly, but in some instances, deferring your own needs and goals may be too high a price for harmony. The loyalty response may also take the form of focusing on what is good and desirable about the relationship and minimizing its problems. Loyalty is silent allegiance that doesn't actively address conflict, so it is a passive response. Because it preserves the relationship, loyalty tends to be constructive, at least in the short term.

Loyalty is most likely to spring from a lose–lose orientation toward conflict. Believing that engaging in overt disagreement only hurts everyone, people may choose to remain loyal to the relationship and not try to work through differences.

Student Voices

Zondomoni:

In South Africa, the tradition is for women not to speak out against their husbands. Women are supposed to support whatever the husband says or does. A woman who speaks out or who disagrees with her husband or any male relative is considered bad; she is behaving inappropriately. But some of us are now challenging this custom. I disagreed with my father about my marriage, and he did not speak to me for many months after. Now he speaks to me again. I also sometimes disagree with my husband. Life is changing in South Africa.

The Voice Response

Finally, the **voice response** addresses conflict directly and attempts to resolve it. People who use the voice response identify problems or tensions and assert a desire to deal with them. Voice implies that people care enough about a relationship to notice when something is wrong and to want to do something to improve the situation. Thus, voice often is the most constructive way of responding to conflict in enduring intimate relationships.

The voice response is most likely to be fostered by a win–win orientation toward conflict. It takes belief in yourself and the other person to give voice to problems and disagreements. Voicing concerns also expresses belief in the relationship. We're unlikely to voice disagreements unless we believe that a relationship can withstand our doing so. Voice may also take the form of genuine apology for behaviour that has hurt another, or explicit acceptance of a partner's apology (Fincham & Beach, 2002; Vangelisti & Crumley, 1998).

Although each of us has developed a preferred response, we can become skillful in other responses if we so choose. Constructive strategies (voice and loyalty) are advisable for relationships that matter to you and that you want to maintain. Exit may be useful as an interim strategy when partners need time to reflect or cool off before dealing with conflict directly. Loyalty may be appropriate in situations where conflict is temporary and provoked by external pressures. Developing skill in a range of responses to conflict increases your ability to communicate sensitively and effectively.

Apply the Idea

ENLARGING YOUR REPERTOIRE OF RESPONSES TO CONFLICT

Identify two responses to conflict that you do not often use. For each one, specify two strategies to increase your skill in using that response.

Example: Voice Response to Conflict	**Strategies for Achieving Competence**
I have trouble talking about conflict.	1. When I feel like avoiding conflict, I will remind myself that avoiding has never made problems go away. 2. When friends ask what's wrong, I will stop saying "Nothing's wrong."

COMMUNICATION PATTERNS DURING CONFLICT

Communication skills shape the process and outcomes of conflict. Thus, we want to understand specific kinds of communication that foster or impede effective conflict. Ineffective communication can hurt individuals, damage relationships, and undermine the possibility of resolving problems. Unproductive communication patterns in managing conflict reflect a preoccupation with self and a disregard for the other. Table 10.1 identifies behaviours that foster constructive and unproductive conflict communication (Gottman, 1993; Gottman, Notarius, Gonso, & Markman, 1976; Gottman, Notarius, Markman et al., 1976; Vangelisti, 1993).

TABLE 10.1

SUMMARY OF CONSTRUCTIVE AND UNPRODUCTIVE COMMUNICATION

Constructive	Unproductive
Validation of each other	Disconfirmation of each other
Sensitive listening	Poor listening
Dual perspective	Preoccupation with self
Recognition of other's concerns	Cross-complaining
Asking for clarification	Hostile mind reading
Infrequent interruptions	Frequent interruptions
Focus on specific issues	Kitchen-sinking
Compromises and contracts	Counterproposals
Useful metacommunication	Excessive metacommunication
Summarizing the concerns	Self-summarizing by both partners

Unproductive Conflict Communication

The Early Stages

The foundation of unproductive conflict is established by communication that fails to confirm individuals. If Vaclav says, "I want us to spend more time together," Anna may reply, "That's unreasonable." This disconfirms Vaclav's feeling and request. Anna could also disconfirm him by not replying at all, which would be a refusal to acknowledge him. During the early stages of conflict, people tend to listen poorly. They may listen selectively, taking in only what they expect or want to believe. They may communicate disdain nonverbally. For instance, Anna could roll her eyes to tell Vaclav his request is outrageous, or she might shrug and turn away to signal that she doesn't care what he wants.

Cross-complaining occurs when one person's complaint is met by a counter-complaint. Anna could respond to Vaclav's request for more time by saying, "Yeah, well, what I want is a little more respect for what I do." That response doesn't address Vaclav's concern; it is an attempt to divert the conversation and to switch the fault from Anna to Vaclav. Poor listening and disconfirmation establish a climate in which dual perspective is low and defensiveness is high.

Negative climates tend to build on themselves. As parties in conflict continue to talk, mind-reading is likely. Instead of offering an explicit apology, Vaclav assumes that Anna knows he is sorry (Vangelisti & Crumley, 1998). Instead of asking Vaclav to clarify or explain his feelings, Anna assumes she knows his motives. Perhaps

olly/Shutterstock

she thinks he wants to divert her from her work so that she won't succeed. If Anna makes this assumption, she discounts what Vaclav wants. Mind-reading in distressed relationships has a distinctly negative tone. The negative assumptions and attributions reflect and fuel hostility and mistrust.

The Middle Stages

Once a negative climate has been set, it is stoked by other unconstructive communication. People often engage in **kitchen-sinking,** in which everything except the kitchen sink is thrown into the argument. Vaclav may add to his original complaint by recalling all sorts of other real and imagined slights from Anna. She may reciprocate by hauling out her own laundry list of gripes. The result is such a mass of grievances that Vaclav and Anna are overwhelmed. They can't solve all the problems they've dragged into the discussion, and they may well forget what the original issue was. Kitchen-sinking is particularly likely to occur when people have a host of concerns they've repressed for some time. Once a conflict begins, everything that has been stored up is thrown in.

The middle stages of unproductive conflict tend to be marked by frequent interruptions that disrupt the flow of talk. Interruptions may also be attempts to derail a partner's issues and reroute discussion: "I don't want to find more time together until we discuss your responsibility for this house." Cross-complaining often continues in this middle stage of the syndrome. Because neither person is allowed to develop thoughts fully (or even to finish a sentence), discussion never focuses on any topic long enough to make headway in resolving it.

The Later Stages

Even if people make little progress in solving their problems, limited time and energy guarantee an end to an episode of conflict. Unfortunately, preceding stages didn't lay the groundwork for effective discussion of solutions. As a result, each person's proposals tend to be met with **counterproposals**. The self-preoccupation that first surfaced in the early phase persists now, so each person is more interested in pushing his or her solution than in considering the other person's. Vaclav proposes, "Maybe we could spend two nights together each week." Anna counterproposes, "Maybe you could assume responsibility for half the chores around here." Her counterproposal fails to acknowledge his suggestion, so her communication does not confirm him. Compounding self-preoccupation is self-summarizing, which occurs when a person keeps repeating what she or he has already said. This egocentric communication ignores the other person and simply restates the speaker's feelings and perspective.

Excessive metacommunication is a final form of negative communication in unproductive conflict. Metacommunication, which we discussed in Chapter 1, is communication about communication. For example, Vaclav might say, "I think we're avoiding talking about the real issue here." This is a comment about the communication that is happening. Metacommunication is used by couples in both unproductive conflict and constructive conflict, but it is used in very different ways (Gottman, Markman, & Notarius, 1977; Gottman, Notarius, Gonso, & Markman, 1976; Gottman, Notarius, Markman et al., 1976).

Junial Enterprises/Shutterstock

In constructive conflict communication, people use metacommunication to keep the discussion on track,

and then they return to the topics at hand. For instance, during a disagreement, Aaron might comment that Norma doesn't seem to be expressing her feelings and invite her to do so. Then, he and Norma would return to their discussion.

In contrast, people who manage conflict unproductively often become embroiled in metacommunication and can't get back to the issues. For example, Norma and Aaron might get into extended metacommunication about the way they deal with conflict and never return to the original topic of conflict. Excessive metacommunication is more likely to block partners than to resolve tensions satisfactorily.

The communication that makes up unproductive conflict reflects and promotes egocentrism and dogmatism because negative communication tends to be self-perpetuating. Egocentrism leads to poor listening, which promotes disconfirmation, which fuels defensiveness, which stokes dogmatism, which leads to hostile mind-reading and kitchen-sinking, which pave the way for self-summarizing.

Each negative form of communication feeds into the overall negative system. Unproductive communication fosters a defensive, negative climate, which makes it almost impossible to resolve conflicts, confirm individuals, or nurture a relationship. When egocentrism prevails, each partner is more interested in getting her or his own

Communication Notes

HOW TO FIGHT

Rules for Fighting Dirty	Rules for Fighting Clean
Apologize prematurely.	Fully express your positive and negative feelings.
Refuse to take the fight seriously.	Define your out-of-bounds areas of vulnerability.
Chain-react by piling on all the issues and gripes (kitchen-sinking).	Paraphrase the other's arguments in your own words and allow the other to do likewise.
Hit below the belt. Use intimate knowledge to humiliate the other person.	Think before fighting, not after fighting. Try not to let your feelings undermine reason and fair play.
Withdraw and avoid confrontation: walk out, be silent.	Consider the merit of the other person's opinions of you before rejecting or accepting them.
Withhold affection, approval, recognition, or material things.	Focus on the other person's behaviour and ideas.
Encourage others to side with you against your partner.	Define what the fight is about and stay within limits.
Play demolition derby with your partner's character—tell the other person what's wrong with him or her, what he or she thinks, feels, means, and so on (mind-reading).	Look for where you and your partner agree, as well as where you disagree.
Demand more—nothing is ever enough. Push to have everything your way.	Decide how each of you can help the other resolve the issue in a way that satisfies him or her.
Attack a person, activity, value, or idea that your partner holds dear.	Avoid discussing a problem or conflict when you are emotionally raw.

REVIEW

Egocentrism leads to poor listening, which promotes disconfirmation, which fuels defensiveness, which stokes dogmatism, which leads to hostile mind-reading and kitchen-sinking, which pave the way for self-summarizing.

way than in creating a solution that both can accept. In addition, unconstructive communication is so disconfirming that it damages individual partners and the long-term health of the relationship. The Communication Notes feature "How to Fight" compares fair and unfair conflict tactics (Bach & Wyden, 1973).

Constructive Conflict Communication

Constructive communication during conflict creates a supportive, positive climate that increases the possibility of resolving differences without harming the relationship. Let's look at how constructive communication plays out in the three phases of conflict.

The Early Stages

The foundation of constructive management of conflict is established long before a specific disagreement is aired. Climate, which is the foundation both of conflict and of the overall relationship, sets the tone for communication during conflict.

To establish a good climate, communicators confirm each other by recognizing and acknowledging each other's concerns and feelings. Returning to our example, when Vaclav says, "I want us to spend more time together," Anna could confirm him by replying, "I wish we could, too. It's nice that you want us to have more time together." Anna's statement communicates to Vaclav that she is listening and that she cares about his concerns and shares them. After she says that, their discussion might go like this:

Vaclav: Yeah, it just seems that we used to spend a lot more time together, and we felt closer then. I miss that.

Anna: I do, too. It sounds as if what's really on your mind is how close we are, not specifically the amount of time we spend together. Is that right?

Vaclav: Yeah, I guess that is more what's bothering me, but I kind of think they're connected, don't you?

Anna: To an extent, but we won't feel closer just by spending more time together. I think we also need some shared interests like we used to have.

Vaclav: I'd like that. Do you have any ideas?

Let's highlight several things in this conversation. First, notice that, when Anna responds directly to Vaclav's opening statement, he elaborates and clarifies what is troubling him. Instead of time per se, the issue is closeness. Listening sensitively, Anna picks up on this and refocuses their conversation on closeness. We should also notice that Anna doesn't mind-read; instead, she asks Vaclav whether she has understood what he meant. When he asks Anna whether she thinks time and closeness are related, Vaclav shows openness to her perceptions; thus, he confirms her and doesn't mind-read. The openness they create clears the way for effective discussion of how to increase their closeness. Once a supportive climate is established, the couple can proceed to the middle stages of conflict knowing they are not fighting each other but working together to solve a problem.

The Middle Stages

The positive groundwork laid in the early phase of conflict supports what happens as people dig into issues. The middle stages of constructive conflict are marked by what Gottman (1993) calls *agenda building,* which involves staying focused on the main issues. When partners keep communication on target, kitchen-sinking is unlikely to derail discussion.

Side issues may come up, as they do in unproductive conflict, but people who have learned to communicate effectively control digressions and stay with their agenda. One useful technique is **bracketing**, which is noting that an issue arising in the course of conflict should be discussed later. Bracketing allows partners to confirm each other's concerns by agreeing to deal with them later. In addition, bracketing topics peripheral to the current discussion allows partners to make progress in resolving the immediate issue.

During the middle stage of constructive conflict, communicators continue to show respect for each other by not interrupting except to get clarification ("Before you go on, could you explain what you mean by closeness?") or to check perceptions ("So you think time together leads to closeness?"). Unlike disruptive interruptions, those that clarify ideas and check perceptions confirm the person speaking by showing that the listener wants to understand the meaning.

Parties in conflict continue to recognize and acknowledge each other's point of view. Rather than the cross-complaining, they acknowledge each other's feelings, thoughts, and concerns. This doesn't mean they don't put their own concerns on the table. Constructive conflict includes asserting our own feelings and needs as part of an honest dialogue. Honouring both ourselves and others is central to good interpersonal communication.

The Later Stages

In the culminating phase, attention shifts to resolving the tension. Whereas in unproductive conflict this involves meeting proposals with counterproposals, in constructive conflict people continue to operate collaboratively.

Keeping in mind that they share a relationship, they continue using dual perspective to remain aware of each other's perspectives. Instead of countering each other's proposals, they engage in **contracting**, which is building a solution through negotiation and the acceptance of parts of proposals. The difference between counterproposals and contracting is illustrated in this example:

Counterproposals

Vaclav: I want us to spend three nights a week doing things together.

Anna: I can't do that right now because we're short-handed at work, and I am filling in nights. Get a hobby so you aren't bored at night.

Vaclav: Not being bored isn't the same as our being close. I want us to spend time together again.

Anna: I told you, I can't do that. Don't be so selfish.

Vaclav: Aren't we as important as your job?

Anna: That's a stupid question. I can't take three nights off. Let's take more vacations.

Contracting

Vaclav: I want us to spend three nights a week doing things together.

Anna: I'm all for that, but right now we're short-handed at work. How about if we use your idea but adjust it to my job? Maybe we could start with one night each week and expand that later.

Vaclav: Okay, that's a start, but could we also reserve some weekend time for us?

Anna: That's a good idea. Let's plan on that. I just can't be sure how much I'll have to work on weekends until we hire some new people. What if we promise to give ourselves an extra week's vacation to spend together when we have full staff?

Vaclav: Okay, that's a good backup plan, but can we take weekend time when you don't work?

Anna: Absolutely. How about a picnic this Sunday? We've haven't gone on a picnic in so long.

Student Voices

Bettina:

My son and I used to argue all the time, and we never got anywhere because we were each trying to get our own way, and we weren't paying attention to the other. Then we went into family counselling, and we learned how to make our arguments more productive. The most important thing I learned was to be looking for ways to respond to what my son says and wants. Once I started focusing on him and trying to satisfy him, he was more willing to listen to my point of view and to think about solutions that would satisfy me. We still argue a lot—I guess we always will—but now it's more like we're working things through together instead of trying to tear each other down.

In the counterproposal scenario, Vaclav and Anna were competing to get their own way. Neither tried to identify workable parts of the other's proposals or to find common ground. Because each adopts a win–lose view of the conflict, it's likely that both of them and the relationship will be losers. A very different tone shows up in the contracting scenario. Neither person represses personal needs, and each is committed to building on the other's proposals.

Specific differences between unproductive and productive conflict can be summarized as the difference between confirming and disconfirming communication. Communication characteristic of unproductive conflict disconfirms both individuals and the relationship. On the other hand, the communication in constructive conflict consistently confirms both people and the relationship.

Conflict Management Skills

Our discussion of constructive and unproductive conflict communication highlights communication skills and attitudes we've emphasized in previous chapters. This is a good time to explicate eight conflict management skills that rely on effective interpersonal communication.

Attend to the Relationship Level of Meaning

Conflict situations, like all other communication encounters, involve both the content level and the relationship level of meaning. Yet many of us tend to focus on the content level of meaning: the issues or the problem.

Focusing on the content level of meaning is understandable, but it's not enough, because it neglects a major dimension of communication. We need to tune into relationship-level meanings also. Who is she saying she is (my friend, my superior, my teacher)? Is he being responsive, showing liking, demonstrating power? What does this suggest about the relationship between us (it is not in jeopardy, its continuation depends on how we resolve this conflict)?

It's equally important to monitor the relationship level of your own communication. Are you saying you care about getting your way more than you care about the relationship or other person? Are you communicating respect, attentiveness, or superiority? Are you attacking a co-worker personally instead of arguing about issues? Are you affirming the relationship, even though there is a difference at the moment? During conflict, it's critical to think carefully about relationship-level messages and meanings.

Communicate Supportively

An important conflict management skill is to monitor your communication to ensure that it encourages a supportive climate that is likely to build a win–win approach to conflict. From our discussion in Chapter 9, you'll recall that supportive interpersonal climates are cultivated by communication that is descriptive, provisional, spontaneous, problem oriented, empathic, and egalitarian. It's also useful to remind ourselves of the kinds of communication that tend to generate defensive climates: evaluation, certainty, strategies, control orientation, neutrality, and superiority. In conflict situations, we may be especially likely to engage in communication that fosters defensiveness and reduces the possibilities for resolving the conflict and sustaining the relationship.

Listen Mindfully

You already know that mindful listening is a very important interpersonal communication skill. This is especially true in conflict because we may not want to consider the other person's ideas or criticisms of our ideas. Even when you disagree with someone's thoughts, actions, goals, or values, you should show respect for the person by paying attention and seeking to understand him or her. That can be really difficult if the other person is not practising effective communication skills.

For example, imagine this scene: One evening, the person you've been dating greets you by griping, "You're late again. Why can't you ever be on time?" That kind of attack tends to make us feel defensive, so a natural reply might be, "What's your problem? Don't make a big deal out of five minutes. Get off my case." However, this kind of retort is likely to fan the flames of discord. A more effective reply would be, "I'm sorry I kept you waiting. I didn't know being on time was so important to you." This response acknowledges your lateness, shows respect for the other person's feelings, and opens the door to a conversation.

Take Responsibility for Your Thoughts, Feelings, and Issues

I language is a cornerstone of effective conflict management. Own your feelings: "I feel angry when you are late" instead of "You make me angry with your lateness." It's also important to own your thoughts and your issues. "We need to keep this apartment cleaner" is a statement that you want the apartment cleaner. The other person may not care, in which case it's not accurate to say, "*We* need to keep this apartment cleaner." The issue is yours, so you should own it by saying, "I am uncomfortable with how messy this place is. Can we figure out a way to deal with this?"

Check Perceptions

Perceptions are easily distorted when conflict is afoot. You may see another person's position as more extreme than it is; you may think someone is immature or unreasonable; you may be inclined to engage in self-serving bias, which we discussed in Chapter 3. During conflict, we need to check our perceptions. Paraphrasing is one effective way to do this: "So you think we should spend every weekend cleaning our apartment?" "Does it seem to you that I'm always late?" We can also check perceptions by asking direct questions, being careful to avoid communication that fosters defensiveness: "What would be clean enough for you?" "Is it the five minutes I'm late that's bothering you, or does lateness mean something else to you?"

Checking perceptions is particularly important in online communication. After reading a classmate's paper at his request, Susan e-mailed a response in which she suggested that he should strengthen one part of his analysis. He replied: "Okay." Susan wondered if the short reply meant that she had offended him with her suggestion, so she called him and said, "I don't know what your 'okay' means. Are you angry about my suggestion?" He replied that he had been rushed and so had typed only a quick response. Paraphrasing and asking questions say, "You matter to me. I'm trying to understand you."

Look for Points of Agreement

During conflict, we tend to focus on disagreements or ways we differ from another person. Although we should acknowledge and deal with real differences, we should also look for points of agreement. You and a friend may disagree on goals, values, or courses of action, but you probably agree on other matters related to a conflict episode. Returning to the previous example, you and your date may disagree on whether being five minutes late is important. However, you may also share a belief that people who care about each other respect each other's feelings. This shared belief is common ground that may help you work out a resolution to the conflict. If we are looking for common ground, we can usually find it. When we do, we're likely to deal with conflict effectively without harming the relationship.

Look for Ways to Preserve the Other's "Face"

In Japan and some other Asian cultures, *face* is a central concept. Your face is the image of yourself that you want others to see and believe (McDaniel & Quasha, 2000). We are embarrassed or ashamed when we lose face. Whereas Western cultures tend to emphasize protecting one's own face, many Asian cultures emphasize the importance of protecting others' faces (Ting-Toomey, 1988; Ting-Toomey & Oetzel, 2001, 2002). The goal is for no one to feel defeated, stupid, or embarrassed.

Protecting others' faces is part of managing conflict effectively. If your point or idea is accepted in an argument, be gracious toward the other person. He or she is likely to feel that face is lost if you say, "I knew you'd come around." If you are committed to protecting the other person's face, you might say, "I appreciate your generosity in understanding how important this is to me." This statement allows the person who may have lost the argument to retain dignity and save face.

Imagine How You'll Feel in the Future

Recall that, in Chapter 5, we noted that one of our symbolic abilities is hypothetical thought. Among other things, this capacity allows us to imagine ourselves in the future and to respond to the future self that we imagine. You can use this ability to help you manage conflict effectively. To illustrate, consider this scenario: A friend has just told you that he borrowed your car without asking and had a minor accident. You feel like shouting and attacking the friend verbally.

Before you say anything, you imagine how you would feel tomorrow or next week or next year if you launched a scathing attack on your friend. Then you imagine how you would feel tomorrow or next week or next year if you expressed your anger calmly yet not aggressively, showed concern about whether your friend was hurt in the accident, and found a way to help your friend save face. You probably prefer the you who behaved considerately to the you who was combative. Taking a moment to imagine yourself after the conflict ends can help you choose to communicate in ways that are ethical, that foster self-respect, and that support the continuation of the relationship.

The eight skills we've discussed translate general communication skills and principles into the specific context of interpersonal conflict. Developing competence in these eight skills will empower you to manage conflict competently, graciously, and effectively. Figure 10.3 summarizes skills for managing conflict productively.

GUIDELINES FOR EFFECTIVE COMMUNICATION DURING CONFLICT

Our study of conflict, along with many of the ideas we've considered in previous chapters, suggests five guidelines for dealing with conflict constructively.

Attend to relationship-level meanings.

Communicate supportively.

Listen mindfully.

Own your feelings, thoughts, and issues.

Check perceptions.

Look for points of agreement.

Look for ways to preserve the other's face.

Imagine how you will feel in the future.

FIGURE 10.3

Conflict Management Skills

Focus on the Overall Communication System

As we noted in Chapter 1, communication is systemic, which means it occurs in contexts, and it is composed of many interacting parts. Applying the principle of systems to conflict, we can see that how we deal with conflict is shaped by the overall systems of relationships and communication.

People who have developed negative interpersonal climates cannot argue constructively simply by practising "good conflict techniques" such as focusing talk and not interrupting. Those techniques occur within larger contexts that affect how they are interpreted. People who have learned to be generally defensive and distrustful are unlikely to respond openly to even the best conflict resolution methods. By the same reasoning, in climates that are generally supportive and confirming, even unconstructive conflict communication is unlikely to derail relationships. Conflict, like all interaction, is affected by the larger contexts in which it takes place.

In other words, conflict is part of a larger whole, and we must make that whole healthy to create a context in which conflict can be resolved without jeopardizing partners or relationships. Keep in mind that conflict always has implications for three parties: you, another person, and the relationship between the two of you. Healthy conflict communication honours all three.

Time Conflict Purposefully

Timing affects how we communicate about conflicts. There are three ways to use chronemics so that conflicts are most likely to be effective. First, try not to engage in serious conflict discussions at times when one or both people will not be fully present psychologically.

Most of us are less attentive, less mindful listeners when we are tired. It's generally more productive to discuss problems in private rather than in public settings (Cupach & Carlson, 2002). If time is limited or if we are rushing, we're less likely to take the time to deal constructively with differences. It's impossible to listen well and respond thoughtfully when a stopwatch is ticking in our minds.

It's also considerate and constructive to deal with conflict when each person is ready to talk constructively about a problem. Of course, this works only if the person who isn't ready agrees to talk about the issue at a later

Student Voices

Stephanie:

I have a really hot temper, so I can cut someone to pieces if I argue when I'm mad. I have hurt a lot of friends by attacking them before I cooled off, and I hate myself when I act like that. I have finally figured out that I can handle fights constructively if I cool down. Now when I'm hot, I tell my friends or my boyfriend that I can't discuss it right then. Later, when I'm calm, I can talk without saying things that hurt them and that I feel bad about.

time. Because research indicates that men are more likely than women to avoid discussing relationship conflicts, they may be especially reluctant to talk about disagreements without first gaining some distance (Beck, 1988; Gray & Foushee, 1997; Rusbult, 1987).

Some people prefer to tackle problems as soon as they arise, whereas others need time to percolate privately before interacting. It's generally a good idea not to discuss conflict in the heat of anger. For the same reason, it's wise to save an e-mail reply you write when angry to see if that's what you want to send when you've cooled down. Constructive, healthy conflict communication is more likely when tempers aren't flaring.

A third use of chronemics to promote positive conflict is bracketing, which we discussed earlier in this chapter. It is natural for a variety of issues needing attention to come up in the course of conflict. If we try to deal with all the sideline problems that arise, however, we can't focus on the immediate problem. Bracketing other concerns for later discussion lets us keep conflict focused productively. Keep in mind, however, that bracketing works only if partners return to the issues they set aside.

Aim for Win–Win Conflict

How you approach conflict shapes what will happen in communication. When conflict exists between two people who care about each other and want to sustain a good relationship, however, the win–win style is usually the best choice. If you enter conflict with the assumption that you, the other person, and the relationship can all benefit from conflict, it's likely that you will bring about a resolution that benefits everyone. Adopting a win–win orientation to conflict reflects a commitment to honouring yourself, the other person, and the integrity of your shared relationship (see Figure 10.4).

To maximize the chance of a win–win conflict resolution, begin by identifying your feelings and your needs or desires in the situation. You may want to review Chapter 4 to remind yourself of ways to clarify your emotions. Understanding what your feelings and desires are is essential to productive conflict communication. Once you figure out what you feel and need, express yourself in clear language. It's not effective to make vague or judgmental statements such as, "I don't like the way you ignore me, and I want you to be more sensitive." It would be more effective to say, "I feel hurt when you don't call, and I want us to find some way that I can be assured of your love without making you feel handcuffed."

The second step is to figure out what the other person feels, needs, and wants. If you don't already know what the other person wants and feels, don't mind-read. Instead, ask the other person what she or he is feeling and what is needed or wanted in terms of a resolution to the conflict. When the other person expresses feelings and preferences, listen mindfully. Resist the temptation to countercomplain. Just listen, and try to understand the other person's perspective as fully as you can. Minimal encouragers and paraphrasing let the other person know you are listening closely and are committed to understanding her or his perspective.

Third, focus on language that promotes cooperation and mutual respect. To do this, rely on supportive communication, and try to avoid communication that fosters a defensive climate. You should also use I language to own your thoughts and feelings. Throughout conflict communication, mindful listening allows you to gain the maximum understanding of the other person's perspective and feelings.

1. **Express your needs:** Identify your own feelings, needs, or desires. Then express yourself clearly, letting your partner know what behaviour is troublesome, how you feel about it, and what you want.
2. **Solicit the needs of the other:** Be mindful, ask questions, paraphrase, encourage, and support to fully understand the needs and feelings of the other.
3. **Negotiate a solution:** Strive for a high-quality solution. Settle for a workable compromise. Be flexible.
4. **Follow-up:** Check in to make sure the solution fits both parties.

FIGURE 10.4

Steps to a Win–Win Conflict

Finally, keep reminding yourself that win–win solutions are most likely when both people balance concern for themselves and concern for each other. On the relationship level of meaning, you want to communicate this message: "I care about you and your feelings and desires, and I know you care about me and how I feel and what I want." If that message underlies your conflict communication, chances are good that you will attain a win–win resolution.

Honour Yourself, Your Partner, and the Relationship

Constructive conflict communication is impossible if we disregard or demean the other person's needs and feelings. Doing so disconfirms the other and sets a win–lose tone for conversation. It is equally undesirable to muffle your own needs and feelings. In fairness to yourself and the other person, you should express your feelings and needs clearly.

In addition to attending to ourselves and others, we must remember that relationships are affected by how we handle conflict. For this reason, win–lose orientations toward conflict should really be called win–lose–lose, because when only one person wins, both the other person and the relationship lose. Win–win orientations and constructive forms of communication make it possible for both individuals and the relationship to win.

Show Grace When Appropriate

Finally, an important principle to keep in mind during conflict is that grace is sometimes appropriate. **Grace** is granting forgiveness or putting aside our own needs when there is no standard that says we should or must do so. Grace is not forgiving when we *should* (for instance, excusing people who aren't responsible for their actions).

Also, grace isn't allowing others to have their way when we have no choice. Instead, grace is unearned, unrequired kindness. For instance, two roommates

Alan and Sandy Carey/Photodisc/Getty Images

Children "let go" and "show grace" more readily than adults.

agree to split chores and one doesn't do her share because she has three tests in a week. Her roommate might do all the chores even though there is no agreement or expectation of this generosity. This is an act of grace. It's also an act of grace to defer to another person's preference when you could hold out for your own. Similarly, when someone hurts us and has no right to expect forgiveness, we may choose to forgive anyway. We do so not because we have to but because we want to. Grace is a matter of choice.

Grace involves the Zen concept of **letting go**, which is to free ourselves of anger, blame, and judgments about another and what she or he did. When we let go of these feelings, we release both ourselves and others from their consequences. Sometimes, we tell a friend that we forgive him for some offense, but then

Communication Notes

THE COMMUNICATION OF FORGIVENESS

What do you do when you feel betrayed by someone with whom you are close? What do you do when you betray someone you love? These questions come up in most relationships that endure over time.

Douglas Kelley (1998) is a communication scholar and a relationship counsellor. In both his research and clinical work, he emphasizes forgiveness as a major influence on how—or whether—relationships progress. Kelley assumes that transgressions both minor and major are inevitable in relationships, so the question becomes: How do couples go forward after harm has been done?

Kelley reports that one crucial dynamic in the forgiveness process is motivations, those of both the transgressor and the forgiver.

Forgiveness is most likely to occur and to allow relationship continuity when both parties are motivated by a desire to restore the well-being of themselves, each other, and the relationship. How willing a person is to forgive a wrong depends in part on what the offender communicates. People are more likely to grant forgiveness to a person who apologizes, expresses remorse, or takes responsibility for the wrong. Kelley also finds that the capacity to forgive is enhanced if the forgiver can reframe the hurtful event by gaining understanding into it, attributing it to factors beyond the offender's control, or viewing it as unintentional.

Finally, Kelley emphasizes that forgiving is a process, not an event that occurs in a single moment. He emphasizes that, even after forgiveness is granted, time is needed to heal a relationship, restore trust, and return to healthy, comfortable interaction.

Adding to Kelley's work is a study by William Cupach and Christine Carlson (2002). They found that forgiveness is more than a set of behaviours and more than efforts to overcome negative feelings, such as wanting revenge. At least as important, they report, is a readiness to forgive—a desire to accept and confirm another, even—or especially—after a transgression of some sort.

The Forgiveness Web's site provides a reading room, message boards, related links, and information about upcoming conferences and workshops: www.forgivenessweb.com.

later we remind him of it. When we hang on to blame and judgment, we haven't really let go, so we have not really shown grace. There's no grace when we blackmail others for our kindness or hang on to hostile feelings.

Grace is given without strings. Arthur Osborne (1996), who believes grace is essential in loving relationships, makes this point clearly when he says, "The person who asks for a reward is a merchant, not a lover" (p. 6). We show kindness, defer our needs, or forgive a wrong without any expectation of reward. Grace isn't doing something nice to make a friend feel grateful or indebted to us. Nor do we act in grace when we do something with the expectation of a payback. To do a favour because you want a reciprocal favour is bargaining, not showing grace. For an act to be one of grace, it must be done without conditions or expectations of return.

Grace is not always appropriate. People can take advantage of grace and kindness. Some people repeatedly abuse and hurt others, confident that pardons will be granted. When grace is extended and then exploited, it may be unwise to extend it again to the same person. However, if you show grace in good faith, and another abuses it, you should not fault yourself. Kindness and a willingness to forgive are worthy ethical values. The richest and most enduring relationships allow room for grace occasionally.

It is important to honour and assert ourselves, as we've emphasized throughout this book. However, self-interest and self-assertion alone are insufficient ethical principles for creating rich interpersonal relationships. None of us is perfect. We all make mistakes, wound others with thoughtless acts, and occasionally do things we know are wrong and hurtful. Sometimes, there is no reason others should forgive us when we wrong them; we have no right to expect exoneration.

R. Walters (1984) offers a moving insight about the role of grace in human relationships. He says, "When we have been hurt we have two alternatives: be destroyed by resentment, or forgive. Resentment is death; forgiving leads to healing and life" (p. 366). For human relationships to live and thrive, there must be some room for redemption, for forgiveness, and for grace.

Apply the Idea

CRITIQUE YOURSELF

Record the details of a specific argument that you've had recently. List the positive points about your role in this argument and also ways in which you might try to handle it differently next time.

Chapter Summary

Because conflicts are normal and unavoidable in any relationship of real depth, the challenge is to learn to manage conflicts effectively. Patterns of conflict are shaped by how people view conflict. We discussed lose–lose, win–lose, and win–win approaches to conflict and explored how each affects interaction. In addition, conflict patterns are influenced by how people respond to tension. Inclinations to exit, neglect, show loyalty, or voice conflict vary in how actively they deal with tension and how constructive they are for relationships. In most cases, voice is the preferred response because only voice allows partners to intervene actively and constructively when conflicts arise.

Communication is a particularly important influence on interpersonal conflict. Communication skills that promote constructive conflict management include being mindful, confirming others, showing dual perspective, listening sensitively, focusing discussion, and contracting solutions, while avoiding mind-reading, interrupting, self-summarizing, and cross-complaining.

We closed the chapter by identifying five guidelines for increasing the productivity of interpersonal conflict. First, we need to remember that conflicts occur within overall systems of communication and relationships. To be constructive, conflict must take place within supportive, confirming climates in which good interpersonal communication is practised. Second, it's important to time conflicts so that those involved have the time they need for private reflection and for productive discussion.

A third principle is to aim for win–win solutions to conflict. Consistent with these three guidelines is the fourth: honouring yourself, your partner and your relationship by working to balance commitments to yourself, others, and relationships when conflict arises. The fifth guideline is to show grace when appropriate. Although grace can be exploited, it can also infuse relationships with kindness and make room for inevitable human errors. It's important to balance the tensions inherent in the notion of grace so that we recognize both its potential values and its dangers.

In the next two chapters, we'll explore the worlds of friendship and romance and of the workplace. As we do, we'll carry forward the information and guidelines we've considered in this chapter, because how we manage conflicts affects the health of our friendships, romantic relationships, and relationships with our co-workers and employers.

Key Concepts

- bracketing
- conflict
- contracting
- counterproposals
- cross-complaining
- exit response
- games
- grace
- kitchen-sinking
- letting go
- lose–lose
- loyalty response
- neglect response
- passive aggression
- voice response
- win–lose
- win–win

For Further Thought and Discussion

1. What ethical principles are implicit in lose–lose, win–lose, and win–win orientations to conflict? Some styles of conflict emphasize fairness, whereas other styles place greater value on cooperation. Do you identify more strongly with either of these value emphases?
2. Think about the ways you typically respond to conflict. Do you tend to rely on one or two of the four responses we discussed (exit, voice, loyalty, neglect)? Are your response tendencies consistent with research findings about women and men, in general?
3. Have you ever been in a relationship in which conflict was stifled? Using the concepts you learned in this chapter, can you now describe how the conflict was repressed? Can you now think of ways you might have engaged in more effective conflict communication in that relationship?
4. Identify one situation in your life in which each orientation to conflict was, or would have been, appropriate. When would lose–lose have been appropriate? When would win–lose have been a reasonable approach? When would win–win have been the best approach?

5. Use your InfoTrac® College Edition to read Esin Tezer's and Ayhan Demir's 2001 article, "Conflict Behaviours Toward Same-Sex and Opposite-Sex Peers Among Male and Female Late Adolescents," published in *Adolescence*. Are the reported differences in males' and females' conflict orientations consistent with your personal experiences and observations?
6. Use your InfoTrac® College Edition to review the tables of content for the five most recent issues of *Journal of Family Practice and Journal of Comparative Family Studies*. Do you find articles that discuss how conflicts affect families or how families can handle conflicts productively?
7. This chapter emphasizes aiming for a win–win approach to conflict in personal relationships. Do you believe that in most cases both people can benefit (or win) if each is committed to honouring one's self and the other?
8. Have you been in relationships in which you felt there was grace? How was grace communicated? What was the impact of grace? Have you extended grace to others? Use your InfoTrac® College Edition to review recent issues of *Religious Studies*. Do authors address issues such as grace, forgiveness, and kindness toward others? How do their views correspond with those in this chapter?
9. To learn about common conflicts in families and ways people deal with them, go to www.suite101.com/welcome.cfm/conflict_resolution. The site provides articles, discussions, and links to other websites.

Chapter 11

Friendships and Romantic Relationships

The most holy bond of society is friendship.

—Mary Wollstonecraft (1792)

A loving person lives in a loving world.

A hostile person lives in a hostile world.

Everyone you meet is your mirror.

—Ken Keys (1984)

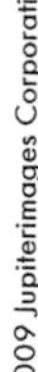

For most of us, friends and lovers are important. Friends help us pass time, grow personally, celebrate moments of joy, and get through the trials and tribulations of everyday life. Romantic partnerships involve romantic and sexual feelings in addition to the sort of love we feel for our friends and family. The intricate design of our lives is made richer by the friendships and intimacies that thread through them.

Across differences in race, gender, class, and sexual preference, most of us expect friends and lovers to invest in us, to provide intimacy, acceptance, trust, practical assistance, and support, and in romantic relationships, passion and commitment. These are common threads in diverse close relationships. However, people differ in how they express these elements.

In this chapter, we explore what friendships are, how they work, and how they differ among people. To launch our discussion, we identify common features of friendship and committed romantic relationships and then point out variations across social communities. We then consider pressures on friendship and how we can deal with them. We will then explore communication and the different styles of loving that people bring to romance. Next, we discuss the developmental pattern that many romantic relationships follow as they grow, stabilize, and sometimes dissolve. Guidelines for effective communication between friends and for communicating effectively to meet challenges that often arise in romantic relationships conclude the chapter.

Student Voices

Will:

It's funny. Kids have ways to symbolize friendship, but adults don't. I remember when Jimmy down the block and I became blood brothers. It was a big, big deal for me at eight. And my sister and her best friend bought matching friendship rings and wore them until their fingers turned green. But what do we have to symbolize friendships when we grow up?

THE NATURE OF FRIENDSHIP

Friendship is a unique relationship. Unlike most relationships, friendship is voluntary. Biology or legal procedures establish relationships between family members, and proximity defines neighbours and co-workers. However, friends come together voluntarily. Unlike marital and family relationships, friendships lack institutionalized structure or guidelines. There are legal and religious ceremonies for marriage and social and legal rules that govern family relationships. We have no parallel ceremonies to recognize friendships and no formal standards to guide interaction between friends.

THE NATURE OF COMMITTED ROMANTIC RELATIONSHIPS

Committed romantic relationships, in Western culture at least, are also voluntary relationships that exist between unique individuals—ones who cannot be replaced. We assume most often that the relationships will be primary and continuing parts of our lives. We invest heavily of ourselves and come to know the other as a completely distinct individual.

Committed romantic relationships are distinct from other close relationships in two ways. First, they involve romantic and sexual feelings in addition to the sort of love we feel for friends and family. Another distinctive quality of romantic relationships is that they are considered primary and permanent in our society. We expect to move away from friends and family, but we assume we'll be

CONCEPTS AT A GLANCE

The Seven Dimensions of Close Relationships

1. Willingness to invest
2. Emotional closeness
   - Closeness through dialogue
   - Closeness through doing
3. Acceptance
4. Trust
5. Support
6. Passion
7. Commitment

permanently connected to a romantic partner. Current divorce rates in Canada, according to the 1998 census, indicate that roughly a third of those who marry will separate, with an even higher rate for those who marry more than once. Even so, we think of romantic commitment (although not every romantic relationship) as permanent, and this makes romantic commitments unique.

DIMENSIONS OF CLOSE RELATIONSHIPS

Seven dimensions of close relationships bear examination, as shown in the Concepts at a Glance feature in the margin. Even though there are no formal standards for friendship, people within a culture hold some fairly consistent ideas about what a friend is and what happens between partners. Regardless of race, sexual orientation, gender, age, and class, Westerners share basic expectations of close relationships.

Student Voices

Lakisha:

I don't know what I'd do without my friends. More than once they've held me together when I had a fight with my Mom or broke up with a guy. When something good happens, it's not quite real until I share it with my friends. I don't think I could be happy without friends.

Willingness to Invest

Most people assume friendships and romantic relationships require personal investments (Duck & Wright, 1993; Monsour, 1992). We expect to invest time, effort, energy, thought, and feeling into our relationships. Women and men of both homosexual and heterosexual orientations report that having friends is important for a fulfilling life (Mazur, 1989; Nardi & Sherrod, 1994; Sherrod, 1989). Although people differ in how they build and experience close relationships, most of us agree they are important.

Emotional Closeness

With friends, we want to feel emotionally close. Emotional **intimacy** grows out of investments, such as time, talk, and shared experiences, and out of becoming familiar and comfortable being together. Although most people agree that closeness is central to close friendships, we have different ideas about what intimacy is. Research on friendship suggests that the biological designation of sex and sociological construct of gender influence how we experience and express intimacy with friends.

Intimacy includes feelings of closeness, connection, and tenderness. Unlike passion and commitment, which are distinct dimensions of romance, intimacy seems to underlie both passion and commitment (Acker & Davis, 1992). Intimacy is related to passion because both dimensions involve feelings. The link between intimacy and commitment is connectedness, which joins partners in romantic relationships not only in the present but also through the past and into the future.

Student Voices

Dennis:

I really count on my buddies to be there for me. Sometimes we talk or do stuff, but a lot of times we just hang out together. That might not sound important, but it is. Hanging out with friends is a big part of my life.

Intimacy is abiding affection and warm feelings for another person. It is why romantic partners are comfortable with each other and enjoy being together even when fireworks aren't exploding. When asked to evaluate various features of love, people consistently rate companionate features such as getting along and friendship as most important. Although passionate feelings also matter, they are

Apply the Idea

YOUR STYLE OF FRIENDSHIP

Before reading further, answer the following questions about how you experience and express closeness with friends. With your closest or best friends, how often do you do the following things?

1. Talk about family problems
2. Exchange favours (provide transportation, lend money)
3. Engage in sports (shoot hoops, play tennis, and so forth)
4. Try to take their minds off problems with diversions
5. Disclose your personal anxieties and fears
6. Talk about your romantic relationships and family relationships
7. Do things together (camp, go to a game, shop)
8. Confide secrets you wouldn't want others to know
9. Just hang out without a lot of conversation
10. Talk about small events in your day-to-day life
11. Provide practical assistance to help friends
12. Talk explicitly about your feelings for each other
13. Discuss and work through tensions in your friendship
14. Physically embrace or touch to show affection
15. Ignore or work around problems in the friendship

Items 1, 5, 6, 8, 10, 12, 13, and 14 have been found to be more prominent in women's friendships. Items 2, 3, 4, 7, 9, 11, and 15 tend to be more pronounced in men's friendships.

less central to perceptions of love than caring, honesty, respect, friendship, and trust (Fehr, 1993; Luby & Aron, 1990).

Closeness through Dialogue

If you found items 1, 5, 6, 8, 10, 12, 13, and 14 in the Apply the Idea exercise above more true of your friendships, then you regard communication as the centrepiece of friendship. This is especially true for people socialized in feminine speech communities, which emphasize talk as a primary path to intimacy. In general, women see talking and listening as the main activities that create and sustain closeness (Aries, 1987; Becker, 1987; Rubin, 1985). Talk between women friends tends to be disclosive and emotionally expressive (Maccoby, 1998). Women discuss not only major issues but also day-to-day activities. This small talk isn't really small at all, because it allows friends to understand the rhythms of each other's lives (Braithwaite & Kellas, 2006; Metts, 2006). Out of intimate conversation, friends build a deep sense of connection.

Margot Petrowski/Shutterstock

A majority of women expect to know and be known intimately by close friends (Johnson, 1996). This is also true of androgynous men, who incorporate both feminine and masculine values into their identities (Jones & Dembo, 1989; Williams, 1985). They want friends to know and understand their inner selves, and they want to know their friends in the same emotional depth.

Student Voices

Lorianne:

My girlfriends and I know everything about each other. We tell all our feelings and don't hold anything back. I mean, it's total knowledge. We give updates on each new episode in our relationships, and we talk about what it means. There's just nothing I wouldn't tell my friends.

Reflecting feminine socialization, communication between women friends typically is responsive and supportive (Chatham-Carpenter & DeFrancisco, 1998; Wright & Scanlon, 1991). Animated facial expressions and head movements convey involvement and emotional response. In addition, women friends ask questions and give feedback to signal that they are following and want to know more. Women friends also tend to give emotional support to one another. They do this by accepting one another's feelings and staying involved in the other's dreams, problems, and lives.

Closeness through Doing

A second way to create and express closeness is by sharing activities. Friends enjoy doing things together and doing things for one another. Items 2, 3, 4, 7, 9, 11, and 15 in the Apply the Ideas exercise on page 311 reflect this approach to intimacy. Closeness through doing often is the primary, but not the only, emphasis in men's friendships (Harris, 1998; Inman, 1996; Metts, 2006; Monsour, in press; Swain, 1989; Wood & Inman, 1993). Given the focus on doing things together, it's not surprising that male friends are more likely to negotiate activities ("Are we going to play racquetball or go skating?") than female friends or male and female friends (Samter & Cupach, 1998). Sharing activities and working toward common goals (winning the game, getting the contract) build a sense of camaraderie (Inman, 1996; Sherrod, 1989).

Student Voices

Josh:

The thing I like about my buddies is that we can just do stuff together without a lot of talk. Our wives expect us to talk about every feeling we have, as if that's required to be real. I'm tight with my buddies, but we don't have to talk about feelings all the time. You learn a lot about someone when you play on a team together or coach Little League.

Josh has a good insight. We reveal ourselves and learn about others by doing things together. In the course of playing football or soccer, teammates learn a lot about one another's courage, reliability, willingness to take risks, and security. Soldiers who fight together also discover one another's strengths and weaknesses. Strong emotional bonds and personal knowledge can develop without verbal interaction (Rubin, 1985). Intimacy through doing also involves expressing care by doing things for friends. Scott Swain (1989) says men's friendships typically involve a give-and-take of favours. Jake helps Matt move into his new apartment, and Matt later helps Jake install a new program on his computer. Perhaps because masculine socialization emphasizes instrumental activities, men are more likely than women to see doing things for others as a primary way to say they care.

Sometimes, different emphases on instrumental and expressive behaviours lead to misunderstandings. If Myra sees intimate talk as the crux of closeness, she may not interpret Ed's practical help in fixing her computer as indicating that he cares about her.

It would be a mistake to conclude that women and men are radically different in how they create intimacy. They are actually more alike than we often think (Canary & Dindia, 1998; Parks & Floyd, 1996b). Although women generally place a special priority on communication, men obviously talk with their friends. Like women, men disclose personal feelings and vulnerabilities. They simply do it less, as a rule, than women. Similarly, although men's friendships may be more instrumental, women friends also do things with and for one another and count these as important in friendship (Duck & Wright, 1993).

To learn more about similarities and differences between women's and men's friendships, use your InfoTrac® College Edition. Into the EasyTrac subject search, type the word *friendship*. Scroll down until you find the article by Roseanne Roy, Joyce Benenson, and Fray Lilly that appeared in 2000 in the *Journal of Psychology*, Volume 134.

Student Voices

Kaya:

My husband's life centres on doing things for me and our kids. He looks for things to do for us. Like when our son came home over break, he tuned up his car and replaced a tire. I hadn't even noticed the tire was bad. When I wanted to return to school, he took a second job to make more money. One day he came home with a microwave to make cooking easier for me. All the things he does for us are his way of expressing love.

Apply the Idea

APPRECIATING TALKING AND DOING IN FRIENDSHIPS

For each of the following scenarios, write out one thing you might say and one thing you might do to show you care about the person described.

1. *Your best friend has just broken up with his/her long-term boyfriend/girlfriend. Your friend calls you and says, "I feel so lonely."*
   You say ____________________
   You do ____________________
2. *A good friend of yours tells you he/she has been cut from the team and won't get to play this year.*
   You say ____________________
   You do ____________________
3. *Your best friend from high school calls and says she/he thinks about you often even though the two of you no longer maintain much contact.*
   You say ____________________
   You do ____________________
4. *A close friend stops you on campus and excitedly says, "I just found out I've been accepted into the law school here. Can you believe it?"*
   You say ____________________
   You do ____________________

Acceptance

A third common expectation of friends and lovers is that they will accept us. Each of us has shortcomings and bad habits, but we count on our intimates and friends to accept us in spite of them. The essence of acceptance is feeling that we are okay as human beings. With people we don't know well, we often feel we need to put on our best face to impress them. With friends, however, we don't want to put up false fronts. If we feel low, we can act that way instead of faking cheerfulness. If we are upset, we don't have to hide it. We expect friends and partners to accept us as we are

Photodisc/Getty Images

Love and friendship

and as we change over time (Adams & Allan, 1999; Yager, 1999).

As we saw with Maslow's hierarchy of human needs in Chapter 1, being accepted by others is important to our sense of self-worth. Most of us are fortunate enough to gain acceptance from family and friends. However, this is not always true. Some parents of gays and lesbians, for example, refuse to validate their children's basic worth.

Because social and familial acceptance sometimes is lacking for them, gay men and lesbians may count on friends for acceptance even more than heterosexuals do (Nardi & Sherrod, 1994; Roberts & Orbe, 1996). Friendships may have heightened importance because they often substitute for families, as reflected in the title of Kath Weston's 1991 book, *Families We Choose*. Although lesbians and gay men may depend more heavily than heterosexuals on friends for acceptance, research has not identified major differences in how their friendships operate. Like heterosexuals, gay men and lesbians value friendship and rely on both talking and doing as paths to intimacy.

Martin and Mattie feel their parents totalize them by focusing on a single aspect of their lives and ignoring everything else about them. They are still students, loving children, people who have dreams, ambitions, hopes, and fears. Yet, they feel that their parents see them only in terms of sexual orientation or interracial dating and disregard everything else about them.

Student Voices

Martin:

It isn't just the homosexual who is outed. Everyone in that person's life is affected when he comes out. My ex-wife was devastated when I told her I was gay. She felt it said something about her as a woman. My father and stepmother are homophobic. They are more fearful of how friends and family will judge them than they are concerned with my issues. My coming out was all about their embarrassment and fear.

Mattie:

I knew my parents wouldn't be pleased that I was seeing someone of another race, but I didn't think they'd go totally into orbit. When I finally got the nerve to tell them about Sheldon, they went nuts. You would have thought I had told them I'd grown a third leg or was hooked on drugs. They yelled at me that they hadn't raised me to "be like that." They threatened to disown me if I didn't stop seeing Sheldon. They said I was immoral and was bringing shame on my whole family. They never even asked what Sheldon is like or what he wants to do or anything about him.

Trust

A key component of close friendships is trust, which has two dimensions. First, trust involves confidence that others will be dependable. We count on them to do what they say and not to do what they promise they won't. Second, trust assumes emotional reliability, which is the belief that a friend cares about us and our welfare. When we feel both dimensions of trust, we feel safe sharing private information with friends, secure in the knowledge that they will not hurt us.

Like most qualities of friendship, trust develops gradually and in degrees. We learn to trust people over time as we interact with them and discover that they do what they say they will and that they don't betray us. As trust develops, friends increasingly reveal themselves to one another. When a high level of trust develops, friends feel less of the uncertainty and insecurity that are natural in early stages of relationships (Boon, 1994).

The level of trust that develops between friends depends on a number of factors. First, our individual histories influence our capacity to trust others. Recalling the discussion of attachment styles in Chapter 2, you'll remember that early interactions with caregivers shape our beliefs about others. For those of us who received consistently loving and nurturing care, trusting others is not especially difficult. On the other hand, some children do not receive that kind of care. If caring is absent or inconsistent, the capacity to trust others is jeopardized.

Family scripts also influence how much and how quickly we trust others. Did your parents have many friends? Did you see them enjoying being with their friends? Were their friends often in your home? How many friends your parents had and how much they seemed to value them may have taught you an early lesson about the importance of friendship in our lives. Basic scripts from families, although not irrevocable, often affect the ease and extent of our ability to trust and our interest in investing in friendships.

Willingness to take risks also influences trust in relationships. In this sense, trust is a leap into the unknown. To emphasize the risk in trusting, it has been said that "trust begins where knowledge ends" (Lewis & Weigert, 1985, p. 462). The risk involved may explain why we trust only selected people.

Student Voices

Sarni:

Trust is the bottom line for friends. It's the single most important thing. It takes me a long time to really trust someone, but when I do, it's complete. I was so hurt when a friend told another person something I told her in confidence. We still get together, but the trust is gone. I don't tell her private things, so there's no depth.

James:

It's tough for me to really trust anybody, even my closest friends or my girlfriend. It's not that they aren't trustworthy. The problem's in me. I just have trouble putting full faith in anyone. When my parents had me, Dad was drinking, and Mom was thinking about divorce. He got into Alcoholics Anonymous and they stayed together, but I wonder if what was happening between them meant they weren't there for me. Maybe I learned from the start that I couldn't count on others.

Support

Communication scholars Brant Burleson and Wendy Samter (1994) report that support is a basic expectation of close relationships. We expect friends to support us in times of personal stress. Once people leave home for college, friends often become the primary people to whom they turn for help and comfort (Adelman, Parks, & Albrecht, 1987).

There are many ways to show support. Common to the various types of support is the relationship message "I care about you." Often, we support friends by listening to their problems. The more mindfully we listen, the more support we provide. How we respond also shows support. For example, it's supportive to offer to help a friend with a problem or to talk through options. Another way we support friends is by letting them know they're not alone. When we say, "I've felt that way too" or "I've had the same problem," we signal that we understand their feelings. Having the grace to accept friends when they err or hurt us is also a way to show support and validate their worth (Burleson, 1984).

Another important form of support is availability. Sometimes we can't do or say much to ease a friend's unhappiness. However, we can be with friends so that at least they have company in their sadness. In one study, young adults said the essence of real friendship was "being there for each other" (Secklin, 1991). Increasingly, when friends can't be there physically, people rely on them for online support (Baym, 2002; Carl, 2006).

Women and men tend to differ somewhat in how they support friends. Because feminine socialization emphasizes personal communication, women generally provide more verbal emotional support than men do (Aries, 1987; Becker, 1987; Duck & Wright,

Student Voices

José:

Last year, my father died, back in Mexico, and I wasn't with him when he died. I felt terrible. My friend Alex spent a lot of time with me after my father died. Alex didn't do anything special, and we didn't even really talk much about my father or how I felt. But he was there for me, and that meant everything. I knew he cared even though he never said that.

Bellino:

A year ago, a friend of mine from back home called me up to ask for a loan. I said, "Sure," and asked what was up. He told me his hours had been cut back and he couldn't buy groceries for his family. I knew the problem was more than paying for groceries. I figured he also couldn't pay for lights and rent and everything else. So I talked with several of his friends in our church, and we took up a collection to help him. Then, I took it over and left it at his house without any note and without saying anything. He didn't have to ask for help, and I didn't have to say anything. What I and the others in our congregation did was to do what was needed to help him.

Student Voices

Rich:

If I don't want to think about some problem, I want to be with a guy friend. He'll take my mind off the hassle. If I'm with a girl, she'll want to talk about the problem and wallow in it, and that just makes it worse sometimes. But when I really need to talk or get something off my chest, I need a girl friend. Guys don't talk about personal stuff.

1993; Johnson, 2000). They are likely to talk in detail about feelings, dimensions of emotional issues, and fears that accompany distress. By talking in depth about emotional troubles, women help one another identify and vent feelings and work out problems.

Men often provide support to friends through "covert intimacy," a term Swain (1989) coined to describe the indirect ways men support one another. Instead of an intimate hug, men are more likely to clasp a shoulder or playfully punch an arm. Instead of engaging in direct and sustained emotional talk, men tend to communicate support more instrumentally. This could mean giving advice on how to solve a problem or offering assistance, such as a loan or transportation. Finally, men are more likely than women to support friends by coming up with diversions (Cancian, 1987; Tavris, 1992). If you can't make a problem any better, at least you can take a friend's mind off it. "Let's go throw some darts" provides a diversion.

Ethnicity also influences orientations toward friendship. In a study of Japanese and Western friendships, Dean Barnlund (1989) found both similarities and differences. Both ethnic groups preferred friends who were similar to them in age and ethnic heritage, and both groups agreed on many of the qualities that describe friends. Commonly valued qualities in friends included understanding, respect, trust, and sincerity. Yet Japanese and Western friends differed in the priority they assigned the qualities. Japanese respondents said togetherness, trust, and warmth were the most important qualities in friendship, whereas Westerners listed understanding, respect, and sincerity as the top qualities. The differences in rankings reflect distinctions between Japanese and Western culture. Interpersonal harmony and collective orientation are central values in Japan, and these are reflected in the qualities Japanese consider most important in friends. Western culture emphasizes individuality, candour, and respect—the very qualities Canadians most prize in friends.

In sum, friendship grows out of investments, intimacy, acceptance, trust, and support. Our membership in different cultures and social communities may lead to variations in how we experience and express these aspects of friendship. However, it seems that these five common expectations (willingness to invest, emotional closeness, acceptance, trust, and support) transcend differences between us.

The last two dimensions of close relationships are found predominantly in committed romantic relationships. Passion and commitment combined with intimacy form a triangle that represents the different facets of what researchers define as love (Acker & Davis, 1992; Hendrick & Hendrick, 1989; Sternberg, 1986). See Figure 11.1.

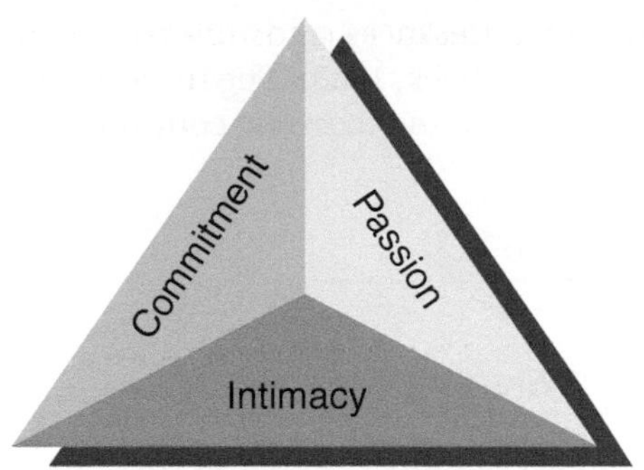

FIGURE 11.1

The Triangle of Love

Passion

For most of us, **passion** is what first springs to mind when we think about romance. Passion is having intensely positive feelings and desires for another person. Passion is not equivalent to sexual or sensual emotions, although these are types of passion. In addition to erotic feelings, passion may involve intense emotional, spiritual, and intellectual attraction. The sparks and emotional high of being in love stem from passion. It's why we feel butterflies in the stomach and fall head over heels.

As much fun as passion is, it isn't the primary foundation for enduring romance. In fact, research consistently shows that passion is less central to how we think about love than are intimacy and commitment. This makes sense when we realize that passion can seldom be sustained for a lifetime. Like other intense feelings, it ebbs and flows. Because passion comes and goes and is largely beyond our will, it isn't a strong basis for long-term relationships. In other words, passion may set romance apart from other relationships, but it isn't what holds romance together. To build a lasting relationship, we need something more durable.

Commitment

The something else needed is **commitment,** the second dimension of romantic relationships. Commitment is an intention to remain with a relationship. As we noted earlier, commitment is not the same thing as love. Love is a feeling based on rewards we get from being involved with a person. Commitment, in contrast, is a decision based on investments we put into a relationship (Lund, 1985). We choose to entwine our life and future with another person's.

In an important study of Western values, Robert Bellah and his colleagues (1985) found that most Westerners want both passion and commitment in long-term romantic relationships. We desire the euphoria of passion, but we know that it won't weather rough times or ensure compatibility and comfort on a day-in, day-out basis. We also want commitment as a stable foundation for a life together. Commitment is a determination to stay together in spite of trouble,

Student Voices

Wade:

I've been married for 15 years, and we would have split a dozen times if love was all that held us together. A marriage simply can't survive on love alone. You can't count on feeling in love or passionate all the time. Lucy and I have gone through spells where we were bored with each other or where we wanted to walk away from our problems. We didn't because we made a promise to stay together "for better or for worse." Believe me, a marriage has both.

REVIEW

Passion is a feeling. Commitment is a choice. Passion may fade, commitment remains steadfast.

disappointments, sporadic restlessness, and lulls in passion. Commitment involves responsibility, not just feeling (Beck, 1988). The responsibilities of commitment are to make a relationship a priority and to invest continuously in it.

Apply the Idea

MEASURING LOVE AND COMMITMENT

Think of a current or past romance to answer these questions (Lund, 1985).

1. *Do you think your relationship will be permanent?*
2. *Do you feel you can confide in your partner about virtually anything?*
3. *Are you attracted to other potential partners or to a single lifestyle?*
4. *Would you be miserable if you couldn't be with your partner?*
5. *Would you find it personally difficult to end your relationship?*
6. *If you felt lonely, would your first thought be to seek your partner?*
7. *Do you feel obligated to continue this relationship?*
8. *Would you forgive your partner for virtually anything?*
9. *In your opinion, do you think your partner intends to continue this relationship?*
10. *Is one of your primary concerns your partner's welfare?*

Commitment is measured by odd-numbered items; love is measured by even-numbered items.

Communication Notes

THE PROTOTYPE OF LOVE

Westerners appear to have a fairly specific prototype of what love is. Research repeatedly reveals that we regard feeling valued by and comfortable with another as more important than passion. Love is typified by feelings such as closeness, caring, and friendship, and by commitment as defined by features such as trust and respect. Intimacy and commitment eclipse passion in importance. Even when people are asked what's most important for "being in love," companionate features have priority.

Do women and men differ in how important they consider the dimensions of love? Although women and men don't differ significantly in what they consider typical of love in general, they do diverge in their personal ideals for love. For both sexes, passion is less salient than companionate features. However, features linked to intimacy and commitment are even more prominent in women's personal ideals of love than in men's. The only feature that men rate higher than women is fantasy. No differences have been found among heterosexuals, gays, and lesbians.

Sources: Button, C. M., & Collier, D. R. (1991, June). *A comparison of people's concepts of love and romantic love.* Paper presented at the Canadian Psychological Association Conference, Calgary, Alberta; Fehr, B. (1993). How do I love thee? Let me consult my prototype. In S. W. Duck (Ed.), *Understanding relationship processes,* 1: Individuals in relationships (pp. 87–122). Newbury Park, CA: Sage; Luby, V., & Aron, A. (1990, July). *A prototype structuring of love, like, and being in love.* Paper presented at the Fifth International Conference on Personal Relationships, Oxford, England; Rousar, E. E., III, & Aron, A. (1990, July). *Valuing, altruism, and the concept of love.* Paper presented at the Fifth International Conference on Personal Relationships, Oxford, England.

Although close relationships reflect the influence of personal experience, gender, and ethnic heritage, there is also much common ground in what people expect and value in these relationships. We expect friends and romantic partners to invest in our relationship and to provide intimacy, acceptance, trust, and support, and in romantic relationships, passion and commitment.

As a result of gender, race, ethnicity, economic class, age, and sexual orientation, we may differ in how we experience and express deep feelings. However, it seems that these seven common expectations transcend differences among us. Yet, it's not enough for us to have these feelings; we must also communicate them. Skills in verbal and nonverbal communication, listening, building climate, and managing conflict contribute to effective expression of friendship and love.

THE DEVELOPMENTAL COURSE OF FRIENDSHIP AND ROMANTIC RELATIONSHIPS

Most friendships develop over time in fairly patterned ways. Although intense bonds are sometimes formed quickly in unusual circumstances such as crises, the majority of friends work out their relationship in a series of stages. Bill Rawlins (1981), an interpersonal communication researcher who focuses on communication between friends, developed a six-stage model of how friendships develop (Table 11.1).

Guidelines for effective communication that we've discussed in other chapters help us deal with tensions in our friendships. For example, it's important to be clear and to rely on *I* language so that you communicate what you feel and want without deflecting responsibility. Sensitive listening and supportive communication are also helpful in keeping a friendship intact while partners address tensions.

TABLE 11.1

THE DEVELOPMENTAL COURSE OF CLOSE RELATIONSHIPS

Phase	Friendships	Romantic Relationships
Growth	Role-limited interaction Friendly relations Moving toward friendship Blossoming friendship	Attraction without interaction Invitational communication Explorational communication Intensifying communication Revising communication Commitment
Navigation	Stabilizing	Managing relational dialectics Rules and rituals Placemaking Everyday interactions
Deterioration	Waning	Dyadic breakdown Intrapsychic phase Dyadic phase Social phase Social support Grave dressing

Communication Notes

FRIENDSHIPS ACROSS THE LIFE SPAN

Friendships vary during the course of life (Blieszner & Adams, 1992; Monsour, 1997; Yager, 1999). Most children begin forming friendships around age two, when they start learning how to communicate with others. Toddlers play primarily side by side, and each is focused more on the activity than on the other person. At the same time, toddlers work to sustain friendships that matter to them, and they sometimes grieve when a friend moves away (Whaley & Rubenstein, 1994).

Children under age six tend to think of friendships primarily in terms of their own needs. As children mature, they develop awareness of norms of friendship, including reciprocity. First-grade friends are less likely to share equally. By the time friends are in third grade, however, they tend to rely on communal norms that lead them to strive for equity with friends (Pataki, Shapiro, & Clark, 1994).

During adolescence, friendship assumes great importance for most people. Having friends is very important, and belonging to friendship cliques is a measure of self-worth. Adolescent boys tend to define their friends as groups of people, usually other boys. Girls, on the other hand, tend to name only one or two peers as close friends.

Sharing personal information and activities are primary criteria for friendships among young adults, who are the group most likely to form and maintain friendships with people of the other sex (Werking, 1997). In adulthood, friendships are more difficult to sustain. People marry, have children, move, and focus on careers. Despite these complications, most adults consider friendships important in their lives.

Later in life, people tend to value long-time friends with whom they can relive events that are part of their shared lives and the era in which they have lived (McKay, 2000). Many friendships between older people were formed between couples or between whole families when each family had young children. Because many older adults are retired and no longer have children at home, friends become an increasingly important source of emotional and instrumental support.

Like friendships, romantic relationships tend to follow a developmental course. Initially, scholars thought relationships move through stages as a result of objective activities such as self-disclosing. More recently, however, we have realized that romance progresses based on how we perceive interaction, not on interaction itself (Honeycutt, 1993). For example, if Terry discloses personal information to Jacquie, then the relationship will escalate if Jacquie and Terry interpret self-disclosure as a move toward greater intimacy. If Jacquie doesn't perceive Terry's disclosure as personal, she's unlikely to feel he has made a move toward greater closeness. It is the meaning they assign to self-disclosing, not the actual act of self-disclosing, that determines how they perceive their level of intimacy.

As we learned in Chapter 3, perceiving is an active process in which we notice, organize, and interpret what goes on around us. We use cognitive schematas and information from past experiences to decide what things mean. The meanings we assign to romance, however, are not entirely individualistic. They also reflect broad cultural beliefs that we internalize as we are socialized. Because members of a society share many views, there are strong consistencies in how we perceive what happens in romantic relationships. Research shows that Western university and college students agree on the script for first dates (Pryor & Merluzzi, 1985).

They also share ideas about how men and women should act. The majority of postsecondary students think men should initiate and plan dates and make decisions about most activities, but women control sexual activity (Rose & Frieze, 1989). In other cultures, different rules prevail. For example, in India, marriages are often arranged by parents; love is understood to be something couples develop after they wed. In Nepal, ritualistic dancing and celebrations are an important part of courtship. Although views of romantic relationships vary among cultures, every culture has shared understandings of what love is and how love develops.

Research on the evolution of romantic relationships has focused on Western society, so we know little about the developmental course of romance in other cultures. Let's now examine the phases of growth, navigation, and deterioration as they relate to romantic relationships. Within these three broad categories, we distinguish a number of more specific stages (see Figure 11.2).

Growth Stages

In moving toward romantic commitment, researchers have identified six stages of interaction that mark progressive intimacy within the three phases. Usually, although not always, these stages occur in sequence.

The first stage is **individuality** in which individuals aren't interacting. We are aware of ourselves as individuals with particular needs, goals, love styles, and qualities that affect what we look for in relationships. Our choices of people with whom to start romance may also be influenced by aspects of ourselves of which we are unaware—for example, attachment styles and the hidden area of the Johari Window. We can call this stage *attraction without interaction*.

The second growth stage is **invitational communication** in which individuals signal they are interested in interacting and respond to invitations from others. "Want to dance?" "Where are you from?" "I love this kind of music," "Hi, my name's Shelby" are examples of bids for interaction. Invitational communication usually follows a conventional script for initial interaction. The meaning of invitational communication is found on the relationship level, not the content level. "I love this kind of music" literally means a person likes the music. On the relationship level of meaning, however, the message is "I'm available and interested. Are you?"

Of all the people we meet, we are attracted to only a few. The three greatest influences on initial attraction are self-concept, proximity, and similarity.

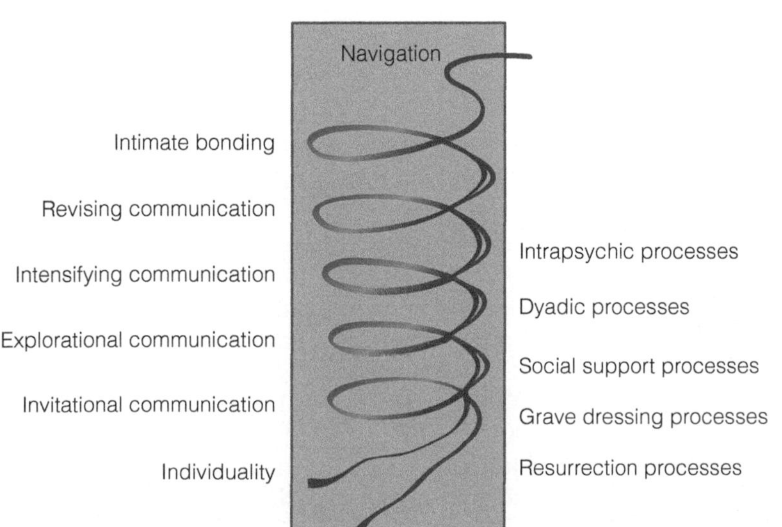

FIGURE 11.2

Developmental Stages in Romantic Relationships

How we see ourselves affects the people we consider candidates for romance. Heterosexuals, lesbians, bisexuals, and gays seek romance with others who share their sexual orientation. The Communication Notes feature "Bases of Romantic Attraction" summarizes research on heterosexual, gay, and lesbian attraction. Social class also influences whom we notice and consider appropriate for us. Most people pair with others of their race and social class. Even with all of the attention to diversity in our era, research indicates that people still seek others who are similar to them. In fact, social prestige influences dating patterns now more than in the 1950s (Whitbeck & Hoyt, 1994). Most college and university students seek to date people who share their social and class backgrounds.

Communication Notes

BASES OF ROMANTIC ATTRACTION

Gay men tend to desire very specific physical characteristics, including an extremely attractive face, a slim and well-conditioned body, and good grooming. In addition, they want partners who are self-sufficient and have prestigious careers that yield good incomes.

Straight men also state that physical attractiveness is very important to them in romantic partners. They report looking for women who are slim and beautiful. Intelligence, status, and personality matter less than physical beauty.

Lesbians generally stress emotional and personal qualities in partners and care little about physical appearance or dress. Although some lesbians admire a "butch" look, others prefer traditional feminine beauty. Lesbians value economic independence in partners, though less so than gays.

Straight women emphasize personal qualities in romantic partners. Warmth, honesty, kindness, and personal integrity are among the qualities straight women consider important. They also value ambition and status in partners.

Sources: Based on Huston, M., & Schwartz, P. (1995). Relationships of lesbians and gay men. In J. T. Wood & S. W. Duck (Eds.), *Understanding relationship processes, 6; Off the beaten track: Understudied relationships*, 89–121. Thousand Oaks, CA: Sage; Sprecher, S. (1989). The importance to males and females of physical attractiveness, earning potential, and expressiveness in initial attraction. *Sex Roles*, 21, 591–607.

In addition to personal identity, proximity and similarity influence initial attraction. We can interact only with people we meet, so where we live, work, and socialize affects the possibilities for relationships. Nearness to others, however, doesn't necessarily increase liking.

Environmental spoiling describes situations in which proximity breeds ill will. This happens when we're forced to be around others whose values, lifestyles, or behaviours conflict with our own. For the most part, we seek romantic partners who are like us. "Birds of a feather" seems to be more true than "Opposites attract." In general, we are attracted to people whose values, attitudes, and lifestyles are similar to ours. Similarity of personality is also linked to long-term marital happiness (Caspi & Harbener, 1990).

Explorational communication is the third stage in the escalation of romance, and it involves exchanging information to explore the possibilities for a relationship. We use communication to announce our identities and to learn about others. In this stage, individuals fish for common interests and grounds for interaction: Are you from the Territories? Do you like blues? What kind of family did you come from? Have you been following the political debates? As we continue to interact with others, both breadth and depth of information increase. Because we perceive self-disclosure as a sign of trust, it tends to escalate intimacy (Berger & Bell, 1988). At this early stage of interaction, reciprocity of disclosure is expected so that one person isn't more vulnerable than the other (Duck, 1992; Miell & Duck, 1986).

If early interaction increases attraction, then individuals may dramatically escalate the relationship. During the fourth growth stage, **intensifying communication,** the partners increase the depth of their relationship by increasing personal knowledge; this allows the couple to begin creating a private culture. During this stage, partners spend more and more time together, and they rely less on external structures such as movies or parties. Instead, they immerse themselves in the budding relationship and may feel they can't be together enough. Further disclosures are exchanged, personal biographies are filled in, and partners increasingly learn how each other feels and thinks. As personal knowledge expands, dual perspective is possible. The Communication Notes feature "The Chemistry of Love" explores the biological basis of attraction between people.

Communication Notes

THE CHEMISTRY OF LOVE

People often talk about the chemistry they have with certain others. Recent research suggests there may be a factual, biological basis to the idea that there is chemistry between people (Ackerman, 1994). Consider:

The cuddle chemical is oxytocin, which is stimulated by either physical or emotional cues. Oxytocin is released when babies nurse, making mothers nuzzle and cuddle them. Oxytocin also pours out during sexual arousal and lovemaking, making lovers want to caress and cuddle one another.

The infatuation chemical is phenylethylamine (PEA). Like amphetamines, PEA makes our bodies tremble when we're attracted to someone and makes us feel euphoric, happy, and energetic when we're in love.

The attachment chemical is really a group of morphine-like opiates that calm us and create feelings of relaxed comfort. This allows couples to form more peaceful, steady relationships than speed-like PEA does. Opiates of the mind promote abiding commitment.

Also characteristic of the intensifying stage are idealizing and personalized communication. Idealizing involves seeing a relationship and a partner as more wonderful, exciting, and perfect than he or she really is (Hendrick & Hendrick, 1988). During euphoria, partners often exaggerate each other's virtues, downplay or fail to perceive vices, and overlook problems in the relationship. It is also during euphoria that partners begin to develop relationship vocabularies made up of nicknames and private codes. Most relationship vocabularies include terms that symbolize important experiences partners have shared. Relationship vocabularies both reflect and fuel intimacy.

Apply the Idea

INTIMATE TALK

Do you and your partner have a private language in your relationship?

- *Do you have special nicknames for each other that others don't have and use?*
- *Do you have special words that you made up to describe experiences, activities, and feelings?*
- *Do you have codes that allow you and your partner to send messages in public that other people don't understand?*
- *How does your special relationship language reflect your relationship? How does it affect the bond?*

Revising communication, although not part of escalation in all romantic relationships, is important. During this fifth stage of romantic relationship growth, partners come down out of the clouds to look at their relationship more realistically. Problems and dissatisfactions are recognized as partners evaluate the relationship's potential to survive. With the rush of euphoria over, partners consider whether this relationship is one they want for the long run. If it is, they work through obstacles to long-term viability. Many couples that fall in love and move through the intensifying stage choose not to stay together. It is entirely possible to love a person with whom we don't want to share our life or to decide that it's better to stay together without formalizing the relationship. Some older couples make this choice, because marrying can decrease their government pension benefits.

The final growth stage is **commitment**, which is a decision to stay with a relationship permanently. This decision transforms a romantic relationship from one based on past and present experiences and feelings into one with a future. Prior to making a commitment, partners don't view the relationship as continuing forever. With commitment, the relationship becomes a given, around which they arrange other aspects of their lives.

Navigating

Navigating is a long-term process. Ideally, a relationship stabilizes in navigating once a commitment has been made. Navigating is the ongoing process of staying committed and living a life together, despite ups and downs and pleasant and unpleasant surprises. Although we hope to stabilize in navigating, the stage itself is full of movement. Couples continuously adjust, work through new problems, revisit old ones, and accommodate to changes in their individual and relational lives. During navigation, partners also continuously experience tension from relational dialectics, which are never resolved once and for all. As partners respond to dialectical tensions, they revise and refine the nature of the relationship itself.

In relationships that do endure, ongoing navigation helps partners avoid dangerous shoals

Student Voices

Esther:

Breaking up with Ted was the hardest thing I ever did. I really loved him, and he loved me, but I just couldn't see myself living with a Christian. My whole heritage is Jewish—it's who I am. I celebrate Hanukkah, not Christmas. Seder, Passover, and Yom Kippur are very important to me. Those aren't part of Ted's heritage, and he wouldn't convert. I loved him, but we couldn't have made a life together.

and keep their intimacy on a good course. To use an automotive analogy, navigating involves both preventive maintenance and periodic repairs (Canary & Stafford, 1994). The goals of navigating are to keep intimacy satisfying and healthy and to remedy any serious problems that arise. To understand the navigating stage, we'll discuss how relational culture is created by managing relational dialectics, rules and rituals, placemaking, and everyday interaction.

The nucleus of intimacy is **relational culture,** which is a private world of rules, understandings, meanings, and patterns of acting and interpreting that partners create for their relationship (Wood, 1982, 1995c). Relational culture includes managing **relational dialectics** which we explored in Chapter 9. Jan and Byron may negotiate a lot of autonomy and little togetherness, whereas Louise and Teresa emphasize connectedness and minimize autonomy. Bobby and Cassandra are very open and expressive, whereas Mike and Zelda preserve more individual privacy in their marriage.

Barbara Penoyar/Photodisc/Getty Images

There are not right and wrong ways to manage dialectics, because individuals and couples differ in what they need. What is most important is for couples to agree on how to deal with tensions between autonomy and connection, openness and privacy, and novelty and routine (Fitzpatrick & Best, 1979; Wood, 1995c).

Relational culture includes rules and **rituals** that partners work out. Couples develop constitutive rules, usually unspoken, about how to show anger, love, sexual interest, and so forth. They also develop routines for contact. Couples reserve weekends for staying in touch. Couples also develop rules for commemorating special times such as birthdays and holidays. Romantic couples develop rituals to structure interaction. Carol Bruess and Judy Pearson (1997) identified seven rituals that are common among married couples. The couples they studied established rules and rituals that partners develop and follow to provide a predictable rhythm for intimate interaction. See Figure 11.3.

Placemaking is the process of creating a personal environment that is comfortable and that reflects the values, experiences, and tastes of a couple (Werner et al., 1993). This can include souvenirs and symbols from travels together, photographs of family and friends, shared music, and mutual decorating decor.

Ryan McVay/Photodisc/Getty Images

Love comes in many forms.

Another important dimension of relational culture is **everyday interaction.** Partners weave the basic fabric of their relationship in day-to-day conversations that realize their togetherness. The Communication Notes feature "Absence Makes the Words Grow Fonder" explores the importance of everyday interaction for couples. Most conversations between intimates aren't dramatic or noteworthy; actually, the majority of interaction is fairly routine and mundane. Yet everyday talk is more important than major celebrations and big crises in creating and sustaining intimacy (Duck, 1994b; Spencer, 1994). Ordinary talk between partners nourishes their interpersonal climate by continuously recognizing and affirming each other.

FIGURE 11.3

The Seven Rituals of Couples

1. Couple time rituals (activities, togetherness, escapes)
2. Symbolic rituals (private codes, play, celebration)
3. Daily routines and tasks
4. Intimacy expressions
5. Communication rituals
6. Patterns, habits, and mannerisms
7. Spiritual rituals

Communication Notes

ABSENCE MAKES THE WORDS GROW FONDER

Couples who have long-distance or commuter relationships face many challenges. Yet what long-distance partners say is most difficult is the loss of daily routines and conversation about everyday matters (Gerstel & Gross, 1985). What they miss most is sharing trivial details of their lives and small talk.

Deterioration

Steve Duck (1998), a scholar of communication in personal relationships, proposed a six-phase model of relational decline. **Dyadic breakdown** is the first phase of relational decay, and it involves degeneration of established patterns, understandings, and routines that make up a relational culture. Partners may stop talking after dinner, no longer bother to call when they are running late, and in other ways neglect the little things that tie them together. As the fabric of intimacy weakens, dissatisfaction intensifies.

There are general gender differences in the causes of dyadic breakdown. For women, unhappiness with a relationship most often arises when communication declines in quality, quantity, or both. Men are more likely to be dissatisfied by specific behaviours. For instance, men report being dissatisfied when their partners don't greet them at the door and make special meals (Riessman, 1990). For many men, dissatisfaction also arises if they have domestic responsibilities that they feel aren't a man's job (Gottman & Carrère, 1994). Many women regard a relationship as breaking down if "We don't really communicate with each other anymore," whereas men tend to be dissatisfied if "We don't do fun things together anymore." Another gender difference is in who notices problems in a relationship. As a rule, women are more likely than men to perceive declines in intimacy. Because women are socialized to take care of relationships, they are more likely than men to notice tensions and early symptoms of problems (Cancian, 1989; Tavris, 1992).

The **intrapsychic phase** involves brooding about problems in the relationship and dissatisfactions with a partner (Duck, 1992). Women's brooding about languishing relationships tends to focus on perceived declines in closeness and intimate communication, whereas men's reflections more often centre on lapses in joint activities and acts of consideration between partners. It's easy for the intrapsychic phase to become a self-fulfilling prophecy: As gloomy thoughts snowball and awareness of positive features of the relationship ebb, partners may actually bring about the failure of their relationship. During the intrapsychic phase, partners may begin to think about alternatives to the relationship.

The **dyadic phase** is the third stage in relational decline, and it doesn't always occur (Duck, 1992). As we saw in Chapter 9, women are more likely to respond to conflict by initiating discussion of problems, and men often deny problems or exit rather than talk about them. Communication scholars report that many people avoid talking about problems, refuse to return calls from partners, and in other ways evade confronting difficulties (Baxter, 1984; Metts, Cupach, & Bejlovec, 1989). Although this is understandable because it is painful to talk about the decline of intimacy, avoiding problems does nothing to resolve them and may, in fact, make them worse. In formal relationships such as marriage, partners must negotiate matters such as division of property and child custody, but they may choose to talk through lawyers rather than directly to each other. What happens in the negotiation phase depends on how committed partners are, whether they perceive attractive alternatives to the relationship, and whether they have the communication skills to work through problems constructively.

If partners lack commitment or the communication skills needed to resuscitate intimacy, they enter the fourth stage, the **social phase** of disintegration, which involves figuring out how to tell outsiders they are parting. Either separately or in collaboration, partners decide how to explain their breakup to friends, children, in-laws, and social acquaintances. When partners don't cooperatively craft a joint explanation for breaking up, friends may take sides, gossip, and disparage one or the other partner as the "bad guy" (La Gaipa, 1982).

Social support is a fifth phase in which partners look to friends and family for support during the breakup. Others can provide support by being available and by listening mindfully. Partners may give self-serving accounts of the breakup in order to save face and secure sympathy and support from others. Thus, Alyssa may portray Janine as at fault and herself as the innocent party in a breakup. During this phase, partners often criticize their exes and expect friends to take their side (Duck, 1992). Although self-serving explanations of breakups are common, they aren't necessarily constructive. It's a good idea to monitor communication during this period so that we don't say things we'll later regret.

Grave dressing is the sixth and final phase in relational decline, and it involves burying the relationship and accepting its end. Like individuals, relationships deserve a proper burial (Duck, 1992). During grave dressing, we work to make sense of

Student Voices

Samantha:

I really hate it when couples in our social circle divorce. It never fails that we lose one of the two of them as a friend, because each of them wants us to take sides. They each blame the other and expect us to help them do that, and you can't do it for both spouses. One of them won't be a friend anymore.

the relationship—what it meant, why it failed, and how it affected us. Usually, individuals need to mourn intimacy that has died. Even if we initiate a breakup, we are sad about the failure to realize what seemed possible at one time. Grave dressing completes the process of relational dissolution by putting the relationship to rest so that partners can get on with their individual lives.

The stages we have discussed describe how most people perceive the course of romance. However, not all couples follow the standard pattern. Some partners skip one or more stages in the typical sequences of escalation or deterioration, and many of us cycle more than once through certain stages. For example, a couple might soar through euphoria, work out some tough issues in revising, and then go through euphoria a second time. It's also normal for long-term partners to depart navigation periodically to experience both euphoric seasons and intervals of dyadic breakdown. Further, because relationships are embedded in larger systems, it's likely that romantic intimacy follows different developmental paths in other cultures.

To add to our understanding of romance, let's now consider the different styles of loving that individuals exhibit.

STYLES OF LOVING

- Does real love grow out of long friendship?
- Should you love someone whose background is similar to yours?
- Would you rather suffer yourself than have someone you love suffer?
- Is love at first sight possible?
- Is the real fun of love getting someone to fall for you rather than becoming seriously involved?

If you were to survey everyone in your class, you'd discover different answers to the above questions. For every person who thinks love grows out of friendship, someone else believes love at first sight is possible. For each of us who considers love the most important focus of life, another person views love as a game.

Although we accept varied tastes in everything from clothes to lifestyle, we seem less open-minded about diversity in love. Whatever we have experienced as love is what we consider "real love." Anything else we discount as "just infatuation," "a sexual fling," or "being a doormat." Yet, it appears people differ significantly in how they love (Lee, 1973, 1988).

Just as there are three primary colours, there are three primary styles of loving. In addition, just as purple is created by blending the primary colours of blue and red, secondary love styles are made by blending primary ones. Secondary styles are as vibrant as primary ones, just as purple is as lovely as red or blue. Figure 11.4 illustrates the styles of love.

Student Voices

Rosa:

When I fall for someone, I fall all the way—like, I mean total and all that. I can't love halfway, and I can't go gradually, though my mother is always warning me to slow down. That's just not how I love. It's fast and furious for me.

Student Voices

Stephen:

Lisa and I have been together for 15 years now, and it's been easy and steady between us from the start. I don't remember even falling in love way back when. Maybe I never did fall in love with Lisa. I just gradually grew into loving her and feeling we belonged to each other.

Primary Styles of Love

The three primary styles of love are eros, storge, and ludus.

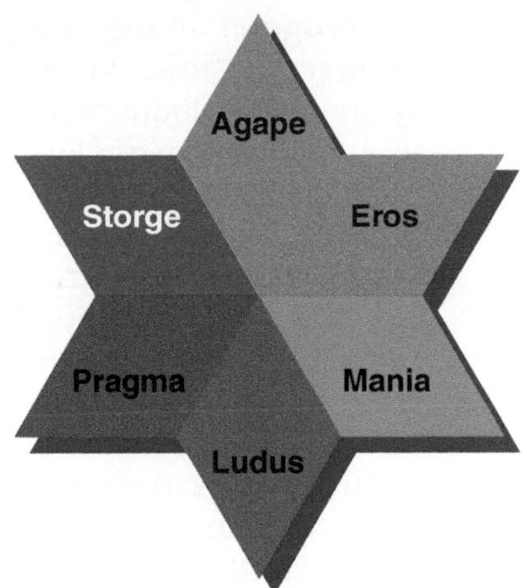

FIGURE 11.4

The Styles of Love

Eros is a powerful, passionate style of love that blazes to life suddenly and dramatically. It is an intense kind of love that may include sexual, spiritual, intellectual, or emotional attraction. Erotic love is the most intuitive and spontaneous of all styles, and it is also the fastest moving. Erotic lovers are likely to self-disclose early in a relationship, be very sentimental, and fall in love hard and fast. Although folk wisdom claims women are more romantic than men, research indicates that men are more likely than women to be erotic lovers (Hendrick & Hendrick, 1996).

Storge (pronounced "store-gay") is a comfortable, even-keeled kind of love based on friendship. Storgic love tends to grow gradually and to be peaceful and stable. In most cases, it grows out of common interests, values, and life goals (Lasswell & Lobsenz, 1980). Storgic relationships don't have the great highs of erotic love, but neither do they have the fiery conflict and anger that erotic people often experience. Steadiness is storge's standard mood.

The final primary style of love is **ludus**, which is playful love. Ludic lovers see love as a game. It's a lighthearted adventure full of challenges, puzzles, and fun, and love is not to be taken seriously. For ludics, commitment is poison. Instead, they like to play the field and enjoy falling in love; they don't seek commitment. Many people go through ludic periods but are not true ludics. After ending a long-term relationship, it's natural and healthy to avoid serious involvement for a while. Dating casually and steering clear of heavy entanglement may be wise and fun. Ludic loving may also suit people who enjoy romance but aren't ready to settle down. Research indicates that more men than women have ludic inclinations when it comes to love (Hendrick & Hendrick, 1996).

Secondary Styles of Love

There are three secondary styles of love: pragma, mania, and agape.

Student Voices

Vijay:

I'm not ready to settle down, and I may not ever be. I really like dating and seeing if I can get a girl to fall for me, but I'm not out for anything permanent. To me, the fun is in the chase. Once somebody falls for me, I kind of lose interest. It's just not challenging anymore.

Student Voices

Ranchana:

I have to think carefully about who to marry. I must go to graduate school, and I must support my family with what I earn when I finish. I cannot marry someone who is poor, who will not help me get through school, or who won't support my family. For me, these are very basic matters.

Student Voices

Pattie:

I never feel sure of myself when I'm in love. I always wonder when it will end, when my boyfriend will walk away, when he will lose interest. Sometimes I play games to see how interested a guy is, but then I get all upset if the game doesn't work out right. Then I just wallow in my insecurities, and they get worse the more I think about them.

Student Voices

Keenan:

My mother is agapic. She has moved more times than I can count because my father needed to relocate to advance. She agreed to the house he wanted and went on the vacations he wanted, even when she had other ideas. There's nothing she wouldn't do for him. I used to think she was a patsy, but I've come to see her way of loving as very strong.

Pragma, as the name suggests, is pragmatic or practical love. Pragma blends the conscious strategies of ludus with the stable, secure love of storge. Pragmatic lovers have clear criteria for partners, such as religious affiliation, career, and family background. Although many people dismiss pragma as coldly practical and not really love, this is a mistake. Pragmatic lovers aren't necessarily unfeeling or unloving at all. For them, though, practical considerations are the foundation of enduring commitments, so these must be satisfied before they let themselves fall in love. Pragmatic considerations also guide arranged marriages in which families match children for economic and social reasons.

Mania derives its name from the Greek term *theia mania,* which means "madness from the gods" (Lee, 1973). Manic lovers have the passion of eros, but they play by ludic rules with results that can be disturbing to them and those they love. Typically unsure that others really love them, manics may devise tests and games to evaluate a partner's commitment. They may also think obsessively about a relationship and be unable to think about anyone or anything else. In addition, manic lovers often experience emotional extremes, ranging from euphoric ecstasy to bottomless despair.

Agape is the final style of love, which is a blend of storge and eros. The term *agape* comes from Saint Paul's admonition that we should love others without expectation of personal gain or return. Agapic lovers feel the intense passion of eros and the constancy of storge. Generous and selfless, agapic lovers will put a loved one's happiness ahead of their own without any expectation of reciprocity. For them, loving and giving to another is its own reward. Agapic love sounds more possible for saints than for mere mortals. Research bears out this insight, because the original studies of love styles found no individuals who were purely agapic. However, many people have agapic tendencies in their style of loving.

In thinking about styles of love, you should keep several points in mind. First, most of us have a combination of styles (Hendrick et al., 1984). So you might be primarily storgic with strong agapic inclinations or mainly erotic with an undertone of ludic mischief. Second, your style of love is not necessarily permanent. Recent studies indicate we learn how to love (Maugh, 1994), so our style of loving may change as we have more experiences in loving.

Third, remember that your love style is part of an overall interpersonal system, so it is affected by all other aspects of your relationship (Hendrick & Hendrick, 1996). Your partner's style of love may influence your own. If you are primarily erotic and in love with a strong ludic, it's possible manic tendencies will be evoked. Finally, we should realize that individual styles of love are not good or bad in an absolute sense; what matters is how partners' styles fit together. An erotic partner's intensity might overwhelm a calm storgic; an agapic person might be exploited by a true ludic; the extremes of mania would clash with the serene steadiness of storge.

Romantic relationships are highlighted by intimacy, passion and commitment. They tend to follow a developmental course, and individuals experience and express romantic intimacy in various styles of loving. Now let's consider thc challenges facing friends and couples in sustaining relationships for the long haul.

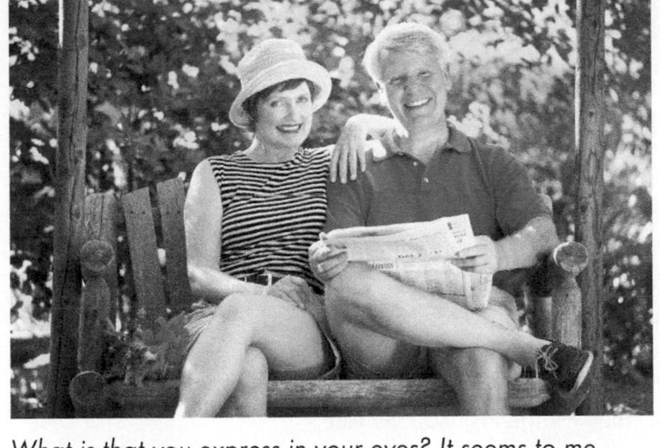

What is that you express in your eyes? It seems to me more than all the words I have read in my life.—Walt Whitman (1855)

CHALLENGES TO SUSTAINING CLOSE RELATIONSHIPS

Like all human relationships, friendships and committed romantic relationships experience pressures and difficulties. Many of the challenges are natural, even inevitable. To understand the strains friends and lovers face, we'll consider the internal tensions and the external constraints that tug at relationships.

CONCEPTS AT A GLANCE

Internal Tensions and External Constraints of Close Relationships

Internal Tensions:

- Relational dialectics
- Diverse communication styles
- Managing sex
- Avoiding violence and abuse

External Pressures:

- Competing demands
- Personal change
- Surviving distance
- Ensuring equity

Internal Tensions

Close relationships, like all personal connections, are vulnerable to tensions inherent in being close. **Internal tensions** are relationship stresses that grow out of individuals and their interaction. We'll consider four of these.

Relational Dialectics

In earlier chapters and in this one, we discussed relational dialectics, which are opposing human needs that create tension and propel change in close relationships. The three dialectics are tension between connection and autonomy, openness and privacy, and novelty and familiarity. These three dialectics punctuate friendships and committed romantic relationships, prompting us to adjust continuously to natural yet contradictory needs.

Dialectics may strain relationships when individuals differ in their needs. For instance, there could be tension if Raj is bored and needing novelty, but his partner Andy is overstimulated and seeking calming routines. Similarly, if Clint has just broken up with a woman, he may seek greater closeness with his friend Mario. When needs collide, we should talk. It's important to be up front about what you need and to be sensitive to what your friend or partner needs. Doing this simultaneously honours yourself, the other, and the relationship. The goal is for friends to express themselves honestly and to engage in dual perspective and sensitive listening within a supportive communication climate. When this occurs, we can usually work out ways to meet each other's needs or at least to understand that differing needs don't reflect unequal commitment to the relationship.

Lana highlights the importance of dual perspective in dealing with tensions caused by relational dialectics. She draws on her own experience of breakups to understand her friends' perspective when they've broken up. This motivates Lana to make time to be with her friends. If she communicates her understanding and acceptance, her friends will feel she supports and cares about them.

Relational dialectics are natural and constructive forces in friendship. They keep us aware of multiple, sometimes clashing needs. In addition, because

Student Voices

Lana:

My girlfriends and I are so often in different places that it's hard to take care of each other. If one of my friends isn't seeing anyone special, she wants more time with me and wants to do things together. If I'm in a relationship with a guy, her needs feel demanding. But when I've just broken up, I really need my friends to fill time and talk with. So I try to remember how I feel and use that to help me accept it when my friends need my time.

we find tension uncomfortable, dialectics motivate us to fine-tune friendships continuously. The strains dialectics spark can be managed by revising friendships and by accepting dialectical tensions as normal, ongoing relationship processes.

Technology's Impact on Personal Relationships

Technology has opened the lines of communication around the world, allowing us to stretch our relationships across time and space through use of the Internet, cellular networks, and other media technologies. Technology brings the world together, enabling us to feel closer to loved ones far away and increasing the frequency of our communication with others.

Personal relationships and friendships can be enriched by many facets of technology. McKenna, Green, & Gleason (2002) found that some relationships can grow through use of the Internet. For example, the Internet offers the advantage of anonymity, thereby reducing the risks often associated with self-disclosure. Many people who have difficulty expressing their true selves in a face-to-face interaction find themselves being truer to their character and freer to express intimate aspects of themselves over the Internet. The study by McKenna and her colleagues argues that this freedom of self-disclosure ultimately builds a stronger foundation for friendships and relationships—their research found that many close Internet relationships were still viable and meaningful two years after the first interaction. Furthermore, they found that self-disclosure became easier online because of the lack of "gating features" such as physical appearance, social anxiety, speech impediments, or apparent shyness that might hinder the development of a relationship.

The Internet also provides an easy way to find people similar to yourself. While in the three-dimensional world it often takes a lot of time and effort to find other people who share your interests, many online chat rooms and newsgroups are dedicated to specific interests. Considering the positive correlation between similarity and compatibility for people in relationships, the Internet can be a powerful matchmaking tool.

Internet Dating

Just as there are many ways to meet someone in real life, there are many ways to make a connection to another online. Some 16.3 million people logged on to Internet dating sites in 2003. *Match.com*, a popular virtual matchmaking and dating website, alone boasts almost 5 million users.

The online dating process is simple. To get started, you either create a profile of yourself using one of the many online dating services, or you can contact a person whose profile already appears on the site. Through e-mail exchanges and, if desired, telephone calls, individuals begin the process of getting to know each other.

Communicating with other people is a vital human need. Social networking sites can offer informal ways to connect people quickly and easily; however it may not always be appropriate for building deep friendships or cultivating and enriching significant intimate relationships in our lives.

Online dating is different from real-life dating because social indicators, gazes, smiles, and physical markers are, of course, not involved. People rely on

Communication Notes

CYBER RELATIONSHIPS

The popularity of the Internet has introduced innovative ways to communicate and develop interpersonal relationships—through e-mails, blogs, and more recently, social networking websites. *Facebook*, launched in 2004, is the second-largest social network on the Web, behind *MySpace* (Yadav, 2006). This enormously successful business connects users with friends, family, and co-workers. Originally founded by a university student as an alternative to the student directory, *Facebook* gives students an opportunity to become familiar and connect with others of similar beliefs, interests, and concerns (Gabbay, 2006).

Facebook has since spread to seven English-speaking countries and includes over 30 000 recognized institutions. It is the sixth most trafficked site in the United States, and according to a 2005 survey, approximately 85 percent of students in colleges had a *Facebook* account, with 60 percent of them logging in daily (Yadav, 2006). The largest network on the website is Toronto, with over 600 000 users (Nimetz, 2007).

A typical *Facebook* profile consists of a number of different sections, including Information, Status, Friends, Photos, Notes, Groups, and The Wall. Users can send both public and private messages to other users and join various groups of individuals that share the same interests, beliefs, and concerns. It offers simple search features to locate and stay in contact with friends and acquaintances. With so many ways to communicate on a daily basis, it is easy to see why websites such as *Facebook* have gained such popularity.

Facebook's main objective is to connect people. Does it really do that? In making communication so rapid and brief, sometimes more important aspects of maintaining relationships are neglected, such as physical closeness, time spent together in shared activities, conveying trust and acceptance, and giving and receiving nonverbal cues like smiles and comforting touches. Far from connecting us, on many levels it can actually disconnect us when we are merely sending instant messages or photos without being in physical contact with other human beings. This isolation can limit the development of close and meaningful relationships with others. The large social network also opens up the risk of cyber bullying and the posting of messages that can be hurtful, discriminatory, or offensive to others.

Also popular are dating and matchmaking sites, which promise to find compatible partners for people without all the awkwardness of live interaction. Some of these sites, such as *eHarmony*, attract people who are looking for long-term relationships, while a growing number appeal to "commitment phobes" and promise "no strings attached" dating hookups. One such site, *OnlineBootyCall*, saw a 38 percent increase in its 3 million members in one month alone in 2009. Critics accuse these sites of damaging family values, destroying relationships, and encouraging infidelity. Proponents suggest they are a place of "refreshing honesty" since users know up front that they cater to people looking for casual encounters (Bielski, 2009).

the online profile and subsequent e-mails to initially form a mental picture of the other. Just as offline couples go on dates, online couples can exchange pictures and arrange meeting times to talk online. These "dates" are often followed by telephone calls. Hearing each other's voice on the phone can deepen an online relationship by igniting sparks between the individuals, and can serve as a steppingstone to meeting in person.

Meeting in person is decisive and can either confirm the relationship one has built online or disconfirm the relationship by exposing fallacies in the information

© iStockphoto.com/sdominick

What are the challenges of cyber relationships?

that the two individuals have exchanged. If there is a successful real-life meeting, couples can continue their relationship in the same manner as offline couples.

Online relationships also have an element of risk, however—in Canada, it is estimated that 18 percent of people using online dating services are married. The Internet makes it easy to attempt to maintain intimate relationships with several people at the same time, meeting different needs through different relationships. Also, people often attach different levels of "realness" to online relationships; for example, an individual in a committed offline relationship who is also pursuing an online relationship may regard the online relationship as not being "real," to justify her or his actions and feelings. These "levels of reality" may get in the way of a person's ability to develop satisfying and supportive relationships either online or offline.

Another drawback of Internet relationships is that the lack of physical presence might cause a person to form an unrealistic image of the other. The online profile and subsequent messages can, of course, be tailored to present a personality or appearance that is most desirable but is not based on fact. High expectations may end in disappointment further into the relationship.

Communication Notes

DESIRE, LOVE, AND BETRAYAL

Julie Albright and Thomas Conran (2003) analyzed narrative data from 314 informants who had been involved in at least one relationship on the Internet. They found that Internet romances seemed to share three common stages:

1. An initial falling in love stage of rapid intimacy, where self-disclosure often proceeds at a rapid, exhilarating pace, like "love at first sight."
2. A meeting of the minds, which often leads to the feeling of a strong "soul mate" connection because interactions are text-based; hearing about who they are as a person, participants expressed a strong sense of getting to know the "inner self" of their lover.
3. A virtual mirror stage of mutual optimization and idealization, in which the screen of the computer becomes a kind of mirror where one throws out a "best self" and sees the reflection of another shaped to one's desires. A partner can be summoned up who instantaneously satisfies all unspoken, conflicting, and fleeting desires—but a partner who is barely known.

Online communication has been called addictive by some researchers and therapists. It seems that "reality checking" is critical before one makes major life-altering decisions.

Diverse Communication Styles

Friendships may also be strained when friends misinterpret each other's communication. The potential for misunderstanding mushrooms as our society becomes increasingly diverse, making it more likely that some of our friends will have cultural backgrounds different from our own. Because how we communicate reflects the understandings and rules of our culture, misinterpretations are likely between friends from different cultures (Wood, 1995a). For instance, in many Asian societies, individuals are socialized to be unassuming and modest, whereas in the West, we encourage assertion and we celebrate ourselves. Thus, a native Japanese might perceive a friend from Ottawa as arrogant for saying "Let's go out to celebrate my acceptance to law school." A Thai woman might not get the support she wants from a friend from Calgary because she was taught not to assert her needs and the Calgary friend was taught that people should speak up for themselves. The Communication Notes feature "Japanese Friendships" explores some of the cultural differences in friendship.

Communication Notes

JAPANESE FRIENDSHIPS

The Japanese distinguish between two types of friendships. *Tsukiai* are friendships based on social obligation (Atsumi, 1980). These usually involve neighbours or work associates and tend to have limited life spans. Friendships based on affection and common interests (*suki*) usually last a lifetime: Personal friendship is serious business. The number of personal friends for many Japanese people is very small and stable, in contrast to friendship patterns in the West. Friendships between women and men are rare in Japan. Prior to marriage, only 20 percent of Japanese say they have close friends of the opposite sex (Mochizuki, 1981).

Misunderstandings also arise from differences among social groups. As a rule, Asian cultures are more communal than Western ones, so taking care of extended family members is a priority over individual needs and desires. Similarly, feminine and masculine communication rules may cause misunderstandings. For example, Ellen may feel that her friend Jed isn't being supportive when instead of empathizing with her problems, he offers advice or suggests they go out to take her mind off her troubles. Yet, he is showing support according to masculine rules of communication. Jed, on the other hand, may feel that Ellen is intruding on his autonomy when she pushes him to talk about his feelings. According to feminine rules of communication, however, Ellen is showing interest and concern.

Differences themselves aren't usually the cause of problems in friendship. Instead, how we interpret and judge others' communication is the root of tension and hurt. What Jed and Ellen did wasn't the source of their frustrations. Jed interpreted Ellen according to his communication rules, not hers, and she interpreted Jed according to her communication rules, not his. Notice that the misunderstandings result from our interpretations of others' behaviours, not the behaviours themselves. This reminds us of the need to distinguish between fact and inference.

Gary Chapman describes in his book *The Five Love Languages* (1995) how people express love differently. Most people look to receive love in the same way they give it, resulting in misunderstandings. Chapman claims that if partners understand each other's love language, they can give and receive love more effectively. Chapman's five love languages are:

- Quality time
- Words of affirmation

- Acts of service
- Physical touch
- Giving gifts

For example, if your primary love language is "acts of service," you might make a special dinner for your partner. If your partner's primary love language is "words of affirmation," she may not view the special dinner as an act of love. She will be wondering why you never tell her how you feel. You must learn to give love in the way your partner understands it and to teach your partner your love language.

Apply the Idea

LOVE LANGUAGES

Identify your love languages and those of your romantic partner in order of importance. Choose from quality time, words of affirmation, acts of service, physical touch, and giving gifts.

You	**Your Partner**
#1 Language ____________	#1 Language ____________
#2 Language ____________	#2 Language ____________
#3 Language ____________	#3 Language ____________

Now examine what you need to do to speak the language of love spoken by your partner.

Managing Sex

Managing sex in relationships can pose challenges. Sexual attraction can cause difficulty between friends. Friendships between heterosexual men and women, or gay men, or lesbians often include sexual tensions. Because Western culture so strongly emphasizes sex, it's difficult not to perceive people in sexual terms (Johnson, Stockdale, & Saal, 1991; O'Meara, 1989). Even if there is no sexual activity between friends, sexual undertones may ripple beneath the surface of their friendships.

Sexual attraction or invitations can be a problem between friends who have agreed not to have a sexual relationship. Tension over sexual attraction or interest can be present in friendships between heterosexual women and men (West, Anderson, & Duck, 1996), as well as in friendships between lesbians and between gay men (Nardi & Sherrod, 1994). Trust may be damaged if someone we consider a friend makes a pass. Further, once a friend transgresses the agreed-upon boundaries of the friendship, it's hard to know how to act with each other or to feel completely comfortable unless the relationship has shifted to a romantic one.

Student Voices

Shasha:

It is so hard to be just friends with guys. When I try to be friends with a guy, he'll hit on me at some point. I tell guys if friendship is all I'm interested in, and they agree, but they hit on me anyway. It's happened so much that by now I feel on guard with guys even before they start anything.

In the HIV/AIDS era, sexual activities pose serious, even deadly, threats to romantic relationships (see the Communication Notes feature "Safe

Communication Notes

JUST FRIENDS?

One study suggests that being "just friends" often includes sexual activity. Walid Afifi and Sandra Faulkner (2000) surveyed 315 women and men in college about their cross-sex friendships. They found that 51 percent of respondents reported having had sex with a friend of the other sex at least once. One-third of respondents said they had repeatedly engaged in sexual activity with friends. Most of the respondents said that sexual activity increased the quality of their friendships, but a few said it harmed the friendships. Perhaps most interesting is the finding that engaging in sexual activity with friends doesn't necessarily—or even usually—change a friendship into a romantic relationship.

At least for the people in Afifi and Faulkner's study, sex was seen as a way to enrich—not recast—the existing relationship. Lee West, Jennifer Anderson, and Steve Duck (1996) emphasize that, if people agree that they have a friendship, not a romance, then specific activities don't necessarily change the definition of the relationship.

Your InfoTrac® College Edition provides the text of a number of articles about sex and friendship. Find these by typing *friendship* into the subject search, then accessing the subdivision analysis.

Sex Still Best Approach"). Despite vigorous public education campaigns, many individuals still don't practise safer sex, which includes abstaining, restricting sexual activity to a single partner who has been tested for HIV, and/or using latex condoms (Reel & Thompson, 1994). Not practising safer sex puts both partners at grave risk for early death.

Communication Notes

SAFE SEX STILL BEST APPROACH

One of the leading researchers in the world in sexually transmitted diseases is Canada's Dr. Robert Brunham (2001), director of the BC Centre for Disease Control. Brunham asserts that frank knowledge about safe sex still offers the best protection for sexually transmitted diseases. Brunham reports that HIV/AIDS continues to be the greatest public health challenge in the world today. While infection rates in Canada are substantially lower than in other parts of the world, it still remains a very serious disease. Sexually transmitted HIV still poses the greatest risk for gay men and for women who have sex with HIV-infected men.

Brunham goes on to say that among other STDs, chlamydia continues to be the most common, with 200 000 new infections occurring in Canada each year. Chlamydia commonly produces asymptomatic infection for prolonged periods of time. Because of this, it can be transmitted unknowingly to sex partners. Screening for infection still remains the best approach to prevention of chlamydia. New infectious agents are being recognized as sexually transmitted ones. The most important of these is the human papillomavirus (HPV) which is demonstrated to be the cause of cervical cancer. It is difficult to recognize and treat.

In light of these findings, says Brunham, safe sex is still the best approach to disease prevention. For current reports and more information, check out www.bccdc.org.

Why don't people who know about sexually transmitted diseases (STDs) consistently follow safer sex techniques? Communication scholars have discovered two primary reasons. First, many individuals find it more embarrassing to talk about sex than to engage in it. They find it awkward to ask direct questions of partners ("Have you been tested for HIV?" "Are you having sex with anyone else?") or to make direct requests of partners ("I want you to wear a condom," "I would like for you to be tested for HIV before we have sex"). Naturally, it's difficult to talk explicitly about sex and the dangers of HIV/AIDS. However, it is far more difficult to live with HIV or with the knowledge that you infected a lover.

A second reason people sometimes fail to practise safer sex is that their rational thought and control are debilitated by drugs, alcohol, or both. In a series of studies of college students' sexual activities, communication researchers Sheryl Bowen and Paula Michal-Johnson (1995) found that safer sex precautions are often neglected when individuals drink heavily. Alcohol and other drugs loosen inhibitions, including appropriate concerns about personal safety. The Communication Notes feature "Reasons Good Enough to Die For?" examines why people do not practise safer sex.

Communication Notes

REASONS GOOD ENOUGH TO DIE FOR?

When students and members of singles organizations were asked about their sexual activities, these were the top five reasons they reported for not practising safer sex (Reel & Thompson, 1994):

1. I knew my partner. We'd discussed our past sexual experiences.
2. I use another form of birth control.
3. A condom wasn't available at the time.
4. Things happened too fast.
5. I didn't feel I was at risk.

Discussing and practising safer sex may be embarrassing, but there is no other sensible option. Principles of effective interpersonal communication we've discussed help ease the discomfort of negotiating safer sex. *I* language that owns your feelings is especially important. It is more constructive to say "I feel unsafe having unprotected sex" than to say "Without a condom, you could give me HIV." A positive interpersonal climate in which to talk about sex is fostered by relational language, such as "we," "us," and "our relationship" (Reel & Thompson, 1994). Individuals who care about themselves and their partners are honest about their sexual histories and careful in their sex practices.

Avoiding Violence and Abuse

Although we like to think of romantic relationships as loving, many are not. Violence and abuse are unfortunately common between romantic partners, and they cut across lines of class, race, and ethnicity (French, 1992; West,

1995). Violence is high not only in heterosexual marriage but also in heterosexual cohabitation. In fact, cohabiting couples have the highest incidence of violence of all couples (Cunningham & Antill, 1995; White & Bondurant, 1996). Cohabiting women suffer 1.5 to 2 times more physical abuse than married women, perhaps because their partners are less committed than husbands (Ellis, 1989). Gay and lesbian relationships are also not immune to abuse.

The majority of detected violence and abuse in intimacy is committed by men against women. In Canada, according to a *Family Violence Report* by Statistics Canada in 2001, over a million women reported violence by a spouse, with aboriginal women reporting more than twice as many violent episodes per population than other Canadian women. Marital separation does not necessarily mark the end of a violent relationship (p. 2). Rape and date rape are escalating, especially when individuals have been drinking ("What Teens Say," 1994). Verbal and emotional abuse cause deep and lasting scars (Vachss, 1994). And dysfunctional relationships, often called "toxic connections," seem to be rising (Wright & Wright, 1995).

Student Voices

Katrina:

It's hard for me to believe now, but I was in an abusive relationship and it took me a long time to get out of it. The first time Ray hit me, I was so surprised I didn't know what to do, so I didn't do anything. The next time, I told him to stop or I'd leave. He said how sorry he was and promised never to hit me again, and then he was real sweet for a long time. I felt like he really did love me, and I felt I should stand by him. And then it happened again. I went to talk to my minister, and he told me my Christian duty was to honour the marriage vows I made before God, so I went back again. Each time Ray beat up on me, he'd follow it with being romantic and sweet, so I'd get sucked back in. I didn't finally leave him until he threw me down some stairs and dislocated my shoulder.

Mental health counsellors who specialize in violence have come to the conclusion that relationships in which men abuse women are not rare but exemplify in extreme form the traditional power dynamics that structure relationships between women and men (Goldner et al., 1990). Men are taught to use power to assert themselves and to compete with others, whereas women are socialized to defer and preserve relationships. When these internalized patterns combine in heterosexual relationships, a foundation exists for men to abuse women and for women to tolerate it, rather than be disloyal (West, 1995).

Violence seldom stops without intervention. Instead it follows a predictable cycle of power and control, just as Katrina describes. Unless those behaviours are changed to more equitable interactions, the violence will continue (see Figures 11.5 and 11.6).

Being loyal in the face of abuse, a response to conflict that we discussed in Chapter 10, is inappropriate because it doesn't protect a victim's safety. Relationships that are violent and abusive are unhealthy for everyone involved. They obviously jeopardize the comfort, health, and sometimes the survival of victims of violence. Less obvious is the damage experienced by abusers. Using physical force against others is a sign of weakness—an admission that a person can't exercise power in intellectual or emotional ways and must resort to the crudest and least imaginative methods of influence. Further, abusers can destroy relationships that they need and want.

Relational dialectics, misinterpretations of different communication styles, sexual tensions, and coping with abuse are sources of internal tension in many close relationships. Usually, straightforward communication, although not always easy, is the best way to deal with these problems and to restore ease. See the guidelines for effective communication at the end of the chapter for ways to improve relationships.

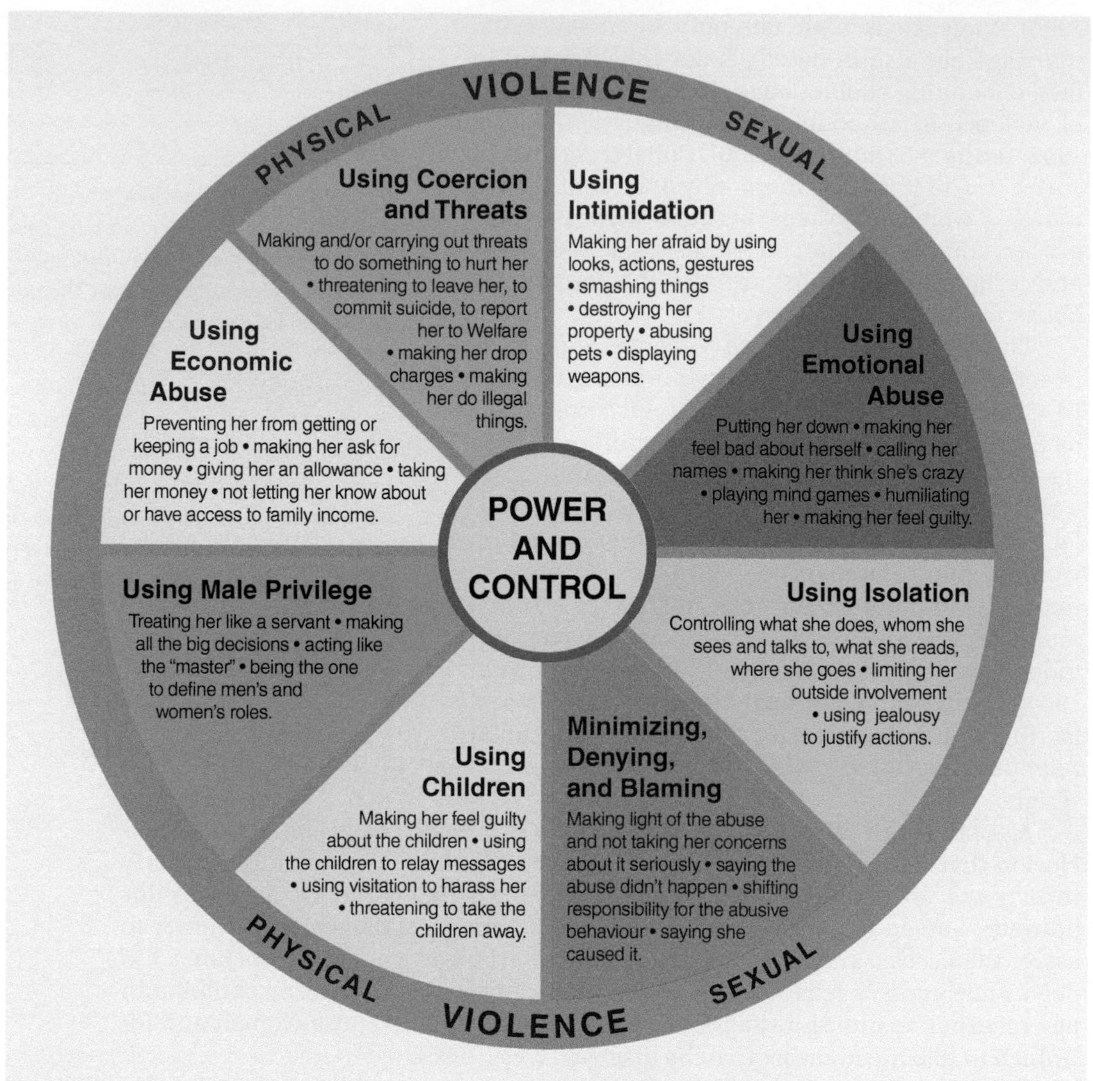

FIGURE 11.5

Power-Based and Control-Based Abuse

Reflective Exercise

Think about your experience with violence, both directly and indirectly. No one should tolerate violence, especially from a person who claims to love you. If you are being abused, seek counselling to discover and think through your options. If you suspect someone you care about is being abused, be a real friend and talk with the person. Too often, signs of abuse are ignored because we find it awkward to talk about violence between intimates. However, standing by and doing nothing is a kind of abuse in itself. If you are abusing someone you care about, get professional help.

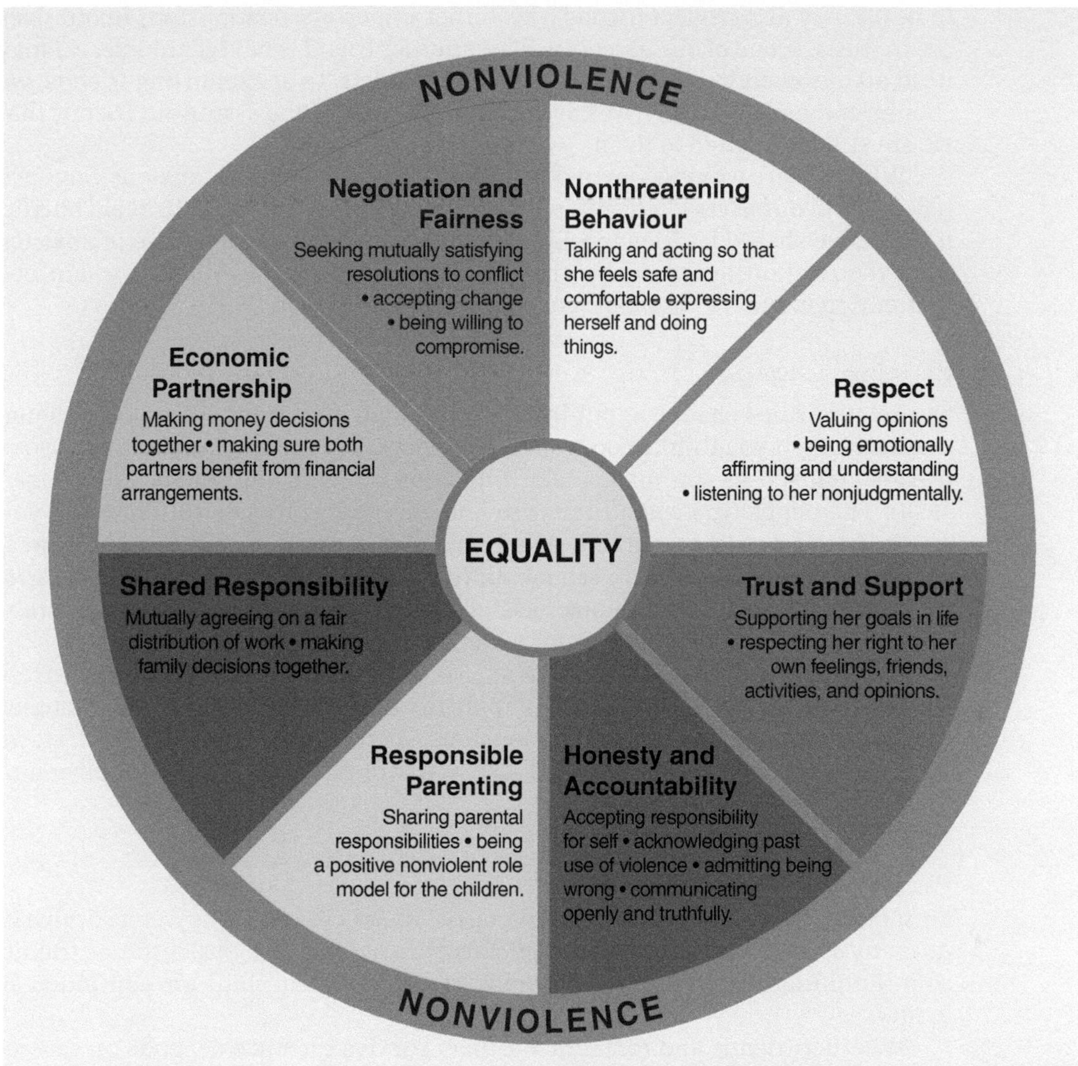

FIGURE 11.6

Equitable Relationship Interactions

External Pressures

In addition to internal tensions, close relationships may encounter pressures from outside sources. Four of these **external tensions** are competing demands, changes, surviving distance, and equity.

Competing Demands

Friendships exist within larger social systems that affect how they function (Allan, 1994). Our work and our romantic relationships tend to be woven into our everyday lives, ensuring that they get daily attention. The early stages of a career take enormous amounts of energy and time. We may not have enough time or energy left to maintain friendships, even those that matter to us (Duck et al., 1991).

We sometimes neglect established friends because of other relationships, especially new ones. When a new romance is taking off, we may be totally immersed in it. We may also neglect friends when other important relationships in our lives are in crisis. If one of our parents is ill or another friend is having trouble, we may need all our energy to cope with the acute situation. To avoid hurting friends, we should let them know when we have to focus elsewhere, and assure our friends that we are still committed to them.

When we are wrapped up in other relationships in happy or anxious ways, we have little of ourselves left to give to those we care about the most. To avoid hurtful feelings, we should let friends and lovers know when we need a leave of absence from the relationship to deal with immediate priorities. If we don't explain our inattention to others, they may feel hurt or rejected (Wood, 1995c).

Personal Changes

Our relationships change as our lives do. Although a few friendships are lifelong, most are not. If you think about your experiences, you'll realize that many of your friends changed as you made major transitions in your life (Allan, 1994; Yager, 1999). The people you spent time with and counted as friends shifted when you started high school, entered college or university, or moved to a new town. They'll change again when you leave school, move for career or family reasons, and perhaps have children. Because one base of friendship is common interests, established friends may not be able to share new interests we develop.

Because our romantic partners are also our friends, many of the same stressors surrounding change in our lives apply to our intimate relationships. Couples often experience strain in their relationships when one goes back to school, starts a new job, or takes on new interests. The new stimulus upsets the equilibrium of the dyad.

Surviving Distance

Most close relationships face the challenge of distance, and many won't survive it. As many as 90 percent of North Americans have at least one long-distance friendship (Rohlfing, 1995). In our highly mobile society, friendships are continuously in flux.

Whether friends and romantic partners survive distance depends on several factors. Perhaps the most obvious influence is how much individuals care about continuing to be close. The greater the commitment, the more likely a relationship will persist despite separation. Geographic distance is the reason the majority of high school friendships dissolve when individuals begin university or college (Rose, 1984). Yet, the likelihood of sustaining a long-distance friendship also depends on other factors, such as socioeconomic class and gender.

Because socioeconomic class profoundly affects who we are and how we live, it's not surprising that it influences the prospect that long-distance friendships will endure. The reason is simple: money. Friendships that survive distance involve frequent phone calls and letters and visits every so often. It takes money to finance trips and long-distance calls. Thus, friends with greater economic resources (in middle and upper socioeconomic classes) are better able to maintain their relationships than are friends with less discretionary income (Willmott, 1987).

A second way in which socioeconomic class affects the endurance of long-distance friendships is flexibility in managing work and family. Middle-class

Student Voices

Ruth:

Sandi and I had been friends for years when I had my first baby. Gradually, we saw less of each other and couldn't find much to talk about when we did get together. She was still doing the singles scene, and I was totally absorbed in mothering. I got to know other mothers in the neighbourhood, and soon I thought of them as my friends. What's funny is that last year Sandi had a baby, and it was so good to get together and talk. We reconnected with each other.

and upper-class individuals usually have generous vacations and flexibility in work schedules, so they can make time to travel. Working-class citizens tend to have less personal control over when they work and how much vacation time they get. Income also affects our ability to pay for baby-sitters who may make it possible for a parent to visit a friend for a weekend.

Gender also affects the endurance of long-distance friendships. There appear to be two reasons why women are more likely than men to sustain ties with friends who live at a distance. First, the sexes differ in how much they value same-sex friendships and how much they give to and get from them. Compared to women, men place less value on their same-sex relationships and invest less in them (Duck & Wright, 1993). This is especially true of married men who often name their wives as their best friends (Rubin, 1985).

Women are also more willing than men to adjust schedules and priorities to make time for friends (Rubin, 1985), and they are more willing to tolerate less than ideal circumstances for being with friends. For example, mothers who sustain long-distance friendships report that when they visit, they are seldom alone, because their children need attention and care. Even though these mothers say they miss the intimacy of uninterrupted conversations, they value each other enough to sustain friendships under the terms that are possible (Rohlfing, 1995). Women also report getting more out of their friendships with women than men report getting out of their friendships with men (Duck & Wright, 1993). For women more than men, friendships are a primary and important thread woven through their lives.

Women can and do sustain ties with important friends by talking on the phone and writing. Men, on the other hand, are more likely to replace friends who have moved away with others who can share activities they enjoy (Rohlfing, 1995). Lillian Rubin's (1985) studies led her to say that women tend to develop **friends of the heart,** who remain close regardless of distance and circumstances. Rubin also noted that many men have **friends of the road,** who change as they move along the road of life and develop new interests and find themselves in new situations. It is easier to replace a friend who was a tennis partner than one with whom we shared intimate feelings and details of our life.

Geographic separation can be even more difficult for romantic couples because Western culture teaches us to expect to live with our partners. The assumption of living together permanently, however, isn't universal. Many immigrants to Canada work several years before bringing spouses and children to join them. Westerners facing long-distance relationships might take heart from the fact that couples in other cultures manage to stay together despite long periods of living apart.

CONCEPTS AT A GLANCE

Three Problems in Long-Distance Relationships

- Loss of daily routines
- Unrealistic expectations of time together
- Unequal investments into the relationship

Many of us will be involved in long-distance romantic relationships because they are increasingly common. The number of long-distance romantic relationships will increase further as more partners pursue independent careers and as extended travel becomes part of more people's jobs. Many couples who share the same home will still be apart a great deal of the time. Researchers have identified three problems, or tensions, commonly experienced in long-distance relationships: loss of daily routines, unrealistic expectations of time together, and unequal investments into the relationship.

Perhaps the greatest problem is the lack of daily sharing of small events. Not being able to share small talk and daily routines is a major loss. As we have seen, sharing the ordinary comings and goings of days helps partners keep their lives woven together. The routine conversations of romantic partners form and continuously reform the basic fabric of their relationship. Everyday talk is how couples connect in countless little moments that shape the overall climate of the relationship.

The lack of routine contact leads to the second problem faced by couples who live apart: unrealistic expectations for time together. Based on 25 years of studying marriages, psychologist and marriage counsellor John Gottman (1997) reports that

Student Voices

Françoise:

When Maurice found a good job outside Quebec, he moved, and both of us thought our relationship would survive. We had talked about marrying when I finished school, so we were pretty serious. At first we did okay, even though it was hard. I would e-mail every day, and he wrote me once or twice each week. One of us called the other every week. Then his messages got less frequent. Then it seemed I was always the one who called him. I told him he was acting like he wasn't committed anymore, but he said he was just busy. I think that was true, but it didn't matter after a while. The upshot is that he was too busy for to keep in touch with me, and I couldn't keep the relationship going on my own.

the mundane, ordinary moments couples share are what build love and establish a positive emotional climate between people. Because partners have so little time together, they often believe every moment must be perfect. They feel that there should be no harsh words or conflict and that they should be happily focused on each other for all the time they have together. Yet, this is an unrealistic expectation. Conflict and needs for autonomy are natural and inevitable in all romantic relationships. They may be even more likely in reunions of long-distance couples, because partners are used to living alone and have established independent rhythms that may not mesh well.

A third common problem in long-distance relationships is unequal effort that the two partners invest in maintaining the connection. According to Vicki Helgeson (1994), one of the major reasons that long-distance couples break up is that one partner is doing most of the work to sustain contact and to take care of the relationship. The inequity in investment creates resentment in the person who is assuming the majority of the work to keep the relationship alive.

The good news is that these problems don't necessarily sabotage long-distance romance. Most researchers report that partners can maintain satisfying commitments despite geographic separation (Rohlfing, 1995). In fact, there are some noteworthy advantages of long-distance relationships. James Reske and Laura Stafford (1990) report that the very everydayness that geographically separated partners miss is a boon to romance. Because couples aren't together continuously, they tend to be more loving when they are together and to feel more passionately about each other. Also, partners who live apart are able to focus on their individual projects and ambitions without the distraction of a constant companion (Gross, 1980).

Some strategies devised by college students (see the Communication Notes feature "Coping with Geographic Separation") provide sound guidelines for sustaining intimacy across distance. Notice that these strategies reflect many of the communication principles we've discussed in this and previous chapters. Because partners don't have the comfort of everyday interaction, it is especially important to build climates that are trusting, open, and honest in long-distance relationships. It's also critical that couples who live apart focus on what is positive and good about the relationship and even the separation.

Ensuring Equity

The last external pressure that challenges close relationships, especially romantic relationships, is ensuring equity within the relationship. Friends may keep a "loose tally" of whose turn it is to do what. In committed romantic relationships, however, perceived equity is very important. **Equity** means fairness, based on the perception that both partners invest relatively equally in a relationship and benefit similarly from their investments. We all want to feel that our partners are as committed as we are and that we gain equally from being together. Although few partners demand moment-to-moment equality, most of us want our relationships to be equitable over time. Inequity tends to breed unhappiness, which lessens satisfaction and commitment and sometimes prompts affairs (Walster, Traupmann, & Walster, 1978).

Equity has multiple dimensions. We may evaluate the fairness of financial, emotional, physical, and other contributions to a relationship. One area that

Communication Notes

COPING WITH GEOGRAPHIC SEPARATION

College students report nine coping strategies they use to sustain intimacy across long distances (Westefield & Liddell, 1982):

1. Recognize that long-distance relationships are common; you're not alone.
2. Create more social support systems (friends) while separated from a romantic partner.
3. Communicate creatively—send videotapes and audiotapes.
4. Before separating, work out ground rules for going out with friends, phoning, visiting, and writing.
5. Use time together "wisely" to be affectionate and to have fun together. Being serious all the time isn't constructive.
6. Maintain honesty. Especially when partners live apart, they need to be straight with each other.
7. Build an open, supportive communication climate so that you can talk about issues and feelings.
8. Maintain trust by abiding by ground rules that were agreed on, phoning when you say you will, and keeping lines of communication open.
9. Focus on the positive aspects of separation.

strongly affects relationship quality is perceived equity in housework and child care, as discussed in the Communication Notes feature "The Second Shift." Inequitable division of domestic obligations fuels dissatisfaction and resentment, both of which harm intimacy (Gottman & Carrère, 1994). Marital stability is more closely linked to perceptions of equitable divisions of child care and housework than to income or sex life (Fowers, 1991; Suitor, 1991).

Communication Notes

THE SECOND SHIFT

In 80 percent of dual-worker families, men work one job and women work two—the second shift begins when they come home (Hochschild with Machung, 1989). Not only do women do more domestic work than men but also work that is less satisfying and more stressful. Women tend to do the day-in, day-out jobs such as cooking, shopping, and helping children with homework. Men more often do domestic work that they can schedule to suit themselves. Mowing the lawn can be scheduled flexibly, whereas fixing meals must be done on a tight timetable. Men also are more likely to take care of occasional and fun child-care activities, such as visiting the zoo, whereas women manage the daily grind of bathing, dressing, and feeding children.

As a rule, women assume psychological responsibility, which involves remembering, planning, and coordinating domestic activities. Parents may alternate who takes children to the doctor, but it is usually the mother who remembers when checkups are needed, makes appointments, and reminds the father to take the child. Birthday cards and gifts are signed by both partners, but women typically assume the psychological responsibility for remembering when birthdays are and for buying cards and gifts.

Student Voices

Cora May:

I said, "Either things are going to change around here or I'm leaving." He didn't believe me, but I stood my ground. For 20 years I had done all of the housework, the cooking, and the child care, while he did none of these. Walter just went to his job each day and came back home for me to wait on him. Well, I went to my job each day too. I worked hard, and I was tired when I got home. You'd think he could figure that out, wouldn't you? It got really bad when I started taking night courses. I need to study at night, not fix meals and do laundry, so I asked him to help out. You'd think he'd been stung by a bee. He said no, so I just quit fixing his meals and left his laundry when I washed my clothes. Finally, he got with the program.

Beginning with the Industrial Revolution, men were assigned responsibility for earning income and women for caring for children and a home. A gendered division of labour no longer makes sense, because most marriages today include two wage earners (Wilkie, 1991). Unfortunately, divisions of family and home responsibilities have not changed in response to changing employment patterns. Even when both partners in heterosexual relationships work outside the home, the vast majority of child care and homemaking is done by women (Nussbaum, 1992; Okin, 1989). In only 20 percent of dual-worker families do men assume equal domestic responsibilities (Hochschild with Machung, 1989). Although many men with partners who work outside the home do contribute, they do less than a fair share. Since the 1950s, the amount of housework and child care that husbands do had risen a scant 10 percent—from 20 to 30 percent—by the mid-1980s (Pleck, 1987).

How are domestic responsibilities managed when both partners are the same sex? Lesbian couples create more egalitarian relationships than either heterosexuals or gays. More than any other type of couple, lesbians are likely to share decision-making and domestic work (Huston & Schwartz, 1995). Consequently, lesbians are least likely to perceive inequity in contributions to home life (Kurdek, 1993). Gay men, like their heterosexual brothers, use the power derived from income to authorize inequitable contributions to domestic life. In gay couples, the man who makes more money has and uses more power, both in making decisions that affect the relationship and in avoiding housework (Huston & Schwartz, 1995). This suggests that power is the basis of gendered divisions of labour and that men, more than women, seek the privileges of power, including evasion of domestic work.

The perception of inequity damages romantic relationships. It creates resentment and anger and erodes love. As resentment eclipses positive feelings, dissatisfaction mushrooms. In addition, there are health consequences. Women who work a second shift are stressed, starved for sleep, and susceptible to illness because they are continuously doing double duty (Hochschild with Machung, 1989). Successful long-term relationships in our era require more equitable divisions of home responsibilities than have been traditional.

CONCEPTS AT A GLANCE

Six Guidelines for Sustaining Close Relationships

- Engage in dual perspective.
- Communicate honestly.
- Grow from differences.
- Show respect and consideration.
- Make daily choices that enhance the relationship.
- Don't sweat the small stuff.

GUIDELINES FOR SUSTAINING CLOSE RELATIONSHIPS

The principles for healthy communication with friends and romantic partners echo the basic principles of good interpersonal communication that we've discussed in preceding chapters. You should be aware that your self-concept and your perceptions influence how you interpret interaction with intimates. It's also important to create a confirming climate by being open, spontaneous, empathic, equal, and nonevaluative. Keeping love and commitment alive for a lifetime is one of the greatest challenges we all face. In addition, you should keep in mind what you have learned about using verbal and nonverbal communication effectively, including when you discuss emotions. Finally, managing conflict constructively is important in all relationships. In addition to these general principles, we can identify six specific guidelines for satisfying communication between friends and romantic partners.

Engage in Dual Perspective

As in all interpersonal relationships, dual perspective is important. To be a good friend and partner we must understand and accept the other's perspectives, thoughts, and feelings. As we've noted before, accepting another person's perspective is not the same as agreeing with it. The point is to understand what the other feels and thinks and to accept that as a reality. Dual perspective helps us to understand others on their terms, not ours.

Two communication principles help us avoid misinterpreting our friends and lovers. First, it's useful to ask questions to find out what others mean. You might ask of a friend, "Why would you want to go out when I said I needed support?" This would allow your friend to explain that he or she was trying to support you in his or her own way by coming up with an activity to divert you from your problems.

Second, we should explain, or translate, our own feelings and needs so that our partners understand what would feel supportive to us. You could say, "What

Apply the Idea

COMMUNICATING NEEDS CLEARLY

Below are three scenarios that describe interactions in which a friend or lover does not initially give the desired response. For each one, write out what you could say to clarify what is wanted.

1. *You just found out that your car needs two new tires and alignment, and you don't have any extra cash. Worrying about money is the last thing you want to do now, with everything else on your mind. You see a friend and tell him what's happened. He says, "Sit down, let's talk about it." You don't want to talk—you want to get your mind off the problem.*

   You say: ______________________________

2. *You are unhappy because your romantic partner is transferring to a university 600 km away. You know that you'll miss each other and you're also worried that the relationship might not survive distance. A friend calls and you mention your concerns. In response, she says, "You can handle this. Just make sure that the two of you have e-mail accounts, and you'll be fine." Although you'd like to believe this, it seems like empty reassurance to you. You'd rather have some help sorting through your feelings.*

   You say: ______________________________

3. *Your live-in partner tells you about being really worried about the job market. As you listen you hear several things: worry about making a living, uncertainty about where you will be living, and doubts about self-worth. You say to your partner, "Sounds as if you are feeling pretty overwhelmed by all of this. Maybe it would help if we took one piece of the problem at a time." Your partner lets out a frustrated sigh and replies, "I don't want to analyze every bit and piece!" You're not sure what it is that your partner wants and how to help.*

   You say: ______________________________

Jack Hollingsworth/Photodisc/Getty Images

would help me most right now is to have a sympathetic ear. Could we just stay in and talk about the problem?" If we make our needs clear, we're more likely to get the kind of support we value.

Communicate Honestly

Honesty is one of the most important gifts friends can give each other. Even when honesty is less than pleasant or not what we think we want to hear, we count on it from friends and loving partners. In fact, people believe that honest feedback is what sets real friends apart from others (Burleson & Samter, 1994). Sometimes it's difficult to be honest with friends and partners. Yet, if we can't count on our friends for honest feedback, then where can we turn for truthfulness? The following three guidelines are helpful for communicating honestly on difficult issues. First, describe your true feelings without condemning the other. Second, tell your friend or partner that you will offer support and love whatever the decision. Finally, suggest that there may be more options than the ones he or she sees.

Many people make the mistake of confusing support with saying only nice things that others want to hear. Yet, this is not the essence of support. The key is caring enough to look out for a person's welfare. Parents discipline children and set limits because they care about their children's long-term welfare. Colleagues who want to help each other give honest, often critical, feedback on work so that others can improve. Romantic partners who are committed tell each other when they perceive problems or when the other isn't being one's best self.

We can be supportive and loving while being honest, but to be less than honest is to betray the trust placed in us. Honesty is part of what it means to care genuinely about another. Although it may be easier to tell friends or lovers what they want to hear or only nice things, genuine friendship and intimacy include honest feedback and candid talk.

Grow from Differences

A third principle for forming rich relationships is to be open to diversity in people. As we learned in Chapter 5, Western culture encourages polarized thinking. We have been socialized to think in either–or terms: either she's like me or she's not; either he acts like I do or he's wrong; either they support me as I want to be supported or they're not real friends. The problem with this either–or thinking is that it sharply limits interpersonal growth.

Egocentric mindsets and either–or thinking limit our horizons. We can't learn and grow if we reject what and who is different simply because they're different. Most of us tend to choose friends and romantic partners who are like us. We feel more immediately comfortable with those who share our values, attitudes, backgrounds, and communication rules. But if we restrict our close relationships to people like us, we miss out on the fascinating variety of people and relationships that are possible. It does take more time and effort to understand and become comfortable with individuals who differ from us, but the dividends of doing so can be exceptional. Forming friendships and entering committed romantic relationships with diverse people facilitates both your growth as an individual and the richness of your interpersonal world.

Show Respect and Consideration

For friendship and romantic intimacy to remain healthy and satisfying, partners need to demonstrate continuously that they value and respect each other. As obvious as this guideline seems, many people don't follow it. Sometimes we treat strangers with more respect and kindness than we offer our closest friends and romantic partners. It's easy to take for granted a person who is a continuing part of our life and to be less loving, respectful, and considerate than we should be.

Communication scholars Gottman, Katz, and Hooven (1996) identify four behaviours that can damage a relationship. They are contempt for the other, constant criticism, defensiveness, and stonewalling or withdrawal.

Gottman and his colleagues focused their research largely on married couples, but the damaging behaviours carry over to friendships and, as we will see in the next chapter, to work relationships.

Consideration and respect don't magically infuse relationships just because we know about interpersonal communication skills, such as those we've discussed in this book. For a respectful, confirming climate to exist, partners must practise effective interpersonal communication in the relationship. We should be as mindful of good communication when we enter a dialogue with close friends and established romantic partners as when we talk with casual acquaintances.

Friends and romantic partners should be respectful of each other, particularly when discussing problems and complaints. Disagreement is natural and often constructive, but how we disagree with a friend or partner is critical. Studies of marriages reveal differences between how satisfied and dissatisfied spouses talk about complaints and problems. Satisfied couples assert grievances and express anger and disagreement. Dissatisfied couples, however, communicate criticism, contempt, and sometimes disgust (Gottman & Carrère, 1994). It would be appropriate for Dimitra to tell Simon, "I feel angry when you smoke in the house because the smell bothers me." However, it would be personally disrespectful for Dimitra to say, "Smoking is a filthy, repulsive habit. Every time you light a cigarette you look revolting." The first statement is a civil complaint about a behaviour; the second statement is a vicious attack on Simon's personal worth.

Both our relationships and our self-respect are at stake in how we act toward close friends and intimate partners. As we learned in Chapter 1, communication is irreversible. Harsh words and personal insults cannot be taken back once we've said them. Neither can we retract sneers, scowls, and other nonverbal behaviours that express contempt. Because we cannot undo communication or its impact, we need to be mindful of what we say and how we say it.

CONCEPTS AT A GLANCE

Four Damaging Behaviours in Close Relationships

- Contempt
- Criticism
- Defensiveness
- Stonewalling (withdrawal)

Make Daily Choices That Enhance Closeness and Intimacy

Perhaps the most important guideline for sustaining close relationships is to be aware that they are creative projects that reflect the choices partners make. Relationships are not things we enter but processes we create and continuously refine. Realizing that we are choice makers enables us to take responsibility for our choices and how they chart the course of intimacy.

Student Voices

Jackson:

One of the things I love most about Meleika is the way she starts each day. Before getting out of bed, she reaches over and kisses my cheek. Then she gets up and showers while I sneak a little more shuteye. When I get up, the first thing she always says is, "Morning, love." That is such a great way to start each day. Even after five years of marriage, she starts each day by letting me know I matter.

The relationships we create reflect a series of personal choices. Although we are not always aware that we are making choices, we continuously choose who we will be and what kind of relationships we will fashion. Intimate partners and close friends choose to sustain closeness or let it wither, to build climates that are open or closed and defensive, to rely on constructive or destructive communication to deal with conflict, to fulfill or betray trust, and to enhance or diminish each other's self-concept.

Too often we focus on large choices such as whether to commit, how to manage a serious conflict, or how to celebrate an anniversary. As important as major choices are, they don't make up the basic fabric of a relationship (Wood, 1995c). Instead, undramatic, day-to-day choices sculpt the quality of intimacy. Do you listen mindfully to a partner or friend when you are tired? Do you continue to invest in intimacy after the initial euphoria has waned? Do you care enough about a relationship to work through crises and conflicts? Do you neglect your partner when you've had a rough day? Do you exert the effort to use dual perspective so that you can understand your friend on her or his terms?

Seemingly small choices like these shape the quality of intimacy and the individuals in it. Although they appear insignificant, our ordinary, daily choices weave the basic fabric of our close relationships. By being aware of the impact of our "small" choices, we can make ones that continuously enhance the quality of intimacy.

Don't Sweat the Small Stuff

Samuel Johnson once remarked that most friendships die not because of major violations and problems but because of small slights and irritations that slowly destroy closeness. Johnson's point is well taken. Certainly, we are going to be irritated by a number of qualities and habits of others. If you are a punctual person, you might be annoyed by a friend who is chronically late. If you are a tidy person (or a neatness fanatic), you might be bothered by your live-in partner leaving the toothpaste cap off the tube. Feeling annoyance is normal in all relationships. What we do with that feeling, however, can make the difference between sustaining a relationship and suffocating it.

One insight into how to let go of small irritations comes from what we've learned about perception. Knowing that perceptions are subjective, you might remind yourself not to fixate on aspects of a friend or intimate that you dislike or find bothersome. There's a big difference between acknowledging irritations and letting them preoccupy us. Is the lateness really more significant than all that you value in your friend? Do your lover's good qualities compensate for the toothpaste mess in the bathroom? You can exercise some control over your perceptions and the weight you attach to them.

Monitoring attributions can also help us avoid sweating the small stuff. You will feel very differently about your best friends or romantic partners if you define irritating behaviour as beyond their control instead of something they are doing to annoy you. It is also important to consider that you may be projecting the very qualities in your own personality that you do not like onto your friends or partners. Perhaps it is your own lateness or your own messiness that bothers you.

Accepting our own failings and those of our partners and responding with grace to small irritations goes a long way to creating harmony in relationships. A valuable practice when the "small stuff" is the focus of conflict between friends and especially live-in partners is to consider that the real issues are not identified yet and the fighting over the toothpaste is simply a cover-up for what is really troubling you.

Chapter Summary

In this chapter, we focused on the dynamics of two kinds of close relationships: friendships and committed romantic relationships. We have seen that close relationships are typified by a willingness to invest, intimacy that is established through dialogue, and intimacy that is established through doing, acceptance, trust, and support, and in the specific case of romantic relationships, passion and commitment. We considered the rules of friendship that are often unspoken and culturally bound. We then examined the development of close relationships through three stages; growth, navigation, and finally deterioration.

Our discussion then focused on six styles of loving; the primary styles of *eros*, *storge*, and *ludus* followed by the secondary styles of *pragma*, *mania*, and *agape*. This led us to examine the challenges inherent in sustaining close relationships. These challenges were identified as either internal or external tensions. The internal tensions were relational dialectics, diverse communication styles, managing sex, and avoiding violence and abuse. The external tensions included competing demands, personal change, surviving distance, and ensuring equity.

We then concluded the chapter with guidelines for communicating effectively with friends and romantic partners. The behaviours for effective communication fell into six helpful categories: engaging in dual perspective, communicating honestly, growing from differences, showing respect and consideration, making daily choices that enhance relationships, and finally, ignoring the small irritations in our relationships. Following these guidelines as well as others identified in previous chapters should enhance your ability to create satisfying friendships and romantic relationships that can stand the test of time.

Key Concepts

- agape
- commitment
- committed romantic relationships
- dyadic breakdown
- dyadic phase
- environmental spoiling
- equity
- eros
- everyday interactions
- explorational communication
- external tensions
- friends of the heart
- friends of the road
- grave dressing
- individuality
- intensifying communication
- internal tensions
- intimacy
- intrapsychic phase
- invitational communication
- ludus
- mania
- navigating
- passion
- placemaking
- pragma
- relational culture
- relational dialectics
- revising communication
- rituals
- social phase
- social support
- storge

For Further Thought and Discussion

1. Think about a friendship you have with a person of your gender and a friendship you have with a person of the other gender. To what extent does each friendship conform to the gender patterns described in this chapter?
2. Review the rules of friendship presented in this chapter. Do these rules show up in your friendships? Are there other rules that you would add based on your personal experiences with friendship?

3. Do you have any long-distance friends? How far away are they? How often do you see them in person? How do you manage to maintain the friendship across the distance?
4. Use your InfoTrac College Edition to read the table of contents for the last year's issues of *Sex Roles*. Read studies that focus on differences and similarities in how women and men engage in close relationships. Are the findings from articles you read consistent with what you've learned in this chapter?
5. Use your InfoTrac®College Edition to look up current information on marriages and divorces in Canada. Access the most recent Statistics Canada census. Can you find statistics on how many people married in the most recent year for which there is a report? What was the average age of women and men who married? How many marriages were first, second, or third marriages? How many divorces were reported in the most recent year for which information is available? Is there information on the average length of marriages that end in divorce?
6. If you have a current romantic partner, can you identify her or his love style? How does it fit with your own love style? Does understanding love styles give you any new insights into dynamics in your relationship?
7. This chapter discussed some gender differences in romantic relationships. Do the differences identified by researchers apply to your own relationships? How do you see gender operating in your romantic relationships?

Chapter 12

Relationships at Work

Ryan McVay/PhotoDisc/Getty Images

Every human has four endowments—self-awareness, conscience, independent will, and creative imagination. These give us the ultimate human freedom ... the power to choose, to respond, to change.

You can't talk your way out of a situation you behave yourself into. ... In the last analysis, what we are communicates far more eloquently than anything we say or do.

I'm convinced that we can write and live our own scripts more than most people will acknowledge. I also know the price that must be paid. It's a real struggle to do it. It requires visualization and affirmation. It involves living a life of integrity, starting with making and keeping promises, until the whole human personality, the senses, the thinking, the feeling, and the intuition are ultimately integrated and harmonized.

—Stephen Covey (1989)

Most of us will spend a large portion of our lives at work. Almost all of those jobs will require us to relate to and communicate with others. The people that inhabit our workplace can include employers, colleagues and co-workers, clients, patients or customers, and the people of other organizations or agencies related to our place of business. We may develop close personal connections with some of these people that approximate the I–Thou relationships we discussed in Chapter 1. We may develop cordial I–You relationships with people we interact with daily, and we may have impersonal I–It relationships with others. Each of these relationships is managed differently. Many of the principles of good interpersonal relationships we have discussed so far will apply to the workplace. There are, however, some important differences.

In this chapter we will examine the communication skills required in the Canadian workplace, the nature of workplace relationships and how they differ from other interpersonal relationships, how communication is established through climate and culture, and the particular challenges and skills of working in teams. Our discussion will then focus on the challenges of communicating effectively in the workplace with particular focus on the conflict issues of dealing with difficult people and harassment. We will conclude with guidelines for improving communication in the workplace to ensure a satisfying work environment.

THE IMPORTANCE OF COMMUNICATION IN THE WORKPLACE

The concept of work can encompass an extremely broad range of tasks and responsibilities, but there is one activity that is common to virtually every job you might think of: communication.

In most jobs, communication is an essential part of day-to-day activity, as well as a defining feature of the settings where work takes place. We interact with others to obtain information, to offer our products and provide services, to share ideas, to make decisions, and to coordinate our activities with others. Even in highly technical positions, the need to interact with others is a critical aspect of getting the work done. For almost all of us, therefore, interpersonal communication is one of the most important work-related skills we can develop.

Leadership authority Stephen Covey highlights communication skills as critical to effectiveness in the workplace (1991). Indeed, employers increasingly insist that communication skills are a basic requirement for most jobs, and that demonstrations of communication expertise, particularly in teamwork, are a key basis for professional advancement. Table 12.1 highlights the importance of communication skills in the modern workplace.

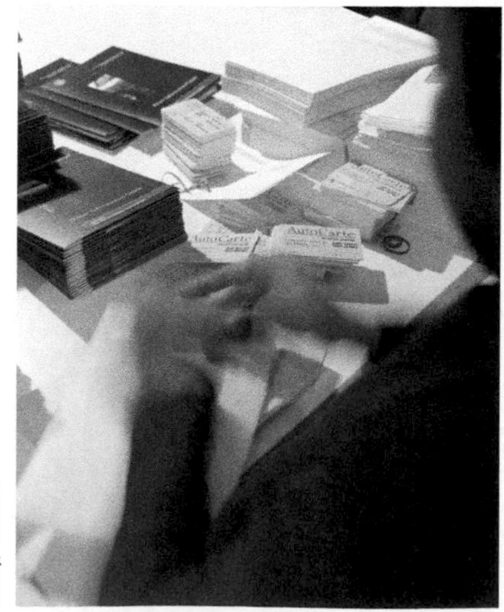
Alamy/GetStock

Even monotonous work is tolerable when there is a climate of respect and team support.

THE NATURE OF WORKPLACE RELATIONSHIPS

Relationships in the workplace are unique. Unlike romantic relationships or friendships, the investments are more about keeping your job and making a satisfying work environment than about sustaining a long-term relationship. People who report having the most satisfying work relationships describe many of the qualities that we have come to enjoy and value in our close relationships. But good working relationships, because of the common focus of accomplishing tasks and striving for the same goal, can be simply

TABLE 12.1

EMPLOYABILITY SKILLS PROFILE: THE CRITICAL SKILLS REQUIRED OF THE CANADIAN WORKFORCE

Academic Skills	**Personal Management Skills**	**Teamwork Skills**
Those skills that provide the basic foundation to get, keep, and progress on a job and to achieve the best results	The combination of skills, attitudes, and behaviours required to get, keep, and progress on a job and to achieve the best results	Those skills needed to work with others on a job and to achieve the best results
Canadian employers need a person who can:	*Canadian employers need a person who can demonstrate:*	*Canadian employers need a person who can:*
Communicate • Understand and speak the languages in which business is conducted • Listen to understand and learn • Read, comprehend, and use written materials, including graphs, charts, and displays • Write effectively in the languages in which business is conducted	**Positive Attitudes and Behaviours** • Self-esteem and confidence • Honesty, integrity, and personal ethics • A positive attitude toward learning, growth, and personal health • Initiative, energy, and persistence to get the job done	**Work with Others** • Understand and contribute to the organization's goals • Understand and work within the culture of the group • Plan and make decisions with others and support the outcomes • Respect the thoughts and opinions of others in the group • Exercise "give and take" to achieve group results • Seek a team approach as appropriate • Lead when appropriate, mobilizing the group for high performance
Think • Think critically and act logically to evaluate situations, solve problems, and make decisions • Understand and solve problems involving mathematics and use the results • Use technology, instruments, tools, and information systems effectively • Access and apply specialized knowledge from various fields (e.g., skilled trades, technology, physical sciences, arts, and social sciences)	**Responsibility** • The ability to set goals and priorities in work and personal life • The ability to plan and manage time, money, and other resources to achieve goals • Accountability for actions taken	
Learn • Continue to learn for life	**Adaptability** • A positive attitude toward change • Recognition of and respect for people's diversity and individual differences • The ability to identify and suggest new ideas to get the job done creatively	

Reprinted with permission of the Corporate Council on Education: The National Business and Education Centre, The Conference Board of Canada, 255 Smyth Road, Ottawa, Ontario K1H 8M7. Copies in English or French can be obtained by calling 1-866-711-2262 or (613) 526-3280, or by faxing (613) 526-4857.

civil and still satisfying. There are also elements in our work relationships that are not present in our other relationships. We will examine four elements that affect communication in the workplace: power, fear of reprisal, task demands, and technology.

CONCEPTS AT A GLANCE

Four Elements of the Workplace That Influence Communication

1. Power
2. Fear of reprisal
3. Task demands
4. Technology

Elements Affecting Communication in the Workplace

Work relationships are not always equal. Regardless of your personal feelings for your boss or your outside-of-work relationship with him or her, you are responsible to that boss and he or she has power over you. Similarly, others may report to you and regardless of your relationship with them, you have power over them. We don't give or get performance appraisals from our friends, lovers, family members, or neighbours.

This difference in power affects our behaviour. First, we may be reluctant to be assertive, for example, for fear of reprisal or job loss. Second, at other times, we recognize the impact of power when decisions are made without our input. The workplace is not always democratic or egalitarian. Third, tasks sometimes demand that our personal feelings be submerged or our issues bracketed in order to meet deadlines. Fourth, technology has affected our workplace relationships by increasing isolation and reliance on electronic means for communicating.

Power

Researchers into leadership and power identify different kinds of power that occur in groups (Brown, 1988; Johnson & Johnson, 1991; Jordan, 1996). The most common kinds of **power** that a leader or group member has are coercive, reward, expert, legitimate, referent, networking, and helplessness (see Table 12.2).

TABLE 12.2

KINDS OF POWER

Kind of Power	Description
Coercive	The ability to punish or withhold resources
Reward	The ability to reward
Expert	Owning special knowledge or expertise
Legitimate	Having authority by virtue of position
Referent	Having personal charisma and charm
Networking	Knowing the right people
Helplessness	Ability to get others to do one's bidding by claiming helplessness or inability

Source: Adapted from French, J., and Raven, B. (1959). The bases of social power. In D. Cartwright (Ed.), *Studies in social power.* Ann Arbor: University of Michigan. Reprinted with permission.

We are often not aware of the power we hold over others. It is sometimes not power we wish to have. For example, teachers must give grades. This is at the same time both reward and coercive power. A co-worker with great technical skill is suddenly a leader in an electrical blackout. This is expert power.

Fear of Reprisal

As we discussed in Chapter 10, the most appropriate response to conflict is assertiveness. This ensures the best possibility for a win–win solution for both parties. In the workplace, however, it may not be wise to be assertive if speaking your mind endangers your job. You are then forced to make an ethical decision about what you are willing to live with and at what price. This is a key difference between workplace relationships and other interpersonal relationships.

Sometimes, because of the power of unions and collective agreements, your job may not be threatened, but the quality of your workplace may be altered. A disgruntled boss could give you the least desirable tasks or "forget" to invite you to the staff party. This kind of passive-aggressive conflict style would be unpleasant to be around but not a breach of a contract.

Task Demands

It isn't always appropriate to bring up irritations or inequities when the tasks required of a work team have stringent restrictions on them. It isn't always timely to engage your team members in discussion about how you feel or where the team is going when task demands are very heavy. In these circumstances, you must bracket personal issues until the task is completed. This is not usually the case in our close relationships. Indeed, the sooner we clear the air on issues that concern us with our friends and partners, the better. In the workplace, we must balance the needs of the people with the demands of the tasks. We'll discuss this in greater length later.

Technology

The increase in new kinds of communication technologies means that the work space and the workday have changed considerably. Many workers are in constant contact with their offices with the aid of computers, laptops, e-mail, fax machines, telephones, and scanners. Telecommunications not only break down distance barriers between the office and employee, but also between the office and the customer. Online shopping has opened up a whole new market for businesses. This technology also has a large impact on service delivery, especially in the health care field. Telemedicine and telehealth allow residents in rural or remote areas of Canada to access primary health care consultation through conferencing technology.

An increasingly large segment of the workforce are telecommuters, who on the one hand enjoy the freedom of being able to work from home or while travelling, but who on the other hand can experience isolation and an invasion of privacy by being on call all the time. The loss of the human element of the workplace, the sense of belonging to a team with shared visions and goals led futurist John Naisbitt to entitle his 1999 book *High Tech High Touch: Technology and Our Search for Meaning.*

The eye scans and fingerprinting techniques that we watch on *CSI* are becoming reality through the technology of biometric systems that identify a person by features such as the retina or iris, hand, fingerprint, or voice. Employers value this method of verification of employees in the workplace because it eliminates stolen or lost identity cards and also keeps accurate track of employee movements. Newer research is exploring ways to identify employees by walking gait and facial recognition.

Although biometric monitoring appeals to businesses, it may seem too invasive to most employees according to University of Toronto researcher David Zweig (2002). He found that workplace monitoring often proves stressful because people reject the notion of monitoring as a violation of their psychological boundaries.

Communication Notes

HEALTH CARE VIRTUAL NETWORK LAUNCHED

On June 26, 2008, the Health Services Virtual Organization (HSVO) under its network-enabled platforms program was launched (CRC, 2008). The goal of HSVO is to create a virtual network designed to link the most advanced medical resources—data, devices, and healthcare experts—to students and health care professionals at widely dispersed locations.

When completed, users will have access to a state-of-the-art virtual network for use in training, patient treatment, and research collaboration. Because the network is "virtual" rather than being based on fixed connections, users can form and create the network connections they require to suit their immediate task, whether that is an anatomy class at dispersed locations or an interaction with a "virtual patient" located at a server in a distant city.

Among the challenges faced to operate such a network is that the resources, whether databases, experts, or interactive surgical mannequins, may be located thousands of kilometres apart. To provide the speed and interactivity the users demand thus requires large amounts of dedicated bandwidth simultaneously linking multiple servers to the users' computers.

To further complicate things, the users are experts in medicine, not computers. They require access to complex services and tools—HD videoconferencing, Canadian Medical Association guidelines, virtual patient simulation—but this access must be seamless and simple, the result of a few clicks of a mouse. Such access has been provided.

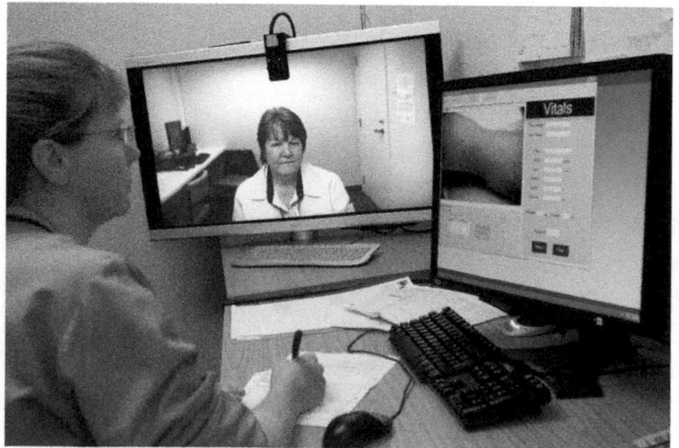

Alamy/GetStock

Technology overcomes geography (telemedicine in Ontario).

Communication Climate and Culture

Organizational scholars have long believed that the overall quality of communication and working relationships in a company has a major impact on both individual and organizational performance. In studying this idea, two concepts have been advanced to help characterize the overall nature of these environments: communication climate and organizational culture.

The overall character and quality of the communication environment of an organization is called the **communication climate**. It is similar to the concept of relationship climates discussed in Chapter 9, although in this case it applies to a larger social group. The climate of a workplace will decide the quality of the communication that takes place there. Interpersonal climate is either confirming (positive, respectful, and supportive) or disconfirming (negative, sometimes punitive, disrespectful, or overly critical). Remember that recognition, acknowledgment, and endorsement are the three key behaviours that establish a confirming climate.

A confirming climate can be established in the ways we greet, involve, and acknowledge the contributions of others. For example, Elias might say to Jane as she enters a meeting, "Glad you could join us, Jane. We were just talking about tomorrow's plans" (recognition). Further evidence of a positive climate is found in statements like "I think Jane was trying to say something. Go ahead, Jane" (acknowledgment) and "That's a very interesting idea. It's an inspired solution. I'm with Jane" (endorsement).

> **Student Voices**
>
> **Keven:**
>
> I am a computer programmer and my job requires me to always be at my desk in front of the monitor. Usually when I need to make any announcements, e-mail is my first choice of communication. There is little physical contact during my day at work—communication occurs through the Internet. But my manager has emphasized the importance of interpersonal communication because we need to work as a team. The manager has arranged monthly group meetings, presentations, and conferences that we must attend to help us with our communication skills.

According to Gerald Goldhaber (1993), the communication climate of an organization is most strongly affected by (1) supportiveness: the degree to which communication relationships foster a sense of personal worth and importance; (2) participation: the degree to which employees feel they can influence decisions that affect them; (3) trust: the extent to which information sources are reliable and believable; (4) openness: the degree to which both supervisors and co-workers are open to participate in communication; and (5) **goal clarity**: the prospect of clear, attainable goals. Where these qualities exist to a high degree, employees tend to have higher levels of job satisfaction. It is unclear if positive climates always lead to increased performance; however, research does indicate that this is true in many cases.

More stress is created in the workplace by interpersonal conflict than by hard work.

Without these five qualities, stressors build. Stressors in the workplace are rarely from the hard work demanded of us. The greatest stressors come from interpersonal conflict with those with whom we are forced to interact. See the Communication Notes feature "Warring Egos, Toxic Individuals, Feeble Leadership."

Organizational Culture

The concept of **organizational culture** provides an alternative way of characterizing the overall quality of an organization. Adapted from anthropology, the concept of culture refers to the overall pattern of beliefs, values, and practices that uniquely characterize a specific social group. Just as individual societies can have unique cultures, organizations have distinct ways of doing things that allow us to identify each as having a unique character. Some companies have a family culture that is expressed by employees' interest in each other's lives. Other organizations have a down-to-business culture reflected by a lot of task communication and little social talk. In each case, the organizational culture is both a reflection and a product of the communication that takes place.

Communication Notes

WARRING EGOS, TOXIC INDIVIDUALS, FEEBLE LEADERSHIP

In a 2009 study, Psychometrics Canada Ltd. identified the causes and effects of workplace conflict in Canada. In many cases, conflict has severely crippling effects on productivity, staff engagement, and working relationships. However, the report also found that when properly managed, conflict actually benefits organizations, leading to major innovations and better solutions to problems.

The study, which polled over 350 human resource (HR) professionals across Canada, identified the causes and effects of workplace conflict. According to the report, almost all HR professionals (99 percent) deal with conflict. The most common causes of conflict are warring egos and personality clashes (86 percent), poor leadership (73 percent), lack of honesty (67 percent), stress (64 percent), and clashing values (59 percent). These conflicts frequently result in negative outcomes. Three out of four (76 percent) have seen conflict result in personal insults and attacks, and 43 percent have witnessed someone being fired. In addition, 81 percent of those surveyed have seen conflict lead to someone leaving the organization, and 77 percent have seen it result in sickness or absence.

The study also uncovered a serious gap between the importance of conflict management skills and the effectiveness of current leaders. Nine out of ten rate the ability to handle conflict as either a very important or critical leadership skill. However, 18 percent of those surveyed indicated that current management and leadership are not at all effective at dealing with conflict, and 63 percent said that they are only somewhat effective.

CONFLICT CAN HAVE BENEFITS IF MANAGED WELL

The study also showed that properly managed conflict benefits organizations. HR professionals have seen conflict lead to better solutions to problems and challenges (57 percent), major innovations (21 percent), increased motivation (31 percent), a better understanding of others (77 percent), and higher work team performance (40 percent).

Recommendations for managers to deal more effectively with conflict included: manage toxic individuals more firmly (75 percent), provide more clarity about their expectations (77 percent), and model appropriate behaviour (84 percent). These recommendations seem to be self-evident, suggesting that when it comes to dealing with conflict, some managers are avoiding an important part of their jobs. If organizations are to turn conflict into improved professional relationships and better organizational performance, they must invest the time to train and coach their employees to deal with different point of views, personalities, and work styles.

To read the complete report, go to www.psychometrics.com/en-us/articles/conflict_study.htm.

CONCEPTS AT A GLANCE

The Elements That Define and Establish Culture in the Workplace

- Vocabulary
- Hierarchical
- Gendered
- Rites and rituals
- Soul

Communication and organizational culture are intertwined. Communication creates, sustains, and sometimes alters organizational culture. At the same time, the culture of business shapes how employees communicate (Pacanowsky, 1989; Van Maanen & Barley, 1985). Let's examine three kinds of communication that express organizational cultures: vocabulary, rites and rituals, and soul in the workplace.

Apply the Idea

What is the culture of your school? Does it portray itself as an institution of higher learning, a place for personal and intellectual growth, or a school devoted to technical excellence? Can you locate documents that express the proclaimed identity of your school?

Now identify specific practices that you and other students engage in that reflect and sustain the identity your school claims to maintain. Going to classes, making notes, studying, taking exams, and so forth are all activities that support a campus's identity as a place in which learning is the preeminent goal.

Vocabulary

Just as the language of an ethnic culture reflects and expresses its history, norms, values, and identity, so does the language of an organization. We will examine the impact of two kinds of language that influence the culture of an organization: hierarchical and gendered language.

Monkey Business Images/Shutterstock

HIERARCHICAL LANGUAGE Many organizations and professions have vocabularies that distinguish levels of status among members. The military, for example, relies on language that continuously acknowledges rank ("Yes sir," "chain of command"), which reflects that status, respect, and privilege are connected to official rank. Rank is also communicated by unequal terms of address. For instance, a corporate CEO may use first names ("Good morning, Jan") when speaking to employees, but unless given permission to use the CEO's first name, lower-status members of a company typically refer to the CEO as Mister, Miss, Sir, or Ma'am. Instructors generally use students' first names, whereas students tend to use titles to address their teachers: Dr. Armstrong, Ms. Armstrong, Mr. Armstrong, or Professor Armstrong.

GENDER DIFFERENCES IN LANGUAGE Perhaps because men have historically outnumbered women in the workplace, language in many organizations emphasizes interests and experiences more typical of men than women. Consider the number of phrases in the working world that are taken from sports (home run, ballpark estimate, touchdown, game plan, team player, starting lineup), military life (battle plan, mount a campaign, plan of attack, under fire, the big guns, defensive move, offensive strike), and typically male sexual references (hit on a person, screw someone, stick it to them, a person has real balls).

Because masculine language legitimizes men's experiences more than those of women, it may foster cultures in which some women feel unwelcome or uncomfortable. Much has been done to emphasize

Student Voices

Daria:

Language really communicates status in the medical world. I worked six years as a nurse in a large hospital, and I never had a doctor call me Ms. Jenkins or address me as Nurse Jenkins. The doctors always used our first names or referred to us as "nurse." But all of us had to call them Dr. So-and-So. And the doctors didn't even bother to learn the names of orderlies and technicians—they just called them "Hey you."

Communication Notes

VENUS, MARS, AND WORKPLACE COMMUNICATION

by Carol Kinsey Goman

We know that men have a different workplace communication style than women—but does "different" mean better?

Well, yes.

And no.

There are obvious strengths and weaknesses in the communication styles of both genders. Based on a recent research project, in which I collected responses from 387 employees and managers in the United States, Canada, and Europe, I found that both sexes identified the same set of strengths and weaknesses in themselves and each other. ...

As you look at the findings below, notice how much of what people call "communication style" is determined not by the words someone is speaking, but what their body is saying. ...

Top Communication Strengths for Females

1. Ability to read body language and pick up nonverbal cues.
2. Good listening skills.
3. Effective display of empathy.

Top Communication Strengths for Males

1. Physical presence.
2. Direct and to-the-point interactions.
3. Body language signals of power

Top Communication Weaknesses for Females

1. Overly emotional.
2. Meandering—won't get the point.
3. Not authoritative.

Top Communication Weaknesses for Males

1. Overly blunt and direct.
2. Insensitive to audience reactions.
3. Too confident in own opinion.

To best understand these findings, however, it's important to consider them in the context of workplace applications and implications.

For example, there is no "best" communication style for all workplace interactions. Women have the edge in collaborative environments (where listening skills, inclusive body language, and empathy are more highly valued), and men are seen to "take charge" more readily (and viewed as more effective in environments where decisiveness is critical).

In all cases, a strength turns into a weakness when overdone. (A female's collaborative style can come across as indecisive and a male's directness can be taken as callousness or disregard for other opinions.)

To a woman, good listening skills include making eye contact and reacting visually to the speaker. To a man, listening can take place with a minimum of eye contact and almost no nonverbal feedback. (Women often cite a lack of eye contact as evidence that their male boss "doesn't value my input."). ...

When a man nods, it means he agrees. When a woman nods, it means she is listening.

Female superiority in reading nonverbal signals during business meetings allows women to accurately assess coalitions and alliances just by tracking who is making eye contact with whom at certain critical points.

Men are judged to be better at monologue—women at dialogue.

Carol Kinsey Goman, Ph.D., is an executive coach and keynote speaker who addresses association, government, and business audiences around the world. Dr. Goman is the author of 10 business books. Her latest is *The Non-verbal Advantage—Secrets and Science of Body Language at Work*. She can reached at CGoman@CKG.com or www.NonverbalAdvantage.com.

Communication Notes

A man's ability to hold his emotions in check and to "keep a poker face"" is viewed as an advantage in business situations. A woman's tendency to show her feelings more outwardly in gestures and facial expressions is perceived as a weakness.

When a woman can't read the person she's talking to, it makes her anxious. Men's ability to mask their facial expressions causes uneasiness in women, who often perceive this as negative feedback. ...

As women make decisions, they tend to process and think of options out loud. Men process internally until they come up with a solution. This can lead to problems if a male thinks that the female's verbal brainstorming means that she's looking for approval rather than just thinking aloud.

Men's discomfort dealing with emotion leads them to believe that there needs to be a solution, rather than understanding that sometimes people just need to be heard. ...

Women are viewed as lacking authority when they try to avoid confrontation and conflict, when they are unnecessarily apologetic, when they are too focused on pleasing others, when they smile excessively or inappropriately, and when they discount their own ideas and achievements.

So Venus or Mars—whichever you are—the trick is to know when your communication style is an aid to success and also when it becomes a deterrent. Comparing your strengths and weaknesses to these generalized gender differences is one place to start. And enlarging your repertoire of communication skills, so you can employ strategies that are most effective under various circumstances, definitely gives you an advantage.

For the full text of this article, which appeared in the April 21, 2009, issue of the *Financial Post*, go to www.financialpost.com/executive/story.html?id=1518761.

more inclusive language in our society. See Table 12.3 for some of the changes that have improved the language of the workplace.

CONCEPTS AT A GLANCE

Four Rites of an Organization

- Rites of passage
- Rites of integration
- Rites of degradation
- Rites of enhancement

Rites and Rituals

Rites and rituals are communication practices that express organizational values and identity. **Rites** are dramatic, planned activities that bring together aspects of cultural ideology into a single event. Harrison Trice and Janice Beyer (1984) identify several kinds of organizational rites. Rites of passage mark entry into different levels in organizations. For example, promotions may be symbolized by larger offices with nicer artwork. Retirements may be acknowledged with banquets and laudatory speeches. Rites of integration affirm and enhance the sense of community in an organization. Holiday parties and annual picnics are common rites of integration.

Organizational cultures include rites that blame or praise individuals and teams. Rites of degradation punish employees and proclaim that the company does not approve of certain identities or activities.

Student Voices

Evangeline:

I had always had male supervisors in the agency I worked for until Julie was hired. On my first visit to her office, I expected the usual lighthearted banter and down-to-business attitude I had engaged in with all my supervisors. But instead, Julie asked me how I was doing and waited for an answer. I replied "Fine," as was our custom in the office. No one really wanted to know the answer. But Julie persisted and said, "No, how are you *really* doing?" I burst into tears. No one had ever asked me how I was really doing before and waited with interest for the answer. It was a breath of fresh air. I realized that feminine communication style was OK in the workplace.

TABLE 12.3

INCLUSIVE LANGUAGE OF THE WORKPLACE

Sexist Language	Gender-Neutral Language
Chairman	Chair, chairperson, chairwoman/chairman
Mailman/postman	Letter carrier
Waiter/waitress	Server
Steward/stewardess	Flight attendant
Secretary	Administrative assistant
Policeman	Officer
Fireman	Firefighter

CONCEPTS AT A GLANCE

Three Rituals of an Organization

1. Personal rituals
2. Social rituals
3. Task rituals

Firings and demotions are the most common degradation rites. Conversely, rites of enhancement praise individuals or teams who represent the organization's self-image. Schools that value teaching, for instance, bestow awards to faculty members who are especially gifted teachers. Many sales companies give awards for productivity (most sales of the month, quarter, year).

Rituals are forms of communication that occur regularly and that employees perceive as familiar and routine parts of organizational life. Rituals are less dramatic and more frequently performed than rites and don't bring together a number of aspects of organizational ideology into a single event. Rather, rituals are repeated communications that express a particular value or role definition. Personal, social, and task rituals are common in organizations.

Personal rituals are activities that individuals routinely engage in to define themselves. In their study of organizational cultures, Michael Pacanowsky and Nick O'Donnell-Trujillo (1983) noted that Lou Polito, the owner of a car company, opened all of the company's mail himself each day. Whenever possible, Polito hand-delivered mail to the divisions of his company to communicate his openness and his involvement with the day-to-day business.

Social rituals are standardized performances that affirm relationships among members of organizations. Some organizations have a company dining room to encourage socializing among employees. Others permit informal interaction during breaks. Tamar Katriel (1990) identified a social ritual of griping among Israelis. *Kiturim,* the name Israelis give to their griping, most often occurs during Friday night social events called *mesibot kiturim,* which means "gripe sessions." Some Jewish families engage in ritualized *kvetching,* which is personal griping that aims to air frustrations but not necessarily to resolve them. The point of the ritual is to complain, not to feel better.

Student Voices

Sharon:

We spend the first half hour or so at work every Monday complaining about what we have to get done that week. Even if we don't have a rough week ahead, we go through the motions, moaning and groaning. It's kind of like a bonding ceremony for us.

Task rituals help members of an organization perform their jobs. A special conference room may be reserved for strategy meetings. In their study of police, Pacanowsky and O'Donnell-Trujillo (1983) identified a ritual that officers are trained to perform when they stop traffic violators. The officers ask questions ("May I see your licence? Do you know why I stopped you? Do you know how fast you were going?") to size up motorists and to decide whether to give them a break.

Eileen points out how effective the rituals are prior to taking part in risky sports. The rituals become the vehicle to pass on values, acknowledge each member of the group, and cheer on the activity ahead.

prism68/Shutterstock

Working in the outdoor recreation industry presents many unusual challenges.

Soul in the Workplace

In 1996, Canadians Lesley Wright and Marti Smye wrote a book called *Civilizing the Workplace*. The book was about corporate abuse, and the authors painted a picture of abusive workplace cultures that they describe as *"soul destroying."* Despite all that we've learned in the past years, chronic job stress is still on the rise.

Soul can be defined as a sense of connectedness and meaning in one's life. In the workplace, it means having a deeper purpose than just receiving a paycheque—it means being regarded as a whole person with a brain, a heart, and a soul. The dilemma of the modern workplace is to not succumb to a world that ignores soul. If we do, we permit our jobs to drain and exhaust our human energies. Ways to bring soul into the workplace include seizing an opportunity for meaningful contribution, innovation, and learning. When the workplace allows for creativity and flexibility, when the communication between the working team is respectful and energetic, when there is opportunity to work with and relate to others in meaningful ways, when we can take part in shaping and actualizing a vision, then we have a sense of soul in our work.

Student Voices

Eileen:

Our white-water kayak instructor began every open-water session with a series of rituals that we all came to love. She would "raft us up" in a group and then each one of us would try our rolls. If successful, the group would all thump the tops of their boats and whoop loudly to signal support. Then we would pass a hug along the line of kayaks. This had an amazing effect of discharging some of our anxiety and making us laugh. The final ritual was a prayer to the "River God" to allow us safe passage over the surface. All of us, regardless of our religious beliefs, took part in this symbolic ritual because it focused our attention on the risks of the sport but also on the respect we owed the river.

In a number of ways, then, organizational cultures provide an important means of shaping communication in the workplace. Cultures provide a common set of rituals and practices that help to give voice to shared beliefs, values, and understanding. They help to define the relational environment of the organization, and to give shape to interactions within it. At the same time, everyday interactions within the organization contribute to the continued shaping and renewal of the culture itself. So, in a sense, communication is shaped by an organization's culture, but it is also the means by which the culture itself is expressed and continuously renewed.

Communicating in Groups and Teams

Groups and teams are central to professional life. Whether you are an attorney working with a litigation team, a health care professional in a health delivery unit, or a factory worker in a group assigned to reduce production time, working with others will probably be a part of your career. Your raises and advancement will likely depend significantly on how effectively you communicate in groups.

CONCEPTS AT A GLANCE

Four Advantages of Groups over Individuals

1. Groups bring a greater range of resources.
2. Groups are more thorough.
3. Groups bring more creativity to solutions.
4. Groups provide enhanced commitment to decisions.

Defining Groups and Teams

What is a group? Are six people standing in line for tickets a group? Are five individuals studying individual materials in a library a group? No—these examples describe collections of individuals, but not groups.

For a group to exist there must be interaction and interdependence among individuals. So, we can define a **group** as three or more individuals who interact over time, who depend on one another, and who communicate to reach a common goal. A **team** is a special kind of group that is brought together for a very specific task and is normally characterized by the distinct and complementary resources of members and by their strong sense of collective identity. Like all groups, teams involve interaction, interdependence, shared rules, and common goals. However, because they are formed with a particular purpose in mind, teams tend to consist of people with specialized and unique skills, and may develop a stronger sense of identity than is typical of most groups (Lumsden & Lumsden, 1997).

Why Organizations Rely on Groups

Organizations have increasingly turned to the use of groups because they offer a number of potential advantages over individuals working alone. For example, compared with individuals' work, groups can bring a far greater range of resources to a task. They have the potential to think through issues more thoroughly, bring heightened creativity to solutions, and often provide enhanced commitment to decisions (Wood, 1992a, 1997a; Yeatts & Hyten, 1998).

A group obviously exceeds any individual in terms of the ideas, perspectives, experiences, and expertise it has to solve a problem. While one member may know technical aspects of a product, another may understand market psychology, a third may be talented in advertising, and so forth. Health care teams consist of doctors, nurses, social workers, and other specialists who combine their knowledge to provide a better level of patient care.

Groups also tend to be more thorough than individuals, probably because members act as a check-and-balance system for each other. Issues one member doesn't understand, another member does; the details of a plan that bore one person interest another; the holes in a proposal that some members overlook are caught by others. Greater thoroughness by groups isn't simply the result of more people working, but reflects interaction among members. Discussion can promote critical and careful analysis because members are stimulated by each other's thinking (Wood, 1997a). **Synergy** is a special kind of energy that enlarges the efforts, talents, and strengths of individual members (Lumsden & Lumsden, 1997).

A third value of groups is that they are generally more creative than individuals. Again, the reason lies in the synergy of groups. When members know how to communicate effectively, they spark good ideas, integrative thinking, and creativity. Any individual eventually runs out of new ideas, but groups have an almost infinite generative ability. As members talk, they build on each other's ideas. They refine proposals and see new possibilities in each

Student Voices

Laura:

When the supervisor said all of us in my department were to meet together to come up with ideas for cutting costs, I thought it was silly. I thought it would be more efficient for each person to submit suggestions individually. But I was wrong. When my group started, each of us had one or two ideas. But the six of us came up with over 25 ideas after we'd talked awhile.

other's comments. The result is often a greater number of overall ideas and more creative solutions.

A final strength of groups is their ability to generate commitment to outcomes. The greater commitment fostered in groups arises from two sources. First, participation enhances loyalty to decisions. Thus, groups with balanced participation build commitment among members, which is especially important if members will be involved in implementing the decision. Second, groups are more likely than individuals to consider the points of view of various people needed to implement a decision. This is critical, since a decision can be sabotaged if the people affected feel their opinions were ignored.

Many of the strengths that groups offer are the result of members' abilities to combine their knowledge, their efforts, and their creativity into a single effort. The synergy that is created by group interaction is available, however, only when group members effectively communicate, share, and merge their ideas. The highest quality outcomes from groups are always the result of the highest quality communication.

Student Voices

Lance:

I used to belong to a creative writing group where all of us helped each other improve our writing. At first, all of us were equally vocal, and we aired different ideas. But then one member of the group had a story accepted by a big magazine, and suddenly we thought of her as a better writer than any of us. She didn't act any different, but we saw her as more accomplished, so when she said something everybody listened and nobody disagreed. It was like a wet blanket on our creativity because her opinion just carried too much weight once she got published.

The Limitations of Groups

Groups enjoy many advantages, but they also have very important limitations, and at times can even generate negative outcomes for organizations. Two of the most significant limitations of group discussion are the time required for group processes and the potential of the pressures of conformity that can interfere with critical, high-quality discussion.

Operating alone, a person can think through ideas efficiently and choose the one he or she considers to be best. In group discussion, however, time is needed so that all members have an opportunity to voice their ideas and respond to ideas put forward by others. Groups also need time to deliberate alternative courses of action. As a result, group discussion is not a wise choice for routine or trivial decisions, where the time required by a group would be wasted. When creativity and thoroughness are important, however, the time that groups require is well spent.

Groups also have the potential to suppress individuals and to encourage conformity. This can happen in two ways. First, pressure for conformity may exist when a majority of members have an opinion different than a minority of members or a single member. It is hard to maintain a point of view when most or all of your peers have a different one. In effective groups, however, all members understand and resist conformity pressures. They realize that the majority is sometimes wrong and the minority, even a single person, is sometimes right. Members have an ethical responsibility to encourage expression of diverse ideas and to foster open debate about different viewpoints.

Conformity pressures may also arise when one member is extremely charismatic or has greater power or prestige than other members. Even if that person is alone in a point of view, other members may conform. Conformity can occur even in the absence of a high-status person. Research on the phenomenon of *groupthink* has shown that ordinary decision-making groups can make extremely poor decisions, even with the presence of top-quality participants and information, when they allow conformity to override common sense (Janis, 1977).

CONCEPTS AT A GLANCE

Group Characteristics

- Groups manage task and maintenance functions.
- Groups go through specific stages of development.
- Members exhibit positive and negative group roles.
- Groups make decisions and solve problems.
- Leadership emerges.

Group Process

What happens when groups go to work? Researchers have found that group processes tend to have several stable characteristics, although the action is sometimes fast and furious. Groups experience both attention to task and attention to the maintenance of the people of the group. Groups tend to go through predictable stages of development. Group members exhibit specific group roles that are both productive and counterproductive to group functioning. Finally, decision making, problem solving, and leadership are all characteristics of groups. Let's examine each one of these group characteristics.

Task and Maintenance

One very consistent finding that students of group behaviour have found is a tendency for the focus of communication to shift back and forth between the task and the maintenance of the group itself. Clearly, in order for a group to work effectively, a good part of its energy has to be directed toward accomplishing its defined goals. However, group members also need to feel that they are included, that their contributions are valued, and that the group as a whole is functioning smoothly.

Although attention to the needs of group maintenance may not appear at first to contribute to the task, these needs permit individuals to develop trust toward the group as a whole and help the group to function smoothly. Groups that fail to look after maintenance needs tend to become ineffective, and often have to return to these important concerns before moving on with a task. Effective group leaders recognize the importance of balancing task and maintenance needs, and often intervene to ensure that these needs are equally met.

Communication Notes

THE FIVE C's OF MANAGING VIRTUAL TEAMS

by Jennifer Rasmussen

Your face-to-face kickoff meeting has just been deemed nonessential travel by the powers that be. The project, however, is just as essential as ever. The team members are scattered in offices all over the country. They've never met, seen, or heard each other, but they need to work as a unit. Getting them to gel together is your challenge.

Even managers who excel at teambuilding in a live environment can find themselves frustrated when faced with a virtual team; yet fostering a strong team dynamic among people who never meet face to face is fast becoming a necessary skill. These five essential best practices will help you do it.

COMMUNICATE

Communication is the most basic of management tools. ... You know you need to include your team in project planning. Your know you need to give timely feedback and immediate updates. But whatever your normal level of communication is, double it with your virtual team.

Clarity, frequency, and responsiveness are the keys. Experts will tell you that anywhere from 65 to 95 percent of communication is nonverbal. Yet for virtual team members, your words are often most or all of what they have to go on. ... So make sure your words are clear, and deliver them often... . [R]egular meetings via conference call or other technology are essential for virtual teams ... Keep the agenda posted electronically in an area the whole team can access, and encourage them to add to it. Finally, make answering your virtual team members' e-mails and phone calls a priority to make up for the fact that they can't drop by your desk or catch you in the hall with a quick question.

CHAT

This is not the same as communication. Communication is professional. Chatting is personal. ... [S]ome level of personal interaction is crucial for team bonding. Virtual teams don't have lunches together. They don't share water coolers. They can't see each other's desks. Chat cannot easily happen organically, so you need to provide a mechanism for it. Have a virtual pizza party: send a pizza to each location at the same time, and get together in an Internet chat session or conference call to gab. Call your team members once in a while just to catch up. There are countless creative ways to introduce chat into your team dynamics, but you must make a conscious effort to do so.

CHANGE IT UP

It's the wealth of technology that we have at our fingertips that makes virtual teaming possible. Telephone and e-mail are far from the only tools at your disposal. Instant messaging systems, collaboration software, group bulletin boards or discussion areas, and chat rooms are all useful for working and meeting together. ... Vary your methods of communicating, and learn which methods work best for which team members. Some people love e-mail; others prefer the phone. Finally, make sure you are using each type of technology appropriately for the purpose it's best suited to. If one e-mail has been forwarded and replied to several times among several people, you'd be better off moving the issue to a conference call or online discussion.

CUT OUT

One of the most often neglected pieces to building a virtual team is providing a safe place for interaction and discussion without the manager. Whether it's a regular conference call, a bulletin board, or a chat session, your team needs a "staff room" that isn't accessible to you. ... Some managers are uncomfortable creating a space that they can't get into, but if you ignore this need you not only eliminate a chance for a more free exchange of ideas, you risk ending up with a team that's bonded well with you, but not with one another.

CELEBRATE

... Accomplishments must be acknowledged and celebrated as a group when possible and appropriate. There are literally hundreds of ways to achieve this. Take the time to create a periodic newsletter and e-mail it or post it; be sure to have a section in it for accolades. Institute a peer-to-peer award system. Send virtual greeting cards or gift certificates from any of the dozens of websites dedicated to these purposes. Send them each a jar of jam when you reach a milestone. However you do it, just make sure you do.

The principles of managing virtual teams well are not much different from the principles of managing anybody or anything well. Apply two more Cs to these five: consistent and conscious. Practice them that way, and it can be virtually painless.

To read the entire 2002 article by Jennifer Rasmussen, go to www.employeedevelopmentsolutions.com/freearticles/virtualteams.htm.

Stages of Group Development

Another consistent observation of group research is that groups pass through regular stages as they mature over time. Although several different formulations have been proposed, the general pattern demonstrates an initial period in which individuals feel each other out and assess if and how they will decide to accept group membership. This is typically followed by a stage of conflict, when individuals vie for control of group topics and procedures; resolution of the conflict finally leads to a period of productive operation, when the group agrees on its own procedures and norms of interaction and is able to work together effectively. These stages are often revisited whenever the group encounters a difficulty or accepts a new member.

Knowledge of these stages of development can help group leaders and members through difficult transitions. In each stage, the group must ensure that certain task or maintenance needs are met. An effective leader can recognize these needs and provide what the group needs to effectively focus its energy and move forward (Sept, 1981).

Effective Member Roles

Throughout its life cycle, each group requires its members to contribute actively and positively to both task and maintenance needs. Of course, every person will make that contribution according to her or his own skills, abilities, and interests. As a result, group members often perform a variety of different roles in order to assist the group to effectively meet its goals.

Several different kinds of member roles have been observed in groups, some of which contribute positively to the groups' progress while others detract. Participation in groups has been classified into four distinct categories, each of which can be associated with a specific type of communication. The first three, task, procedural, and climate communication, are constructive because they foster healthy working relationships and productivity. The fourth category, egocentric communication, detracts from a healthy culture and good decision making. Figure 12.1 illustrates several communication behaviours in each of these categories.

Task communication focuses on the problem, issue, or information. It provides ideas and information, clarifies understanding, and critically evaluates ideas. Task contributions may include initiating ideas, responding to others' ideas, or providing critical evaluation of information. Task comments also include asking for ideas and criticism from others.

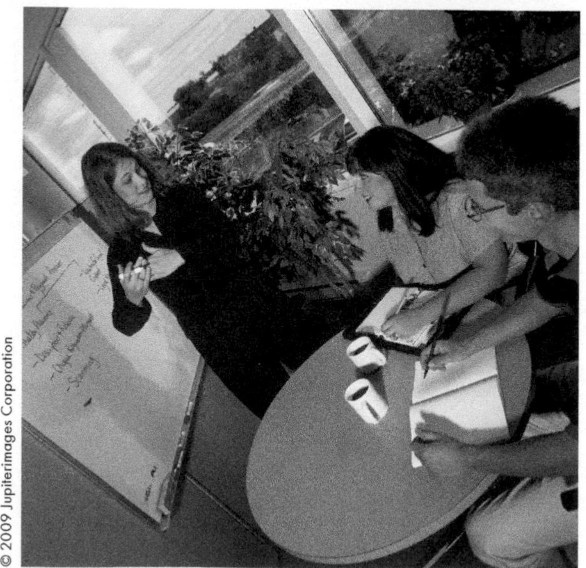

What roles do you play in groups?

If you've ever participated in a disorganized group, you understand the importance of **procedural communication,** which helps a group get organized and stay on track in its decision making. Procedural contributions establish an agenda, coordinate comments of different members, and record group progress. In addition, procedural contributions may curb digressions and tangents, summarize progress, and regulate participation so that everyone has opportunities to speak and nobody dominates.

Climate communication focuses on creating and maintaining a constructive climate that encourages people to contribute freely and to evaluate ideas critically. Climate comments emphasize strengths and progress, recognize others' contributions, reconcile conflicts, and build enthusiasm for the organization and its work.

Task Communication
Initiates ideas Seeks information Elaborates ideas Gives information Evaluates, offers critical analysis
Procedural Communication
Establishes agenda Provides orientation Curbs digression Guides participation Coordinates ideas Records group progress Summarizes others' contributions
Climate Communication
Establishes and maintains healthy climate Energizes group process Recognizes others Harmonizes ideas Reconciles conflicts Builds enthusiasm for group
Egocentric Communication
Aggresses toward others Blocks ideas Seeks personal recognition Dominates interaction Pleads for special interests Disrupts the task Devalues others Trivializes group's work Confesses, self-discloses, seeks personal help

FIGURE 12.1

Communication Roles in Groups

The final kind of communication is not recommended, but it sometimes surfaces in organizational contexts. **Egocentric communication,** or dysfunctional communication, is used to block others or to call attention to oneself. Examples of egocentric talk include devaluing another person's ideas, trivializing group efforts, acting aggressively toward others, bragging about personal accomplishments, dominating, disrupting group work, and pleading for special causes that don't advance organizational goals.

Task, procedural, and climate communication work together to foster productive and comfortable interaction. Egocentric communication, if not checked, can damage an organization's climate and hinder goal achievement. As an illustration, the Apply the Idea discussion "Analyzing Communication in Groups" shows how various contributions to a group discussion can be coded in terms of the kinds of communication just discussed. Notice how the combination of task, procedural, and climate communication helps to move the group forward in its task.

Decision Making and Problem Solving

Most groups in the workplace concentrate on solving problems or making decisions—that is, after all, what they do best. We have already said that groups can

Apply the Idea

ANALYZING COMMUNICATION IN GROUPS

The following excerpt from a group discussion allows you to assess your understanding of the four kinds of communication we've discussed:

Ed: Let's start by talking about our goals. [**procedural**]
Jan: That's a good idea. [**climate**]
Bob: I think our goal is to come up with a better meal plan for students on campus. [**task**]
Ed: What do you mean by "better"? Do you mean cheaper, or more variety, or more tasty? [**task**]
Ann: I think it's all three. [**task**]
Ed: Well, we probably do care about all three, but maybe we should talk about one at a time so we can keep our discussion focused. [**procedural**]
Bob: Okay, I vote we focus first on taste—like it would be good if there was some taste to the food on campus! [**task and climate (humour)**]
Jan: Do you mean taste itself or quality of food, which might also consider nutrition? [**task**]
Bob: Pure taste! When I'm hungry, I don't think about what's good for me, just what tastes good. [**task**]
Jan: Well, maybe we want the food service to think about nutrition since we don't. [**task**]
Bob: If you're a health food nut, that's your problem. I don't think nutrition is something that's important in the food service on campus. [**task; possibly also egocentric if his tone toward Jan was snide**]
Ed: Let's do this: Let's talk first about what we would like in terms of taste itself. [**procedural**] Before we meet next time, we can talk with the cafeteria staff to see if they have to meet any nutritional guidelines in what they serve. [**task**]
Ann: I'll volunteer to do that. [**task**]
Ed: Great. Thanks, Ann. [**climate**]
Bob: I'll volunteer to do taste-testing! [**climate (humour)**]
Jan: With your weight, you'd better not. [**egocentric**]
Bob: Yeah, like you have a right to criticize me. [**egocentric**]
Ann: Look, none of us is here to criticize anyone else. We're here because all of us care about food service on campus. [**climate**] We've decided we want to focus first on taste [**procedural**], so who has an idea of how we should go about studying that? [**task**]

produce highly creative decisions and solutions. But to do so, their communication must provide for an orderly and coherent working process in order to harness a group's creative power and apply it effectively to the problem at hand.

Decisions are made and problems solved by using steps similar to the problem-solving model used for interpersonal conflict. First, the problem must be defined, then analyzed and assessed; solutions are generated and evaluated; and an action plan is implemented and followed up (Dewey, 1910; Wood, 1997a). This works exceedingly well as long as interpersonal conflict is not part of the mix. We'll discuss this more thoroughly when we examine conflict.

Leadership

To be effective, groups and organizations need leadership. For decades, it was assumed that leaders were individuals with special qualities. Research, however, shows that leadership can be provided by one or more people. Strong leadership exists when one person (or more) communicates to establish a good working climate, organizes collective efforts, ensures that discussion is substantive, and

Communication Notes

OUT OF THE BOX: COACHING WITH THE ENNEAGRAM

The Enneagram is a diagnostic tool that helps individuals identify which one of the nine different approaches that they use to habitually view the world. Mary Bast & Clarence Thomson (2004), experts in corporate behaviour, are convinced that once we recognize our usual responses, we can break out of the box of life-long patterns and strengthen personal qualities that will transform our lives. Here is a sample of Enneagram leadership styles.

Leadership Style	Description
The Idealists	Are wise, tolerant, and generally balanced, but their fixation on perfection can lead these leaders to be preachy and to be resentful when tasks are not done to their expectations.
The Mentors	Are interpersonally orientated, caring leaders who derive satisfaction from the development of others. However, they may use manipulation to influence others.
The Stars	Are unreserved, risk-taking go-getters who ensure high productivity for their organizations. They are efficient, goal-orientated, and good at self-promotion. These forces may cause these leaders to be vain and self deceptive.
The Innovators	Are able to view things from alternative perspectives, and are not bound by tradition. However, they are very in touch with feelings, which may lead them to be moody.
The Synthesizers	Are able to take in the whole picture and put the smaller pieces of the whole together in creative ways. They are strategists and visionaries who influence others through their knowledge. They are likely to be very independent and tend to hoard.
The Partners	Since they are team-orientated, they make excellent managers who bring out the best in others; nonetheless, they may have underlying fear or self doubt.
The Futurists	Are very optimistic and focus on long-term possibilities but may be egotistical and oversimplify difficulties.
The Advocates	Are able to handle a lot of responsibility without having to control everything by being soft-hearted and confident, but they may have the need to "fix" everything.
The Diplomats	Are serene, centred, cooperative, able to deal with others' problems, and build consensus, but run the risk of being out of touch with their own wishes.

Student Voices

Krystal:

The most effective group I've ever been in had three leaders. I understood our task best, so I led the way in analyzing information. Belinda kept us organized. She could get us off tangents and move us from one stage of work to the next. She also pulled our ideas together. Kevin was the climate leader. He could tell a joke if things got tense, and he was the best person I've ever seen for recognizing everyone's contributions. I couldn't point to any one leader in that group, but we sure did have good leadership.

controls disruptive people. You may have noticed that leadership parallels the types of participation we just discussed. Leadership, in that sense, is effective participation.

When a single person provides leadership, she or he takes responsibility for managing everything. In other cases, several people share leadership responsibilities. Sometimes one person provides guidance on a task and another person leads in building a healthy climate. Different people may provide leadership at different times. The individual who guides at the outset may not be the one who is most effective in bringing a project to its conclusion. Even when an official leader exists, other people may contribute much of the communication that provides leadership. The most effective group members are those who can identify what the group needs at any given time and provide the skills or information that will help move the group forward.

Whether provided by one or several people, effective leadership involves communication that advances tasks, organizes deliberations, controls disruptions, and fosters a constructive climate.

CHALLENGES TO COMMUNICATING IN THE WORKPLACE

CONCEPTS AT A GLANCE

Challenges in the Workplace

1. Managing conflict
   - Conflict resolution style
   - Dealing with difficult people
   - Tactical communication
   - Harassment
2. Managing intimacy
3. Managing complexity

The workplace poses many challenges. We will examine three that cause much stress for employees and employers alike. The most distressing and conversely the most exhilarating challenge in the workplace is managing conflict. Certainly, dealing with difficult people can create much stress in our lives. Successfully resolving differences on the other hand can be very satisfying and creative. Inherent in the discussion of conflict in the workplace is the issue of harassment. We will also visit alternative communication approaches. Our discussion will then move to the two areas of managing intimacy and managing complexity in the workplace.

Managing Conflict in the Workplace

Our discussion in Chapter 10 on managing conflict provides us with the basis of sound conflict resolution. There are some changes we will make to the approach to conflict that take into account the various people we deal with and our investment in those relationships.

Conflict is natural and can be productive. In the workplace, conflict can also have a number of positive spinoffs if it is managed effectively. For example, the presence of mild conflict can stimulate thinking, help people search for more information, and seek better solutions to problems. The challenge of conflict often spurs people to be more creative in addressing issues in order to come up with the best possible solution. Mild conflict also gives voice to diverse perspectives on issues, and allows minority views to be expressed in ways that otherwise might not be possible. To the extent that conflict brings about a more open sharing and discussion of issues, it can lead to increased understanding of problems, assignments, and decisions.

To achieve these goals, however, conflict must be managed carefully so that it enriches an organization's ability to achieve its goals rather than getting in the way. Conflict can be allowed to exist as a creative tension between individuals or groups, but it must be carefully monitored to ensure that it does not get out of hand. Opposing groups or individuals should be encouraged to seek positive means of addressing the issue—seeking new information, clearly expressing viewpoints, seeking creative solutions, and so on—rather than attempting to harm or undermine the other person. Conflicts that begin to cross the line and become destructive may require intervention, such as some form of mediation or third-party settlement, so that they do not negatively affect others in the organization.

Student Voices

Troy:

I used to think conflict was terrible and that it hurt groups, but last year I was on a committee that had no—I mean, zero—conflict. A couple of times I brought up a reservation about what the committee was doing, but the others squelched my ideas. Everyone was determined to agree and to get along. When our recommendation was put into practice, it bombed. We could have foreseen and avoided the failure if we had been willing to argue and disagree in order to develop a sound proposal.

Troy's commentary is instructive. Although many of us don't enjoy conflict, we can nonetheless recognize its value—even its necessity—in the workplace. The challenge is to harness the positive potentials of conflict. To encourage constructive conflict, communication should demonstrate openness to different ideas, willingness to alter opinions when good reasons exist, and respect for the integrity of other people and the views they express. Constructive conflict allows people to broaden their understanding and to subject their ideas to careful, cooperative analysis.

Constructive conflict is most likely to occur when the appropriate groundwork has been established by creating a supportive and open climate of communication. A positive climate is built throughout the life of a group, beginning with the first meeting among members. Thus, it is important to communicate in ways that build a strong climate from the start so that it has been established when conflict arises.

Conflict Resolution Model

As we discussed in Chapter 10, sometimes it is not worth resolving conflict because we have little investment in a relationship. A server in a restaurant for example, although irritated or frustrated with an insensitive diner, is not likely to invest in resolving conflict in the same manner that he or she does with a co-worker. Similarly, a merchant who relies heavily on word of mouth for business is going to shrug off or accommodate behaviour that he or she would not tolerate from an intimate partner or a friend. A police officer or youth worker might use humour or might ignore troublesome behaviour in order to diffuse hostility.

Let's examine the similarities and differences in conflict resolution of interpersonal relationships and workplace relationships (see Table 12.4). As we discussed earlier, the basic process of problem solving is defining, analyzing, generating solutions, implementing, and following up. Note the variations when more difficult interpersonal conflict is encountered.

A conversation about conflict might sound something like this: "I am concerned about ..." (raise the issue). "When this happens, the result is ..." and "How do you see the situation?" and "Then, from your perspective ..." (describe your experience, solicit response from the other, paraphrase). "In the future, how can we ..." (request a change in behaviour). "OK, so I'll ... and you'll ..." (agree on an action plan). "When can I expect to see some change?" (make plans to follow up). There is certainly much similarity in style between the two relationship approaches, but there is evidence of the power differences in the workplace scenario.

TABLE 12.4

COMPARISON OF CONFLICT RESOLUTION STYLES

Interpersonal Relationship Conflict Resolution Model	Workplace Relationship Conflict Resolution Model
Step 1: Express your needs	Step 1: Raise the issue
Step 2: Solicit the needs of the other	Step 2: Describe the specifics
Step 3: Negotiate a solution	Step 3: Request a change in behaviour
Step 4: Follow up	Step 4: Agree on an action plan
	Step 5: Make plans to follow up

Dealing with Difficult People

Sometimes our best conflict resolution efforts do not work because the people with whom we are in conflict are not invested in a win–win solution. Usually difficult people are invested in a win–lose solution. Table 12.5 identifies six types of personalities that frequently present conflict for us, along with some suggested responses.

TABLE 12.5

DEALING WITH DIFFICULT PEOPLE

Type	Problem	Action	Sample Responses
Procrastinators/ perfectionists	They get paralyzed by a belief that work must be perfect. They miss deadlines.	• Encourage • Create the structure they lack • Help break down tasks • Validate the good work they do	Try: "There are two standards; acceptable and excellence. Maybe this task can be just acceptable." "Not everything has to be perfect." "You do such good work that your acceptable will be excellent to others."
Verbally abusive people	They violate others' rights: • the right to be treated with respect • the right to express oneself • the right to one's body, time, and space	• Set limits • Remove yourself if it's unsafe • Listen, let them vent a bit • Ask them what they want • Agree with any truth in their rantings	Try: "You don't have to yell at me to make me listen to you. I want to hear what you have to say but not when you abuse me with your words." "I am going to leave if you don't lower your voice and take your hand off my shoulder." "What exactly do you want?" (After you've talked) "Your concerns are important to me, but the next time something's bothering you, please get rid of some of that anger before you walk in here. Do not yell at

Type	Problem	Action	Sample Responses
			me, shake your fist at me, poke my shoulder, or stand too close. It makes me very uncomfortable."
Complainers and "Yes but-ters"	They focus on the negative and are not committed to solving problems. By complaining, they don't have to endorse a project or policy. They undermine the climate of the workplace.	• Make the distinction between complaining and problem solving • Identify your desire to hear about problems and to engage in problem solving • Model good problem solving • Teach problem-solving skills	Try: "I'm not interested in your complaints but I am very interested in solving problems. Let's define the problem." "I want to hear your good ideas, not complaints."
Egocentric self-summarizers	They have difficulty with dual perspective. They constantly bring issues, topics around to their needs, wants. They are insensitive to time-sharing. They often lead the discussion off topic.	• Interrupt their monologues • Set time limits on self-disclosures • Ask for dual perspective • Get them to bracket irrelevant or tangential issues	Try: "We need to move on; who else would like to speak?" "I think I understand your point (short paraphrase). I'd like to hear from others." "I see your position, could you summarize others' positions for us?" "That issue will have to wait for another time. Let's confine our discussion to this issue."
Noncommittal "I don't know" people	They are often afraid to an voice opinion. They may be approval-seeking. They may be sabotaging the efforts of the team by covert fighting.	• Force commitment to one side of the issue or the other • Validate their position on the team • Set limits • Call out their indirect hinting behaviour	Try: "If you did know, what would it be?" "Use the 49/51 rule: Be on one side or the other. You cannot choose 50/50." "I really want to know what you want, your thoughts are important to me."
Smarmy, manipulative people	They believe they cannot be straightforward in getting what they want so they use flattery or hinting. They want to catch you off-guard. Their orientation to conflict is win-lose.	• Set limits • Call out their indirect hinting behaviour	Try: "You seem to want something, what might that be?" "I get the feeling something else is bothering you, that we're not talking about the real issue yet. Would you be more direct please." "It's hard for me to accept your kind words when there's a 'but' coming. What is it you want?"

Tactical Communication

Police officers and mediators have long been acquainted with tactical communication to diffuse potentially hostile situations. Communication scholars use the term "verbal judo" or "tongue fu" (Horn, 1996; Thompson & Jenkins, 1993) to describe this alternative to the common conflict resolution approach of voice or assertiveness. Because our work lives bring us into contact with people we might never choose to have a relationship with, it is valuable to have some alternative communication abilities for difficult situations.

Horn identifies four behaviours to diffuse, deflect, or disarm verbal conflict—agree, apologize, act, appreciate. For example, a salesperson might say to a complaining abusive customer, "You're right, those shoes should have lasted longer" (agree). "I'm sorry you have had so much trouble with them" (apologize). "I'll personally get the rep to send you a new pair" (act). "I'm so glad you came back and let us straighten this out. We appreciate your business" (appreciate).

The above tactic works very well in the customer service domain, but there are some situations when clear limits need to be set with hostile people. The respectful *I* language that is so important in civil interpersonal interchanges might need to be replaced with stronger *You* language to stop abusive people. So instead of saying "I'm uncomfortable with you shouting like that," you might need to use the stronger language of "You need to lower your voice when you are speaking to me." Abusive people frequently do not hear the subtle language cues of civil speech. Try the Apply the Idea exercise "Diffusing Conflict" to practise deciding what kind of tactical communication might be most effective. Remember that the goal is to diffuse conflict and open the door to conflict resolution.

Apply the Idea

DIFFUSING CONFLICT

Examine the following four scenarios and decide whether to use the four steps of agree, apologize, act, and appreciate, or the stronger *You* language to create suitable responses to the following situations. Once you have written your responses, choose a partner and put into practice your new verbal behaviours.

Scenario One:

You are the receptionist at a community recreation centre, and a hostile mother comes in claiming to have been bumped off the waiting list for a set of lessons for her child.

You say: ______________________________

Scenario Two:

You are a nurse on a ward with restricted patient-visiting privileges. A distraught family member has been refused entry into his loved one's room.

You say: ______________________________

Scenario Three:

You are a cashier in a college cafeteria, and an angry student demands money back from a vending machine that ran out of his selection.

You say: ______________________________

Scenario Four:

You are a teacher in an elementary school, and an angry father demands to be able to sit in on his child's classes even though his presence is disruptive.

You say: ______________________________

There is no magic solution for dealing with difficult people. The situation, the goals you wish to achieve, the state of mind of the adversarial person, and the resources you have at hand will determine whether you act assertively, with humour, aggressively, or by simply ignoring the situation. Sometimes the high ground in a difficult situation is to walk away.

CONCEPTS AT A GLANCE

Dealing with Harassment

- Tell the harasser to stop.
- Keep notes.
- Seek the assistance of a supervisor, counsellor, or union representative.
- File a human rights claim.

Harassment

Harassment is a common problem in the workplace. Harassment can be based on a person's race, colour, place of origin, sexual orientation, religion, or ability. The outcome of harassment in the workplace is costly. It contributes to increased absenteeism, lack of productivity, and personal health deterioration. Sexual harassment has become recognized as one of the most common barriers to equality experienced by women in the workplace. Sexual harassment is also experienced by men, but less often.

Harassment is any uninvited, unwelcome conduct that poisons the work environment. Harassment is an abuse of power, and the person who is harassed frequently suffers personal feelings of anger, frustration, and loss of self-esteem. If you experience harassment in your workplace, follow the four-step response in the Concepts at a Glance feature in the margin.

Harassment is a serious issue in the workplace, not only for the one being harassed but also for anyone who feels falsely accused of harassing. The first line of defence against a poisoned workplace is clear, respectful communication. Remember that we all have the right to our bodies, to our time, to our space, to express ourselves, and to be treated with respect. When our actions violate the rights of another, conflict results.

Student Voices

Kirk:

Everyone thinks that harassment just happens to women, gay men, or visible minorities. But I'm a married man working in a sheet-metal shop, and I have to put up with disgusting crude behaviours from the guys I work with, including the boss, all day long. They are constantly making sexist derogatory remarks about women.

To get along, I laugh with them and just try to keep separate from it all. But it takes a toll on me. When I come home to my beautiful wife and three little daughters, I feel irritated and angry and depressed. My wife has stopped asking me how my day was or what is wrong with me. She knows I need to be alone for a good half-hour to let the grunge of my work fall off me before I feel human enough to interact with her and the girls. I feel harassed!

Managing Intimacy in the Workplace

A second challenge of communication in the workplace involves participating in relationships that are simultaneously personal and professional. In a study entitled "Bosses and Buddies," Ted Zorn (1995) noted that close relationships between people who work together are commonplace. Since most adults work at least 40 hours a week, personal relationships on the job are inevitable.

Friendships between co-workers or between supervisors and subordinates can be difficult. A supervisor may have trouble fairly evaluating a subordinate who is also a friend. The supervisor might overrate the subordinate's strengths or might be overly harsh to compensate for personal affection. Friendship may also make it difficult to give negative feedback, which is essential to effective performance on the job (Larson, 1984). On the positive side, personal relationships may enhance commitment to a job and communication between co-workers (Zorn, 1995).

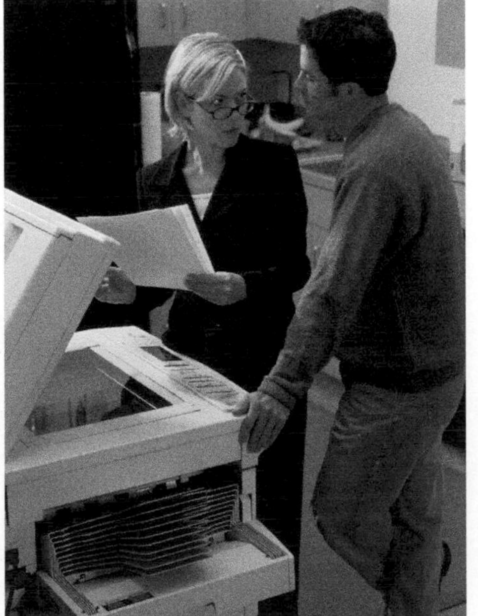

Ryan McVay/Photodisc/Getty Images

Harassment in the workplace: What can you do?

Student Voices

Mandy:

It's hard for me now that my best friend has been promoted over me. Part of it is envy, because I wanted the promotion, too. But the hardest part is that I resent her power over me. When Billie gives me an assignment, I feel that as my friend she shouldn't dump extra work on me. But I also know that as the boss she has to give extra work to all of us sometimes. It just doesn't feel right for my best friend to tell me what to do and to evaluate my work.

Student Voices

Eugene:

Once, I got involved with a girl where I was working. We were assigned to the same team and really hit it off, and one thing led to another and we were dating. The problem came when we broke up. It's impossible to avoid seeing your ex when you work together in a small office, and everyone else walked on eggshells around us. When she quit, I could feel tension drain out of everyone in our office.

Romantic relationships between people who work together involve many of the tensions that operate in friendships between co-workers. In addition, romantic relationships may especially cause resentment and discomfort for others in the workplace. Romantic breakups also tend to be more dramatic than ended friendships. Thus, when a romance dies, there may be repercussions in workplace relationships and climate (Dillard & Witteman, 1985).

It's unrealistic to think we won't form personal relationships with co-workers. The challenge is to manage those relationships so that the workplace doesn't interfere with the personal bond, and the intimacy doesn't jeopardize professionalism. Friends and romantic partners may need to separate personal and work roles so that on-the-job communication doesn't reflect favouritism and privileges that could cause resentment in co-workers. When away from the job, they may have to curb shop talk.

Managing Complexity in the Workplace

Today's workplaces are increasingly complex in personnel, roles, and supporting structures. We will look briefly at each of these areas. First, consider the following descriptions of individuals who work in one company:

- Eileen is a 28-year-old, single, bilingual Jewish woman who is the primary caregiver for her disabled mother.
- Frank is a 37-year-old, married European Canadian man whose wife is a full-time homemaker and mother for their two children. He is especially skilled in collaborative team-building.
- Denise is a 30-year-old European Canadian single mother of a 4-year-old daughter. Denise has expertise as a public speaker.
- Sam is a 59-year-old African Canadian who has two grown children; his wife is an accountant. He is widely regarded as supportive and empathic.
- Ned is a divorced First Nations man who is 42 years old and who just had a heart bypass operation.
- Vinh is a 23-year-old Asian Canadian. He and his wife, who works full-time, are expecting their first child.

Eileen, Frank, Denise, Sam, Ned, and Vinh illustrate the diversity of people, life situations, and needs that characterizes the modern workplace. Organizations need to adapt to the needs of an increasingly complex workforce. Eileen and Denise need flexible working hours so that they can manage caregiving responsibilities. Eileen may also expect her employer to allow her to respect Rosh Hashanah, Yom Kippur, and Hanukkah. Ned may need extended disability leave and a period of part-time work while he recuperates from his heart surgery. Vinh may want parental leave when his child is born. Each of these individuals is likely to bring diverse values, skills and expectations to their workplace.

Secondly, many workers not only have work roles in their employment or profession but often need to function toward multidisciplinary tasks on interdisciplinary teams or on transdisciplinary teams. **Interdisciplinary** usually refers to a group of individuals from distinct disciplines sharing the same space but functioning with separate goals. For example, a hospital team may have nurses, doctors, surgeons, and X-ray and lab technicians; each person has specific roles and provides input from her or his vantage point.

Transdisciplinary teams, on the other hand work toward mutual goals and have overlapping responsibilities (Mullins, Balderson, & Chaney 1999). An example of a transdisciplinary team would be a fully integrated health care team working together to manage serious rehabilitation situations. This team would share mutual goals and have overlapping roles and responsibilities. This group would need to demonstrate a high level of communication and balance of power, and make concerted efforts to enhance team functioning and integrated patient care.

The third area of complexity revolutionizing work life is that of changes in the physical supporting structures. Much is lost and gained as we communicate in the electronically connected workplace. As more people telecommute, managers will need to learn how to lead employees who work in different locations and at different hours. Project teams may interact through e-mail bulletin boards more often than they interact face to face. The organizations that survive and thrive in the years ahead will be those that adapt effectively to meet the expectations and needs of different workers. By extension, individuals who succeed will be comfortable with a stream of changes in people and in ways of working.

GUIDELINES FOR EFFECTIVE WORKPLACE COMMUNICATION

In this chapter, we have discussed the nature of relationships in the workplace and the specific challenges that surround our communication with others in this specialized context. To conclude our discussion, we will examine several guidelines that help improve and maintain effective communication in the workplace. Several of the guidelines will now look familiar as they have occurred in many of the preceding chapters. This underscores the basic elements of interpersonal communication. The contexts may change, but the abiding principles of good communication remain.

CONCEPTS AT A GLANCE

Four Guidelines for Effective Workplace Communication

1. Participate effectively.
   - Use dual perspective.
   - Listen mindfully.
   - Avoid damaging relationship behaviours.
   - Monitor self.
   - Provide leadership.
2. Use celebration and humour.
3. Be equally responsible for task and people.
4. Bring soul to the workplace.

Participate Effectively

We have seen how organizations rely very heavily on communication to perform all of their complex functions. Participating effectively in such an environment has several dimensions. First, it is important to realize that, despite all the complexity of the organization, most work is accomplished through basic interpersonal exchanges—the kind we have been exploring throughout this book. You can enhance your workplace communication—and your value to the organization—by honing your own personal communication skills.

Use dual perspective in your dealings with others, practise mindful listening, be clear and precise in your spoken communication, and watch and understand nonverbal cues. Understanding is the prelude to action (Covey, 1991). You cannot make accurate, effective decisions if you have not first understood the needs of others. All of the basic skills of interpersonal communication touched on earlier in this book are the basic tools of effective workplace communication. Use them.

Student Voices

Don:

I realized all too late that I fell into all four of the damaging relationship behaviours. I was irritated when I went to one of our team meetings because we were behind schedule. I began the meeting by saying sarcastically "How hard can it be to get a two-page report in?" (contempt). Then I criticized and challenged everyone's work commitment (criticism). When people tried to explain why there had been holdups in the schedule and how they needed more support, I became defensive (defensiveness) and then I withdrew and got silent, refusing to participate in further discussion (stonewalling).

Needless to say, the meeting didn't go well. Back at my office, I realized how ineffective I had been and how damaging my behaviour had been to the team. I had lots of repairing to do.

Practising effective interpersonal communication may also help your co-workers to become clear about their own information and communication needs on the job, and may provide a model for others to follow. Being clear and effective in your interpersonal communication can help others understand the benefits of high-quality communication, and may inspire them to improve their own communication skills. In group settings, effective participation often includes monitoring yourself by being aware of the roles that you play. Knowing your own strengths as a communicator, as well as the strengths of others, will help you to know when to actively step in and when to sit back and allow others to contribute. Understanding the key aspects of the group process can help you contribute more positively as an equal member.

Critical to the smooth functioning of relationships in the workplace is avoiding damaging relationship behaviours. Recall in Chapter 11 that the four most damaging behaviours to relationships according to Gottman, Katz, and Hooven (1996) are contempt, criticism, defensiveness, and stonewalling. Just as these behaviours stress and damage friendships and romantic relationships, so do they damage workplace relationships. Too late, Don recognized the impact of his damaging behaviours in a meeting.

Beyond participating as an individual, you may also be called on to provide leadership**.** We have seen that, especially in group settings, leadership may come from a number of sources, and it does not always require a formal title or position. Occasionally, contributing effectively as a group member may mean that you take charge and offer your own ideas about how to approach a task, suggest procedures, assist other members to bring forth their contributions, and so on. By being aware of roles that are not being fulfilled and by stepping in to provide the needed action, you can provide helpful leadership for the group, even if you are not designated as a leader. In interview settings, either as interviewer or interviewee, you can assist others by recognizing how the communication process is unfolding and offering information or other help to move the process forward.

Whenever you use your knowledge of communication to facilitate more effective working relationships, you will be exercising effective leadership. And if your boss is paying attention, you may be rewarded with recognition and opportunities for advancement.

Use Celebration and Humour

As we discussed earlier in the chapter, the culture of an organization affects communication. If there is a culture of celebration, where small and large accomplishments are recognized, where personal events are punctuated (birthdays and anniversaries, etc.), where even creative acts that fail are acknowledged, then there is a climate of acceptance, openness, and support. When we are encouraged by humour instead of punished by criticism, there is a climate of risk-taking and ingenuity. These are worth cultivating in the workplace.

Be Equally Responsible for Task and People

© 2009 Jupiterimages Corporation

Every group is charged with completing tasks and managing the people of the working team. With increased emphasis in our modern work life to work in teams, each member must become responsible for contributing to the health of the team. That is accomplished when there is equal attention to the demands of the tasks and to the needs of the people. This does not happen simultaneously. Sometimes it is necessary to stop working toward completion of a task in order to sort through group members' feelings or concerns that are getting in the way. Sometimes this requires leaving the workplace and truly having a break. At other times, it is evident that everyone must bracket their personal issues and needs for the sake of making a pressing deadline.

The important communication imperative is to watch that both task and people are being attended to. To be completely task-oriented would result in bullying. To be completely people-oriented would result in work stoppage. Balance and self-monitoring are the keys.

Brenda Carson/Shutterstock

The face of the Canadian workplace is changing.

Bring Soul to the Workplace

The final guideline in this chapter and, fittingly, in the book, is to bring soul to the workplace. Our earlier discussion of soul identified the need to treat individuals as whole people with minds, bodies, hearts, and souls. This requires the employer to make opportunities for flexibility, innovation, connectedness, vision, and contribution. This requires the employee to seek ways to create meaning in the workplace and to respect and honour relationships. Our connectedness to ourselves, the people around us, and the physical environment we inhabit is the essence of soul.

Chapter Summary

Our examination of communication in the workplace has led us to identify the importance of communication in creating satisfying work relationships and in creating effective organizations. Communication skills and the ability to work in teams ranks highest in the sought-after employability skills of the Canadian workforce. We then defined the nature of the relationships we create and sustain in the workplace. Four elements that affect these relationships are power, the fear of reprisal, task demands, and technologies.

We focused our discussion on the climate and culture of organizations and how each is created. A positive climate is typified by supportiveness, participation, trust, openness, and goal clarity. Culture is created by the vocabulary we use, which has been influenced by a hierarchical and masculine language style. Modern workplaces require a de-sexing of that language. Culture is also created by the rites and rituals that take place in an organization. Finally, infusing the workplace with soul creates a positive, healthy work environment.

The last of the topics under the nature of relationships in the workplace explored teamwork and groups. We discussed the nature of groups and the roles individuals play in groups. We then focused our discussion on the several challenges that are inherent in communicating in the workplace. Three specific challenges were identified; managing conflict, managing intimacy, and managing the complexity created by diversity and change. The discussion of conflict embraced differing conflict resolution styles, dealing with difficult people, tactical communication, and harassment.

The chapter concluded with four guidelines for effective communication in the workplace. Participating effectively by using dual perspective, mindful listening, avoiding damaging relationship behaviours, monitoring self, and providing leadership was the first guideline. This was followed by the power of celebration and humour. Thirdly, we emphasized the responsibility of each to manage equally both tasks and people. We concluded the chapter with the need to bring soul to the workplace.

Key Concepts

- climate communication
- communication climate
- egocentric communication
- goal clarity
- group
- harassment
- interdisciplinary
- organizational culture
- personal rituals
- power
- procedural communication
- rites
- rituals
- social rituals
- soul
- synergy
- task communication
- task rituals
- team
- transdisciplinary

For Further Thought and Discussion

1. Visit your local police academy and interview officers about their specialized training in tactical communication. Identify the ways in which police officers defuse difficult situations with verbal communication skills.
2. Use your InfoTrac® College Edition to look up current information on soul in the workplace.
3. Use your InfoTrac® College Edition to look up current information on the changing shape of the North American workforce. What is the impact of immigration patterns and the aging baby boomers on the future of work in Canada?
4. Search your province's Human Rights Commission for the latest publications on harassment in the workplace. Look up a recent decision by your province's Human Rights Tribunal and determine the nature and implications of communication practices in the workplace.
5. Examine two groups to which you belong in terms of the roles you and others play in maintaining or sabotaging the task and people functions of the group. Choose one group that is largely cooperative in nature and a second that is largely competitive in nature. Compare the two.
6. Examine the rites and rituals of one of the places in which you have worked. How do these behaviours contribute or detract from a healthy communication climate in that workplace?

Epilogue

CONTINUING THE CONVERSATION

Although *Everyday Encounters* is drawing to a close, the conversation we've launched in these pages will continue—interpersonal communication will be central to your life in the years ahead. There have been three predominant themes in the 12 chapters: Communication creates and reflects identity, interpersonal communication is central to relationships, and interpersonal communication takes place in a diverse world.

Communication Creates and Reflects Identity

Communication is both an important source of personal identity and a primary means by which we express who we are. Our sense of personal identity grows directly out of interpersonal communication. We enter the world without any clear sense of self, and we look to others to tell us who we are. Parents, grandparents, siblings, and others who are significant in our first years of life provide us with reflected appraisals that express how they see us and our value. Family members also shape our attachment styles and the scripts we follow in dealing with conflict, expressing emotions, and engaging in other forms of interpersonal communication.

As we venture beyond the confines of family, we continue to learn from others and to see ourselves through the eyes of others. Peers, teachers, friends, and romantic partners communicate their views of us, and those become part of how we see ourselves and how we define our paths of personal growth. They also provide us with additional scripts and perspectives that we may rely on in our interpersonal communication.

Identity not only grows out of interpersonal communication but also is expressed in communication. How we communicate expresses who we are. Verbally and nonverbally, we announce that we are dominant or deferential, outgoing or introverted, caring or indifferent, emotionally expressive or reserved, egotistical or interested in others, assertive or passive, accepting or judgmental, and so forth.

Interpersonal Communication Is Central to Relationships

Communication is the heart of personal relationships. The health and endurance of personal relationships depends in large measure on our ability to communicate effectively. For relationships to be satisfying, we need to know how to express our feelings, needs, and ideas in ways that others can understand. We also need to know how to listen sensitively and responsively to people in our lives so that they feel safe in being open and honest with us. Interpersonal communication skills also allow us to create climates that are supportive and affirming, so that our relationships are healthy. Communication is the basis of meaning in human relationships, and it is the primary way we build, refine, sustain, and transform close connections with others.

Interpersonal Communication Takes Place in a Diverse World

A third theme of this book is that social diversity shapes and is reflected in communication. We've seen that our social standpoints affect how we communicate and how we interpret the communication of others. What is normal or desirable in one social group may be offensive or odd in other communities. Once we understand that standpoints shape communication, we are able to see that there are no absolutely right or wrong styles of communicating. Our ways of communicating, then, reflect not only our individual identities but also standpoints that are shaped by the social groups to which we belong.

Diverse cultures and the communication styles they cultivate offer rich opportunities to learn about others and ourselves. The more we interact with people whose backgrounds, beliefs, and communication styles differ from our own, the more we will grow as individuals and as members of a common world.

What you've studied about interpersonal communication should give you insight into how each of these themes applies in your current life. Let's now consider how they pertain to our personal and collective future.

THE ROAD AHEAD

Interpersonal communication will be as much a part of your everyday life in the future as it is today, although it may assume different forms and functions in the years ahead. The skills and perspectives we've discussed in this book will serve you well in meeting the challenges that will accompany changes in yourself, relationships, and society.

In the coming years, your interpersonal relationships will change in both anticipated and surprising ways. Some of the friends you have today will still be close in years to come, whereas others will fade away and new people will assume importance in your life. Some romances of the moment will flourish and endure, and others will wither. New people will come into your life, and familiar ones will leave. Each person who enters or exits your life will affect your personal identity.

There will also be changes and surprises in how people go about the process of forming and sustaining relationships. The trend toward long-distance romances and friendships will grow as more individuals who care about each other find they cannot live or work in the same location. Technology will also alter how we communicate with friends and romantic partners. Increasingly, we will rely on electronic forms of communication to sustain important personal relationships. Most of us rely on technology to communicate daily with parents, siblings, friends, partners, work associates, and leisure groups. In the future, friends, romantic partners, and family members will make increasing use of technology to stay in touch.

Finally, interpersonal communication and relationships will evolve in response to changes in the larger society. Medical advances will stretch the average life span further, so that a promise to stay together "'til death do us part" will involve a greater time commitment than it does today. Longer lives will also increase the number of older people in society and the opportunities for them to be part of our friendships and families. Relationship forms that are not always recognized or approved of today may be accepted more widely in the future. Interaction with an increasing diversity of people will change our perspective of what relationships are and how to sustain them. In addition, diversity will broaden the options we recognize for creating our own relationships.

We cannot foresee what lies ahead for us and for our world. However, we can predict with assurance that there will be changes in us, others, and cultural life. Whatever changes we experience, we can be sure that interpersonal communication will continue to be central to our happiness and effectiveness.

In *Everyday Encounters* and the course it accompanies, you have learned much about interpersonal communication. The understandings you've gained and the skills you've acquired will be valuable to you in the years ahead. If you commit to practising and continuously expanding on the principles and skills introduced in this book, then you are on the threshold of a lifelong journey that will enrich you and your relationships with others.

Glossary

A

abstract Removed from concrete reality. Symbols are abstract because they are inferences and generalizations abstracted from a total reality.

agape A secondary style of loving that is selfless and based on giving to others, not receiving rewards or returns from them. Agape is a blend of eros and storge.

aggression Form of overt conflict expressed in an act or attitude of hostility.

ambiguous Unclear meaning. Symbols are ambiguous because their meanings vary from person to person, context to context, and so forth.

ambushing Listening carefully for the purpose of attacking a speaker.

analogical and inductive reasoning Reasoning that takes us beyond the confines of current knowledge to conclusions about the unknown. Induction is employed, for example, in using specific propositions such as: This child likes to play (or: All children I have ever known liked to play) to infer general propositions such as: All children like to play. An analogy relies on the inference that attributes are known to be shared. Analogical reasoning is very frequent in common senss. Time-oriented individuals are likely to wear and to check watches.

anxious/ambivalent attachment style A mode of relating characterized by preoccupation with relationships and inconsistent behaviour toward the partner. Develops in childhood when a caregiver behaves inconsistently toward a child—sometimes being loving and other times being rejecting or neglectful.

arbitrary Random or unnecessary. Symbols are arbitrary because there is no necessary reason for any particular symbol to stand for a particular referent.

artifacts Personal objects we use to announce our identities and personalize our environments.

assertion Clearly and nonjudgmentally stating what we feel, need, or want. Assertion is not synonymous with aggression because aggression involves putting our needs ahead of, and sometimes at the cost of, others' needs.

attachment styles Patterns of parenting that teach children who they are, who others are, and how to approach relationships.

attending Nonverbal listening behaviours that let the speaker know we are being mindful. Captured by the acronym FELOR.

attributions Causal accounts that explain why things happen and why people act as they do.

B

bracketing Noting an important issue that comes up in the course of discussing other matters and that needs to be discussed at a later time. Bracketing allows partners to stay effectively focused on a specific issue at one time but to agree to deal with other issues later.

C

chronemics A type of nonverbal communication concerned with how we perceive and use time to define identities and interaction.

climate The dominant feeling between people who are involved with each other.

climate communication Group communication that focuses on creating and maintaining a constructive climate that encourages people to contribute freely and to evaluate ideas critically.

cognitive complexity Determined by the number of constructs used, how abstract they are, and how elaborately they interact to create perceptions.

cognitive CQ A person high in cognitive CQ has extensive rote learning about the beliefs, customs, and taboos of other cultures.

cognitive labelling view of emotions Theory that claims what we feel is shaped by how we label physiological responses.

collectivism One of Hofstede's five dimensions of culture in which individuals are integrated into strong cohesive in-groups that offer protection in exchange for unquestioning loyalty. Rules promote order, obedience, and cooperation.

commitment A decision to remain with a relationship. Commitment is one of three dimensions of enduring romantic relationships, and it has more impact on relationship continuity than does love alone. It is also an advanced stage in the process of escalation in romantic relationships.

committed romantic relationships Voluntary connections we presume will be primary and continuing parts of our lives. Committed romantic relationships include three dimensions: intimacy, passion, and commitment.

communication climate The overall character and quality of the communication investment of an organization.

communication devices Signals that define beginnings and endings of interaction episodes in a conversation, such as speed, pacing, pausing, overlap, and interruption.

communication rules Shared understandings of what communication means and what behaviours are appropriate in various situations.

conflict Exists when individuals who depend on each other express different views, interests, or goals and perceive their differences as incompatible or as opposed by the other.

constitutive rules Communication rules that define what communication means by specifying how certain communicative acts are to be counted.

constructivism Theory that states that we organize and interpret experience by applying cognitive structures called *schemata*.

content level of meaning Refers to the content or denotative information in communication. Content-level meanings are literal.

contracting Building a solution through negotiation and acceptance of parts of proposals for resolution. Contracting is usually present in the later stages of constructive conflict.

counterfeit emotional language Communication that seems to express feelings but doesn't actually describe what a person is feeling.

counterproposals A proposal made in response to another proposal instead of serious consideration of the first.

cross-complaining Occurs when one person's complaint is met by a countercomplaint; unproductive conflict response.

cultural anthropology Describes and seeks to explain similarities and differences in thought and behaviour among groups of humans.

cultural intelligence (CQ) Understanding why people from different backgrounds act as they do, so that we can improve how we relate to one another.

culture Beliefs, understandings, practices, and ways of interpreting experience that are shared by a number of people.

D

deep acting Management of inner feelings.

defensive listening Perceiving personal attacks, criticisms, or hostile undertones in communication when none are intended.

direct definition Communication that explicitly tells us who we are by specifically labelling us and reacting to our behaviours. Direct definition usually occurs first in families and also in interaction with peers and others.

dismissive attachment style Promoted by caregivers who are disinterested, rejecting, or abusive toward children. Unlike people who develop fearful attachment styles, those experiencing a dismissive style do not accept the caregiver's view of them as unlovable. Instead, they dismiss others as unworthy and thus do not seek close relationships.

downers People who communicate negatively about us and reflect negative appraisals of our self-worth.

dual perspective The ability to understand both your own and another's perspective, beliefs, thoughts, and feelings.

dyadic breakdown The first stage of relational decay. Dyadic breakdown involves degeneration of established patterns, understandings, and routines that make up a relational culture and that sustain intimacy on a day-to-day basis.

dyadic phase Stage of relational deterioration that involves discussing problems and negotiation.

E

ego boundaries Define where an individual stops and the rest of the world begins.

egocentric communication Dysfunctional group communication that blocks others and calls attention to the individual. Egocentric communication aggresses toward others, disrupts the task, devalues others, trivializes the group's work, and is self-serving.

emotion work Effort invested to make ourselves feel what our culture defines as appropriate and to not feel what our culture defines as inappropriate in particular situations.

emotional intelligence The ability to recognize which feelings are appropriate in which situations and the skill to communicate those feelings effectively.

emotions Processes that are shaped by physiology, perceptions, social experience, and language.

empathy Ability to feel with another person; to feel what she or he feels in a situation.

environmental racism A pattern whereby toxic waste dumps and hazardous plants are disproportionately located in lower-income neighbourhoods.

environmental spoiling Process by which proximity breeds ill will.

equity Fairness, based on the perception that both partners invest relatively equally in a relationship and benefit similarly from their investments. Perceived equity is a primary influence on satisfaction with relationships.

eros A powerful, passionate style of love that blazes to life suddenly and dramatically. Eros is one of the three primary styles of loving.

ethics Branch of philosophy that deals with moral principles and codes of conduct. Interpersonal communication involves ethical issues.

ethnic group Functions within a society to maintain a subculture based on religion, language, common origin, or ancestral traditions.

ethnocentrism The assumption that our culture and its norms are the only right ones. Ethnocentric communication reflects certainty, which tends to create defensive communication climates.

everyday interaction The way in which partners weave the basic fabric of their relationship in day-to-day conversations that realize their togetherness.

exit response One of four ways of responding to conflict. The exit response is to leave conflict either psychologically (by tuning out disagreement) or physically (by walking away or even leaving the relationship). The exit response is active and generally destructive.

explorational communication The third stage in relational escalation, which involves exchanges of information to check out the possibilities of a relationship.

external tensions Relationship stresses derived from competing demands, personal change, surviving distance, and ensuring equity.

F

fearful attachment style Cultivated when the caregiver in the first bond communicates in consistently negative, rejecting, or even abusive ways to a child.

feedback Responses to messages. Feedback may be verbal, nonverbal, or both; it may be intentional or unintentional.

feeling rules Culturally based guidelines that tell us what we have a right to feel or are expected to feel in specific situations.

framing rules Culturally based guidelines that define the emotional meaning of situations and events.

friends of the heart Friends who remain close, regardless of distance and changes in individuals' lives.

friends of the road Friends who are temporary and with whom intimacy is not sustained when one of the friends moves or changes occur.

fundamental attribution error Overestimating the internal causes of others' behaviour and underestimating the external causes.

G

games Interactions in which the real conflicts are hidden or denied and a counterfeit excuse is created for arguing or put-downs.

generalized other One source of social perspectives that people use to define themselves and guide how they think, act, and feel; our perception of the views, values, and perspectives that are endorsed by society as a whole.

goal clarity The prospect of clear attainable goals.

grace Granting forgiveness or putting aside personal needs when it is not required or expected. Grace reflects generosity of spirit.

grave dressing The final phase in relational decline, it involves burying the relationship and putting it to rest.

group Three or more individuals who interact over time.

H

haptics The sense of touch and what it means. Haptics is one form of nonverbal communication.

harassment Any uninvited, unwelcome conduct that poisons the work environment.

hate speech Language that radically dehumanizes others.

hearing A physiological activity that occurs when sound waves hit our eardrums. Unlike listening, hearing is a passive process.

high context Refers to societies or groups with close connections over a long period of time, and where relationships are more important than tasks. Words themselves have little meaning until placed in the context of people, relationships, and histories.

I

identity scripts Guides to action based on rules for living and identity. Initially communicated in families, scripts define our roles, how we are to play them, and basic elements in the plot of our lives.

I–It communication Impersonal communication in which individuals are treated as objects or instruments for our purposes.

***I* language** Language that takes personal responsibility for feelings by using words that own the feelings and do not project the responsibility for feelings onto others.

implicit personality theory Assumptions about which qualities fit together in human personalities. Implicit personality theories are often unconscious.

indexing Technique to remind us that evaluations are not static, not unchanging. Indexing links evaluations to specific times and/or circumstances.

individualism One of Hofstede's five dimensions of culture in which ties between individuals are loose; everyone is expected to look after oneself. Rules promote independence, choices, and freedom.

individuality The first stage of interaction marking progressive intimacy in which we are aware of ourselves as individuals with particular needs, goals, love styles, and qualities that affect what we look for in relationships. This stage can also be called "attraction without interaction."

intensifying communication Stage in the escalation of romantic relationships that increases the depth of a relationship by increasing personal knowledge and allowing a couple to begin creating a private culture. Also called *euphoria*.

interactive models Models that represent communication as a process in which listeners are involved in sending messages back to speakers through feedback.

interactive view of emotions Claims that social rules and understandings shape what people feel and how they do or don't express feelings.

interdisciplinary Refers to a group of individuals from distinct disciplines sharing the same space but functioning with separate goals.

internal tensions Relationship stresses that grow out of individuals and their interaction.

interpersonal climate The overall feeling, or emotional mood, of a relationship.

interpersonal communication A selective, systemic, ongoing process in which unique individuals interact to reflect and build personal knowledge and to create meanings.

interpersonal communication competence Communication that is interpersonally effective and appropriate. Competence includes abilities to monitor oneself, engage in dual perspective, enact a range of communication skills, and adapt communication appropriately.

interpretation The subjective process of evaluating and explaining perceptions.

intimacy Includes feelings of closeness, connection, and tenderness between lovers. Intimacy is one of three dimensions of committed romantic relationships.

intrapsychic phase The second phase in disintegration of romantic relationships, this involves brooding about problems in the relationship and dissatisfactions with a partner.

investment Something put into a relationship that cannot be recovered should the relationship end. Investment, more than rewards and love, increases commitment.

invitational communication The second stage in the escalation phase of romantic relationships. In this stage, individuals signal they are interested in interacting and respond to invitations from others.

I–Thou communication Fully interpersonal communication in which individuals acknowledge and deal with each other as unique individuals who meet fully in dialogue.

I–You communication Interaction that is midway between impersonal and interpersonal communication. In I–You relationships, communicators acknowledge each other as human beings but do not know and act toward each other as unique individuals in their totalities.

J

Johari Window A model of different sorts of knowledge that affect self-development; created by Joseph Luft and Harry Ingham.

K

kinesics Body position and body motions, including those of the face.

kitchen-sinking Unproductive form of conflict communication in which everything except the kitchen sink is thrown into the argument.

L

letting go To free ourselves of anger, blame, and judgments about another and what she or he did. Letting go of these feelings is part of showing grace.

linear models Models that represent communication as a one-way process that flows in one direction—from sender to receiver. Linear models do not capture the dynamism of communication or the active participation of all communicators.

listening A complex process that consists of being mindful, hearing, selecting and organizing information, interpreting communication, responding, and remembering.

listening for information One of three goals of listening. Listening for information focuses on gaining and evaluating ideas, facts, opinions, reasons, and so forth.

listening for pleasure One of three goals of listening. Listening for pleasure is motivated by a desire to enjoy rather than to gain information or support others.

listening to support others One of three goals of listening. Listening to support others focuses more on the relationship level of meaning than on the content level of meaning. It aims to understand and respond to others' feelings, thoughts, and perceptions in ways that affirm them.

literal listening Listening only to the content level of meaning and ignoring the relationship level of meaning.

loaded language An extreme form of evaluative language that relies on words that strongly slant perceptions and, thus, meanings.

long-term orientation One of Hofstede's five dimensions of culture; refers to the degree to which a society values long-term commitments and respect for tradition.

lose–lose An orientation toward conflict in which it is assumed that nobody can win and everyone loses from engaging in conflict.

low context Refers to societies and groups where people tend to have many connections but of shorter duration or for some specific reason. Beliefs tend to be more explicit, rule-oriented, and task-centred. Literal meanings of words are emphasized.

loyalty response One of four ways of responding to conflict. The loyalty response consists of silent allegiance to a relationship and a person when conflict exists. Loyalty is passive and tends to be constructive.

ludus One of three primary styles of love. Ludus is playful love, in which the goal is not commitment but to have fun at love as a game or a series of challenges and manoeuvres.

M

mania One of three secondary styles of loving made up of eros and ludus. Mania is passionate, sometimes obsessive love that includes emotional extremes.

masculinity One of Hofstede's five dimensions of culture; refers to the distribution of social gender roles that are clearly distinct. The culture is more conducive to dominance, assertiveness, and the acquisition of things.

metacommunication Communication about communication. When excessive, as in unproductive conflict interaction, metacommunication becomes self-absorbing and diverts partners from the issues causing conflict.

mindfulness A concept from Zen Buddhism that refers to being fully present in the moment. Being mindful is the first step of listening and the foundation for all others.

mind-reading Assuming we understand what another person thinks or how another person perceives something.

minimal encouragers Communication that gently invites another person to elaborate by expressing interest in hearing more.

model A representation of what something is and how it works.

monitoring The capacity to observe and regulate your own communication.

monopolizing Continuously focusing communication on ourselves instead of on the person who is talking.

motivational CQ A person high in motivational CQ is confident of being able to understand people from unfamiliar cultures.

N

navigating After relationships have escalated to commitment, partners navigate continuously, adjusting and reworking interaction to keep a relationship satisfying and healthy. Ideally, this stage lasts a lifetime.

neglect response One of four ways of responding to conflict. The neglect response is to deny or minimize problems. The neglect response is passive and tends to be destructive.

noise Anything that distorts communication so that it is more difficult for individuals to understand each other.

nonverbal communication All forms of communication other than words themselves. Nonverbal communication includes inflection and other vocal qualities as well as several other behaviours.

O

organismic view of emotions Theory that external phenomena cause physiological changes that lead us to experience emotions. Also called *James-Lange view of emotions.*

organizational culture The overall pattern of beliefs, values, and practices that are uniquely characteristic of a specific organization.

P

paralanguage Communication that is vocal but not verbal.

paraphrasing A method of clarifying another's meaning by reflecting our interpretations of his or her communication back to him or her.

particular others One source of social perspectives that individuals use to define themselves and guide how they think, act, and feel. The perspectives of particular others are the viewpoints of specific individuals who are significant to the self.

passion Intensely positive feelings and desires for another person. Passion is based on rewards from involvement and is not equivalent to commitment. It is one of three dimensions of enduring romantic relationships.

passive aggression Attacking while denying doing so. Passive aggression is a means of covertly expressing conflict, anger, or both.

perception An active process of selecting, organizing, and interpreting people, objects, events, situations, and activities.

perceptual view of emotions Theory that claims subjective perceptions shape what external phenomena mean and what emotions we associate with external phenomena. Also called *appraisal theory*.

personal constructs Bipolar mental yardsticks that allow us to measure people and situations along specific dimensions of judgment.

personal rituals Activities that individuals routinely engage in to define themselves.

person-centredness Ability to perceive individuals as unique and to differentiate them from social roles and generalizations based on membership in social groups.

physical CQ Actions and demeanour that show we are ready to enter the world of another culture.

placemaking Process of creating a physical environment that is comfortable and that reflects the values, experiences, and tastes of individuals. Physical environment is part of relational culture, which is the nucleus of intimacy.

power A dimension of relationship-level meanings, often expressed through nonverbal communication, which indicates the influence and control that one person has over another.

power distance Defined by Hofstede as "the extent to which the less powerful members of institutions and organizations within a country expect and accept that power is distributed unequally."

pragma A secondary style of loving that is pragmatic or practical in nature. Pragma is a blend of storge and ludus.

procedural communication Group communication that helps keep a group organized and on track. Procedural communication establishes the agenda, provides orientation, curbs digression, guides participation, coordinates ideas, records group process, and summarizes contributions.

process An ongoing, continuous, dynamic flow that has no clear-cut beginning or ending and that is always evolving and changing. Interpersonal communication is a process.

prototypes Knowledge structures that define the clearest or most representative examples of some category.

proxemics A type of nonverbal communication that includes space and how we use it.

pseudolistening Pretending to listen.

R

rational-emotive approach to feelings Approach that emphasizes using rational thinking to challenge and change debilitating emotions that undermine self-concept and self-esteem.

reflected appraisal Process of seeing and thinking about ourselves in terms of the appraisals of us that others reflect.

regulative rules Communication rules that regulate interaction by specifying when, how, where, and with whom to talk about certain things.

relational culture A private world of rules, understandings, and patterns of acting and interpreting that partners create to give meaning to their relationship. Relational culture is the nucleus of intimacy.

relational dialectics Opposing forces, or tensions, that are normal parts of all relationships. The three relational dialectics are autonomy/intimacy, novelty/routine, and openness/closedness.

relationship meaning Refers to what communication expresses about the relationship between communicators. Three dimensions of relationship-level meanings are liking or disliking, responsiveness, and power (control).

remembering The process of recalling what you have heard. This is the sixth part of listening.

responding Symbolizing your interest in what is being said with observable feedback to speakers during the process of interaction. This is the fifth of six elements in listening.

revising communication A stage in the escalation of romantic relationships that many, but not all, couples experience. Revising involves evaluating a relationship and working out any obstacles or problems before committing for the long term.

rites Communication practices that express organizational values and identity through dramatic, planned activities that bring together aspects of cultural ideology into a single event.

rituals Communication practices that express organizational values and identity. They occur regularly, and members of an organization perceive them as familiar and routine parts of organizational life.

S

scripts One of four cognitive schemata. Scripts define expected or appropriate sequences of action in particular settings.

secure attachment style The most common and most positive attachment style. This style develops when the caregiver responds in a consistently attentive and loving way to a child.

selective listening Focusing on only selected parts of communication. We listen selectively when we screen out parts of a message that don't interest us or with which we disagree, and also when we rivet attention on parts of communication that do interest us or with which we agree.

self A multidimensional process that involves forming and acting from social perspectives that arise and evolve in communication with others and ourselves.

self-disclosure Revealing personal information about ourselves that others are unlikely to discover in other ways.

self-fulfilling prophecy Acting in ways that bring about expectations or judgments of ourselves.

self-sabotage Self-talk that communicates we are no good, we can't do something, we can't change, and so forth. Self-sabotaging communication undermines belief in ourselves and motivation to change and grow.

self-serving bias Tendency to attribute our positive actions and successes to stable, global, internal influences that we control, and to attribute negative actions and failures to unstable, specific, external influences beyond our control.

self-talk Ways that we communicate with ourselves that affect how we feel and act. Self-talk is intrapersonal communication.

social comparison Involves comparing ourselves with others to form judgments of our own talents, abilities, qualities, and so forth.

social phase Part of relational disintegration in which partners figure out how to inform outsiders that the relationship is ending.

social rituals Standardized performances that affirm relationships among members of organizations.

social support Phase of relational decline in which partners look to friends and family for support during the trauma of breaking up.

soul A sense of connectedness and meaning in one's life.

speech community Group of people who share norms, regulative rules, and constitutive rules for communicating and interpreting the communication of others.

standpoint A point of view shaped by awareness of the material, social, and symbolic conditions common for members of a social group.

static evaluation Assessments that suggest something is unchanging. "Bob is impatient" is a static evaluation.

stereotypes Predictive generalizations about people and situations.

storge A comfortable, friendly kind of love, often likened to friendship. It is one of three primary styles of loving.

subculture A particular mix of shared understandings held by groups within a larger society.

summarizing A paraphrase that captures all the thoughts, feelings, and actions that the speaker has shared.

surface acting Controlling outward expression in inner feelings.

symbols Abstract, arbitrary, and ambiguous representations of other phenomena, including feelings, events, ideas, relationships, situations, and individuals.

synergy A special kind of energy that enlarges the efforts, talents, and strengths of individual group or team members.

systemic A quality of interpersonal communication that means it takes place within multiple systems that influence what is communicated and what meanings are constructed. Examples of systems affecting communication are physical context, culture, personal histories, and previous interactions between people.

T

task communication Group communication that focuses on the problems, issues, or information needed to accomplish group business. Task communication initiates ideas, seeks information, elaborates on ideas, gives information, and offers critical analysis.

task rituals Behaviours that help members perform the tasks of their jobs.

team A special kind of group that is brought together for a special task and is characterized by distinct and complementary resources of members, and by a strong sense of collective identity.

totalizing Responding to a person as if one aspect of him or her is the total of who he or she is.

transactional models Models that represent communication as a dynamic process that changes over time and in which participants assume multiple roles.

transdisciplinary Refers to a group of individuals working from distinct disciplines toward mutual goals and having overlapping responsibilities.

trust Entails two factors: (1) belief in another's reliability (he or she will do what is promised); (2) emotional reliance on another to care about and protect our welfare. Trust is believing that private information about us is safe with another person because she or he cares for us and will look out for our welfare.

U

uncertainty avoidance One of Hofstede's five dimensions of culture; describes society's tolerance for uncertainty and ambiguity and indicates to what extent a culture programs its members to feel either comfortable or uncomfortable in unstructured situations.

uppers People who communicate positively about us and who reflect positive appraisals of our self-worth.

V

voice response One of four responses to conflict. The voice response involves communicating about differences, tensions, and disagreements. Voice responses are active and can be constructive for individuals and relationships.

vultures An extreme form of downers. They not only communicate negative images of us but also attack our self-concepts.

W

win–lose An orientation toward conflict that assumes one person wins at the expense of another person whenever conflict arises.

win–win An orientation toward conflict that assumes everyone can win, or benefit, from engaging in conflict and that it is possible to generate resolutions that satisfy everyone.

Y

***you* language** Language that projects responsibility for feelings or actions onto other people. You language is not recommended for interpersonal communication.

References

Acitelli, L. (1988). When spouses talk to each other about their relationship. Journal of Social and Personal Relationships, 5, 185–199.

Acitelli, L. (1993). You, me, and us: Perspectives on relationship awareness. In S. W. Duck (Ed.), Understanding relationship processes, 1: Individuals in relationships (pp. 144–174). Newbury Park, CA: Sage.

Acker, M., & Davis, M. H. (1992). Intimacy, passion and commitment in adult romantic relationships: A test of the triangular theory of love. *Journal of Social and Personal Relationships,* 9, 21–51.

Ackerman, D. (1994). *A natural history of love.* New York: Random House.

Adams, R., & Allan, G. (Eds.). (1999). *Placing friendship in context.* Cambridge, England: Cambridge University Press.

Adelman, M. B., Parks, M. R., & Albrecht, T. L. (1987). Supporting friends in need. In T. L. Albrecht, M. B. Adelman, & Associates (Eds.), *Communicating social support* (pp. 105–125). Beverly Hills, CA: Sage.

Adler, R., & Towne, N. (1993). *Looking out/looking in* (7th ed.). Fort Worth, TX: Harcourt Brace Jovanovich.

Afifi, W., & Faulkner, S. (2000). On being "just friends": The frequency and impact of sexual activity in cross-sex friendships. *Journal of Social and Personal Relationships,* 17, 205–222.

Ainsworth, M. D. S., Blehar, M. C., Waters, E., & Wall, S. (1978*). Patterns of attachment: A psychological study of the strange situation.* Hillsdale, NJ: Erlbaum.

Albright, J., & Conran, T. (2003, Fall). Desire, love, and betrayal: Constructing and deconstructing intimacy online. *Journal of Systemic Therapies,* 22(3), 41. New York: Guilford Publications.

Alexander, E. R., III. (1979). The reduction of cognitive conflict: Effects of various types of communication. *Journal of Conflict Resolution,* 23, 120–138.

Allan, G. (1994). Social structure and relationships. In S. W. Duck (Ed.), *Understanding relationship processes, 3: Social context and relationships* (pp. 1–25). Newbury Park, CA: Sage.

Allport, G. W. (1954). The Nature of Prejudice. Reading, MA: Addison-Wesley Pub. Co.

Almany, A., & Alwan, A. (1982). Communicating with the Arabs. Prospects Heights, IL: Waveland.

Altemeyer, B., & Hunsberger, B. (1992). Authoritarianism, religious fundamentalism, quest, and prejudice. *International Journal for the Psychology of Religion,* 2, 113–133.

Anders, G. (1997, September 4). Doctors learn to bridge cultural gaps. *The Wall Street Journal,* pp. B1, B4.

Andersen, M. L., & Collins, P. H. (Eds.). (1992). *Race, class, and gender: An anthology.* Belmont, CA: Wadsworth.

Andersen, M. L., & Collins, P. H. (Eds.). (1998). *Race, class, and gender: An anthology* (3rd ed.). Belmont, CA: Wadsworth.

Andersen, P. (1999). *Nonverbal communication: Forms and functions.* Mountain View, CA: Mayfield.

Andersen, P., Hecht, M., Hoobler, G., & Smallwood, M. (2002). Nonverbal communication across cultures. In W. Gudykunst & B. Mody (Eds.), *The handbook of international and intercultural communication* (2nd ed.). Thousand Oaks, CA: Sage.

Anderson, K., & Leaper, C. (1998). Meta-analyses of gender effects on conversational interruption: Who, when, where, and how? *Sex Roles,* 39, 225–252.

Anderson, P., & Guerrero, L. (Eds.). (1998). *Handbook of communication and emotion.* San Diego, CA: Academic Press.

Angelou, M. (1990). *I shall not be moved.* New York: Random House.

Arenson, K. (2002, January 13). The fine art of listening. *Education Life,* pp. 34–35.

Argyle, M., & Henderson, M. (1985). The rules of relationships. In S. W. Duck & D. Perlman (Eds.), *Understanding personal relationships: An interdisciplinary approach* (pp. 63–84). Beverly Hills, CA: Sage.

Aries, E. (1987). Gender and communication. In P. Shaver (Ed.), *Sex and gender* (pp. 149–176). Newbury Park, CA: Sage.

Aries, E. (1996). *Men and women in interaction: Reconsidering differences.* New York: Oxford University Press.

Arnett, R. C. (1986). The inevitable conflict and confronting in dialogue. In J. Stewart (Ed.), *Bridges, not walls* (4th ed., pp. 272–279). New York: Random House.

Artz, Sibylle. (1998). *Sex, power and the violent school girl.* Toronto: Trifolium Books.

Atsumi, R. (1980). Patterns of personal relationships. *Social Analysis,* 5, 63–78.

AXIS Center for Public Awareness of People with Disabilities, 4550 Indianola Avenue, Columbus OH 43214.

Axtell, R. (1990a). *Do's and taboos around the world* (2nd ed.). New York: Wiley.

Axtell, R. (1990b). *Do's and taboos of hosting international visitors.* New York: Wiley.

Ayres, J., Keereetaweep, T., Chen, P., & Edwards, P. (1998). Communication apprehension and employment interviews. *Communication Education, 47*, 1–17.

Ayto, J. (Ed.). (1999). *Twentieth century words.* Oxford, UK: Oxford University Press.

Bach, G. R., & Wyden, P. (1973). *The intimate enemy: How to fight fair in love and marriage.* New York: Avon.

Bachen, C., & Illouz, E. (1996). Imagining romance: Young people's cultural models of romance and love. *Critical Studies of Mass Communication, 13*, 279–308.

Bailey, P. (1998, September 29). Daily bread. *Durham Herald Sun,* p. C5.

Bargh, J. (1999, January 29). The most powerful manipulative messages are hiding in plain sight. *Chronicle of Higher Education,* p. B6.

Barker, L., Edwards, R., Gaines, C., Gladney, K., & Holley, F. (1981). An investigation of proportional time spent in various communication activities by college students. *Journal of Applied Communication Research, 8*, 101–109.

Barnlund, D. (1989). *Communication styles of Japanese and Americans: Images and reality.* Belmont, CA: Wadsworth.

Bartholomew K., & Horowitz, L. M. (1991). Attachment styles among young adults: A test of a four-category model. *Journal of Personality and Social Psychology, 61*, 226–244.

Basketball Nova Scotia Code of Conduct. Retrieved June 7, 2009, from www.basketball.ns.ca/Policies.htm.

Basow, S., I., & Rubenfeld, K. (2003). "Troubles talk": Effects of gender and gender-typing. *Sex Roles, 48*, 183–187.

Bass, A. (1993, December 5). Behavior that can wreck a marriage. *Raleigh News and Observer,* p. 8E.

Bast, M., & Thomson, C. (2004). *Out of the box: Coaching with the Enneagram.* Portland, OR: Metamorphous Press.

Bates, E. (1994, Fall). Beyond black and white. *Southern Exposure,* pp. 11–15.

Bateson, M. C. (1990). *Composing a life.* New York: Penguin/Plume.

Baxter, L. A. (1984). Trajectories of relationship disengagement. *Journal of Social and Personal Relationships, 7*, 141–178.

Baxter, L. A. (1985). Accomplishing relational disengagement. In S. Duck & D. Perlman (Eds.), *Understanding personal relationships: An interdisciplinary approach* (pp. 243–265). Beverly Hills, CA: Sage.

Baxter, L. A. (1987). Self-disclosure and relationship disengagement. In V. Derlega & J. H. Berg (Eds.), *Self-disclosure: Theory, research, and therapy* (pp. 155–174). New York: Plenum.

Baxter, L. A. (1988). A dialectical perspective on communication strategies in relationship development. In S. W. Duck, D. F. Hay, S. E. Hobfoll, W. Iches, & B. Montgomery (Eds.), *Handbook of personal relationships* (pp. 257–273). London: Wiley.

Baxter, L. A. (1990). Dialectical contradictions in relational development. *Journal of Social and Personal Relationships, 7*, 69–88.

Baxter, L. A. (1993). The social side of personal relationships: A dialectical perspective. In S. Duck (Ed.), *Understanding relationship processes, 3: Social context and relationships* (pp. 139–165). Newbury Park, CA: Sage.

Baxter, L. A., & Montgomery, B. M. (1996). *Relating: Dialogues and dialectics.* New York: Guilford.

Baxter, L. A., & Simon, E. P. (1993). Relationship maintenance strategies and dialectical contradictions in personal relationships. *Journal of Social and Personal Relationships, 10*, 225–242.

Baym, N. (2002). Interpersonal life online. In L. Lievrouw & S. Livingstone (Eds.), *The handbook of new media* (pp. 62–76). Thousand Oaks, CA: Sage.

Be civil. (1994, July 5). *The Wall Street Journal,* p. A1.

Beck, A. (1988). *Love is never enough.* New York: Harper & Row.

Becker, C. S. (1987). Friendship between women: A phenomenological study of best friends. *Journal of Phenomenological Psychology, 18*, 59–72.

Begley, S. (1997, Spring/Summer special issue). How to build a baby's brain. *Newsweek,* pp. 27–30.

Bellah, R., Madsen, R., Sullivan, W., Swindler, A., & Tipton, S. (1985). *Habits of the heart: Individualism and commitment in American life.* Berkeley, CA: University of California Press.

Bellamy, L. (1996, December 18). Kwanzaa cultivates cultural and culinary connections. *Raleigh News and Observer,* pp. 1F, 9F.

Belsky, J., & Pensky, E. (1988). Developmental history, personality, and family relationships: Toward an emergent family system. In R. A. Hinde & J. Stevenson-Hinde (Eds.), *Relationships within families: Mutual influences* (pp. 193–217). Oxford: Clarendon.

Benenson, J., Apostoleris, N., & Parnass, J. (1997). Age and sex differences in dyadic and group interaction. *Developmental Psychology, 33*, 538–543.

Benjamin, B., & Werner, R. (2004). Touch in the Western world. *Massage Therapy Journal, 43*, 28–32.

Benjamin, D., & Horwitz, T. (1994, July 14). German view: "You Americans work too hard—and for what?" *The Wall Street Journal,* pp. B1, B6.

Berg, J. H. (1987). Responsiveness and self-disclosure. In V. J. Derlega & J. H. Berg (Eds.), *Self-disclosure: Theory, research, and therapy.* New York: Plenum.

Berger, C. R., & Bell, R. A. (1988). Plans and the initiation of social relationships. *Human Communication Research, 15*, 217–235.

Bergstrom, M., & Nussbaum, J. (1996). Cohort differences in interpersonal conflict: Implications for older patient–younger care provider interaction. *Health Communication*, 8, 233–248.

Bernard, E. (2004). *Some of my best friends: Writing on interracial friendships.* New York: Harper-Collins-Amistad.

Berne, E. (1964). *Games people play.* New York: Grove.

Bernstein, B. (1974). *Class, codes, and control: Theoretical studies toward a sociology of language* (rev. ed.). New York: Shocken.

Best, J. (1989). *Images of issues: Typifying contemporary social problems.* New York: Aldine de Gruyter.

Bielski, Zosia. (2009, April 9). *One Click Stands. The Globe and Mail*, p. L1.

Bippus, A., & Young, S. (2005). Owning your emotions: Reactions to expressions of self-versus other-attributed positive and negative emotions. *Journal of Applied Communication Research*, 33, 26–45.

Birdwhistell, R. (1970). *Kinesics and context.* Philadelphia: University of Pennsylvania Press.

Bites. (1998, September 30). *Raleigh News and Observer*, p. 1F.

Blieszner, R., & Adams, R. (1992). *Adult friendship.* Newbury Park, CA: Sage.

Blumstein, P., & Schwartz, P. (1983). *American couples: Money, work, and sex.* New York: William Morrow.

Bolton, R. (1986). Listening is more than merely hearing. In J. Stewart (Ed.), *Bridges, not walls* (4th ed., pp. 159–179). New York: Random House.

Boon, S. (1994). Dispelling doubt and uncertainty: Trust in romantic relationships. In S. W. Duck (Ed.), *Understanding relationship processes, 4: Dynamics of relationships* (pp. 86–111). Thousand Oaks, CA: Sage.

Bordo, S. (1999). *The male body: A new look at men in public and in private.* New York: Farrar, Straus & Giroux.

Bosmajian, H. (1974). *The language of oppression.* Washington, DC: Public Affairs Papers.

Bowen, S. P., & Michal-Johnson, P. (1995). Sexuality in the AIDS era. In S. W. Duck & J. T. Wood (Eds.), *Understanding relationship processes, 5: Relationship challenges* (pp. 150–180). Thousand Oaks, CA: Sage.

Bowlby, J. (1973). *Separation: Attachment and loss* (Vol. 2). New York: Basic.

Bowlby, J. (1988). *A secure base: Parent–child attachment and healthy human development.* New York: Basic.

Bozzi, V. (1986, February). Eat to the beat. *Psychology Today*, p. 16.

Brace C. L. (2001). "Debunking biological theories of race." Review of *The Emperor's New Clothes: Biological Theories of Race at the Millennium*, by Joseph L. Graves, Jr. *The American Scientist*, 89:277.

Bradbury, T. N., & Fincham, F. D. (1990). Attributions in marriage: Review and critique. *Psychological Bulletin*, 107, 3–33.

Braithwaite, C. (1990). Communicative silence: A cross cultural study of Basso's hypothesis. In D. Carbaugh (Ed.), *Cultural communication and intercultural contact* (pp. 321–327). Hillsdale, NJ: Erlbaum.

Braithwaite, D. (1996). "Persons first": Exploring different perspectives on the communication of persons with disabilities. In E. B. Ray (Ed.), *Communication and disenfranchisement: Social health issues and implications* (pp. 449–464). Hillsdale, NJ: Erlbaum.

Braithwaite, D., & Kellas, J. K. (2006). Shopping for and with friends: Everyday communication at the shopping mall. In J. T. Wood & S. Duck (Eds.), *Composing relationships: Communication in everyday life* (pp. 86–95). Belmont, CA: Wadsworth.

Brazelton, T. B. (1997, Spring/Summer special issue). Building a better self-image. *Newsweek*, pp. 76–77.

Brehm, S. (1992). *Intimate relations* (2nd ed.). New York: McGraw-Hill.

Brooks, D. (2001, April 30). Time to do everything except think. *Newsweek*, p. 71.

Brooks, R., & Goldstein, S. (2001). *Raising resilient children.* New York: Contemporary Books.

Bruess, C., & Hoefs, A. (2006). The cat puzzle recovered: Composing relationships through family ritual. In J. T. Wood & S. Duck (Eds.), *Composing relationships: Communication in everyday life* (pp. 65–75). Belmont, CA: Wadsworth.

Bruess, C., & Pearson, J. (1997). Interpersonal rituals in marriage and adult friendship. *Communication Monographs*, 64, 25–46.

Brunham, Robert. (August 7, 2001.) Personal communication.

Buber, M. (1957). Distance and relation. *Psychiatry*, 20, 97–104.

Buber, M. (1970). *I and thou* (Walter Kaufmann, Trans.). New York: Scribner.

Buckley, M. (1992). Focus on research: We listen a book a day; we speak a book a week: Learning from Walter Loban. *Language Arts*, 69, 622–626.

Burgoon, J. K., Buller, D. B., Hale, J. L., & deTurck, M. A. (1984). Relational messages associated with nonverbal behaviors. *Human Communication Research*, 10, 351–378.

Burgoon, J. K., Buller, D. B., & Woodhall, G. W. (1989). *Nonverbal communication: The unspoken dialogue.* New York: Harper & Row.

Burgoon, J. K., & LePoire, B. (1999). Nonverbal cues and interpersonal judgments: Participant and observer perceptions of intimacy, dominance, composure, and formality. *Communication Monographs*, 66, 105–124.

Burgoon, J. K., Stern, L., & Dillman, L. (1995). *Interpersonal adaptation: Dyadic interaction patterns.* New York: Cambridge University Press.

Burleson, B. R. (1984). Comforting communication. In H. E. Sypher & J. L. Applegate (Eds.), *Communication by children and adults: Social cognitive and strategic processes* (pp. 63–104). Beverly Hills, CA: Sage.

Burleson, B. R. (1987). Cognitive complexity. In J. C. McCroskey & J. A. Daly (Eds.), *Personality and interpersonal communication* (pp. 305–349). Newbury Park, CA: Sage.

Burleson, B. R. (1994). Comforting messages: Features, functions, and outcomes. In J. A. Daly &J. M. Wiemann (Eds.), *Strategic interpersonal communication* (pp. 135–161). Hillsdale, NJ: Erlbaum.

Burleson, B. R., & Samter, W. (1994). A social skills approach to relationship maintenance: How individual differences in communication skills affect the achievement of relationship functions. In D. J. Canary & L. Stafford (Eds.), *Communication and relational maintenance.* Orlando: Academic.

Burley-Allen, M. (1995). *Listening: The Forgotten Skill.* New York: John Wiley & Sons Inc.

"Business Bulletin." (1996, July 18). *The Wall Street Journal,* p. A1.

Butterfield, F. (1982). *China: Alive in the bitter sea.* New York: Times Books.

Button, C. M., & Collier, D. R. (1991, June). *A comparison of people's concepts of love and romantic love.* Paper presented at the Canadian Psychological Association Conference, Calgary.

Caldera, Y. M., Huston, A. C., & O'Brien, M. (1989). Social interactions and play patterns of parents and toddlers with feminine, masculine, and neutral toys. *Child Development,* 60, 70–76.

California Department of Education. *Inside the Teenage Brain*: pubs.cde.ca.gov/tcsii/ch4/adlescntcharactr.aspx.

Campbell, S. M. (1986). From either–or to both–and relationships. In J. Stewart (Ed.), *Bridges, not walls* (4th ed., pp. 262–270). New York: Random House.

Canary, D., & Dindia, K. (Eds.). (1998). *Sex differences and similarities in communication.* Mahwah, NJ: Erlbaum.

Canary, D., & Stafford, L. (Eds.). (1994). *Communication and relational maintenance.* New York: Academic.

Cancian, F. (1987). *Love in America. Cambridge,* MA: Cambridge University Press.

Cancian, F. (1989). Love and the rise of capitalism. In B. Risman & P. Schwartz (Eds.), *Gender in intimate relationships* (pp. 12–25). Belmont, CA: Wadsworth.

Canfield, Jack (Ed.). (1996, November). Chicken soup for the soul at work: 101 stories of courage, compassion and creativity in the workplace. *Health Communications.*

Capella, J. N. (1991). The biological origins of automated patterns of human interaction. *Communication Theory,* 1, 4–35.

Carl, W. (1998). A sign of the times. In J. T. Wood, *But I thought you meant ...: Misunderstandings in human communication* (pp. 195–208). Mountain View, CA: Mayfield.

Carl, W. (2006). <where r u?><here u?>: Everyday communication with relational technologies. In J. T. Wood & S. Duck (Eds.), *Composing relationships: Communication in everyday life* (pp. 96–109). Belmont, CA: Wadsworth.

Caspi, A., & Harbener, E. S. (1990). Continuity and change: Assortive marriage and the consistency of personality in adulthood. *Journal of Personality and Social Psychology,* 58, 250–258.

Cassirer, E. (1944). An essay on man. New Haven, CT: Yale University Press.

Cathcart, D., & Cathcart, R. (1997). The group: A Japanese context. In L. Samovar & R. Porter (Eds.), *Intercultural communication: A reader* (8th ed., pp. 329–339). Belmont, CA: Wadsworth.

Caughlin, J., Afifi, W., Carpenter-Theune, K., & Miller, L. (2005). Reasons for, and consequences of, revealing personal secrets in close relationships: A longitudinal study. *Personal Relationships,* 12, 43–59.

Chapman, Gary. (1995). *The five love languages: How to express heartfelt commitment to your mate.* Chicago: Northfield Pub.

Chatham-Carpenter, A., & DeFrancisco, V. (1998). Women construct self-esteem in their own terms: A feminist qualitative study. *Feminism and Psychology,* 8, 467–489.

Chodorow, N. (1989). *Feminism and psychoanalytic theory.* New Haven, CT: Yale University Press.

Cissna, K. N. L., & Sieburg, E. (1986). Patterns of interactional confirmation and disconfirmation. In J. Stewart (Ed.), *Bridges, not walls* (4th ed., pp. 230–239). New York: Random House.

Civickly, J. M., Pace, R. W., & Krause, R. M. (1977). Interviewer and client behaviors in supportive and defensive interviews. In B. D. Ruben (Ed.), *Communication yearbook,* 1 (pp. 347–362). New Brunswick, NJ: Transaction.

Clark, R. A. (1998). A comparison of topics and objectives in a cross-section of young men's and women's everyday conversations. In D. Canary & K. Dindia (Eds.), *Sex differences and similarities in communication: Critical essays and empirical investigations of sex and gender interaction* (pp. 303–319). Mahwah, NJ: Erlbaum.

Cloven, D. H., & Roloff, M. E. (1991). Sense-making activities and interpersonal conflict: Communicative cures for the mulling blues. *Western Journal of Speech Communication,* 55, 134–158.

Coates, J., & Cameron, D. (1989). *Women in their speech communities: New perspectives on language and sex.* London: Longman.

Coleman, J. (2000, March 27). My turn: Is technology making us intimate strangers? *Newsweek,* p. 12.

Collins, P. H. (1998). *Fighting words: Black women and the search for justice.* Minneapolis: University of Minnesota Press.

Condry, S. M., Condry, J. C., & Pogatshnik, L. W. (1983). Sex differences: A study of the ear of the beholder. *Sex Roles,* 9, 697–704.

Conference Board of Canada. Corporate Council on Education. (1992). *Employability Skills Profile.* Ottawa: Conference Board of Canada.

Conrad, C., & Poole, M. S. (2002). *Strategic organizational communication* (5th ed.). Fort Worth, TX: Harcourt.

Cooley, C. H. (1961). The social self. In T. Parsons, E. Shils, K. D. Naegele, & J. R. Pitts (Eds.), *Theories of society* (pp. 822–828). New York: Free Press.

Cooper, L., Seibold, D., & Suchner, R. (1997). Listening in organizations: An analysis of error structures in models of listening competency. *Communication Research Reports,* 14, 3.

Copeland, L., & Griggs, L. (1985). *Going international.* New York: Random House.

Corballis, M. C. (2002). *From hand to mouth: The origins of language.* Princeton, NJ: Princeton University Press.

Covey, Stephen (1989). *The seven habits of highly effective people.* New York: Free Press.

Covey, Stephen R. (1991). *Principle-centered leadership.* New York: Fireside.

Cozart, E. (1996, November 1997). Feng shui. *Raleigh News and Observer,* p. D1.

Crane, Frank. (1919). *Four Minute Essays* (Vol. V). New York: Wm. H. Wise & Co., Inc.

Crane, Frank. (1927). *Everyday Wisdom.* New York: Wm. H. Wise & Co.

CRC (Communications Research Centre Canada). (2008). *Eye on Technology:* www.crc.gc.ca/en/html/crc/home/mediazone/eye_on_tech/2008/issue9/hsvo.

Crockett, W. (1965). Cognitive complexity and impression formation. In B. A. Maher (Ed.), *Progress in experimental personality research,* 2. New York: Academic.

Cronen, V., Pearce, W. B., & Snavely, L. (1979). A theory of rule-structure and types of episodes and a study of perceived enmeshment in undesired repetitive patterns ("URPs"). In D. Nimmo (Ed.), *Communication yearbook,* 3. New Brunswick, NJ: Transaction.

Cross T., Bazron, B., Dennis, K., and Isaacs, M. (1989). *Towards a culturally competent system of care: A monograph on effective services for minority children who are severely emotionally disturbed* (Vol. I). Washington, DC: Georgetown University Child Development Center.

Crossen, C. (1997, July 10). Blah, blah, blah. *The Wall Street Journal,* p. 1A, 6A.

Culture at Work. *Communicating across cultures*: www.culture-at-work.com/highlow.html.

Cunningham, J. A., Strassberg, D. S., & Haan, B. (1986). Effects of intimacy and sex-role congruency on self-disclosure. *Journal of Social and Clinical Psychology,* 4, 393–401.

Cunningham, J. D., & Antill, J. K. (1995). Current trends in nonmarital cohabitation: The great POSSLQ hunt continues. In J. T. Wood & S. W. Duck (Eds.), *Understanding relationship processes, 6: Off the beaten track: Understudied relationships* (pp. 148–172). Thousand Oaks, CA: Sage.

Cupach, W. R., & Carlson, C. (2002). Characteristics and consequences of interpersonal complaints associated with perceived face threat. *Journal of Social and Personal Relationships,* 19, 443–462.

Cutler, B., & Penrod, S. (1995). *Mistaken identification: The eyewitness, psychology, and the law.* Cambridge, England: Cambridge University Press.

Cutrona, C. E. (1982). Transitions to college: Loneliness and the process of social adjustment. In L. A. Peplau & D. Perlman (Eds.), *Loneliness: A sourcebook of current theory, research, and therapy* (pp. 291–309). New York: Wiley Interscience.

Cyberscope, (1996, December 23). *Newsweek,* p. 10.

Dainton, B. (2006). *Stream of Consciousness* (2nd ed.). Routledge: London.

Davis, K. (1940). Extreme isolation of a child. *American Journal of Sociology,* 45, 554–565.

Davis K. (1947). A final note on a case of extreme isolation. *American Journal of Sociology,* 52, 432–437.

Davis, S., & Kieffer, J. (1998). Restaurant servers influence tipping behaviors. *Psychological Reports,* 83, 223–236.

Deal, T., & Kennedy, A. (1999). *The new corporate cultures: Revitalizing the workplace after downsizing, mergers, and reengineering.* Reading, MA: Perseus Books.

de Becker, G. (1997). *The gift of fear: Survival signals that protect us from violence.* New York: Little Brown.

DeFrancisco, V. (1991). The sounds of silence: How men silence women in marital relations. *Discourse and Society,* 2, 413–423.

de Frane, Gordon. (2000). *Spirituality and generosity: An understanding of the sacred men and women in aboriginal societies of the Americas.* Unpublished manuscript.

Delia, J., Clark, R. A., & Switzer, D. (1974). Cognitive complexity and impression formation in informal social interaction. *Speech Monographs,* 41, 299–308.

Dentan, R. (1995). Bad day at Bukit Pekan. *American Anthropologist,* 97, 225–231.

Derlega, V. J., & Berg, J. H. (1987). *Self-disclosure: Research, theory, and therapy.* New York: Plenum.

Dewey, J. (1910). *How we think.* Boston: D.C. Heath

Dews, B., & Law, C. (Eds.). (1995). *This fine place so far from home: Voices of academics from the working class.* Philadelphia: Temple University Press.

Dickson, F. (1995). The best is yet to be: Research on long-lasting marriages. In J. T. Wood & S. Duck (Eds.), *Understanding relationship processes, 6: Understudied relationships* (pp. 22–50). Thousand Oaks, CA: Sage.

DiFranco, Ani (singer–songwriter). (1994). Overlap. Album: *Out of Range.*

Dillard, J. P., & Witteman, G. (1985). Romantic relationships at work: Organizational and personal influences. *Human Communication Research,* 12, 99–116.

Dindia, K. (1994). A multiphasic view of relationship maintenance strategies. In D. Canary & L. Stafford (Eds.), *Communication and relational maintenance* (pp. 91–112). New York: Academic.

Dindia, K., & Fitzpatrick, M. A. (1985). Marital communication: Three approaches compared. In S. Duck & D. Perlman (Eds.), *Understanding personal relationships: An interdisciplinary approach* (pp. 137–157). Newbury Park, CA: Sage.

Dixson M., & Duck, S. W. (1993). Understanding relationship processes: Uncovering the human search for meaning. In S. W. Duck (Ed.), *Understanding relationship processes, 1: Individuals in relationships* (pp. 175–206). Newbury Park, CA: Sage.

Dolan, R. E., & Worden, R. L. (Eds.). (1992). *Japan: A country study.* Washington, DC: Library of Congress.

Dubos, Rene. (1981). *Celebrations of Life.* New York: McGraw-Hill.

Duck, S. W. (1985). Social and personal relationships. In M. L. Knapp & G. R. Miller (Eds.), *Handbook of interpersonal communication* (pp. 655–686). Beverly Hills, CA: Sage.

Duck, S. W. (1990). Relationships as unfinished business: Out of the frying pan and into the 1990s. *Journal of Social and Personal Relationships,* 7, 5–24.

Duck, S. W. (1992). *Human relationships* (2nd ed.). Newbury Park, CA: Sage.

Duck, S. W. (1994a). *Meaningful relationships.* Thousand Oaks, CA: Sage.

Duck, S. W. (1994b). Steady as (s)he goes: Relational maintenance as a shared meaning system. In D. Canary & L. Stafford (Eds.), *Communication and relational maintenance* (pp. 45–60). New York: Academic.

Duck, S. W. (2006). The play, playfulness, and the players: Everyday interaction as improvised rehearsal of relationships. In J. T. Wood & S. Duck (Eds.), *Composing relationships: Communication in everyday life* (pp. 15–23). Belmont, CA: Wadsworth.

Duck, S. W., Rutt, D. J., Hurst, M. H., & Strejc, H. (1991). Some evident truths about conversation in everyday relationships: All communications are not created equal. *Human Communication Research,* 18, 228–267.

Duck, S. W., & Wright, P. H. (1993). Reexamining gender differences in same-gender friendships: A close look at two kinds of data. *Sex Roles,* 28, 709–727.

Dyson, M. (1995). The plight of black men. In M. L. Andersen & P. H. Collins (Eds.), *Race, class, and gender: An anthology* (2nd ed., pp. 136–146). Belmont, CA: Wadsworth.

Eadie, W. F. (1982). Defensive communication revisited: A critical examination of Gibb's theory. *Southern Speech Communication Journal,* 47, 163–177.

Earley, P. C., & Mosakowski, E. (2004, October). Cultural intelligence. *Business Review,* 00178012, 82(10), 130–146.

Eaves, M., & Leathers, D. (1991). Context as communication: McDonalds vs. Burger King. *Journal of Applied Communication,* 19, 263–289.

Eckman, P., Friesen, W., & Ellsworth, P. (1971). *Emotion in the human face: Guidelines for research and an integration of findings.* Elmsford, NY: Pergamon.

Ehrenreich, B. (1995). The silenced majority: Why the average working person has disappeared from American media and culture. In M. L. Andersen & P. H. Collins (Eds.), *Race, class, and gender: An anthology* (2nd ed., pp. 147–148). Belmont, CA: Wadsworth.

Eichenbaum, L., & Orbach, S. (1987). *Between women: Love, envy, and competition in women's friendships.* New York: Viking.

Eisenberg, N. (2002). Empathy-related emotional responses, altruism, and their socialization. In R. J. Davidson & A. Harrington (Eds.), *Voices of compassion: Western scientists and Tibetan Buddhists examine human nature* (pp. 131–164). London: Oxford University Press.

Ekman, P. & Davidson, R. (Eds.) (1994). *The nature of emotions: Fundamental questions.* New York: Oxford University Press.

Ellis, A. (1962). *Reason and emotion in psychotherapy.* New York: Lyle Stuart.

Ellis A., & Harper, R. (1975). *A new guide to rational living.* Englewood Cliffs, NJ: Prentice-Hall.

Ellis, D. (1989). Male abuse of a marriage or cohabiting female partner. *Violence and Victims,* 4, 235–255.

Emmons, S. (1998, February 3). The look on his face: Yes, it was culture shock. *Raleigh News and Observer,* p. 5E.

Erbert, L. (2000). Conflict and dialectics: Perceptions of dialectical contradictions in marital conflict. *Journal of Social and Personal Relationships,* 17, 638–659.

Estes, W. K. (1989). Learning theory. In A. Lessold & R. Glaser (Eds.), *Foundations for a psychology of education.* Hillsdale, NJ: Erlbaum.

Etcheverry, P. E., & Le, B. (2005). Thinking about commitment: Accessibility of commitment and prediction of relationship persistence, accommodation, and willingness to sacrifice. *Personal Relationships,* 12, 103–123.

Fadiman, A. (1997). *The spirit catches you and you fall down.* New York: Farrar, Straus & Giroux.

Fantini, A. E. (1991). Bilingualism: Exploring language and culture. In L. Malave & G. Duquette (Eds.), *Language, culture, and cognition: A collection of studies on first and second language acquisition* (pp. 110–119). Bristol, PA: Multilingual Matters, Ltd.

Fehr, B. (1993). How do I love thee: Let me consult my prototype. In S. W. Duck (Ed.), *Understanding relationship processes, 1: Individuals in relationships* (pp. 87–122). Newbury Park, CA: Sage.

Fehr, B., & Russell, J. A. (1991). Concept of love viewed from a prototype perspective. *Journal of Personality and Social Psychology,* 60, 425–438.

Feigenson, N. (2000). *Legal blame: How jurors think and talk about accidents.* Washington, DC: American Psychological Association.

Ferrante, J. (1992). *Sociology: A global perspective.* Belmont, CA: Wadsworth.

Ferrante, J. (1995). *Sociology: A global perspective* (2nd ed.). Belmont, CA: Wadsworth.

Fincham, F. D. (2000). The kiss of the porcupines: From attributing responsibility to forgiving. *Personal Relationships,* 7, 1–23.

Fincham, F. D., & Beach, S. (2002). Forgiveness in marriage: Implications for psychological aggression and constructive communication. *Personal Relationships,* 9, 239–251.

Fincham, F. D., & Bradbury, T. N. (1987). The impact of attributions in marriage: A longitudinal analysis. *Journal of Personality and Social Psychology,* 53, 510–517.

Fincham, F. D., Paleari, G., & Regalia, C. (2002). Forgiveness in marriage: The role of relationship quality, attributions, and empathy. *Personal Relationships,* 9, 27–37.

Finkel, E., Rusbult, C. E., Kumashiro, M., & Hannon, P. (2002). Dealing with betrayal in close relationships: Does commitment promote forgiveness? *Journal of Personality and Social Psychology,* 82, 956–974.

Finkelstein, J. (1980). Considerations for a sociology of emotions. *Studies in Symbolic Interaction,* 3, 111–121.

Fisher, B. A. (1987). *Interpersonal communication: The pragmatics of human relationships.* New York: Random House.

Fisher, J. D., & Byrne, D. (1975). Too close for comfort: Sex differences in response to invasions of personal space. *Journal of Personal and Social Psychology,* 32, 15–21.

Fitzpatrick, M. A. (1988). *Between husbands and wives: Communication in marriage.* Newbury Park, CA: Sage.

Fitzpatrick, M. A., & Best, P. (1979). Dyadic adjustment in relational types: Consensus, cohesion, affectional expression and satisfaction in enduring relationships. *Communication Monographs,* 46, 167–178.

Fleishman, J., Sherbourne, C., & Crystal, S. (2000). Coping, conflictual social interactions, social support, and mood among HIV-infected persons. *American Journal of Community Psychology,* 28, 421–453.

Fletcher, G. J., & Fincham, F. D. (1991). Attribution in close relationships. In G. J. Fletcher & F. D. Fincham (Eds.), *Cognition in close relationships* (pp. 7–35). Hillsdale, NJ: Erlbaum.

Fletcher, G. J., Fincham, F. D., Cramer, L., & Heron, N. (1987). The role of attributions in the development of dating relationships. *Journal of Personality and Social Psychology,* 51, 875–884.

Floyd, K., & Parks, M. (1995). Manifesting closeness in the interactions of peers: A look at siblings and friends. *Communication Reports,* 8, 69–76.

Forbes, G. B. (2001). College students with tattoos and piercings: Motives, family experiences, personality factors, and perception by others. *Psychological Reports,* 89, 774–786.

Fowers, B. J. (1991). His and her marriage: A multivariate study of gender and marital satisfaction. *Sex Roles,* 24, 209–221.

Fox, L., & Frankel, H. (2005). *Breaking the code: Two teens reveal the secrets of better parent-child communication.* New York: Penguin-New American Library.

Fox-Genovese, E. (1991). *Feminism without illusions.* Chapel Hill: University of North Carolina Press.

French, J. R .P. and Raven, B. (1959). The bases of social power, in D. Cartwright (Ed.), *Studies in social power,* Ann Arbor: University of Michigan.

French, M. (1992). *The war against women.* New York: Summit.

Fresener, Scott, (1995). *The T-Shirt Book.* Layton, UT: Gibbs M. Smith Inc.

Fridlund, A. J. (1994). *Human facial expression.* San Diego: Academic.

Friesen, M., Fletcher, G., & Overall, N. (2005). A dyadic assessment of forgiveness in intimate relationships. *Personal Relationships,* 12, 61–77.

Frijda, N. H. (1986). *The emotions.* Cambridge, U.K.: Cambridge University Press.

Gabbay, Nisan. (2006). *Facebook* Case Study: Offline Behaviour Drives Online Usage. *Startup Review*: www.startup-review.com/blog/facebook-case-study-offline-behavior-drives-online-usage.php.

Gaines, S., Jr. (1995). Relationships among members of cultural minorities. In J. T. Wood & S. W. Duck (Eds.), *Understanding relationship processes, 6: Off the beaten track: Understudied relationships* (pp. 51–88). Thousand Oaks, CA: Sage.

Gangopadhyay, M., & Mandal, K. M. (2008). Emotional intelligence: A universal or cultural-specific construct? In R. J. Emmerling, V. K. Shanwal & M. K. Mandal (Eds.), *Emotional intelligence: Theoretical and cultural perspectives* (pp. 115–134). New York: Nova Science.

Gangwish, K. (1999). *Living in two worlds: Asian-American women and emotion.* Paper presented at the National Communication Convention, Chicago.

Gerstel, N., & Gross, H. (1985). *Commuter marriage.* New York: Guilford.

Gibb, J. R. (1961). Defensive communication. *Journal of Communication,* 11, 141–148.

Gibb, J. R. (1964). Climate for trust formation. In L. Bradford, J. Gibb, & K. Benne (Eds.), *T-group theory and laboratory method* (pp. 279–309). New York: Wiley.

Gibb, J. R. (1970). Sensitivity training as a medium for personal growth and improved interpersonal relationships. *Interpersonal Development,* 1, 6–31.

Gibran, Kahlil. (1926). *Sand and Foam.* New York: Knopf.

Gilman, S. (1999a). *Creating beauty to cure the soul: Race and psychology in the shaping of aesthetic surgery.* Durham, NC: Duke University Press.

Gilman, S. (1999b). *Making the body beautiful: A cultural history of aesthetic surgery.* Princeton, NJ: Princeton University Press.

Goldhaber, G. M. (1993). *Organizational communication* (6th ed.). Dubuque, IA: Wm. C. Brown & Benchmark.

Goldin-Meadow, S. (2004). *Hearing gesture: How our hands help us think.* Cambridge, MA: Harvard University Press.

Goldner, V., Penn, P., Sheinberg, M., & Walker, G. (1990). Love and violence: Gender paradoxes in volatile attachments. *Family Process,* 19, 343–364.

Goldsmith, D., & Fitch, K. (1997). The normative context of advice as social support. *Human Communication Research,* 23, 454–476.

Goldsmith, D., & Fulfs, P. (1999). You just don't have the evidence: An analysis of claims and evidence in Deborah Tannen's *You just don't understand.* In M. Roloff (Ed.), *Communication Yearbook,* 22 (pp. 1–49). Thousand Oaks, CA: Sage.

Goleman, D. (1995a). *Emotional intelligence.* New York: Bantam.

Goleman, D. (1995b, November–December). What's your emotional intelligence? *Utne Reader,* pp. 74–76.

Goleman, D. (1998). *Working with emotional intelligence.* New York: Bantam.

Goleman, D., Boyatzis, R., & McKee, A. (2002). *Primal leadership: Realizing the power of emotional intelligence.* Cambridge, MA: Harvard Business School Press.

Goman, C. K. (2009, April 21). Venus, Mars and workplace communication. *Financial Post.*

Goode, T. D., Dunne, M. C., & Bronheim, S. M. (2006). *The evidence base for cultural and linguistic competency in health care.* Washington, DC: Georgetown University Child Development Center.

Good-looking lawyers make more money, says a study by economists. (1996, January 4). *The Wall Street Journal,* p. A1.

Gottman, J. (1993). The roles of conflict engagement, escalation or avoidance in marital interaction: A longitudinal view of five types of couples. *Journal of Consulting and Clinical Psychology,* 61, 6–15.

Gottman, J. (1997, May). *Findings from 25 years of studying marriage.* Paper presented at the Conference of the Coalition of Marriage, Family and Couples Education, Arlington, VA.

Gottman, J., & Carrère, S. (1994). Why can't men and women get along? Developmental roots and marital inequities. In D. J. Canary & L. Stafford (Eds.), *Communication and relational maintenance* (pp. 203–229). New York: Academic.

Gottman, J., Katz, L., and Hooven, C. (1996). *Meta-emotions: How families communicate emotionally.* Hillsdale, NJ: Lawrence Erlbaum Assoc.

Gottman, J., Markman, H. J., & Notarius, C. (1977). The topography of marital conflict: A sequential analysis of verbal and nonverbal behavior. *Journal of Marriage and the Family,* 39, 461–477.

Gottman, J., Notarius, C., Gonso, J., & Markman, H. J. (1976). *A couple's guide to communication.* Champaign, IL: Research Press.

Gottman, J., Notarius, C., Markman, H., Banks, S., Yoppi, B., & Rubin, M. E. (1976). Behavior exchange theory and marital decision making. *Journal of Experimental Social Psychology,* 34, 14–23.

Gottman, J., & Silver, N. (2000). *The seven principles for making marriage work.* Three Rivers, MI: Three Rivers Press.

Gravois, John. (2005, April 8). "Teach impediment: When the student can't understand the instructor, who is to blame?" *The Chronicle of Higher Education.*

Gray, H., & Foushee, V. (1997). Adolescent dating violence: Differences between one-sided and mutually violent profiles. *Journal of Interpersonal Violence,* 12, 126–141.

Greenberg, S. (1997, Spring/Summer special issue). The loving ties that bind. *Newsweek,* pp. 68–72.

Greene, J., & Burleson, B. (Eds.). (2003). *Handbook of communication and social interaction skills.* Mahwah, NJ: Erlbaum.

Griffin, D., and Bartholomew, K. (1994). The metaphysics of measurement: The case of adult attachment. *Advances in Personal Relationships,* 5, 17–52.

Gross, H. E. (1980). Couples who live apart: Time/place disjunctions and their consequence. *Symbolic Interaction,* 3, 69–82.

Gross, M. (2000, June). The lethal politics of beauty. *George,* pp. 53–59, 99–100.

Gudykunst, W., & Lee, C. (2002). Crosscultural communication theories. In W. Gudykunst & B. Mody (Eds.), *The handbook of international and intercultural communication* (2nd ed., pp. 25–50). Thousand Oaks, CA: Sage.

Gueguen, N., & De Gail, M. (2003). The effect of smiling on helping behavior: Smiling and good Samaritan behavior. *Communication Reports,* 16, 133–140.

Guerrero, L. (1996). Attachment style differences in intimacy and involvement: A test of the four-category model. *Communication Monographs,* 63, 269–292.

Hakuta, K. (1986). *Mirror of language: The debate on bilingualism.* New York: Basic.

Hall, E. T. (1966). *The hidden dimension.* New York: Anchor.

Hall, E. T. (1968). Proxemics. *Current Anthropology,* 9, 83–108.

Hall, E. T. (1976). *Beyond culture.* New York: Doubleday.

Hall, E. T. (1983). *The dance of life: The other dimension of time.* New York: Anchor.

Hall, J. A. (1978). Gender effects in decoding nonverbal cues. *Psychological Bulletin,* 85, 845–857.

Hall, J. A. (1987). On explaining gender differences: The case of nonverbal communication. In P. Shaver & C. Hendricks (Eds.), *Sex and gender* (pp. 177–200). Newbury Park, CA: Sage.

Hall, J. A., Carter, J. D., & Horgan, T. G. (2000). Gender differences in nonverbal communication of emotion. In A. H. Fischer (Ed.), *Gender and emotion: Social psychological perspectives* (pp. 97–117). Cambridge, England: Cambridge University Press.

Hallstein, L. (2000). Where standpoint stands now: An introduction and commentary. *Women's Studies in Communication*, 23, 1–15.

Hamachek, D. (1992). *Encounters with the self* (3rd ed.). Fort Worth: Harcourt Brace Jovanovich.

Hansen, J. E., & Schuldt, W. J. (1984). Marital self-disclosure and marital satisfaction. *Journal of Marriage and the Family*, 46, 923–926.

Haraway, D. (1988). Situated knowledges: The science question in feminism and the privilege of partial perspective. *Signs*, 14, 575–599.

Harding, S. (1991). *Whose science? Whose knowledge? Thinking from women's lives*. Ithaca, NY: Cornell University Press.

Harris, J. (1998). *The nurture assumption*. New York: Simon & Schuster/Free Press.

Harris, M., Walters, L., & Waschall, S. (1991). Gender and ethnic differences in obesity-related behaviors and attitudes in a college sample. *Journal of Applied Social Psychology*, 21, 1545–1566.

Harris, T. J. (1969). *I'm OK, you're OK*. New York: Harper & Row.

Hasserbrauck, M., & Aaron, A. (2001). Prototype matching in close relationships. *Personality and Social Psychology Bulletin*, 27, 1111–1122.

Healy, J. (1990). *Endangered minds: Why children don't think and what we can do about it*. New York: Simon & Schuster.

Hecht, M. L., Marston, P. J., & Larkey, L. K. (1994). Love ways and relationship quality in heterosexual relationships. *Journal of Social and Personal Relationships*, 11, 25–44.

Heider, F. (1958). *The psychology of interpersonal relations*. New York: Wiley.

Heise, D. (1999). Controlling affective experience interpersonally. *Social Psychology Quarterly*, 62, 4–11.

Helgeson, V. (1994). Long-distance romantic relationships: Sex differences in adjustment and breakup. *Personal and Social Psychology Bulletin*, 20, 254–266.

Hendrick, C., & Hendrick, S. (1988). Lovers wear rose-colored glasses. *Journal of Social and Personal Relationships*, 5, 161–184.

Hendrick, C., & Hendrick, S. (1989). Research on love: Does it measure up? *Journal of Personality and Social Psychology*, 56, 784–794.

Hendrick, C., & Hendrick, S. (1996). Gender and the experience of heterosexual love. In J. T. Wood (Ed.), *Gendered relationships*. Mountain View, CA: Mayfield.

Hendrick, C., Hendrick, S., Foote, F. H., & Slapion-Foote, M. J. (1984). Do men and women love differently? *Journal of Social and Personal Relationships*, 2, 177–196.

Henley, N. M. (1977). *Body politics: Power, sex and nonverbal communication*. Englewood Cliffs, NJ: Prentice-Hall.

Henry, F. (2002). Canada's contribution to the "management" of ethno-cultural diversity. *Canadian Journal of Communication*, 27, 2.

Hewes, D. (Ed.). (1995). *The cognitive bases of interpersonal perception*. Mahwah, NJ: Erlbaum.

Hickson, M., Stacks, D., & Moore, N. (2004). *Nonverbal communication: Studies and applications*. Los Angeles, CA: Roxbury.

Hochschild, A. (1979). Emotion work, feeling rules, and social structure. *American Journal of Sociology*, 85, 551–575.

Hochschild, A. (1983). *The managed heart*. Berkeley: University of California Press.

Hochschild, A. (1990). Ideology and emotion management: A perspective and path for future research. In T. Kemper (Ed.), *Research agendas in the sociology of emotions* (pp. 117–142). New York: State University of New York Press.

Hochschild, A. (1997). *The time bind: When work becomes home and home becomes work*. New York: Metropolitan Books.

Hochschild, A., with Machung, A. (1989). *The second shift*. New York: Viking.

Hofstede, G. (1980). *Explanation of cultural dimensions*: www.12manage.com/methods_hofstede.html.

Hofstede, G. (1991). *Cultures and organizations: Software of the mind*. London: McGraw Hill.

Hofstede, G. (2001). *Cultures' consequences: Comparing values, behaviors, institutions, and organizations across nations*. Thousand Oaks, CA: Sage Publications.

Hoijer, H. (1994). The Sapir–Whorf hypothesis. In L. Samovar & R. Porter (Eds.), *Intercultural communication: A reader* (7th ed.). Belmont, CA: Wadsworth.

Hojat, M. (1982). Loneliness as a function of selected personality variables. *Journal of Clinical Psychology*, 38, 136–141.

Honeycutt, J. M. (1993). Memory structures for the rise and fall of personal relationships. In S. W. Duck (Ed.), *Understanding relationship processes, 1: Individuals in relationships* (pp. 30–59). Newbury Park, CA: Sage.

Honeycutt, J. M., Woods, B., & Fontenot, K. (1993). The endorsement of communication conflict rules as a function of engagement, marriage and marital ideology. *Journal of Social and Personal Relationships*, 10, 285–304.

Honoré, C. (2004). *In praise of slowness*. San Francisco: Harper.

Honoré, C. (2005). *In praise of slowness: Challenging the cult of speed.* San Francisco: HarperCollins.

Horn, Sam. (1996). *Tongue Fu!* New York, NY: St. Martin's Griffin.

Houston, M. (2004). When black women talk with white women: Why dialogues are difficult. In A. González, M. Houston, & V. Chen (Eds.), *Our voices: Essays in culture, ethnicity, and communication* (4th ed., pp. 119–125). Los Angeles: Roxbury.

Howard, J. W., & Dawes, R. M. (1976). Linear prediction of marital happiness. *Personality and Social Psychology Bulletin,* 2, 478–480.

Huitt, W. (1999, March 1). *Becoming a brilliant star.* Paper presented at the Tenth Annual Youth-At-Risk Conference, Savannah, GA. Available online: http://chiron.valdosta.edu/whuitt/brilstar.html.

Human Rights Watch. (1999). *Broken people: Caste violence against India's untouchables.* Washington, DC: Author.

Hunsberger, B. (1996). Religious fundamentalism, right-wing authoritarianism, and hostility towards homosexuals in non-Christian religious groups. International Journal for the Psychology of Religion, 6, 39–49.

Huston, M., & Schwartz, P. (1995). Relationships of lesbians and gay men. In J. T. Wood & S. W. Duck (Eds.), *Understanding relationship processes, 6: Off the beaten track: Understudied relationships* (pp. 89–121). Thousand Oaks, CA: Sage.

Huston, T. L., McHale, S. M., & Crouter, A. C. (1985). When the honeymoon is over: Changes in the marriage relationship over the first year. In R. Gilmour & S. Duck (Eds.), *The emerging field of personal relationships* (pp. 109–132). Hillsdale, NJ: Erlbaum.

Hymowitz, C. (2000, February 8). Racing onto the Web, one manager's secret is simple: Listening. *The Wall Street Journal,* p. B1.

Imperato, G. (1999, May). The email prescription. *Fast Company,* pp. 90–92.

Inman, C. (1996). Friendships among men: Closeness in the doing. In J. T. Wood (Ed.), *Gendered relationships* (pp. 95–110). Mountain View, CA: Mayfield.

International Listening Association (ILA). (1995, April). An ILA definition of listening. *ILA Listening Post,* 53, p. 4.

Isaacs, W. (1999). *Dialogue and the art of thinking together.* New York: Broadway Business.

Izard, C. E. (1991). *The psychology of emotions.* New York: Plenum.

Jacobson, N., & Gottman, J. (1998). *When men batter women.* New York: Simon & Schuster.

James, C. (1999). *Seeing ourselves: Exploring race, ethnicity and culture.* (2nd ed.). Toronto: Thompson Ed. Pub.

James, W. (1890). *Principles of psychology,* 2 vols. New York: Henry Holt Company.

James, W., & Lange, C. B. (1922). *The emotions.* Baltimore: Williams and Wilkins.

Janis, I. L. (1977). *Victims of group-think.* Boston: Houghton-Mifflin.

Jhally, S., & Katz, J. (2001, Winter). Big trouble, little pond. *Umass,* pp. 26–31.

Johannesen, R. (1996). *Ethics in human communication* (4th ed.). Prospect Heights, IL: Waveland.

Johnson, C. B., Stockdale, M. S., & Saal, F. E. (1991). Persistence of men's misperceptions of friendly cues across a variety of interpersonal encounters. *Psychology of Women Quarterly,* 15, 463–465.

Johnson, D., and Johnson, F. (1991). *Joining together: Group theory and group skills* (4th ed.). Englewood Cliffs, NJ: Prentice Hall.

Johnson, F. L. (1989). Women's culture and communication: An analytic perspective. In C. M. Lont & S. A. Friedley (Eds.), *Beyond the boundaries: Sex and gender diversity in communication* (pp. 301–316). Fairfax, VA: George Mason University Press.

Johnson, F. L. (1996). Friendships among women: Closeness in dialogue. In J. T. Wood (Ed.), *Gendered relationships* (pp. 79–94). Mountain View, CA: Mayfield.

Johnson, F. L. (2000). *Speaking culturally: Language diversity in the United States.* Thousand Oaks, CA: Sage.

Johnson, M. (in press). Gendered communication and intimate partner violence. In B. Dow & J. T. Wood (Eds.), *Handbook of gender and communication.* Thousand Oaks, CA: Sage.

Jones, E., & Gallois, C. (1989). Spouses' impressions of rules for communication in public and private marital conflicts. *Journal of Marriage and the Family,* 51, 957–967.

Jones, G. P., & Dembo, M. H. (1989). Age and sex role differences in intimate friendships during childhood and adolescence. *Merrill-Palmer Quarterly of Behavior and Development,* 35, 445–462.

Jones, S., & Burleson, B. R. (2003). Effects of helper and recipient sex on the experience and outcomes of comforting messages: An experimental investigation. *Sex Roles,* 48, 1–19.

Jones, W. H., & Moore, T. L. (1989). Loneliness and social support. In M. Hojat & R. Crandall (Eds.), *Loneliness: Theory, research, and applications* (pp. 145–156). Newbury Park, CA: Sage.

Jordan, D. J. (1996). *Leadership in leisure services: Making a difference.* State College, PA: Venture Publishing, Inc.

Kagan, J. (1998). *Three seductive ideas.* Cambridge, MA: Harvard University Press.

Katriel, T. (1990). Griping as a verbal ritual in some Israeli discourse. In D. Carbaugh (Ed.), *Cultural Communication and Intercultural Contact* (pp. 99–113). Hillsdale, NJ: Lawrence Erlbaum Associates.

Kaye, L. W., & Applegate, J. S. (1990). Men as elder caregivers: A response to changing families. *American Journal of Orthopsychiatry,* 60, 86–95.

Keeley, M. P., & Hart, A. J. (1994). Nonverbal behavior in dyadic interaction. In S. W. Duck (Ed.), *Understanding relationship processes, 4: Dynamics of relationships* (pp. 135–162). Thousand Oaks, CA: Sage.

Kelley, D. (1998). The communication of forgiveness. *Communication Studies,* 49, 1–17.

Kelley, H. H. (1967). Attribution theory in social psychology. In D. Levine (Ed.), *Nebraska symposium on motivation* (vol. 15, pp. 192–238). Lincoln: University of Nebraska Press.

Kelly, C., Huston, T. L., & Cate, R. M. (1985). Premarital relationship correlates of the erosion of satisfaction in marriage. *Journal of Social and Personal Relationships,* 2, 167–178.

Kelly, G. A. (1955). *The psychology of personal constructs.* New York: Norton.

Kemper, T. (1987). How many emotions are there? Wedding the social and autonomic components. *American Journal of Sociology,* 93, 263–289.

Keyes, R. (1992, February 22). Do you have the time? *Parade,* pp. 22–25.

Kilpatrick, J. (2000, June 12). Computers, et al., churn out new words. *Raleigh News and Observer,* p. 11A.

Keys, Ken. (1984). *Handbook to Higher Consciousness.* Coos Bay, OR: Love Line Books.

Kleinke, C., Peterson, T., & Rutledge, T. (1998). Effects of self-generated facial expressions on mood. *Journal of Personality and Social Psychology,* 74, 272–279.

Knapp, M. L. (1972). *Nonverbal communication in human interaction.* New York: Holt, Rinehart & Winston.

Kohlberg, L. (1958). *The development of modes of thinking and moral choice in the years 10 to 16.* Unpublished doctoral dissertation, University of Chicago.

Korzybski, A. (1958). *Science and sanity* (4th ed.). Lakeville, CT: International Non-Aristotelian Library Publishing Company.

Kovecses, Z. (1990). *Emotion concepts.* New York: Springer-Verlag.

Kupfer, D., First, M., & Regier, D. (2002). *A research agenda for DSM-V.* Washington, DC: American Psychiatric Press.

Kurdek, L. A. (1993). The allocation of household labor in gay, lesbian, and heterosexual married couples. *Journal of Social Issues,* 49, 127–139.

Kwanzaa. The official Kwanzaa website: www.official-kwanzaawebsite.org/index.shtml. Labov, W. (1972). *Sociolinguistic patterns.* Philadelphia: University of Pennsylvania Press.

Lacher, I. (2005, March 3). In new book, professor sees a "mania" in U.S. for possessions and status. *The New York Times,* pp. A15, A21.

La Gaipa, J. J. (1982). Rituals of disengagement. In S. W. Duck (Ed.), *Personal relationships, 4: Dissolving personal relationships.* London: Academic.

Laing, R. D. (1961). *The self and others.* New York: Pantheon.

Lakoff, G., & Johnson, M. (1980). *Metaphors we live by.* Chicago: University of Chicago Press.

Lane, R. (2000). *The loss of happiness in marketplace democracies.* New Haven, CT: Yale University Press.

Langer, S. (1953). *Feeling and form: A theory of art.* New York: Scribner.

Langer, S. (1979). *Philosophy in a new key: A study in the symbolism of reason, rite, and art* (3rd ed.). Cambridge, MA: Harvard University Press.

Langston, D. (1992). Tired of playing monopoly? In M. L. Andersen & P. H. Collins (Eds.), *Race, class, and gender: An anthology* (pp. 110–119). Belmont, CA: Wadsworth.

Larson, J. R. (1984). The performance feedback process: A preliminary model. *Organizational Behavior and Human Performance,* 33, 42–76.

Lasswell, M., & Lobsenz, N. M. (1980). *Styles of loving.* New York: Doubleday.

Laswell, H. (1948). The structure and function of communication in society. In L. Bryson (Ed.), *The communication of ideas.* New York: Harper & Row.

Leaper, C. (Ed.). (1994). *Childhood gender segregation: Causes and consequences.* San Francisco: Jossey-Bass.

Leaper, C., Breed, L., Hoffman, L., & Perlman, C. A. (2002). Variations in the gender-stereotyped content of children's television cartoons across genres. *Journal of Applied Social Psychology.* 32, 1653–1662.

Leaper, N. (1999). How communicators lead at the best global companies. *Communication World,* 16, 33–36.

Leathers, D. G. (1986). *Successful nonverbal communication: Principles and applications.* New York: Macmillan.

Lee, J. A. (1973). *The colours of love: An exploration of the ways of loving.* Don Mills, Ontario, Canada: New Press.

Lee, J. A. (1988). Love styles. In R. J. Sternberg & M. L. Barnes (Eds.), *The psychology of love* (pp. 38–67). New Haven, CT: Yale University Press.

Lee, W. S. (1994). On not missing the boat: A processual method for intercultural understanding of idioms and lifeworld. *Journal of Applied Communication Research,* 22, 141–161.

Lee, W. S. (2000). That's Greek to me: Between a rock and a hard place in intercultural encounters. In L. Samovar & R. Porter (Eds.), *Intercultural communication: A reader* (9th ed., pp. 217–224). Belmont, CA: Wadsworth.

LePoire, B. A., Shepard, C., & Duggan, A. (1999). Nonverbal involvement, expressiveness, and pleasantness as predicted by parental and partner attachment style. *Communication Monographs,* 66, 293–311.

Levine, R. (1988). The pace of life across cultures. In J. McGrath (Ed.), *The social psychology of time* (pp. 39–60). Newbury Park, CA: Sage.

Levine, R., & Norenzayan, A. (1999). The pace of life in 31 countries. *Journal of Cross Cultural Psychology,* 30, 178–205. Levy, G. (1999). Gender-typed and nongender-typed category awareness in toddlers. *Sex Roles,* 39, 851–861.

Lewis, J. D., & Weigert, A. J. (1985). Social atomism, holism and trust. *Sociological Quarterly*, 26, 455–471.

Lim, T. (2002). Language and verbal communication across cultures. In W. Gudykunst & B. Mody (Eds.), *The handbook of international and intercultural communication* (2nd ed., pp. 69–88). Thousand Oaks, CA: Sage

Lohmann, A., Arriaga, X., & Goodfriend, W. (2003). Close relationships and placemaking: Do objects in a couple's home reflect couplehood? *Personal Relationships*, 10, 437–449.

Longatan, N. (2008). *Hofstede's five dimensions of culture: Global business communication determined by five variables:* workabroadtravel.suite101.com/article.cfm/hofstedes_five_dimensions_of_culture.

Lorde, A. (1992). Age, race, class, and sex: Women redefining difference. In M. L. Andersen & P. H. Collins (Eds.), *Race, class, and gender: An anthology* (pp. 495–502). Belmont, CA: Wadsworth.

Luby, V., & Aron, A. (1990, July). *A prototype structuring of love, like, and being in-love.* Paper presented at the Fifth International Conference on Personal Relationships, Oxford, England.

Luft, J. (1969). *Of human interaction.* Palo Alto, CA: National Press Books.

Lumsden, G., & Lumsden, D. (1997). *Communicating in groups and teams.* Belmont, CA: Wadsworth.

Lund, M. (1985). The development of investment and commitment scales for predicting continuity of personal relationships. *Journal of Social and Personal Relationships*, 2, 3–23.

Lytton, H., & Romney, D. M. (1991). Parents' differential socialization of boys and girls: A meta-analysis. *Psychological Bulletin*, 109, 267–296.

Maccoby, E. (1998). *The two sexes: Growing up apart, coming together.* Cambridge, MA: Harvard University Press.

MacGeorge, E. L., Gillihan, S. J., Samter, W., & Clark, R. A. (2003). Skill deficit or differential motivation? Accounting for sex differences in the provision of emotional support. *Communication Research*, 30, 272–303.

MacGeorge, E. L., Graves, A. R., Feng, B., Gillihan, S. J., & Burleson, B. R. (2004). The myth of gender cultures: Similarities outweigh differences in men's and women's provision of and responses to supportive communication. *Sex Roles*, 50, 143–175.

MacNeil, S., & Byers, E. S. (2005). Dyadic assessment of sexual self-disclosure and sexual satisfaction in heterosexual dating couples. *Journal of Social and Personal Relationships*, 22, 169–181.

Mahany, B. (1997, August 7). A hands-on study of language. *Raleigh News and Observer*, pp. 1E, 3E.

Main, M. (1981). Avoidance in the service of attachment. In K. Immelmann, G. Barlow, L. Petrenovich, & M. Main (Eds.), *Behavioral development: The Beilfield interdisciplinary project.* New York: Cambridge University Press.

Major, B., Schmidlin, A. M., & Williams, L. (1990). Gender patterns in social touch: The impact of setting and age. In C. Mayo & N. M. Henley (Eds.), *Gender and nonverbal behavior* (pp. 3–37). New York: Springer-Verlag.

Malandro, L. A., & Barker, L. L. (1983). *Nonverbal communication.* Reading, MA: Addison-Wesley.

Maltz, D. N., & Borker, R. (1982). A cultural approach to male–female miscommunication. In J. J. Gumpertz (Ed.), *Language and social identity* (pp. 196–216). Cambridge, England: Cambridge University Press.

Mangan, K. (2002, July 5). Horse sense or nonsense? Critics decry what they consider the "softening" of medical education. *Chronicle of Higher Education*, pp. A8–A10.

Manning, A. (1996, March 6). Signing catches on as a foreign language. *USA Today*, p. 4D.

Margolis, Phillip. (1999). *Random House Webster's Computer and Internet Dictionary* (3rd ed.). New York: Random House Reference.

Markman, H. J. (1981). Prediction of marital distress: A 5-year follow-up. *Journal of Consulting and Clinical Psychology*, 49, 760–762.

Markman, H. J. (1990). *Advances in understanding marital distress.* Unpublished manuscript. University of Denver.

Marks, Jonathan. (2006, June 7). "The realities of races." Published by the Social Science Research Council Web forum, *Is race "real"?*: raceandgenomics.ssrc.org/Marks.

Martin, C., Fabes, R., Evans, S., & Wyman, H. (2000). Social cognition on the playground: Children's beliefs about playing with girls versus boys and their relations to sex segregated play. *Journal of Social and Personal Relationships*, 17, 751–771.

Maslow, A. H. (1954/1970). *Motivation and personality* (3rd ed.). New York: Harper & Row.

Maslow, A. H. (1959/1970). *New knowledge in human values.* Chicago: H. Regnery.

Maslow, A. H. (1968). *Toward a psychology of being.* New York: Van Nostrand Reinhold.

Masters, W. H., & Johnson, V. E. (1979). *Homosexuality in perspective.* Boston: Little, Brown.

Matsumoto, D., Franklin, B., Choi, J., Rogers, D., & Tatani, H. (2002). Cultural influences on the expression and perception of emotion. In W. Gudykunst & B. Mody (Eds.), *The handbook of international and intercultural communication* (2nd ed.). Thousand Oaks, CA: Sage.

Maugh, T., II. (1994, November 26). Romantics seem to be bred, not born. *Raleigh News and Observer*, pp. 1A, 4A.

Mayes, Linda, & Cohen, Donald. (2002). *The Yale child study center guide to understanding your child.* Little, Brown & Co.

Mazur, A, (1989) United States trends in feminine beauty and over adaption. *Journal of Sex Research*, 22, 281–303.

Mazur, E. (1989). Predicting gender differences in same-sex friendships from affiliation motive and value. *Psychology of Women Quarterly*, 13, 277–291.

McCormick, J., & Begley, S. (1996, December 9). How to raise a tiger. *Newsweek*, pp. 52–59.

McCroskey, J. C., Richmond, V. P., & McCroskey, L. L. (2006). *An introduction to communication in the classroom: The role of communication in teaching and training.* Boston, MA: Allyn & Bacon.

McCullough, M., & Hoyt, W. (2002). Transgression-related motivational dispositions: Personality substrates of forgiveness and their links to the big five. *Personality and Social Psychology Bulletin*, 28, 1556–1573.

McDaniel, E., & Quasha, S. (2000). The communicative aspects of doing business in Japan. In L. Samovar & R. Porter (Eds.), *Intercultural communication: A reader* (9th ed., pp. 312–324). Belmont, CA: Wadsworth

McIntosh, P. (1995). White privilege and male privilege: A personal account of coming to see correspondences through work in women's studies. In M. L. Andersen & P. H. Collins (Eds.), *Race, class, and gender: An anthology* (2nd ed., pp. 94–105). Belmont, CA: Wadsworth.

McKay, V. (2000). Understanding the co-culture of the elderly. In L. Samovar & R. Porter (Eds.), *Intercultural communication: A reader* (9th ed., pp. 180–189). Belmont, CA: Wadsworth.

McKenna, K., Green, A., & Gleason, M. (2002). Relationship formation on the Internet: What's the big attraction? *Journal of Social Issues*, 58, pp. 9–31.

McKinney, B., Kelly, L., & Duran, R. (1997). The relationship between conflict message styles and dimensions of communication competence. *Communication Reports*, 10,185–196.

McLemee, S. (2003, February 21). Getting emotional. *Chronicle of Higher Education*, pp. A14–A16.

McNeill, D. (1992). *Hand and mind: What gestures reveal about thought.* Chicago: University of Chicago Press.

Mead, G. H. (1934). *Mind, self, and society.* Chicago: University of Chicago Press.

Meeks, B., Hendrick, S., & Hendrick, C. (1998). Communication, love and satisfaction. *Journal of Social and Personal Relationships*, 15, 755–773.

Mehrabian, A. (1981). *Silent messages: Implicit communication of emotion and attitudes* (2nd ed.). Belmont, CA: Wadsworth.

Metts, S. (2006). Hanging out and doing lunch: Enacting friendship closeness. In J. T. Wood & S. W. Duck (Eds.), *Composing relationships: Communication in everyday life* (pp. 76–85). Belmont, CA: Wadsworth.

Metts, S., Cupach, W. R., & Bejlovec, R. A. (1989). "I love you too much to ever start liking you": Redefining romantic relationships. *Journal of Social and Personal Relationships*, 6, 259–274.

Miell, D. E., & Duck, S. W. (1986). Strategies in developing friendship. In V. J. Derlega & B. A. Winstead (Eds.), *Friendship and social interaction* (pp. 129–143). New York: Springer-Verlag.

Milardo, R. (1986). Personal choice and social constraint in close relationships: Applications of network analysis. In V. Derlega & B. Winstead (Eds.), *Friendship and social interaction* (pp. 145–166). New York: Springer-Verlag.

Miller, G. R., & Parks, M. R. (1982). Communication in dissolving relationships. In S. W. Duck (Ed.), *Personal relationships, 4: Dissolving personal relationships* (pp. 127–154). London: Academic.

Miller, J. B. (1993). Learning from early relationship experience. In S. W. Duck (Ed.), *Understanding relationship processes, 2: Learning about relationships* (pp. 1–29). Newbury Park, CA: Sage.

Miller, W. I. (1993). *Humiliation.* Ithaca: Cornell University Press.

Miller, W. I. (1998). *The anatomy of disgust.* Cambridge, MA: Harvard University Press.

Miller, W. I. (2003). *Faking it.* UK: Cambridge University Press.

Min, P. (Ed.). (1995). *Asian Americans: Contemporary trends and issues.* Thousand Oaks, CA: Sage.

Mochizuki, T. (1981). Changing patterns of mate selection. *Journal of Comparative Family Studies*, 12, 318–328.

Molloy, B., & Herzberger, S. (1998). Body image and self-esteem: A comparison of African-American and Caucasian women. *Sex Roles*, 38, 631–643.

Monastersky, R. (2001, July 6). Look who's listening. *Chronicle of Higher Education*, pp. A14–A16.

Monkerud, D. (1990, October). Blurring the lines: Androgyny on trial. *Omni*, pp. 81–86.

Monsour, M. (1992). Meanings of intimacy in cross- and same-sex friendships. *Journal of Social and Personal Relationships*, 9, 277–295.

Monsour, M. (1997). Communication and cross-sex friendships across the life cycle: A review of the literature. In B. Burleson (Ed.), *Communication Yearbook*, 20 (pp. 375–414). Thousand Oaks, CA: Sage.

Monsour, M. (in press). Communication and gender among adult friends. In B. Dow & J. T. Wood (Eds.), *Handbook of gender and communication.* Thousand Oaks, CA: Sage.

Montgomery, B. M. (1988). Quality communication in personal relationships. In S. W. Duck (Ed.), *Handbook of personal relationships* (pp. 343–366). New York: Wiley.

Morreale, S. (2001, May). Communication important to employers. *Spectra*, p. 8.

Morreale, S. (2004, December). Accounting graduates need better listening skills and correct grammar. *Spectra*, p. 7.

Morris, T., Gorham, J., Cohen, S., & Huffman, D. (1996). Fashion in the classroom: Effects of attire on student perceptions of instructors in college classes. *Communication Education*, 45, 135–148.

Mosley-Howard, S., & Evans, C. (1997). *Relationships in the African American family.* Paper presented at the 1997 Conference of the International Network on Personal Relationships, Oxford, Ohio.

Muehlhoff, T., & Wood, J. T. (2002). Speaking of marriage: The marriage between theory and practice. *Journal of Social and Personal Relationships,* 19, 613–619.

Mulac, A., Wiemann, J. M., Widenmann, S. J., & Gibson, T. W. (1988). Male/female language differences and effects in same-sex and mixed-sex dyads: The gender-linked language effect. *Communication Monographs,* 55, 315–335.

Mullins, L., Balderson, B., & Chaney, J. (1999, Winter). Implementing team approaches in primary and tertiary care settings: Applications from the rehabilitation context. *Families, Systems & Health,* 17(4), 413–426.*Multiculturalism Act: Annual report on the operation of the Canadian Multiculturalism Act, 2007–08*: www.cic.gc.ca/english/resources/publications/multi-report2008/index.asp.

Mustard, F. (1994). The contribution of the community to the competence and resilience of children. *Bulletin of the Sparrow Lake Alliance,* 5(1), 8–10.

Mwakalye, N., & DeAngelis, T. (1995, October). The power of touch helps vulnerable babies survive. *APA Monitor,* p. 25.

Naisbitt, J. (1999). *High tech high touch: Technology and our search for meaning.* New York, NY: Broadway Books.

Nanda, S., & Warms, R. (1998). *Cultural anthropology* (6th ed.). Belmont, CA: West/Wadsworth.

Nardi, P. M., & Sherrod, D. (1994). Friendship in the lives of gay men and lesbians. *Journal of Social and Personal Relationships,* 11, 185–199.

Narem, T. R. (1980). Try a little TLC. *Science,* 80, 15.

Netspeak. (2000, August–September). *bLink,* p. 19. Pasadena, CA: Earthlink.

Nettle, D., & Romaine, S. (2000). *Vanishing voices: The extinction of the world's languages.* Oxford, England: Oxford University Press.

Neuliep, J. W., & McCroskey, J. C. (1997). The development of intercultural and interethnic communication apprehension scales. *Communication Research Reports,* 14, 145–156.

Newman, P. (1964, February). "Wild man" behavior in New Guinea Highlands community. *American Anthropologist,* 66, 1–19.

Neyer, F. (2002). The dyadic interdependence of attachment security and dependency: A conceptual replication across older twin pairs and younger couples. *Journal of Social and Personal Relationships,* 19, 483–503.

Nimetz, Jody. (2007). The Facebook Years: Everything You Need to Know About Facebook. *Marketing Jive*: seo space.blogspot.com/2007/09/facebook-years-everything-you-need to html.

Noller, P. (1986). Sex differences in nonverbal communication: Advantage lost or supremacy regained? *Australian Journal of Psychology,* 38, 23–32.

Noller, P. (1987). Nonverbal communication in marriage. In D. Perlman & S. Duck (Eds.), *Intimate relationships: Development, dynamics, and deterioration* (pp. 149–176). Newbury Park, CA: Sage.

Notarius, C. I. (1996). Marriage: Will I be happy or will I be sad? In N. Vanzetti & S. Duck (Eds.), *A lifetime of relationships* (pp. 265–289). Pacific Grove, CA: Brooks/Cole.

Nunberg, G. (2003, May 29). *Fresh Air* [radio interview]. Cited in R. West & L. Turner, (2006). *Understanding interpersonal communication* (p. 164). Belmont, CA: Wadsworth.

Nussbaum, J. E. (1992, October 18). Justice for women! *New York Review of Books,* pp. 43–48.

Nyquist, M. (1992, Fall). Learning to listen. *Ward Rounds* (pp. 11–15). Evanston, IL: Northwestern University Medical School.

Okin, S. M. (1989). *Gender, justice, and the family.* New York: Basic.

O'Meara, J. D. (1989). Cross-sex friendship: Four basic challenges of an ignored relationship. *Sex Roles,* 21, 525–543.

Omohundro, J. T. (2008). *Thinking like an anthropologist: A practical introduction to cultural anthropology* (pp. 27–29). New York: McGraw-Hill.

O'Neill, M. (1997, January 12). Asian folk art of feng shui hits home with Americans. *Raleigh News and Observer,* p. 6E.

Orbuch, T., & Eyster, S. (1997). Division of household labor among black couples and white couples. *Social Forces,* 76, 301–322.

Orbuch, T., & Veroff, J. (2002). A programmatic review: Building a two-way bridge between social psychology and the study of the early years of marriage. *Journal of Social and Personal Relationships,* 19, 549–568.

Orbuch, T., Veroff, J., & Hunter, A. (1999). Black couples, white couples: The early years of marriage. In E. Hetherington (Ed.), *Coping with divorce, single parenting, and remarriage* (pp. 23–43). Mahwah, NJ: Erlbaum.

Ornish, D. (1998). *Love and survival: The scientific basis for the healing power of intimacy.* New York: HarperCollins.

Ornish, D. (1999). *Love and survival: 8 pathways to intimacy and health.* New York: HarperCollins.

Osborne, A. (1996, Summer). The paradox of effort and grace. *Inner Directions,* pp. 4–6.

Otnes, C., & Lowrey, T. (Eds.). (2004). *Contemporary consumption rituals.* Mahwah, NJ: Erlbaum.

Pacanowsky, M. (1989). *Creating and narrating organizational realities.* In B. Dervin, L. Grossberg, B. O'Keefe, & E. Wartella (Eds.), *Rethinking communication: Paradigm exemplars.* Newbury Park, CA: Sage. 250–257.

Pacanowsky, M., & O'Donnell-Trujillo, N. (1983). Organizational communication as cultural performance. *Communication Monographs,* 30, 126–147.

Parks, M., & Adelman, B. (1983). Communication networks and the development of romantic relationships: An expansion of uncertainty reduction theory. *Human Communication Research,* 10, 55–79.

Parks, M., & Floyd, K. (1996a). Making friends in cyberspace. *Journal of Communication,* 46, 80–97.

Parks, M., & Floyd, K. (1996b). Meanings for closeness and intimacy in friendship. *Journal of Social and Personal Relationships,* 13, 85–107.

Parks, M., & Roberts, L. (1998). Making MOOsic: The development of personal relationships online and a comparison to their offline counterparts. *Journal of Social and Personal Relationships,* 15, 517–537.

Pataki, S., Shapiro, C., & Clark, M. (1994). Children's acquisition of appropriate norms for friendships and acquaintances. *Journal of Social and Personal Relationships,* 11, 427–442.

Patterson, M. L. (1992). A functional approach to nonverbal exchange. In R. S. Feldman & B. Rime (Eds.), *Fundamentals of nonverbal behavior* (pp. 458–495). New York: Cambridge University Press.

Pearce, W. B., Cronen, V. E., & Conklin, F. (1979). On what to look at when analyzing communication: A hierarchical model of actors' meanings. *Communication,* 4, 195–220.

Pearson, J. C. (1985). *Gender and communication.* Dubuque, IA: Brown.

Peck, M. Scott. (2000). *Abounding grace: An anthology of wisdom.* New York: Andrews McMeel Publishing.

Pennebaker, J. W. (1997). *Opening up: The healing power of expressing emotions* (rev. ed.). New York: Guilford.

Perry, J. (1996, Summer). Applying meditation to everyday life. *Inner Directions,* pp. 21–23, 26.

Petersen, W. (1997). *Ethnicity counts.* New York: Transaction.

Petronio, S. (1991). Communication boundary management: A theoretical model of managing disclosure of private information between married couples. *Communication Theory,* 1, 311–335.

Pettigrew, T. F. (1967). Social evaluation theory: Consequences and applications. In D. Levine (Ed.), *Nebraska symposium on motivation* (pp. 241–311). Lincoln: University of Nebraska Press.

Philippot, P., & Feldman, R. (Eds.). (2004). *The regulation of emotion.* Mahwah, NJ: Erlbaum.

Phillips, G. M., & Wood, J. T. (1983). *Communication and human relationships.* New York: Macmillan.

Piaget, J. (1932/1965). *The moral judgment of the child.* New York: Free Press.

Pierson, J. (1995, November 20). If sun shines in, workers work better, buyers buy more. *The Wall Street Journal,* pp. B1, B8.

Planalp, S. (1997, September). Personal correspondence.

Planalp, S., & Fitness, J. (2000). Thinking/feeling about social and personal relationships. *Journal of Social and Personal Relationships,* 16, 731–750.

Pomerleau, A., Bolduc, D., Malcuit, G., & Cossette, L. (1990). Pink or blue: Environmental stereotypes in the first two years of life. *Sex Roles,* 22, 359–367.

Popenoe, D. (1996). *Life without father.* New York: Free Press.

Porchia, A. *Voices.* (1943). (W. S. Merwin, Trans.). Port Townsend, WA: Copper Canyon Press.

Potter, W. J. (2001). *Media literacy* (2nd ed.). Thousand Oaks, CA: Sage.

Price, R. (1994). *A Whole New Life.* New York: Scribner.

Proctor, R. (1991). *An exploratory analysis of responses to owned messages in interpersonal communication.* Doctoral dissertation. Bowling Green University, Bowling Green, Ohio.

Pryor, J. B., & Merluzzi, T. V. (1985). The role of expertise in processing social interaction scripts. *Journal of Experimental Social Psychology,* 21, 362–379.

Raphael, M. (1997, May 13). It's true: Drivers move slowly if you want their space. *Raleigh News and Observer,* p. 1A.

Rankin, J., Quinn, J., Shephard, M., Duncanson, J., & Simmie, S. (2002, October 20). Police target black drivers, *Toronto Star.*

Rasmussen, J. (2002). *The five Cs of managing virtual teams*: www.employeedevelopmentsolutions.com/freearticles/virtualteams.htm.

Rawlins, W. K. (1981). *Friendship as a communicative achievement: A theory and an interpretive analysis of verbal reports.* Doctoral dissertation. Temple University, Philadelphia.

Rawlins, W. K. (1994). Being there and growing apart: Sustaining friendships during adulthood. In D. Canary & L. Stafford (Eds.), *Communication and relational maintenance* (pp. 275–294). New York: Academic.

Reel, B. W., & Thompson, T. L. (1994). A test of the effectiveness of strategies for talking about AIDS and condom use. *Journal of Applied Communication Research,* 22, 127–141.

Reis, H. T., Senchak, M., & Solomon, B. (1985). Sex differences in the intimacy of social interaction: Further examination of potential explanations. *Journal of Personality and Social Psychology,* 48, 1204–1217.

Reisenzaum, R. (1983). The Schachter theory of emotion: Two decades later. *Psychological Bulletin,* 94, 239–264.

Remen, R. N. (1997). Just Listen. *Kitchen Table Wisdom.* New York: Riverhead Trade.

Remland, M. (2000). *Nonverbal communication in everyday life.* Boston: Houghton-Mifflin.

Reske, J., & Stafford, L. (1990). Idealization and communication in long-distance premarital relationships. *Family Relations,* 39, 274–290.

Ribeau, S. A., Baldwin, J. R., & Hecht, M. L. (1994). An African-American communication perspective. In L. Samovar & R. Porter (Eds.). (2000). *Intercultural communication: A reader* (7th ed., pp. 140–147). Belmont, CA: Wadsworth.

Richmond, V., & McCroskey, J. (2000). The impact of supervisor and subordinate immediacy on relational and organizational outcomes. *Communication Monographs,* 67, 85–95.

Riessman, C. (1990). *Divorce talk: Women and men make sense of personal relationships.* New Brunswick, NJ: Rutgers University Press.

Robarchek, C., & Dentan, R. (1987). Blood drunkenness and the bloodthirsty Semai: Unmaking another anthropological myth. *American Anthropologist,* 89, 356–363.

Roberts, G., & Orbe, M. (1996, May). *Creating that safe place: Descriptions of intergenerational gay male communication.* Paper presented at the annual meeting of the International Communication Association, Chicago.

Robinson, J. (2000, September–October). 4 weeks vacation for everyone! *Utne Reader,* pp. 49–54.

Rohlfing, M. (1995). Doesn't anybody stay in one place anymore? An exploration of the understudied phenomenon of long-distance relationships. In J. T. Wood & S. W. Duck (Eds.), *Understanding relationship processes, 6: Off the beaten track: Understudied relationships* (pp. 173–196). Thousand Oaks, CA: Sage.

Root, M. P. P. (1990). Disordered eating habits in women of color. *Sex Roles,* 22, 525–536.

Roper Starch poll (1999). How Americans communicate: http://www.natcom.org/research/Roper/how_americans_communicate.htm.

Rose, A., & Asher, S. (2000). Children's friendships. In C. Hendrick & S. Hendrick (Eds.), *Close relationships: A sourcebook* (pp. 47–57). Thousand Oaks, CA: Sage.

Rose, S., & Frieze, I. H. (1989). Young singles' scripts for a first date. *Gender and Society,* 3, 258–268.

Rose, S. M. (1984). How friendships end: Patterns among young adults. *Journal of Social and Personal Relationships,* 1, 267–277.

Rosenberg, M. (1979). *Conceiving the self.* New York: Basic.

Rosenwein, B. (1998). *Anger's past: The sacred uses of emotion in the Middle Ages.* Ithaca, New York: Cornell University Press.

Rothwell, J. D. (2004). *In the company of others.* New York: McGraw-Hill.

Roux, A. (2001). Rethinking official measures of poverty: Consideration of race, ethnicity, and gender. In D. Vannoy (Ed.), *Gender mosaics* (pp. 290–299). Los Angeles: Roxbury.

Rowland, D. (1985). *Japanese business etiquette.* New York: Warner.

Ruberman, T. R. (1992, January 22–29). Psychosocial influences on mortality of patients with coronary heart disease. *Journal of the American Medical Association,* 267, 559–560.

Rubin, L. (1985). Just friends: The role of friendship in our lives. New York: Harper & Row.

Ruddick, S. (1989). *Maternal thinking: Towards a politics of peace.* Boston: Beacon.

Rusbult, C. (1987). Responses to dissatisfaction in close relationships: The exit–voice–loyalty–neglect model. In D. Perlman & S. W. Duck (Eds.), *Intimate relationships: Development, dynamics, and deterioration* (pp. 109–238). London: Sage.

Rusbult, C. E., Johnson, D. J., & Morrow, G. D. (1986). Impact of couple patterns of problem solving on distress and nondistress in dating relationships. *Journal of Personality and Social Psychology,* 50, 744–753.

Rusbult, C. E., & Zembrodt, I. M. (1983). Responses to dissatisfaction in romantic involvement: A multidimensional scaling analysis. *Journal of Experimental Social Psychology,* 19, 274–293.

Rusbult, C. E., Zembrodt, I. M., & Iwaniszek, J. (1986). The impact of gender and sex-role orientation on responses to dissatisfaction in close relationships. *Sex Roles,* 15, 1–20.

Rusk, T., & Rusk, N. (1988). *Mind traps: Change your mind, change your life.* Los Angeles: Price, Stern, Sloan.

Ryan, R., La Guardia, J., Solky-Butzel, J., Chirkov, V., & Kim, Y. (2005). On the interpersonal regulation of emotions: Emotional reliance across gender, relationships, and cultures. *Personal Relationships,* 12, 145–163.

Saarni, C. (1990). Emotional competence: How emotions and relationships become integrated. In R. A. Thompson (Ed.), *Socioemotional development: Nebraska symposium on motivation* (pp. 115–182). Lincoln: University of Nebraska Press.

Saarni, C. (1999). *The development of emotional competence.* New York: Guilford.

Sallinen-Kuparinen, A. (1992). Teacher communicator style. *Communication Education,* 41, 153–166.

Salopek, J. (1999). Is anyone listening? *Training and Development,* 53, 58–59.

Samover, L., & Porter, R. (1994). *Intercultural communication: A reader* (7th ed.). Belmont, CA: Wadsworth.

Samter, W., & Cupach, W. (1998). Friendly fire: Topical variations in conflict among same- and cross-sex friends. *Communication Studies,* 49, 121–138.

Scarf, M. (1987). *Intimate partners.* New York: Random House.

Schachter, S. (1964). The interaction of cognitive and physiological determinants of emotion states (pp. 138–173). In P. Leiderman & D. Shapiro (eds.), *Psychobiological approaches to social behavior.* Stanford, CA: Stanford University Press.

Schachter, S., & Singer, J. (1962). Cognitive, social, and physiological determinants of emotional state. *Psychological Review,* 69, 379–399.

Schiminoff, S. B. (1980). *Communication rules: Theory and research.* Newbury Park, CA: Sage.

Schmanoff, S. (1985). Expressing emotions in words: Verbal patterns of interactions. *Journal of Communication,* 35, 16–31.

Schmanoff, S. (1987). Types of emotional disclosures and request compliance between spouses. *Communication Monographs,* 54, 85–100.

Schneider, A. (1999, March 26). Taking aim at student incoherence. *Chronicle of Higher Education,* pp. A16–A18.

Schramm, W. (1955). *The process and effects of mass communication.* Urbana: University of Illinois Press.

Schutz, A. (1999). It was your fault! Self-serving bias in the autobiographical accounts of conflicts in married couples. *Journal of Social and Personal Relationships,* 16, 193–208.

Schutz, W. (1966). *The interpersonal underworld.* Palo Alto, CA: Science and Behavior Books.

Schwartz, T. (1989, January–February). Acceleration syndrome: Does everyone live in the fast lane nowadays? *Utne Reader,* pp. 36–43.

Scott, C., & Meyers, K. (2005). The socialization of emotion: Learning emotion management at the fire station. *Journal of Applied Communication Research,* 33, 67–92.

Seay, E. (2004, February 11). Lost city, lost languages. *Princeton Alumni Weekly,* pp. 17, 43.

Sebeok, T. A., & Rosenthal, R. (Eds.). (1981). *The Clever Hans phenomenon: Communication with horses, whales, apes and people.* New York: New York Academy of Sciences.

Secklin, P. (1991, November). *Being there: A qualitative study of young adults' descriptions of friendship.* Paper presented at the Speech Communication Association Convention, Atlanta.

Sedgwick, E. K. (1995). *Shame and its sisters: A Silvan Tomkins reader.* Durham, NC: Duke University Press.

Sedikides, C., Campbell, W., Reeder, G., & Elliott, A. (1998). The self-serving bias in relational context. *Journal of Personality and Social Psychology,* 74, 378–386.

Segrin, C. (1998). Interpersonal communication problems associated with depression and loneliness. In P. Andersen & L. Guerrero (Eds.), *Communication and emotion: Theory, research, and applications* (pp. 215–242). San Diego, CA: Academic Press.

Seligman, M. E. P. (1990). *Learned optimism: How to change your mind and your life.* New York: Simon & Schuster/Pocket Books.

Seligman, M. E. P. (2002). *The authentic self.* New York: Free Press.

Sellnow, D., & Sellnow, T. (2001). The "illusion of life" rhetorical perspective: An integrated approach to the study of music as communication. *Critical Studies in Media Communication,* 18, 295–415.

Sept, R. (1981). *Bridging theory and practice in laboratory education: An heuristic model for intervention in human relations training groups.* Unpublished thesis, Simon Fraser University, Vancouver.

Servaes, J. (1988). Cultural identity in East and West. *Howard Journal of Communications,* 2, 58–71.

Shannon, C., & Weaver, W. (1949). *The mathematical theory of communication.* Urbana: University of Illinois Press.

Sharlet, J. (1999, July 2). Beholding beauty: Scholars nip and tuck at our quest for physical perfection. *Chronicle of Higher Education,* pp. A15–A16.

Shaver, P., Schwartz, J., Kirson, D., & O'Connor, C. (1987). Further explorations of a prototype approach. *Journal of Personality and Social Psychology,* 52, 1061–1086.

Shaver, P., Wu, S., & Schwartz, J. (1992). Cross-cultural similarities and differences in emotion and its representation: A prototype approach. In M. S. Clark (Ed.), *Emotion* (pp. 175–212). Newbury Park, CA: Sage.

Shenk, D. (1997). *Data smog.* New York: Harper-Edge.

Sherrod, D. (1989). The influence of gender on same-sex friendships. In C. Hendrick (Ed.), *Close relationships* (pp. 164–186). Newbury Park, CA: Sage.

Shillington, R. (2000, March 19). *Adding social condition to the Canadian Human Rights Act: Some issues.* Report for the Canadian Human Rights Act Review Panel: www.shillington.ca/rights/chra-rp.pdf.

Shott, S. (1979). Emotion and social life: A symbolic interactionist analysis. *American Journal of Sociology,* 84, 1317–1334.

Shotter, J. (1993). *Conversational realities: The construction of life through language.* Newbury Park, CA: Sage.

Simmons, L. (2002). *Odd girl out: The hidden culture of aggression in girls.* Orlando, FL: Harvest Books.

Simmons, L. (2004). *Odd girl speaks out: Girls write about bullies, cliques, popularity, and jealousy.* Orlando, FL: Harvest Books.

Simon, S. B. (1977). *Vulture: A modern allegory on the art of putting oneself down.* Niles, IL: Argus Communications.

Smith, A. D. (2005, March 21). *Standing in the shadows: Wide awakeness counts.* The 2005 Weil Lecture on American Citizenship. Chapel Hill: University of North Carolina at Chapel Hill.

Snell, W. E., Jr., Hawkins, R. C., II, & Belk, S. S. (1988). Stereotypes about male sexuality and the use of social influence strategies in intimate relationships. *Journal of Clinical and Social Psychology,* 7, 42–48.

Spain, D. (1992). *Gendered spaces.* Chapel Hill: University of North Carolina Press.

Sorrentino, R., Cohen, D., Olson, J., & Zanna, M. (Eds.). (2005). *Culture and social behavior: The Ontario Symposium.* Mahwah, NJ: Erlbaum.

Spear, W. (1995). *Feng shui made easy: Designing your life with the ancient art of placement.* New York: HarperCollins.

Spencer, T. (1994). Transforming relationships through ordinary talk. In S. W. Duck (Ed.), *Understanding relationship processes, 4: Dynamics of relationships* (pp. 58–85). Thousand Oaks, CA: Sage.

Spitzack, C. (1990). *Confessing excess.* Albany: State University of New York Press.

Spitzack, C. (1993). The spectacle of anorexia nervosa. *Text and Performance Quarterly,* 13, 1–21.

Spousal Violence: www.statcan.ca/english/freepub/85-224-XIE/free.htm.

Stacey, J. (1996). *In the name of the father: Rethinking family values in a postmodern age.* Boston: Beacon.

Stafford, L., Dutton, M., & Haas, S. (2000). Measuring routine maintenance: Scale revision, sex versus gender roles, and the prediction of relational characteristics. *Communication Monographs,* 67, 306–323.

Stearns, C., & Stearns, P. (1986). *Anger: The struggle for emotional control in America's history.* Chicago: University of Chicago Press.

Steiner-Pappalardo, N., & Gurung, R. (2002). The femininity effect: Relationship quality, sex, gender, attachment, and significant-other concepts. *Personal Relationships,* 9, 313–325.

Stephenson, S. J., & D'Angelo, G. (1973). *The effects of evaluative/empathic listening and self-esteem on defensive reactions in dyads.* Paper presented to the International Communication Association. Montreal, Quebec, Canada.

Sternberg, R. J. (1986). A triangular theory of love. *Psychological Review,* 93, 119–135.

Stewart, J. (1986). *Bridges, not walls* (4th ed.). New York: Random House.

Stewart, L. P., Stewart, A. D., Friedley, S. A., & Cooper, P. J. (1990). *Communication between the sexes: Sex differences and sex role stereotypes* (2nd ed.). Scottsdale, AZ: Gorsuch Scarisbrick.

Swain, S. (1989). Covert intimacy: Closeness in men's friendships. In B. Risman & P. Schwartz (Ed.), *Gender and intimate relationships* (pp. 71–86). Belmont, CA: Wadsworth.

Sypher, B. (1984). Seeing ourselves as others see us. *Communication Research,* 11, 97–115.

Tannen, D. (1990). *You just don't understand: Women and men in conversation.* New York: William Morrow.

Tannen, D. (1995). *Talking nine to five.* New York: William Morrow.

Tannen, D. (2001). *Talking from 9 to 5: Women and men at work.* New York: Harper Collins.

Tannen, D. (2002). *Talking to Your Parents, Partner, Sibs, and Kids When You're All Adults.* New York: Random House.

Tavris, C. (1989). *Anger: The misunderstood emotion.* New York: Simon & Schuster.

Tavris, C. (1992). *The mismeasure of woman.* New York: Simon & Schuster.

Taylor, S. (2002). *The tending instinct: How nurturing is essential for who we are and how we live.* New York: Times Books.

Teachers' words may clash with cultures. (2000, February 23). *Raleigh News and Observer,* p. 4E.

Thomas, V. G. (1989). Body-image satisfaction among black women. *Journal of Social Psychology,* 129, 107–112.

Thompson, G., and Jenkins, J. (1993). *Verbal judo: The gentle art of persuasion.* New York, NY: William Morrow.

Tillich, Paul. (1963). *The Eternal Now.* New York: Scribners.

Ting-Toomey, S. (1991). Intimacy expressions in three cultures: France, Japan, and the United States. *International Journal of Intercultural Relations,* 15, 29–46.

Ting-Toomey, S. (1988). Intercultural conflict styles: A face-negotiation theory. In Y. Kim & W. Gudykunst (Eds.), *Theories in intercultural communication* (pp. 213–235). Newbury Park, CA: Sage.

Ting-Toomey, S., & Oetzel, J. (2001). *Managing intercultural conflict effectively.* Thousand Oaks, CA: Sage.

Ting-Toomey, S., & Oetzel, J. (2002). Cross-cultural face concerns and conflict styles. In W. Gudykunst & B. Mody (Eds.), *Handbook of international and intercultural communication* (2nd ed., pp. 143–163). Thousand Oaks, CA: Sage.

Tolhuizen, J. H. (1989). Communication strategies for intensifying dating relationships: Identification, use, and structure. *Journal of Social and Personal Relationships,* 6, 413–434.

Treichler, P. A., & Kramarae, C. (1983). Women's talk in the ivory tower. *Communication Quarterly,* 31, 118–132.

Trice, H., & Beyer, J. (1984). Studying organizational cultures through rites and ceremonials. *Academy of Management Review,* 9, 653–669.

Trotter, R. J. (1975, October 25). The truth, the whole truth, and nothing but . ... *Science News,* 108, 269.

Turner, L. H., & Shutter, R. (2004). African American and European American women's visions of workplace conflict: A metaphorical analysis. *Howard Journal of Communication,* 15, 169–183.

Ueland, B. (1992, November/December). Tell me more: On the fine art of listening. *Utne Reader,* pp. 104–109.

Underwood, A., & Adler, J. (2005, April 25). When cultures clash. *Newsweek,* pp. 68–72.

Underwood, M. (2003). *Social aggression among girls.* New York: Guilford.

University College Cork: www.ucc.ie/ucc/equalcom/language.html.

Urgo, J. (2000). *The age of distraction.* Jackson: Mississippi University Press.

Vachss, A. (1994, August 28). You carry the cure in your own heart. *Parade,* pp. 4–6.

Van Maanen, J., & Barley, S. (1985). *Cultural organization; Fragments of a theory.* In P. J. Frost et al. (Eds.) Organizational culture. Beverly Hills, CA: Sage, 31–54.

Vangelisti, A. (1993). Couples' communication problems: The counselor's perspective. *Journal of Applied Communication Research,* 22, 106–126.

Vangelisti, A., & Crumley, L. (1998). Reactions to messages that hurt: The influence of relational context. *Communication Monographs,* 65, 173–196.

Van Styke, E. (1999). *Listening to conflict: Finding constructive solutions to workplace disputes.* New York: AMA Communications.

Vanyperen, N. W., & Buunk, B. P. (1991). Equity theory and exchange and communal orientation from a cross-national perspective. *Journal of Social Psychology,* 131, 5–20.

Varkonyi, C. (1996, June 22). Color code. *Raleigh News and Observer,* pp. 1–2E.

Veroff, J. (1999). Marital commitment in the early years of marriage. In W. Jones and J. Adams (Eds.), *Handbook of interpersonal commitment and relationship stability* (pp. 149–162). New York: Plenum Press.

Vickers, S. (1999). *Native American identities: From stereotype to archetype in art and literature.* Albuquerque: University of New Mexico Press.

Villarosa, L. (1994, January). Dangerous eating. *Essence,* pp. 19–21, 87.

Vobejda, B., & Perlstein, L. (1998, June 7). Girls catching up with boys in ways good and bad, study finds. *Raleigh News and Observer,* 1A, 14A.

Vocate, D. (Ed.). (1994). *Intrapersonal communication: Different voices, different minds.* Hillsdale, NJ: Erlbaum.

Walker, M. B., & Trimboli, A. (1989). Communicating affect: The role of verbal and nonverbal content. *Journal of Language and Social Psychology,* 8, 229–248.

Walster, E., Traupmann, J., & Walster, G. W. (1978). Equity and extramarital sexuality. *Archives of Sexual Behavior,* 7, 127–141.

Walters, R. (1984). Forgiving: An essential element in effective living. *Studies in Formative Spirituality,* 5, 365–374.

Waner, K. (1995). Business communication competencies needed by employees as perceived by business faculty and business professionals. *Business Communication Quarterly,* 58, 51–56.

Watzlawick, P., Beavin, J., & Jackson, D. D. (1967). *Pragmatics of human communication.* New York: Norton.

Weiner, N. (1967). *The human use of human beings.* New York: Avon.

Weiner, N. (1997). *The human use of human beings.* New York: Avon.

Weiss, S. E. (1987). The changing logic of a former minor power. In H. Binnendijk (Ed.), *National negotiating styles* (pp. 44–74). Washington DC: U.S. Department of State.

Werking, K. (1997). *We're just good friends: Women and men in nonromantic relationships.* New York: Guilford.

Werner, C. M., Altman, I., Brown, B. B., & Ginat, J. (1993). Celebrations in personal relationships: A transactional/dialectical perspective. In S. W. Duck (Ed.), *Understanding relational processes, 3: Social context and relationships* (pp. 109–138). Newbury Park, CA: Sage.

Werner, C. M, Altman, I., & Oxley, D. (1985). Temporal aspects of homes: A transactional perspective. In I. Altman & C. M. Werner (Eds.), *Home environments: Vol. 8. Human behavior and environment: Advances in theory and research* (pp. 1–32). Beverly Hills, CA: Sage.

Werner, C. M., & Haggard, I. M. (1985). Temporal qualities of interpersonal relationships. In G. R. Miller & M. L. Knapp (Eds.), *Handbook of interpersonal communication* (pp. 59–99). Beverly Hills, CA: Sage.

West, J. (1995). Understanding how the dynamics of ideology influence violence between intimates. In S. W. Duck & J. T. Wood (Eds.), *Understanding relationship processes, 5: Confronting relationship challenges* (pp. 129–149). Thousand Oaks, CA: Sage.

West, L., Anderson, J., & Duck, S. (1996). Crossing the barriers to friendship between men and women. In J. T. Wood (Ed.), *Gendered relationships.* Mountain View, CA: Mayfield.

Westefield, J. S., & Liddell, D. (1982). Coping with long-distance relationships. *Journal of College Student Personnel,* 23, 550–551.

Weston, K. (1991). *Families we choose: Lesbian, gays, kinship.* New York: Columbia University Press.

Wexner, L. B. (1954). The degree to which colors (hues) are associated with mood-tones. *Journal of Applied Psychology,* 38, 432–435.

Whaley, K., & Rubenstein, T. (1994). How toddlers "do" friendship: A descriptive analysis of naturally occurring friendships in a group child care setting. *Journal of Social and Personal Relationships,* 11, 383–400.

Whan, K. (1997, August 10). UNC study observes link between health, loving support. *The Chapel Hill Herald,* p. 7.

What teens say about drinking. (1994, August 7). *Parade,* p. 9.

Wheatley, M. (2002). *Turning to one another.* San Francisco: Berrett-Koehler.

Whitbeck, L. B., & Hoyt, D. R. (1994). Social prestige and assortive mating: A comparison of students from 1956 and 1988. *Journal of Social and Personal Relationships,* 11, 137–145.

White, B. (1989). Gender differences in marital communication patterns. *Family Process,* 28, 89–106.

White, J., & Bondurant, B. (1996). Gendered violence in intimate relationships. In J. T. Wood (Ed.), *Gendered relationships.* Mountain View, CA: Mayfield.

Whitman, Walt. (1855/1983). *Leaves of Grass.* New York, NY: Bantam Books, lines 226–227.

Whorf, B. (1956). *Language, thought, and reality.* New York: MIT Press/Wiley.

Wiemann, J. M., & Harrison, R. P. (Eds.). (1983). *Nonverbal interaction*. Beverly Hills, CA: Sage.

Wilkie, J. R. (1991). The decline in men's labor force participation and income and the changing structure of family economic support. *Journal of Marriage and the Family,* 53, 111–122.

Williams, D. G. (1985). Gender, masculinity–femininity, and emotional intimacy in same-sex friendship. *Sex Roles,* 12, 587–600.

Williams, R., & Williams, V. (1998). *Anger kills.* New York: HarperPerennial.

Willmott, P. (1987). *Friendship networks and social support.* London: Policy Studies Institute.

Winsor, J., Curtis, D., & Stephens, R. (1997). National preferences in business and communication education: An update. *Journal of the Association for Communication Administration,* 3, 170–179.

Winzeler, R. (1990). Amok: Historical, psychological, and cultural perspectives. In W. J. Karim (Ed.), *Emotions of culture: A Malay perspective* (pp. 97–122). Oxford, England: Oxford University Press.

Wittgenstein, Ludwig. (1922). *Tractatus Logico-Philosophicus.* London: Routledge.

Wollstonecraft, Mary. (1792). *A Vindication of the Rights of Woman*. Boston: Peter Edes (1792); New York: Bartleby (1999).

Woo, E. (1995, December 18). Stereotypes may psych out students. *Raleigh News and Observer,* pp. 1A, 10A.

Wood, J. T. (1982). Communication and relational culture: Bases for the study of human relationships. *Communication Quarterly,* 30, 75–84.

Wood, J. T. (1986). Different voices in relationship crises: An extension of Gilligan's theory. *American Behavioral Scientist,* 29, 273–301.

Wood, J. T. (1992a). *Spinning the symbolic web.* Norwood, NJ: Ablex.

Wood, J. T. (1992b). Telling our stories: Narratives as a basis for theorizing sexual harassment. *Journal of Applied Communication Research,* 4, 349–363.

Wood, J. T. (1993). Engendered relations: Interaction, caring, power, and responsibility in intimacy. In S. W. Duck (Ed.), *Understanding relationship processes, 3: Social context and relationships* (pp. 26–54). Newbury Park, CA: Sage.

Wood, J. T. (1994a). Engendered identities: Shaping voice and mind through gender. In D. Vocate (Ed.), *Intrapersonal communication: Different voices, different minds* (pp. 145–167). Hillsdale, NJ: Erlbaum.

Wood, J. T. (1994b). Gender and relationship crises: Contrasting reasons, responses, and relational orientations. In J. Ringer (Ed.), *Queer words, queer images: The construction of homosexuality* (pp. 238–265). New York: New York University Press.

Wood, J. T. (1994c). Gender, communication, and culture. In L. Samovar & R. Porter (Eds.), *Intercultural communication: A reader* (7th ed., pp. 155–164). Belmont, CA: Wadsworth.

Wood, J. T. (1994d). *Gendered lives: Communication, gender, and culture.* Belmont, CA: Wadsworth.

Wood, J. T. (1994e). *Who cares? Women, care, and culture.* Carbondale: University of Southern Illinois Press.

Wood, J. T. (1995a). Diversity in dialogue: Communication between friends. In J. Makau & R. Arnett (Eds.), *Ethics of communication in an age of diversity.* Urbana: University of Illinois Press.

Wood, J. T. (1995b). Feminist scholarship and research on relationships. *Journal of Social and Personal Relationships,* 12, 103–120.

Wood, J. T. (1995c). *Relational communication*. Belmont, CA: Wadsworth.

Wood, J. T. (Ed.). (1996). *Gendered relationships.* Mountain View, CA: Mayfield.

Wood, J. T. (1997a). Clarifying the issues. *Personal Relationships,* 4, 221–228.

Wood, J. T. (1997b). *Communication in our lives.* Belmont, CA: Wadsworth.

Wood, J. T. (1997c). *Gendered lives,* 2nd ed. Belmont, CA: Wadsworth.

Wood, J. T. (1998). *But I thought you meant ...: Misunderstandings in human communication.* Mountain View, CA: Mayfield.

Wood, J. T. (2000a). *Relational communication* (2nd ed.). Belmont, CA: Thomson/Wadsworth.

Wood, J. T. (2000b). That wasn't the real him: Women's dissociation of violence from the men who enact it. *Qualitative Research in Review,* 1. 1–7.

Wood, J. T. (2005). *Gendered lives: Communication, gender, and culture* (7th ed.). Belmont, CA: Thomson/Wadsworth.

Wood, J. T. (2006). Chopping the carrots: Creating intimacy moment by moment. In J. T. Wood & S. Duck (Eds.), *Composing relationships: Communication in everyday life* (pp. 24–35). Belmont, CA: Thomson/Wadsworth.

Wood, J. T., Dendy, L., Dordek, E., Germany, M., & Varallo, S. (1994). Dialectic of difference: A thematic analysis of intimates' meanings for differences. In K. Carter & M. Presnell (Eds.), *Interpretive approaches to interpersonal communication* (pp. 115–136). New York: State University of New York Press.

Wood, J. T., & Inman, C. C. (1993). In a different mode: Masculine styles of communicating closeness. *Journal of Applied Communication Research,* 21, 279–295.

Word for Word. (2005, March 6). *The New York Times,* p. WK 7.

Wren, C. S. (1990, October 16). A South Africa color bar falls quietly. *The New York Times,* pp. Y1, Y10.

Wrench, J. S., Corrigan, M. W., McCroskey, J. C., & Punyanunt-Carter, N. M. (2006). Religious fundamentalism and intercultural communication: The relationships among ethnocentrism, intercultural communication apprehension, religious fundamentalism, homonegativity, and tolerance for religious disagreements. *Journal of Intercultural Communication Research,* 35:1 March 2006, 23–44.

Wrench, J. S., & McCroskey, J. C. (2003). A communibiological explanation of ethnocentrism and homophobia. *Communication Research Reports,* 20, 24–33.

Wright, L., & Smye, M. (1996). *Civilizing the Workplace. Toronto:* Key Porter Books.

Wright, P. H., & Scanlon, M. B. (1991). Gender role orientations and friendship: Some attenuation but gender differences still abound. *Sex Roles,* 24, 551–566.

Wright, P. H., & Wright, K. (1995). Codependency: Personality syndrome or relationship process? In S. Duck & J. T. Wood (Eds.), *Understanding relationship processes, 5: Confronting relationship challenges* (pp. 109–128). Thousand Oaks, CA: Sage.

Yadav, Sid. (2006). Facebook—The Complete Biography. *Mashable: The Social Media Guide*: mashable.com/2006/08/25/facebook-profile.

Yager, J. (1999). *Friendshifts.* Stamford, CT: Hannacroix Creek.

Yamamoto, T. (1995). Different silence(s): The poetics and politics of location. In W. L. Ng, S. Chin, J. Moy, & G. Okihiro (Eds.), *Reviewing Asian America: Locating diversity* (pp. 132–145). Pullman: Washington State University Press.

Yeatts, D. E., & Hyten, C. (1998). *High-Performing Self-Managed Work Teams.* Thousand Oaks, CA: Sage.

Yerby, J., Buerkel-Rothfuss, N., & Bochner, A. (1990). *Understanding family communication.* Scottsdale, AZ: Gorsuch Scarisbrick.

Yum, J. (1987). Korean philosophy and communication. In D. Kincaid (Ed.), *Communication theory: Eastern and Western perspectives* (pp. 71–86). London: Academic Press.

Zhang, Y. B., Harwood, J., & Hummert, M. L. (2005). Perceptions of conflict management styles in Chinese intergenerational dyads. *Communication Monographs,* 72, 71–91.

Zorn, T. (1995). Bosses and buddies: Constructing and performing simultaneously hierarchical and close friendship relationships. In J. T. Wood & S. W. Duck (Eds.), *Understanding relationship processes, 6: Off the beaten track: Understudied relationships* (pp. 122–147). Thousand Oaks, CA: Sage.

Zweig, D., & Jane Webster. (2002) Where is the line between benign and invasive? An examination of psychological barriers to the acceptance of awareness monitoring systems. *Journal of Organizational Behavior,* 23,605–633.

Credits

This page constitutes an extension of the copyright page. We have made every effort to trace the ownership of all copyrighted material and to secure permission from copyright holders. In the event of any question arising as to the use of any material, we will be pleased to make the necessary corrections in future printings. Thanks are due to the following authors, publishers, and agents for permission to use the material indicated.

Chapter 1. 4: Reprinted by permission of Dr. William G. Huitt. **12:** Adapted from Shannon & Weaver, 1949 **13:** Adapted from Schramm, 1955.

Chapter 2. 41: Vachss, A. (1994, August 28). "You carry the cure in your own heart." *Parade,* 4–6. **49:** Griffin, D.W. and Bartholomew, K. (1994) "The Metaphysics of Measurement: The Case of Adult Attachment" in K. Bartholomew and D. Perlman, *Attachment Processes in Adulthood.* London: Jessica Kingsley Publishers, p. 51. Reproduced by permission of the author.

Chapter 4. 103: Reprinted by permission of the author. **127:** *Anger Kills* (1998), Redford Williams and Virginia Williams, pp. 5-11.

Chapter 5. 139: The Council for Canadian Unity. Retrieved July 3, 2001, from www.ccu-cuc.ca/en/library/bill_101.html. **141:** *Non-Sexist Language: A Guide* by the Committee on Equality of Opportunity, p. 4, © 1994, University College Cork

Chapter 6. 164: Seboek, T. A., and Rosenthal, R. (Eds). (1981). *The Clever Hans phenomenon: Communication with horses, whales, apes and people.* New York: New York Academy of Sciences. **167:** Raphael, M. (1997, May 13). "It's true: Drivers move slowly if you want their space." *Raleigh News and Observer,* p. 1A. **172:** "Be civil." (1994, July 5). *The Wall Street Journal,* p. A1; Basketball Nova Scotia Code of Conduct. Retrieved April 10, 2001, from www.basketball.ns.ca/Codeofconduct.html. **173:** Courtesy of the National Institute on Deafness and Other Communication Disorders **176:** Business bulletin. (1996, July 18). *The Wall Street Journal,* p. A1. **178:** Bellamy, L. (1996, December 18). "Kwanzaa cultivates cultural and culinary connections." *Raleigh News and Observer,* pp. 1F, 9F; George, L. (1995, December 26). "Holiday's traditions are being formed." *Raleigh News and Observer,* pp. C1, C3; Kwanzaa. Retrieved May 2, 2001, from http://cbc.ca/onair/specials/holidays/kwanzaa.html. **179:** Varkonyi, C. (1996, June 22). "Colourcode." *Raleigh News and Observer,* pp. 1E–2E; Wexner, L. B. (1954). "The degree to which colours (hues) are associated with mood-tones." *Journal of Applied Psychology,* 38, 432–435. **180:** Pierson, J. (1995, November 20). "If sun shines in, workers work better, buyers buy more." *The Wall Street Journal,* pp. B1, B8.

Chapter 7. 194: *Cognitive Evolution: The Biological Imprint of Applied Intelligence,* by Alice Travis **195:** *Annual Report on the Operation of the Canadian Multicultural Act,* 2007-8. (http:/www. pch.gc.ca) **195:** Data is derived from Statistics Canada, "Ethnic Origin and Visible Minorities, 2006 Census," catalogue 97-562, Released April 2, 2008. **196:** Reproduced by permission from the California Department of Education, CDE Press, 1430 N Street, Suite 3207, Sacramento, CA 95814. **199:** Swenson, David. The College of St. Scholastica. Culture maps. Retrieved March 25, 2005, from faculty.css.edu/users/dswenson/web/CULTURE/CULTMAPS.HTM. Used by permission. **201:** Adapted from Benjamin, D., & Horwitz, T. (1994, July 14). "German view: "You Americans work too hard—and for what?"" *The Wall Street Journal,* pp. B1, B6. Reprinted with permission of *The Wall Street Journal,* Copyright © 2004 Dow Jones & Company, Inc. All Rights Reserved Worldwide. **205:** John Borovilos, ed., (1990). *Breaking through: A Canadian literary mosaic.* Scarborough, Ontario: Prentice-Hall, pp.181-82. Reprinted with permission of David Suzuki. **206:** Reprinted by permission of *Harvard Business Review.* Excerpted from "Cultural Intelligence" by Earley, P. Christopher, Mosakowski, Elaine, Vol. 82, Issue 10, Oct. 2004. Copyright © 2004 by the Harvard Business School Publishing Corporation; all rights reserved. **207:** Adapted from *Canadian Forces Journal,* Vol. 9, No. 3, http://www.journal.dnd.ca/vo9/no3/05-scoppio-eng.asp **208:** Reprinted by permission of *Harvard Business Review.* Exhibit from "Cultural Intelligence" by Earley, P. Christopher, Mosakowski, Elaine, Vol. 82, Issue 10, Oct. 2004. Copyright © 2004 by the Harvard Business School Publishing Corporation; all rights reserved. **210:** Reprinted by permission of *Harvard Business Review.* Exerpt from "Cultural Intelligence" by Earley, P. Christopher, Mosakowski, Elaine, Vol. 82, Issue 10, Oct. 2004. Copyright © 2004 by the Harvard Business School Publishing Corporation; all rights reserved. **211:** National Center for Cultural Competence, http://www.commonwealthfund.org. Used by permission of The Commonwealth Fund. **212:** Cross, Bazron, Dennis & Isaacs,1989; Goode, Dunne, Bronheim, 2006

Chapter 8. 223: Carl, W. (1998). "A sign of the times." In J. T. Wood, *But I thought you meant...: Misunderstandings in human communication* (pp. 95–208). Mountain View, CA: Mayfield; Manning, A. (1996, March 6). "Signing catches on as a foreign language." *USA Today,* p. 4D. **225:** Crossen, C. (1997, July 10).

"Blah, blah, blah." *The Wall Street Journal*, pp. 1A, 6A. **227:** Bolton, R. (1986). Listening is more than merely hearing. In J. Stewart (Ed.), *Bridges, not walls* (4th ed., pp. 159–179). New York: Random House. **235:** Crossen, C. (1997, July 10). "Blah, blah, blah." *The Wall Street Journal*, pp. 1A, 6A; Nyquist, M. (1992, Fall). *Learning to listen. Ward Rounds*. Evanston, IL: Northwestern University Medical School, pp. 11–15.

Chapter 9. 253: Lund, M. (1985). "The development of investment and commitment scales for predicting continuity of personal relationships." *Journal of Social and Personal Relationships*, 2, 3–23. **257:** Canary, D., & Dindia, K. (Eds.). (1998). "Sex differences and similarities in communication," Mahwah, NJ: Erlbaum; Floyd, K., & Parks, M. (1995). "Manifesting closeness in the interactions of peers: A look at siblings and friends." *Communication Reports*, 8, 69–76; Wood, J. T., & Inman, C. C. (1993). "In a different mode: Masculine styles of communicating closeness." *Journal of Applied Communication Research*, 21, 279–295. **261:** Rankin, J., Quinn, J., Shephard, M., Duncanson, J., & Simmie, S. (2002, October 20). "Police Target Black Drivers." *Toronto Star*. Retrieved from www.thestar.com. **262:** Adapted from AXIS Centre for Public Awareness of People with Disabilities, 4550 Indianola Avenue, Columbus, OH 43214.

Chapter 10. 287: Weiss, S. E. (1987). "The changing logic of a former minor power." In H. Binnendijk (Ed.), *National negotiating styles* (pp. 44–74). Washington, DC: Department of State. **295:** Adapted from Bach, G. R., & Wyden, P. (1973). *The intimate enemy: How to fight fair in love and marriage*. New York: Avon.

Chapter 11. 318: Based on Lund, M. (1985). "The development of investment and commitment scales for predicting continuity of personal relationships." *Journal of Social and Personal Relationships*, 2, 15. **318:** Button, C. M., & Collier, D. R. (1991, June). "A comparison of people's concepts of love and romantic love." Paper presented at the Canadian Psychological Association Conference, Calgary, Alberta; Fehr, B. (1993). "How do I love thee: Let me consult my prototype." In S. W. Duck (Ed.), *Understanding relationship processes, 1: Individuals in relationships* (pp. 87–122). Newbury Park, CA: Sage; Luby, V., & Aron, A. (1990, July). "A prototype structuring of love, like, and being in love." Paper presented at the Fifth International Conference on Personal Relationships, Oxford, England; Rousar, E. E., III, & Aron, A. (1990, July). "Valuing, altruism, and the concept of love." Paper presented at the Fifth International Conference on Personal Relationships, Oxford, England. **322:** Based on Huston, M., & Schwartz, P. (1995). "Relationships of lesbians and gay men." In J. T. Wood & S. W. Duck (Eds.), *Understanding relationship processes, 6; Off the beaten track: Understudied relationships* (pp. 89–121). Thousand Oaks, CA: Sage; Sprecher, S. (1989). "The importance to males and females of physical attractiveness, earning potential, and expressiveness in initial attraction." *Sex Roles*, 21, 591–607. **323:** Ackerman, D. (1994). *A natural history of love*. New York: Random House. **326:** Gerstel, N., & Gross, H. (1985). *Commuter marriage*. New York: Guilford. **334:** JOURNAL OF SYSTEMIC THERAPIES by /STORM, CHERYL. Copyright 2003 by GUILFORD PUBLICATIONS INC. Reproduced with permission of GUILFORD PUBLICATIONS INC in the format Textbook via Copyright Clearance Center. **335:** Atsumi, R. (1980). "Patterns of personal relationships". *Social Analysis*, 5, 63–78; Mochizuki, T. (1981). "Changing patterns of mate selection." *Journal of Comparative Family Studies*, 12, 318–328. **335:** Excerpt from *The Five Love Languages* by Gary Chapman. (1992). Reprinted with permission **337:** Personal communication with Dr. Robert Brunham, August 7, 2001. **338:** Reel, B. W., & Thompson, T. L. (1994). "A test of the effectiveness of strategies for talking about AIDS and condom use." *Journal of Applied Communication Research*, 22, 127–141. **340:** Domestic Abuse Intervention Project, 202 E. Superior Street, Duluth, MN 55802, 218-722-2781, www.duluth-model.org **341:** Domestic Abuse Intervention Project, 202 E. Superior Street, Duluth, MN 55802, 218-722-2781, www.duluth-model.org **345:** Based on Hochschild, A., with Machung, A. (1989). *The second shift*. New York: Viking Press. **345:** Westefield, J. S., & Liddell, D. (1982). "Coping with long-distance relationships." *Journal of College Student Personnel*, 23, 550–551. **349:** "Four Damaging Behaviours in Close Relationships" from META-EMOTION: HOW FAMILIES COMMUNICATE EMOTIONALLY by J. Gottman, L. Katz and C. Hooven. Reprinted by permission of Lawrence Erlbaum Associates.

Chapter 12. 353: Employability Skills 2000+ Brochure 2000 E/F (Ottawa: The Conference Board of Canada, 2000). **356:** Adapted from J. French and B. Raven. (1959). "The bases of social power," in D. Cartwright (Ed.), *Studies in social power*. Ann Arbor: University of Michigan. Reprinted with permission **358:** CRC among Pioneers of Healthcare Virtual Network (*Eye on Technology* Issue 9), www.crc.gc.ca/en/html/crc/home/mediazone/eye_on_tech/2008/issue9/hsvo, Communications Research Centre Canada, 2008. Reproduced by permission of the Minister of Public Works and Government Services, 2009. **360:** Adapted from *Warring Egos, Toxic Individuals, Feeble Leadership*, http://www.psychometrics.com/docs/conflictstudy_09.pdf. Used by permission of Psychometrics Canada. **362:** Carol Kinsey Goman, Ph.D., is an executive coach and keynote speaker who addresses association, government, and business audiences around the world. Dr. Goman is the author of 10 business books. Her latest is *The Non-verbal Advantage - Secrets and Science of Body Language at Work*. She can reached at CGoman@CKG.com or www.NonverbalAdvantage.com. **368:** Jennifer Rasmussen, www.rasmussencentral.com, http://www.employeedevelopmentsolutions.com/freearticles/virtualteams.htm **373:** May R. Bast, Ph.D., Out of the Box Coaching, www.breakoutofthebox.com

Index

D

E

F

G

H

I

J

K

L

M

N

O

P

Q

R

S

T

U

V

W

Y

Z